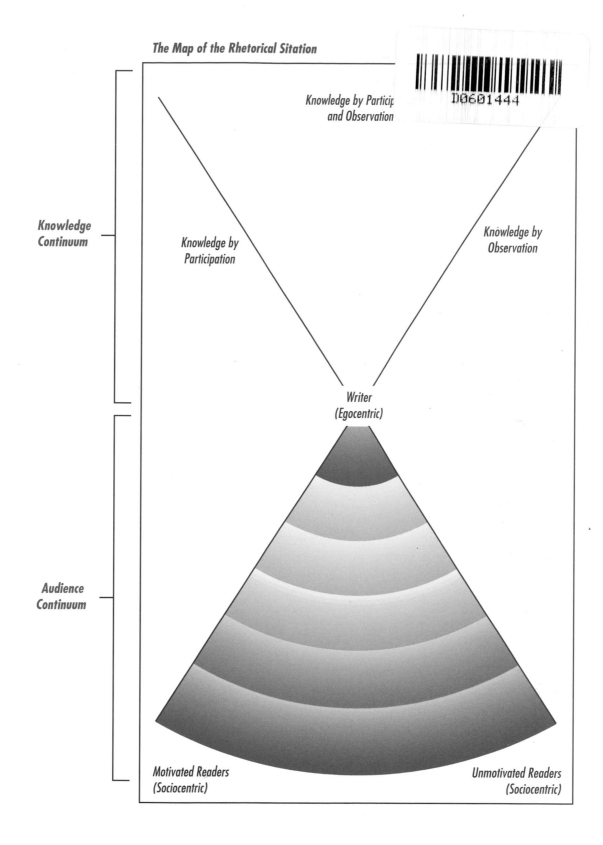

The Map of the Rhetorical Sitation

Knowledge
Continuum

Knowledge by Particip
and Observation

Knowledge by
Participation

Knowledge by
Observation

Writer
(Egocentric)

Audience
Continuum

Motivated Readers
(Sociocentric)

Unmotivated Readers
(Sociocentric)

$\mathcal{A}$ $\mathcal{W}$RITER'S $\mathcal{R}$EPERTOIRE

A Writer's Repertoire

GWENDOLYN GONG
Texas A & M University

SAM DRAGGA
Texas Tech University

LONGMAN

An imprint of Addison Wesley Longman, Inc.

New York • Reading, Massachusetts • Menlo Park, California • Harlow, England
Don Mills, Ontario • Sydney • Mexico City • Madrid • Amsterdam

Senior Acquisitions Editor: Jane Kinney
Project Editorial Manager: Melonie Parnes
Design Manager: Lucy Krikorian
Text Designer: Circa 86, Inc.
Cover Design: John Callahan
Cover Illustration: Judy Pedersen
Art Studio: Vantage Art, Inc.
Electronic Production Managers: Laura Chavoen/Susan Levine
Desktop Administrator: Laura Leever
Manufacturing Manager: Willie Lane
Electronic Page Makeup: Circa 86, Inc.
Printer and Binder: R.R. Donnelley & Sons Company
Cover Printer: Coral Graphics Services, Inc.

A Writer's Repertoire

Library of Congress Cataloging-in-Publication Data

Gong, Gwendolyn.
    A writer's repertoire / Gwendolyn Gong, Sam Dragga.
       p. cm.
    Includes index.
    ISBN 0-321-08441-1
       1. English language—Rhetoric. 2. English language—Grammar. 3.
College readers. I. Dragga, Sam. II. Title.
PE1408.G5734   1995
808' .042—dc20   94-13236
                                                          CIP

00 01 02 03-DOC-5 4 3 2 1

To our students,
our teachers,
and our families

Brief Contents

Detailed Contents

A Writer's Repertoire is a text of exploration and opportunity. In these pages, you will explore key concepts and strategies about writing and have frequent opportunities to apply them in the creation of your own texts. We have chosen two metaphors to guide you on this expedition: *repertoire* and *journey.*

The first metaphor appears in our title. The term *repertoire* refers to the storehouse of approaches and abilities that an individual either possesses or has the potential to develop; we use this metaphor to describe a writer's competence in using language to think critically and in translating that reasoning into appropriate, meaningful messages for others. Repertoire also encompasses the available resources of information that a writer draws on to gain understanding about a subject. These resources can be experience based (direct) or source based (indirect). In keeping with our metaphor, we present writing as both a solo (individual) and an ensemble (collaborative) activity. And we include responses to writing tasks that have been composed by student writers like you—in effect, members of our repertory company.

A Writer's Repertoire is divided into ten major sections, progressively enabling you to develop your basic writing repertoire and challenging you to expand it by composing essays for a wide range of audiences and in a variety of rhetorical situations.

Part I, "Understanding the Subject of Writing," provides a general overview of essential rhetorical terms and concepts, information that is applied in writing situations throughout the book. Writers need opportunities not only to engage in writing (the *how* of writing) but also to understand something about writing as a discipline (the *what* and *why* of writing). In Chapter 1, "Rhetoric and Writing: Background and Concepts," we define the rhetorical *canons* or major divisions of rhetoric (invention, arrangement, style, memory, and delivery) in terms of contemporary writing theory and practice. Another key feature of this chapter is the introduction of the distinction between *knowledge by participation* (personal experience) and *knowledge by observation* (oral and written sources of information). This distinction enables writers to recognize how they have obtained information and helps them to identify which of their ideas require documentation. In addition, we explain the concept of *rhetorical situation*—the tension among writer, reader, and subject—as well as *aims* and *purposes* of writing.

In Chapter 2, "Composing Processes," we discuss the complex act of writing, exploring how writing processes interact with the rhetorical canons. We also address various internal and external constraints such as attitude, motive, fatigue, environment, computer hardware and software and their effects on writers.

Chapter 3, "Collaborative Writing," covers both *sequential collaboration*—writers working on different tasks at different times—and *simultaneous collaboration*—writers working on the same task at the same time. We offer guidelines for effective collaboration, including creating heterogeneous groups, developing a group identity, establishing procedures for fair and considerate participation, and avoiding a rush to consensus.

Part II, "Developing a Writer's Repertoire: Strategies and Techniques" explores the rhetorical canons in greater detail. We have developed Chapter 4 on invention in terms of the knowledge continuum, the spectrum that illustrates the way information is discovered: by participation (brainstorming, visualizing, and computer-assisted invention) and by observation (interviews, questionnaires, and library sources).

In Chapter 5, "Arrangement," we consider the traditional areas of rhetorical modes and organization. We also introduce some theoretical contributions to writing theory, such as discourse blocs, cohesion techniques, and the verbal and visual representation of ideas. Discourse blocs are units in the structure of a piece of writing that share a common purpose. These units represent how a writer develops ideas and consist of one or more paragraphs. To augment our discussion of discourse blocs, we examine cohesion techniques (ways to make sentences and ideas fit together effectively) and the verbal and visual representation of ideas (ways that words and graphics work together to clarify a writer's meaning).

Chapter 6, "Style," offers guidance on adapting verbal and visual expression to the subject, audience, aim, and purpose of the text. We cover such issues as formal versus informal usage, simple versus complex sentences, and passive versus active voice; in addition, this chapter discusses the influences on the ways we express ideas in language.

Chapter 7, "Memory and Delivery," updates and expands the writing process by examining the design of a physical text. By considering research developments in reading theory, cognitive psychology, and computer technology, we identify ways that writers can use these new insights to strengthen their understanding of their audiences and their strategies for communicating with them.

Parts III–V contain a total of ten chapters that present strategies and techniques as well as opportunities to compose essays for different situations, purposes, and audiences. Each section begins with an introductory chapter on a particular aim of writing—expressive, referential, or persuasive—discussing the processes for composing each kind of essay. The remaining chapters within each section present tasks and subjects across the disciplines for you to respond to, as well as strategies and techniques for you to refine. We also feature individually and collaboratively authored sample essays that student writers in our repertory company have produced. Student writers present their writing processes from invention to delivery, narrating and explaining their rhetorical choices, decisions, and outcomes in their journal entries.

Parts VI–X present five special reference sections:

- Part VI, "Readings," contains 12 essays published by professional writers. These essays illustrate writing in a variety of rhetorical situations and complement the student responses to writing tasks in Parts III–V.

- Part VII, "A Guide to Logic and Reasoning," supplements Chapter 14, which focuses on persuasive aim writing, by offering an examination of formal logic—deductive logic, inductive logic, and logical fallacies—and Toulmin's practical reasoning.

- Part VIII, "A Guide for Writing Essay Examinations," introduces strategies for taking timed writing tests. This section shows how and why composing processes for essay examinations differ from out-of-class essays. Responses to specific essay questions are included and analyzed.

- Part IX, "A Guide for Documenting Knowledge by Observation," covers recording, examining, and documenting information. Included are detailed examples of the MLA, APA, IEEE, and CBE documentation styles.

- Finally, Part X, "A Guide to Classroom English," presents brief, descriptive information and examples concerning words, sentences, punctuation, spelling, and usage. At the end of this section, we identify and explain ten cautions for writers.

The journey motif serves as our second metaphor. We invite you to join us as we travel the terrain of rhetoric, identifying, explaining, developing, and expanding your repertoire. We will act as guides who have planned our sojourn and made all the necessary arrangements. We have mapped the itinerary, booked the accommodations along the way, scheduled activities for each stop, and even arranged for you to meet other student writers who are developing, applying, and expanding their own writing repertoire.

But who are we, your traveling companions? We are spouses, parents, siblings, and our parents' children. One of your guides, Sam Dragga, is of

Sicilian descent, an Italian American born and reared in Cleveland, Ohio. Your other guide, tracing her origins back to Canton in Southern China, is Gwendolyn Gong, a Chinese American born and reared approximately three miles from Cleveland, Mississippi. Though markedly different, we are, nevertheless, both "Clevelanders" of sorts, and more. We are also writers and writing teachers, fascinated by the prospect of sharing with you our professional, academic understanding of writing, complemented by the perspectives our own distinct cultural and ethnic backgrounds have afforded us. As a consequence, we will begin many chapters of *A Writer's Repertoire* with narratives that connect our memories of language—the Midwest and the Deep South, Sicily and Canton, Europe and Asia—to the contemporary theory and practice of writing in our shared world now.

Collaborating on this book has enabled us to expand our writing repertoire and explore the power of language. It has also helped us realize that our collaboration extends well beyond our own ideas, conversations, and drafts. And we would now like to acknowledge those who have made *A Writer's Repertoire* possible and to whom this book is dedicated.

Sincere appreciation goes to the students in our writing classes. Our students have shared our commitment to understanding more about writing as a subject and a practical art. They have expected us to give them our best instruction about how and why we write; they have encouraged us to test how compatible theory and practice are in the classroom; and they have given us a forum to converse and negotiate what, how, and why we teach writing as we do. For their active participation in our daily lives, we thank our students. We wish to offer special acknowledgement to those whose work appears in *A Writer's Repertoire:* Tonya Armstrong, Elaine Barton, Elizabeth Branan, Karyn E. Bratz, Matthew Coplen, Rochelle Davis, LaRae Carole Fischer, Kenneth J. Fontenot, Tricia Goodwin, Jason L. Graves, Wendy Greener, Christina Griffith, Lisa Haley, Hayley Hamby, Michelle Y. Harris, Krista Hierholzer, Ursula Houston, Tamara Jones, Angela E. Jordan, Stacy Kaaz, Kristine L. Koenig, Hector Longoria, Laura Lott, Michelle Mauldin, Melissa McDaniels, Robin L. Moore, Karen A. Phillips, Kate Satterwhite, Stephanie M. Sellers, Melissa A. Smith, Melissa Walton, Christine Wilson, and Suzanne Young. We have occasionally modified their essays and accompanying materials in order to identify or emphasize rhetorical principles and composing processes. We would also like to thank the students at Bowling Green State University, Kansas State University, the University of Oklahoma, William Paterson College, and Wright State University who provided us with useful feedback on an early version of *A Writer's Repertoire.*

As lifelong students, we would also like to acknowledge our teachers who have helped us to recognize the power of language and communication as well as to value knowledge and ways of knowing. Among our teachers are reviewers, class-testers, and editors who have participated in the development of this text: James Barszcz, William Paterson College; Melody Bowden, University of Oklahoma; Richard Bullock, Wright State University; Suzanne L. Bunkers, Mankato State University; Margaret

Dahlberg, University of North Dakota; Linda J. Daigle, Houston Community College System; Carrie Krantz Fischer, Bowling Green State University; Judith E. Funston, SUNY–Potsdam; David W. Furniss, University of Wisconsin; Christopher Gould, University of North Carolina; Alfred Guy, New York University; Stephen Hahn, William Paterson College; Dawn Hubbel-Staeble, Bowling Green State University; Maurice Hunt, Baylor University; Linda Klabunde, Kansas State University; Charles Kostelnick, Iowa State University; Stephanie Lyman, University of New Orleans; David Mair, University of Oklahoma; Wanda Martin, University of New Mexico; Delma McLeod-Porter, McNeese State University; Elizabeth Metzger, University of South Florida; Walter E. Meyers, North Carolina State University; Shirley Rose, Purdue University; Barbara Saez, University of Rhode Island; Thomas E. Schirer, Lake Superior State University; Lana Lake Schnauder, McNeese State University; J. Blake Scott, University of Oklahoma; David W. Smit, Kansas State University; Maggy Smith, University of Texas; Charlotte Smith, Virginia Polytechnic Institute; John Taylor, South Dakota State University; Michael T. Warren, Wright State University; Heide Marie Weider, Tennesse Tech University; Beth Wharton, Wright State University; and Linda Woodson, University of Texas–San Antonio. We would also like to thank Adrienne Gardner for her useful comments on using the library in Chapter 4. For their early support of this project, James L. Kinneavy from the University of Texas–Austin, W. Ross Winterowd from the University of Southern California, and Charles I. Schuster from the University of Wisconsin–Milwaukee deserve special thanks.

Our thanks go to our collaborators and close friends at Longman: Jane Kinney, our greatest creative resource, for "living" this book with us for the past two years; Laurie Likoff, for her support and belief in this project; Carla Samodulski and Marian Wassner for their keen editorial guidance; and Melonie Parnes, for her expert production of the text. We would also like to thank Ann Stypuloski for her imaginative marketing strategies. Many heartfelt thanks go to our Texas-based Longman supporters: Laura Stowe, Greg Odjakjian, Sharon Noble, Ben Jordan, and Shane Stagg. The Longman staff in New York and Texas have become members of our extended family.

We are especially privileged, however, to acknowledge our families for their unwavering love and support: our parents, Kung Woo and Lee Chiles Sit Gong and Sam and Theresa Dragga; our spouses, John Powers and Linda Dragga; and our children, Devereux Gong Powers and Timothy and Nicholas Dragga. We are grateful for their hugs and smiles, love and encouragement, and patience and understanding as we wrestled with how best to express the ideas trapped inside our heads.

While developing this book, we have experienced lots of joy in discovering and articulating our ideas about writing theory and the teaching of writing. We hope our joy comes through in our words.

Gwendolyn Gong
Sam Dragga

We would like to take this opportunity to welcome you to *A Writer's Repertoire*. Based on our experiences with communication and writing, both inside and outside the classroom, we have put together what we hope is a "next generation" rhetoric, a book that looks at both the how and the why of writing. We discuss not only practical approaches to writing, but the theoretical foundations for those approaches.

During the course of *A Writer's Repertoire,* we will travel some new terrain in the teaching of composition and revisit some rhetorical concepts from earlier times. We look back at the rhetorical canons as first introduced in ancient Greece, but also integrate the discoveries of contemporary rhetoricians. We explain ways of thinking about audience and purpose and ways of thinking about the writer's knowledge of his or her subject.

In addition, we examine different types of writing and provide assignments and sample student essays to demonstrate the actual processes of writing. At every turn, we offer suggestions for group work and opportunities for students to write collaboratively. Throughout the text, we encourage both students and instructors to develop and expand their own repertoires by looking at writing in new ways.

As your traveling companions and guides in this journey of exploration, we hope that you will find this experience to be as rewarding and as empowering as we feel it has the potential to be. If you have any comments or questions about our text, please feel free to contact us.

Gwendolyn Gong/Sam Dragga
c/o Ann Stypuloski
Addison-Wesley Educational Publishers
College Marketing, Twenty fifth Floor
1185 Avenue of the Americas
New York, NY 10036

Gwendolyn Gong   Sam Dragga

ABOUT THE AUTHORS...

Gwendolyn Gong received her Ph.D. at Purdue University and is an associate professor of English at Texas A&M University. She has served as the director of Freshman English Studies, preparing high school and college writing teachers to be facilitators and administrators in educational and corporate settings. Gong has taught a wide range of undergraduate and graduate academic, business, and technical writing courses. She has also taught writing and reading courses at the Institut Teknologi MARA in Shah Alam, Malaysia, and is currently on a research leave in Hong Kong. In addition, she is a consultant for the Center for Executive Development at Texas A&M as well as for various colleges and universities.

Sam Dragga is an associate professor of English at Texas Tech University. He has a B.A. in English from the University of Dayton and an M.A. and Ph.D. in English from Ohio University. Dragga is a member of the executive board of the Association of Teachers of Technical Writing and is co-editor of the ATTW bulletin. He won the ATTW's 1991 best article award for "Responding to Technical Writing." He also designed and edited the ATTW publication *Technical Writing: Student Samples and Teacher Responses*. In addition, he has published articles on visual communication, business correspondence, collaboration, grading practices, computer-based instruction, and biblical literature.

Sam Dragga and Gwendolyn Gong are the co-authors of *Editing: The Design of Rhetoric* (Baywood, 1989) which received the 1990 NCTE Achievement Award for Technical and Scientific Writing in the category of "Best Book of the Year."

A WRITER'S REPERTOIRE

Rhetorical Canons

In Part I, *AWR* defines the rhetorical canons—**invention**, **arrangement**, **style**, **memory**, and **delivery**—in terms of contemporary writing so students will come to understand writing as a discipline. Defining the canons allows students to appreciate the importance of writing as a social act that enables them to find, create, and communicate knowledge.

Rhetoric and the Canons in Classical Times

If you were a student of rhetoric in classical times, you would focus on three types of oratory, arising from various social contexts: policy speaking, legal speaking and debating, and special occasion speaking. *Policy oratory* strives to persuade listeners to act in a certain manner or to adopt the speaker's point of view. It involves decisions and events that lie in the future and require some course of action: to go to war, to levy taxes, to enact legislation, or to vote for specific candidates in an upcoming election. *Legal speaking and debating* are used in court settings. Speakers rely on factual arguments as well as precedents (rulings and evidence borne out from past cases) in order to persuade. *Special occasion oratory* refers to speeches of praise or blame made at weddings, award ceremonies, funerals, Congressional hearings, political "roasts," and the like. As such, this third type of oratory is concerned with events and people in the present—the here and now.

In your study of these three types of oratory, you might analyze, compose, and make speeches by following the approach of *Cicero* (106-43 B.C.E.), a Roman philosopher, orator, and teacher. Cicero wrote treatises on the persuasive effects of speech and is credited with dividing rhetoric into five parts, or *canons*, for educational efficiency: *invention, arrangement, style, memory,* and *delivery* (Corbett 22).

Invention

The first canon of rhetoric, *invention* or *inventio*, concerns the discovery of arguments and other means of persuasion that may be effective in convincing an audience. Following the teaching of the Greek philosopher and rhetorician *Aristotle* (384-322 B.C.E.), you would be instructed to use both inartistic and artistic proofs to find your evidence. *Inartistic proofs* refer to external sources that require you to consult other knowledge bases such as the testimony of witnesses, information provided by interviewees, and research results in empirical and laboratory reports. In *A Writer's Repertoire*, we will refer to evidence gained from external sources as *knowledge by observation*.

On the other hand, *artistic proofs* refer to rhetorical strategies that enable you to use evidence gained from personal experience. The two major categories of artistic proofs are the topics and the three appeals. The *topoi* or *topics* help you discover good reasons for arguments. Some common topoi are definition, classification and division, comparison and contrast, and cause and effect. In *A Writer's Repertoire*, we will call evidence gained from personal experience *knowledge by participation*.

Another artistic proof you would rely on to help you find evidence would be the three types of appeals: ethos, logos, and pathos. *Ethos* or *ethical appeal* refers to a speaker's character and credibility. As a speaker, you must realize that *who* says something is often more influential than *what* is said. If your listeners perceive you to be honest and qualified to

"Repertoire" Chapters

Parts III-V, Expanding Your Repertoire, address students' actual composing processes by presenting strategies and techniques as well as opportunities to compose **expressive, referential,** and **persuasive** writing. Each part contains an introduction to a particular aim of writing, a discussion of the processes for composing each kind of text, student-written essays representing each form of writing, and cross-curricular writing tasks for students to complete.

REPERTOIRE WRITING TASK: EXPLANATION

Select a subject that interests you and that will appeal to either readers much like you; a general college audience; a general adult readership; or a specific campus, community, or professional group. Consider carefully what your readers already know about this idea or object and how your essay might further their understanding of its relevance or importance.

Three variations of this writing task follow, based upon the different ways you can "know" about your subject:

Knowledge by Participation

Write an essay that explains the meaning, influence, and significance of a key idea or object that you came to know about through direct experience.

Knowledge by Observation

Write an essay that explains the meaning, influence, and significance of a key idea or object that you came to know about through indirect means (through interviews, reading, television, or another medium). Your subject should be one that others have written about, yielding some form of published biographical, social, or historical information that you can integrate into your essay.

Knowledge by Participation and Observation

Write an essay that explains the meaning, influence, and significance of a key idea or object that you came to know about through direct experience as well as through indirect means (through interviews, reading, television, or another medium). Your subject should be one that others have written about, yielding some form of published biographical, social, or historical information that you can integrate into your essay.

REPERTORY COMPANY OF STUDENT WRITERS: RESPONSES TO THE WRITING TASK

...about this writing task, you may find it helpful to ...ers and read their essays, written in response to ...all of these student writers worked within their ...es or groups; their groups met regularly to talk, ...ith one another. They also reviewed their journal ...nts in Chapters 1-7—responses that may have ...g ideas. Interacting within their writing communi-...nged ideas and strengthened their sense of what

---

In your community organization, you might propose additional legislation on drunk driving to your local representative. On the job, you might propose to your boss that the company adopt a new vacation policy for part-time sales clerks.

In writing proposals, you will try to prove to your audience that your solution is appropriate. It is especially important, therefore, that you discuss and answer possible objections to your solution.

REPERTOIRE WRITING TASK: PROBLEM-SOLUTION

Define and explain the problem clearly, and propose your solution as the most feasible, developing a reasoned argument for it. Be certain to make your argument convincing by analyzing your audience carefully, using rhetorical appeals judiciously, as well as providing sound, sufficient evidence and counterarguments. Because this is persuasive aim writing, consider carefully what your readers already know about this subject, what their perceptions and attitudes may be about it, and why.

Here are three variations of this writing task, based upon the different ways you may "know" about your subject:

Knowledge by Participation

Write an essay proposing a solution to a problem faced by your community or by a group to which you belong, and address your proposal to one or more members of the community or group. The problem you select should be one that you know about through personal experience.

Knowledge by Observation

Write an essay proposing a solution to a problem that your community or group is coping with and that you came to know of through indirect means (through interviews, reading, television, or another medium). Your subject should be one that others have written about informally or formally, yielding some form of published biographical, social, or historical information that you can integrate into your essay. Address your proposal to one or more members of the community or group.

Knowledge by Participation and Observation

Write an essay proposing a solution to a problem that your community or group is coping with and that you came to know of through direct experience and indirect means (through interviews, reading, television, or another medium). Your subject should be one that others have written about informally or formally, yielding some form of published biographical, social, or historical information that you can

AWR enables students to differentiate among three kinds of knowledge: **knowledge by participation**—information gained from personal experience; **knowledge by observation**—information obtained from oral and written sources; **knowledge by participation and observation**—information learned from both experience and outside sources. These concepts describe how writers come to know and write about ideas, people, places, and things, therefore making it easier for students to decide whether their work requires documentation.

Our perceptions of ourselves and our world are shaped by familiar people and places. For example, we know about the roles and responsibilities of family members through our personal interaction with our own relatives. We may know about famous and not-so-famous landmarks—local, national, or foreign—because we actually visited those places. This knowledge may be augmented by understanding gained from sources such as other people, books, articles, films, television, radio, and newspapers.

It has been said that each person is the sum of his or her experiences. Whether or not your life experiences are direct, indirect, or some combination thereof, they surely contribute to making you who you are. One of the most effective ways to examine the significance that people and places have for you is to write about them. The writing task in this chapter asks you to discover or rediscover a particular character or place that has made such a contribution.

REPERTOIRE WRITING TASK: CHARACTERS AND PLACES

Describe a character or place using specific, vivid details to create a dominant impression, so that your audience can understand your subject and its importance to you. Your audience may be readers much like you; a general college audience; a general adult readership; or a specific campus, community, or professional group.

Below are three variations of this writing task, based upon the different ways you may "know" about the character or place that you focus on:

Knowledge by Participation

Write an essay about an individual or place that you know personally and explain his, her, or its impact on you. How has this person or location changed or affected you?

Knowledge by Observation

Write an essay about an individual or place that you know indirectly (through interviews, reading, television, or another medium) and explain his, her, or its impact on you. This person or location should be one that others have written about either formally or informally, yielding some form of published biographical, social, or historical information that you can integrate into your essay. How has this person or location changed or affected you?

Knowledge by Participation and Observation

Write an essay about an individual or place that you know about directly and indirectly (through interviews, reading, television, or another medium), and explain his, her, or its impact on you. This person or location should be one that others have written about either

Knowledge Continuum and Audience Continuum

Students are asked to visualize each rhetorical situation—the tension among writer, reader, and subject—using an innovative mapping apparatus. The upper portion of the map represents the **knowledge continuum** where students identify information about their subject and distinguish the way(s) they have learned about the subject. The lower portion of the map represents the **audience continuum**, which helps students analyze their readers: how similar or different they are from the student writers and how interested or disinterested they may be in the subject.

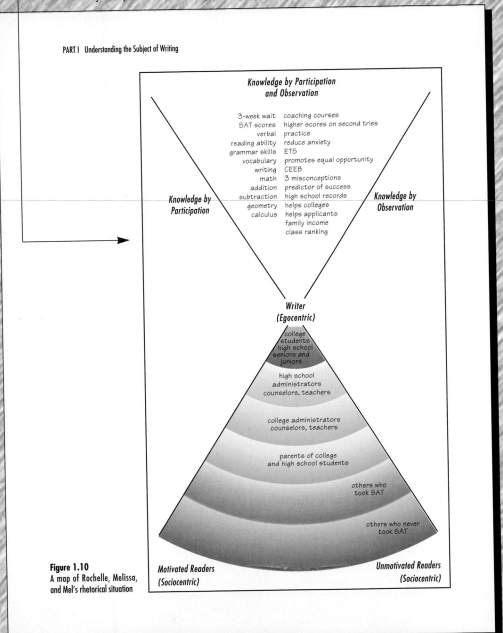

Figure 1.10
A map of Rochelle, Melissa, and Mel's rhetorical situation

Journal Keeping

Students are encouraged throughout the text to keep a **writing journal**, providing them with additional practice in composing various forms of writing, and offering them an opportunity to develop a resource book and personal memoir focusing on writing.

Journals may include entries on any subject concerning writing, as well as:
- responses to **Issues for Writing**
- identification and rationale for writing decisions
- reflections on the writing tasks
- completed essays

Reviewing Journal Entries

Christine's journal entries for "Filthy Grins" are very different from Karen's. While Karen writes full sentences and seems to enjoy recording her thoughts in her journal, Christine uses her journal to jot down ideas and lists of things to do. Only after her paper is completed does she write in full sentences and paragraphs. In a sense, Christine's entries during her writing processes represent an extension of her invention and planning strategies; the entries written after she's finished her essay represent her evaluative and reflective commentary.

Journal

My concerns about my paper:

> *my characters need more development*

> *more action and description*

> *more interaction with the children—show contrast better between sad house, happy kids*

> *conclusion needs more*

Anyone's paper should

> *catch the reader in the beginning*

> *give some action*

> *develop characters so reader can identify with them*

Introduction—dialogue
Middle of paper—description of the situation
Conclusion—outcome of family
> *personal significance to me*

> *Overall, I'm happy with the way it turned out. I tried to write this paper on the computer, but I couldn't do it because of the nuisance of the quotes. With pen and paper I could get my ideas out better. Also my creativity is highest in the evening when I don't have access to a computer.*
> *The style is flowing but could use more coherence. There are no hangups for readers in the reading except the transition at the end.*
> *The invention was hard at first but once I got my pen moving it came easier than I thought. I started writing about the family but wrote more about the house, the setting. Writing so many different drafts helped me to see more structural awkwardness and stumbling blocks for readers.*
> *I would've liked to be able to talk more about the mother and the kids but I couldn't figure out how to ask the case worker at Child Protective Services. That would've been difficult and inconvenient for her. She already*

AWR contains a separate chapter that actually teaches students *how* to collaborate by providing them with ample opportunities to problem-solve and compose together. Covering both **sequential collaboration**—writers working on different tasks at different times—and **simultaneous collaboration**—writers working on the same task at the same time—the text offers guidelines for effective collaboration.

INDIVIDUAL WRITING VERSUS COLLABORATIVE WRITING

Much of the writing that you do in school and later on the job will be individual: from start to finish you will be the only writer involved. You will come up with the ideas, organize them yourself, compose the first draft, revise it to your liking, and design the final document for your readers. Often, however, you will need to share the responsibilities for creating your research report, book review, essay, or proposal. Sometimes, the collaboration will be extensive: you will work with other writers from start to finish. At other times, you will brainstorm and outline ideas with others, but do most of the writing and editing yourself. That is, individual writing and collaborative writing are not two different types of writing processes, but two different points on a continuum of writing processes.

If you are to collaborate effectively, we think it is important that you understand a few things about collaborative processes:

- Collaboration has two basic orientations: simultaneous and sequential.
- You already have experience with collaborative communication.
- Collaborative writing improves individual writing abilities.
- Computers have enhanced collaboration.
- Trust is essential to effective collaboration.
- Collaboration is difficult, but worthwhile.

Two Orientations of Collaboration

Collaborative writing has two basic orientations: simultaneous and sequential. In *simultaneous collaboration*, the writers work together at the same time on the same task, usually sitting in the same room. In sequential collaboration, the writers divide the tasks: for example, he does the research, she composes, he revises, she edits. Often collaboration involves a mix of the two types: for example, the writers might research and compose separately, then edit together. In writing this book, we adopted a mix of simultaneous and sequential collaborative processes, but the collaboration with the editors and designers at HarperCollins was usually sequential. Before we wrote a chapter, for example, the editors did research on how particular subjects were covered in other composition textbooks. With this information, we would write each chapter, trying to be distinctive, but comprehensive. After we finished a chapter, the editors would offer suggestions and ask questions. And then we would revise. Occasionally, however, we would fly to New York City to sit face

Student Sample Essays

Tracing the composing processes from first draft to completed essays, *AWR* demonstrates how various student writers working alone or in groups responded to the writing tasks presented in the *Repertoire* chapters. These samples include excerpts from students' **journals**, their **maps** of the rhetorical situation, **notes**, **outlines**, **rough drafts**, and **final drafts** of their essays.

motivated to tackle it, so he wisely changes his focus. But, as he says in one of his entries: "Time's a killer."

Journal

This is not going to be pretty. Here it is three days before the essay is due, and I just changed my subject. I wanted to do something on multicultural education because I had already had the research for it. But I couldn't find anything really controversial that I wanted to follow up on now. So I decided to change my subject to the NEA.

I just got back from the library where I got more research than I'll ever need, but it's all from newspapers. I need to go back tomorrow and try to get some articles from journals.

I had an argument today with one of my conservative friends about the NEA. This should be an interesting paper.

Well, I must admit—I'm a little disappointed in myself. I don't think this paper is really up to par. I've already thought of two counterarguments I didn't discuss. And I think I should have argued just one thing (the NEA should not be restricted) instead of two (and the NEA should not be abolished) because the paper is really too long for a persuasive paper, especially considering I didn't talk about two points that I should have. Since I changed my subject, I only had one day to write it and nobody to read it. Too late to meet with my group. I think it is well written in the sense that it flows, but I don't think it was very well conceived. I don't think that I would want my conservative friend to read it simply because it is not as strong an argument as it should be. Time's a killer.

Mapping Kenneth's Persuasive Rhetorical Situation

Kenneth's knowledge of the NEA is gained by observation, so he lists his details on the "knowledge by observation" side of the continuum (see Figure 16.3).

Knowledge by Participation and Observation

art
obscenity
censorship
Jesse Helms
government subsidies
$0.64 of tax money
museum support
peer review
attract corporate sponsors
$175 million budget
85,000 grants
Serrano
Mapplethorpe
1989 fight
legal restrictions
defining obscenity
self-censorship

Knowledge by Participation

Knowledge by Observation

Writer
(Egocentric)

liberals

Who'll Decide for You
What's Art and What's Obscenity?

(Draft 2—Final Draft)

What is art? It's a difficult question to answer, isn't it? Despite the trouble people have defining it, a handful of representatives in Congress think they know what art is. They may not be able to give you a definition of it, but they know it when they see it. Not only do they know what it is, but they also know what it is not. Moreover, they know what's obscene. At least, this is what they would have you believe. In fact, they'd like to decide for the whole country what's art and what's obscenity.

With communism collapsing around the world, it is truly ironic that, in the so-called land of the free, artists can be subjected to censorship by the U.S. government. However, this has happened thanks to Jesse Helms and other members of Congress. Reacting to two National Endowment for the Arts (NEA) funded projects that they deemed obscene, Helms led the charge to place restrictions on the NEA in 1989. And what's more, if certain people have their way, the NEA will be abolished altogether. It is vital to America that the NEA not only remain in existence, but also be able to operate without Congressional content restrictions on prospective project grants.

There are some who believe that it's not the job of the government to patronize the arts, but that it's up to the private sector. Their simple reasoning is that they shouldn't have to pay for endowments to the arts through the government because they don't want to. The arts, they contend, are [illegible] military, and [illegible]

Professional Essays

AWR also contains twelve essays authored by professional, multicultural writers in ***Part VI: Readings***, which illustrate writing in a variety of rhetorical situations and complement the student responses to writing tasks in Parts III–V.

Life on the Global Assembly Line

by Barbara Ehrenreich and Annette Fuentes

Barbara Ehrenreich is a journalist whose works include these co–authored books: The American Health Empire *(1970),* Witches, Midwives and Nurses: A History of Women Healers *(1972), and* For Her Own Good: 150 Years of the Experts' Advice to Women *(1979); in addition, she has written* Re-Making Love: The Feminization of Sex *(1986), and* Fear of Falling *(1986).*

Like Ehrenreich, Annette Fuentes is also a journalist concerned with women's issues. She serves as the editor of Sisterhood Is Global.

"Life on the Global Assembly Line" was published in Ms. *magazine. In this essay, Ehrenreich and Fuentes question the effects of large corporations when they locate businesses in developing countries and employ laborers—usually women who work for extremely low wages in dangerous workplaces and jobs. As journalists, Ehrenreich and Fuentes draw from their own knowledge of women's jobs and wages in the American workplace and investigate numerous sources to write this essay. In writing for the general readers of* Ms., *the authors document their sources by identifying them within their text (i.e., tagging) rather than by using footnotes, endnotes, or formal bibliographies.*

In Ciudad Juarez, Mexico, Anna M. rises at 5 A.M. to feed her son before starting on the two hour bus trip to the maquiladora (factory). He will spend the day along with four other children in a neighbor's one-room home. Anna's husband, frustrated by being unable to find work for himself left for the United States six months ago. She wonders, as she carefully applies her new lip gloss, whether she ought to consider herself still married. It might be good to take a night course, become a secretary. But she seldom gets home before eight at night, and the factory, where she stitches brassieres that will be sold in the United States through J.C. Penney, pays only $48 a week.

In Penang, Malaysia, Julie K is up before the three other young women with whom she shares a room, and starts heating the leftover rice from last night's supper. She looks good in the company's green-trimmed uniform, and she's proud to work in a modern, American-owned factory. Only not quite so proud as when she started working three years ago—she thinks as she squints out the door at a passing group of women. Her job involves peering all day through a microscope, bonding hair-thin gold wires to a silicon chip destined to end up inside a pocket calculator, and at 21, she is afraid she can no longer see very clearly.

Every morning, between four and seven, thousands of women like Anna and Julie head out for the day shift. In Ciudad Juarez, they crowd

I arrived early for my interview. I presented extra copies of my cover letter and résumé to the receptionist and waited for my name to be called. Dressed in a blue suit and armed with a briefcase full of sample materials and letters to substantiate my teaching experience and educational background, I was confident about my chances of being selected. Summer teaching jobs were hard to come by, and summer teaching jobs in special programs for writing teachers were even harder to find and compete for. But here I was at the interview, certain of my qualifications to be just the kind of writing instructor this program was seeking.

The receptionist called my name, handing me a folder with my name typed in the upper tab. "You'll need to present this file for your interview. Go right in." His tone was matter-of-fact, shaking my confidence a bit. Reminding myself of my purpose and abilities, however, I regained my sense of self and stepped into the office.

Behind a large desk sat a portly man, engaged in a telephone conversation. As he turned and looked up at me, I handed my folder to him. The man grinned broadly. "I'll call you back later," he said excitedly to the person on the phone. "The answer to my problem has just walked in the door!"

"Come in and have a seat," invited my interviewer.

I was so relieved. Obviously, here was a person who had seen my file and knew a qualified candidate when he saw one. Both my self-confidence as well as my faith in this interviewer's judgment were growing. I sat down in a chair in front of the desk, pleased with the way things were going.

The interviewer held my folder and located my name, typed in capital letters across the tab label. "I am so happy to see you. I can tell you right now that you are the answer to our prayers. We have had lots of applicants for these positions, but this year we need additional teachers and tutors. I know you are qualified because you made the interview; my staff screens and verifies your experience and background, you know."

I was speechless. It seemed apparent that I was in: I had landed this job without saying a word about myself. My thoughts were interrupted by this warm job offer: "Welcome to our summer staff. You'll love teaching college algebra and trigonometry to our students."

"College algebra and trigonometry?" I asked. I could feel the blood rushing to my face. Surely he was joking.

Unfortunately, he was serious. He assumed that I taught [mathemat]ics—a subject area in which they obviously needed extra ins[tructors. Real]izing that something was amiss, he opened my folder, scann[ing my] application, and immediately began to explain his confusion[. "Have we ever interviewed any English teachers who are Asia[n? No,] you're a first, I believe. Of course, we've had numerous Asia[n math and] science teachers. So, you see why I thought. . . ." (GG)

Opening Vignettes

AWR includes chapters that open with brief, **autobiographical vignettes** from the authors' lives. These stories introduce and illustrate key ideas of language, composing, and rhetoric, thus making abstract ideas more concrete and relevant to students.

Did You Know Boxes

These sections feature interesting **facts and tips about writing**, along with advice for collaborative work and brief biographies of key rhetorical figures of the ancient world: Plato, Aristotle, Cicero, and Quintillion.

In an article in the *Los Angeles Times*, Irene Lacher reports on the importance of good book titles. Here is an excerpt:

Six million softcovers ago, Judith Krantz's first paperback publisher had scruples about the title of her new romance.

The hitch was that his secretary considered *Scruples* a lousy title for a book. After all, what on earth were scruples?

"I asked him if he knows what unscrupulous means," Krantz recalls. "This was the Nixon era. He said, 'Yes.' I said, 'Anyway, I'm not worried about your secretary's understanding. That is the title that's destined for the book. Nobody can make me change it.'"

Destiny? Maybe. If success is destiny's watermark, Krantz's subsequent cavalcade of monster best sellers would indicate that fate—like many publishers—favors short and snappy titles.

More prosaically, a book's title is where poetry, wit and commerce converge. It's the first line of defense in the publishing industry's war of the words. In a publisher's fondest dream, it's the distinctive snippet that will grab you by the lapels and prompt you to buy that one book among many, the catchy phrase that will dance to your lips when you ask if the book is in stock.

. . . Remember that fine classic *Trimalchio in West Egg?* Or the legendary *Tote the Weary Load?* Those misguided early titles were scratched for the more mellifluous—and memorable—*The Great Gatsby* and *Gone With the Wind*, respectively.

. . . For an author, "it's like naming your baby," says Stuart Applebaum, vice president of Bantam Books. "It may have a wonderful importance and resonance for you and your family but be a complete head-scratcher to the world at large.

"While the act of writing may be a monastic one, the act of publishing it—which includes marketing—is very much a collaborative one. So you have a lot of different opinions, which may and may not conform to the author's."

That is precisely what *New York Post* reporter Randall Pierson was up against when he handed in his investigative tome on Leona Helmsley's tax woes. Pierson wanted to call it *Woman on Trial*, which his editors found lackluster.

"We were ready to pull our hair out," says Applebaum. "It was in one of these brainstorming sessions where [Pierson] wasn't present that my colleague Steve Rubin blurted out, 'How about *The Queen of Mean?*'"

Voila.

1. In your journal, write your own opening narrative for this chapter. Your story should focus on a specific time when you were first learning to write. To capture this memory, begin by making lists, taking notes, and outlining the information you can remember. Try to recall as much about your first rhetorical situation as you can: where you were at the time, who was with you, who helped you or offered you feedback, what age you were, why you were writing. Also try to remember the writing instrument and the kind of paper you used. If you can, ask family or friends what they remember about your learning to write. Did being able to write affect you and your perception of language then? Your narrative should describe and explain this first writing experience.

2. Reread the opening story and your own narrative. Make a list of the ways in which the description of learning to write Chinese is similar to and different from your first memories about writing.

3. Share your list in response to 2 with members of your focus group. In your journal, identify and explain how similar and different the group members' accounts of their writing experiences were.

Write More About It

These two Issues for Writing may provide you with essay subjects in later chapters. In Chapter 9, you will tell the story of a meaningful event, and your response to 1 may provide useful notes and a good preliminary narrative to develop further for that writing task. In Chapter 13, you will analyze a historical event, social or cultural trend, technological innovation, or artistic work. Your response to 2—the analysis of your first writing experience as compared to that described in the opening narrative in this chapter—may be a workable subject for the writing task in Chapter 13.

Composing Processes and the Canons

Until 1971, when researcher and teacher Janet Emig published her study on composing, writing was described as one process that occurred in three stages: prewriting, writing, and rewriting. As this model suggests, each stage was perceived as distinct and separate from the other stages. For example, writers would first prewrite (i.e., think or plan to prepare them to write); then, they would write straight through from beginning to end; last, writers would revise (i.e., edit and proofread, rather than making substantive changes in meaning and organization). Notice that this linear model represents a lock-step procedure, precluding interaction among the various stages.

Issues for Writing

These writing suggestions provide individual and collaborative exercises and activities for students to record in their journals.

Write More About It

These sections forecast how students' responses to the *Issues for Writing* exercises may be pertinent to specific writing tasks in later chapters.

Read More About It

These marginal cross-references point students to other chapters where there is additional material on the subject.

Read More About It
See Chapter 4, pp. 94–115.

Your information is **pertinent** if you focus the audience's attention on your thesis and avoid unnecessary details or digressions. Once again, you need to be sensitive to your audience as you decide which information is essential and which is distracting, which information clarifies your explanation or analysis and which interferes with your audience's understanding. If you were explaining wireless telegraphy to engineering majors, you might briefly identify its inventor, Guglielmo Marconi. You probably would not need to mention his receipt of the 1909 Nobel Peace Prize, however, because this information does little to improve your audience's understanding of wireless telegraphy.

Motivating Your Audience

In addition to establishing credibility and developing a thesis, you also have to solicit the audience's attention to your explanation or analysis. Readers will not automatically examine every piece of referential writing that is offered to them. Your job is to motivate your audience to read your explanation or analysis and add it to their previous knowledge of the subject. You motivate your audience to do so by emphasizing the simplicity and the significance of your information; that is, you have to show that your explanation or analysis is easy to read and important to know.

To emphasize the simplicity of your explanation or analysis, offer examples and illustrations. By making your ideas vivid and easily accessible, examples and illustrations improve the clarity and memorability of your explanation or analysis. **Examples** identify practical applications or specific occurrences. **Illustrations** display vital characteristics of your subject. For example, if you were analyzing your company's economic situation, you might give examples of this year's major successes and failures and design tables and figures to display appropriate statistics. If you were explaining the meaning of the word *acronym* (a word derived by combining the initial letters of a series of words), you might give examples such as *scuba* or *radar* and illustrate their derivation by highlighting the pertinent letters (*self-contained underwater breathing apparatus; radio detecting and ranging*).

Similarly, **narratives** dramatize and personalize your information, making your explanation or analysis easier to understand and remember. If you were describing the operation of a commercial printing company, for example, you might describe how a particular book was printed, guiding your readers through each stage of the printing process.

You might also **compare and contrast** your subject to one that is more familiar to your audience, thus simplifying your discussion and easing understanding. You could, for example, explain how a color photocopier is similar to and different from a black-and-white photocopier.

Or you might consider **division** of the subject to allow your audience to digest it more easily. For example, if you discussed the printing

Inductive Logic

The **inductive** relationship points only to the probability of truth. If the premises are true, it is likely that the conclusion is also true. Induction is predictive: that is, given evidence of yesterday's conditions and today's conditions, you try to predict tomorrow's conditions. Inductive logic is thus the basis of scientific reasoning. The inductive relationship of the premises to the conclusion is either categorical, statistical, or analogous.

In a **categorical** relationship, the premises describe specific examined cases and the conclusion offers a prediction regarding all cases:

All the patients we have admitted to the clinic have survived; therefore, we believe all the patients are likely to survive.

In a **statistical** relationship, the premises describe a specific fraction of examined cases and the conclusion offers a prediction regarding a specific equal fraction of all cases:

Because 90 percent of the patients we have injected with this new drug have improved, we believe that this drug has promise for 90 percent of all patients.

If the relationship is **analogous**, the premises describe specific examined cases and the conclusion offers a prediction regarding specific unexamined cases. Analogous relationships are either categorical or statistical:

All of the cancer patients admitted to the clinic have survived. Bill is a cancer patient and thus is likely to survive.

Of the cancer patients admitted to the clinic, 75 percent have survived. Bill has cancer and so there's a 75 percent probability that he'll survive also.

Erroneous premises and invalid inductive relationships lead to fallacious or deceptive reasoning. Such mistakes of logic are called **logical fallacies**.

Composition is the claim that a characteristic of each part is necessarily a characteristic of the whole:

Sooner or later humanity will die off because all human beings are mortal.

This claim is fallacious because the mortality of individual humans is different from the extinction of the human species.

Division is the claim that a characteristic of the whole is necessarily a characteristic of each part.

Part VII: A Guide to Logic and Reasoning

This section focuses on persuasive writing by examining **formal logic**—deductive logic, inductive logic, and logical fallacies—and Toulmin's practical reasoning.

Examinations

essay examinations, your writing is subject to a variety of influ-. Specifically, because the essay examination is a testing situation, might be anxious or nervous. A night of studying might also leave physically tired. In addition, because essay examinations are timed situations, you ordinarily have little opportunity to revise your or to consider issues of style, memory, and delivery. Your focus is lly on invention and arrangement: retrieving information appropri- the question and organizing that information logically.

PLANNING YOUR ANSWERS

Because the essay examination is timed writing, you might be tempted to read the question and immediately start writing your answer to it. Resist this temptation. You are more likely to write a satisfactory answer if you do a little quick planning.

Dedicate ten minutes at the beginning of the examination period to planning your answers to all the questions. If you do your thinking at the beginning of the examination period—while you are still alert—you are more likely to compose answers of uniform quality. In a one-hour examination, for example, after you have been writing for thirty minutes, you are likely to be tired and, as a consequence, thinking less clearly. Such fatigue often causes the later answers on essay examinations to be inferior to the earlier ones. If your essay examination has several questions, divide the time available to you according to the complexity or weight of the questions. For example, a question that is 25 percent of the examination deserves approximately 25 percent of your time.

Start your planning by reading each question critically to determine the appropriate way to answer it. Is the question asking you for a summary, evaluation, or analysis? If a question asks you to analyze or evaluate a subject and you only summarize it, your answer is inappropriate and thus unsatisfactory. Questions that ask you to summarize assess your ability to retrieve and discuss information covered during class or by assigned readings. Evaluative questions ask you to judge the merits of a subject, weigh advantages and disadvantages, or choose among alternatives. Analytical questions assess your ability to recognize similarities and differences, determine causes, perceive influences, interpret results, consider implications, explain significance, or apply knowledge to specific situations. Consider, for example, the following examination questions:

Sample Examination Questions	Explanations of Questions
Identify and briefly discuss three examples of unsatisfactory hospitality in Homer's *Odyssey*?	This question asks you to summarize. Your task is to choose three episodes and offer sufficient details to prove the episodes are

Part VIII: A Guide for Writing Essay Examinations

This part introduces strategies that students can use when taking timed writing tests. It shows *how* and *why* different composing processes may be developed for **writing exams**.

Book, one author:
Crosby, Faye J. *Relative Deprivation and Working Women.*
  New

    York: Oxford UP, 1982.

Book, two authors:
Larson, Carl E., and Frank M. J. LaFasto. *Teamwork: What
  Must Go
    Right, What Can Go Wrong.* Newbury Park: Sage, 1989.

Book, three authors:
Stanley, Linda C., David Shimkin, and Allen H. Lanner. *Ways
  to
    Writing: Purpose, Task, and Process.* New York: Macmil-
    lan, 1985.

Book, four or more authors:
Johansen, Robert et al. *Leading Business Teams.* Reading:
  Addi-

    son-Wesley, 1991.

Book, edited:
Barker, Thomas T., ed. *Perspectives on Software Documentation:

    Inquiries and Innovations.* Amityville: Baywood, 1991.

Book, edition other than the first:
Lannon, John. *Technical Writing.* 6th ed. New York: Harper

    Collins, 1994.

Book, translation:
Vygotsky, Lev. *Thought and Language.* Trans. Eugenia Hanfman
  and

    Gertrude Vakar. Cambridge: MIT, 1962.

Essay or article in a book:
Van Pelt, William, and Alice Gillam. "Peer Collaboration
  and the

    Computer-Assisted Classroom: Bridging the Gap Betwe
    Academia and the Workplace." *Collaborative Writing
    Industry: Investigations in Theory and Practice.* Ed
    Mary M. Lay and William M. Karis. Amityville: Baywo
    1991. 170-205.

Part IX: A Guide for Documenting Knowledge by Observation

This section covers recording, examining, and documenting information and includes detailed examples of the **MLA**, **APA**, **IEEE**, and **CBE** documentation styles.

PART X: A Guide to Classroom English

This **brief handbook** section presents descriptive information and examples on grammar, mechanics, punctuation, spelling, and usage.

Verbals

Verbals are verbs that function as nouns or adjectives. Similar to verbs, verbals are either transitive (acting on objects) or intransitive (acting without objects). Verbals are of four types:

Verbal Type	Function	Example
infinitive (*to* + verb)	noun	She asked <u>to leave</u> the room.
	adverb	<u>To please</u> his sister, he washed the dishes.
gerund (verb + *-ing*)	noun	His job is <u>repairing</u> small appliances.
present participle (verb + *-ing*)	adjective	<u>Running</u> all the way, he arrived at his office before nine o'clock.
past participle (verb + *-ed/-t*)	adjective	Often he would sleep through class, <u>exhausted</u> from his job as a waiter.
(verb + vowel mutation)		<u>Rung</u> each morning and evening for fifty years, the school bell cracked.
(verb + *-n/-en*)		We could be allies, <u>given</u> the right conditions.
(verb + vowel mutation + *-n/-en/-t*)		<u>Kept</u> from his friends, the boy was always lonely.
(verb mutation)		The vicious criminal, finally <u>caught</u> by the police, admitted his guilt.
(verb)		<u>Hit</u> by a hurricane, the city was severely damaged.

Often a participle has a subject, creating a verbal phrase that modifies the remainder of the sentence:

<u>The sun starting to shine</u>, she closed the umbrella.

The city was again quiet, <u>the police officers having stopped the riot</u>.

<u>His shirt [being] dirty</u>, the man decided to leave. (The word *being* is optional.)

<u>His reputation [being] damaged</u>, the man quit his job. (The word *being* is optional.)

Adverbs

Adverbs modify verbs, adjectives, adverbs, and sentences. Adverbs modify from several positions within a sentence:

At Addison-Wesley Educational Publishers, we are always interested in hearing your feedback. To improve our textbooks, we revise them every few years, taking into account the experiences both instructors and students have with the previous editions. Please take a moment to fill out this brief questionnaire.

Name_____ Phone _____

School _____

City _____ State _____ Zip _____

Course _____ Instructor _____

Other books required _____

Did you enjoy reading the vignettes from the author's lives that opened several chapters? ❏ Yes ❏ No
Why or why not?
_____
_____

Did you find the audience and knowledge continuums helpful? ❏ Yes ❏ No Why or why not?
_____
_____

Did you benefit from reading the materials produced by student writers featured in *A Writer's Repertoire*?
❏ Yes ❏ No Why or why not?
_____
_____

Do you feel more knowledgeable about the theory of writing as a result of what you learned in *A Writer's Repertoire*? ❏ Yes ❏ No Why or why not?
_____
_____

Do you feel that you're a better writer as a result of what you learned in *A Writer's Repertoire*?
❏ Yes ❏ No Why or why not?
_____
_____

Did you enjoy working in groups and collaborating with your peers on some of the assignments?
❏ Yes ❏ No . Why or why not?
_____
_____

On the whole, what was your opinion of *A Writer's Repertoire* ?
_____
_____

Please return this questionnaire to: Ann Stypuloski
College Marketing, Twenty fifth Floor
Addison-Wesley Educational Publishers
1185 Avenue of the Americas
New York, NY 10036

A Writer's Repertoire

PART I

Understanding the Subject of Writing

Rhetoric and Writing: Background and Concepts

*I*t was a typical sultry afternoon in August, and our family was finally moving into the house we'd been assigned by the Institut Teknologi MARA (ITM) administrators. The Boehme family had occupied this domain for the past three years, and they were still packing their belongings when we arrived to pick up the key. Elizabeth Boehme, excited about going home to Kingsville, Texas, invited us in. John and I noticed our hostess was barefoot, so we took off our shoes at the door, placing them beside the front step. From our orientation workshop for visiting faculty, we knew that it is customary in Malaysia to remove footwear before entering others' homes. Practically speaking, this habit reduces the amount of dirt that can be tracked in. For the superstitious, taking off one's shoes means that you leave any bad fortune at the door.

Joe Boehme was seated on one of two broad, low, bamboo chairs with floral-patterned cushions; the couch matched the chairs, complete with a rectangular glass coffee table. "Please, sit down," Joe urged. We carefully sat on several square pillows on the floor, tucking our feet underneath us; it is considered rude to expose the soles of your feet to another in Malaysia. Joe had been an engineering professor at ITM, so we had much to discuss: teaching at the university, the students, Malaysia and Malaysians, customs, the house and landlady, transportation, the exchange rate of the ringgit (Malaysian currency) versus the U.S. dollar, and the like.

As we talked, I repositioned my daughter, Devereux, in my lap. "How old is your little girl?" inquired Elizabeth, with warm interest. I told her about Devereux and my nervousness about finding someone to take care of her during the week. Elizabeth perked up, almost as if an alarm had sounded. In a matter of minutes, she had arranged for a woman named Uma to come for an interview later that afternoon.

The intervening hours passed quickly. John and I listened as Joe and Elizabeth advised us on how to adjust to life in a Muslim country, an educational system established in the British colonial tradition, as well as the social, religious, and political interaction among the three main racial groups in Malaysia: indigenous Malays, Indians, and Chinese. As the Boehmes talked, we both took notes. Suddenly, we heard the putt-putt of a small motorcycle, followed shortly by a brisk rap at the screen door.

It was Uma. Joe left the room to do some last-minute packing; Elizabeth, John, and I rose to greet the visitor, who had already removed her sandals. Uma was slightly taller than I and spoke with a British accent. She wore a beautiful turquoise sari elaborately embroidered with gold thread. The four of us talked, trying not to stare at one another too obviously. We learned that Uma, 27, was the mother of three children and had been a nanny since she was 9. In addition to finding out about her work experience, we discovered Uma knew Tamil (her native Indian language), Malay (the national language of Malaysia), English, and Mandarin. John and I were definitely impressed and hired her.

That was a month ago, when all was fine. Now, Uma seemed to be defying me by ignoring my instructions. "Feed Devereux baby food; she's too young for table food." I'd gone over this information with Uma; she always nodded and said "Yes? Try," so she must have heard what I'd said. (Sometimes she responded, "Yes. Can." Weren't those two responses synonymous?) Why, I'd even highlighted the appropriate sections of books by experts like Benjamin Spock, T. Berry Brazelton, and Penelope Leach and put them in conspicuous places for Uma to find. Why didn't she follow their instructions about feeding? Why didn't she ask me questions about the baby food, then?

I eventually confronted Uma about this matter. Why didn't she follow the directions as I had instructed her? Her response was simple: She could not read English. In fact, though she could speak four languages fluently, she could read only Tamil. I felt embarrassed, and so did Uma. Why hadn't I asked her about her reading knowledge of English? Why hadn't she volunteered this information? How could I, an English professor, have overlooked the possible differences between orality and literacy in this rhetorical situation? I had simply taken for granted that, because Uma could speak English, she could also read it. I had obviously misunderstood this particular aspect of the rhetorical, linguistic, and cultural context in which I was now living. (GG)

This story illustrates my own initiation into a new context: I had shifted from College Station, Texas, in the American Southwest, to Shah Alam, Malaysia, in Southeast Asia. To prepare myself for this dramatic change, I read travel books, studied the ITM faculty handbook, and participated in a day-long orientation workshop in Austin, Texas, designed especially for those of us headed for Malaysia. All of this information represented *knowledge by observation:* that is, knowledge obtained from others' experiences. Based on that reading, I began to create my own database about Malaysia well before I ever journeyed there. I continued to build my knowledge structure as I interviewed others by telephone and met with Malaysian students attending Texas A&M. My knowledge about Malaysian life came from those outside sources—sources that collectively formed a knowledge continuum. The continuum extended from my personal perspective as an Asian-American woman investigating Southeast Asia, to informal conversations, to formal interviews where I'd pose a specific set of questions, to the diverse selection of library reference materials I had read. Undoubtedly, I learned much from other people who passed along their insights about Malaysia's customs (e.g., taking off my shoes before entering homes, handling and eating food only with my right hand), peoples (i.e., Malays, Chinese, and Indians), languages (i.e., Malay, Cantonese, Mandarin, Tamil, English), and many religious beliefs (e.g., Islam, Christianity, Buddhism, Taoism, Hinduism, Sikhism).

When I arrived in Shah Alam, I learned first-hand about my new *rhetorical situation:* speaker (who I was: Chinese woman, English professor from the United States), audience (who I was interacting with: Malaysians, as well as other expatriates), and subject (what I was focusing on: my family's daily life in Malaysia). Understanding acquired in this first-hand way is called *knowledge by participation.* For example, I am an American-born Chinese who grew up in a bilingual home where both English and Cantonese were spoken; my background and life experiences prior to going to Malaysia served as a primary type of knowledge by participation. This knowing was increased by my witnessing how American faculty adopted Malaysian cultural habits in their daily lives (e.g., sitting on the floor, covering the soles of the feet when seated, eating with the right hand) even in the privacy of their own homes.

Living in Shah Alam and working at ITM, however, I began to realize that much of my understanding about my context was a blend of both *knowledge by participation and observation.* That is, after a while, my discoveries about people, places, events, and ideas—derived from my reading or talking with others—were augmented by my personal experience. For example, the students, ITM, the house and the landlady, shopping, the *ringgit,* eating papayas, and so on were things I came to know about from a wide array of sources, and I too was among those valuable sources.

Unfortunately, my knowledge base was inadequate when it came to Uma. As I have recounted, I used both knowledge by observation and knowledge by participation: I got recommendations from the university and others about her; I interviewed her; I observed how she and Devereux interacted; I checked her work record, salary, references. What my external sources couldn't tell me and what I neglected to ask was so obvious in retrospect: Can you read? Being so overwhelmed by Uma's knowing four languages, I simply forgot my environment: Malaysia, a country of many peoples whose native languages differ. It is a relatively oral culture, where speaking rather than writing is often the key to a person's livelihood. It is common for people living there to speak a number of languages and dialects fluently; furthermore, it is just as common for them not to read in all of those languages and dialects. As an English language and writing teacher, I perhaps should have known this fact. I should have realized the difference between *try* and *can* when Uma said those words. I should have analyzed my audience better, taking my rhetorical situation into account more carefully. And that's what this chapter is about.

A Writer's Repertoire is designed to help you understand how to use language effectively. We begin to do so in this chapter by reviewing our rhetorical tradition and some key concepts that will make your learning easier.

1. In your journal, write an opening narrative for this chapter, recalling a time when you, a family member, or a close friend either visited or lived in an unfamiliar place (e.g., a college dormitory, an apartment, a sorority or fraternity house, a commune, another region of this country, or a foreign country). Analyze that cultural and social context by considering the following questions:

   a. Who lived there? Identify the cultural and ethnic groups that were represented there.

   b. What languages or dialects did people speak?

   c. What were some of their customs, dress, or foods? Which customs, dress, or foods were similar to yours? Which were different?

   d. What had you read or heard about this place before going there? How did you imagine these impressions would affect the way you'd interact with people there? Now that you've learned more about this new place, do you think your initial impressions were accurate? Explain why or why not.

   e. What were people's initial impressions about you, the member of your family, or your close friend upon arriving in this new place? Identify and describe them. Do you think their impressions were accurate? Explain why or why not.

   f. If you were in that place now, what would people's perceptions of you be? How would they react to your background, speech, customs, dress, and so on?

2. Exchange your narrative with a classmate. How do his or her responses to the questions compare with your own? Are they similar or different?

3. Write about a time when you misjudged your rhetorical situation in a new environment—perhaps you wore inappropriate clothing to a restaurant, for example, or offered meat to a vegetarian. Was the outcome awkward, sad, or funny? What did you learn from the experience? Try to describe what happened and analyze why it happened.

4. Have you ever known someone who never learned to read or write? How did you first discover this information and how did you respond when you realized this? How did that person respond to you afterward? Why? Did you develop a different perspective about literacy afterward? In retrospect, what did this person say or do that may have indicated that he or she was unable to read or write? Using your responses to these questions, write a brief narrative about this person. Incorporate specific details into your story so that your reader can relive your experience and learn about this person through your words. Your reader for this story is a close friend.

> ### Write More About It
>
> Each of these **Issues for Writing** provides you with possible essay subjects in later chapters. For example, in Chapter 9, you will be asked to tell the story of a meaningful event. Your responses to questions (1) and (3) may provide useful notes and drafts for essays about experiences in which other people's languages or dialects, ability to read or write, customs, dress, foods, music, pastimes, and so on were different from yours. In Chapter 10, you will be asked to describe a significant person or place. The stories and descriptions you write in response to questions (1), (2), and (4) may give you strong subjects to develop further in Chapter 10.

THE TERRITORY OF RHETORIC

What do the Declaration of Independence, the Voting Rights Act of 1965, Anita Hill's and Clarence Thomas's testimony regarding sexual harassment, AIDS prevention procedures published for health care workers, Mikhail Gorbachev's resignation speech, obituaries, movie reviews, articles in research journals, and CNN reporter Peter Arnett's accounts of the bombing of Baghdad have in common? All are examples of **rhetoric**. Just what is rhetoric?

During the past 2500 years, the word *rhetoric* has been construed in a great many ways. For some, the term suggests a certain eloquence. For others, it means deceptive ornamentation, as is evident in comments such as "All show, but no substance" and "empty bombast." Passing remarks like these are often attributed to unfulfilled campaign promises made in political speeches, slick use of language and image in advertising, or eyeball-busting research articles written by scholars whose intent seems more to impress than to inform (Lindemann 35).

Perhaps one of the most objectionable examples of deceptive language is **doublespeak**, a term formed from the combination of *newspeak* and *doublethink*. William Lutz, chair of a committee formed by the National Council of Teachers of English to identify contemporary examples of doublespeak, describes this use of rhetoric: "Doublespeak is language which makes the bad seem good, something negative appear positive, and something unpleasant appear attractive, or at least tolerable" (Lutz 17). He cites examples such as the use of *air support* for *bombing*, *energetic disassembly* for *nuclear explosion*, *rapid oxidation* for *nuclear fire*, *unlawful or arbitrary deprivation of life* for *killing*, and *crew transfer containers* to refer to the coffins of the *Challenger* space shuttle astronauts (Lutz 30–43). These uses of rhetoric are dishonest and assume a gullible, docile audience.

Examples of the negative connotations of rhetoric are abundant, but so are the positive meanings associated with the term. As mentioned earlier, historically rhetoric has referred to a person's ability with using language. For instance, the Declaration of Independence is a document that

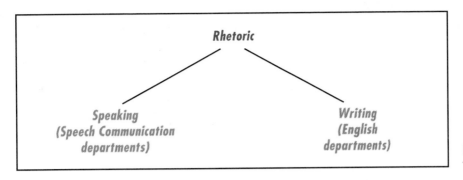

Figure 1.1
Two branches of rhetoric

expresses the American people's common agreement to support certain self-evident truths. People have continued to use language to reveal insights gained from human experience, to report about our world and ourselves, and to persuade people to support ideas and causes (Linde-mann 35–36).

Is rhetoric good or bad? As a discipline (an academic subject of study) and as a skill (an ability, craft, or art), it is neither. The positive and negative connotations of rhetoric arise from the way language is used to express, inform, and persuade others. One person may use doublespeak to misrepresent someone or something, whereas another may use direct, clear language to present accurate information about the subject under discussion. In essence, rhetoric reflects the intent of those who study and use it; if rhetoric is honestly practiced, it is a just and noble art. It is this practice of rhetoric that *A Writer's Repertoire* seeks to teach.

Does rhetoric refer to speaking or writing? In contemporary times, rhetoric encompasses both oral and written language. In fact, today there are rhetoricians who focus only on speech, while others devote their full attention to written texts. You may recognize this dichotomy in the courses offered at your university. As a discipline, rhetoric can be divided into two branches: speaking, and writing or composition, as shown in Figure 1.1.

In antiquity, rhetoric referred only to spoken language; after the Middle Ages, however, as writing became more common, rhetoric included both speaking and writing. Eventually, these two branches became distinct subjects in their own right and thus were commonly taught in different departments in universities, much as they are taught today. As a consequence, if you study the art of speaking in a speech communication course, you may examine the theory and practice of rhetoric as oral language. On the other hand, if you study the art of writing in an English department, you may explore research and theories concerning nonfiction writing, as well as develop your own writing abilities. *A Writer's Repertoire* fits into the latter scenario, for the word *rhetoric* can also refer to books designed to teach students like you about rhetorical principles—both their theories and their applications in a wide range of writing situations.

So, what exactly does *rhetoric* mean? As slippery as the term may be, you will need to understand it in all of its complexity to derive the most benefit from this exploration of rhetoric and writing. The following list gives the function and scope of rhetoric:

1. Rhetoric is both a field of humane study and a pragmatic art; that is, we can read about it as well as practice it.

2. The practice of rhetoric must be viewed as a culturally determined, inter-disciplinary process. Rhetoric enables writers and speakers to design messages for particular audiences and purposes. Since people in various cultures and historical periods are likely to adopt different perspectives on what makes communication effective, rhetoric will accommodate the needs of those who practice it....

3. When we practice rhetoric, we use language, either spoken or written, to "induce cooperation" in an audience.

4. The purpose of rhetoric, inducing cooperation, involves more than mere persuasion, narrowly defined. Discourse which affects an audience, which informs, moves, delights, and teaches, has a rhetorical aim....

5. Rhetoric implies choices, for both the speaker or writer and the audience. When we practice rhetoric we design the message, first by making decisions about our subject, audience, point of view, and purpose. Then, we select our best ideas, the best order in which to present them, and the best resources of language to express them. In other words, we develop strategies for creating an effect in our audience. However, the notion of choice carries with it an important ethical responsibility. Our strategies must be reasonable and honest. Furthermore, the audience must have a choice in responding to the message, must be able to adopt, modify, or reject the message. A burglar who holds a gun to my head and calmly expresses an intention to rob me may induce my cooperation, but not by means of rhetoric. (Lindemann 36–37)

While rhetoric does refer to the study and production of oral and written language, rhetoric in *A Writer's Repertoire* pertains specifically to writing and written texts. (We will, however, trace historical developments in rhetoric that require us to refer to speaking and/or writing. In these cases, we will explicitly identify the change in meaning.) We believe the study of rhetoric allows you to expand your **repertoire**—your storehouse of approaches and abilities—for the writing you will do both in school and on the job.

1. *Rhetoric* has many meanings. Recall two examples of times when you perceived the term in a positive way and two instances when you thought of it in a negative way. Describe each situation, explaining why you interpreted *rhetoric* as either "good" or "bad."

2. In class, form groups of three to five students. Interview two people outside of class as a group to determine what their definition of *rhetoric* is. You might talk with acquaintances or people you know well: professors or students in other courses, co-workers, family members, neighbors, and so on. Be sure to ask your interviewees to give you key examples that illustrate their meaning. Write a group summary of your findings, and make copies of your summary to place in your journal and to distribute to other groups. In class, discuss these summaries. Did interviewees view *rhetoric* as good or bad? Were there key examples that interviewees commonly mentioned? How were their perceptions formed (e.g., from politicians, classical studies, newspapers, television, writing class)?

Write More About It

In Chapter 12, you will explain a key idea or object, and in Chapter 13, you will analyze a historical event, social or cultural trend, technological innovation, or artistic work. Your response to question (2) may help you develop an essay in which you explain or analyze the slippery term *rhetoric*.

THE CANONS OF RHETORIC

Now that you have some ideas about what we mean by rhetoric, we need to turn our attention to the rhetorical canons. To give you some sense of the rich historical tradition of rhetoric and the canons, let's travel back in time to the classical age in Greece and Rome. At that time, rhetoric referred only to speech and was defined primarily as the art of persuasion (Aristotle; Corbett). Although we cannot cover every key idea of rhetoricians such as Aristotle and Cicero, we can selectively discuss some of their major contributions as they relate to the development of the canons.

Rhetoric and the Canons in Classical Times

If you were a student of rhetoric in classical times, you would focus on three types of oratory, arising from various social contexts: policy oratory, legal speaking and debating, and special occasion oratory. These types of oratory still exist today. **Policy oratory** strives to persuade listeners to act

Did you know?

As a discipline and a practical art, rhetoric has had a long and honorable tradition in Western culture. Below are four major classical figures who have made significant contributions to the evolution of rhetoric as we understand it today.

Plato (427–347 B.C.E.) was a Greek philosopher and rhetorician. He wrote a great many works in the form of dramatic dialogues, which illustrate Plato's emphasis on style—the eloquent use of language. His most familiar writings include the *Apology, Phraedrus, Gorgias, Meno, Republic,* and *Epistles.*

A Greek philosopher, psychologist, political thinker, and biologist, **Aristotle** (384–322 B.C.E.) is perhaps best known as the inventor of the science of logic, the father of the syllogism, and the founder of literary criticism. Among his numerous works are the *Rhetoric, Poetics, Nichomachean Ethics, Politics,* and *De anima.*

Cicero (106–43 B.C.E.) was a Roman orator, statesman, barrister, scholar, and writer. Through his writings, he is remembered for his command of Latin and for making contributions in areas such as rhetoric with *De Oratore;* political philosophy with *De Republica;* speculative philosophy with *De Finibus;* and theology with *De Natura Deorum.*

Born in Spain, **Quintilian** (35–95? C.E.) was a Roman writer whose work on rhetoric is one of the most valuable contributions of the ancient world to educational theory and to literary criticism. His most important text is the *Institutio oratoria,* which offers a comprehensive course of instruction for a student from infancy to the time when the student becomes a "complete orator." Quintilian's goal was to mold the virtuous character (ethos) as well as train the mind (logos) and eloquence (pathos) of his students.

in a certain manner or to adopt the speaker's point of view. It involves decisions and events that lie in the future and require some course of action: to go to war, to levy taxes, to enact legislation, or to vote for specific candidates in an upcoming election. **Legal speaking and debating** are used in courtroom settings. Speakers rely on factual arguments as well as precedents (rulings and evidence borne out from past cases) in order to persuade. **Special occasion oratory** refers to speeches of praise or blame made at weddings, award ceremonies, funerals, Congressional hearings, political "roasts," and the like. As such, this third type of oratory is concerned with events and people in the present—the here and now.

In your study of these three types of oratory, you might analyze, compose, and make speeches by following the approach of Cicero (106–43 B.C.E.), a Roman philosopher, orator, and teacher. Cicero wrote treatises on the persuasive effects of speech and is credited with dividing rhetoric into five parts, or **canons,** for educational efficiency: *invention, arrangement, style, memory,* and *delivery* (Corbett 22).

Invention

The first canon of rhetoric, **invention** or **inventio,** concerns the discovery of arguments and other means of persuasion that may be effective in convincing an audience. Following the teaching of the Greek philosopher and rhetorician Aristotle (384–322 B.C.E.), you would be instructed to use both inartistic and artistic proofs to find your evidence. **Inartistic proofs** refer to external sources that require you to consult other knowledge bases such as the testimony of witnesses, information provided by interviewees, and research results in empirical and laboratory reports. In *A Writer's Repertoire,* we will refer to evidence gained from external sources as *knowledge by observation.*

On the other hand, **artistic proofs** refer to rhetorical strategies that enable you to use evidence gained from personal experience. The two major categories of artistic proofs are the topics and the three appeals. The *topoi* or topics help you discover good reasons for arguments. Some common topio are definition, classification and division, comparison and contrast, and cause and effect. We will call evidence gained from personal experience *knowledge by participation.*

Three types of appeals—ethos, logos, and pathos—are another artistic proof you might rely on to help you find evidence. **Ethos** or **ethical appeal** refers to a speaker's character and credibility. As a speaker, you must realize that *who* says something is often more influential than *what* is said. If your listeners perceive you to be honest and qualified to comment on a subject, then your audience considers you to have ethos. When you create a realistic persona whose words "sound" authentic in your speech, your audience views you as both trustworthy and believable.

Logos or **logical appeal** refers to the accuracy and clear reasoning of the speaker. While ethos may overshadow logos on occasion, it actually is established through a speaker's presentation of evidence: to be considered a reasonable, ethical person, you must present reasonable, logical ideas.

So far, we have considered the need for ethical speakers to present reasonable ideas. But to whom do speakers address their speeches? They address the people in their audience, listeners who are not only logical but also emotional. **Pathos** or **emotional appeal** thus refers to information that stirs feelings of joy, sorrow, anger, disgust, and so on in listeners. This appeal involves others in what a speaker is saying. At times, emotional appeals can increase listeners' ability and desire to remember vivid details and repeat key ideas.

Crucial to invention is audience analysis, for without an audience to persuade, you would have no one to affect with your oratory. Analyzing your audience requires that you investigate, for example, the education, age, social background, and professional experience of your listeners. Having gathered all of this evidence, your next task would be to assess your audience's viewpoints against your available evidence to determine which arguments to use in your speech. At this point, you would be ready to consider the next rhetorical canon: arrangement.

Arrangement

After identifying the most appropriate arguments, you would consider the canon of **arrangement (dispositio),** strategies for organizing your ideas according to your audience's needs and expectations. Aristotle taught that texts should have a beginning, middle, and end; more specifically, he wrote that arguments should possess four major sections: the introduction, the outline or narration of the subject (statement of the case), the proofs or arguments for and against the case, and the summary. Cicero later expanded the parts of an argument into the introduction; the background of the issue to be resolved; the argument or outline of the thesis to be proven; proofs or arguments asserting the speaker's position; proofs refuting the opponent's arguments; and a conclusion that reviews the main argument and makes a final appeal to the audience.

Style

Next, you would be instructed to consider your **style** or **elocutio:** that is, your word choice, sentence structure, and sentence length. Just as *rhetoric* means different things to different people, so does *style*. As a student in ancient Greece or Rome, your perception of style would depend on who your teacher was. For example, if you were a student of the Greek philosopher and rhetorician Plato (427–347 B.C.E.), you would be instructed to privilege style. Plato viewed style as the use of "deceitful flattery" (Lindemann 37). Consequently, for Plato effective rhetoric was persuasive because it impressed and moved listeners through the orator's use of emotional, embellished language (pathos).

In contrast, if you were a student of Aristotle, you would be taught that a speech persuades because it is logical and reasonable and makes use of a natural, dignified, and appropriate style; it never calls attention to itself. Aristotle valued evidence (logos) above a style characterized by fancy word choices and elaborate sentences (pathos). If you were a student of the Ciceronian tradition that followed Aristotle, however, you would be taught that your knowledge of your subject (logos) as well as your understanding of human experience and emotion (pathos) would be central to producing effective rhetoric.

If the Roman rhetorician Quintilian (35–95? C.E.) were your teacher, you would view effective rhetoric as that which strikes a balance among logos, pathos, and ethos. That is, Quintilian builds on the Ciceronian tradition by stressing the relationship between good rhetoric (the text) and the good rhetorician (the ethos of the orator). According to Quintilian, being an ethical person (ethos) is as important as marshalling sound evidence (logos) and appealing to your audience's emotions (pathos).

Memory

To give your speech effectively, you would need to commit it to memory, so that your presentation would be smooth, natural, and convincing. As a part of the canon of **memory** or **memoria,** orators established mnemonic devices to enable them to memorize outlines, key words, and difficult phrases in their speeches. A telephone number that spells a pertinent word like 1-800-FLOWERS is a contemporary example of a mnemonic device. Similarly, we are all familiar with abbreviations and acronyms that make it easier to remember long names or titles (NASA for National Aeronautics and Space Administration, AIDS for acquired immunodeficiency syndrome, UNICEF for United Nations International Children's Emergency Fund).

Delivery

Delivery, or **actio,** is the fifth canon; it refers to the dramatic and effective use of gestures, facial expressions, and voice when presenting or giving a speech. Depending on which definition of rhetoric you embrace (honest arguments or deceptive language), delivery can take on a very different emphasis. If you were a student of Plato, the quality of your words would be judged in light of your dramatic performance or the execution of your speech, as well as your verbal embellishment.

Continuing our journey through time, we now catch a glimpse of the influences of classical rhetoric on the medieval and Renaissance ages and beyond.

Redefining the Canons: From Orality to Literacy

In medieval and Renaissance times in Europe, priests used rhetoric to teach listeners about Christianity. In their secular and ecclesiastical courts, the clergy also applied rhetoric in their correspondence to keep records of transactions. In these contexts, the canons of style and delivery gained prominence. Invention was downplayed: the clergy did not see the need for invention to search for arguments; the truths of the Church were clear. In a further shift, medieval and Renaissance clergy and scholars also became concerned with how to apply rhetorical principles to writing. The classical tradition dominated by **orality,** the spoken word, was beginning to yield to **literacy,** the written word (Lindemann 39).

With the advent of the printing press in the fifteenth century, the importance of writing increased rapidly. With the movement from orality to literacy, the ways in which knowledge was recorded, scrutinized, retrieved, and passed on were altered and advanced. Information no longer was transferred from speakers to audiences in speeches or as oral histories. People no longer had to memorize and retell stories to both preserve and pass on secular, religious, and cultural information concerning people and places, fact and fancy, lore and tradition. No longer were selected texts written by hand, requiring long, painstaking efforts. The printing press made mass production of written texts possible, giving large numbers of people access to information as never before, and the spread of education gave them the ability to read. More and more, audiences owned and read written documents such as the Bible. This ascension of the "technologizing of the word" (Ong) would eventually make the canons of memory and delivery irrelevant in the world of the written word. This trend has certainly affected the study of rhetoric and writing—until now.

Rhetoric and the Restoration of the Canons in Contemporary Times

To see how the rhetorical canons have changed in our own time, let's first consider what *rhetoric* means in the twentieth century. In our contemporary culture and community, *rhetoric* refers to "the art or the discipline that deals with the use of [language], either spoken or written, to inform or persuade or motivate an audience, whether that audience is made up of one person or a group of persons" (Corbett 3).

And what of the canons? As stated earlier, the five canons traditionally provided orators with a common set of terms to describe the different aspects of a speech—its planning, production, and analysis. With the development of the printing press, the ways of referring to spoken language were transferred to writing, and the canons of memory and delivery became virtually extinct in modern discussions of rhetoric and writing.

In the move from orality to literacy, the need for memory is either eliminated or absorbed by delivery. For example, the canon of memory reappears in such written forms as highlighted key terms or descriptive words in titles—forms that are associated with delivery. The burden of storing information in the human mind is offset: now information can be written or printed on paper or saved in a computer's memory for long-term storage.

Because computer technology gives many writers the ability to change the appearance of their text (e.g., type design, type size) and to integrate graphics into their page designs, the canon of delivery warrants restoration in contemporary rhetoric and writing (Dragga and Gong 11–15). When we consider how people read, how written documents can be designed, and how technology allows us to produce sophisticated documents, the need to reintegrate delivery into the practice of rhetoric becomes apparent. This is especially true when we consider interactive technological advances in computer hardware and software that enable us to design and manipulate words and illustrations on a page. In *A Writer's Repertoire,* we make a clear distinction between style (i.e., word choice and sentence structure) and delivery (i.e., the appearance of type and illustrations in a text).

In the "contemporary" canons of rhetoric and writing, delivery is restored, and invention no longer entails the discovery of available arguments exclusively. We have access to many types of information, but no two people have exactly the same knowledge, as was assumed in classical times. As a result, invention now refers to the discovery and generation of ideas about a subject, as well as to the various ways that language users come to know those ideas. It is a powerful and crucial canon that we will consider further in Chapter 4. Arrangement (Chapter 5) now involves the organization of a text's major parts—the beginning, middle, and end—as well as the way the sentences within these parts cohere. As we perceive rhetoric and writing today, style entails the standard examination of diction, sentence structure, and sentence length, complemented in Chapter 6 by factors such as subject and audience that influence our ways of expressing ideas. And in Chapter 7, "Memory and Delivery," we consider how the visual representation of words (e.g., type design, type size) and illustrations can enhance the reader's ability to read, comprehend, and recall the meaning of a text.

THE RHETORICAL SITUATION: WRITER, READER, SUBJECT

Writing always occurs in and responds to a rhetorical situation. The **rhetorical situation** represents the dynamic relationship among the subject, writer, and reader that makes communication purposeful and necessary. The **communication triangle** shown in Figure 1.2 illustrates this important rhetorical concept.

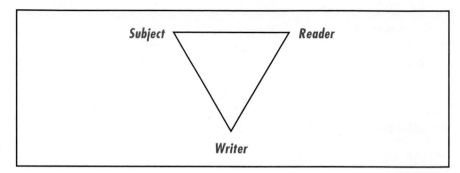

Figure 1.2
The communication triangle
and the rhetorical situation

As you can see, the writer, reader, and subject constitute the three points of the communication triangle; they also constitute the necessary elements in any rhetorical situation. Whenever a writer, reader, and subject interact, they provide a tension or dynamic, creating a rhetorical situation that compels everyone involved to respond.

In identifying a rhetorical situation, let's begin by considering the writer. The **writer** experiences a need or sense of urgency to respond to a situation (Bitzer 6). This response may or may not be rhetorical. For the response to be rhetorical, the writer must have the opportunity to modify the subject or audience in some way. For example, the seasons, death, and natural disasters are all exigencies, certainly, but they cannot be altered by the use of language and thus aren't rhetorical. A writer may propose to abolish tornadoes to no avail: tornadoes will inevitably happen; as a consequence, this proposal is not rhetorical. However, making apologies for the foreboding weather is rhetorical. Likewise, floods and earthquakes are natural disasters that cannot be stopped by words; yet using language to console the survivors of these natural disasters is rhetorical.

Two other elements are necessary for a rhetorical situation. First, the dynamic requires a **reader** or *audience* capable of reading the writer's words and in some way being affected by them—edified, provoked to thought or action, entertained. Situations in which the audience is given no viable choice are not rhetorical. Recall the example of the burglar who holds the gun to your head; this situation is not rhetorical at all. But your testimony at the criminal's trial is rhetorical.

The **subject** completes the rhetorical situation. Simply put, information about a subject compels the writer to discover and communicate that information to the reader. When you see an ad picturing a starving, homeless child, you experience a need to respond in some way. You might contemplate the misery of this child's circumstances. You might investigate how to provide food and shelter for this or some other needy youngster. Or you might take specific action by mailing a check to the organization that ran the ad, by giving time and money as a volunteer for a local children's advocacy group, or by participating in a foster parent, big brother, or big sister program.

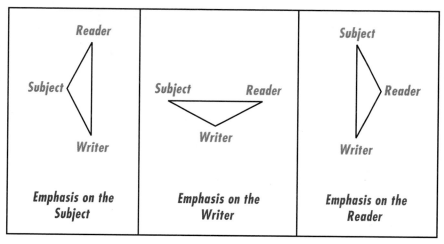

Figure 1.3
Variations in the rhetorical situation

When all three elements of the rhetorical situation interact together in "a proper balance," **rhetorical stance** is achieved (Booth 141). The rhetorical situation can be compared to a rubber band connecting the three parts in the communication triangle. The elasticity of the band makes it possible for each corner to expand and contract, usually accommodating the entire area, no matter how symmetrical or asymmetrical the design. In Figure 1.2, the three corners of the communication triangle are in equilibrium. However, Figure 1.3 illustrates variations in emphasis on the writer, reader, and subject—configurations that are more likely to reflect most rhetorical situations.

The tension created by the rubber band results in the shape that the rubber band assumes. In addition, because of this tension, the rubber band responds flexibly to any shifts in dynamics. In other words, if one corner requires greater area, the tension among all three corners of the triangle is affected, requiring a response that fits the newly defined dimensions of the angles. But that response depends upon the tension created by the design of the three corners. If the rubber band is stretched unreasonably and can't naturally accommodate the distention, it breaks, destroying the basis for a workable rhetorical stance. In this case, the triangle ceases to exist; similarly, if the reader, writer, or subject is removed, the rhetorical situation and the possibility for ethical communication cease as well.

AIMS AND PURPOSES OF WRITING

In classical times, you would analyze, imitate, and produce speeches of persuasion: policy speaking, legal speaking and debating, as well as speeches for special occasions. But, as you know, our notion of rhetoric is quite different. First of all, rhetoric is no longer considered to be exclu-

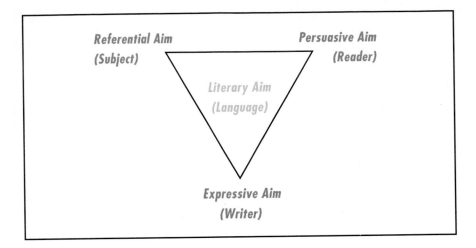

Figure 1.4
Aims and the communication triangle

sively the oral and persuasive use of language. Second, rhetoric isn't classified in terms of policy-making, judicial, and special occasion speeches. Instead, rhetoric in our time is usually classified according to its aims and purposes, as explained by theorist James L. Kinneavy in *A Theory of Discourse.*

For Kinneavy, there are four **aims of writing:** *expressive, referential, persuasive,* and *literary* (18–19, 37–40). These aims derive from the communication triangle—*writer, reader,* and *subject*—which is expanded to include **language**, as illustrated in Figure 1.4 (Kinneavy; Jakobson).

We can illustrate the principle of aims by returning to the rubber band comparison used to illustrate the rhetorical situation. As before, the rubber band extends around the three corners of the communication triangle; its elasticity makes it possible for each corner to expand and contract, usually accommodating the entire area, no matter how symmetrical or asymmetrical the design (see Figure 1.3). The tension created by the rubber band yields various aims of writing.

When a rhetorical situation calls for an emphasis on the writer corner, the *writer* angle becomes wider than the other corners, and the writing aim is expressive. **Expressive aim** writing allows you to explore, define, and refine your own values. For example, suppose your political science professor asks you to write an essay about how you participated in some way in a governmental process or function. After much thought, you decide to compose a personal essay, narrating what you did and saw while you were a college campus volunteer for a candidate running for national office. In addition, you interpret what you were thinking and feeling at that time. Your own perceptions of actually meeting a viable national candidate and of being actively involved in a grassroots political movement represent your personal reality, and the purpose of your essay is to express that reality to your professor.

In writing your essay, you learn of two other classmates who also were volunteers for that candidate and have written about their own experiences on the campaign trail in their hometowns. Your political science professor overhears the three of you comparing stories, anecdotes that illustrate the advantages and disadvantages of the American election process. Your professor joins your discussion and suggests that you work together and collaboratively write another essay in which the three of you analyze and synthesize your various observations and insights. The single-authored essay represents expressive aim writing; the multiple-authored essay does, too. In sum, the purpose of this type of writing is to express—to reflect on and relive the experience and its significance to you.

When the angle of the *subject* corner widens, the situation calls for referential aim writing. **Referential aim** writing, sometimes called expository writing, informs or teaches readers, chiefly by explaining and analyzing its subject. *A Writer's Repertoire* is an example of referential aim writing.

If the *reader* is emphasized, the situation requires **persuasive aim** writing. Almost all writing may be seen as persuasive to some degree; however, when the primary focus is on the reader, the writing is considered primarily persuasive. For the most part, the purpose of persuasive writing is to reveal an individual's position on an issue, propose a solution to a problem, or present an evaluation or assessment of a situation. Persuasive aim texts attempt to convince an audience to view an issue in a certain light, or even to take action on it. For a hostile audience, persuasion may actually convert readers to a different opinion on a subject; for a neutral audience, persuasion may offer readers perspective and a point of view on a subject; and for a friendly audience, persuasion may simply confirm or strengthen readers' convictions and beliefs about an issue.

Literary aim writing comes about when *language* is emphasized rather than the *writer, subject,* or *audience* corners of the triangle. Short stories, poetry, drama, jokes and limericks, and novels are illustrations of this type of "artistic" writing.

Though many consider only literary texts to be *literature,* we make this distinction: all writing, regardless of its aim, is literature. This means that you can be asked to "review the literature" in your field of study, be it the arts, humanities, business, sciences, or engineering. Literature, therefore, is not restricted to "artistic" forms; but writing with a literary aim is. The writer of a literary work is concerned with the effect of language on the reader and therefore attempts above all else to perfect the form that language takes.

As is evident in our rubber band comparison, the shape of the triangle can serve as a visual representation of a particular piece of prose. More specifically, the angles of the three corners can illustrate the **dominant aim**—the corner with the widest angle—and the **subordinate aims**—those corners with narrower angles. In other words, while the basic aims of writing are expressive, referential, persuasive, and literary, these aims may overlap. A referential description of the Civil Rights Institute in Birmingham, Alabama, may include the writer's personal insights and experiences in addition to the impressions of a random sampling of visitors. It may even have persuasive overtones: readers who have never traveled to the museum before may be drawn to its exhibits as a result of reading the personal anecdotes in the description and may add this site to their list of places to visit next summer. Even when aims overlap, however, one aim will emerge as dominant.

For Kinneavy, aims can be likened to general "categories" of writing, somewhat similar to literary genres such as poetry, drama, and fiction. Accordingly, aims possess certain distinctive features. In the chapters that follow, we will identify and explain key features of expressive, referential, and persuasive aim writing.

1. Make a list of three documents that you have written over the past year. Were these texts written for school, for work, or for your personal needs or interests? Identify the primary and subordinate aims of each document.

2. Exchange the list you completed for exercise (1) with someone else in class. If you are working collaboratively in a group, compile your group's lists and swap them with another group's. What various aims are listed? By collecting data in this fashion, are you gaining knowledge by participation, knowledge by observation, or knowledge by participation and observation? Explain your answer.

THE KNOWLEDGE CONTINUUM

Have you ever wondered how you came to know a person, place, or thing? Your mind is like a repository of information with infinite storage space. Comparable to a library or a computer disk, your mind files all of the data you have absorbed through experience. Somehow you manage to retrieve that knowledge when you need it, use new information to modify your ideas, and replace obsolete ideas with fresh ones. But how is it that you can alter and expand your store of knowledge? Throughout recorded history, philosophers of knowledge have grappled with *epistemology,* the nature and origin of knowledge. Rhetoricians have also speculated on the nature of the knower and the known. For Plato, the ornamentation of language made the integrity of the message secondary to the execution or performance of it; that is, the presentation of the message was more important than the message itself. For Aristotle, logic was central to the nature of knowledge. In modern times, psychologists grapple with epistemic issues when they investigate intellectual development, the behaviors and processes that enable organisms to come to know.

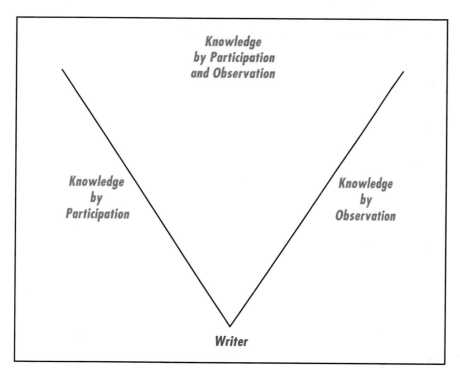

Figure 1.5
The knowledge continuum

While we cannot cover both the philosophy of knowledge and cognitive psychology in their full complexity here, we can help you see their importance to the act of writing by visualizing the sources of knowledge through our **knowledge continuum,** as shown in Figure 1.5 (cf. Bakhtin; Bruner; Piaget; Polyani; Russell; and Vygotsky).

The knowledge continuum is V-shaped and illustrates the spectrum of knowledge structures from the writer's knowledge by participation (the left line) to knowledge by observation (the right line). In this continuum, all knowledge is seen as it relates to the writer, who appears at the intersection of the two lines of knowledge. The world is full of information or knowledge—some discovered, some in the process of being discovered or being revised, and some yet to be discovered. Given the dynamic nature of knowledge (the fact that what we know today may change in light of what we learn tomorrow), how the writer interacts with and acquires data—how the writer comes to know—is crucial. If the writer's search for understanding is inappropriate or inadequate, he or she will probably have difficulty in reasoning and in conveying meaning to others.

Knowledge by participation is information gained from a writer's first-hand experience. In essays informed by this kind of knowing, the main character will be you, for it is through your own experience that you can write about this topic with authority and credibility. You know about your subject through direct, personal interaction, and consequently, you write your essay from the perspective or point of view of a participant.

Knowledge by observation refers to information that a writer gleans from other people's experiences. Such external sources include data collected in interviews, polls and surveys, journal articles, research and annual reports, legislative records, and books. Because you rely purely on the ideas of experts in such essays, those authorities and their findings are often the voices that emerge more prominently than your own. You know about your subject through other people, and consequently, you write your essay from the standpoint of an observer.

The midpoint of the continuum symbolizes the blending of both "internal" and "external" means of finding information. This midpoint represents **knowledge by participation and observation**. This way of knowing is perhaps the most common means by which we learn and generate information.

Whether you gain knowledge of your subject by participation, observation, or both, you may write independently or in collaboration with others. Your decision to single- or coauthor a text will also open up rhetorical choices for the point of view or voice in the resulting essay.

You can visualize how you know and what you know about your subject by listing key words associated with the subject in the appropriate domain on the knowledge continuum. For example, you would record data gained through personal experience in the area to the left; information gained through consulting outside sources would appear in the area to the right. You would list key ideas gained from both participation and observation toward the center. The completed map would represent your field of knowledge about a particular subject.

Figure 1.6 is a map of the knowledge continuum that student writers Rochelle, Melissa, and Mel completed when they wrote "Scholastic In-Aptitude Test," an essay featured in Chapter 16. These collaborators were writing an essay about the SAT, a subject that they know about from personal experience as well as through outside sources. In other words, these writers explored their knowledge by both participation and observation; as a consequence, they recorded what they know about the SAT along the midline, between the participation domain (the left line) and the observation domain (the right line).

Although they are located in the domain of both participation and observation, notice that the key words and ideas are carefully grouped either to the left or right side, suggesting either knowledge by participation or knowledge by observation. By referring to their map, these coauthors could easily determine the quality and quantity of information they discovered about the SAT.

In the writing that you do in response to tasks in the following chapters, we suggest that you use the knowledge continuum to map your key

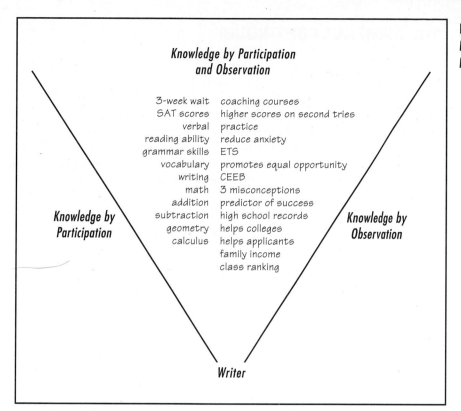

Figure 1.6
Map of Rochelle, Melissa, and Mel's knowledge continuum

ideas so that you can see what types of invention—resources for discovering information—you will require. Moreover, these "illustrations" of your writing will enable you to review your progress throughout the course and thereby provide a means of charting your journey as you develop and expand your writing repertoire.

As you move from the participation end of the continuum to the participation-observation intersection and on to the observation end, you will see the importance of this movement itself. It provides a tangible way of representing and generating different kinds of knowledge; it offers a concrete illustration of the different ways you come to know and thus expand your own databases; it allows you to select a specific strategy in pictorial form so that you can locate the point at which you leave your personal domain of understanding and enter others' domains. It is important to know when this transition has occurred, for when you use the knowledge conceived of and reported by others, you need to document these sources by including in-text parenthetical notes, footnotes, or endnotes as well as bibliographic citations. The knowledge continuum depicts the rich combinations of ways we obtain and meaningfully use our knowledge in the world in which we live, our "universe of discourse" (Moffett).

THE AUDIENCE CONTINUUM

We've referred to the concept of audience throughout this chapter. It is now time to turn our full attention to it and its importance for you as a writer. While there are some theorists who contend that writers needn't concern themselves with audience until the later stages of composing—if even then—there is a broad consensus that writers must be concerned with audience from the outset. Do you consider who will read your writing? If you do, then when do you analyze your readers—before, during, or after you begin writing? How do you analyze your audience? If you don't consider who your readers are, why don't you? In order for you to respond to these questions, you need to take into account how you conceptualize your audience, a question that has long intrigued rhetoricians.

Among the various ways that rhetoricians and writers have conceptualized audience, three key perspectives emerge. You will find that you use these three concepts of audience in isolation or combination at various times throughout your life as a writer (Ede and Lunsford; Kroll).

The first perspective is the **classical view**. This perspective originated in Aristotle's time when orators addressed their speeches directly to their audiences, selecting and arranging ideas primarily for these known listeners. The classical view suggests that readers are external and identifiable, so much so that writers can analyze them in terms of demographic data—classifying them according to their ages, educational levels, socioeconomic conditions, cultural backgrounds, beliefs and attitudes, professional experience, and so on. Whether you write for familiar audiences (i.e., people you know) or for unfamiliar audiences (i.e., people you don't know), you can benefit greatly by adopting the classical perspective. That is, you can analyze specific known individuals in a familiar audience or representative members of an unfamiliar audience.

The **cognitive view**, the second major perspective, is concerned with the way writers transfer their ideas successfully to readers' minds. Instead of analyzing their audience demographically, writers who take the cognitive perspective analyze how people read and process information. In addition, these writers consider their audience's level of motivation: are readers approaching the text with enthusiasm or indifference? As a consequence, these writers focus on strategies that provide memory cues, forecasts of the information to come, "chunking" of ideas into manageable units, signposts such as headings, colors, typefaces, type sizes, and so on, all of which may serve as clues to text content. Any strategy that helps readers to process information appropriately falls within the purview of the cognitive perspective. For example, the chapters in this book contain headings and use different colors to aid you in reading. Each heading forecasts what the particular section or "bloc" of writing is about and indicates how the various sections are ordered to make a logical whole.

Because the goals of this textbook are primarily to inform and educate a large audience of student writers, we as authors cannot possibly know each of you personally. Given the aim of this text and its diverse readership, the book must adopt and reflect the cognitive perspective as well as the classical view.

According to the third perspective, the **social view** of audience, people are engaging in a social act when they write. Writers attempt to communicate with others in their community—their shared world (Britton; Moffett; Piaget; Lunsford; Vygotsky). From birth, we all move through developmental linguistic stages that seem to gain momentum by virtue of the fact that we are social beings. We need interaction with others, and language is one way we can satisfy that need. In our early years, we may seem **egocentric**; we talk about things that we are interested in and in a way that we alone can understand. Egocentric language is language for communicating with yourself and others like you.

As we grow up, we begin to "decenter"—to move outside ourselves so that we can gear our communication to other individuals. **Decentering**, sometimes called **distancing**, allows us to move gradually from audiences who are mirror images of ourselves to audiences who may be only products of our imaginations, readers we don't or can't yet know. We thus progress from being egocentric to **sociocentric**: from speaking with and writing for audiences we know to those we do not know. For this reason, our language development is enhanced significantly when we speak and write in social contexts and in groups. According to theorist Barry Kroll, we can develop a sixth sense—a sharp sense of audience—by interacting with readers and listeners, internalizing their responses. In the chapters to come, you will have the opportunity to write for audiences whose relationship to you ranges from readers who are like you (egocentric) to readers from different cultural, economic, academic, and professional backgrounds (sociocentric).

The **audience continuum** (see Figure 1.7) was designed to help you envision your audience and its relationship to you as a writer. This continuum is a series of arcs that indicate the *proximity* of readers to you, the writer. The smaller arcs positioned close to the writer represent readers like you; the larger, more distant arcs represent readers different from you. As you analyze your audience, you can classify and list your readers according to your shared characteristics, roles, or expertise; then you can "map" your list of readers, placing them in the arc that best approximates their distance from you. In addition, each arc allows you to identify your readers' *level of motivation*, from those who are highly motivated to those with little or no motivation.

Figure 1.8 shows Rochelle, Melissa, and Mel's analysis of the audience for their persuasive essay on the SAT. They consider members of the university and local community to be likely readers of their essay, which argues against the widespread use of the SAT as a key measure for college admissions.

Figure 1.7
The audience continuum

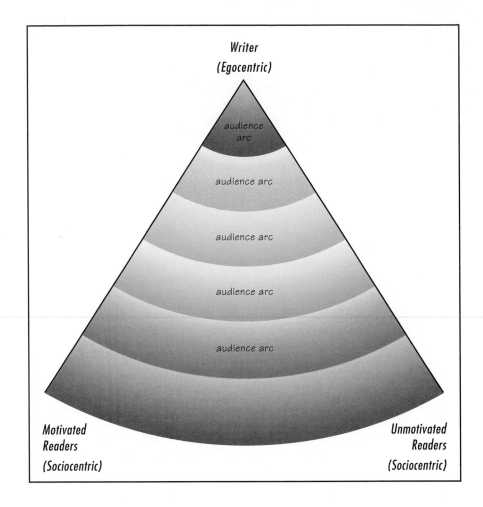

Observe how these coauthors have broken down their audience: first-year college peers as well as high school seniors and juniors; high school administrators, counselors, and teachers; college administrators, counselors, and teachers; parents; those who have taken the SAT; those who have never taken the SAT. The three writers have placed their readers on the audience continuum according to how alike or different these readers may be from them: the more like the writers the readers may be, the closer these readers are to the writer on the map. To complete their map of the audience continuum, the student writers considered their readers' motives or interest level in the SAT. As you can see, they thought that college and high school students would be the most concerned about this subject, and this group was therefore charted on

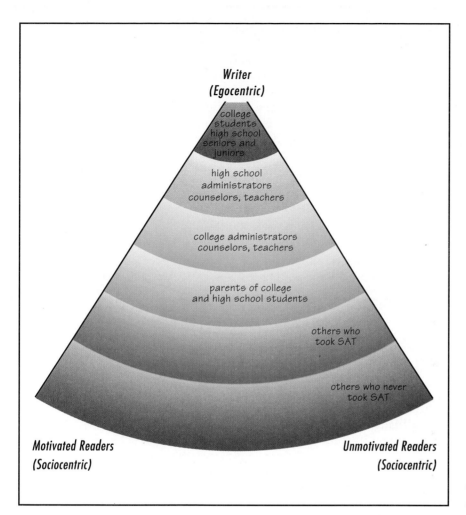

Writer
(Egocentric)

college
students
high school
seniors and
juniors

high school
administrators
counselors, teachers

college administrators
counselors, teachers

parents of college
and high school students

others who
took SAT

others who never
took SAT

Motivated Readers
(Sociocentric)

Unmotivated Readers
(Sociocentric)

Figure 1.8
Map of Rochelle, Melissa, and
Mel's audience continuum

the left side of the audience continuum. On the other hand, those read-ers who have never taken the SAT were projected to be the least moved by this subject and were placed far to the right to suggest their probable lack of interest.

The audience continuum accommodates all three audience perspec-tives—the classical, the cognitive, and the social—and enables you to visualize your readers. Specifically, **mapping** the audience continuum for an essay offers you a means of analyzing your audience in two distinct ways every time you plan and write: your audience's proximity to you and your audience's motivation or interest level toward your subject.

1. Identify three documents that you wrote last week. Your list might include personal, school, and work documents such as forms, letters, homework assignments, tests, and essays. For each item, identify the audience for whom you were writing. Were those readers you knew by name, had worked or socialized with, or met before? Were there some readers you didn't have any clue about, readers you needed to fictionalize or imagine? Were there readers you analyzed according to their individual or group differences (i.e., demographics)? Considering how you conceptualized your audience, how successful do you think each of your documents was? Explain your assessment.

2. Review the list of three documents that you created in question (1). If you are working collaboratively, combine your lists, select two examples of expressive, referential, and persuasive aim writing, and interview the writer of each to determine the following information:

   a.   the rhetorical situation (writer, reader, subject)
   b.   the aim(s) of the writing (expressive, referential, persuasive)

VISUALIZING AND MAPPING THE RHETORICAL SITUATION

Imagine that you are holding two identical paper triangles together, one directly on top of the other. The triangle shape represents the communication triangle, illustrating the dynamic relationship among the key elements of any rhetorical situation—writer, reader, and subject. Now lift the top triangle and flip it downward, as shown in Figure 1.9.

When you "open" the communication triangle in this fashion, you create a way of **visualizing the rhetorical situation**. Derived from the communication triangle, this *map of the rhetorical situation* resembles an hourglass: the top triangle represents the knowledge continuum, and the lower one depicts the audience continuum. The writer is located at the intersection of the two triangles.

On the knowledge continuum, you record what and how you know about your subject; on the audience continuum, you record who your readers are, what their relationship to you may be, and how interested those readers are in your subject. Your knowledge of a subject is filtered through you to your readers. And that's exactly what Rochelle, Melissa, and Mel set out to do when they completed their knowledge and audience continua, shown in Figures 1.6 and 1.8. Figure 1.10 shows what happened when they put their two continua together.

When Rochelle, Melissa, and Mel combined the knowledge continuum and the audience continuum into one graphic, they completed a map of their rhetorical situation: writers, readers, and subject—in this case, knowledge about the SAT. This full map of the rhetorical situation, which originates from the communication triangle, enabled the writers to analyze their list of key words and ideas (subject) in terms of their audience (readers). Does the information in the knowledge continuum reflect a balance of viewpoints and good reasoning? Is the information relevant and logical? How would the specific readers identified on the audience continuum respond to the list of key words in the knowledge continuum? With great enthusiasm? Kind neglect? Open hostility? Given the range of anticipated reader responses, do the writers need to supplement their research? By examining the

Figure 1.9
Visualizing the rhetorical situation

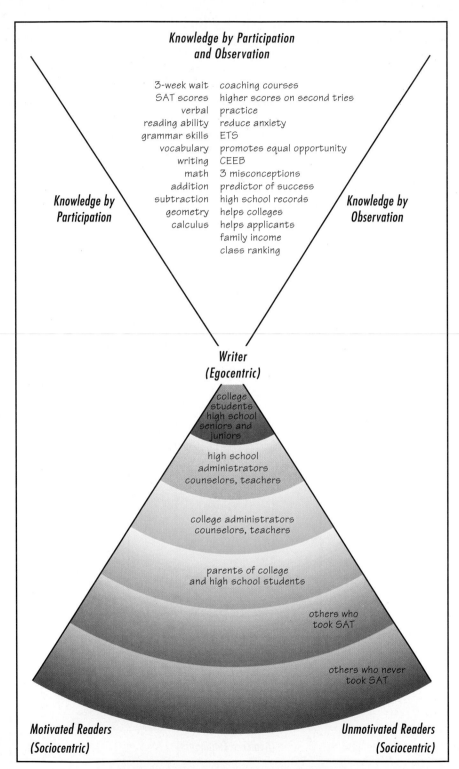

Figure 1.10
A map of Rochelle, Melissa, and Mel's rhetorical situation

In *The Power of Maps* (New York: Guilford Press, 1992), Denis Wood explains and analyzes how realities are created through the construction of maps. According to Wood, when we draw plans for a house, a city, or a landscape, we use them to visualize that structure or space and eventually to guide architects in its development. From mental pictures come maps, and from maps come tangible constructs. Put simply, map making and map reading enable people to construct realities—both imagined and real. Wood writes:

> The world we take for granted—the real world—is made like this, out of the accumulated thought and labor of the past. It is presented to us on the platter of the map, *presented,* that is *made present,* so that whatever is invisible, unattainable, erasable past or future can become part of living . . . *now* . . . *here.* . . . (p. 7)

Past, present, and future knowledge and knowing come together through "the grace of the map" (p. 7).

For example, the Nobel prize–winning novelist William Faulkner created his Yoknapatawpha County in Mississippi by drawing a map of the geographic area with his words. Literary scholars have studied Faulkner's descriptive accounts to construct maps of this rural county. Although Yoknapatawpha was based on landmarks and locations in an actual town—Oxford, Mississippi, in Lafayette County—Faulkner's county is a fiction, a place founded in his imagination. Through their map making, however, readers and scholars have transformed Faulkner's fictional world—everything and everyone there—into a seemingly real place. Such is the power of maps.

Did you know?

dynamics between potential readers and the subject, Rochelle, Melissa, and Mel can start to get a sense of why and how their information must be adjusted so that their essay appeals to readers effectively.

As you engage in your composing processes in the following chapters, you can refer to this map of the rhetorical situation to remind yourself of how important your writing context is. (See Chapters 9–10, 12–13, and 15–17 for additional maps of rhetorical situations.) Map every writing task so that you have a visual conceptualization to guide you as you think, plan, write, rethink, plan, rewrite, and so on. The succession of diagrams will correspond to the various essay drafts and final copies that you produce in this course. It's a good idea to keep all of your diagrams and essays in a file folder, envelope, or binder. Together they will provide you with a record of your travels in the expansive territory called rhetoric.

Issues for Writing

1. Read the following essays: "Twenty-five Steps Away" (Chapter 9); "Discovering Yourself with Myers-Briggs" (Chapter 12); and "Scholastic In-Aptitude Test" (Chapter 16). For each essay, record the following information in your journal:

   a. the rhetorical situation (writer, reader, subject)

   b. the aim(s) of the writing

   c. the particular knowledge structure or way of knowing that the writing would require (knowledge by participation, observation, or participation and observation)

   Look at the maps for these essays. Write a brief journal entry in which you explain these maps of the rhetorical situation to a classmate.

2. In your focus group, select and read an essay from Part VI, identifying the following information:

   a. the rhetorical situation (writer, reader, subject)

   b. the aim(s) of the writing

   c. the particular knowledge structure or way of knowing that the author uses (knowledge by participation, observation, or participation and observation)

   Construct a map of the rhetorical situation for this essay. Your group should be prepared to present and justify your map to your classmates. If your essay was also selected by another group, identify and explain the similarities and differences in your maps.

Write More About It

These **Issues for Writing** may provide you with essay subjects in Chapter 13, where you will be asked to explicate and analyze a historical event, a social or cultural trend, technological innovation, or an artistic work.

---

knowledge by participation and
    observation p. 24
knowledge continuum p. 23
language p. 20
legal speaking and debating p. 13
literacy p. 16
literary aim p. 21
logos or logical appeal p. 14
mapping p. 29
memory or memoria p. 15
orality p. 16
pathos or emotional appeal p. 14
persuasive aim p. 21
Plato p. 12
policy oratory p. 11
Quintilian p. 12

reader p. 18
referential aim p. 21
repertoire p. 8
rhetoric p. 8
rhetorical situation p. 6
rhetorical stance p. 19
social view of audience p. 27
sociocentric p. 27
speaker p. 6
special occasion oratory p. 13
style or elocutio p. 14
subject p. 6
subordinate aims p. 21
visualizing the rhetorical situation
    p. 30
writer p. 18

Works Cited

Aristotle. *Rhetoric.* Trans. W. R. Roberts. New York: The Modern Library, 1954.

Bakhtin, M. M. *The Dialogic Imagination: Four Essays.* Trans. Caryl Emerson and Michael Holquist. Austin: University of Texas, 1981.

Bitzer, Lloyd F. "The Rhetorical Situation." *Philosophy and Rhetoric* 1 (1968): 1–14.

Booth, Wayne. "The Rhetorical Stance." *College Composition and Communication* 14 (1963): 139–145.

Britton, James, et al. *The Development of Writing Abilities* (11–18). London: Macmillan, 1979.

Bruner, Jerome S. *On Knowing.* Cambridge: Harvard, 1979.

Corbett, Edward P. J. *Classical Rhetoric for the Modern Student.* 3rd ed. New York: Oxford, 1990.

Dragga, Sam, and Gwendolyn Gong. *Editing: The Design of Rhetoric.* Amityville: Baywood, 1989.

Ede, Lisa S., and Andrea Lunsford. "Audience Addressed/Audience Invoked: The Role of Audience in Composition Theory and Pedagogy." *College Composition and Communication* 35 (1984): 155–171.

Jakobson, Roman. "Linguistics and Poetics." *Essays on the Language of Literature.* Ed. Seymour Chatman and Samuel L. Levin. Boston: Houghton Mifflin, 1967. 296–322.

Kinneavy, James L. *A Theory of Discourse.* New York: Norton, 1971.

Kroll, Barry. "Writing for Readers: Three Perspectives on Audience." *College Composition and Communication* 35 (1984): 172–185.

Lindemann, Erika. *A Rhetoric for Writing Teachers.* 2nd ed. New York: Oxford, 1987.

Lunsford, Andrea A. "Cognitive Development and the Basic Writer." *College English* 41 (1979): 39–46.

Lutz, William. "Notes Toward a Description of Doublespeak" (Revised). *Doublespeak: A Brief History, Definition, and Bibliography, with a List of Award Winners, 1974–1990.* Ed. Walker Gibson and William Lutz. NCTE Concept Paper No. 2. Urbana: NCTE, 1991.

Moffet, James. *Teaching the Universe of Discourse*. Upper Montclair: Boynton/ Cook, 1983.

Ong, Walter J., S.J. *Orality and Literacy: The Technologizing of the Word*. New York: Methuen, 1982.

Piaget, Jean. *Psychology of Intelligence*. Trans. Malcolm Peircy and D.E. Berlyne. London: Routledge and Paul, 1950.

Polyani, Michael. *Personal Knowledge*. New York: Harper and Row, 1958.

Russell, Bertrand. *The Problems of Philosophy*. London: Oxford, 1959.

Vygotsky, Lev S. *Thought and Language*. Trans. Eugenia Hanfmann and Gertrude Vakar. Cambridge: MIT, 1962.

Wood, Denis. *The Power of Maps*. New York: Guilford Press, 1992.

Composing Processes

*C*hinese School was offered at the Cleveland Chinese Baptist Church every summer. Every weekday morning, school-age Chinese youths from all over the Mississippi Delta congregated in the sandy gravel parking lot between the sanctuary and the Sunday School building, resulting in a class of roughly fifteen students. Parents and children dutifully sat in their cars, windows and doors wide open, until Chan Mook Slew, the preacher and schoolteacher, appeared in the school doorway, smiling and beckoning his students inside.

The day usually began in the "big room," where we all gathered to sing and recite in Chinese. We sang "Yay-Su Oy Gnor" ("Jesus Loves Me") or some other hymns. We repeated in unison some Chinese poetry or scriptures that we had read or memorized for homework. Chan Mook Slew often provided phonetic transcriptions of each character; these English "translations" helped us pronounce the sounds uniformly, but they couldn't mask our Southern accent. And they couldn't accelerate our vocabulary growth, so when we didn't know the Chinese word, we resorted to substituting the English word plus "ah" ("television-ah"), spoken with a Chinese accent. As children, we developed an ear for our own brand of Southern Cantonese dialect. Ironically, we spoke Chinese with an American Southern accent, interspersed with "English-ah" additions, while many of our parents spoke English with Chinese accents.

After our oral lesson, the whole group moved to a small classroom that was perpendicular to the "big room." Here our different ages, competencies, and grade levels were subtly ignored. We sat at desks and were assigned basically the same types of activities. We had more sessions on sounds and learned new vocabulary words. Then, we prepared to write.

Writing in Chinese was like painting to me, and I found myself mesmerized by it. No crayons, pencils, or ballpoint pens needed here; instead, I gingerly removed my brush and inkwell. Chan Mook Slew distributed mimeographed sheets of writing exercises, each page resembling a blank calendar—plain, empty boxes blocked out on the white paper. As we wrote, he would stop at each student's desk, checking the condition of our writing implements, critiquing the position of the hand holding the brush, and demonstrating the type and order of brush strokes for a particular Chinese character in one of the empty spaces on the page. Over and over again, we imitated Chan Mook Slew's brush strokes, and he examined our technique and accuracy.

As we sweated in the Mississippi heat and swatted flies and mosquitoes, our hands swept our brushes across the paper, creating thin and thick lines that eventually would combine to form a character, a Chinese word. Our teacher explained that Chinese characters represent words and ideas that can be combined to create new words and ideas. There is no Chinese alphabet. Instead, pictographs (simple drawings to represent concrete *objects, people, and things) and ideographs (more complex drawings to represent abstract concepts) are used as a system for writing. For example, the character for female or woman is 女 . When combined with the character for child, 子 a new character or symbol is created: 好 , meaning "good."*

For the first time in my young life, I understood how important my marks on a page could be. Although I had been writing English letters, numbers, and words since I was three or four years old, I had never really thought about them as meaning-making symbols before. For some reason, the mechanics of putting letters together to form words did not capture my imagination; but making brush strokes come together to mean something fascinated me. I felt power in my hand, fingers, and brush. (GG)

1. In your journal, write your own opening narrative for this chapter. Your story should focus on a specific time when you were first learning to write. To capture this memory, begin by making lists, taking notes, and outlining the information you can remember. Try to recall as much about your first rhetorical situation as you can: where you were at the time, who was with you, who helped you or offered you feedback, what age you were, why you were writing. Also, try to remember the writing instrument and the kind of paper you used. If you can, ask family or friends what they remember about your learning to write. Did being able to write affect you and your perception of language then? Your narrative should describe and explain this first writing experience.

2. Reread the opening story and your own narrative. Make a list of the ways in which the description of learning to write Chinese is similar to and different from your first memories about writing.

3. Share your list in response to (2) with members of your focus group. In your journal, identify and explain how similar and different the group members' accounts of writing experiences were.

Issues for Writing

Write More About It

These **Issues for Writing** may provide you with essay subjects in later chapters. In Chapter 9, you will tell the story of a meaningful event, and your response to (1) may provide useful notes and a good preliminary narrative to develop further for that writing task. In Chapter 13, you will analyze a historical event, social or cultural trend, technological innovation, or artistic work. Your response to (2)—the analysis of your first writing experience as compared to that described in the opening narrative in this chapter—may lead you to a workable subject for the writing task in Chapter 13.

COMPOSING PROCESSES AND THE CANONS

Until 1971, when researcher and teacher Janet Emig published her study on composing, writing was described as one process that occurred in three stages: prewriting, writing, and rewriting. As this model suggests, each stage was perceived as distinct and separate from the other stages. For example, writers would first prewrite (i.e., think or plan to prepare them to write); then, they would write straight through from beginning to end; last, writers would revise (i.e., edit and proofread, rather than make substantive changes in meaning and organization). Notice that this **linear model** represents a lock-step procedure, precluding interaction among the various stages.

From your own research on writing, does this model accurately represent your composing process? Does it fairly depict the writing processes of people you have interviewed or observed? Our guess is that your response is a resounding "no." This linear model presents writing as a simple, straightforward series of physical behaviors; nothing could be further from the truth.

Composing is not a single, linear process. Instead, composing can more realistically be understood as three overlapping and ongoing processes (a modified version of Flower and Hayes) that interact with the rhetorical canons, as shown in Figure 2.1.

In this model of composing, you can see the relationship between the processes that writers go through when writing (planning, translating, and reviewing) and the divisions of rhetoric (invention, arrangement, style, memory, and delivery). These composing processes are highly **recursive,** which means that

- *Writing processes occur more than once.* For example, writers return to invention frequently to do more planning.

- *More than one process happens at the same time.* Writers will often return to invention to translate and review ideas simultaneously.

The rhetorical canons have already been discussed in Chapter 1 and will be covered in detail in Chapters 4–7; now it's time to focus on composing processes. What do planning, translating, and reviewing entail? Let's take a closer look.

Planning

Planning is a composing process during which you generate information and strategies, as well as set goals and solve problems. To begin, you

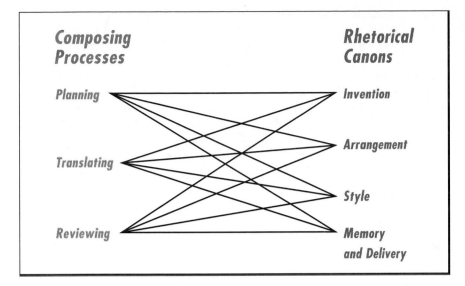

Figure 2.1
Writing: An interactive series
of processes

identify and investigate the rhetorical situation: the writer, the subject, and the audience. In other words, you analyze your writing task. Why are you writing? Who are your readers? Why are your readers interested in this subject? Once you've explored these concerns, you can begin to develop plans for invention, arrangement, style, memory, and delivery as necessary.

For example, when applied to invention, planning allows you to determine strategies for accomplishing the following tasks.

- assessing your knowledge bases (i.e., knowledge by participation, observation, participation and observation)
- retrieving data gained through personal experience
- locating and critically reading available background references
- posing questions and discussing ideas
- conducting informal experiments
- note taking

When applied to arrangement, planning enables you to develop outlines and diagrams; in this way, you can determine how appropriate and logical the information and its organization may be for your readers and your purpose. The planning process also helps you to imagine how to integrate illustrations and use white space to clarify the presentation of your ideas as well as to increase readers' ability to remember your ideas. Generally, planning refers to a continual discovery of your thoughts about a task and the various choices for writing about them.

What are some ways you can go about planning? Perhaps the best way to answer this question is to look at the diverse approaches of other writers. Some write their thoughts out in silence; some talk to themselves; some record their thoughts on a tape recorder; some initiate a dialogue or collaborate with others; others punch their thoughts out on a keyboard to see ideas on a computer screen; still others make handwritten lists or draw pictures of their ideas while watching television. However you prefer to plan is your choice. As a writer, you will think, decide, then think some more. The time you devote to planning will vary from task to task. There may be times when you seem to do very little conscious planning (e.g., while writing essay tests); however, these instances are the exception rather than the rule. What is important is to recognize planning as a process that you—indeed all writers—rely on. Thinking about your options and pondering your approach to planning are a part of this process that you may return to many times while writing.

Translating

Planning generates information, strategies, and goals for composing; in addition, it is a process conducted by and for the writer. Consequently, the planning process may yield **writer-based prose.** On the other hand, the goal of the translating process is to produce writing that is tailored to readers' needs and expectations: **reader-based prose. Translating** refers to the execution of plans into writing that others will understand. It also refers to rewriting or retranslating parts or entire drafts of a paper. Why is this movement from writer-based to reader-based activities so important? How do these two activities differ? In Table 2.1, we've compared them for you (Flower).

Writer-based prose and reader-based prose enjoy a symbiotic relationship. That is, one needs the other to exist and have purpose. While your goal as a college writer is to produce reader-based prose, you shouldn't underestimate the value of writer-based prose. Writer-based prose may contain code words that only you can decipher, chaotic outlines or random notes that only you can organize, and grammatical constructions that you use as informal shorthand; but that's all right. You're writing for yourself—establishing a dialogue with yourself. But your conversation doesn't end here. It extends to your readers. To communicate effectively with others, you must find ways to express your thoughts in language that your readers will find meaningful and that will accurately reflect your ideas.

Table 2.1 Writer-Based Prose to Reader-Based Prose

Writer-Based Prose	Translating Process	Reader-Based Prose
Writing by a writer to and for self	translates Function to →	Writing that represents a conscious attempt to communicate something to readers
Example: "Can't breathe—someone's sitting on my chest. It's gotta work out, or I'll never look them in the eyes again."		"I just completed my midterm exams and I'm so nervous about how well I did on them. If I don't make at least a B in every course, I'll probably lose my scholarship. And if that happens, I'll never be able to look in my parents' eyes again without feeling like a failure."
Chronological order or narrative organization used frequently without regard to rhetorical situation	translates Structure to →	Logical and hierarchical organization of ideas based on rhetorical situation
Example: "I went to the library, met some friends, and read for my history class. Then I saw the time and decided to have a burger for lunch. I went to the food court and noticed some people I knew. They were standing at the pizza counter. I ordered a large pepperoni and never made it back to the library."		"Two places where I always find friends are the library and the food court. Whenever I go to the library to read for my history class, I meet other students in that course. Our professor keeps all of the readings for the class in the Reserved Reading Room, so it's inevitable that I'll visit with someone from that class. And it's inevitable that I'll end up in the food court for lunch or a snack. I'm a member of a support group for first-year students that meets there regularly. As a result, if I go there to eat, I probably won't eat by myself. I'll probably order something that I can share with other group members— usually a large pizza; a burger isn't as easy to divide."
Underdeveloped, ambiguous terms that may hold personal meaning for the writer, not the readers; choices of words and phrases reflect what's going on inside writer's head	translates Language →	Precise and carefully explained word choices that create a shared context with readers
Example: "I brought six heads to your scene. Two were mad-fat, two were T's, and two were punks. The mad-fats got locked. All they said to me was, 'We're Audi.'"		"I brought six people to your party. Two were very popular at school, two were very bookish, and two were rather prudish. The popular, in-group guests became inebriated. As they put on their coats for the long walk home, they nonchalantly informed me that they were leaving."

Like planning, translating is a very flexible and recursive process. Translating does not simply refer to transcribing thought into visible language—words on a page. Translating involves constant experimentation with making meaning—creating sense out of ideas that may come from many sources and take a wide range of forms: intuition, memories, mental pictures, research notes, pencil drawings, tables, and figures. When speaking to other writers about how and when they actually draft, you may recognize some common patterns that link planning and translating. During the planning process, some writers may jot down key phrases or sentences that they want to remember. When their planning seems to be done, they take these ideas and develop them for readers; for these writers, those key ideas provide the foundation for their papers. Other writers report that they just sit down and write their papers from beginning to end, concurrently translating their thoughts into words on the page as they think. Others write preliminary outlines and notes; having worked out their plans, these writers place them out of sight and then begin the task of translating their strategies and goals from memory, reviewing their outlines and notes only when they get stuck. Still other writers report following their extensive outlines point by point when drafting. Some writers proceed very slowly, scrutinizing and refining every word as they write (see "Reviewing" in the next section).

Traditionally, when thinking about translating or drafting, you would automatically think of putting pen to paper. Nowadays, however, you may translate your thoughts into words by typing them into a computer and printing them out. Either way, you produce a "hard copy." What can you realistically expect computers and word processors to do for you? To be candid, they probably won't make you a better writer or thinker; however, they may enhance the way you think or translate thoughts into words. Using a computer may help you to think and write more efficiently, saving time and effort in making your ideas "visible." And, if you're a good typist, you can "translate" at about the same speed as you think or speak.

If translating is the ongoing conversion of writer-based prose into reader-based prose, then how do you know when to translate further or when to stop? We turn to the reviewing process to respond to this question.

Reviewing

Reviewing is a process during which you evaluate ongoing writing plans and translations. When you review your writing, an internal monitor or "inspector" checks what is happening in the writing process and provides feedback that enables you to move from writer-based to reader-based prose. For example, your "inspector" might ask: Is this word too difficult? Is this sentence clear? How can I change the way this section sounds?

During the reviewing process, you read and reread what you are writing to examine your choices in invention, arrangement, style, memory, and delivery. You can add, delete, and rearrange material to produce writing that is more effective for your readers. For many writers, reviewing begins as soon as they start planning. They plan and translate their thought into words; then, in scanning or reviewing what they've written, they retranslate that thought again or move on. Planning and translating work together, one making the other possible. Reviewing triggers the back-and-forth movement between these writer-based and reader-based concerns.

The reviewing process may lead you to revise your purpose in your paper, move "chunks" of writing to other places, scrap some sections, or add new material to others. Or it may lead you to edit wordy sentences and change words and phrases. Reviewing may also lead you to proofread for typographical inconsistencies and errors. Most writers put off most proofreading concerns until after they have attended to their planning and translating processes. Whatever the case, reviewing is a critical process and one that you can refine as you gain experience writing. Why and how is this so? As a writer, your internal monitor gives you a sense of how effective and appropriate your writing is; that is, you develop a sense of how and why a piece of writing may be effective. The sharper your monitor in the reviewing process is, the stronger your reading and writing skills become.

As a result, you may wish to explore how using computers can sharpen your reviewing abilities. Rather than scanning barely legible handwritten pages, you can either review and replan and retranslate as you look at a computer screen, or you can carry out these processes on a printout. After entering changes, you can produce your revised paper, avoiding the burden of retyping it entirely.

In addition, you may also use computer programs that scan your writing, providing data that you can use when revising. For example, some computer programs can flag biased or offensive words, unconventional punctuation and spelling, and jargon (technical or specialized words). And some programs can identify the passive voice or calculate readability scores so that you can replan and possibly retranslate certain sentence structures or rework sentence lengths and word choices to make your writing more accessible for your particular readers.

Whether or not you choose to use computers and software that "review" your writing, it is important that you have a sense of what you can and cannot gain by using this technology. You can gain time, efficiency, and clean hard copies without having to retype earlier drafts. By activating your software's "monitor," you can gain another source of feedback to strengthen your confidence and ability to read and develop your own monitor. This feedback can free you to turn your attention to the operation that computers can't do: thinking.

1. Below is an excerpt from a student writer's journal:

   What a bummer roomie. How did I get a cellmate like Books? Luck of the draw? Lotto, not-o. Books is getting next to me. All Books wants to do is books. And how can I veg-out all night, every night, doing books? I want to party, big time. Books rags about making the marks, making the grades. But, hey, life's gotta have gusto, too. Books gets high from books, and books bring me down. Mutt and Jeff, or what?

   As you can tell, this passage is an example of writer-based prose, full of ambiguous slang and code words. Translate this passage into reader-based prose. In class, compare your translation to your classmates' revisions. How similar are your translations? Based on the translations of this passage, what are some basic distinctions between writer-based and reader-based prose?

2. In your focus group, take turns describing how each of you has typically written formal essay assignments in other classes. As you recall your writing processes, consider the following questions: How did you plan, translate, and review? Did you draft or translate first and then review? Did you make extensive plans first? Did you review and revise on a computer or manually on paper? What did you do when you had trouble getting started? Did you ask other people to read or listen to what you were writing? From this discussion, write a journal entry that summarizes what you learned about your group's writing processes.

3. Describe how you wrote your opening narrative for this chapter. Were your composing processes different because you were writing a personal story in your journal instead of a formal essay assignment? Why or why not?

Write More About It

Exercises (2) and (3) may provide you with essay subjects in later chapters. For example, in Chapter 12, you will explain a key idea or object, and in Chapter 13, you will analyze a historical event, social or cultural trend, technological innovation, or artistic work. Your explanation (Chapter 12) and comparative analysis (Chapter 13) of your writing processes may be promising subjects for these upcoming writing tasks.

While writing can be studied from a predominantly historical perspective (history of writing), there are other perspectives as well. For example, another type of inquiry focuses on writing processes (how people write) and is referred to as **research on composing**. Here are some examples that illustrate some of the different approaches researchers have taken to study writing processes.

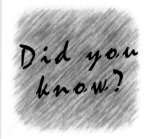

Did you know?

American writer Gertrude Stein collaborated with Leon Solomons to learn more about the relationship between language and the subconscious. Influenced by Harvard psychologist William James, they conducted a study on automatic writing, using a planchette (a triangular board with a pointer supported by two casters and a vertical pencil), which is said to spell out messages from the subconscious as the user lightly grasps it. You can learn more about their findings in their article, "Normal Motor Automatism," published in the September 1896 issue of *The Psychological Review.* (Solomons and Stein; Meyerowitz 14).

Janet Emig used the case-study approach to investigate writing processes. Case studies focus on a limited number of subjects and require a variety of data-gathering methods. In her case study, Emig examined eight high school seniors. Her research data included taped comments of the students, who talked about their thoughts and feelings as they wrote specific assignments; "writing autobiographies," or recollections about reading experiences and writing instruction; and taped interviews on students' "stimulating or traumatic" past writing experiences (v–vi). Emig's study, *The Composing Processes of Twelfth Graders,* represents the first true research on student writing processes. It is a publication of the National Council of Teachers of English (Urbana, 1971).

Sondra Perl examined the writing processes of 20 writing teachers who were enrolled in one of her courses at New York University. Perl gave a writing subject to these writing teachers/students in the morning. Then she asked them to locate a comfortable place where they wouldn't be distracted and to tape their thoughts as they composed aloud later in the day. This assignment provided Perl with oral and written data about these subjects' writing processes; perhaps more important, however, this assignment gave the subjects the chance to discuss and analyze their own writing strategies in subsequent class meetings. Perl's description of her study and observations (e.g., writing is not a regularized, lock-step process) appears in "Understanding Composing," in *College Composition and Communication* 31.4 (1980): 363–369.

George H. Jenson and John K. DeTiberio have explored how a writer's personality type affects his or her writing and learning processes. Jenson and DeTiberio use the Myers-Briggs Type Indicator (MBTI), a psychological instrument that can identify a writer's personality type. The MBTI reveals four basic bipolar dimensions: extroversion-introversion (ways of focusing energy); sensing-intuition (ways of perceiving); thinking-feeling (ways of making decisions); and judging-perceiving (ways of approaching tasks in the outer world). These four types yield sixteen combinations or possible personality types. Jenson and DeTiberio maintain that when student writers know their personality types, they and their teachers can appreciate the different ways these writers compose and learn. Moreover, teachers can adapt their instructional approaches to match their students' different needs more effectively. For a descriptive account of this system and its application, read "Personality and Individual Writing Processes," published in *College Composition and Communication* 35.3 (October 1984): 285–299.

INFLUENCES ON COMPOSING PROCESSES

Have you ever noticed that in your entire life as a writer, rarely have any two writing experiences and processes been exactly the same? Granted, there may have been similarities and some overlap. For every writing task, a writer may automatically practice certain writing habits or rituals such as sharpening a favorite pencil or making a cup of coffee, but the composing processes—their order and frequency—will vary, task to task (McLeod). Why does this happen? Writing always exists in a context, a rhetorical situation. Writers do not compose in a vacuum and readers do not read that writing in a vacuum. As a consequence, composing processes are affected by two types of factors: internal and external influences (see Table 2.2).

Table 2.2 Influences on Composing

Internal Influences	External Influences
physical condition	readers
attitudes and emotional state	task
knowledge	time
	environment
	technology
	collaborators/coauthors

Internal Influences

Internal influences are factors that exist within the writer. No matter how experienced or inexperienced writers may be, they and their composing processes may be either advanced or hampered by their physical, emotional, and intellectual condition at the time of writing (McLeod). Here are some questions associated with these three internal influences:

Physical Condition

- Are you healthy? Do you have a cold, allergies, headache, or some other ailment at the time you're trying to write?
- Is your writing hand sore or cramping?
- If you're typing, are your fingers and wrists tired?
- Are you well rested or fatigued?
- Is there a time of day when you think you write best?
- Is your vision clear or blurry from staring at a computer screen for long periods of time?
- Are your eyes tired from reading?
- Are you hungry or too full?
- Have you consumed high-caffeine products (chocolate, tea, or coffee) that have left you feeling jittery or light-headed?

Attitudes and Emotional State

- Are you excited, neutral, or disinterested in what you're writing?
- Are you confident or apprehensive about this task or about your ability to do this task?
- Do you find yourself daydreaming instead of writing?
- Are you worried or anxious about some person, place, idea, task, and so on?
- Do what you believe and what you have learned from your research correspond? If not, is this a problem for you?

Knowledge

- Do you have enough information to write effectively on your subject?
- Is your research (knowledge by participation, observation, or participation and observation) accurate and thorough?
- Are you familiar with your subject?
- Can you talk extemporaneously about your subject with your peers?

Read More About It

See Chapter 1, pp. 23–24.

External Influences

Writing is a social act. This statement reinforces the notion that the writer, reader, and subject always exist in a rhetorical situation or context. All rhetorical situations suggest a world outside of the writer: **external influences.** Here is an inventory of some external influences that can have an impact on the way a writer composes:

Readers

- Who are your readers? Are they professors, peers, family members, employers, community members?
- Why is your audience going to read your writing?
- What kinds of feedback will readers offer, if any?
- What do your readers already know?
- What kinds of education, work experience, cultural background, socioeconomic status, values, age levels, and so on do your readers have?

Task

- Is your writing task clear?
- Do you consider the task manageable?
- Have you ever responded to a writing task similar to this one? If you have, how did you approach it and how effective was your writing?
- How will that previous experience (or any others) influence you this time?

Time

- How long do you have to complete this writing task?
- If the deadline is near, how will it affect how you plan, translate, and review your writing?
- Does having time limits help or hinder you? How?

Environment

- Are you writing in a familiar or comfortable setting?
- Is there music, talking, street sounds, laughter, crying, or coughing in the background? How does this noise affect you?
- Is the temperature in the room where you are writing too cold or too hot?
- Do you have ample space to write?
- Do you have enough light?

Technology

- Do you prefer to compose by hand or on a typewriter or computer?
- If you prefer to use a computer, is the word processing program you're using user-friendly? Why or why not?
- Are you familiar with the keyboard?
- Does the computer screen seem too bright, producing glare?
- What kind of printer are you using, and how user-friendly is it?
- Have you lost what you've been writing on the computer recently? How often and why?

Collaborators/Coauthors

- Do you like to research and write with others? Why or why not?
- Have you researched or written with these particular people before? What kind of experience was it?
- What are your coauthors' attitudes about working collaboratively?
- What strengths do your collaborators contribute to your group?
- Are your coauthors from cultural and socioeconomic backgrounds different from your own?

So far we've seen that writing may be a different experience for you every time you compose. You, your composing processes, and the text that you produce are continually affected by your rhetorical situation, internal influences, and external influences. Do the following comments sound familiar to you? "It's not my day." "If I had more time to write this. . . ." "I'm taking some medicine for this cold, and I just can't seem to focus." "I'm just not interested in writing about this subject." Such comments reflect how involved you become when you write. At this point, you may be wondering, "If there's no regularity to my writing processes—if I'm going to be subject to influences beyond my control—then why study writing?" This is a fair question.

First, there are some operations that all writers practice. For instance, as a writer, you engage in three basic, ongoing, recursive composing processes: planning, translating, and reviewing. No matter how formal or informal your college writing may be, you will use all three processes. Second, these processes always interact—although freely—with the canons of invention, arrangement, style, memory, and delivery. Third, you can analyze your external and internal influences and, most of the time, alter or realistically cope with them so that they won't significantly impede your writing processes.

As a writer in the act of composing, you are like a ship in the ocean. You float in the water and become a part of the sea, yet you are a separate, independent entity. The waves, wind, and weather help and hinder your progress more at one moment than another. And the way you set your sails and steer, for example, also affects you. For the most part, you stay your course, constantly reviewing your position in case you need to adjust your plans and revise your route. To navigate well, you must recognize sailing processes as well as the dynamic relationship between nature and your ship. Just as a navigator can't predict or control the weather, you can't always control factors that affect you as you write. But being aware of those factors can empower you as a writer: you can anticipate and compensate for them and reach your intended destination.

Issues for Writing

1. Reread the narrative at the beginning of this chapter, and analyze the internal and external influences that may have affected the writer and her writing processes.

2. In a brief essay, describe your own writing rituals or habits. Explain how the internal and external influences listed in Table 2.2 affect you when you write. If there are influences that distract you (e.g., a talkative roommate, poor lighting, confusion about your task), what can you do to alter or compensate for them the next time you write? In your focus group, read your essays and suggest coping strategies for the particular internal and external influences that you have identified.

Index of Key Terms

Works Cited

Emig, Janet. *The Composing Processes of Twelfth Graders*. Urbana: National Council of Teachers of English, 1971.

Flower, Linda. "Writer-Based Prose: A Cognitive Basis for Problems in Writing." *College English* 41.5 (1979): 19–37.

---, and John R. Hayes. "A Cognitive Process Theory of Writing." *College Composition and Communication* 32.4 (1981): 365–387.

Jenson, George H., and John K. DeTiberio. "Personality and Individual Writing Processes." *College Composition and Communication* 35.3 (1984): 285–299.

Lauer, Janice M., and J. William Asher. *Composition Research: Empirical Designs*. New York: Oxford UP, 1988.

McLeod, Susan. "Some Thoughts about Feelings: The Affective Domain and the Writing Process." *College Composition and Communication* 38.4 (1987): 426–435.

Meyerowitz, Patricia, ed. *Gertrude Stein: Writings and Lectures 1909–1945*. Baltimore: Penguin, 1967.

Ong, Walter J., S. J. *The Presence of the Word.* Minneapolis: U of Minnesota P, 1967.

Perl, Sondra. "Understanding Composing." *College Composition and Communication* 31.4 (1980): 363–369.

Smagorinsky, Peter. "The Reliability and Validity of Protocol Analysis." *Written Communication* 6.4 (1989): 463–479.

Solomons, Leon M., and Gertrude Stein. "Normal Motor Automatism." *The Psychological Review* 3 (1896): 492–512.

Collaborative Writing

In my Italian family, during holiday dinners my grandparents and aunts and uncles and cousins would all linger at the table after we finished eating. It was a time for telling stories about their lives and I would listen eagerly, trying to picture my parents as children and my grandparents as parents. For me, the stories described an unfamiliar world. But for the adults, the telling of stories was never only to convey information to the young; it was the opportunity to live through the experience again together, to share once more the memories and the emotions of the event. If my grandfather started to tell a story, such as the time he bought a live turkey for Thanksgiving dinner, but then grew fond of it and refused to kill it, my grandmother or mother or uncle would often interrupt him. Each would offer an important detail that he had omitted. The telling of the story was thus collaborative: my grandfather was the major narrator, but he received assistance (sometimes unwanted assistance) from his family. Because each of them had lived through this same experience or had heard this story many times before, each was able to contribute to the telling.

But after dinner, when my grandfather and I sat alone together on the back porch, he would tell me stories without interruption, narrating individually. I was not a participant in the events he would describe and I had never heard him talk of these things before (such as his immigration to America, his wedding, the birth of my mother). I could contribute nothing to his storytelling, except a pair of big and curious eyes. (SD)

This episode illustrates the difference between collaborative writing and individual writing. If others have participated in the experience that you are discussing, collaborative writing is possible. If others have observed the subject you have observed, collaborative writing is possible. But if you have participated in the experience alone or observed the subject alone, you are the only one who can write about it.

And just as with my grandfather's storytelling, collaborative writing has its advantages and disadvantages. At the dinner table, because the members of my family could contribute important details or clarify the chronology of his narrative, I received a more precise and thorough understanding of the events he described. But often, the adults all spoke at the same time, offering conflicting accounts of the same events, trying to sort out for themselves from their differing recollections what had actually happened years ago. I was left confused. Sometimes, the story remained unfinished, trailing off into a disagreement on a minor issue. Then I was left dissatisfied. On the back porch, with my grandfather narrating alone, I received a coherent and complete story, but I could never be entirely confident that he was remembering correctly or including all the important details.

Issues for Writing

1. In your journal, write a narrative that describes a particular family holiday tradition. On holidays, do you have dinner with your immediate family only? Or do you have friends and relatives as guests? What are the typical subjects of dinner conversation? Who leads or monopolizes the conversation? How is this dinner conversation different from the individual conversations you might have before or after dinner?

2. Answer the following questions: Which holiday dinner do you most look forward to? Which do you least look forward to? Why? How would your answers differ if you were collaborating with members of your family?

Write More About It

In Chapter 9, we will ask you to tell the story of a meaningful event. And in Chapter 10, we will ask you to describe a significant person or place. If you choose to write from knowledge by participation, this exercise could help you to generate ideas for either or both of those essays. For example: Which holiday dinner sticks in your mind as particularly important or enjoyable? Who do you enjoy talking to or listening to during dinner? Who do you try to avoid? Do you go to a special place for holiday dinners?

Collaborative writing also involves different forms and degrees of participation. For example, we—Gwendolyn Gong and Sam Dragga—coauthored this book. We wrote collaboratively, but that collaboration differed from chapter to chapter, and section to section. On some chapters, we wrote the initial version individually—she, in her office at Texas A&M University in College Station, writing one chapter; and I, in my office at Texas Tech University in Lubbock, writing another chapter. We then mailed each other paper and disk versions of the chapters we had written. She edited and revised my materials, and I edited and revised what she had written. We also talked on the telephone frequently, discussing the chapters that we were each working on. And we used electronic mail, sending messages and sections of chapters from one computer to the other. In addition, I would occasionally fly to College Station or Gwen would come to Lubbock to review and revise chapters together as well as to design appropriate exercises and assignments. So although I wrote the first draft of this chapter, the version you are reading represents our combined effort as authors; the same is true of chapters for which Gwen wrote the first draft.

But the collaboration on this book did not stop there. We also received guidance from our editor at HarperCollins College Publishers. She read every word we wrote, editing thoroughly and offering suggestions for revision. A big part of her job was to ensure that this book has a consistent tone and style, even though it was written by two authors. That is, the book needed to read smoothly from chapter to chapter and give the impression of a single voice or at least two harmonious voices. She also mailed each chapter to a board of reviewers—instructors of composition courses at public and private colleges and universities—for their observations and suggestions regarding what we had written. She then compiled and summarized their commentary for us, noting any differences of opinion among the reviewers and drawing up a set of recommendations based, whenever possible, on the opinion of the majority. We, in turn, read both the reviews and the editor's analysis of them and carefully evaluated each of the suggestions. Sometimes we agreed with her analysis and followed her recommendations. At other times we did not agree, and the three of us discussed our differing viewpoints until we arrived at a solution to the problem that we all found satisfactory. As an example of the changes that can occur through this collaborative process, we reprint below the original version of the paragraph you are reading:

> But the collaboration on this book did not stop there. We also received guidance from our editor. Once we were satisfied with a chapter, we sent it to our editor at HarperCollins College Publishers. She read every word we wrote, editing thoroughly and offering suggestions for revision. A big part of her job is to insure that this book, even though it is written by two authors, nevertheless has a consistent tone and style. That is, the book needs to read smoothly from chapter to chapter and give the impression of a single voice or at least two harmonious voices. She also mailed each chapter to a board of ten reviewers at colleges and universities across America for their observations and suggestions regarding what we had written. She then compiled their commentary and summarized it for us. We took this commentary, noted any differences of opinion among the reviewers, evaluated carefully each of the suggestions, and adopted the majority.

But the collaboration did not stop there, either. HarperCollins's sales representatives discussed introductory composition with writing instructors at universities, colleges, and community colleges across the United States; in doing so, the sales representatives gathered suggestions from these instructors regarding subjects that ought to be covered in the ideal composition textbook. Undoubtedly, the instructors developed their suggestions by observing and talking to their students.

We also asked instructors from a variety of schools and geographical regions to use an early version of this book to teach their composition classes for one semester. During and after the course, the instructors and their students provided us with valuable insights on what worked well and what still needed work. Here are some examples of their comments:

"I really like the way this chapter is formatted (boxes, lists, etc.), and I like the diagrams, especially the maps. But I'd like to see more on computers and collaboration."

"This chapter has a lot of difficult material. Include more examples and writing exercises."

"The little stories at the beginning of each chapter give me the feeling that the authors are really speaking to me and sharing themselves with me. It makes the reading more enjoyable and less like a textbook."

"There's a lot of repetition of major points. Is this necessary?"

"The reading here is accessible, but challenging enough that I know I'm actually working with intellectually significant materials. I especially like the explanations of the terminology and theories of writing."

Designers also collaborated on this book. Working individually and collectively, they developed graphics, selected type styles, and laid out the material on each page. Their objective was to make this book a better instructional resource by making it easy to read and easy to use. We also contributed to the design of the book by offering ideas for the cover as well as for appropriate tables and figures.

From start to finish, writing this book has been a collaborative process. And the collaboration is ongoing. Already we are working on a revised version, using the reactions of readers like you to improve our explanations and examples.

1. In your journal, start recording your observations about this book. Identify what you like or dislike. Which explanations did you understand and which confused you? Which examples helped you and which did you consider unnecessary? Be as specific as possible: identify chapters and page numbers.

2. Discuss your observations with the members of your focus group. How do their observations differ from yours? Does this discussion change your opinion of the book?

Write More About It

In the Epilogue, we will ask you to use your observations to write a letter to us—Gwendolyn Gong and Sam Dragga, c/o HarperCollins College Publishers, 10 East 53rd Street, New York, New York 10022-5299—with your suggestions on how we might improve this book.

INDIVIDUAL WRITING VERSUS COLLABORATIVE WRITING

Much of the writing that you do in school and later on the job will be individual: from start to finish you will be the only writer involved. You will come up with the ideas, organize them yourself, compose the first draft, revise it to your liking, and design the final document for your readers. Often, however, you will need to share the responsibilities for creating your research report, book review, essay, or proposal. Sometimes, the collaboration will be extensive: you will work with other writers from start to finish. At other times, you will brainstorm and outline ideas with others, but do most of the writing and editing yourself. That is, individual writing and collaborative writing are not two different types of writing processes, but two different points on a continuum of writing processes.

If you are to collaborate effectively, it is important that you understand a few things about collaborative processes:

- Collaboration has two basic orientations: simultaneous and sequential.
- You already have experience with collaborative communication.
- Collaborative writing improves individual writing abilities.
- Computers have enhanced collaboration.
- Trust is essential to effective collaboration.
- Collaboration is difficult, but worthwhile.

TWO ORIENTATIONS OF COLLABORATION

Collaborative writing has two basic orientations: simultaneous and sequential. In **simultaneous collaboration,** the writers work together at the same time on the same task, usually sitting in the same room. In **sequential collaboration,** the writers divide the tasks (for example, he does the research, she composes, he revises, she edits). Often collaboration involves a mix of the two types. For example, the writers might research and compose separately, then edit together. In writing this book, we adopted a mix of simultaneous and sequential collaborative processes, but the collaboration with the editors and designers at HarperCollins was usually sequential. Before we wrote a chapter, for example, the editors did research on how particular subjects were covered in other composition textbooks. Using this information, we tried to make each chapter distinctive from other books, but comprehensive. Once we finished a chapter, the editors offered suggestions and asked questions. Then we revised. Occasionally, however, we would fly to New York City to sit face to face with the editors and review a particularly difficult chapter, revising it together. It is thus important to emphasize that simultaneous collaboration and sequential collaboration are two different points on a continuum of collaborative processes as opposed to two different types of collaboration.

YOUR EXPERIENCE WITH COLLABORATION

Collaboration is not something new or something with which you have no experience. Every time you have a conversation, face to face or on the telephone, you are engaging in simultaneous collaboration. You and each of the other participants share the responsibility for creating the conversation, like the narratives a family might compose during a holiday dinner. You each act as speaker and listener, together composing a discussion of a subject or series of subjects.

In collaborative writing, the conversation focuses on composing a written discussion of a subject. A lot of talking occurs, a lot of thinking aloud, and a portion of this talking is recorded in writing. Some of the talking is about how to write the essay—how to start it, how to organize it, what points to cover. Some of the talking is about what to write, that is, voicing the words that will compose the written essay. Collaborative writing is thus a complex conversation, but a conversation nevertheless.

Sequential collaboration is something that you have also experienced. If you have ever written something, given it to others to read, and then asked them what they thought about it, you have engaged in sequential collaboration. Or if you have suggested subjects for a friend to write about or edited something that he or she wrote, then you have engaged in sequential collaboration. Sequential collaboration is a tidy process, with clearly identified tasks divided across space and time. For example, he does the writing today in his office, and she does the editing tomorrow in her office. And because collaborators are not required to come together in the same place at the same time, sequential collaboration is often convenient for all participants.

1. Record a conversation with a friend, with his or her permission. Afterward, write out your portion of the conversation. What did you contribute to the conversation? What did your friend contribute? Did either of you dominate the conversation? How? Why? What does this exercise show you about simultaneous collaboration?

2. Ask a friend to revise a paragraph that you have written. What changes does your friend recommend? Do you like or dislike the changes? Why? Or try revising a paragraph that your friend has written. Does he or she like or dislike the changes you recommend? Why? What does this exercise show you about sequential collaboration?

Issues for Writing

COLLABORATION AND INDIVIDUAL WRITING ABILITIES

Collaborative learning has a positive influence on individual abilities. Consider, for example, M. L. J. Abercrombie's research on the training of medical students at the University of London during the 1950s and 1960s. The traditional teaching practice was individualized: that is, each medical student would examine a patient and offer his or her diagnosis to the instructing physician for correction. In *Anatomy of Judgment,* Abercrombie explains how she required medical students to work together in their examination of patients and to develop a single diagnosis through consensus. She discovered that students taught to diagnose patients collaboratively developed good medical judgment more quickly than did students trained in the traditional manner of individual diagnosis. This process of collaborative learning has been adopted by writing teachers and adapted to their classrooms with impressive success (Bruffee; Elbow; Hawkins). Today, students like you are learning to research, organize, write, revise, and edit collaboratively as well as individually.

COMPUTERS AND COLLABORATION

Like almost everything else about writing, collaboration has been considerably improved by the use of computers (Van Pelt and Gillam 186–187), which allow collaborators to communicate their ideas in written language with all the immediacy of spoken language. The earliest human communication was oral, that is, a simultaneous collaboration of speakers and listeners. Without a written language, people communicated ideas through face-to-face conversations. The opportunity to collaborate sequentially depended on the evolution of a written language. With a written language, a writer could compose a rough version of a narrative on Monday, give it to a friend to review on Tuesday, and revise it on Wednesday. While writing permitted sequential collaboration, it also hindered simultaneous collaboration: that is, it was virtually impossible to collaborate *while* writing. Writing was a tedious process of putting words on paper, either manually with a pen or pencil or mechanically with a typewriter. It was a communication process that required more time and more physical and intellectual energy than speaking. And integrating the ideas of two people who were simultaneously writing (composing on different typewriters) could be accomplished only through sequential collaboration and a laborious process of physically cutting apart and piecing together a written document. With written language, as a consequence, the image of the individual man or woman composing in isolation was the dominant perception of how writing occurred. This solitary writer replaced the earlier image of the composer as a speaker, singing songs, reciting stories, or discussing ideas among a gathering of listeners.

The invention of the personal computer has radically altered this association of spoken language with simultaneous collaboration and written language with sequential collaboration. Through what has come to be labeled *groupware* (software and hardware designed for groups), collaboration is possible in each of four situations: collaborators in the same place at the same time, in the same place at different times, in different places at the same time, and in different places at different times (Johansen et al. 16). Today, for example, it is possible through a network of electronically linked computers to carry on a written conversation with a collaborator. Gwen composing at her computer in College Station can send electronic written messages (e-mail) in a matter of seconds to me composing at my computer in Lubbock, and vice versa. And integrating what she writes on her computer with what I write on mine is as simple and quick as a couple of clicks of the mouse button.

Moreover, in a networked computer classroom operating on a system like Daedelus® or Close-Up®, each student can compose at a computer and see scrolling across his or her computer screen everything that everybody else in the class is composing. As the composing continues, the written classroom conversation scrolls on. Students can read what others are writing and then offer their commentary. They can scroll up to an earlier point in the ongoing discussion, responding to that point. They can create smaller conversations among a group of writers interested in a particular issue raised in the classroom conversation. This interchange is a simultaneous written collaboration that is possible only with the computer.

The tedious mechanical process of putting words on paper is thus virtually disappearing. Replacing it is the lightning-quick process of putting words on a computer screen: electronic words are easy to insert, delete, move, copy, and edit. Electronic written words are almost as easy to manipulate as spoken words, thereby eliminating a major hindrance to simultaneous written collaboration.

COLLABORATION AND TRUST

Much of what is known about collaboration has been learned from watching groups in business and industry and learning from their successes and failures (e.g., Ede and Lunsford). The chief lesson of such observations is that trust is critical to a group's success for four reasons (Larson and LaFasto 88–93):

1. Trust keeps a group focused on its objective. If the members of your group trust each other, you can all dedicate yourselves without reservation to the completion of your project.
2. Trust leads to more efficient communication and better cooperation among group members. If you trust your collaborators, you are more willing to speak candidly and directly, without worrying that you or your ideas might be ridiculed.

3. Trust improves the quality of the group's work. If your group establishes a trusting and supportive relationship, you are more likely to inspire and invigorate each other—to bring out the best in each other.

4. Trust encourages members of the group to compensate for each other's weaknesses. If you trust the members of your group, you are confident that each will contribute his or her fair share to the completion of the project; as a consequence, you are more willing to come to each other's aid on difficult jobs.

For example, if your writing group is asked to compose a movie review, you might decide to go to the film together. Sharing this experience will serve to unify your group and build trust. You will all have to trust each other to come to the movie theater on time, each with enough money for his or her ticket. You will all have to trust each other to give the film your complete attention instead of talking or sleeping through it.

You will all have to exchange your opinions of the film, trusting that all insights and interpretations will be genuinely appreciated and seriously considered. And you will have to compose your review, trusting each other to contribute equally to its completion.

With trust, your group's collaboration will be a stimulating and satisfying experience. You will compose a review offering ideas that you would never have discovered or developed individually. Your composing processes will also be more efficient because you will divide the jobs of editing, typing, and duplicating.

Without trust, however, you will be worried. You will worry that your group will be late to the theater. You will be anxious while watching the film, worried that your group is failing to view it closely and critically. You will hesitate to offer your opinions of the film, especially opposing opinions, afraid that your group will dismiss or despise your ideas. You will be suspicious of your group's dedication, worried that you might have to do all the typing if your review is going to be finished by the deadline. And all your worries will leave you distracted—while you view and discuss the film as well as while you compose your review, edit it, type it, and duplicate it. You and your group, as a consequence, will be neither as perceptive nor as efficient as you could be.

THE COMPLEXITIES OF COLLABORATION

Collaboration is often difficult. And because it is difficult, you might be tempted to avoid it. But resist this temptation. In college and on the job, you will be assigned to projects that require the cooperation of a number of individuals—projects that are simply too big for you alone to complete satisfactorily in the time available. Learning to write collaboratively, therefore, is essential to your academic and professional success.

Research on groups in business and industry has helped to identify 12 characteristics of effective teams (Parker 33):

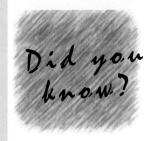

1. Clear purpose: Each member of the team understands the mission or objective, and the team has a plan of action.
2. Informality: The working environment is informal. Team members feel comfortable with the project and with each other. No one is tense or bored.
3. Participation: Discussions are lively and each member of the team has a chance to participate.
4. Listening: Team members listen to each other. They summarize, paraphrase, or ask questions in order to encourage explanation or elaboration.
5. Civilized disagreement: Team members feel comfortable disagreeing with each other. Disagreements are polite and friendly.
6. Consensus decisions: The team arrives at its decisions through discussion of each member's ideas. Team members avoid both formal voting and easy compromises.
7. Open communication: Team members tell each other how they feel about the team's project and the team's operation. They have no secrets or ulterior motives.
8. Clear roles and work assignments: Each member of the team understands the job that he or she is expected to do. Work assignments are fairly distributed and promptly completed.
9. Shared leadership: The responsibilities of leadership rotate periodically among the members of the team.
10. External relations: The team develops a working relationship with the supervisor and with other teams. It displays to those outside the team a distinct identity.
11. Diverse responsibilities: Each member of the team has a special emphasis. The team includes members who emphasize the quality of the document, the setting of objectives, the process of investigating alternatives and building consensus, and the administration of the team.
12. Self-assessment: The team does periodic self-examinations. Each member of the team evaluates how effectively the team is functioning and recommends how it might improve.

In business and industry, you will find three different types of teams operating (Larson and LaFasto 66–69):

1. **tactical teams,** completing a specific task (e.g., construction workers building a bridge)

Issues for Writing

1. Recall your own experiences of working in a group or on a team. Which of the 12 characteristics did your team possess? Which was it missing? What happened as a consequence? Discuss your recollections in your focus group.

2. Make a list of additional characteristics that you think are necessary for groups to function. Discuss your list in your focus group. Develop a list of all the characteristics that your group considers necessary for groups to function.

Write More About It

In Chapter 13, we will ask you to analyze a subject. Your analysis of a team or group might be a good subject. If you write using knowledge by participation and observation, this exercise will help you to generate appropriate information. Your experiences in a group or on a team constitute knowledge by participation, and Parker's list of 12 characteristics is knowledge by observation.

2. **problem-solving teams,** devising solutions to particular problems (e.g., a personnel committee investigating a case of sexual discrimination)
3. **creative teams,** developing new products or services (e.g., engineers designing a new automobile)

Members of tactical teams must be committed to completion of the task, action-oriented, possessed by a sense of urgency, and quickly responsive. Members of problem-solving teams must be conceptual, analytical, practical, and sensitive. And creative team members must be innovative and independent thinkers. A collaborative writing group is especially complex because it incorporates the characteristics of all three types of teams. A writing group is like a tactical team: it has a specific writing assignment to complete by a designated deadline. A writing group is also like a problem-solving team: it has to figure out the most effective way to address the audience and achieve the purpose of the document. And a collaborative writing group is like a creative team, putting together information obtained through experience and observation to compose a written product that did not exist before.

You will also need to know the abilities that are appropriate at each point in the collaborative process; that is, collaborating is neither static nor uniform. It is a dynamic process and typically includes five different operations (Malone 112):

1. defining the issues and objectives
2. developing criteria by which to weigh the alternatives

3. generating alternatives
4. weighing the alternatives against the criteria
5. recording the decision

The different characteristics of the three types of teams are more helpful for some of these operations and less helpful for others (Malone 112–113). In recording the decision, for example, your commitment to completion and your orientation to action are desirable traits. But such characteristics are less important during the careful deliberations over issues and objectives. For that operation, as well as for weighing alternatives, your conceptual and analytical abilities are needed. For devising criteria and generating alternatives, your creativity is important.

An additional complication is that these five operations may occur in a variety of sequences. You might perform the operations in the order listed, but such a simple and linear collaborative process would be unusual. More often, you will cycle through and shift among the five operations several times during the course of your collaboration; that is, the process is recursive. For example, if your group was asked to develop a smoking policy for campus residence halls, it would probably start by defining the issue. Does the policy cover the smoking of cigarettes, cigars, and pipes? Or cigarette smoking only? Will the policy apply to all residence halls or only the residence halls that have received complaints regarding smoking? Your group decides that the smoking policy will cover all types of smoking and all residence halls.

Next your group considers the criteria by which it will assess the alternatives, devising the following list:

1. Is the policy fair to nonsmokers?
2. Is the policy fair to smokers?
3. Does the policy contribute to a healthful environment?
4. Does the policy contribute to a safe environment?

As you consider the criteria, however, you realize that the six new residence halls have sealed windows and centralized air conditioning and the six old residence halls have windows that open and individual heating/cooling room units. It could be fair to nonsmokers to allow smoking in a building with windows that open, but unfair in a building with sealed windows. So your group reviews the objective and decides that it will devise a two-track smoking policy to accommodate the new and old residence halls. You continue creating your criteria and add the following:

5. Does the policy save the school money?
6. Is the policy easy to enforce?

With the criteria established, your group starts to think of alternatives, discussing and investigating available options. One member speaks to a friend at a college that has a smoking policy. Other members go to the library and locate several magazine articles on companies that have instituted smoking policies. From this reading, one member discovers a company that instituted a complicated smoking policy that it later simplified because employees had trouble understanding when and where smoking was prohibited and when and where it was permitted. As a consequence, your group decides to add a new criterion:

7. Is the policy easy to understand?

At this point your group realizes that fairness, a safe and healthful environment, and ease of understanding are more important than money and ease of enforcement. You also estimate that there are more non-smokers than smokers living in campus residence halls. Your group, therefore, organizes the list of criteria according to the following order of importance:

1. Does the policy contribute to a healthful environment?
2. Does the policy contribute to a safe environment?
3. Is the policy fair to nonsmokers?
4. Is the policy fair to smokers?
5. Is the policy easy to understand?
6. Does the policy save the school money?
7. Is the policy easy to enforce?

Your group weighs the alternatives according to each of the seven criteria and arrives at a decision—to recommend that smoking be prohibited in all new residence halls and permitted in all old residence halls. As your group starts to compose the report of its recommendations, one member raises a question regarding the specific number of smokers in campus residence halls. After several telephone calls to the housing office and a quick poll of your residence hall, you estimate that only 15 percent of the men and women in campus residence halls are smokers. Several members of your group claim that distributing this 15 percent throughout the six old residence halls is unfair to the nonsmokers in those buildings. At this point, the writing stops and discussion starts again as your group considers new alternatives and new information. Reviewing all the information your group has collected, you discover that two of the old residence halls constitute approximately 15 percent of the available dormitory rooms on campus. Your group decides, therefore, to recommend that smoking be restricted to these two residence halls. Finally your group writes its report. As it does so, it cycles through the five operations again and again, continuously reviewing its earlier decisions. The process of collaborative writing is thus complex, usually messy, and often frustrating, but it is equally stimulating and satisfying.

1. Which types of groups have you joined (e.g., athletic teams, campus committees, community groups)? How were the groups similar? How did the groups differ? Consider such issues as each group's objective, organization, membership, effectiveness, and location and frequency of meetings. Discuss your recollections in your focus group. Make a list of any similarities or differences among the experiences of your group.

   ### Write More About It

   In Chapter 12, we will ask you to explain the meaning of a subject, such as the term *team*. This exercise will help you to generate ideas using knowledge by participation (your experiences) and knowledge by observation (the experiences of your group's members).

2. If your focus group were asked to review your school's admissions policy, how would you proceed? How would you divide your duties? How would you determine your objectives or develop your criteria? Which of you would do the research? The writing? The editing?

GUIDELINES FOR EFFECTIVE COLLABORATION

To develop the 12 characteristics of effective groups, adopt the following practices:

- Appreciate diversity within your group.
- Develop a group identity.
- Establish fair and considerate participation.
- Avoid a rush to consensus.

Appreciate Diversity Within Your Group

A serious obstacle to effective collaboration is the tendency of participants to establish homogeneous groups. A group of similar individuals with similar experiences is more likely to come to consensus quickly, but possibly hastily. The similarity of the participants signals a similarity of knowledge; each collaborator virtually knows what the others are thinking. This shared perspective and common understanding, however, might also blind the collaborators to opposing opinions or alternative ideas. A group consisting entirely of men, for example, might be insensitive to the views of women, or vice versa. It is therefore important to establish groups comprising men and women of different ethnic and racial heritage as well as different religions and academic fields. Ordinarily, the more diverse the collaborators, the more productive is their collaboration. Each participant brings to the group the unique knowledge that he or she has acquired through participation and observation. The more diverse that knowledge is, the more likely it is that the group will consider a variety of perspectives, investigate all avenues, and identify appropriate solutions (Morgan and Murray 79). For example, among a group of English majors, the student with a business minor or job experience at a copy service might offer a critical insight to the group's discussion of copyright laws. The variety of knowledge and opinions, however, often slows the collaboration process, with more information to exchange, more views to explain and to consider, and more room for differences of opinion. Patience and perseverance are thus critical.

Develop a Group Identity

A group identity or a commitment to the group is essential to effective collaboration. In sequential collaboration, because you have participated in only a portion of the required tasks, it is possible to lose sight of your collaborators' contributions or to consider your efforts the most important contribution to completing the project. Effective collaboration, however, requires that you be sensitive to your collaborators. If you are practicing sequential collaboration, it is often helpful to meet with all participants at the start of the project in order to identify common objectives, determine a satisfactory timetable, build trust, develop an understanding and appreciation of each other, and thereby establish a cohesive writing group that will work harmoniously even though its members will not work together. It is also useful to give your group a name, making this simple problem the first issue that your group addresses. Naming the group might seem silly to you, but giving the participants a common identity helps the group to bond in a small but important way. Moreover, the personality of a group is often different from that of its individual participants and the name the group chooses will often characterize its collective personality. What do you think of a group, for example, that calls itself The Research Group? Sounds serious, doesn't it? What do you think of a group that titles itself Amigos Incorporated? Sounds friendly, doesn't it?

Establish Fair and Considerate Participation

Without fair and considerate participation, collaboration is virtually impossible. In simultaneous collaboration, sometimes a single person dominates the conversation, refusing to share the job of speaking and listening and thus imposing his or her ideas on the other participants. This situation is a monologue as opposed to a genuine dialogue. But typically the most productive conversations allow each participant the opportunity to contribute his or her unique perspective. If you are practicing simultaneous collaboration, give each person a chance to speak and a chance to lead the discussion. You might periodically ask each member to summarize the group's progress and specify the group's direction. It is also important to give each member a chance to record the discussion: it is the person holding the pen or sitting at the keyboard who has the ultimate power to decide which words out of all the talking are recorded in writing.

Equally critical is polite and perceptive listening. Look at the speaker while he or she is speaking. Avoid interrupting. People are more willing to contribute to a discussion if you show that you are paying attention to their opinions. As soon as the speaker is finished, summarize his or her ideas, ask questions, or offer suggestions.

In sequential collaboration, similarly, each collaborator must contribute his or her fair portion to the project. Attention to deadlines is especially important. If the writers miss their deadline, the editors might have to hurry through their editing. Or if the editors are slow to complete their job, the writers might not have enough time to complete the necessary revisions.

If your job is to edit or review the writing, it is essential that you be supportive. Keep your objective in mind: you are trying to guide the writer or writers to improve their writing. If you leave writers feeling humiliated or discouraged, you contribute to discord within your group and diminish the likelihood of a satisfactory revision. In responding to writing, identify passages you like as well as passages you dislike. Explain why you think the passage is effective or ineffective. A writer's successes are potentially as instructive as his or her failures. Avoid comments such as "I like this!" Instead, be specific: "I like the way your words paint a vivid picture!" Similarly, avoid saying "I don't understand this sentence!" Instead, try to specify the cause of your confusion: "In this sentence, I can't tell who the word *he* is referring to."

If you dislike a passage, ask questions or offer the writer suggestions as to how you think it might be changed: "Could this paragraph offer evidence to support your opinion?" or "I think it might help if this paragraph described the house a bit before telling us who lives there."

If possible, avoid you-assertions such as "You've lost me here." Instead, offer I-assertions such as "I'm confused here." You-assertions accuse the writer, whereas I-assertions describe the reader's ability to interpret and appreciate the writing.

In addition, try to direct positive comments to the writer and negative comments to the writing. For example, avoid saying "This is a clear explanation!" Instead, focus on the writer's success: "I think you've done a terrific job of explaining this difficult idea." Similarly, avoid comments such as "I think you need to include more examples." Instead, focus on the failure of the writing: "I think this passage would be easier for me to understand if it included more examples."

Avoid a Rush to Consensus

Effective collaboration is unlikely if you rush to consensus. Often, collaborative groups seize on the first idea mentioned and never consider a second or third idea. Because of their desire to avoid the social discomfort of disagreements, members are often unwilling to criticize the first idea mentioned or offer any alternatives. The result is that the group comes to a quick consensus, but often an unsatisfactory or undeveloped solution to the problem. According to writing researcher Timothy Weiss, "difference and struggle are inherently part of the bridge-building of understanding" (46). If your group is to be genuinely productive, you will need to recognize that conflicting opinions and attitudes within a group are a normal and often beneficial condition. You will also need to distinguish among the three types of group conflict: affective, procedural, and substantive (Putnam).

Affective conflicts are disagreements among incompatible personalities. Social or political differences, for example, might lead to personal hostilities that disrupt or divide your group. Your group can minimize affective conflict by focusing members on their common objectives, by identifying the specific strengths and weaknesses of each group member, and by establishing guidelines for group interaction. For example, your group might start each meeting with a reminder of its task and a review of its accomplishments. You might also ask each member to list his or her strengths and weaknesses as a writer. This self-evaluation process serves as a reminder to the group that everybody is strong in some areas and weak in others and that by working together group members can compensate for each other. Or your group might regulate the opportunity to speak during meetings by passing a pencil among the members: whoever is holding the pencil has the right to speak. This procedure eliminates impolite or unfriendly interruptions and emphasizes the importance of genuine listening. If you allow affective conflicts to divide and disrupt the group, you jeopardize its creativity and productivity.

Procedural conflicts are disagreements about how the business of the group is conducted. Does the group decide issues by a majority vote or by achieving unanimity? Does the group have a leader? Is this a rotating position? Who records the decisions of the group? You should keep in mind that unresolved procedural conflicts can cause or contribute to affective conflicts. Moreover, procedural conflicts are often a mask for affective conflicts; that is, some members of your group may feel more comfortable arguing with each other about what time to hold meetings than airing their private grievances in front of the other members of the group. The easiest way to eliminate procedural conflict is to address policy issues at the first meeting of your group. Allow each member to contribute his or her ideas and arrive at a consensus on policies and procedures with which you can all live and work, including a method for periodically evaluating the group's progress. This important meeting, however, will probably not resolve all procedural conflicts. Other problems that you never anticipated will undoubtedly arise. You should realize that this situation is likely to occur. It does not mean that your group has failed. It does indicate that your group has entered new territory. Before you continue, you should establish a new policy or procedure to guide you.

Substantive conflicts are disagreements regarding the writing project itself. As opposed to affective or procedural conflict, substantive conflict is potentially productive. Your collaborators might have different notions of who the audience is, what the purpose of the document is, which information to include, how to organize that information, which sources to cite, how to phrase a particular idea, or even where to position the page numbers. A disagreement within your group about the appropriate organization of information, for example, will lead your group to consider alternative ways of organizing the ideas. Out of such a consideration of alternatives could come a more appropriate organization as well as a richer understanding of the principles of organization. Without such differences of opinion, your group might have ignored the available alternatives. Voicing substantive disagreements is important to the effectiveness of your group and the success of its collaborative writing. If you dislike a decision of your group, therefore, say so. Your silence contributes nothing. Explain your difference of opinion and why you disagree. Ask your collaborators to explain their ideas, to elaborate, to clarify. Perhaps you will convince them of your solution, perhaps they will convince you of theirs, or perhaps you will all arrive at a new and better solution.

As you explain and negotiate, the following techniques will help you to explore and resolve substantive conflict (Sullivan).

1. *Review your audience.* Sometimes your group will get so caught up in the details of the subject that you will lose your sense of who the readers are, how much they already know about the subject, and how much more they want to know. Reminding yourselves of the readership is often enough to help the group decide, for example, which words to use, how to organize the paragraph, or where to put the definitions.

2. *Review your objective.* As with the sense of audience, it is easy to get so involved in the processes of writing, revising, and editing your document that you lose sight of what you want it to accomplish. If your group is trying to decide, for example, which information to add or delete, you might stop to review your objective. Are you writing to inform your readers of a problem? Are you recommending a solution? Are you trying to inspire action? Such a reminder may help your group arrive at the appropriate decision.

3. *Outline your document.* If you create a model of the document by outlining it, you will help your group to focus on the big picture and the relationship of each part to the whole. Each collaborator will understand how each section should fit with the other sections to create a coherent and cohesive piece of writing. Having a model also allows your group to keep things in perspective; seeing the skeletal

structure of the document makes it easy to remember that negotiating the issue of organization is more important than a disagreement over individual words.

4. *Compare and contrast.* If you compare and contrast your document with similar documents, you can often find solutions to particular problems in the document that your group is writing. If you are trying to persuade your audience that smoking ought to be illegal, for example, it is often instructive to examine documents that make the same or opposing arguments or that discuss the legality or illegality of various other practices. How do these other documents cite sources? How do they start? How do they conclude? What kind of language do they use? How do they handle the transitions between paragraphs? Are these other documents effective? Why or why not? Comparing and contrasting does not mean copying everything from other documents. You will find some techniques that you want to imitate and others that you want to avoid, some that will fit your purpose and audience, and others that will not. You will need to look carefully and choose wisely.

Whenever a disagreement in your group is not quickly resolved, you should determine whether the problem is affective, procedural, or substantive (Burnett). How you resolve your disagreement will depend on the type of conflict you confront.

We will have more suggestions for you in later chapters about how to collaborate effectively on specific documents and during different stages of your writing. We hope this brief introduction to the subject has given you a better understanding of how to work in groups and prepared you for the collaborative writing you will do in school and on the job.

Summary of Guidelines for Effective Collaboration

- Appreciate diversity within your group.

- Develop a group identity.
  Meet with all participants.
  Give your group a name.

- Establish fair and considerate participation.
  Give each person a chance to speak and a chance to lead the discussion.
  Ask each member to summarize the group's progress and specify the group's direction.
  Give each member a chance to record the discussion.
  Look at the speaker.
  Avoid interrupting.

Summarize the speaker's ideas, ask questions, offer suggestions.
Edit and review by making specific and supportive comments that
identify effective as well as ineffective passages.

- Avoid a rush to consensus.
Start each meeting with a reminder of the group's task and a
review of its accomplishments.
Ask each member to list his or her strengths and weaknesses as a
writer.
Regulate the opportunity to speak within the group.
Address policy issues at the first meeting of your group.
Explain your differences of opinion and why you disagree.
Ask your collaborators to explain their ideas, to elaborate, to
clarify.

---

1. In your focus group, consider at least 10 different names for the group. Make a list of all the names you consider. For each name you reject, explain why you reject it. For the name you choose, explain why you chose it.

2. In your focus group, make a list of all the ways in which group members are different from each other. Make a second list of all the ways in which the members of your group are similar to each other. Is your group more heterogeneous or homogeneous?

Issues for Writing

Write More About It

In Chapter 13, we will ask you to compose an analysis of a subject; one subject you might consider is your focus group. This exercise will help you to generate ideas for that analytical essay.

3. In Chapter 9, examine the journal entries of Angela Jordan, Hector Longoria, and Stephanie Sellers, the authors of "United We Stand, Separately We React." What advice would you offer this group of writers?

4. Make a list of your strengths and weaknesses as a member of your focus group. What are the areas of knowledge or expertise that you can contribute to the group? What are the areas where you hope to rely on the knowledge or experience of others? Share your list with the other members of your focus group.

Write More About It

In Chapter 15, we will ask you to assess a subject. You might write a self-evaluation of your contribution to your focus group. This exercise will help you to generate ideas for that essay.

Index of Key Terms

affective conflicts p. 72
creative teams p. 66
problem-solving teams p. 66
procedural conflicts p. 72

sequential collaboration p. 60
simultaneous collaboration p. 60
substantive conflicts p. 73
tactical teams p. 65

Works Cited

Abercrombie, M. L. J. *Anatomy of Judgment*. Harmondsworth, Eng.: Penguin, 1964.

Bruffee, Kenneth. *A Short Course in Writing: Composition, Collaborative Learning, and Constructive Reading*. 4th ed. New York: HarperCollins, 1993.

Burnett, Rebecca E. "Substantive Conflict in a Cooperative Context: A Way to Improve the Collaborative Planning of Workplace Documents." *Technical Communication* 38.4 (1991): 532–539.

Ede, Lisa, and Andrea Lunsford. *Singular Texts, Plural Authors: Perspectives on Collaborative Writing*. Carbondale: Southern Illinois UP, 1990.

Elbow, Peter. *Writing Without Teachers*. New York: Oxford UP, 1973.

Hawkins, Thom. *Group Inquiry Techniques for Teaching Writing*. Urbana: NCTE, 1976.

Johansen, Robert et al. *Leading Business Teams*. Reading: Addison-Wesley, 1991.

Larson, Carl E., and Frank M.J. LaFasto. *Teamwork: What Must Go Right, What Can Go Wrong*. Newbury Park: Sage, 1989.

Malone, Elizabeth L. "Facilitating Groups through Selective Participation: An Example of Collaboration from NASA." *Collaborative Writing in Industry: Investigations in Theory and Practice*. Ed. Mary M. Lay and William M. Karis. Amityville: Baywood, 1991. 109–119.

Morgan, Meg, and Mary Murray. "Insight and Collaborative Writing." *Collaborative Writing in Industry: Investigations in Theory and Practice*. Ed. Mary M. Lay and William M. Karis. Amityville: Baywood, 1991. 64–81.

Parker, Glenn M. *Team Players and Teamwork: The New Competitive Business Strategy*. San Francisco: Jossey-Bass, 1990.

Putnam, Linda L. "Conflict in Group Decision-Making." *Communication and Group Decision-Making*. Ed. Randy Y. Hirokawa and Marshall Scott Poole. Beverly Hills: Sage, 1986. 175–196.

Sullivan, Patricia. "Collaboration Between Organizations: Contributions Outsiders Can Make to Negotiation and Cooperation During Composition." *Technical Communication* 38.4 (1991): 485–492.

Van Pelt, William, and Alice Gillam. "Peer Collaboration and the Computer-Assisted Classroom: Bridging the Gap between Academia and the Workplace." *Collaborative Writing in Industry: Investigations in Theory and Practice*. Ed. Mary M. Lay and William M. Karis. Amityville: Baywood, 1991. 170–205.

Weiss, Timothy. "Bruffee, the Bakhtin Circle, and the Concept of Collaboration." *Collaborative Writing in Industry: Investigations in Theory and Practice*. Ed. Mary M. Lay and William M. Karis. Amityville: Baywood, 1991. 31–48.

PART II

Developing a Writer's Repertoire: Strategies and Techniques

Invention

My family operated a mom-and-pop general store in a rural town called Boyle in the Mississippi Delta, a 185-mile stretch of flat land that extends from Memphis, Tennessee, to Vicksburg, Mississippi. Our store was sandwiched between two unpaved alleys where most of the African-Americans in town lived and owned small businesses, and it faced the post office, City Hall, and the defunct fire station and train depot. Not only did my whole family work in the store, but we also lived in adjoining quarters—quarters connected to the store by a long, narrow kitchen. In a way, the kitchen was the culinary and cultural "bridge" between our Asian world and the Southern world of Caucasians and African-Americans. For it was in our kitchen that Mama prepared dishes from recipes she learned when she was a schoolgirl in Canton, China; and it was in this same kitchen that Mama learned sumptuous Deep South cooking.

In the store, Mama would smile at and chat with customers as she totalled their bills and sacked their items. While customers were paying her, Mama would casually ask them what they were planning to make with the ingredients they were buying. If a customer said these were the fixings for some common dish that Mama already knew or had a recipe for, she'd hand over that person's change directly. However, if a customer revealed that these items were going to be used to make foods that Mama either didn't know how to make or wanted another variation of, she'd slowly hand over the customer's receipt and change, lean over the counter and continue the conversation by asking more about that recipe. If the patron had time, Mama would escort him or her around the store, gathering the ingredients needed to make that particular dish. Then, she'd invite the customer into our kitchen to show her how to make it—right then and there.

This is how Mama learned to cook Southern. Mrs. Velma Lamberson, who ran the café by the bayou, taught Mama how to make the moistest homemade white layer cake covered with slabs of seven-minute frosting and freshly grated coconut, as well as deep-dish Georgia peach pie. Mr. Lester Jones, a retired cotton gin supervisor, showed Mama how to cook venison stew so that it was tender and didn't have a "wild" meat flavor. Mrs. Viola Spurgeon, who once cooked for some of the "old money" families in town, gave Mama lessons on making angel biscuits, iron skillet cornbread, mixed greens and smoked hog jowls, crackling bread, Southern fried chicken, fried catfish, and strawberry-fig preserves. As these folks demonstrated, Mama watched, listened, and asked questions.

After they left, she sometimes wrote down or drew pictures of what she could remember; then, she'd go over to her rack of cookbooks and compare her version to published ones. From that point, she would make these dishes from her memory, cryptic notes and sketches, and senses. She'd carefully examine the texture of whatever she was making, trying to recall how it *tasted, smelled, looked, and felt when Mrs. Lamberson or Mr. Jones or Mrs. Spurgeon made the recipe. In her attempts to figure out how to cook these dishes exactly as others had done in her kitchen, Mama experimented over and over again, modifying ingredients ever so slightly with each try. As a result, she never really made any dish exactly as her mentor did; instead, she prepared dishes in her distinctive way, creating "new" versions of those traditional recipes.*

Mama had a variety of sources and strategies for discovering information about how to prepare Southern cuisine. She learned by watching, interviewing, notetaking, drawing, listening, tasting, smelling, feeling, reading, and doing. She also learned by sharing what she had cooked with other people. (GG)

Similarly, my mother learned to cook by following different sources of information. For example, my mother cooks rice the way she cooks spaghetti. She fills a pot with water, brings it to a boil, and pours in the desired quantity of rice, stirring it occasionally. She samples the rice periodically to determine if it is ready to serve; as soon as it is, she drains the rice through a strainer. She cooks rice in this manner because this is the way her mother cooked rice. The directions on the rice package stipulate using 2 cups of water for each cup of rice, no stirring, cooking until the rice absorbs the water, and no draining, but my mother prefers her mother's method.

For making cannoli (a fried cylinder of sweet dough with a cream filling), however, my mother uses a different source of information. My grandmother rarely bothered with desserts and never with cannoli. The package of cannoli tubes (aluminum cylinders around which the dough is wrapped before immersion in hot oil for frying) offered no recipes for making cannoli—either for the dough or the filling. So my mother relied on the instructions of a neighbor. Over the years she has modified the recipe for the cream filling as she has tasted other people's cannoli and experimented with cookbook or magazine recipes.

For pizzelles (a thin, sweet waffle), my mother uses a third source of information—the package directions. She started making pizzelles before her neighbors, friends, and relatives did. So without a teacher to offer instruction, she used the recipe that arrived with the pizzelle iron (a small appliance similar to a waffle iron). She has sampled other people's pizzelles over the years, but swears that the recipe she uses—the recipe on the package—is superior. (SD)

These were our mothers' invention strategies for expanding their cooking repertoires—interactive ways of knowing that are similar to ones you can use to expand your writing repertoire.

1. In your journal, write your own opening narrative about a member of your family or a friend who has a special talent. How has that person developed that ability? Through knowledge by participation? Observation? Participation and observation? In your essay, be sure to explain the significance of this talent to you and that relative.

2. In your focus group, make a list of the different factors that each of you considered and the various strategies you used in deciding to enroll in the school you're now attending. How did your current rhetorical situations affect your decision making? Were there any factors or strategies that others considered or used that you might use in making future decisions? Were there any friends or family members who helped you make your decision? Explain your response in your journal.

Write More About It

In Chapter 10, you'll write about a character and his or her significance to you. And in Chapters 12 and 13, you'll explain and analyze a subject. Your responses to these two exercises may be developed into a fuller essay for these writing tasks, or it may lead you to consider other subjects to write about.

This chapter focuses on the canon of invention. **Invention** is the art of discovering and generating information about a subject. Before you can generate information, of course, you need to find a subject to write about. You've probably heard the adage: You write best about subjects that you know well. In Chapters 8, 11, and 14, you'll learn more about how to select subjects to write about—subjects that you have prior knowledge about as well as subjects that are brand new to you. You'll practice choosing ideas to write about based on different writing situations that we'll identify and describe for you.

But for now, how do you come to know and thus to write about different subjects? As the knowledge continuum presented in Chapter 1 reveals, your knowledge may derive from firsthand experience (knowledge by participation), outside sources (knowledge by observation), or a combination of both (knowledge by participation and observation).

Invention, however, involves more than the knowledge continuum. It also refers to the discovery and generation of information within a context—a rhetorical situation. Invention requires you to do the following:

- identify your aim and purpose
- analyze and map your rhetorical situation (the knowledge continuum and the audience continuum)
- research and discover information about your subject

This information will constantly be shaped by your recursive writing processes (planning, translating, and reviewing). Here is an example of how writing processes interact with the canon of invention. Invention guides you to locate and retrieve data concerning your aim and purpose, readers, and appeals. You *review* information generated by invention and *plan* an outline or organization for writing; with this tentative plan in mind, you may *translate* or incorporate that information into your text. The ongoing interaction among these three writing processes and invention continues until you either finish your text or submit it to someone else to read and comment on. As you gather more information and evaluate it, you will continue to revise the corresponding maps of the knowledge continuum.

We turn now to examine the three requirements for invention so you can add them to your repertoire.

AIM AND PURPOSE

As we pointed out in Chapter 1, everything you write has **aim** and **purpose.** You respond to a rhetorical situation by creating a text whose intended goal is to achieve some effect on its readers. Table 4.1 outlines three aims that a text can have, along with the different purposes of each aim.

The majority of the writing that you will do in college and in your professional life has at least one of these three aims. As a college student, you may write a journal entry or a letter to your family, recounting how challenged you felt when you attended your first college class (expressive). Or you may write an essay for a class, describing and explaining recent satellite photographs that provide support for the Big Bang theory of the universe (referential). Or, as a college student, you may propose

Table 4.1 Writing Aims and Purposes

Aim	Purpose
Expressive (stress on the writer corner)	To communicate to readers the value or significance that a writer attributes to a person, place, thing, or event
Referential (stress on the subject corner)	To inform or teach readers by reporting, explaining, or analyzing ideas, people, places, things, events
Persuasive (stress on the audience corner)	To convince readers to support a certain position on an issue, proposed solution to a problem, or evaluation of a person or situation

measures to discourage teenagers from bringing weapons to public school, thus decreasing violence there (persuasive). As a professional, you may write similar kinds of texts: an entry in your sales log, describing how you felt after visiting a new customer; a progress report, presenting the status of a project to computerize a hospital's pharmaceuticals and prescriptions; or a feasibility study, recommending the best location for a new community center. Of course, in your daily life as a citizen in your community, you have many opportunities to tell stories, give directions, explain ideas, and champion causes. No matter who you are, you will most likely write expressive, referential, and persuasive documents (Kinneavy 6).

Except for expressive aim writing, these aims and purposes frequently occur in combination. For example, you may write a persuasive letter to the editor of your campus newspaper, calling for readers to protest proposed tuition increases; however, to make your case, you explain the history and meaning of the proposal (referential) as well as tell a personal story about the hardships previous tuition hikes have caused (expressive). While your letter would be primarily persuasive, it would also have subordinate referential and expressive aims. And these subordinate aims would affect the type and amount of information you would include in your letter. In this case, your persuasive text would include many objective facts as well as some personal information.

Identifying the **dominant and subordinate aims** and purposes of your text answers the key question: Why are you writing? By asking this question and checking your response to it throughout your writing processes, you can better maintain your focus. At the outset of a project, you may be uncertain of your reason for writing; as you learn more about your subject, your purpose may change, and you may develop a different subordinate aim as your subject becomes clearer. Like your writing processes, your commitment to aim and purpose needs to be flexible. However, we have discovered that when writers begin by identifying their aims and purposes as well as developing maps of their knowledge continuum for writing tasks, they usually compose more effectively and efficiently.

1. What kinds of writing tasks are assigned in the other courses you are taking? What are the aims and purposes of these assignments? Compare some sample assignments with those of the other members of your focus group.

2. Read the following essays: "The Wall" (Chapter 10), "Stress and the College Student" (Chapter 12), and "Shelter Is Available" (Chapter 16). Identify the dominant aims, subordinate aims (as applicable), and purposes of these essays.

THE RHETORICAL SITUATION

When you write, you are responding to a **rhetorical situation.** Writing tasks often suggest possible aims, purposes, subjects, and readers. Once these elements are identified, you begin to develop your response to that context. You start to consider what you know about your subject and audience; moreover, you analyze how you can find out more about them. Situation is central to the development of your response and your need to search for information about your subject. Consequently, for any writing task, first analyze your rhetorical situation informally *before* you begin to research your subject formally. Researching without understanding your context is like responding before you know your assignment. As you learn more about your subject and readers, you will have a clearer idea about how to evaluate the quality and quantity of your information.

To clarify your relationship with your subject and readers in a concrete way, try **mapping your rhetorical situation.** As you learn more about your subject and readers and as you compose working drafts of your text, you can continue to revise your map. Throughout your writing processes, use the **knowledge continuum** to locate your subject and ways of researching it, and chart your readers and their motivation by using the **audience continuum.** When the knowledge continuum and audience continuum are consolidated into one graphic, they create a picture of the rhetorical situation: writer, knowledge about a subject, and readers.

Figure 4.1 is a map of a student writer's rhetorical situation, in this case the context for "Filthy Grins," an essay about a child custody case, written by Christine Wilson, that we feature in Chapter 9.

After several revisions, Christine produces this map of the audience continuum for her essay. "Filthy Grins" is written for an audience of general adult readers. Christine analyzes her readers by classifying them according to their educational levels. In discussing her readers with her group, she divides them as follows: those with no high school education, those with some high school education, high school graduates, those with some college education, and college graduates. To Christine, it seems that college students (who are in close proximity and similar to the writer) and high school graduates won't ordinarily be much interested in the subject of child custody. To reach these readers, Christine realizes she must work hard to motivate them by using a catchy title, an inviting introduction, vivid details, and fully developed characters. According to this map, high school students and college graduates—those readers in the arcs more distant from Christine—might best identify with or be compelled by the conditions and plight of this family. As her analysis of the rhetorical situation becomes clearer, Christine refines her map of the audience continuum, a picture of her readers' proximity to her as well as their potential interest in her subject.

Figure 4.1
The continua combined: A map of Christine's rhetorical situation

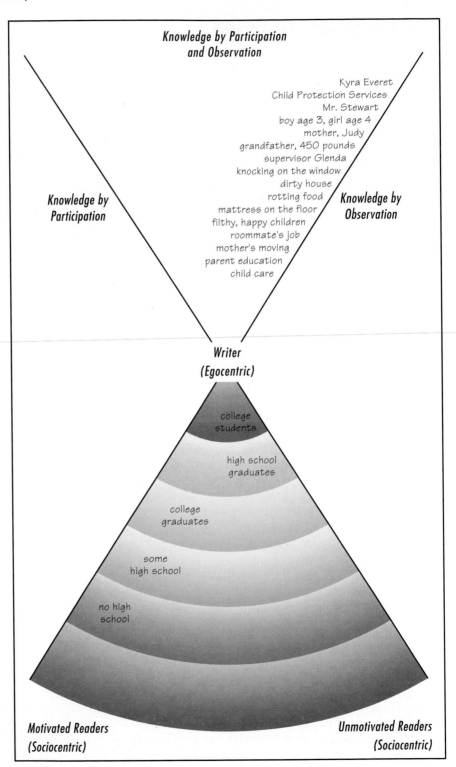

Knowledge by Participation
and Observation

Kyra Everet
Child Protection Services
Mr. Stewart
boy age 3, girl age 4
mother, Judy
grandfather, 450 pounds
supervisor Glenda
knocking on the window
dirty house
rotting food
mattress on the floor
filthy, happy children
roommate's job
mother's moving
parent education
child care

Knowledge by
Participation

Knowledge by
Observation

Writer
(Egocentric)

college students

high school graduates

college graduates

some high school

no high school

Motivated Readers
(Sociocentric)

Unmotivated Readers
(Sociocentric)

As Figure 4.1 shows, Christine uses the upper portion of the map to focus on and make a list of key words as she goes through the process of learning and generating information about her subject. She could have chosen to research this Child Protective Services case in a number of ways. For instance, she could have grounded her knowledge base in participation, employing actual field work, or in participation and observation, combining direct and indirect ways of knowing. Instead, however, Christine researches this case by observation exclusively: she interviews others and reads a newspaper article. As she reviews her list of key words, Christine can check to see that the information on the "knowledge by observation" side of her map originates from outside sources. In addition, as she revises and refines her map, she can evaluate the quality and quantity of the key terms or ideas on the observation side of the continuum. That is, Christine can see who her readers are, how interested they are in this subject, and how similar to or different from her they may be. Then, she can take the information in her knowledge continuum and ask herself some key questions:

- Have I provided enough background and new information for these readers?

- Which key terms or key ideas do readers probably already know about?

- Which key terms or key ideas are new and might augment readers' current understanding of this subject?

- Does this information create in readers a need to know more about this subject?

- If I were a representative member of these different groups of readers, what questions or information needs would I want the writer to address?

By examining how readers on her audience continuum might respond to the available information on her knowledge continuum, Christine can expand her research efforts to include direct experience (knowledge by participation) or investigate additional external sources such as pamphlets or brochures from the Department of Human Services. If the key words on the map don't come from outside sources, she can move the ideas to the "knowledge by participation" side.

By combining her knowledge and audience continua, Christine has created a complete map that presents the possible interaction among herself, her readers, and her knowledge about her subject. Like Christine, you can also develop maps of your rhetorical situations.

The ongoing process of mapping the rhetorical situation for a writing task allows you to do the following:

- analyze your readers (who they are and what their relationship to you may be)

- discover strategies for knowing about your subject (how you know about your subject)

- generate and review key ideas pertaining to your subject (what you know about your subject)

- determine writing strategies and appeals, based on how readers (audience continuum) might respond to information about your subject (knowledge continuum)

As you compose, create a map of your rhetorical situation, and refer to it to remind yourself of your writing context. So that you can get a better sense of how to use the continua to develop a map of the rhetorical situation, let's consider each continuum further.

Read More About It

See Chapter 1, p. 23.

Your Subject and the Knowledge Continuum

The knowledge continuum illustrates the spectrum of knowledge structures, from the writer's knowledge by participation to knowledge by observation. In the continuum, all knowledge (i.e., information about subjects) is seen as it relates to the writer, who is situated at the intersection of the two lines of knowledge.

To review, **knowledge by participation** refers to information gained from a writer's firsthand experience or direct, personal interaction. If you write about a subject that you know so well that no external or outside sources are needed, then you would record details about your subject in the knowledge by participation domain.

Knowledge by observation refers to information that a writer gleans from other people's experiences or outside sources. If you write about a subject that you understand exclusively through external sources, then you would locate your subject in the knowledge by observation domain.

Likewise, if you write about a subject that you understand through both direct and indirect means, then you would graph that information in the center domain. That is, you would map the subject somewhere in the midpoint along the continuum. This center domain symbolizes the combination of "internal" and "external" ways of understanding called **knowledge by participation and observation.** This way of knowing is perhaps the most common means by which we learn and generate information.

The knowledge continuum helps you visualize *how you know* and *what you know* about your subject. For example, in Figure 4.2, we review Christine's map of the knowledge continuum.

Christine gained her knowledge about this particular Child Protection Services case by observation, so she lists the key words pertaining to this subject in the observation domain. Christine researched this story without having actually been at the scene where the incident took place. She interviewed her roommate—a social worker for Child Protection Services—and her roommate's supervisor. She also read a newspaper article about this

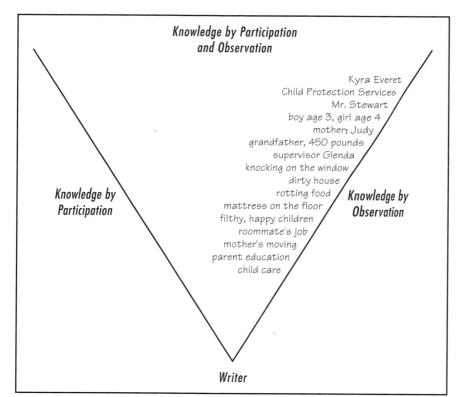

*Knowledge by Participation
and Observation*

Kyra Everet
Child Protection Services
Mr. Stewart
boy age 3, girl age 4
mother; Judy
grandfather, 450 pounds
supervisor Glenda
knocking on the window
dirty house
rotting food
mattress on the floor
filthy, happy children
roommate's job
mother's moving
parent education
child care

*Knowledge by
Participation*

*Knowledge by
Observation*

Writer

Figure 4.2 Christine's map of the knowledge continuum

custody case. Mapping the knowledge continuum in this way allows Christine to see not only what she knows about her subject, but how she gained that knowledge. Thus, she can determine whether or not she has any gaps in her research. And, when she combines her knowledge and audience continua, Christine can consider how her readers might respond to the information in her map. She can see how she might arrange her key ideas in her essay and analyze how they will further her readers' knowledge and interest in this subject.

Your Readers and the Audience Continuum

A text's intended audience influences its aim and purpose, for all writing is produced for some readership. It is thus important for you to analyze your readers carefully. In Chapter 1, we introduced three perspectives on audience: *classical, cognitive,* and *social.* Before going further, let's review in Table 4.2 the meaning of the three perspectives (Kroll) and some of the strategies they suggest.

The three views of audience listed in Table 4.2 require you to identify your readers in some way. As the classical perspective implies, you can write for specific known individuals in a familiar audience or representative members of an unfamiliar audience. For example, let's suppose you are writing a letter to four of your high school friends who decided to attend a college different from yours. You and your readers share experiences, education, age, interests, acquaintances, and so on.

Table 4.2 Perspectives on Audience

Audience Perspective	Meaning and Recommended Strategies
Classical Perspective	Assumes that you may personally know your readers; they are like you, or they are people you know by name, have met, or have worked or socialized with. *Suggests you analyze demographics of identified readers.*
Cognitive Perspective	Considers how your audience reads and processes the text. *Suggests you provide memory cues, forecast information, organize information in manageable units or chunks, integrate illustrations, and use visual signposts such as headings, colors, type designs, type sizes.*
Social Perspective	Posits that you may not personally know your readers; they may be different from you, and they may be a heterogeneous collection of individuals. *Suggests you role play, imagining these readers' informational needs, motives or reasons to read your text, ways of reading.*

Use the audience continuum to visualize this audience and its relationship to you. The audience continuum contains a series of arcs that indicate the proximity of readers to the writer. When you are similar to your readers, you map the audience within the smaller arcs. When you are different from your readers, you map the audience within the larger arcs. You also gauge how motivated your audience is by locating more enthusiastic readers toward the left side of the arc and less enthusiastic readers toward the right.

The audience continuum that illustrates your four high school readers and their relationship to you might look like Figure 4.3.

If you don't really know your audience, however, identify your readership by classifying them as representative members of a certain group. You can analyze your readers according to their shared characteristics,

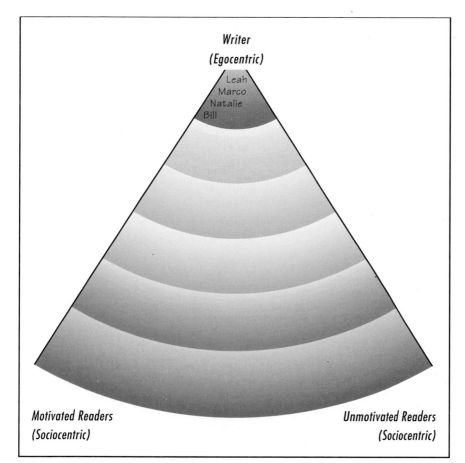

Figure 4.3 Mapping a familiar audience

occupation, professional affiliation, gender, or ethnicity (Ong). For example, a university audience may be classified in terms of their roles as
undergraduates, graduate students, professors, or administrators. Again,
you should also gauge their level of motivation. If you are discussing
security in your dormitory, the audience continuum might look something
like the one in Figure 4.4.

Another way of identifying a university audience may be according to
their expertise in a subject area: general readers have little or no background; novices are taking or have taken some courses in the subject
area; experts teach and conduct research in this subject area. Imagine that
in your economics class, you're writing in support of free trade, and you
need to judge the level of motivation of your audience. In this case, general readers may be less enthusiastic than either novices or experts. The
audience continuum could look like the one in Figure 4.5.

In technical writing, readers are commonly differentiated by their
varying levels of expertise and job responsibilities: experts, technicians,
operators, managers, lay readers. In this scheme, experts possess both a

theoretical and practical understanding of their field; they rarely have difficulty deciphering jargon, abbreviations, or abstract concepts. Technicians have a basic theoretical and practical knowledge; in their daily lives, they may apply theory to calibrate equipment, prepare lab experiments, collect data for studies. Operators typically have no theoretical background, but have extensive practical experience; for example, they carry out procedures (input data, assemble parts). Managers are often supervisors and executives who have technical expertise in other professional fields. Because these readers usually have job responsibilities in complementary departments or divisions within the organization, managers are concerned with how information in a document may affect these departments (budget and finance, research and development, communications, sales, production). Finally, lay readers have little or no specialized background in the subject area. These readers often are interested people outside of the organization proper; they may be stockholders, government representatives, or accreditation officials. This collective set of readers is diverse and

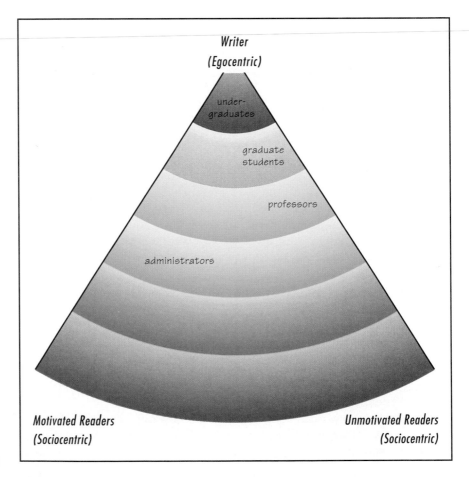

Figure 4.4 Mapping unfamiliar audiences by roles

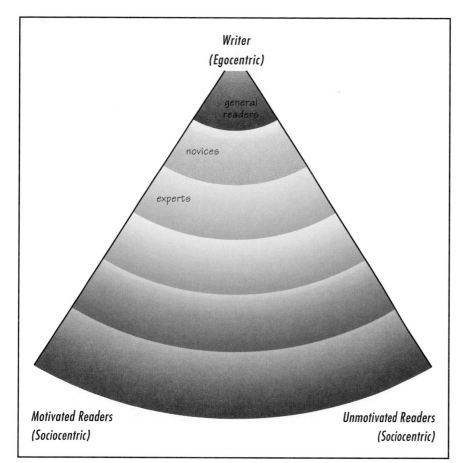

Figure 4.5 Mapping unfamiliar audiences by expertise

complex. A writer can develop a profile of such a mixed group of readers by analyzing them from the classical, cognitive, and social perspectives.

The classification systems we have used in our examples give you some sense of how you can "see" the people you are writing to. Obviously readers can fit into numerous groupings, depending on how you decide to envision your audience. Once you've established who your readers are in a general way and have located them on the audience continuum, you can analyze them in more detail.

Audience analysis enables you to develop a text that is sensitive to readers' purposes for reading. It recognizes readers as individuals with both distinct and shared characteristics (classical and social perspectives) and encourages you to seek strategies to make reading easier for your audience (cognitive perspective). Throughout your writing processes, the map helps you to keep your audience in mind as you locate and retrieve information about your subject.

Issues for Writing

1. If you have written your own opening narratives for certain chapters, select one of your stories and analyze the audience for that essay by classifying and mapping the readers on the audience continuum.

2. Read the following essays and the audience continuum maps for each one:

   "Kyle Field: Home of Dreams" (Chapter 10)

   "The Unique Relationship of Elizabeth Bennett and Her Father" (Chapter 13)

   "Poverty in the Inner City" (Chapter 17)

   In your group, identify the way the writers classified and mapped their readers for these assignments. Do you agree or disagree with their audience analysis? How do you think that the writers' perception of their readers influenced the kind of information as well as the arrangement of the information in these essays? Collaboratively write a journal entry of your responses. Delegate one person to photocopy and distribute copies to group members the next time you meet.

INFORMATION: RESEARCH AND DISCOVERY

One of the primary purposes of the knowledge continuum is to offer writers some research strategies for finding and generating information about a subject. Writing and researching naturally belong together because every text you write needs to contain evidence that develops and supports your main idea. You may be thinking, "How do I research a subject? The only research I've done and written about was for a high school term paper." Relax. You're probably not alone. If you informally polled your peers, you'd likely find that many share your concerns. (Incidentally, your poll would represent a type of research.)

As a college student, you will conduct research that moves far beyond what you presently know. The classes that you're taking now and will take in the coming months will require you to explore what you know about certain subjects (knowledge by participation) and to examine what others know about those subjects as well (knowledge by observation). For example, you may be required to locate and generate knowledge in different disciplines, as these writing assignments suggest:

- In your history class, you've read about the Watts Riots in 1965, as well as the South Central Riots in 1992, that occurred in Los Angeles, California. Interview several people who remember both events. Analyze these riots and the possible causes for them.

- Write a case history of a child you've been assigned to observe for your social work class.

- Report the findings of a study on sibling rivalry conducted by you and two other classmates for a child psychology course.
- Prepare a lab report for your biology class.
- Evaluate the current status of the Florida Everglades to determine whether or not federal and state agencies should take additional measures to preserve them.
- Write a proposal to study costs and savings for a recycling program on campus.
- Argue for or against compensating victims of radiation experiments.
- Write a psychological analysis of a character in a novel you've read in your science fiction survey course.
- Define and explain value-based marketing as it can be applied to the beef industry.
- Design an after-school program for children at a local elementary or middle school.
- Explain the concept of a *maquiladora*. Do you think *maquiladoras* are good for the national economy? Why or why not?

As appropriate, you may research and write about some of these subjects in this class. You can determine a subject's appropriateness by considering such questions as "How does this subject fit the writing task?" "What perspective may my audience have on the subject?" "What kinds of knowledge do the task and subject require of me?"

In addition to these questions, you may also consider guidelines that your instructor has provided. For example, you may be advised to consult with your instructor before writing about "too recent" topics because information may be scarce or unavailable at this time, and overused or "hot" topics (e.g., abortion, capital punishment, funerals, religion, politics). We encourage you to discuss your writing ideas with your instructor and your classmates, regardless of your subject. (Note that the writing tasks in Parts III through V are designed so that you can research and write about subjects in a wide range of areas, including business, education, fine arts, government, history, humanities, sciences, and social sciences.)

When we use the term **researching,** we are referring to **knowing.** We have introduced the knowledge continuum to illustrate three ways that writers can search for information: by participation, by observation, as well as by participation and observation. When you write, you convey your understanding of a subject. You discover information about that subject by using one of these three ways of knowing and the research strategies they imply.

Knowledge by Participation

Knowledge by participation refers to firsthand information derived from personal experience. For many writers, this way of knowing is the most natural starting point to explore a subject. To determine what knowledge you may have about your subject, you can use a wide array of research strategies. We present six possible approaches: *personal records, brainstorming, pentad, classical topics, visualizing,* and *computer-assisted invention.*

We recommend that you experiment with these strategies to learn which ones you think work best for different types of writing tasks. For example, marketing executives report that brainstorming is one of the most effective ways to discover fresh ideas about or "angles" for advertising a new product. Engineers, on the other hand, often prefer graphic techniques to visualize their subject. Still other writers use a combination of strategies, insisting that they can analyze their subject more effectively if they use the pentad as well as brainstorming or journal writing. As you gain experience as a writer, you will eventually be able to identify your "favorite" strategies for different writing situations—ones that consistently work best for you. In fact, the writing tasks in Parts III through V will offer you many opportunities to experiment with these strategies. As you become comfortable with certain strategies, however, don't stop trying others. You have choices. Let's see what they include.

Personal Records

Personal records are documents that chronicle firsthand information. Whenever you preserve information, you are actually creating future sources for writing. Examples of personal records are travel logs, lab notebooks, and field journals. The journal that you've been keeping is another example. It contains your thoughts and responses to the subject of writing and to this course—potential content for future essays. To ensure that entries in your records are accurate and reliable, always write down dates, times, names, places, references, and so on. As we mentioned in the Prologue, your journal can be an important resource for finding and researching writing subjects.

Brainstorming

Brainstorming is a spontaneous way of generating information about a subject. Just jot down what you know about your subject. Don't worry about the order or logic of your ideas while brainstorming. Simply relax and list all related thoughts that come to mind about your writing topic. Some writers brainstorm aloud. That is, instead of writing down their thoughts, they tape record them. Because formulating ideas and speaking come so naturally and involuntarily, thinking aloud can be an effective and easy way to brainstorm. An important collaborative strategy widely used in business and industry, brainstorming in small groups enhances creativity, as one person's ideas stimulate the ideas of others in the group.

Pentad

The **pentad** consists of five key topics: act (*what* was done?), scene (*when* or *where* was it done?), agent (*who* did it?), agency (*how* was it done?), and purpose (*why* was it done?). These topics and their resulting questions guide you in your information search. The pentad is the contribution of rhetorician Kenneth Burke (155–156) and is often associated with the familiar set of questions that journalists use in news writing: who? what? when? why? where? how? This strategy is useful because it enables you to focus on specific facts about your subject.

Classical Topics

Read More About It

See Chapter 5, pp. 132–134.

Aristotle developed the **classical topics** as a guide for analyzing a subject from different perspectives: definition, classification and division, process, cause-effect, and comparison and contrast. Suppose you're researching preregistration at your university. Using the classical topics, you can generate important information:

- Define preregistration.
- Give examples of different preregistration systems.
- Compare and contrast different aspects of preregistration or preregistration systems.
- Analyze causes for preregistration problems and their effects.
- Divide the preregistration process into steps or stages.
- Categorize or classify different registration systems.
- Identify problems preregistration creates and solve them.

Like the pentad, the topics direct your research energy in a deliberate and thorough manner. They also can provide ways of organizing ideas in an essay.

Visualizing

When you write words, you are making your ideas "visual." However, we mean something more when we use the term **visualizing.** Have you ever heard someone say, "I need to see the big picture before I can really understand what you're saying"? What this person wants is a sense of how the parts form a whole. This sense may be conveyed in many ways: through contrasting examples, chronology, and so on. Taken literally, the big picture may be conveyed as a diagram that clearly shows each part in relation to all of the others.

Visualizing includes numerous types of diagrams and illustrations that can help you:

- to generate and analyze information about your subject.
- to narrow your subject.

Figure 4.6 shows how you can draw *flow charts* to identify stages in a process. To make a flow chart, write down the steps in a process, and draw circles around each step; next, draw arrows to connect the circles, making certain that the arrows indicate the direction of movement appropriately.

Figure 4.7 is an example of clustering. Clustering helps you "see" associations among ideas; by thinking of ideas that are related to your subject, you can narrow your focus and develop ideas related to that focus. To try clustering, write down your subject in the middle of a piece of paper. Then jot down words that you associate with your subject. Circle the words, and connect them to the words that triggered them. In the example, the subject is Mary Shelley's *Frankenstein*. The writer associates *characters, setting,* and *narrators* with this subject; these words, in turn, trigger other clusters of ideas.

Organizational charts, sometimes called tree diagrams, clarify hierarchical relationships by arranging each position in a separate group, as shown in Figure 4.8. To make an organizational chart, write down the subject and areas related to it. The figure is an organizational chart of the field of advertising, showing the horizontal and vertical relationships of the different branches such as television, radio, and newspapers and magazines.

Venn diagrams, like Figure 4.9, identify similarities and differences. These diagrams are especially useful when you want to generate and analyze similarities and differences between related ideas, people, places, objects, and so on. To begin, draw two overlapping circles. Now record information about each subject in the circles, placing the similarities in the middle area where the circles intersect.

Storyboards trace the development of an idea, person, place, or thing by combining pictures and words. Writers frequently find storyboards useful for composing narratives. You can see how to construct a storyboard by looking at Figure 4.10. This example chronicles major developments in the life of the writer Christine De Pizan. The six frames provide an outline that helps the writer to focus on a manageable number of key events and to sequence them accurately.

Have you ever tried to use visualizing to help generate information about a subject or organize your thoughts? If so, which types of diagrams or illustrations did you use? Why? If you haven't experimented with visualizing, we encourage you to give it a try. Sometimes when you conceptualize ideas graphically, you develop a clearer sense of those ideas. And this is the true strength of this kind of technique.

Figure 4.6 Flow chart

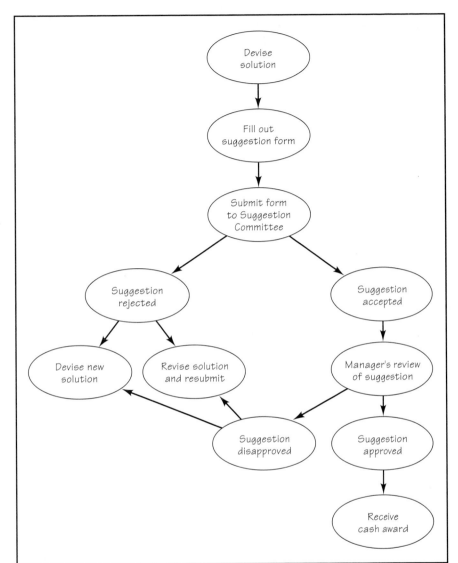

Figure 4.7 Clustering

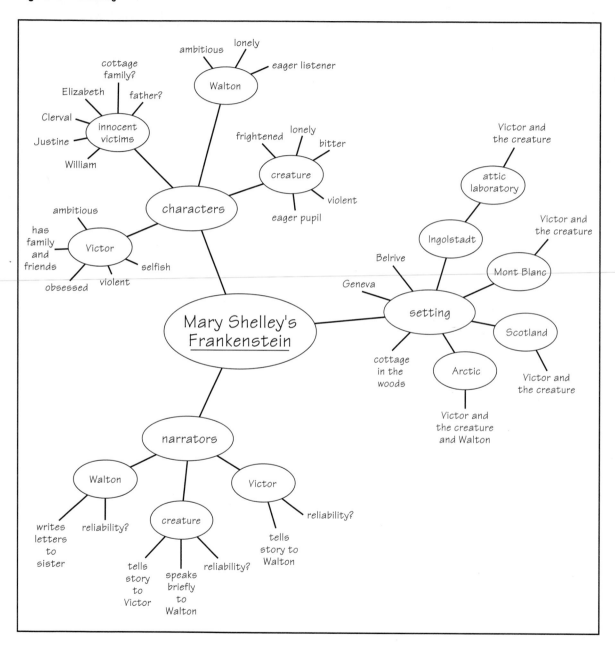

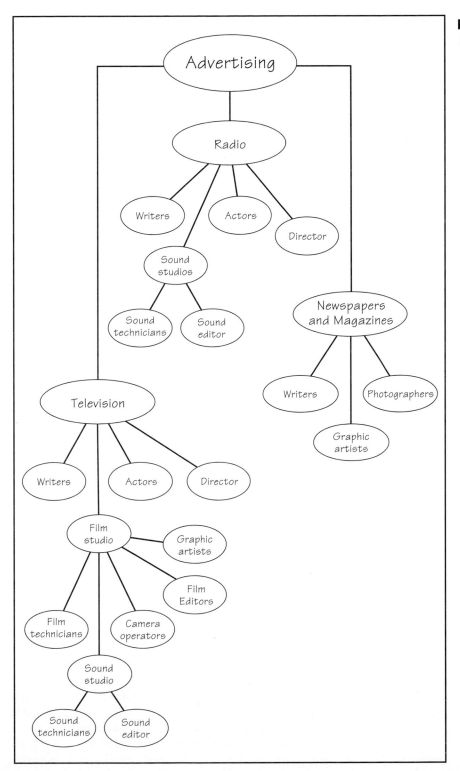

Figure 4.8
Organizational chart

Figure 4.9
Venn diagram

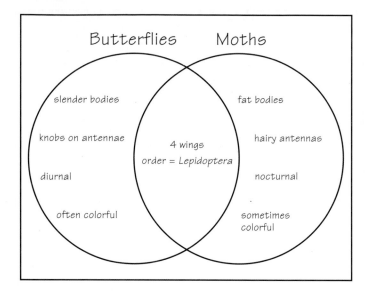

Figure 4.10
Storyboard

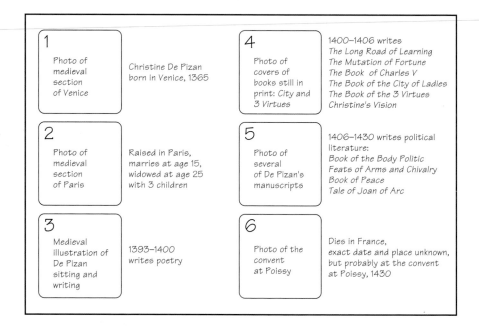

Computer-Assisted Invention

Computer-assisted invention can aid you in exploring and recording information. You can discover and generate data about a subject by using any of the invention programs designed to help writers think and plan. For example, you can keep your personal records (journal or log) in designated files in your computer. To maintain a consistent form for your entries, you can even program particular formats. In this way, when a journal file is opened, a preset "form" (similar to a memo heading: date, time, subject) appears on the screen; you fill in the information and write your journal or log entry. Using either commercial software programs or a do-it-yourself program, you can also brainstorm on the computer; the computer screen may ask you to type in your topic, main idea, or key question. Then, you are free to key in everything that comes to mind. If you're a good typist, you can generate pages and pages of ideas using your computer. Another strategy involves brainstorming on the computer with the screen turned off or completely darkened. Some writers find that their fluency and creativity increase when they can't see what they are writing.

The pentad and the classical topics are common strategies found in computer-aided invention programs. Frequently, both the pentad and the topics are phrased as questions. When you open a file, you see one question at a time (What happened? How is your subject defined?); when you've responded to the question, you press certain keys and a new question appears. These strategies can be quite effective because their question-answer format engages you in a sort of dialogue with the computer.

While you can "converse" with a computer, you can also visualize by designing illustrations on its screen. Instead of drawing flow charts, trees, Venn diagrams, and storyboards manually, you can create them on the computer. In most instances, you select a basic illustration. Then you revise its form, labeling as you go.

We recommend that you try computer-assisted invention software, if you can. You may find it frees you to think and write down ideas. In fact, some writers insist it helps them avoid writers' block and reduces their writing anxiety or fear of the blank page. People who write with a computer report feeling empowered because they can add, delete, substitute, copy, and move their thoughts easily on the screen. Furthermore, they can save their work in the computer's memory and print a hard copy as well. Invention software is typically easy and fun to use. You can also use your word processing program to try these invention strategies. While it won't automatically provide the cues or illustrations that invention programs will, it can still help you generate information quickly and effectively.

These six strategies can help you to research what you personally know about your subject. Just as important, they can also help you discover what you don't know. Let's return to the preregistration topic. If your writing task indicates that you should be able to write about a subject without researching external sources, then preregistration may be a good topic, especially if you're interested in it. However, suppose you didn't generate much information about it, no matter which strategy you tried. There were huge gaps when you used the pentad and the classical topics. You didn't have enough information to draw a flow chart of the process itself. Should you pursue preregistration as your subject for this particular writing task and situation? Probably not. Perhaps this subject would be more appropriate for a writing task that requires you to try another research approach: knowledge by observation.

Constructing a map of the knowledge continuum enables a writer to take information and contextualize it. After using one or more of these invention strategies, map that research information on the knowledge continuum and visualize how workable your subject will be. If your map is full of key terms and key ideas that readers will find interesting, you may sense that you have lots of information on a very good subject; however, if your map contains scanty information that readers will not find compelling, you have two choices: identify which areas to research further or consider a new subject to research. In the latter case, the invention strategies that you'd already used would show you where information deficits were; as a consequence, you would use some of the research strategies in this next section to locate missing information.

Issues for Writing

1. Select one of the following subjects to brainstorm about:

   my proudest moment

   the most unforgettable person I've ever known

   the place I'd like to visit again

   my favorite sport or hobby

   television violence

   U.S. foreign policy

   safety in the workplace

   After you've finished brainstorming about your subject, try the classical topics to generate information about it. Which strategy was more effective? Which strategy do you prefer? Had you ever used this strategy before? If so, was it effective then? Would you try the other strategy again? Explain your answer.

2. Look through your journal entries. Locate an entry that you would like to develop into an essay. Write a new entry in your journal that lists additional information about your subject, audiences, aims, and purposes for that essay.

3. In your focus group, create a rhetorical situation (select a subject that you all know something about and identify your readers) that would require that you write a letter collaboratively. Working together, use visualizing strategies or computer-assisted invention to generate information for your letter.

Write More About It

In Chapters 9 and 10, you'll write about the personal significance of an event, character, or place. And in Chapters 12 and 13, you'll explain and analyze a subject. Your responses to these exercises may be developed into a fuller essay for these writing tasks, or it may lead you to consider other subjects to write about—individually or collaboratively.

Knowledge by Observation

When your research efforts extend beyond your personal domain of knowing, you are researching knowledge by observation, information that you learn from others. Because you can't directly interact with the subject to learn about it, you interact with other people to learn about their experiences and accounts pertaining to the subject. As a consequence, when you use knowledge by observation, you must document any information derived from these sources and must include them in the bibliography at the end of your text. Three strategies that can help you research the knowledge of others are interviews, surveys or polls, and library resources.

Interviews

Interviews may help you gather new information that doesn't appear in any publication or interpret existing information from a different perspective. Being a good interviewer, however, requires much preparation and skill.

First of all, you need to know as much as possible about your subject and your interviewee. Ask yourself these questions:

- What do I know about this subject?
- What additional information should I gather before the interview?
- What do I know about the interviewee?
- What do I expect to learn from him or her?
- How should I address the interviewee?

In addition, you need to decide on how, where, and when it would be best to conduct the interview.

Preparation for the interview is not enough, however; you will also need some interviewing skill. For example, if you pose "yes-no" questions, your interviewee will probably respond in monosyllables. Here are some guidelines to follow as you develop your interview strategy:

- Pose questions whose answers require definition, explanation, or evaluation rather than yes or no responses. For example, ask "How many confidential sources have contributed to this news story?" rather than "Have any confidential sources contributed to this news story?"

- Design follow-up questions or rephrase your questions to encourage explanation or analysis. This is especially important when respondents' answers are brief or unclear. For example, ask "As a journalist, how far do you think a reporter should go to protect the identity of confidential sources?" Follow that question with "What are some specific cases that illustrate your view? Which contradict or challenge your view?"

- Phrase questions specifically to maintain the focus of the interview on your purpose. "As you know, I'm researching the ethics of reporters who protect their confidential sources. What is the professional and ethical responsibility of a reporter to his or her confidential source?"

- Ask one question at a time. Instead of asking a three-part question, for example, break your queries into three separate questions. This will help your respondent provide more complete answers and remember your questions better. For example, you might preface your questions in this way: "I have a question and a follow-up question for you. . . ."

- Include questions that refer to any research (published or unpublished) that your interviewee has conducted. These questions show that you've done your homework; they also demonstrate your interest in both the research subject and researcher. "In *Ethics and Jailed Journalists,* you state that the number of reporters jailed for refusing to disclose their informants' names have tripled over the past five years. How do you explain or account for this increase?"

Interviews can be conducted in person or by telephone. If your interviewee agrees to a personal interview, you may, with permission, tape-record the session. Be sure to write down key information about the interview: name, date, location, time, and so on. And, after either a personal or telephone interview, write a thank-you letter, acknowledging your interviewee for his or her assistance.

Questionnaires

When you invite written comments or responses about a subject, you usually do so by surveying or polling people. Five basic types of **questionnaires** are used in surveys and polls: either/or, multiple choice, rank order, continuum, and essay.

Questionnaire	Example
Either/Or	Did you vote in the last general election? (yes/no)
Multiple Choice	Which candidate do you support? (Martha, Jerome, Jaime, Lane)
Rank Order	Identify how you spend your money (1 = most, 5 = least): food, entertainment, school supplies, housing, transportation

Continuum	On a scale from 1 to 10 (1 = unhealthy, 5 = neutral, 10 = extremely healthy), how would you rate your eating habits?
Essay	Describe your impression of our customer service department.

Questionnaires for surveys or polls must be carefully designed and distributed. Questions that include bias jeopardize the reliability of the responses. For example, how would you respond to this question: Given the detrimental effects of passive smoke, what is your position on ordinances banning smoking in public buildings? Chances are, you might indicate that you support antismoking laws, even though you might really believe otherwise. The question conveys a certain attitude, and most respondents are usually subconsciously swayed by it. If you can, test your questionnaire on others (friends, relatives, roommates) and revise it before giving it to respondents.

Data can also be biased if questionnaires are not distributed to appropriate respondents. For instance, assume that your research purpose is to determine whether or not most first-year college students support an ordinance banning smoking in public buildings. You distribute your questionnaire at the student bookstore; when you receive your responses, however, you notice that only 20 percent were completed by first-year students. Obviously, this information may be of limited use: too few first-year students responded to the questionnaire for you to draw conclusions from the data.

1. If you were going to write a referential aim essay that identifies and explains the greatest concerns of college seniors at your school, would you use interviews or some kind of survey or poll? Would you use a combination? Why or why not? Explain your choice.

2. If you were going to use interviews to collect data, would you give your interviewees a copy of your questions beforehand? Why or why not?

3. In your focus group, develop a questionnaire to learn the demographics (age, gender, ethnicity, citizenship, education, and so on) of your classmates. After you have finished writing your questionnaire, meet with another group and compare your two questionnaires. In what ways are they alike or different? Why? How would you revise your questionnaire? How would you suggest that the other group revise theirs?

Issues for Writing

Write More About It

In Chapters 12 and 13, you'll explain and analyze a subject. Your responses to exercise (1) may be developed into a fuller essay for these writing tasks or may lead you to consider other subjects to write about—individually or collaboratively.

Library Resources

Another way you can gain insights into your subject is by consulting *primary and secondary sources*. **Primary sources** are original research or creations, such as diaries, notes, letters, interviews, autobiographies, recordings, and musical scores. **Secondary sources** discuss existing research and creations. Some examples of secondary sources are critical reviews, biographies, journal articles, newspaper stories, and television commentaries.

To illustrate the relationship between primary and secondary sources, consider the following scenario. Imagine we are biologists. We've conducted original research and written about our findings. Our report is considered a primary source, for it contains our original research data. However, suppose you interview us about that research. Then you write an article in which you use information from our original research report as well as your interview. The transcript of your interview would be a primary source. Your article, discussing and analyzing your interview with us as well as evaluating our original research, would be a secondary source. Table 4.3 provides a general overview of primary and secondary sources that shows how these important kinds of knowledge by observation compare.

You probably will be able to find almost any primary or secondary source that you will need for the writing you do for this course in your campus library; however, sometimes you may need to locate and retrieve sources from other libraries using electronic databases.

College writing will require you to develop your library research skills. Regardless of the library and the task, you can always recruit the help of research and staff librarians. These librarians can work with you to locate and retrieve sources. If time permits, some librarians can assist in determining whether or not your subject is workable, how you might narrow your research focus, and what general research plan for checking sources you might follow. Besides the library personnel, there are six basic **library resources** that you can rely on when exploring your subject and locating sources: **reference works, card catalog, periodical indexes, newspaper indexes, government documents,** and **computerized sources.**

REFERENCE WORKS

In the reference section of your library, you can locate a vast amount of information to begin your review of published materials. In addition to containing college catalogs, almanacs, and telephone directories, the reference section also houses specialized encyclopedias, handbooks, dictionaries, and bibliographies.

Table 4.3 Research and Knowing by Observation

Subject Area	Primary Sources (original research or creations)	Secondary Sources (discussion of existing research or creations)
Business	research studies, marketing campaigns, management models, memoranda, letters, and financial data	discussion of business issues in newspapers, magazines, journals, government documents, and books
Education	testing and measurement research studies, materials, curricular designs and goals	analyses and assessments of ideas and data in reports, journals, books, and monographs
Fine Arts	originals and reproductions of films, paintings, music, and sculptures	analyses and evaluations of earlier works in journals, articles, critical reviews, and biographies
Government, Political Science, History	historical and political texts, i.e., speeches, legislation, and memoirs	summaries and analyses in newspapers, magazines, journals, newsletters, and books
Literary Subjects	poems, plays, short stories, novels, autobiographies, manuscripts	interpretation and critical analyses of works and authors
Hard Sciences	feasibility studies, procedures, testing methods, outcomes	discussions of data and findings in journals and books
Social Sciences	case studies, diagnostic reports, statistical analyses, research models, procedures, studies of survey data	analyses and assessments in reports, journals, and books

---

If you need an overview of your subject, consult **specialized encyclopedias.** In these sources, you can find summaries of essential facts and theories about a subject, and this information can provide a good starting point for doing more focused library research and for narrowing your topic. Some commonly used encyclopedias are listed below:

American Medical Association Encyclopedia of Medicine

Cambridge Guide to World Theater

Encyclopedia of American History

Encyclopedia of Computer Science and Technology

Encyclopedia of Philosophy

Encyclopedia of Physics

Encyclopedia of Psychology

Encyclopedia of Religion and Ethics

Encyclopedia of World Art

Encyclopedia of World Crime

Encyclopedia of World Cultures

Encyclopedia USA

International Encyclopedia of Education

International Encyclopedia of Astronomy

International Encyclopedia of the Social Science

McGraw-Hill Encyclopedia of Science and Technology

Reader's Encyclopedia

The reference section also houses specialized handbooks and dictionaries. **Handbooks** are compact reference works that provide current factual information in numerous areas such as accounting, astronomy, biology, chemistry, computer science, education, engineering, mathematics, and physics, to name only a few.

Specialized dictionaries typically focus on technical terms and their meanings. Here are some examples:

- *Dictionary of the History of Ideas*
- *Penguin Dictionary of Science*
- *Dictionary of Art Terms*
- *Dictionary of Philosophy*

However, some dictionaries are collections of other kinds of specialized information, as these titles suggest:

- *Acronyms, Initialisms and Abbreviations Dictionary*
- *Dictionary of Scientific Biography*
- *New Grove Dictionary of Music and Musicians*
- *Oxford Dictionary of Quotations*
- *World Almanac Dictionary of Dates*

THE CARD CATALOG

The *card catalog* is a listing of all books, bound volumes of periodicals, as well as microfiche, maps, video tapes, films, audio recordings, and computer software that a library houses. The card catalog is in file drawers containing thousands of three-by-five-inch cards. Increasingly, libraries have computerized catalogs that let you search for information by entering subject, author, or title information. When you do, the "card" containing all of the standard information will appear on the screen.

Every item in a library has a call number, a set of letters and numbers that identifies its location. Call numbers are based on one of two systems: the **Dewey decimal system,** which divides books into 10 categories, or the **Library of Congress system,** which divides books into 21 categories. Usually public libraries use the Dewey decimal system, and university libraries use the Library of Congress system. You can use the Library of Congress Subject Headings (LCSH) to identify other research topics that are related to your subject and to narrow your subject. Learning how books are classified and shelved in your library allows you to go to a particular area and browse. Browsing can be a relaxing and enjoyable way to discover sources if you can afford the time.

If you don't have time to browse, however, go directly to the card catalog. You will find that each volume has been cross-referenced in three different ways on separate cards: title, author, subject. Each card contains standard information:

- call number
- author(s) or editor(s)
- title, including any subtitle, and edition
- place of publication, publisher, and date of publication
- physical description, including number of pages, size, and type of illustrations
- other information about content, such as whether the item has an index or bibliography
- headings under which the item is cross referenced in the subject catalog

Figure 4.11 shows a sample screen from an on-line card catalog.

BIBLIOGRAPHIES AND INDEXES FOR BOOKS AND PERIODICALS

While books in your library can be located by using the card catalog, articles in magazines and journals can't. Nor can books your library doesn't own. To find these materials, you need to consult **bibliographies** and **indexes.** There are bibliographies and indexes for almost any subject you may research. We've listed some below:

Applied Science and Technology Index
Accountants' Index
Art Index
Biography Index
Biological and Agricultural Index
Business Index

```
AUTHOR          Halpern, Jeanne W.
TITLE:          Computers & composing: how the new technologies are
                changing writing
PUBLICATION:    Carbondale: Southern Illinois University Press, c 1984
DESCRIPTION:    xii, 144p.; 22cm
    Library of Congress subject headings:
                        English language–Rhetoric–Study and teaching
                        English language–Rhetoric–Data processing
                        Authorship–Data processing
                        Word processing
OTHER AUTHORS: Liggett, Sarah
OTHER TITLES: Computers and composing
NOTES: "Published for a Conference on College Composition and
        Communication"
                        Bibliography: p. <137>-144
SERIES:         Studies in writing & rhetoric
LOCATION:       CALL NUMBER         STATUS/DUE DATE:
Stacks          PE1404 .H34 1984    Charged, 10/08/94
```

Figure 4.11 On-line card catalog sample

Computer Literature Index
Cumulative Index to Nursing Literature
Current Index to Journals in Education
Engineering Index
Essay and General Literature Index
Facts on File
General Science Index
Humanities Index
Index of Economic Articles in Journals and Collective Volumes
Index to Art Periodicals
Index to Legal Periodicals
Index to Scientific Reviews
*MLA International Bibliography of Books and Articles on the Modern
    Languages and Literatures*
Readers' Guide to Periodical Literature
Social Sciences Index

While each index has its special focus, all indexes have some features in common. All generally categorize information by subject, include full bibliographic citations, and provide instructions on how to use that index. Some indexes also have abstracts or summaries of articles; however, you should know that abstract indexes are also published. By scanning these abstracts and summaries, you can determine whether or not you need to look further at certain articles. Some examples of these **special indexes** include:

- *Biological Abstracts*
- *Dissertation Abstracts International*

- *Historical Abstracts*
- *Journal of Human Services Abstracts*
- *Oceanic Abstracts*
- *Personnel Management Abstracts*
- *Pollution Abstracts*
- *Sociological Abstracts*
- *Water Resources Abstracts*

NEWSPAPER INDEXES

To trace public events and figures, you may research *newspaper indexes.* Only a few newspapers are completely indexed. The most widely used newspaper indexes in the United States are the *New York Times Index* and the *Wall Street Journal Index.* A computerized index that is gaining users is *NewsBank,* a compilation of articles from over one hundred newspapers on major issues and public figures.

GOVERNMENT DOCUMENTS

The Government Printing Office (GPO) in Washington, DC, and the Congressional Research Service of the Library of Congress publish numerous indexes, abstracts, and reports. Here are a few examples:

- *American Statistics Index*
- *Index to Government Periodicals*
- *Congressional Quarterly Almanac*
- *Index to U.S. Patent Classification*
- *Monthly Catalog of U.S. Government Publications*

Government documents also include any documents that your state and local governments may print. Consult with your reference librarian to learn more about GPO publications.

COMPUTERIZED SOURCES

Many libraries have CD-ROM indexes that not only allow you to search sources but also print a copy of your bibliography. Here is a list of some **computerized indexes** you may ask your reference librarian about:

business	ABI/Inform
current events/news/ events/contemporary life/general information	NewsBank; InfoTrac
economics/public affairs	PAIS
education	ERIC
literary subjects	MLA International Bibliography
mathematics	MathSci disc
medicine	MEDLINE
psychology	PsycLIT
science	SciTech Reference Plus
social science	Social Sciences Citation Index

Using computerized sources enables you to research subjects quickly. You may discover that there are long lines of people waiting to use terminals, and computers may be inoperative for some reason. In these cases, remember that these computerized sources usually duplicate information your library houses elsewhere.

Knowledge by Participation and Observation

As a college student, you will have the opportunity to do many different kinds of writing tasks. Some of your assignments will require you to explore and discuss what you know about a subject now. What would be the effects of a state lottery on your city or town? How did you decide on your major or minor field of study? Who has influenced your attitude about education most, and how? These questions focus on you, the writer. Knowledge that springs from your thoughts, feelings, and personal experience is powerful. But college writing doesn't stop there. It broadens your base of knowledge beyond knowledge by participation.

As we have seen, college writing will also call on you to research the contributions others have made to your field of study. For example, you may write reviews of literature and annotated bibliographies of published studies by scholars. The more you take specialized courses in your major, the more you'll study the ideas and research of key figures in that field. As a consequence, your storehouse of ideas will be enriched by another way of learning: knowledge by observation.

Perhaps the most representative type of learning and writing you may do as an undergraduate, however, is knowledge by participation and observation. For example, you may write about your own and others' perceptions of a state lottery, incorporating other people's voices and ideas with your own and creating a text that contains some documentation. Or you and two other students in your major may research and write collaboratively, each telling a story about why he or she has chosen this area of study; in the introduction and conclusion of your text, you collectively summarize and analyze how different people with different experiences can share a common goal or interest. Or you may write an essay in which you compare and contrast your view of education to that of a peer or a famous educator. In each of these instances, the content of the essay is generated by a combination of personal knowledge and experience and knowledge gleaned from the research and the experience of others.

Writing requires that you learn by both participation and observation. When you read about what we know about writing, you are learning indirectly from others (knowledge by observation). When you apply what we tell you about how to write, you are learning by doing (knowledge by participation). As you can see in Table 4.4, in each of these cases you come to understand not only by articulating your own knowledge of something, but also by integrating other people's words and ideas into your writing.

Table 4.4 Researching and Knowing

Way of Knowing	Description of the Research Approach
Knowledge by Participation	Firsthand information; research your personal experience about a subject. You gain understanding of people, places, things, events, concepts, etc. through direct interaction. *Research strategies: personal records, brainstorming, pentad, classical topics, visualizing, and computer-assisted invention.*
Knowledge by Observation	Secondhand information; research other people's experience and published materials about a subject. You gain understanding of people, places, things, events, concepts, etc. through indirect interaction. *Research strategies: interviews, questionnaires, and library resources.*
Knowledge by Participation and Observation	Both firsthand and secondhand information; research your own and others' experiences and understandings of a subject. *Research strategies: combination of those identified above.*

---

1. Choose three topics from the following list.

Standardized tests	Voting rights
Mexico	Local police
Quebec	Deforestation
World population	Budgeting money
Anorexia	Hunting
Rap music	Time management
Recycling	Nutrition
Desktop publishing	Medical ethics
Skydiving	Immigration
Prison parole	Athletic scholarships
Fast food	Puerto Rico
National Service	Gardening

Issues for Writing

How do you have knowledge of each topic? From participation? From observation? From participation and observation?

2. Imagine that you have been asked by the campus newspaper to write a guest editorial. Make a list of three topics that you might write about from personal experience (knowledge by participation). Make a list of three topics that would require you to interview sources and conduct library research (knowledge by observation). Take turns reading your lists to group members so that they can recommend possible invention strategies for researching the topics.

3. Which techniques of participation are you most familiar with? Which techniques of observation are you most familiar with? Which techniques have you never tried? Why? Compare your experience with that of your focus group.

4. Choose a writing assignment from one of the other courses you are taking. In your planning for this assignment, use one technique of participation or one technique of observation that you have never tried before. In your journal, discuss your experience with this "new" way of knowing.

Invention Guide

Aim and Purpose

1. What is your writing task?
2. Are you writing individually or collaboratively?
3. What is the text's dominant aim? Expressive? Referential? Persuasive?
4. Are there subordinate aims? What are they and how do they affect the information in the text?
5. What is your purpose for writing? What specifically do you want your text to accomplish? Does your purpose satisfy the requirements of your writing task?
6. Are there subordinate purposes? What are they and how do they affect the information in the text?

Mapping the Rhetorical Situation: Subject and the Knowledge Continuum

1. What is your subject?
2. What is your relationship to the subject? That is, will your point of view in your essay be that of a participant, observer, or participant-observer?
3. Map your knowledge on the knowledge continuum by listing key words about your subject. Mapping is an ongoing process: continue to revise and refine your map as you learn more about your subject.

Figure 4.12
Invention guide

Figure 4.12
Invention guide
(continued)

Mapping the Rhetorical Situation: Readers and the Audience Continuum

1. What is the demographic profile of your readers (age; gender; social, economic, and educational levels; personal and professional backgrounds and experiences; cultural and situational factors and contexts)? How will their profile affect their responses to the subject and text?

2. Select representative members of your audience, and role play to determine the following:

    - readers' motives for reading your text

    - readers' enthusiasm about your subject

    - readers' sense that your subject is timely

3. How can you help readers to process and interpret your text more effectively (organization, memory cues, language, and visual signposts)?

4. Map your readers on the audience continuum. Mapping is an ongoing process: continue to revise and refine your map as you learn more about your audience.

Information: Research and Discovery

1. What kind of knowledge does your writing task require?

    Knowledge by participation (personal records, brainstorming, pentad, classical topics, visualizing, and computer-assisted invention)—documentation and bibliography usually unnecessary

    Knowledge by observation (interviews, questionnaires, and library resources)—documentation and bibliography usually necessary

    Knowledge by participation and observation (combination of sources identified above)—documentation and bibliography usually necessary

2. Which research strategies will you use to locate and generate information? Why?

3. How will you establish your credibility?

4. How will you provide specific and accurate details for the text's distinctive features?

Index of Key Terms

Works Cited

Aristotle. *Rhetoric*. Trans. W. R. Roberts. New York: The Modern Library, 1954.

Burke, Kenneth. "The Five Key Terms of Dramatism." *Contemporary Rhetoric*. Ed. W. Ross Winterowd. New York: Harcourt, 1975. 183–199.

Kinneavy, James L. *A Theory of Discourse*. New York: Norton, 1971.

Kroll, Barry. "Writing for Readers: Three Perspectives on Audience." *College Composition and Communication* 35 (1984): 172–185.

Ong, Walter J., S. J. "The Writer's Audience Is Always a Fiction." *Publication of the Modern Language Association* 90 (1975): 9–21.

Arrangement

K. W. Gong & Co. was the name of our family business, a general store that reflected my father's ideas about the world. Daddy held that everything—from groceries to dry goods—had its place and purpose. The overall layout of the four walls was strategic, and every item needed to be thoughtfully and carefully organized according to aisle and shelf.

Along the front wall, lined by large untinted windows, Daddy positioned long freezers and refrigerators that contained items our patrons frequently requested: milk, butter, prepackaged meats, eggs, frozen vegetables, TV dinners, pizzas, and ice cream. He believed that the "cold" items somehow neutralized the hot sunshine that beamed in through the large window panes; the large refrigerators and freezers also served as a pseudo-wall that robbers would have to get past should they try a nighttime break-in.

Opposite the front wall, Daddy placed two more freezers, full of hens, ducks, whiting fish, chitlings, ox and pig tails, beef roasts, slabs of pork ribs, and the like. Out of sight, on the other side of the freezers, he placed large kegs of loose nails and staples that we sold by the pound. In addition, he lined the back wall with household items such as dishwasher powders, bath soaps, scrubbing pads, drain cleaners, bathroom tissue, and insecticides. These were items that had strong smells and that customers did not routinely buy every time they came to the store.

The side walls of the store were logical extensions of Daddy's mind, too. From back to front, the right-hand wall of the store featured canned goods—coffee, fruits, vegetables, evaporated milk, fish, and meat—as well as boxed goods, such as tea, oatmeal, grits, and other breakfast cereals. The front part of that side wall, however, housed a large cooler full of fresh vegetables: greens, carrots, beets, rutabagas, cabbages, celery, tomatoes, and lettuce. Daddy was adamant that perishables should be arranged near the front of the store so that we could "push" them and monitor them for freshness. Consequently, the left-hand side wall was lined with coolers full of wax-covered cheese wheels, whole "sticks" of sandwich meats, whole chickens, ground beef, pork loins, slabs of bacon and salted fatback, and link sausages that we would slice or package for customers upon request. Beside these meat coolers were two adding machines atop a long checkout counter wide enough to accommodate two customers at a time. The counter was conveniently located near the front doors, and behind this counter area were tobacco products, medicines, toothpastes, shoe polish and laces, penny candies and gum, shaving cream, razor blades, and hardware supplies (locks, nuts, bolts, extension cords, and light sockets).

Every aisle within these store "walls" was likewise planned and stocked from front to back according to each item's shelf-life, customer demand, size, smell, as well as type (vegetable, detergent, meat, etc.). From the front of the store, aisle 1 contained cases of fresh apples, oranges, white and *sweet potatoes, and onions, as well as displays of fresh bananas, watermelons, and grapes. In addition, crackers, cookies, chips, nuts, and soft drinks were placed here. Aisle 2 housed fresh breads, rolls, and cakes; spices, pickles, shortening, sugar, flour, corn meal, and cake mixes. Aisle 3 held rice, noodles, dried beans, canning supplies, and light bulbs. In aisle 4, you could find shoes, oil cloth, 100-pound sacks of corn feed, pet food, dish towels, cotton hose, work gloves, scarves, handkerchiefs, dress patterns with pre-cut fabrics, sewing notions, linoleum flooring, cane fishing poles, and various sizes of wash tubs. And aisle 5 provided customers with mops, brooms, plates, bowls, silverware sets, cast iron skillets, aluminum pots and pans, and an assortment of household utensils. (GG)*

In arranging the store, Daddy kept in mind what kind of store and goods we offered (aim and purpose) and what kinds of customers frequented our business (audience). Then, he decided that the key organizing principles should be from front to back, perishable to nonperishable, most to least frequently sold, types and packaging of goods, and so on. Daddy's way of envisioning products and consumer needs resulted in a blueprint and consistent logic for everything in our store. And that logic provided my siblings and me with a mental map that showed us where to stack new inventory. Also, it gave us—and our regular patrons—the ability to figure out the approximate location of any item in the store. Everything had its place.

Just as arranging the merchandise in his store was a crucial concern for Daddy in the opening narrative, arrangement is an essential consideration for writers. When you write, you need to provide a logical way of ordering ideas in your text, based on your aim, purpose, audience, and available evidence. That is, while many different ways of organizing ideas may be logical, only a few ways may be appropriate for a particular rhetorical context. Arrangement, the structuring of information in your writing, can help you discover and select effective patterns for your ideas and situation. In addition, arrangement can help readers to anticipate and follow your reasoning effectively and efficiently.

We begin our discussion with some preliminary considerations regarding research and thesis development. Then we move on to examine three key areas of arrangement: *unity, development,* and *cohesion.* We cover **unity** by exploring how the main idea (thesis) and the principles of organization convey to readers the same message. We look at **development** by explaining parts of a text (discourse blocs), their functions, and methods for generating them. We then explore **cohesion,** strategies used to link words and ideas logically and smoothly, and we review ways in which computers and outlining can be useful aids for arrangement. We conclude this chapter by presenting some strategies that you can use to strengthen the structure and development of your texts.

1. In your journal, write an opening narrative for this chapter. Do you or does someone you know have a passion for orderliness as Daddy in this story does? Describe something or someplace that reflects your or that person's sense of arrangement ("Everything had its place"). Through your description, you'll not only be recreating a visual picture, but you'll also be revealing an important characteristic of you or that other individual.

2. Using the description of the store in the opening narrative, draw a map that customers might use to find items. How might this map be used to strengthen a writer's ability to arrange ideas logically?

Write More About It

In Chapter 10, you'll write about a character or place and its significance to you. Your response to this exercise may be developed into a fuller essay for that writing task, or it may remind you of another subject to write about.

REVIEWING AND ORGANIZING EVIDENCE

While gathering information about a subject, you are simultaneously beginning to sort and organize your research material. That is, the processes of planning, translating, and reviewing operate constantly as you scrutinize and select your data. Four important considerations emerge:

- sufficiency and relevance of the research
- rhetorical appeals
- thesis statement
- organization of information

Sufficiency and Relevance of the Research

Has your exploration of your subject yielded **sufficient** and **relevant information?** Have you discovered and generated enough data to understand your subject? Do you have relevant information to fulfill your dominant aim and purpose (expressive aim: narrate an event, describe a person or place; referential aim: explain or analyze; persuasive aim: evaluate, take a position, or propose a solution)? If not, what additional research do you need to undertake? This issue of sufficiency and relevance is a good litmus test to help you examine your subject objectively: Should you pursue this subject further, or should you research another one? Asking yourself these kinds of questions fosters critical thinking about your subject, tentative plans about arrangement, and acute awareness of particular strengths and weaknesses of your research data.

Rhetorical Appeals: Ethos, Logos, and Pathos

Three **rhetorical appeals** are important to varying degrees in any piece of writing: **ethos** (how ethical and credible the information is); **logos** (the soundness of your evidence and reasoning); and **pathos** (whether your information stirs readers' emotions). How do your research data reflect these rhetorical appeals? As you review the information generated by your research, analyze each bit of data and each source to determine its appeal; using a pencil or highlighter, you might even identify and label the type of appeal each piece of information best illustrates. As you proceed to organize your ideas and draft your essay, be sure you're using a mixture of the appeals, relying most heavily on logos, or logical appeal, to craft a text with an appropriate **rhetorical stance** (Booth).

Examine the ethos (ethical appeal) of your evidence by asking these kinds of questions:

- Are your sources reliable and respected authorities on the subject?
- Will their credibility instill in your readers a sense of trust in you?

Note that you can also establish your ethos by using evidence fairly and thoughtfully.

To determine logos (logical appeal), consider these queries:

- Is your information sound and reasonable?
- Are the ideas in your sources objectively explained and supported with facts, statistics, and examples?

For pathos (emotional appeal), analyze each piece of information for its effect on readers:

- Will it move readers to feel joy, pain, anger, despair, happiness, horror, or respect?

You may find that most of your evidence will reflect dominant and subordinate appeals, much as the aims of writing do. In other words, a research article may provide rational, clear evidence (logos) in addition to being written by a reputable scholar (ethos). However, if you learn from your analysis that emotional appeals outnumber logical appeals, you need to review your subject and evidence once more. This imbalance may indicate that you need to conduct additional research on your current subject or research a new one.

Thesis Statement

How does your research shape your **thesis statement**? Given that your research is sufficient and represents the appeals appropriately, you can now begin developing and refining your thesis. But what is a thesis?

A **thesis** is the controlling or central idea of a text. Unlike the subject of your writing, which gives your research direction, the thesis provides your text with a clear focus. It states your view on a subject. For example, the *subject* of your writing may be recycling; however, your *thesis* might be that the community can develop a cooperative plan with the city for recycling aluminum cans, glass, and newspapers. Depending on the aim of your writing, a thesis can have a personal, impartial, or persuasive tone.

Personal tone (expressive):   While working in the local animal shelter, I began to understand why animal cruelty laws exist.

Impartial tone (referential):   Animal cruelty laws protect animals from outright abuse and improper care.

Persuasive tone (persuasive): We should support animal cruelty laws.

As we mentioned at the beginning of this section, you may begin to develop your thesis while you research your subject. Or, you may discover it after you assemble all of your information, honing it as you draft—as you plan and translate supporting ideas. Regardless of when you start to identify your controlling idea or how tentative it is, it is important for you to articulate your thesis.

Your essay may have an **explicit thesis** (overt and direct) or an **implicit thesis** (implied or indirect); we have found that many writers prefer to compose explicit ones. Whichever you choose, present your thesis statements as declarative assertions instead of questions. Questions can be effective setups preceding your thesis, however. For example, if you pose a question at the beginning of an essay, your response could be seen as the entire essay. In this instance, your thesis would be implicitly rather than explicitly stated, for your readers must infer your thesis. In contrast, you can also pose the question and then immediately follow it with a response that conveys the explicit thesis.

When experimenting with implicit thesis statements, be aware of two possible pitfalls. First, implicit thesis statements sometimes cause readers to either miss or misunderstand your implied thesis. Second, implicit thesis statements may lead readers to believe that you don't really know your position on the subject—if you don't articulate your thesis plainly, is it because you won't or can't? Given these two problems, you can see why many writers prefer to use explicit thesis statements.

How do you know if you've written a good thesis statement? Here are some characteristics that usually indicate clear controlling ideas:

- Thesis statements are specific and concrete.
- Thesis statements are focused and feasible.
- Thesis statements stimulate readers' interests.

Thesis statements are specific and concrete. Resist the temptation to use generalities, obvious assertions, and clichés. For example, avoid this type of vague claim: "Happiness means different things to different people." Also avoid the "middle of the road" type of thesis: "Many people support the new tax code, but many others don't." As you can see, a weak thesis statement provides no clear main or controlling idea for either the reader or writer. In contrast, a strong thesis statement consists of a main assertion that may also include specific limiting or clarifying information. For example, suppose your main assertion is "Vote to support strip mining in our local wildlife preserve." To this assertion, add this qualifying information: "because we have been assured the latest reclamation techniques will be used." Your thesis statement now becomes "Vote to support strip mining in our local wildlife preserve because we have been assured the latest reclamation techniques will be used." In your essay, you might support this thesis statement through a series of accompanying sentences that define and explain the terms *strip mining, wildlife preserve,* and *reclamation techniques.*

Thesis statements are focused and feasible. In a way, thesis statements promise to do something. For example, suppose your thesis leads readers to expect an explanation of the nature and history of strip mining (referential aim); however, instead of providing that explanation, you write an essay that advocates strip mining (persuasive aim). In this case, you've failed to deliver on your promise and damaged your credibility (ethos). To restore your credibility, you have two options. You can either revise your thesis to reflect your persuasive case in favor of strip mining, or you can keep your original thesis and conduct further relevant research that would enable you to provide the expository presentation your thesis promises. As this example illustrates, thesis statements should be perceived as tentative assertions that will be developed and refined throughout your composing processes.

Thesis statements stimulate readers' interest. In composing your tentative thesis, seek ways to engage your readers—to make them want to know more about your message. Be creative when you state your main idea; entice your readers to read on. If they are indifferent to the subject and your slant on it, you'll be writing for nobody rather than writing meaningfully to readers about your thesis statement. For example, which of the following theses would tempt you to read further? "Every child deserves an education" or "A mind is a terrible thing to waste"? "Teen pregnancies are on the rise" or "Our children are having children—taking home newborn babies instead of high school diplomas, assuming the roles of parents instead of graduates"?

Finally, we need to distinguish between *thesis statements* and *statements of purpose*. A formal **statement of purpose** serves as a reminder of what you are setting out to do. The classic statement of purpose reads as follows: "The purpose of this essay is to . . . in order to. . . ."

Statements of purpose are commonly used in technical reports; they may also be found in articles in professional journals. In essays, however, readers usually expect originality of expression and consider formulaic statements of purpose to be dull and mechanical. Employ statements of purpose judiciously, therefore, taking care not to substitute them for thesis statements.

Issues for Writing

1. Bring to class a copy of a newspaper editorial and analyze it. Locate the thesis statement. Is it effective? Does it have sufficient and relevant information? Which rhetorical appeals does the writer use (ethos, logos, and pathos)? How? How might the editorial be improved? Using the information in the editorial, write your own editorial taking a different position on the issue.

2. Bring one example of the following types of articles from your school or local newspaper to your focus group:

    advice column

    editorial

    movie, music, or restaurant review

    letter to the editor

    sports feature

    national news feature

    Using a pencil or highlighter, identify the aim, purpose, audience, and thesis for each article. Then, identify and label the type of appeals in each piece. Do some articles have more emotional appeal (pathos) than logical (logos) or ethical (ethos) appeal? Which ones? Why do you think this is so?

Write More About It

In Chapter 16, we will ask you to take a position on an issue. If you choose to write from knowledge by participation and observation, exercise (1) could help you to generate ideas for this essay. Refer to exercise (2) when you consider subjects to analyze in Chapter 13. In Chapter 15, you will be asked to evaluate a subject, and exercise (2) could help you to develop assessment criteria for this essay.

3. Formulate three thesis statements in your group. First, choose three subjects and compose your main assertions. Then add specific limiting or clarifying information. Evaluate your explicit theses. Are they

clear? Do they make readers want to know more about the subject? If not, how can you revise your thesis statements to be more interesting?

Principles of Organization

Organizational patterns give your writing unity—a sense that all of the ideas in your text coalesce. They aid you in arranging information so that your readers can follow your logic and approach to your subject and your thesis. Like a road map, these patterns provide a sound strategy for converting thinking that makes sense to you (writer-based thinking) into thinking that will also make sense to others (reader-based thinking). Inexperienced travelers may need more signposts or more explicit directions than their tour guides. If you don't provide clear directions, your travelers may strike out on their own and get lost; similarly, if you don't organize your ideas well, readers may be forced to create a structure for your text on their own.

Whenever you pass the responsibility for arrangement to your readers, you take some unnecessary risks. You gamble that readers will be able to grasp your meaning accurately, to trust your ethos and logos on the subject, and to tolerate doing your "thinking" for you. Organizational patterns should be a means of unifying and communicating your meaning—from you to your text and from your text to your readers. The arrangement of a text represents the cognitive connection—a bridge of understanding—between you and your readers. There are two major **principles of organization** that can serve as cognitive connections: **sequential** and **categorical.**

Sequential Organization

When you arrange ideas sequentially, you use *chronological, spatial,* or *hierarchical patterns* to organize your information. A feature common to these three patterns is predictability. That is, readers can use the initial piece of information in the sequence to predict or anticipate how the subsequent piece of information will connect to it.

CHRONOLOGICAL PATTERNS

Chronological patterns are appropriate when you want to arrange ideas according to time. For example, texts that tell a story, narrate a process, or explain a procedure occur along a time line. One act or activity makes the next one possible and logical. Chronological patterns move either forward (natural order) or backward through time (reverse order or flashback technique).

If you're recounting an event or writing a set of instructions, you may instinctively develop your information in chronological order. As an alternative, you can start in the present and then flash back to the past, when

Read More About It

See Chapter 8,
p. 253.

the actual incidents in the story occurred. If you use the flashback technique, you'll need to give readers a clear sense of transition and time reference in the text. A type of document that would require reverse chronological order is the résumé. A résumé provides readers with a chronology of a person's life history (e.g., education, work experience, and abilities) that is organized according to reverse order—from most to least recent.

You can reinforce chronological patterns by integrating visuals into your texts such as numbered or alphabetized lists, flow charts, storyboards, line graphs, time-lapse photos, and sequential drawings.

SPATIAL PATTERNS

When your aim and purpose for writing requires description, your choice for arranging details is a **spatial pattern.** When you use this organizational pattern, you progress in a single direction, either moving from the top to the bottom of the object, from left to right, east to west, or north to south. By moving in one direction as you describe the object, you make it easy for readers to understand and assimilate the specific details you are presenting. Each new piece of information extends the preceding piece of information in a predictable and linear way.

If you violate this expectation, you make it more difficult for readers to understand your document. Moreover, you probably appear somewhat confused and confusing, jeopardizing your ethos and logos in readers' minds. If, for example, you describe an object by first focusing on the middle, then moving to the top, then down to the bottom, then up to the top again, then down to the middle again, readers would find it impossible to anticipate which portion of the object you would describe next. Notice how the narrative at the beginning of this chapter arranges information spatially, describing the store by beginning at the front, then moving to the back, right, and left walls, and finally each aisle from front to back.

Some of the most common visuals that suggest spatial patterns are photographs, blueprints, organizational charts, and representational drawings. These illustrations reinforce spatial patterns of organization in your writing.

HIERARCHICAL PATTERNS

When you use **hierarchical patterns** of organization, you move in either ascending or descending order of importance. Hierarchical patterns are appropriate for texts that present recommendations and conclusions, such as evaluations, proposals, position papers, and development plans. For example, if you need to identify the factors that justify why you should receive a college scholarship, you might list your achievements in ascending order of importance, culminating in the most impressive and persuasive accomplishments. Or, in a letter that lists grievances about conditions at your dormitory, you might begin with your most serious complaint for dramatic emphasis and end with the least serious. Again, by moving in one direction, from most important to least important or vice versa, you can signal to readers what each new piece of information contributes to previous data. Especially in persuasive texts, hierarchical patterns effectively guide readers to anticipate the logical relationship between ideas (e.g., causes and effects; costs and benefits; similarities and differences; and advantages and disadvantages).

What would happen if you didn't use some type of hierarchical pattern in a text that contained recommendations and conclusions? Your document's thesis would be supported less effectively and clearly. For example, suppose you are writing an evaluation of the local school board's decision to cancel all extracurricular activities such as chorus, band, and art because of budget cutbacks. If you present your information about the advantages and disadvantages of having a "no-frills" curriculum in random order, your readers will find it difficult to determine which criteria and recommendations you consider more important or urgent than others. Consequently, they would be forced to assume your responsibility as the writer and determine the importance of your evidence, no matter how unwilling or unable they are to make these judgments effectively. In this situation, readers may feel frustrated or burdened and may question your credibility and competence altogether.

Visuals that can complement hierarchically arranged texts are numbered or alphabetized lists, pie charts, bull's-eye charts, and multiple line graphs.

Categorical Organization

Using categorical patterns of organization allows you to design comparative or causal patterns of information. When you use this principle of organization, you classify information into "categories" (similarities and differences, causes and effect, advantages and disadvantages) and then either discuss one category at a time or alternate between the categories, covering one piece of information from each category until you have presented all the evidence. For example, if you were arranging information about heart-valve surgery and coronary artery bypass surgery, two of the most common types of open heart surgery done today, you might choose to discuss valve surgery and all its advantages and disadvantages first; then you would examine the advantages and disadvantages of bypass surgery. This type of categorical organization is called a whole-to-whole pattern. If instead you arranged your ideas by considering the advantages of each procedure, followed by the disadvantages of each, you would be using a part-to-part pattern. Here is how these two basic patterns can be outlined:

Whole-to-Whole Pattern	*Part-to-Part Pattern*
Valve Surgery	Advantages
Advantages	Valve Surgery
Disadvantages	Bypass Surgery
Bypass Surgery	Disadvantages
Advantages	Valve Surgery
Disadvantages	Bypass Surgery

Categorical organization might also be combined with sequential organization: you discuss all the advantages in order of importance, and then all the disadvantages in order of importance. Frequently, readers find categorical organization more difficult or demanding to process than the single linear direction of sequential organization. For this reason, it is especially important that you provide clear transitional words and phrases to guide your readers.

Categorical organization can be reinforced in your writing through illustrations such as paired listings (as shown in the example above), or paired photos, drawings, tables, and bar graphs.

Texts can be developed according to a simple principle of organization (chronological, spatial, hierarchical, or categorical). Or they can be arranged according to a complex principle of organization (hierarchical-chronological, hierarchical-spatial, hierarchical-categorical).

Issues for Writing

1. Bring to class a copy of a textbook used in one of your other courses. In your group, analyze the preface of each textbook for its principles of organization. Is information organized sequentially or categorically? Is the organization effective? How might each preface be improved?

2. Read the following student essays:

   "Birds in the Tabernacle" (Chapter 10)

   "Who'll Decide for You What's Art and What's Obscenity" (Chapter 16)

   "A Solution to the Problem" (Chapter 17)

   "Changing the Future with Preventive Discipline" (Chapter 17)

   Identify the aim, purpose, audience, and thesis statement for each of these essays. Then analyze the principle of organization in each. Is information organized sequentially or categorically? Is the organization effective? Imagine you are classmates of these writers. What advice would you offer them about the arrangement of information in each essay?

3. Find a journal entry and analyze its principle of organization. Why did you arrange the information in this way? What would you change if you were going to rewrite this entry? Why? Rewrite the entry, using your own advice to guide you.

DISCOURSE BLOCS

Just as there are strategies that help you create an effective overall structure for your writing, there are means to assist you in developing these internal components of your essay. We begin our discussion of these means by explaining what the internal components, or discourse blocs, are. Then, we present the modes of development, different ways of converting ideas into a meaningful series of sentences. Finally, we turn our attention to the functions that discourse blocs can serve in a text.

Discourse Blocs and Idea Development

Traditionally, writers have been taught that individual **paragraphs** are the basic units of any text. In this view, every paragraph contains a topic sentence that states the purpose of the paragraph, one idea, and some specific number of sentences (Shearer). What are some of the rules that you can recall learning about the paragraph?

To be fair, for every "rule" about the paragraph, there probably is a reasonable explanation. For example, you might remember being told that every paragraph should have seven sentences. If you were to count the sentences in paragraphs found in this book and others, however, you'd see that this "rule" may be more aptly termed a "myth." Did your teachers mislead you or, worse, outright lie to you? Probably not. Teachers who advocated the seven-sentence paragraph may have decided to provide you with a concrete guideline concerning paragraph length—a guideline that would force you to specify an idea and develop it more fully. These teachers had good intentions; they found this teaching strategy effective in making you aware of **paragraph development.**

But we would like to direct your attention to a unit of composition beyond the paragraph: the discourse bloc (Rodgers; Pitkin). **Discourse blocs** are units in the structure of a text; they may consist of one or more paragraphs, all sharing a common purpose that is stated in the topic sentence for that discourse bloc. Rather than thinking of a text in terms of paragraphs, we encourage you instead to see the **internal components** of a piece of writing as a series of discourse blocs. Figure 5.1 shows the components of a written text.

How do writers create discourse blocs? A *discourse bloc* consists of a **topic sentence** that identifies the purpose of the entire bloc, whatever its size (one paragraph or more). Every paragraph within the discourse bloc contributes to the development of that topic sentence. In other words, the paragraphs in a discourse bloc explain, illustrate, and support the same topic sentence. The discourse bloc begins with an introductory paragraph that gives the unit focus and direction by means of a topic sentence, contains a series of supporting paragraphs, and concludes with a summary or transitional paragraph.

Text

Discourse blocs (one or more paragraphs)

Sentences or clauses

Phrases

Words

Figure 5.1 Components of a text

Paragraphs within a bloc may also contain their own explicit topic sentences. However, not every paragraph within a bloc needs to have its own topic sentence. In studies focusing on the frequency and placement of topic sentences, researchers have contradicted the common belief that all paragraphs have topic sentences (Braddock). Instead, while key introductory paragraphs within a bloc consistently present topic sentences, supporting paragraphs in the bloc may continue to develop that idea rather than present new or different ones. Consequently, supporting paragraphs may not require their own topic sentences.

Understanding the internal components of a text as discourse blocs can help you in several important respects. First, it allows you to think analytically about your subject; you are free to develop ideas within your writing, creating as many paragraphs as you deem necessary. Second, using discourse blocs skillfully gives you a text structure that clearly reflects your logic—the relationship and ordering of major and minor supporting evidence. Third, this concept enables you to read your blocs critically to ensure that their arrangement, purpose (unity), and development are strong.

Rhetorical Modes: Methods of Development for Discourse Blocs

Discourse blocs represent key parts of a text. Writers typically compose these parts using various **rhetorical modes** or methods of development. What exactly are the rhetorical modes? Rhetoricians have historically divided the modes into four general categories: **narration, description, exposition,** and **persuasion.** In the following list we briefly define each of the four categories and their subcategories:

Narrative Mode of Development

narration   recounting events in a chronological
                               order; telling a story

Descriptive Mode of Development

description   giving specific and concrete details that
                               appeal to the five senses about a person,
                               place, thing, or idea

Expository Modes of Development

exemplification   including one or more examples that
                               illustrate or support the idea or point
                               being made

process   identifying and explaining, in chronologi-
                               cal order, the steps or stages in how
                               something is made or done, how some-
                               thing works, or how some outcome is
                               achieved

comparison/contrast   pointing out similarities, pointing out dif-
                               ferences, or doing both

analogy   making extended comparisons between
                               two different yet related people, places,
                               things, or ideas to make the "unfamiliar"
                               or unknown understandable by setting it
                               alongside the "familiar" or known

analysis   examining a subject's component parts
                               and showing the relationship among
                               them

classification   sorting items into logical categories,
                               groups, and divisions

enumeration   listing items or examples in a series

causation   examining the reasons for a specific phe-
                               nomenon or event

effects   explaining or predicting the conse-
                               quences or outcomes of a specific phe-
                               nomenon or event

definition	delineating the meaning of a term or concept
negative definition	delineating the meaning of a term or concept by explaining what it is not

Persuasive Mode of Development

persuasion	convincing readers that a certain stand or view on an issue is appropriate or that a particular solution to a problem is logical and feasible; refuting opposing arguments and evidence; convincing readers to take specific action

To form solid discourse blocs and a well-developed text, you may combine different modes of development. Your strategy for selecting the appropriate modes will depend on your dominant and subordinate aims and purpose, audience, subject, and thesis. For example, to define and explain the concept of year-round school to high school students, you might choose modes from all four categories, as in the following annotated essay, written by Stacy Kaaz and Laura Collins Lott.

As you can see, the modes provide these writers with a way of developing discourse blocs. And these discourse blocs create a sense of movement or progression of information to help readers understand year-round school. What kind of overall organization do you think Stacy and Laura use? Why do they integrate the exemplification of a case in the conclusion? Is this an effective strategy? Why or why not?

Discourse Bloc, Title

Classes for All Seasons

Discourse Bloc, Introduction

Driving back to college after spending my Thanksgiving holiday with my family, I felt agitated. The visit had gone well. I had gorged myself on Mom's home cooking, gone on a shopping spree with my sister, and attended several parties with my high school friends. So why was I feeling uneasy? As odd as it seemed, I was upset about the new school calendar that my high school was going to start next year. My friends called it year-round school. I was determined to understand what was happening at my school, an institution that I thought would never change. Before the school board convened again, I was determined to find out what this year-round school was so that I could fight against it. After all, to defeat the enemy, you must know it. So, when I got back to my dorm and unpacked my suitcase and duffel bag, I grabbed my backpack and jacket and

Narration

dashed over to the library to research my foe. Reading for hours in the library stacks, I soon realized the enemy was an interesting and often misunderstood concept.

Discourse Bloc, introducing and explaining the term

Year-round school is a calendar variation of the traditional school year that involves school being in session every season of the year. This calendar takes the traditional school calendar, a September to June term with one long vacation, and redistributes class time into several shorter terms with three or four weeks of vacation between each. This variation keeps the school doors open more days of the year – 240 compared to 180 days – and relieves overcrowding since the student population is put on various "tracks" (Glines 35). For example, a certain percentage of the population (Track A) is in school for a few consecutive terms and then released for a term while Track B and Track C have supplementing schedules that allow them long vacations at different times. In other words, students do not attend school all year long, but rather they are divided into groups that start school sessions at staggered dates during the year. Students attend a required minimum number of school days each year, and school facilities are open and in full use all year long (Shepard 1).

Definition

Comparison and Contrast

Exemplification

Discourse Bloc, comparing year-round to other types of school calendars

Year-round school should not be confused with either the extended school year or summer school. All three of these types of school calendars or programs are deviations from the traditional school year, but there are important distinctions to be made.

Negative Definition

Comparison and Contrast

The extended school year calendar involves an actual increase in the amount of time each year that students would spend in school. For example, students in an extended program would attend school for ten or eleven months out of a year rather than the standard nine. This deviation from the traditional school year is often used to increase students' educational achievement (Shepard 2).

Definition

Exemplification and Process

Summer school is a program that offers remedial or accelerated work during the summer months when regular school is not in session. Summer school does not offer

Definition and

the full range of courses available during regular school terms, and the courses that are offered can be either mandatory or voluntary (Shepard 2).

Negative definition

Year-round school does not involve an increase in the time that students attend each year, nor does the regular year-round calendar offer special remedial or accelerated courses not required for all students. As stated earlier, the student body is divided into groups that start mandatory school sessions at staggered dates. The school year may be divided into three, four, five, or six equal parts, with students required to attend two, three, four, or five of these sections (Shepard 1-2).

Negative definition; process

Discourse Bloc, explaining the logical development of the traditional calendar

The traditional school calendar that lasts from September through June developed during a time when American society was primarily agrarian, and children were needed on the farm from planting season through harvest time. Schools were closed from spring until mid-fall. The standard September through June calendar that is used today grew out of a compromise between the agrarian needs and the longer school calendar utilized in urban areas (Shepard 2-3).

Causation

Effects

In recent years, schools have been faced with problems such as overcrowding and teacher shortages, and there has been increasing interest in maximizing the use of school facilities. There has also been interest in competing with other countries such as Japan, which already offers year-round education to its students. The school calendar based on an agrarian economy is outdated. The year-round school calendar could be an answer to some of the problems of modern schools (Shepard 9).

Effects

Persuasion

Discourse Bloc, illustrating how different year-round school can be implemented

There are six basic types of year-round school calendars. These are the 45-15 School Year, the Quarter School Year, the Concept 6 School Year, the Quinmester School Year, the Trimester School Year, and the Flexible Year-Round School Year. Each involves having at least some portion of students at any given time during the year while the rest are on vacation (Shepard 9).

Classification; enumeration

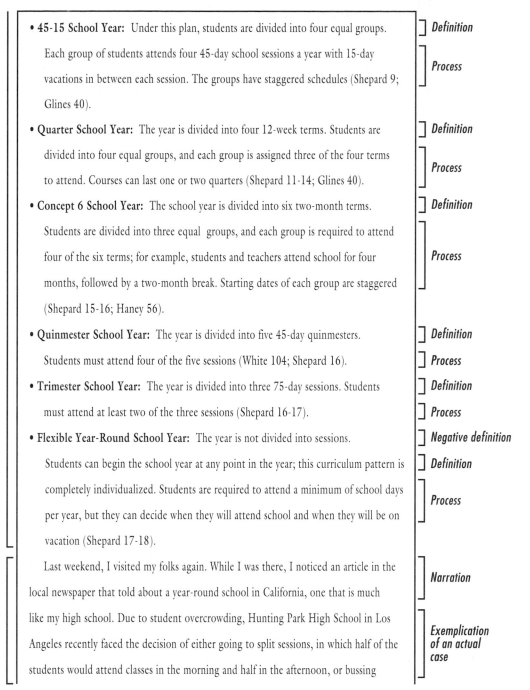

- **45-15 School Year:** Under this plan, students are divided into four equal groups. *Definition*

  Each group of students attends four 45-day school sessions a year with 15-day *Process*

  vacations in between each session. The groups have staggered schedules (Shepard 9;

  Glines 40).

- **Quarter School Year:** The year is divided into four 12-week terms. Students are *Definition*

  divided into four equal groups, and each group is assigned three of the four terms

  to attend. Courses can last one or two quarters (Shepard 11-14; Glines 40). *Process*

- **Concept 6 School Year:** The school year is divided into six two-month terms. *Definition*

  Students are divided into three equal groups, and each group is required to attend

  four of the six terms; for example, students and teachers attend school for four *Process*

  months, followed by a two-month break. Starting dates of each group are staggered

  (Shepard 15-16; Haney 56).

- **Quinmester School Year:** The year is divided into five 45-day quinmesters. *Definition*

  Students must attend four of the five sessions (White 104; Shepard 16). *Process*

- **Trimester School Year:** The year is divided into three 75-day sessions. Students *Definition*

  must attend at least two of the three sessions (Shepard 16-17). *Process*

- **Flexible Year-Round School Year:** The year is not divided into sessions. *Negative definition*

  Students can begin the school year at any point in the year; this curriculum pattern is *Definition*

  completely individualized. Students are required to attend a minimum of school days

  per year, but they can decide when they will attend school and when they will be on *Process*

  vacation (Shepard 17-18).

Discourse Bloc,
Conclusion

Last weekend, I visited my folks again. While I was there, I noticed an article in the *Narration*

local newspaper that told about a year-round school in California, one that is much

like my high school. Due to student overcrowding, Hunting Park High School in Los *Exemplification*
of an actual
case

Angeles recently faced the decision of either going to split sessions, in which half of the

students would attend classes in the morning and half in the afternoon, or bussing students to other areas in the city. School officials decided instead to keep the school open all year long. Students were able to continue their daily routines, although they had to give up their long summer break for two shorter ones in the fall and spring. Huntington is now able to handle 3650 students in buildings designed to accommodate only 2400 (Year-round 5A). The Huntington case is only one example of how schools around the country are using the year-round school calendar to alleviate a host of problems relating to money, personnel, student needs, and facilities.

Driving back to college, I felt contented. The visit had gone well. As usual, I feasted on my Mom's cooking, shopped with my sister, and met with old friends for movies, late-night card games, and gossip. When I talked with my friends about the big change at the high school – the new calendar, I was confident and clear about what year-round school was and would require. And I was able to help my friends understand the idea better, too. I conveyed what I had learned in my college library to my friends, and we all came to understand that the year-round school was not an enemy to defeat as we had once thought; instead, it was a viable solution to the changes that our school needed to adjust to. As I pulled into my dorm parking lot, I experienced a great sense of satisfaction: changes require changes, and change is what growing up is all about.

Narration

Works Cited

Glines, Don. "Schools That Don't Close." <u>California School Boards Journal</u>
  Summer 1987: 35–40

Haney, David. "What About My Summer Vacation?" <u>Thrust</u> Summer 1990:
  55-57

Newman, Michael. "Summertime Blues?" <u>California School Boards Journal</u>
  Summer 1990: 50–54

Shepard, Morris A., and Keith Baker. <u>Year-Round Schools</u>. Lexington, MA:
  Lexington Books, 1977.

White, William D. "Year-Round High Schools: Benefits to Students, Parents,
  and Teachers." <u>NASSP Bulletin</u> January 1988: 103–106

"Year-Round School Has Wide Appeal." <u>Bryan-College Station Eagle</u> 23 March
  1991, sec. A:5.

In an article in the *Los Angeles Times,* Irene Lacher reports on the importance of good book titles. Here is an excerpt:

Did you know?

> Six million softcovers ago, Judith Krantz's first paperback publisher had scruples about the title of her new romance.
>
> The hitch was that his secretary considered *Scruples* a lousy title for a book. After all, what on earth were scruples?
>
> "I asked him if she knows what unscrupulous means," Krantz recalls. "This was the Nixon era. He said, 'Yes.' I said, 'Anyway, I'm not worried about your secretary's understanding. That is the title that's destined for the book. Nobody can make me change it.'"
>
> Destiny? Maybe. If success is destiny's watermark, Krantz's subsequent cavalcade of monster best sellers would indicate that fate—like many publishers—favors short and snappy titles.
>
> More prosaically, a book's title is where poetry, wit and commerce converge. It's the first line of defense in the publishing industry's war of the words. In a publisher's fondest dream, it's the distinctive snippet that will grab you by the lapels and prompt you to buy that one book among many, the catchy phrase that will dance to your lips when you ask if the book is in stock.
>
> . . . Remember that fine classic *Trimalchio in West Egg?* Or the legendary *Tote the Weary Load?* Those misguided early titles were scratched for the more mellifluous—and memorable—*The Great Gatsby* and *Gone With the Wind,* respectively.
>
> . . . For an author, "it's like naming your baby," says Stuart Applebaum, vice president of Bantam Books. "It may have a wonderful importance and resonance for you and your family but be a complete head-scratcher to the world at large.
>
> "While the act of writing may be a monastic one, the act of publishing it—which includes marketing—is very much a collaborative one. So you have a lot of different opinions, which may and may not conform to the author's."
>
> That is precisely what *New York Post* reporter Randall Pierson was up against when he handed in his investigative tome on Leona Helmsley's tax woes. Pierson wanted to call it *Woman on Trial,* which his editors found lackluster.
>
> "We were ready to pull our hair out," says Applebaum. "It was in one of these brainstorming sessions where [Pierson] wasn't present that my colleague Steve Rubin blurted out, 'How about *The Queen of Mean?*'"
>
> Voila.

Functions of Discourse Blocs

While the purposes of discourse blocs are to support and develop topic sentences, they also provide certain structural functions in a text. Texts typically consist of a beginning, middle, and end. But what exactly does that statement mean?

In considering the structure of a text, we discuss the special **functions of discourse blocs** in more detail. We define and explain four major blocs and their roles in a text: *titles, introductions, transitional blocs,* and *conclusions*. Knowing their special functions can clarify and strengthen your judgment concerning the arrangement and development of these discourse blocs.

Titles

Titles are classified as discourse blocs because they initiate the rapport between writer and reader, indicating the focus of the text. Accordingly, the function of a title, the first words that readers see, cannot be undervalued. Boring titles usually result in boring reading. To prove this point, examine the table of contents for a magazine or journal. Which articles tempt you to read them? What are the titles of the pieces you glossed over? If you wouldn't even bother to flip to the first page of these pieces, then we can assume that you will probably never read these texts. A text relies largely upon the interest that a title—the first impression—stirs in readers.

Effective titles are informative and inviting. Review the list of articles you would turn to and read. Why do you think they appealed to you? Often, writers attempt to make their titles "catchy" by using alliteration (repetition of vowel or consonant sounds), turns of phrase, and emotional language. When you compose a title, you want to entice people to read the text—to go beyond the title; however, remember that you also want your title to reflect the tone of your text. Avoid using confusing or sensational titles—no matter how clever or alluring—at the expense of your text's message. If you create a rather obscure or imaginative title, however, add a subtitle that will provide readers with a clearer sense of your focus.

When should you write your title for a text? It depends. Some writers report that they can't write until they've come up with a title; others say the title is the very last matter they attend to; still others admit they alternate between these two approaches. Each writer may express different preferences at different times, depending upon the internal and external influences on them during composing. You are no exception.

Introductions

Introductions serve many functions. Like titles, **introductions** establish a writer's rapport with readers, engaging them and suggesting the subject and focus of a text. In addition, the beginning of a text may accomplish the following functions:

- state or limit the thesis, or both
- provide context or background information
- reveal your credentials to write on this subject
- preview the organization of the document
- define key terms

Not every introduction needs to achieve all of these functions. To design an introduction, consider the nature and length of the document you are writing. The more complex the subject, the longer your text may be; likewise, the longer your text, the longer your introduction may need to be. Practically speaking, the opening discourse bloc for a text should be proportionate to the other major sections within it. The introduction for a book may be an entire chapter; the beginning of a research essay may take up one to four paragraphs, and the opening for a short, informal essay may be completed in a direct, succinct paragraph.

Besides subject and document length, consider also the field or discipline that you are writing in and about. Authors of essays appearing in newspapers or magazines typically get to the point quickly by using some clever or emotional anecdote, statement, question, opinion, or quotation. In this case, the writer needs to grab the attention of an audience whose members expect a text to inform and entertain them. Readers' expectations and their willingness to expend effort are quite different for more formal technical and academic writing. These readers expect introductions to be informative reviews of research literature or descriptive backgrounds of histories and problems. They may also expect these introductory discourse blocs to contain an overview paragraph that clearly forecasts the arrangement of ideas to come.

Some ideas for developing introductions are listed here, followed by several writing strategies:

- Use pathos to stimulate readers' interest and curiosity.

   a dramatic scenario, narrating and describing the situation you wish to focus on

   an anecdote

   a shocking or humorous statement or opinion

- Use ethos to engage your readers by showing the subject's relevance to them.
- Use quotations by respected authorities on the subject.

   a personal, honest account of something related to your subject

   a self-introduction (identify yourself, your background, and your personal involvement with the subject)

- Use logos to establish the importance and urgency of your subject:

  a rhetorical question

  an immediate articulation of your thesis, followed by supporting data

  facts and figures, followed by your thesis

  a review of the literature (historical, social, economic background)

  a description of the problem

  a classification of the subject

  a process description (overview and steps)

  a definition of key terms

You can use any of these strategies to begin your text. However, there are pitfalls that you should be aware of.

- An **inconsistent opening** doesn't match the tone and style of the rest of your document. If the beginning and the rest of your text don't match, your writing may sound as if two different people have composed it. You may lose your credibility and confuse your readers unnecessarily.

- Always compare your introduction to your conclusion to verify that the two discourse blocs correspond in meaning and emphasis. If they don't, your text may convey a **divided thesis**—two different main ideas.

- "Since the beginning of time," "From the dawn of civilization," "Throughout history," "In today's world," "In today's modern society," "From time immemorial"—all are overused statements that will evoke yawns from your readers. Such a **"beginning of time" opening** also suggests that your essay lacks a clear focus.

- "Love has many meanings to many people," "Some people agree with . . . while others disagree," "People are complex because they are different and yet similar." As you can see, the **"empty" opening** provides readers with no direction or sense of the writer's commitment to anything. Instead, this opening signals that the writer has little if anything important to say, is unmoved by the subject, and is trying to mask his or her lack of information. Consequently, readers may become impatient and hostile to the text and the writer; readers suspect that the empty opening statement is mere padding, a waste of their time. What's the solution to this type of opening? Get to the point.

Transitional Discourse Blocs

Transitions are words, phrases, and sentences that help writers and readers move from one idea to another. Similarly, **transitional discourse blocs** are paragraphs that act as bridges from one discourse bloc to another. They signal the end of discussion about one idea and provide a smooth and logical start for the next. Typically, a transitional discourse bloc is a brief paragraph. Long transitional paragraphs can defeat their function as bridges: they interrupt readers' concentration and convey a sense of the separateness of, rather than unity between, discourse blocs.

Conclusions

Conclusions provide writers with graceful exits from the text and give readers a satisfactory sense of closure or completion that both complements and strengthens the thesis. There are numerous ways to fulfill these responsibilities:

- Echo the introduction (a dramatic scenario, anecdote, shocking or humorous climactic statement or opinion, quotations, personal account).
- Recommend a plan of action.
- Summarize the significance of a process or event.
- Outline alternatives and invite readers to choose.
- Offer a solution to a problem.
- Review advantages and disadvantages.
- Respond to the rhetorical question posed in the introduction.
- Predict negative consequences if your recommendation or judgment is ignored.
- Serve as peacemaker, showing how ideas, people, things, and so forth are more similar than different (encourage readers to see their cups as half full instead of half empty).
- Keep lines of communication open (call for reader commitment and participation).
- Relate the implications of your message to other situations.

Conclusions serve as final impressions and thus should be more than vague "decorations" or afterthoughts. Here are three common pitfalls to avoid:

- If you write a conclusion that either undermines your thesis or introduces a different one, you will confuse your reader.
- Resist the temptation to repeat your introduction. Granted, reiterating almost verbatim your opening does guarantee that your closing will match, not contradict, it. However, a blatant cut-and-paste repetition will likely leave your readers cold; they may sense that you are indifferent or condescending to them and the subject. There's nothing wrong with reminding readers of key information presented in the introduction, but you should augment the summary with new ideas that have been advanced and supported within the body of your essay.

- Unless you're writing a very long, complicated text, try not to begin your concluding discourse bloc with clichéd and obvious phrases such as "in conclusion," "in sum," "in closing," and so on. While these signposts are necessary cues in speeches, they seem insulting and unsophisticated in written texts. If you find yourself resorting to these kinds of phrases on occasion, don't worry. The real danger occurs when writers routinely and predictably conclude their texts this way. Just as introductions need to be creative, provocative, and informative, so too do conclusions.

Issues for Writing

1. Bring to class a magazine article to analyze. What methods of development does the writer use? Which methods of development occur most often? Which occur least often? Is the title of the article effective? Why? What kind of introduction and conclusion does it have? How would you improve this text if you were writing it?

2. If you haven't written your own opening narrative for this chapter, compose one now so that you can share it with your group. For each narrative, your group should do the following:

   - identify its aim, purpose, audience, and thesis
   - analyze the function and development of these four discourse blocs: title, introduction, transitional blocs, and conclusion.

   What changes in these discourse blocs would your group suggest? Why? Consider your group's advice and rewrite your narrative in your journal.

Write More About It

In Chapter 13, you'll analyze a historical event, social or cultural trend, technological innovation, or artistic work. Your analysis of a magazine article may give you some useful practice to draw upon when you respond to this upcoming writing task. Or your analysis of this article may become a fuller essay for that writing task.

COHERENCE AND COHESION

The thesis and overall organization of your text should reflect its *unity,* and the arrangement of discourse blocs can reveal its *development.* The third key area of the canon of arrangement is *coherence.* To say writing has **coherence** means that all of the sentences within a particular text are logically related and create a whole. Readers process sentences in sequential order as they appear, unconsciously asking: "What is the meaning of this sentence?" and "What is the relationship between this sentence and the earlier sentences?" Usually, the longer it takes readers to answer both questions, the more difficult the sentence is to understand.

You can connect sentences by using these strategies:

- repetition
- substitution
- parallelism
- transitions

These strategies for creating coherence in a text are called **cohesive devices.** While *coherence* refers to the related meaning of sentences within the overall structure of a text, *cohesion* refers to the presence in each sentence of one or more of these four strategies that link one sentence to the next (Halliday and Hasan).

Repetition

One of the easiest ways to show how one sentence relates to another is by using repetition. **Repetition** means using the same word or words to reinforce, explain, or develop ideas mentioned earlier. The first two sentences in this paragraph illustrate how writers can reiterate a term to connect two sentences; the first sentence introduces the notion of *repetition,* and the second sentence picks up the term and expands on its meaning.

Substitution

Cohesion can be achieved by using a variation of pure repetition called **substitution.** Instead of repeating a word or phrase exactly, you use pronouns and synonyms to refer to previously mentioned ideas. For example, if we were discussing a *computer display unit,* we might refer to it as the *screen, TV monitor, display unit, computer monitor, TV screen, display screen, cathode ray tube,* or *CRT.* And, as you can see, we might also refer to the monitor using the pronoun *it.*

Pronouns and synonyms are effective only if the words for which they substitute or to which they refer are immediately clear to readers. If you are unsure of your readers' familiarity with your substitutions or if you are not certain of the connotation (associated or emotional meanings) of a synonym, use repetition. Avoid sacrificing clarity and accuracy for variety's sake.

Parallelism

Read More About It

See Part X, p. 744.

Ideas or items that share grammatical form and function are said to be **parallel elements.** Words, phrases, and clauses can be developed into parallel elements. Here are some examples of **parallelism:**

Words	The *pitcher, catcher,* and *shortstop* were selected to the all-star team.
Phrases	Before the baseball game started, the mayor *sang the national anthem with the high school choir, delivered a welcoming speech to the crowd,* and *threw the first pitch to the catcher.*
Clauses	*Not only did pitcher Greg Maddox throw a no-hitter, but catcher Damon Berryhill also hit a grand slam.*

This similarity in the arrangement and grammatical structure of ideas or items suggests to readers their similar meanings. As a consequence, parallelism serves as a cohesive strategy that can create coherence when you write.

Transitions

Read More About It

See Part X, p. 697.

When you saw the words *coherence* and *cohesion,* you probably immediately thought of transitional words and phrases. Without question, transitions are popular means of "gluing" one sentence to the next. **Transitions** reinforce both the meaning of and organizational patterns in a text, as the following list illustrates:

additive:	in addition, also, moreover, furthermore
temporal:	meanwhile, while, before, during, after, since
locative:	above, below, adjacent to, perpendicular to
enumerative:	first, second, last, finally
comparative:	similarly, likewise, in the same manner
contrastive:	however, on the other hand, although, whereas, while

causal:	therefore, as a consequence, hence, thus, since, because
illustrative:	for example, namely, such as, thus
explanatory:	that is, in other words
summative:	to summarize, finally, in short, in conclusion

As mentioned before, cohesive devices can clarify relationships among ideas at all levels in a text: sentences, paragraphs, and discourse blocs. And transitional words and phrases are especially effective strategies for achieving this objective.

1. Write a summary of the section on coherence and cohesion. Then analyze your summary by locating specific examples of these cohesive devices: repetition, substitution, parallelism, and transitions.
2. Read "I'm So Hungry, I'm Starving to Death" (Chapter 12). In your group, identify examples of repetition, substitution, parallelism, and transitions in that essay.

Issues for Writing

OUTLINING

Another strategy for arranging information is **outlining.** Outlines are similar to itineraries that chronicle the sequence of activities or places you plan to visit; as a result, outlines help writers logically to plan and double-check their courses of action, ensuring that their progression of ideas has unity, development, and coherence.

Should you always outline before you begin writing? The answer depends on your needs and preferences. You may be a writer who can't begin writing without a detailed working blueprint. In this case, the answer is obvious: start with an outline. However, as you write your rough drafts, remember that you may alter that working blueprint; an outline isn't a fixed entity during the planning, translating, and reviewing processes of writing. On the other hand, you may be a writer who produces outlines only after you've completed a draft of a text. Perhaps you find it easier to get out what you need to say first, outlining afterward to determine and refine the design and development of your document. And you may be one of the many writers who report that they do both: sometimes they construct outlines before they draft, sometimes after.

The type of outline that you write depends not only on your needs but also the nature of your writing task. For example, if you're composing a short text, you probably can work from a topic outline. However, when writing a long, formal text, you may profit by producing a more elaborate, careful, and detailed sentence outline. The aim and purpose of your writing influence how elaborate and formal your outline needs to be.

No matter when you choose to outline or what type of outline you produce, it is important that you eventually write one. Outlining allows you to review and analyze the information you have presented. A good outline will help you determine whether your document achieves these important objectives:

- Your main idea is clear.
- Your ideas are relevant and logically ordered.
- Your key points are all covered.
- Your development of ideas is sufficient and proportionate to their difficulty and importance in the text.
- Your readers can understand and follow your presentation of ideas.

In a way, an outline serves as an informal table of contents. Like a table of contents, it provides a preview of the information contained in the pages to follow, and this type of preview can be invaluable to writers as they read, think, evaluate, and revise.

Conventions for Outlines

An **outline** provides a visual overview of the relationship among ideas in a text. For example, indentation signals that one idea is subordinate to another. To compose an outline, first write your thesis statement at the left-hand margin. Next, list major and minor points, systematically indenting as you move from main topics to subtopics. Ideas that share the same relative importance in the same way should be indented the same number of spaces; moreover, like ideas should be expressed in parallel form, which reinforces their similarity.

Indentation and parallelism are further reinforced by the use of a consistent numbering and lettering system that reflects the logical sequence of ideas, as follows:

- Capital roman numerals (I, II, III, IV) indicate main ideas.
- Capital letters (A, B, C, D) indicate subordinate ideas.
- Arabic numerals (1, 2, 3, 4) introduce the next level of subordination.
- Lowercase letters (a, b, c, d) signal another level of specificity.
- Lowercase roman numerals (i, ii, iii, iv) signal minor points.

Clearly, ideas with the same level of importance should have the same kind of numeral or letter and be indented in the same way. (Remember that if you divide a section of your outline into subsections, you must have at least two subsections: if you have an A, you must have a B, and so on.)

Types of Outlines

Let's see how these conventions are used in topic outlines, sentence outlines, and computer outliners.

Topic Outlines

A **topic outline** is a general description of the main points in a text. This type of outline is usually rather informal, including the thesis statement, introduction, major and minor points, and the conclusion. Below is an example of a topic outline:

Thesis: Outlines are similar to itineraries that chronicle the sequence of activities or places you plan to visit; as a result, outlines help writers logically plan and double-check their courses of action, ensuring that their progression of ideas has unity, development, and coherence.

   I. Outlining
      A. Time to outline
      B. Kinds of outlines
      C. Objectives of outlining
  II. Conventions for Outlines
      A. Ideas in outlines
         1. Thesis statement
         2. Major points
         3. Minor points
      B. Presentation of ideas in outlines
         1. Thesis at the beginning
         2. Indentation
         3. Parallelism
         4. Lettering
            a. Capital roman numerals for main ideas
            b. Capital letters for subordinate ideas
            c. Arabic numerals for next level of subordination
            d. Lowercase letters for the next level of specificity
            e. Lowercase roman numerals for minor points
 III. Types of Outlines
      A. Topic outlines
      B. Sentence outlines
      C. Computer outliners

Topic outlines take little time to write and are effective for short, simple texts. However, for longer documents, you will probably need to develop a formal or sentence outline.

Sentence Outlines

In these outlines, you write in complete sentences. Unlike a topic outline that doesn't force you to reveal specific details, a **sentence outline** requires you to articulate complete thoughts. Here is an example:

Thesis: Outlines help writers logically plan and double-check their courses of action, ensuring that their progression of ideas has reasonable unity, development, and coherence.

   I. Outlining is a strategy for arranging information.
     A. Many writers report that they construct outlines at different times in their composing processes: before, during, and after.
     B. The kind of outline that you write depends on your needs and the nature of your writing task.
     C. Outlining allows you to review and analyze the information you have presented and serves as an informal table of contents.
  II. An outline provides a systematic, visual overview of the relationship among ideas in a text.
     A. The ideas in an outline are presented in hierarchical order.
       1. The thesis statement is the most important information in the outline; everything in the outline should be related to and support it.
       2. The major points follow the thesis.
       3. The major points are broken down into logical minor points.
     B. The ideas in an outline are designed according to formatting conventions.
       1. The thesis statement appears at the beginning of the outline.
       2. The indentation of ideas signals their level of importance and specificity.
       3. Parallelism helps reinforce the fact that ideas are similar.
       4. Lettering indicates the order and importance of ideas.
         a. Capital roman numerals are used for main ideas.
         b. Capital letters are used for subordinate ideas.
         c. Arabic numerals are used for the next level of subordination.
         d. Lowercase letters introduce the next level of specificity.
         e. Lowercase roman numerals introduce minor points.
 III. Writers use three basic types of outlines.
     A. Most writers use topic outlines, general descriptions of the major and minor points in a text.
     B. Sentence outlines require the articulation of complete thoughts.
     C. Computer outliners allow writers to indent, number, and letter items, as well as rearrange headings and content to improve organization, automatically.

This sentence outline is a logical extension of the writer's thinking on the topic and is very close to the text that it describes. Because it is so much more complete than the topic outline, this type of outline is particularly valuable as a guide for both writing and revising. And, with the development of computer programs that have outlining functions, even sentence outlining can be quick and easy. The next section discusses computer outliners in more detail.

Computer Outliners

Word processing programs are constantly becoming more powerful and sophisticated. One specific example that supports this observation is computer outliners. **Computer outliners** allow you to indent, number, and letter items automatically. That is, simple commands indent text swiftly and easily to the right or "outdent" it from the left. "Cut" and "paste" functions let you rearrange headings to improve organization. "Insert" and "delete" functions let you develop and change the content of your outline. Finally, *windows* that can be opened simultaneously let you move interactively between your invention notes and outline; you can save yourself work by copying or moving text from one window to another. If your program doesn't have multiple windows, you can still copy from one file (document) to another.

In addition, you can use your computer outliner to accomplish the following special functions:

Split-screen viewing. **Split-screen viewing** allows you to see your text and outline at once on two different windows on your computer monitor. As a consequence, you can move back and forth between your draft and outline, making corresponding changes in both places in a fluid and natural way.

Hidden annotations. Some computer outliners permit you to embed annotations (comments and explanations for your eyes only) after headings; these private notes can be "hidden" so that, while they appear on your computer screen, they do not appear in your printed copy. **Hidden annotations** help you remember key information and develop the ideas in your outline and draft more fully.

Sorting. A **sorting** function automatically groups information alphabetically or numerically for your entire outline or for individual parts. The advantage of sorting is that it enables you to organize different levels of information and check the logical order of your ideas in a systematic and thorough manner.

Issues for Writing

1. What function does outlining serve for you? Do you outline before, during, or after you write? Does outlining help you to draft or to revise? Do you prefer topic or sentence outlines? Why? Discuss your answers with your group.

2. Make a topic and sentence outline of one of the essays in Part VI, Readings. What advantages and disadvantages do you think outlines provide for writers? What advantages and disadvantages do outlines provide for readers?

OVERALL TEXT STRUCTURE AND DISCOURSE BLOCS: WRITERS' COMMON CONCERNS

The more you write, the more you will discover strategies that work well for you; in addition, you'll experience writing situations that challenge and confound you. To help you with these situations, we've compiled some common concerns about the structure of texts. Notice that our responses to these problems are computer oriented; however, they may be done with pen and paper as well. While you may not always compose on a computer from start to finish, you may wish to experiment by using it intermittently during your planning, translating, and reviewing processes. Consider our troubleshooting advice when you have concerns about the following problems.

Divided Thesis

When your text advances two different main points or theses, it has a **divided thesis.** One of the quickest ways to detect this problem is by comparing your introduction and conclusion. Often, writers compose conclusions days or weeks after they've written the openings and bodies of their texts. As they wrote, however, they began to analyze their data differently. Because of this, either the conclusion now differs from the earlier parts, or the opening conflicts with the body and conclusion. This incongruity is a normal, even beneficial process that occurs in writing; it is part of the discovery and creation of meaning that makes writing such a powerful act. While this shift in your thinking helps you work through ideas as you write, it may confuse or frustrate readers.

To avoid this pitfall, use the split-screen function on your computer so that you can see both the introduction and conclusion on the screen. Read them in order. Do they correspond? Do the tone, level of formality, and types of details seem consistent? Does the ending fulfill what the opening promised? If not, reread the entire text to determine which discourse bloc or blocs—the introduction or conclusion, or perhaps both—need to be revised.

The Five-Paragraph Theme

A **five-paragraph theme** is a traditional arrangement consisting of a thesis statement with three points. The thesis is presented in the first paragraph and basically tells what the writer is going to say. In mechanical fashion, the body of the essay says what the writer said he or she promised to say. That is, paragraph 2 covers the first point, paragraph 3 discusses the second point, and paragraph 4 explains the last point. Paragraph 5 summarizes what has just been said.

While this essay structure is direct and easy for most writers and readers to follow, it has limited use in college or professional writing situations where you are focusing on complex, specialized subjects. In these instances, readers expect more depth and details in a text: a three-point, five-paragraph essay may suggest to readers that the discussion is simplistic, or that the writer isn't knowledgeable about the subject, or that the writer is "talking down" to readers. As an effective writer, you want to avoid any arrangement that can foster these misperceptions. Most ideas can't be broken down into three points, yet even if they logically can, each point can't always be adequately developed in a single paragraph. That's why we urge writers to think of idea units as discourse blocs, not as paragraphs.

Here's a general troubleshooting strategy that may help you to move beyond the five-paragraph theme. Type your five paragraphs into the computer. Place a page break after each paragraph so that you now have a document that is five pages long. Then closely examine your first paragraph to find your thesis. Isolate the thesis by changing it from plain type to boldface. Is it accurate? Do you have enough information to support it? Rather than presenting a thesis that lists three things to cover, how can you present a main idea that offers an overview of the subject? (See "Thesis Statement," p. 124.) Does this introduction need to be developed further, or is a single paragraph sufficient to interest readers and provide an overview of the subject? Now, reread the section on introductions that appears earlier in this chapter to consider ways to enhance and hone this discourse bloc.

Once you have examined the introduction, turn to pages 2, 3, and 4 of your document, copying the boldfaced thesis at the top of each page. If you are satisfied with the key ideas and organization, begin analyzing the discourse blocs to see if they are too broad and underdeveloped (see "Underdeveloped Discourse Blocs," p. 155). Revise accordingly. You may be surprised at how much longer and more fully developed these discourse blocs become as you attend to them, one by one; you may find, for example, that you offer more details and integrate transitional blocs. The purpose of this review is to make certain that your ideas support your thesis and are expressed in focused, well developed discourse blocs.

Now go back to page 1, and reread your introduction in light of the revisions you've made to the body of your essay. What changes are necessary? Why? Do you need to replace your original thesis in your introduction with a revised one? If so, revise your thesis and introduction. Keep your thesis in boldface. Copy your revised introductory discourse bloc onto your last page of the document, where your conclusion appears. Compare the two discourse blocs. Do they correspond? Is one paragraph sufficient to give readers a sense of closure and clarity at the end of the essay? Would a longer conclusion belabor the point or be construed as padding? Review the strategies for writing endings presented earlier in this chapter to discover ways of strengthening this discourse bloc.

Read More About It

See Part VIII.

Using the computer to view each discourse bloc allows you to see how the parts combine to support the whole; that is, the body must justify the introduction and conclusion. This approach invites you to develop ideas by generating fuller discussions of them, thereby making a five-paragraph theme virtually impossible.

The five-paragraph structure is appropriate in certain situations: for example, in timed essay exams. Essay tests are usually designed to showcase students' abilities to provide specific information. Consequently, the predictable organization of the five-paragraph theme readily displays to the test evaluator what you know. It also can make composing your answer relatively fast and automatic. Obviously, before approaching an essay test in this way, you would need to analyze the rhetorical situation: the subject, level of the class, type of essay examination (timed or take-home), your expertise, and the test question itself.

Chronological or Writer-Based Arrangement

Chronological organization is sometimes referred to as **writer-based prose** because it centers around you and your account of how you did or knew something. Narratives and processes require you to follow sequences in time; chronological order meets both your and your readers' needs and expectations. However, for many other types of documents, unfolding ideas along a time line is inappropriate, giving readers information that they neither need nor want.

Arranging your writing into chronological order every time would be a mistake for other reasons as well. It would arbitrarily privilege time over other important principles of organization and meaning, such as spatial, hierarchical, and categorical patterns. If you use chronological order to the exclusion of other organizing principles, your writing may become repetitive, and you risk losing your readers' interest. It is better to think creatively about your ideas and be open to a variety of arrangements for your text, as appropriate to your rhetorical situation and choices (aim and purpose, subject, audience, writer, principles of organization). For example, in texts that evaluate an issue, take a position on an issue, and propose a solution to a problem, it may be important to build tension or to construct your arguments progressively; these rhetorical considerations might not be well served by a chronological arrangement.

One way to resist the temptation to rely exclusively on chronological arrangements is to type your text into the computer and then classify ideas. Then, you can organize them further according to similarities or differences, advantages or disadvantages, greatest to least importance or frequency, and so on. If your computer has the capacity, try producing a graphic (tree diagram, organizational chart) to visualize the kind and amount of information you have gathered. Then you can begin to explore different methods of arrangement that will better support your thesis and respond more directly to your rhetorical situation.

Unfocused Discourse Blocs

Have you ever written a discourse bloc of one or more paragraphs that seemed disjointed or unrelated when you reread it? The discourse bloc contained interesting and important points, but the ideas didn't quite come together. The paragraphs weren't different enough to represent different discourse blocs, yet they weren't purposefully associated. This is a description of an **unfocused discourse bloc.**

To address this problem, call up this discourse bloc on your computer screen. Then identify the overall topic sentence that best reflects the purpose of this part of your text; if you can't find a strong topic sentence, compose one and put it at the beginning of the bloc. Format this sentence in boldface or all capital letters so that it appears prominently on the screen. Ask yourself what principle of organization and which modes might best develop this point; plan to try several. Write, integrating into your selected patterns any sentences from your previous draft that work effectively in your current draft. After you've finished the various versions, identify and underline sentences in each paragraph within the discourse bloc that either narrow or illustrate supporting ideas of the topic sentence. Then, compare each of these underlined sentences with your overall topic sentence (in bold or all capital letters). Are they all related? Do they follow some logical principle of organization? If they don't, revise these sentences as needed. Then review each paragraph to ensure that every sentence is related to its topic sentence and overall thesis statement. Using this approach to unfocused discourse blocs will help you to design paragraphs and sentences that support and illustrate your meaning.

Underdeveloped Discourse Blocs

If your discourse blocs consist of short paragraphs that contain noticeably fewer words and sentences than those around them, they may represent **underdeveloped discourse blocs.** There are two ways to address this concern.

Scroll to this discourse bloc, and, using the "copy" function on your word processing program, duplicate the bloc. In this way, you maintain the original version and have a copy to experiment with. Now you're ready to review and revise.

The first consideration should be whether or not you have segmented the discourse bloc into too many paragraphs, resulting in choppy or thin paragraphs. To check this, delete all paragraph indentations in this bloc. Now read. Experiment with the sentences and words: move sentences, delete any repetitions, and rework transitions as necessary. In combining several short paragraphs, have you created a more focused and developed one? Discourse blocs may contain one or more paragraphs, so if this bloc is more effective as a single, longer paragraph rather than a series of skimpy ones, that's fine.

If combining the paragraphs within the discourse bloc isn't the answer, ask yourself three questions: "Is the purpose of each paragraph within this bloc clear?" "Are the paragraphs logically ordered and effective?" "What other information can I integrate into these paragraphs to make them stronger?"

Find your overall topic sentence for this discourse bloc, and format it in boldface; for each of the paragraphs within the bloc, locate and underline sentences that indicate their purposes or rhetorical justification. Read the entire discourse bloc again. Move the boldfaced and underlined material onto one place on your computer screen. Read it to see how the sentences are related.

If you're satisfied with the key ideas and their ordering, consider how you can add more concrete details, examples, case studies, facts, statistics, quotations, paraphrases, or summaries to make the paragraphs in the discourse bloc more specific. Because you are working on a copy of the discourse bloc, experiment freely; you can always recall your original discourse bloc.

To generate more information within discourse blocs, you can use a strategy called **TRIPSQA** (pronounced *tripskuh*). This acronym stands for topic, restriction, illustration; problem, solution; question, answer. Each letter can represent one or more full paragraphs in a discourse bloc, or each grouping (TRI, PS, QA) may be used to develop a one-paragraph discourse bloc (Young and Becker). The complexity of your subject and the nature of your writing task will determine the type of internal structure your discourse blocs will require. How does TRIPSQA work? Label each sentence or group of related sentences on your computer screen according to function; then diagram the various options each may offer you as you analyze and revise your discourse bloc. Here are some examples.

Topic sentence	states the main idea. *"When we think of dinosaurs, we often imagine the meat-eating Tyrannosaurus Rex; however, most dinosaurs were plant eaters."*
Restriction	narrows the focus of the topic sentence. *"One of the most interesting plant eaters*

was the maiasaur, a 25-foot-long duck-billed dinosaur."

Illustration

adds specific support (examples, concrete details, facts, etc.) to the idea expressed in the topic sentence. *"Maiasaurs lived on a diet of dogwoods, evergreens, and berry bushes. Their babies were also nourished on these plants. For example, a duckbill parent would chew and swallow berries, seeds, and grass that grew near its nest and then regurgitate this repast into the mouths of the hungry baby maiasaurs."*

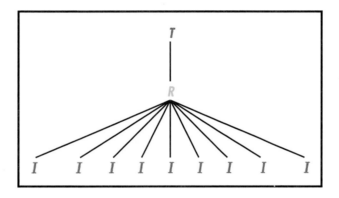

Problem

identifies the history or context of the conflict or dilemma. *"How can we verify the theory that maintains that dinosaurs were some sort of prehistoric bird?"*

Solution

names, explains, and justifies a proposed plan of action to address the problem. *"According to dinosaur researchers, we can take the dinosaur leg bones (for example, those of the troodon, the herrerasaurus, or the comsognathus) and compare them to the leg bones of chickens and other birds to determine their similarities in structure and position. From this very elementary comparative anatomy, we should be able to either prove or disprove this theory."*

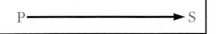

Question   frames the conflict or dilemma in question form, suggesting a dialogic tone. *"Should we believe the old myths that suggest that dinosaurs were slow, clumsy, lumbering, cold-blooded meat eaters?"*

Answer   responds to the question with specific details and plans. *"We think not. If we examine the footprint fossils and calculate their running speed and musculature for supporting their bodies, we know dinosaurs were rather agile and fast. And by studying the trekking and migration patterns of dinosaurs, we can also conclude that they were hot-blooded reptiles, some carnivores and some herbivores, with high metabolism rates."*

TRIPSQA focuses your reader and you on the key information in the discourse bloc. And this attention to the relationship among your ideas prohibits you from padding your discourse blocs with extraneous details. When writers try to develop their ideas further, they sometimes overcompensate, leading to the next pitfall: sprawling discourse blocs.

Sprawling Discourse Blocs

What do you do if your paragraphs extend to one or two pages at times? What you have before you is *sprawl;* that is, multiple paragraph discourse blocs are consolidated into a massive paragraph that contains more words and sentences than other blocs with similar purposes in your text. **Sprawling discourse blocs** are disproportionate to other discourse blocs in a document and are difficult to read. They need to be revised.

To address this problem, read the bloc to determine its topic, and always make a copy of this discourse bloc before you begin revising. Use the "underline" function on your computer to identify key ideas within the passage. Begin a new paragraph for each underlined sentence. To analyze your passage, you might try identifying sentences according to the TRIPSQA strategy. Each letter in the acronym may indicate the need for a paragraph break. As always, delete unrelated or repetitive material.

Topic Headings

Depending on the purpose, audience, and type of text that you are writing, using headings to signal discourse blocs may or may not be appropriate. Headings are routinely used in professional and academic publications. For college writing tasks, it's a good idea to ask your instructor before including them.

Topic headings can indicate the overall text structure, summarize the topics and purposes of each discourse bloc, and provide transitions between blocs. Not only do they serve an organizational function, but they also can help writers analyze their discourse blocs to determine whether a bloc is underdeveloped or sprawling.

When you include headings, remember these guidelines:

- Headings should be succinct, clear, and parallel. If one heading is in question form, all should be interrogatives.

- Headings should be brief, logical, and parallel. Double-check for these criteria by creating a table of contents from your headings. If you are using a computer, use the table of contents function of your word processing program.

- Even though headings provide transitions between discourse blocs, sentences that precede headings should serve this function as well.

- The first sentence after a heading should not depend on the heading for its meaning: "This is a good topic. . . ." What does "this" refer to? Would readers know the sentence's meaning if the heading were deleted?

If used appropriately, headings can be powerful aids for readers and writers.

---

1. Using TRIPSQA, compose a discourse bloc on one of the following topics: food labeling, child care facilities, telephone answering machines, endangered species, intramural sports, violence on television.

2. In your group, compile a list of all the advice you have been given over the years regarding the structure and organization of essays. What advice is common to all group members? How does this advice compare with the guidelines in this chapter?

3. Locate a news magazine article that uses headings. Do the headings improve your ability to see the logical sequence of thought? Why?

4. Either compose or find an example of one of the following:

   - divided thesis
   - five-paragraph theme
   - chronological or writer-based arrangement
   - unfocused discourse bloc
   - underdeveloped discourse bloc
   - sprawling discourse bloc

   In your journal, revise your discourse bloc. First, identify which kind of discourse bloc you have produced or found, and then use the strategies in this chapter to revise.

Issues for Writing

The arrangement guide in Figure 5.2 summarizes the principles of arrangement presented in this chapter. You'll find this guide especially useful as you respond to the writing tasks in Chapters 8–17.

Figure 5.2 Arrangement guide

Arrangement Guide

Evidence: Establishing Unity

1. Has your research yielded sufficient, plausible, and pertinent information to support your thesis?
2. How do your research data reflect the three rhetorical appeals: ethos, logos, and pathos?
3. How does your research shape your thesis statement ? Is your thesis statement specific and concrete? Focused and feasible? Interesting?
4. How do the patterns of organization in your text help readers see and follow the logic and approach to your subject? Have you chosen sequential organization (chronological, spatial, hierarchical), categorical organization, or a mix of the two? Why?

Discourse Blocs: Developing Ideas

1. What is the internal structure of your text? Identify and outline the discourse blocs in your essay.
2. What modes of development have you used within the discourse blocs? Why?
3. What functions do the various discourse blocs serve (title, introduction, transitional blocs, conclusions)?

Coherence and Cohesion: Making Connections

1. Have you connected sentences by using repetition, substitution, and transitions?
2. Have you used parallelism for coordinated and listed items? To reinforce ideas of equal importance or similar meaning?

Outlining: Tracing Your Path

1. Have you written an outline, either before or after you've drafted your text? Does it seem logical and clear?
2. How will you refine the design and development of your text in the next draft?

Works Cited

Booth, Wayne. "The Rhetorical Stance." *College Composition and Communication* 14 (1963): 139–145.
Braddock, Richard. "The Frequency and Placement of Topic Sentences in Expository Prose." *Research in the Teaching of English* 3 (1974): 287–304.
Halliday, M. A. K., and Ruqaiya Hasan. *Cohesion in English*. London: Longman, 1976.

Lacher, Irene. "Book Title That Sells Is Elusive But Crucial." *Los Angeles Times* 12 Jan. 1992, G1+.

Pitkin, Willis L. "Discourse Blocs." *College Composition and Communication* 20 (1969): 138–148.

Rodgers, Paul C., Jr. "The Stadium of Discourse." *College Composition and Communication* 18 (1967): 178–185.

Shearer, N. A. "Alexander Bain and the Genesis of Paragraph Theory." *Quarterly Journal of Speech* 58 (1972): 399–408.

Young, Richard E., and Alton L. Becker. "Toward a Modern Theory of Rhetoric: A Tagmemic Contribution." *Harvard Educational Review* 35 (1965): 450–468.

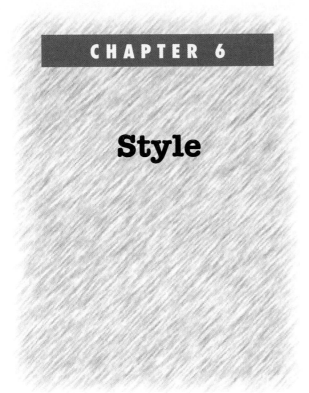

CHAPTER 6

Style

Both of my parents are children of Italian immigrants. Both were born and raised in Cleveland, Ohio, and still live there. As I was growing up, I learned particular ways of saying things that were peculiar to my environment, though I never realized this at the time. For example, whenever members of my family visited friends and relatives and were offered something to eat or drink, my father and mother would always answer, "Oh, I don't care." Their meaning was something like "Please don't go to any trouble just for me because I am but a guest and this is your house and I am already imposing on you just by my visit, but if you are getting something to eat or drink for yourself or if something is already prepared, then yes I would be most grateful, but only if it is not inconvenient for you." This is the humble perspective of immigrants—new arrivals who see themselves imposing on the hospitality of their adopted land and its people— and I am sure my parents learned this style from their parents, as I learned it from my parents.

The feigned indifference of the expression "I don't care" essentially relieved the host of the social obligation to serve food or drink to the guest. It also allowed the host to display the sincerity and generosity of his or her hospitality: that is, the host would always serve the food or drink in spite of the guest's expression of indifference. This habit was so ingrained that it was the typical reply to all offers of food and drink, even within my immediate family. If I asked my mother, "Would you like a cup of tea?" she would answer, "Oh, I don't care." I used this expression all through childhood, adolescence, my four years of college, and two years as a professional writer/editor—always responding to offers of food or drink with what I was raised to believe was the polite reply: "Oh, I don't care."

On the day I started graduate school, I met the woman I would marry. Linda is from Syracuse, New York. She is of English heritage: her father's parents immigrated from England, and her mother's family was here before the American Revolution. Linda's family, as a consequence, developed a different perspective on social obligations. In Linda's family, it is the host's obligation to satisfy the guest and the guest's only obligation is to display satisfaction. If offered food or drink, the polite reply is "Oh yes, that would be nice."

As you might guess, this difference of style caused us a little difficulty at the beginning. We would have conversations like the following:

"Sam, would you like a cup of coffee?"

"Oh, I don't care."

"Oh, well, how about some tea?"

"I don't care."

"Hot chocolate?"

"I don't care."

"Do you want anything?"

"I don't care."

> *"I'm getting myself some water. How about if I get you a glass too?"*
> *"Okay."*
> *While I thought I was being a polite guest, Linda believed that I was saying I was dissatisfied with the type of drink she was offering. She also thought my expression of indifference was ungracious and offensive. Nevertheless, she believed that she was obliged as a host to keep looking for a drink that I would consider satisfactory. (SD)*

I thus discovered that my "Oh, I don't care" was neither always polite nor always impolite. It was a question of style—of appropriate or inappropriate—as opposed to a question of right or wrong. If I was speaking to my family, "Oh, I don't care" was effective communication of my gratitude. If I was addressing my wife's family, however, my expression of feigned indifference communicated dissatisfaction. I also discovered that my expression was peculiar to my ethnic and regional dialect. I questioned my colleagues; the majority thought "I don't care" was impolite. As a consequence, today I avoid "I don't care" unless I am speaking to my family.

Similarly, it is important for you to adjust your style of speaking or writing to suit your audience and purpose. Learning to adjust your style—developing the ability to choose the appropriate style—is critical to the effective communication of your ideas.

Issues for Writing

1. In your journal, write your own opening narrative for this chapter. In your story, describe your experience with a misunderstanding caused by language—a time when you said or wrote something that was misinterpreted or a time when you misinterpreted something said or written to you. How did this misunderstanding occur? Was it serious or comic?

2. Share your narrative with the other members of your focus group. How is the misunderstanding you describe similar to theirs? How is it different? Do you think such misunderstandings could have been avoided? Explain your answer.

Write More About It

In Chapter 10, we will ask you to tell the story of a significant event. If you choose to write from knowledge by participation, this exercise could help you generate ideas for this essay. For example: How did the misunderstanding start? What was said or written? How was it interpreted? Who was the speaker/writer and who was the listener/reader? Where did the misunderstanding occur? When? What were the consequences?

WHAT IS STYLE?

Style is the way you speak or write. It includes your choice of words, your manner of putting words together to compose sentences, and your handling of the mechanical issues of oral communication, like pronunciation, or of written communication, like spelling and punctuation. Your vocabulary might be simple (e.g., *I will try to find out the truth of this claim*) or complicated (e.g., *I will endeavor to ascertain the veracity of this assertion*). You might depend chiefly on nouns and verbs to communicate your message or use lots of adjectives, adverbs, and prepositional phrases. You might compose simple sentences or complex sentences. You might spell words according to the way you pronounce them (e.g., *vittles*) or adopt the dictionary's spelling (e.g., *victuals*). You might capitalize words you consider important (e.g., *I visit my Mother once a week*) or comply with the guidelines of a typical style manual (e.g., *I visit my mother once a week*). However you do it, this is your style.

Different writers have different writing styles. In writing this book, for example, we have discovered that we have different styles. Look at the brief narratives at the beginning of Chapter 1 and Chapter 3: Notice that Gwen's narrative of her experience in Malaysia is highly descriptive and includes direct quotations, whereas Sam summarizes his family's typical holiday dinner, stripping the narrative to its essential ingredients. Each style is distinctive. You might like Gwen's style and dislike Sam's, or vice versa, but neither style is necessarily right or wrong.

No writing style is correct or incorrect. Instead, a writer's style is more or less appropriate, more or less effective. And your audience and purpose determine how appropriate or how effective your style is. In the previous paragraph, for example, we directed you to look at the *narratives* at the beginning of Chapter 1 and Chapter 3. We originally thought of referring to such narratives as *vignettes* because that was the word we used for these autobiographical pieces whenever we discussed them with each other. (A *vignette* is literary terminology for a narrative of a brief occurrence or incident.) We chose to use the word *narrative* here because we realized that you might be unfamiliar with the word *vignette*. And we thought that if we stopped to define the word *vignette,* we would distract you from the issue we were trying to emphasize—the different writing styles of the two narrative passages. Thus *narrative* was the more appropriate, more effective word for us to use because of who we were writing for and why we were writing.

INFLUENCES ON YOUR STYLE

According to language researchers David Crystal and Derek Davy, a number of factors influence your style, including the following:

- your individual style choices
- the period of time during which you speak or write as well as your age and your audience's age
- the dialect of your geographical and social groups
- collaborative composing
- the discipline or field of your subject
- the type of document you compose
- your relationship with your audience

Individuality

Because you are a unique individual, you speak or write in distinctive ways. For example, you might use *since* instead of *because* or *while* instead of *whereas*. You might avoid particular words or use a favorite word again and again. You might enjoy composing complicated sentences or joining two sentences with a semicolon instead of starting a new sentence. You might maximize adjectives and minimize adverbs, or vice versa. You might like *preventative* and dislike *preventive*, spell *judgment* as *judgement*, or prefer *sulfur* to *sulphur*. Your choices might be idiosyncratic and peculiar or familiar and common. Your choices might be conscious or unconscious, important or unimportant, but each is the echo of your individual language experiences, and each contributes to your style.

Time

The period of **time** during which you write or speak influences your style. As society changes so does the language that people use to discuss their lives within that society. Technological innovations, for example, require new technical terminology. Thus the *ice box* gives way to the *refrigerator* and the *record* and the *record player* give way to *CDs* and *CD players*. If your essay mentions *carbon copies,* this usage signals to readers either that you are discussing a time before the invention or wide availability of copy machines or that you are using virtually antiquated terminology.

Time also influences the meaning of words. For example, during World War II, a *blockbuster* was a big bomb that could destroy a full city block. Today, to the majority of people, a *blockbuster* is quite the opposite of a *bomb:* it is a movie that is explosive at the box office, selling lots of tickets and making lots of money.

Your age and the age of your audience are also important indicators of the influence of time. If you were writing on the subject of war for a group of retired citizens, for example, you might choose your evidence and examples from World War II, using the terminology characteristic of that war (e.g., *displaced persons, blitzkrieg*); if you were also a retired citizen, you would be quite familiar with this terminology. If you are a young man or woman addressing other young men and women on the subject of war, however, you might be more likely to adopt the language of later wars (e.g., *ethnic cleansing, surgical bombing*).

Occasionally, the spelling of a word changes over time; for example, yesterday's *aeroplane* is today's *airplane*. The way we capitalize words also changes. If you pick up a copy of *Gulliver's Travels* (published in 1727), you will notice that virtually every noun is capitalized. Today we capitalize words more selectively.

Time also influences the phrasing of ideas. In earlier times, writers often used numerous adjectives and adverbs, a complicated vocabulary, and long and complex sentences. This **elaborate style** developed partially because the ability to read and write was a rarity: people with academic training were a fraction of the population, and people with a university education were a fraction of that fraction. The ability to write was evidence of the writer's level of education, and the more elaborate the writing, the more educated the writer was perceived to be. Only a small number of people could write, and the technology for publication and distribution was slow and expensive. Available reading material was quite limited; as a consequence, people could give each piece of reading material a lot of time and attention and thus could easily tolerate the elaborate style.

Today, a clear majority of Americans read and write, and people with a college education compose 20 percent of the population. The importance or desirability of writers displaying their level of education through elaborate wording and phrasing has thus diminished. In addition, more writers are creating more reading material for more readers, and the technology of publishing and disseminating information has undergone extraordinary advances. People have more and more rapid access to more and more information, more and more reading to do, and less and less time to do it. One consequence of these educational and technological changes is that people today prefer a plain writing style; that is, people like writing that avoids unnecessary words, that is direct, straightforward, and crisp, using simple and common words instead of complicated and fancy words. **Plain style** is considered easier to read and to write and thus more efficient for both reader and writer.

Elaborate and plain style, however, are two opposing orientations to style as opposed to two different types of style. And although the plainer style is dominant, writers and speakers often adopt a more elaborate style. The ceremonial language of wedding invitations and the impassioned language of political campaign speeches are examples of this more elaborate style. Consider the following address:

> The people of this rich and beautiful land have articulated time and time again their inexorable desire to create a shining example for the millions of people who inhabit this delicate world, a shining

example of all that is glorious, all that is miraculous, all that a democratic community might achieve by simply and patiently working together with generosity of spirit, purity of heart, and nobility of mind. This desire finds its most treasured expression among the indefatigable pioneers of our nation's history, those men and women who toiled so vigorously to establish human virtue as the timeless foundation of civic governance. Our collective task today is to give equally poetic, equally enduring expression to this basic national objective.

In plain style, this is a less stirring paragraph:

The people of this nation have said again and again that they would like to show the rest of the world that democracy can bring out people's best qualities. The people who founded this nation probably said this best. They worked hard to make virtue the basis for our laws. Our job today is to repeat this same message to the people of the world.

The language of bureaucracy also illustrates a more elaborate style. This is a style of writing, however, that is ordinarily criticized because it obscures ideas and inflates the importance of the writer and his or her subject. It is fancy language without passion, inspiration, or a ceremonial motivation. It has been denounced as "the official style" (Lanham) because it is often the language of civic, military, and business officials. This elaborate style uses complicated words and long and sprawling sentences so that small and simple ideas seem big and complex. Consider, for example, the following:

At the present time, it is of utmost importance that the determination and dissemination of all additional policies and procedures regarding any quantifiable or nonquantifiable subject be hereafter terminated at the earliest possible opportunity.

The plain English version is considerably easier:

Stop making rules.

Dialect

Social, regional, and ethnic **dialects** also influence your style. If you live in Texas, for example, you might speak or write using expressions like *I was fixing to paint the house*. If you live in West Virginia you might adopt expressions like *The house needs painted*. **Local dialects** are characteristic of a specific group and carry prestige only within that group. If you are addressing a specific group, it is often appropriate to use the local dialect to communicate your message. **Universal dialects** have a wider currency and carry prestige across specific groups. Such is the case with a dialect of

Read More About It

See Part X.

English that might be called **classroom English.** This is the dialect, for example, of schoolteachers, businesspeople, and journalists; it is the dialect of dictionary spellings and grammar books. In classroom English, *fixing to* would be *going to* or *getting ready to* and *needs painted* would be *needs painting* or *needs to be painted*. If your audience is composed of different groups, using the local dialect of your social, ethnic, or regional group might be distracting and thus inappropriate. To communicate your message effectively, you might choose a dialect that has a wider currency. Often, classroom English is this dialect.

Collaboration

The way you speak is different from the way you write. In speaking, you and your audience are often together in the same place at the same time, and you take turns speaking and listening. If your wording is ambiguous, your listeners might interrupt you to ask questions or look at you quizzically to solicit a clearer explanation. In writing, however, you and your audience are often in different places, and your writing and their reading typically occur at different times. Ordinarily, the responsibility for composing lies exclusively with the writer: while you are writing, you have to anticipate the questions that your readers might ask, and you have to determine if your explanation is clear. In writing, as a consequence, you try to word your ideas as precisely as possible, erring on the side of caution, elaborating and specifying in order to minimize the possibility of misunderstanding.

Collaboration, however, serves to bridge this opposition of speaking versus writing because, like speaking, collaborative writing is interactive. If you write collaboratively, your coauthors and editors ask you questions, identify confusing passages, and offer suggestions for revision. Together, through discussion and cycles of reviewing, editing, and revising, your collaborators influence your style and you influence theirs.

Subject

Your **subject** also influences your style. Technical terminology, for example, differs across disciplines, leading to differences of wording and phrasing. In the field of accounting, for example, your writing might incorporate a lot of numerical information, especially dollar figures. In the field of history, however, chronological and geographical information prevails. Similarly, the language of lawyers and the field of law is quite unlike the language of doctors and the field of medicine, musicians and the field of music, or electrical engineers and the field of electrical engineering.

Different disciplines also have different ways of addressing mechanical issues such as citing sources of information (see Part IX, A Guide for Documenting Knowledge by Observation). In the social sciences, for example, the usual way for you to cite a source is to identify the author's last name and the year of publication. You enclose this information in parentheses immediately after the material that you paraphrased:

(Smith, 1992)

If you quote, you also identify the page number—abbreviated *p.* or *pp.*—of the quoted material:

(Smith, 1994, p. 156)

In the typical humanities citation, you also use parentheses and give the author's last name, but you omit the year of publication and always identify the page number—without the abbreviation—for the material that you are quoting or paraphrasing:

(Smith 156)

Science prizes new information and thus accords importance to identifying the year of publication. In the humanities, however, ancient ideas and new ideas might be equally valid and thus the year of publication is of lesser importance. In addition, books and articles in the humanities are ordinarily longer than studies in the sciences, but illustrations and headings occur less often. Therefore, a reader looking for the passage you cited has a lot of pages to examine and the pages look a lot alike. Because you include the page number in the citation of your source, you genuinely help the interested reader locate the passage you cited.

Thus, learning the specialized communication practices of a discipline is a necessary price of admission to that discipline. It is impossible to be a physicist, for example, unless you are familiar with the language of physicists as well as the particular habits and techniques of using language that are characteristic of physicists.

Type of Document

Your style is also influenced by the **type of document** that you compose. The style of a business letter, for example, is different from the style of a persuasive essay. The essay has no addresses, no salutation, and no signature, and the business letter ordinarily is brief and to the point.

In writing essays, you typically avoid using particular words again and again, unless emphasis is necessary, because readers usually consider such repetition boring. A diverse vocabulary is more likely to keep their attention. Consider, for example, the following paragraphs with and without a varied vocabulary:

Individual writing and collaborative writing are opposite points on a continuum instead of two distinct types of composing processes. For example, writers can compose for themselves as well as for others. But when they write for others, they are inevitably influenced by their readers or by their perception of their readers.

The writing is thus no longer entirely the work of a single individual. Even those who write only for themselves are always influenced in varying degrees by their society.

Individual writing and collaborative writing are opposite points on a continuum instead of two distinct types of writing. For example, writers can write for themselves as well as for other people. But when writers write for other people, they are inevitably influenced by these other people or by their perception of these other people. The writing is thus no longer entirely the writing of a single individual writer. Even individual writers who write only for themselves are inevitably influenced in varying degrees by their society.

Notice that even the paragraph with a varied vocabulary uses several words at least twice (*individual, writing, write, influenced, themselves*). Such repetition is necessary to keep the passage coherent and cohesive; that is, the selective repetition of words helps readers to comprehend the meaning of the sentences and to recognize that the sentences all address a common subject (see "Coherence and Cohesion," Chapter 5 p. 144). Ideally, your essay displays neither boring repetition nor bewildering variation.

If you are writing instructions, however, the repetition of words is critical, boring though it might be. For example, if you are directing a reader to press the *shift* key on a computer keyboard, you might stick with the word *press* so that your readers understand that the same action is required each time. If you switch arbitrarily from *press* to *push, hit,* or *strike,* your readers might think that these four different words refer to four different actions of increasing physical intensity. Thus, if you are writing instructions, a diverse vocabulary increases the likelihood of misunderstanding.

Relationship to Audience

The relationship you have with your reader or listener influences the way you write or speak. This **relationship to audience** guides the formality/informality of your language. If you are addressing your teacher or boss, for example, you are likely to be fairly formal in your expression (*Yes, Ms. Smith*). If you are speaking or writing to a friend, however, you are likely to use informal language (*Yeah*). Or if you wish your readers to perceive you as a figure of authority, a formal expression of your ideas might be appropriate (*We have a number of tasks to complete*). If you wish your readers to perceive you as their equal, however, informal language could be effective (*We've got a lot of things to do*).

The difficulty here is learning the characteristics of formal language versus informal language. For example, a universal dialect like classroom English is usually considered more formal and a local dialect more informal. A dictionary spelling of a word is formal, whereas a unique or creative spelling is informal (*light* versus *lite*, *barbecue* versus *bar-b-q*). Contractions are often judged informal. Polysyllabic words are more typical of formal writing. In addition, different audiences have different opinions of formality and informality. For example, you might have friends who consider the absence of obscene or vulgar words enough to constitute formal language. Or you might speak informally to a colleague on the job, but still avoid the extraordinary informality of obscenity or vulgarity.

Issues for Writing

1. In your journal, discuss your earliest awareness of the subject of style as it applies to writing, clothing, automobiles, houses, music, painting, or dance.

   Write More About It

   In Chapter 9 we will ask you to remember an event. If you choose to write from knowledge by participation, this exercise could help you to generate ideas for this essay. For example, how did you arrive at your awareness of style? When and where did this occur? How old were you? Who was with you at the time?

2. In your focus group, answer the following questions: How have clothing styles changed during your lifetime? How have styles of automobiles, houses, music, painting, or dance changed? Why?

   Write More About It

   In Chapter 12, we will ask you to explain a subject. If you choose to write from knowledge by participation, this exercise could help you to generate ideas for this essay. For example, what is the meaning of style as it applies to writing, clothing, automobiles, houses, music, painting, or dance? Is it possible to develop a single definition of style that applies to all fields?

DEVELOPING YOUR STYLE

Your writing style is thus the consequence of a variety of influences. You might think of writing style as similar to clothing styles. The way you dress is also subject to various influences. You have individual likes and dislikes regarding clothing (e.g., striped shirts versus solid shirts) and fashions change with the times (e.g., wide neckties versus narrow neckties, long skirts versus short skirts). If you live in Oklahoma, you might often wear cowboy boots, but if you live in Minnesota, you might often wear snow boots; if you are Chinese, you might wear a lot of red because it is the color of good luck, but if you are Irish, you might prefer the color green. If you are going to a wedding with a friend, the two of you might coordinate your clothing to avoid a hideous clash such as brown plaid and pink paisley. If you have a job as a restaurant cook, your uniform includes a hat and apron, but if you are a lifeguard at a swimming pool, you wear a swimsuit and a whistle. If you are visiting friends, you might slip on a pair of old jeans, but if you are going to a job interview, you would likely choose a new suit.

In the same way that you develop a sense of appropriate style regarding clothing, you also develop a sense of writing style. The more familiar you are with each influence on your style, the more aware you will be of your style and the more easily and effectively you will adjust your style to your audience and purpose. You acquire knowledge of your writing style the way you acquire all knowledge: through participation and observation.

Participation: Developing Your Style Through Reading and Writing

The more you read, the more familiar you are with the possible variations of writing style. You experience personally the individuality, dialect, and time of other writers. You see the impact of collaboration, subject, type of document, and relationship to audience on the way other writers communicate their ideas. And consciously or unconsciously you perceive the similarities and differences between their style and yours. Similarly, the more you write, the more you discover different ways of communicating your ideas, learning through trial and error to identify styles appropriate to different aims and audiences.

Issues for Writing

1. Choose a passage from a favorite book or essay. Keep a copy for yourself and exchange a copy with a member of your group. Compare and contrast the writing style of your passage with that of the passage you are given. Are the words and sentences typically short and simple or long and complicated? Do you consider the writing style to be formal or informal? Which passage is easier to read? Which passage do you prefer? Explain your answers.

2. Choose two expressive essays from Part III, two referential essays from Part IV, or two persuasive essays from Part V. What similarities and differences of writing style do you notice?

3. Choose two expressive, two referential, or two persuasive essays from Part VI. What similarities and differences of writing style do you notice?

4. Exchange copies of a sample of your writing with two members of your group. Compare and contrast the writing style of the two samples you are given. How do their styles differ from yours?

Observation: Developing Your Style by Examining Usage Guides and Style Manuals

It is also possible to acquire knowledge of style through observation: a wide variety of books have been written on the subject of style, offering advice or giving specifications on such issues as word choice, phrasing, punctuation, spelling, and citation of information sources (see Figures 6.1 and 6.2).

Figure 6.1 Usage Guides

Bernstein, Theodore M. *The Careful Writer.* New York: Atheneum Press, 1977.

Bryant, Margaret M. *Current American Usage.* New York: Funk & Wagnalls, 1962.

Cook, Clair K. *The MLA's Line by Line: How to Edit Your Own Writing.* Boston: Houghton, 1985.

Copperud, Roy H. *American Usage and Style: The Consensus.* New York: Van Nostrand Reinhold, 1980.

Follett, Wilson. *Modern American Usage: A Guide.* New York: Hill, 1966.

Fowler, Henry W. *A Dictionary of Modern English Usage.* 2nd ed. Rev. by Sir Ernest Gowers. Oxford : Oxford UP, 1983.

Lanham, Richard A. *Revising Prose.* 3rd ed. New York: Macmillan, 1992.

Miller, Casey, and Kate Swift. *The Handbook of Nonsexist Writing for Writers, Editors, and Speakers.* 2nd ed. New York: Harper, 1988.

Strunk, William Jr., and E. B. White. *The Elements of Style.* 3rd ed. New York: Macmillan, 1979.

Williams, Joseph M. *Style: Ten Lessons in Clarity and Grace.* 4th ed. New York: HarperCollins, 1994.

Zinsser, William K. *On Writing Well: An Informed Guide to Writing Nonfiction.* 4th ed. New York: HarperCollins, 1991.

Figure 6.2 Style Manuals

General

The Chicago Manual of Style. 14th ed. Chicago: U of Chicago P, 1993.

Specific

Agriculture and Agronomy

Publications Handbook and Style Manual. Madison: American Society of Agronomy, 1988.

Biology

CBE Style Manual: A Guide for Authors, Editors, and Publishers in the Biological Sciences. 5th ed. Chicago: Council of Biology Editors, 1983.

Chemistry

Dodd, Janet S. *The ACS Style Guide: A Manual for Authors and Editors.* Washington: American Chemical Society, 1986.

Handbook for AOAC Members. 6th ed. Washington: Association of Official Analytical Chemists, 1989.

Education

NEA Style Manual for Writers and Editors. Rev. ed. Washington: National Education Association, 1974.

Engineering

Information for IEEE Transactions and Journal Authors. New York: Institute of Electrical and Electronics Engineers, 1989.

Geology

Cochran, Wendell, Peter Fenner, and Mary Hill, eds. *Geowriting: A Guide to Writing, Editing, and Printing in Earth Science.* 4th ed. Alexandria: American Geological Institute, 1984.

Journalism

Goldstein, Norm. *Associated Press Stylebook and Libel Manual.* Rev. ed. Reading: Addison, 1992.

Holley, Frederick S. *Los Angeles Times Stylebook: A Manual for Writers, Editors, Journalists and Students.* New York: NAL, 1981.

Jordon, Lewis. *The New York Times Manual of Style and Usage.* New York: Quadrangle/New York Times Book Company, 1976.

Language and Literature

Achtert, Walter S., and Joseph Gibaldi. *The MLA Style Manual.* New York: Modern Language Association, 1985.

Law

A Uniform System of Citation. 15th ed. Cambridge: Harvard Law Review Association, 1991.

Mathematics

A Manual for Authors of Mathematical Papers. 9th ed. Providence: American Mathematical Society, 1990.

Physics

AIP Style Manual. 4th ed. New York: American Institute of Physics, 1990.

Psychology

Publication Manual of the American Psychological Association. 3rd ed. Washington: American Psychological Association, 1983.

1. Examine two style manuals. (You should be able to find most of these at your library.) List the similarities that you notice in the guidelines of the two books. Also list the differences that you notice. For example, consider the directions for wording, punctuation, spelling, capitalization, italics, abbreviations, headings, tables and figures, and citing and listing sources of information.

Issues for Writing

Write More About It

In Chapter 12, we will ask you to analyze a subject. If you decide to write from knowledge by observation, this exercise could help you generate ideas for this essay. For example, you might discuss how the writing style of your academic major differs from the writing style of your academic minor. Examine the style manuals of your major and minor fields to determine the similarities and differences. You might also interview professors from your major and minor fields to observe their styles of writing.

2. Make copies of your list of similarities and differences for your focus group. How are your two books similar to their books? How do your two books differ from theirs? Why?

Observation: Developing Your Style by Considering Twelve Style Issues

Style manuals and usage guides differ from writer to writer and discipline to discipline; however, all give similar advice on basic issues. The following suggestions apply to a wide variety of writing situations.

Simple Words

Consider using short, simple, common words whenever possible because readers are more likely to be familiar with such words and are more likely to appreciate your writing. Avoid using long, complicated, uncommon words unless you think it is necessary to do so; such words are more difficult for readers to understand and are more likely to cause confusion, misinterpretation, and frustration (Zipf 19–22; Becker; Dobbs, Friedman, and Lloyd; Hudson and Bergman). For example, look at the two lists of words in Table 6.1.

Notice that the words in the column on the right are all shorter and more readily understood. The words in the column on the left are longer and quite unlike the vocabulary of typical speakers and writers. If you are discussing a relatively simple subject, consider using words that are simple. If your subject is complicated, you might use a complicated vocabulary, but only if your readers are likely to tolerate the additional difficulty either because of their familiarity with your subject, their advanced level of education, or their enthusiasm for your subject. If your readers have lit-

Table 6.1 Complicated versus Simple Words

Complicated	Simple
Nouns:	
aggregate	total
assemblage	crowd
compilation	list
conceptualization	idea
entities	things
parameters	limits/conditions
predisposition	tendency
ramification	impact
Verbs:	
abort	stop
ascertain	find out
consolidate	combine
fabricate	make
disseminate	distribute
effectuate	cause
endeavor	try
enhance	improve
expedite	speed up
facilitate	ease
formulate	create
implement	carry out
initiate	start
modify	change
operationalize	start
prioritize	rank
terminate	stop/fire
utilize	use
Adjectives:	
cognizant	aware
erroneous	wrong
mendacious	false
optimum	best
perspicacious	perceptive
sentient	conscious
sufficient	enough
Adverbs:	
frequently	often
infrequently	rarely
presently	now
previously	earlier
subsequently	later

tle knowledge of your subject, perceive it as difficult, or think it is boring, a simple vocabulary is likely to clarify your message and encourage your readers to pay attention to you.

Keep in mind that the difficulty with using long and complicated words is rarely with a particular word, but with the tendency to use lots of such words together so that a clear expression like *I checked the truth of his story* or even *I investigated the accuracy of his story* deteriorates to the obscure *I conducted a comprehensive investigation regarding the veracity of his narrative explication of previous occurrences.*

Complicated Words

Often you will choose to use a more complicated vocabulary. You might, for example, wish to avoid repetition. Instead of using the same simple word again and again, you introduce a little variety to your writing by occasionally substituting a synonym. (See "Coherence and Cohesion," Chapter 5, p. 144.) This synonym, however, could be a more complicated word. To minimize the chances of misunderstanding, verify that the meaning of the synonym is as close as possible to the original word, including its denotation (its strict dictionary definition) and its connotation (its psychological associations). The words *kill* and *assassinate,* for example, have similar denotations, but different connotations. You might write *The governor was killed in an automobile accident,* but *The governor was assassinated in an automobile accident* is unsatisfactory as a substitute. The word *assassinate* implies that the governor was the victim of a treacherous individual or group who deliberately caused the accident. Similarly, you might write *The thief killed the sales clerk,* but *The thief assassinated the sales clerk* is unsatisfactory because the word *assassinate* implies that the victim is a person of political, social, or religious importance.

You might also choose complicated words in order to establish credibility (ethos) with your readers by demonstrating that you are a highly literate individual who uses big words appropriately. A little of this verbal display, however, is usually enough to do the job. If you keep doing it, you call attention to what you are trying to do and you lose credibility. Instead of seeming comfortable with your subject and confident of your knowledge, you seem anxious to prove your credibility. Your audience is also more likely to be impressed by your ability to communicate effectively than by big words: that is, the way to establish credibility with your audience is by understanding your subject matter and by making it as easy as possible for others to understand.

Specialized Terminology

Use **specialized terminology** or technical language selectively. Consider using common words whenever possible. If your writing includes a lot of specialized words, your readers will be less likely to start reading and more likely to stop reading as soon as difficulties arise.

You will have to use specialized terminology, however, if your objective is to educate your readers and learning the special words is essential to their education. If you are discussing the subject of human language, for example, it might be important for you to introduce your readers to words like *syntax* and *semantics*. This introduction would include a definition of each word. You would also have to determine how important each word is to their understanding of your writing and thus how detailed a definition is necessary. Often a brief parenthetical definition is sufficient: for example, *syntax* (the arrangement of words in phrases and sentences) and *semantics* (the study of meaning in language).

Specialized terminology is also necessary if no satisfactory alternative is available. This is often the case with technological innovations. For example, if you are referring to a *digital scanner,* you have no choice but to introduce the specialized words and, if appropriate, a definition.

You also have the choice of using specialized terminology if your readers are familiar with it. If you have such readers, using the specialized language allows you to demonstrate your familiarity with your subject and thus establish credibility (ethos) with your readers. If your readers know the terminology, they will expect you to use it. Your failure to do so could lead them to conclude that you are unfamiliar with it, and you would therefore lose credibility.

Specific and Sensory Words

Consider using specific words that speak to the five senses whenever possible. Avoid generalized abstractions. **Specific and sensory language** give readers a more complete picture of your subject—a full-color portrait—whereas generalizations and abstractions offer only a silhouette (see Table 6.2).

The specific sentence is much more vivid, interesting, and memorable. It has a vitality that gives you the impression you have personally witnessed this episode. The generalized sentence, while considerably shorter, is also much less meaningful, chiefly because it is a generic, one-size-fits-all description. This same sentence might be used to describe a number of quite different schoolbus accidents. It offers nothing that is tailored to this accident, nothing that helps readers to paint a mental picture of this occurrence.

In choosing words and phrases that address the sense of sight, consider details such as the size, color, and shape of your subject or the speed and direction of its motion. To address the sense of hearing, think of the noises, music, or language characteristic of your subject and its surroundings: specify how loud or quiet and how frequent or infrequent the sounds are. For the sense of touch, choose details regarding the texture, solidity, weight, or temperature of your subject. If appropriate, address the senses of taste and smell by identifying flavors and odors characteristic of your subject and its surroundings; explain also how pleasing or offensive and how strong or weak the flavors or odors are.

Table 6.2 General, Abstract Language versus Specific, Sensory Language

Type of Information	General and Abstract	Specific and Sensory
Who	A youngster	A 10-year-old boy
What	rescued some children	saved five first-graders from drowning
When	after their bus had an accident	after their yellow schoolbus swerved to avoid crushing a small dog, overturned, and plunged through the steel guard rail
Where	on the way to school.	on Red River Bridge.

Simple Verbs

Consider using **simple verbs** to describe actions. Avoid turning simple verbs into complicated noun phrases (see Table 6.3) because such a practice raises the number of your words without adding to your meaning. The consequence is that you have to write and your readers have to read a lot of unnecessary words. If you stick with simple verbs, your writing will be more crisp and clear. For example, instead of *I will make a decision later* you could write *I will decide later.* Or instead of *She will conduct the distribution of the prizes,* you could write *She will distribute the prizes.* Why write four words (verb + article + noun + preposition) if a single word (verb) communicates your message?

Table 6.3 Complicated Verb Phrases versus Simple Verbs

Complicated	Simple
direct an allocation of	allocate
conduct an assessment of	assess
make an assignment of	assign
give assistance to	assist
practice avoidance of	avoid
exercise compliance with	comply
give consideration to	consider
manage the conversion of	convert
make a decision about	decide
give a description of	describe
make a determination about	determine
engage in a discussion about	discuss
undertake the distribution of	distribute
direct an evaluation of	evaluate
offer an explanation of	explain
present a justification for	justify
provide for the maintenance of	maintain
obtain redemption of	redeem
furnish specifications for	specify
pursue a verification of	verify

Concise Wording

Offer maximum meaning from minimum reading by choosing **concise wording** whenever possible. **Repetitious wording** (redundancy) is inefficient because instead of using a single appropriate word, you use two words with similar meanings; instead of two words, you write five. You write *dead corpse* instead of *corpse* (a corpse is always dead); you write *visible to the eye* instead of *visible* (the eye is the only organ of vision). Soon you have pages of unnecessary words, using paper and killing trees without adding to the meaning of your message (see Table 6.4).

Table 6.4 Repetitious Wording versus Concise Wording

Repetitious	Concise
absolutely essential	essential
absolutely certain	certain
advance planning	planning
ask a question	ask
at the present moment in time	at present
basic essentials	basics
brief moment	moment
close scrutiny	scrutiny
completely eliminate	eliminate
completely stop	stop
consensus of opinion	consensus
cooperate together	cooperate
dangerous killer	killer
freezing cold	freezing
harmonize together	harmonize
personal opinion	opinion
particular individuals	individuals
specific examples	examples
specific details	details
terrible calamity	calamity
totally isolated	isolated
yellow in color	yellow
whisper quietly	whisper

Unbiased Language

If your language discriminates according to people's race, religion, ethnic heritage, sex, sexual orientation, or physical disabilities, you risk offending your readers and interfering with their ability to receive your message. You also lose credibility and damage your reputation for being fair. **Biased language** reinforces negative images that divide and antagonize people. Biased language distorts understanding instead of improving it. For example, the word *policemen* implies that police are rightfully men, that policing is a man's job, and that a woman doing this job is peculiar, is doing a man's job, or is trying to be a man. The title *police officers,* however, carries none of this bias: it implies neither that being a man nor that being a woman is a superior or necessary qualification for the job.

The word *man* itself is often said to include women. Such usage, however, is also biased. For example, if you were to ask people to paint a picture of *the evolution of man,* it is likely that the majority would paint a picture of a *man.* That is, people perceive the word *man* as referring primarily to a *man* and only secondarily to a *woman* (Schneider and Hacker). Or consider the following two sentences:

Man is a strange animal: just look at Randolph Jones.

Man is a strange animal: just look at Gertrude Smith.

In the two sentences, is the word *man* equally satisfactory? If the word *man* described men and women equally, you would perceive no difference between the two sentences. Using the words *man, men,* or *mankind* to refer jointly to men and women is thus a usage that privileges men. The words *people, persons, individuals, human beings,* or *humanity* avoid this bias.

Similarly, if a noun has no specified gender, using the pronouns *he, his, him,* and *himself* is biased language (Martyna). Consider, for example, the following sentences:

Each doctor I interviewed said he was satisfied with the medical profession.

A doctor will often instruct his patients to exercise.

I observed each doctor to see how much the patients liked him.

Every doctor considers himself lucky to practice medicine.

If you were to ask people to paint pictures of each sentence, the majority would be likely to paint pictures of a man as the doctor. Again, people typically perceive the words *he, his, him,* and *himself* as referring primarily to men and only secondarily to women. Using such words to refer to men and women together is thus unequal and unfair. To avoid this bias, you could substitute *he or she, his or her, him or her,* and *himself or herself,* or you could switch the nouns, pronouns, and verbs to the plural:

All of the doctors I interviewed said they were satisfied with the medical profession.

Doctors will often instruct their patients to exercise.

I observed all of the doctors to see how much the patients liked them.

All doctors consider themselves lucky to practice medicine.

Or you might revise the wording to avoid unnecessary pronouns:

Each doctor I interviewed was satisfied with the medical profession.

A doctor will often instruct patients to exercise.

I observed each doctor to see how appreciative the patients were.

Every doctor considers it a privilege to practice medicine.

In addition, if you refer to Randolph Jones as *Jones,* also refer to Gertrude Smith as *Smith* instead of as *Gertrude* or *Ms. Smith.* That is, if gender is not a factor in your identification of Jones, it should not be a factor in your reference to Smith. Similarly, if you identify basketball played by women as *women's basketball,* also refer to basketball played by men as *men's basketball.* If gender is important to your identification of the women's game, it is also important to your identification of the men's game. If you refer to the women's game as *women's basketball* and the men's game as *basketball,* you imply the superiority of the men's game; you identify the men's game as "genuine basketball" and the women's game as a version of it.

Essentially, if you consider and address people equally, without privilege or prejudice, you avoid biased language (see Table 6.5).

Table 6.5 Biased versus Unbiased Language

Biased	Unbiased
chairman	chairperson/chair
congressman	representative
craftsman	craftsperson/artisan
fireman	firefighter
fisherman	fisher
manhole cover	sewer cover
mankind	humanity/people
mailman	mail carrier/postal worker
man the office	staff the office
manmade	artificial/synthetic
newsman	news reporter
policeman	police officer
salesman	salesperson/sales clerk
weatherman	weather forecaster
Jones and Ms. Smith	Jones and Smith
Mr. Jones and Jane Smith	Mr. Jones and Ms. Smith
two nurses and a woman doctor	two nurses and a doctor
two women and two African-American men	two women and two men
a writer and two Jewish artists	a writer and two artists
two judges and a Polish thief	two judges and a thief
a man and two lesbians	a man and two women
two dancers and a blind singer	two dancers and a singer

Simple, Compound, and Complex Sentences

Use simple sentences to emphasize your ideas. Use compound and complex sentences to identify or clarify relationships among your ideas.

A **simple sentence** is a single independent clause. A clause has a subject (a noun or pronoun) and a predicate (a verb, verb + object, or verb + complement). The predicate offers information about the subject. A clause is independent if it communicates a complete idea by itself:

> subject   predicate (verb)
> *My writing improved* on the computer.

> subject   predicate (verb + object)
> *Writers* normally *use their computers* instead of their typewriters.

> subject   predicate (verb + complement)
> *The computer is a valuable writing tool.*

If a specific idea deserves the reader's undivided attention, use a simple sentence.

A **compound sentence** has at least two independent clauses. The relationship of the clauses is coordinated, that is, of equal importance:

> subject   predicate   compound subject
> *My writing improved* on the computer, and *my editing and revising*

> predicate
> *accelerated.*

> subject   compound predicate   subject
> *Writers* normally *use computers and avoid typewriters,* but *editors*

> predicate
> *like pens or pencils.*

> subject   predicate   subject   predicate
> *The computer is a valuable writing tool,* or *it is a terrible nuisance.*

Notice that the coordinated clauses of a compound sentence are divided by a comma and joined by a coordinating word (*and, but, nor, or, yet*). To divide a reader's attention equally among several ideas, use a compound sentence.

A **complex sentence** also has at least two clauses, but of unequal importance. The **main clause** is independent, but the other clause or clauses are subordinate to the main clause and depend on it to communicate a complete idea:

> main clause   subordinate clause
> *My writing improved on the computer before my revising and editing accelerated.*

> subordinate clause   main clause
> *After my writing improved on the computer, my revising and editing accelerated.*

> main clause   subordinate clause
> *Writers and editors normally use their computers because their typewriters are virtually obsolete.*

subordinate clause   main clause
Because writers and editors normally use their computers, their typewriters are virtually obsolete.

main clause   subordinate clause
The computer is a valuable writing tool, although it is often a terrible nuisance.

subordinate clause   main clause
Although the computer is a valuable writing tool, it is often a terrible nuisance.

Notice that the **subordinate** (or dependent) **clause** is always separated from the main (or independent) clause by a comma if the subordinate clause comes before the main clause. If the subordinate clause comes after the main clause, the comma is often omitted. Subordinating words (*after, as soon as, although, because, before, if, since, though, unless, until, when, whereas, while*) serve to introduce and identify the subordinate clause.

To divide a reader's attention unequally among several ideas, use a complex sentence. Use the subordinate clause for the less important idea and the main clause for the more important idea. If the subordinate clause comes before the main clause, this division of importance is emphasized. In the preceding list of examples, notice that the second sentence in each pair of sentences is more emphatic than the first.

Readability of Sentences

In starting a sentence, readers unconsciously look for the subject. The longer it takes them to find it, the more difficult the sentence is for them to understand. That is, long introductory phrases or subordinate clauses increase the level of reading difficulty. As soon as readers locate the subject, they start looking for the verb. Again, the longer it takes them to find the verb, the more difficult the sentence is for them to understand. That is, phrases and clauses between the subject and the verb raise the level of reading difficulty. If the verb uses a direct object, readers start looking for the object; the longer it takes them to locate it, the more difficult the sentence is for them to understand. In other words, phrases and clauses between the verb and its object increase reading difficulty. Once readers have located the subject and the verb or the subject, verb, and object, then additional phrases and clauses contribute little to the difficulty of the sentence.

Imagine that each sentence you write has either three or four slots:

_____ subject _____ verb _____

or

_____ subject _____ verb _____ object _____

Consider the following sentences:

                                     subject   verb

On the afternoon of April 2, 1981, Timothy arrived.

subject   **verb**

The thief, who was dodging traffic and running from the police, tripped.

subject   verb

Nicholas smiled at the thought of winning the 1995 soccer championship.

subject verb   **object**

She delivered to the offices on the fifth floor a box of apples, cherries, grapes, oranges, and peaches.

subject   verb   object

Devereux discovered the spider on a window on the side of the house.

The more slots you fill, the more difficult your sentence is. Filling the final slot contributes the least to reading difficulty. Ordinarily, you will fill one or two of the slots, but the readability of your sentences will be seriously jeopardized if you always fill all the slots (Felker et al. 45–47).

You will also have to choose which slots to fill. Earlier we said that a main clause is more emphatic if the subordinate clause precedes it. In such a sentence, the subordinate clause fills the slot before the subject, increasing the level of reading difficulty:

    subordinate clause subject _____ verb _____ object _____.

As a writer, you have to decide if the improved emphasis justifies the added difficulty of the sentence.

Keep in mind also that variety of sentences is usually a desirable characteristic. If all of your sentences start with subordinate clauses, for example, readers might think that the rhythmical repetition is either boring or irritating and you could lose their attention or approval.

Active Voice

In **active voice** sentences, the subject of the sentence is active:

    Linda repaired the computer.

In this sentence, the subject is Linda and she is performing the repairs to the computer.

In a **passive voice** sentence, however, the subject of the sentence is a passive recipient of the action:

    The computer was repaired by Linda.

In this sentence, the original subject, *Linda,* is shifted to a position following the verb and the word *by* is inserted. Often, this original subject is simply omitted (e.g., *The computer was repaired*.). The object of the original sentence is shifted to the subject position. The verb changes to *be* + verb + *ed/en* ending: for example, *describe* changes to *is described; give* changes to *are given*. The new subject is passive: it receives the action of repairing as opposed to doing the repairs.

Passive voice sentences are more difficult to understand (Gough; Savin and Perchonock) because readers normally expect to find active voice sentences. That is, upon locating the subject of a sentence, readers typically assume that the subject is active. Operating on this assumption, they proceed to look for the verb of the sentence. If the verb is active voice, their impression of the subject is verified and their reading continues without interruption. If the verb is passive voice, however, they realize that their original impression of the subject was incorrect: the subject is receiving the action instead of initiating it. Readers are thus compelled to stop momentarily to revise their interpretation of the subject before continuing with their reading of the sentence. Passive voice sentences thus slow reading.

Passive voice, however, is appropriate if the agent of action is unimportant. Consider, for example, the following active voice sentence:

HarperCollins published this book in 1995.

This sentence emphasizes the publisher and the year of publication. If you choose to emphasize the year of publication only, you might change this sentence to passive voice, omitting the agent of action:

This book was published in 1995.

In the fields of science and engineering, similarly, the agent of action is often unimportant. Consider, for example, the following sentences:

Active Voice: The researcher observed the chemical reaction.

Passive Voice: The chemical reaction was observed by the
                researcher.

To the scientist, it is unimportant who observed the chemical reaction: only the observation itself is vital. Thus the active voice sentence is inappropriate. In the passive voice sentence, the inclusion of the agent of action contributes little to the meaning. In this situation, passive voice and the omission of the agent of action are justified:

The chemical reaction was observed.

Whenever you use passive voice sentences, keep in mind that such sentences raise the level of reading difficulty. Analyze your audience, especially their level of motivation. Motivated readers are more likely to tolerate difficult reading. In complex sentences or sentences using complicated words or a specialized terminology, avoid passive voice. Such sentences are difficult enough without passive voice adding to their difficulty.

Positive Sentences

Negative sentences are more difficult for readers to understand (Gough; Just and Carpenter; Savin and Perchonock; Wason) because a negative sentence asks readers to consider two ideas: a positive assertion and its negation. Consider, for example, the following sentence:

> I recommend that you do not replace the existing system.

Understanding this sentence requires that you first think of its positive version (*I recommend that you replace the existing system*) and then negate or reject this assertion. It is easier for your readers if you phrase your ideas positively:

> I recommend that you keep the existing system.

In addition to slowing the reading process, negative sentences often contribute to misinterpretation or misunderstanding. Consider, for example, the following hypothetical advertising slogan:

> No other pesticide is more effective than Exterminaid.

A quick reading of this sentence might lead you to the impression that Exterminaid is more effective than any other pesticide, especially because you see the words *more effective.* This reading, however, is incorrect. The assertion here is only that no other pesticide is more effective; in other words, Exterminaid is at least as effective as other pesticides. A **positive sentence** like *Exterminaid is at least as effective as other pesticides* is unlikely to sell a lot of Exterminaid. If Exterminaid were genuinely more effective, a positive phrasing would be clear, crisp, and emphatic:

> Exterminaid is more effective than any other pesticide.

You will have to use negative sentences occasionally. Whenever you do, keep in mind that such sentences raise the level of reading difficulty. Analyze your audience and assess their ability to tolerate this added difficulty. Readers who are motivated, educated, or familiar with your subject are more likely to tolerate and decipher difficult reading. If possible, avoid negating passive voice sentences, complex sentences, or sentences with complicated or specialized vocabulary. Such sentences already have a high level of reading difficulty; if you negate such sentences, you multiply their difficulty.

Spelling and Punctuation

Dictionaries give the traditional spellings of universal dialects such as classroom English. Such spellings communicate effectively across local dialects to a wide variety of individuals from different academic fields. In addition, because of their wide usage, dictionary spellings are less subject to the influence of time.

Unique or creative spellings (e.g., *laff, tonite*) are occasionally appropriate to your aim and audience. In advertising materials, for example, writers might incorporate such spellings to gain attention or arouse curiosity. Ordinarily, however, unique or creative spellings are potentially distracting or annoying. And if such spellings imply that you are unfamiliar with the dictionary spellings, you could damage your credibility.

Grammar books identify traditional punctuation practices, including guidelines regarding commas, periods, colons, semicolons, dashes, apostrophes, quotation marks, brackets, and parentheses. Again, your familiarity with traditional usage serves to establish your credibility, whereas unique or creative usage could be distracting or disorienting. Analyze your aim and audience to determine if traditional usage is appropriate. Consider especially your relationship to your audience: unique or creative usage signals informality.

In addition to dictionaries and grammar books, however, also check the style manual of your academic field. Guidelines on such issues as hyphenation, capitalization, or abbreviation often differ from field to field. The style manual of the American Psychological Association (APA), for example, advises using words for the numbers zero through nine and numerals for all higher numbers. The style manual for the Modern Language Association (MLA) also has this guideline. If your discussion includes little numerical information, however, MLA allows you to substitute words for all numbers that might be spelled as one or two words (e.g., nineteen, thirty-five, sixty-five million). APA gives you no such option.

Summary of Suggestions on Style

1. Use simple words.
2. Use complicated words selectively.
3. Use specialized terminology selectively.
4. Use specific and sensory words.
5. Use simple verbs.
6. Use concise wording.
7. Use unbiased language.
8. Use simple sentences to emphasize your ideas. Use compound and complex sentences to identify or clarify relationships among your ideas.
9. Consider the readability of your sentences.
10. Use active voice.
11. Use positive sentences.
12. Adopt traditional and uniform habits of spelling and punctuation.

ANALYZING YOUR STYLE

Analysis of your writing style integrates knowledge by participation and knowledge by observation. Your direct experience of different styles through your reading and writing and your investigation of style manuals together offer you a variety of insights on effective writing style—a repertoire of style choices and style guidelines. This knowledge allows you to adapt your style to specific writing situations. If you also identify the distinctive characteristics of your style and the major influences on your style, you will advance your knowledge of your writing style and thereby improve your ability to adjust your style. In this analysis of your writing style, you both participate (as the writer) and observe (as the investigator of your writing style). Figure 6.3 is designed to guide you through this stylistic analysis of your writing.

Figure 6.3 Style guide

Style Guide

1. *Individuality.* How much of you is in this writing sample? What features of your style indicate your likes and dislikes regarding wording, sentence structure, spelling, and punctuation?

2. *Time.* How does the time period during which you are writing influence your style? Does your age or your audience's age influence your style? How?

3. *Dialect.* Are you using a local dialect or a universal dialect? Why? What features of style are characteristic of the dialect you are using?

4. *Collaboration.* Is your writing collaborative? How do editors and coauthors influence your style?

5. *Subject.* What is the subject of your writing? What special words or phrases are typical of writing on this subject? How does this subject influence the spelling and punctuation?

6. *Type of Document.* What type of document are you composing? What is its aim and purpose? How will your audience use this document? What features of style are characteristic of this type of document?

7. *Relationship to Audience.* What is your relationship with your audience? Is a formal or informal style appropriate? What is the appropriate degree of formality or informality? How does this degree of formality or informality influence your style?

The following, for example, is Sam's stylistic analysis of the narrative passage at the beginning of this chapter:

1. Individuality: I think there is a lot of me in this passage, probably because I am talking about myself and my family instead of a more abstract subject like writing. This passage also shows how I tell a

story: narrative interspersed with explanation and critical analysis. I like my stories to include conversations: thus the dialogue section. I also like to use colons to introduce examples or explanations. This passage has three such sentences. And I identify my wife as being of *English* heritage. People often think of *English* and *British* as synonymous, but I prefer the word *English* because of its associations with the language and because it serves to distinguish among the English, the Scottish, and the Welsh. In addition, I use the word *while* instead of *although* to start the final paragraph. I do this even though I was the copyeditor of a journal that uses APA style. According to APA style, the word *while* is never used unless it refers to a time period (e.g., *While he was sleeping, the package arrived.*). After five years of copyediting, I have adopted this practice and use *although* automatically, but here I deliberately chose *while* because I thought the two clauses of the sentence implied a relationship of time as well as opposition.

2. Time: The time period during which I am writing has little influence on this passage: no new words or expressions occur. What is more important probably is my age versus the age of the majority of likely readers. Because many members of my audience are age eighteen and nineteen, and because I am at least twice that age, I considered it important to adopt a plain style and clean the narrative of all potentially distracting language that might identify the period of time—language that might interfere with my reader's ability to appreciate my plight. Thus I never identify the year of birth of either of my parents, nor the years during which I was raised. I also omit the year I started graduate school and never mention the music that was playing on the radio while my wife and I were having that conversation years ago. The narrative gives the impression, as a consequence, that my realization regarding style could have occurred yesterday.

3. Dialect: I have aimed here for a universal dialect because I am also aiming for the widest possible audience. Thus I avoid language characteristic of specific geographical regions or social classes. Because I teach writing, I am familiar with classroom English and thus readily adopt its wording and phrasing. I also use a computerized spelling checker to verify the spelling of all words as dictionary spellings. In addition, I adopt the American practice of using double quotations (". . ." instead of '. . .') and always putting periods inside the quotation marks.

4. Collaboration: This book's editor has reviewed my earlier opening narratives and offered commentary that has influenced my style. Specifically, the editor advised me to keep the narratives relatively brief, the style plain, and the wording and sentences fairly simple for maximum readability. I have tried to adopt the editor's guidelines, especially the advice to keep the sentences simple. My usual habit is to link two sentences together using a colon. For example, I would ordinarily have written the following two sentences as a single sentence:

> In Linda's family, it is the host's obligation to satisfy the guest and the guest's only obligation is to display satisfaction. If offered food or drink, the polite reply is "Oh yes, that would be nice."

However, the editor's commentary guided my decision to divide the two sentences. I do, however, include a particularly complex 70-word sentence:

> Their meaning was something like "Please don't go to any trouble just for me because I am but a guest and this is your house and I am already imposing on you just by my visit, but if you are getting something to eat or drink for yourself or if something is already prepared, then yes I would be most grateful, but only if it is not inconvenient for you."

I think this sentence, comprising several coordinated and subordinated clauses, is justified because it imitates the complexity of thought and emphasizes all the ideas that the brief "Oh, I don't care" summarizes.

5. Subject: The subject of this passage is a personal experience regarding language and especially the issue of style. Because of this subject, the passage includes quotations and uses such words as *ask, answer, conversations, expression, reply, saying,* and *style*. Because I am discussing style, it is especially important to my credibility that my style be effective. I have to exhibit, for example, my familiarity with grammar book guidelines on how to incorporate direct quotations within sentences. I have also tried to keep the sentences simple and the wording familiar so that readers will be comfortable with this subject.

6. Type of Document: This is a brief essay designed to emphasize that the issue of style is a question of appropriate or inappropriate choices as opposed to a question of right or wrong. Ideally, the readers of this essay will use it as a starting point for more serious and difficult thinking and reading on this subject. Important characteristics of this type of writing include such techniques as a striking or intriguing opening, direct quotations, and variety of word choice. My opening two sentences, for example, are designed to solicit the reader's attention:

> Both of my parents are children of Italian immigrants. Both were born and raised in Cleveland, Ohio, and still live there.

Each sentence is simple (subject + predicate and subject + compound predicate, respectively) and each is short (nine and twelve words, respectively), thus offering the easiest possible reading. Both start with the word *both,* thus emphasizing their common subject. Both offer quite ordinary biographical information, and the simplicity and brevity of the sentences emphasize this. But together the sentences might arouse a reader's curiosity as to why this information is being offered. The third sentence of the essay (*As I was growing up, . . .*) starts the narrative that uses this biographical information as its basis. Ideally, the narrative quickly will engage the reader and satisfy his or her curiosity.

The essay also uses direct quotations, and the word choice is diverse; however, I do notice that I use the word *expression* a lot and ought to substitute synonyms occasionally or revise the phrasing to eliminate the repetition. Because it is a narrative of a personal experience, I also have to consider the issue of using past tense and present tense consistently. I use past tense to describe things that are finished (e.g., *were born and raised*) and present tense for things that are ongoing (e.g., *still live there*).

7. Relationship to Audience: My relationship to my readers is essentially a teacher-student relationship, and thus my style is fairly formal. As a teacher, my style has to be as effective as possible so that I have credibility on the subject of writing and writing style. I am also addressing college students who have knowledge of my subject and its specialized terminology through their earlier writing classes and writing experiences. Nevertheless, their knowledge is limited. I thus have to communicate my authority on this subject while also emphasizing the accessibility of this subject; that is, my writing has to demonstrate that I have knowledge of a difficult subject and thus deserve my readers' attention, but I also have to be certain that my subject is easily understood. This is a difficult and delicate balance to achieve. Formality heightens my authority, but informality improves accessibility. As a consequence, this passage displays simple sentences and familiar wording (a higher degree of informality) while adopting dictionary spellings and traditional guidelines on punctuation practices (a higher degree of formality). I also avoid contractions, unless offering a direct quotation. And I use a diverse vocabulary and a variety of simple and complex sentences to prove my writing ability and to avoid insulting college students with a style that is simplistic or condescending.

You will learn more about style as you compose, revise, and edit individually and collaboratively. Learning the characteristics of your style is a process that never stops because style is dynamic; your writing style changes as your knowledge of style develops, as you discover the influences on your style, and as you build your repertoire of deliberate stylistic choices.

Issues for Writing

1. Analyze the style of a sample of your writing. What characteristics of the style do you notice? To which of the influences on style might you attribute each of the characteristics that you notice? Was the style of this piece appropriate to your audience and purpose? Explain.

2. Exchange writing samples among the members of your group. Do a stylistic analysis of their writing, investigating influences on their style. How is your analysis of your writing similar to their analysis? How does it differ?

Works Cited

Becker, Curtis A. "Allocation of Attention During Visual Word Recognition." *Journal of Experimental Psychology: Human Perception and Performance* 2 (1976): 556–566.

Crystal, David, and Derek Davy. *Investigating English Style.* Bloomington: Indiana UP, 1969.

Dobbs, A. R., Alinda Friedman, and Julie Lloyd. "Frequency Effects in Lexical Decisions: A Test of the Verification Model." *Journal of Experimental Psychology: Human Perception and Performance* 11 (1985): 81–92.

Felker, Daniel B. et al. *Guidelines for Document Designers.* Washington, DC: American Institutes for Research, 1981.

Gough, Philip B. "Grammatical Transformations and Speed of Understanding." *Journal of Verbal Learning and Verbal Behavior* 4 (1965): 107–111.

Hudson, Patrick T. W., and Marijke W. Bergman. "Lexical Knowledge and Word Recognition: Word Length and Word Frequency in Naming and Decision Tasks." *Journal of Memory and Language* 24 (1985): 46–58.

Just, Marcel Adam, and Patricia A. Carpenter. "The Relation Between Comprehending and Remembering Some Complex Sentences." *Memory and Cognition 4.3* (1976): 318–322.

Lanham, Richard A. *Revising Prose.* 3rd ed. New York: Macmillan, 1992.

Martyna, Wendy. "Beyond the He/Man Approach." *Signs* 5 (1980): 482–293.

Savin, Harris B., and Ellen Perchonock. "Grammatical Structure and the Immediate Recall of English Sentences." *Journal of Verbal Learning and Verbal Behavior* 4 (1965): 348–353.

Schneider, Joseph W., and Sally L. Hacker. "Sex Role Imagery and Use of the Generic 'Man' in Introductory Texts: A Case in the Sociology of Sociology." *American Sociologist* 8.1. (1973): 12–18.

Wason, P. C. "The Processing of Positive and Negative Information." *Quarterly Journal of Experimental Psychology* 11 (1959): 92–107.

Zipf, George Kingsley. *Human Behavior and the Principle of Least Effort.* Cambridge: Addison-Wesley, 1949.

Memory and Delivery

*M*y wife and I were married in September 1977 in Fayetteville, New York. Linda had just received her master's degree in speech and language pathology and was starting her first job as a professional. I was still in graduate school, starting my studies for a doctoral degree in English.

Linda was from Syracuse, New York, and I was from Cleveland, Ohio. Unlike my family, Linda's family was small: her father had a younger brother and a younger sister, and her mother had two older sisters. Linda was the younger of two daughters.

My family, however, was quite a bit bigger. My mother was the oldest of three children; my father had six older brothers and sisters and a younger brother. I had one older sister and one younger brother. In addition, numerous cousins, cousins of cousins, and children of cousins as well as cherished immigrant friends and friends from the inner city neighborhood all lived in Cleveland.

Linda and I decided to have two receptions for the two families: we would be married in Fayetteville, with a reception immediately following the ceremony for Linda's family and my immediate family, and a week or so later we would have a Cleveland reception for my family's relatives and friends.

Linda's family is of English heritage. Her mother's family immigrated before the American Revolution, and her father's father arrived in the early 1900s. While the wide circle of my Italian family and their equally wide circle of friends were given to the decorative and the demonstrative, Linda's family believed quiet simplicity was ideal. Considering this heritage and the size of Linda's family, we decided that a small and simple wedding was appropriate. Linda and I chose plain gold bands for wedding rings. We decided to have no bridesmaids or ushers; Linda's sister and my brother would be the two witnesses. The men would wear dark blue suits; the women would wear long dresses of various colors. The wedding would be a brief 20-minute ceremony, including traditional vows and classical music.

We designed the wedding invitation to communicate this ideal of simplicity (see Figure 7.1). Notice that the invitation is quite plain: cursive type on ivory paper. No embossing of flowers or angels, no pictures of wedding bells. It was important to us how the invitation looked; if it was plain and simple, it would promise a plain and simple affair.

The Fayetteville reception was equally simple: 100 wedding guests gathering for champagne and finger sandwiches. The Cleveland reception was relatively simple for Italian families: 200 guests drinking, eating, and dancing. (SD)

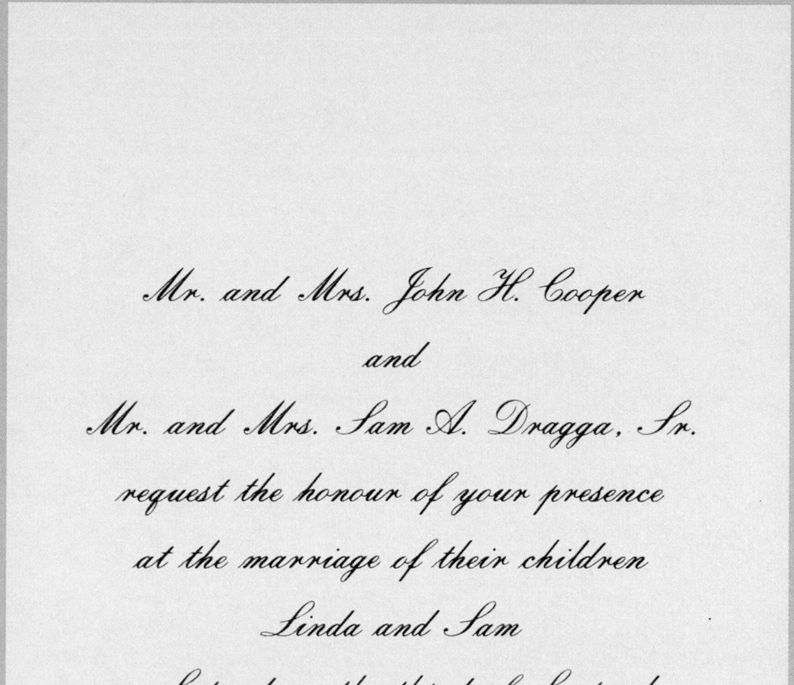

Mr. and Mrs. John H. Cooper

and

Mr. and Mrs. Sam A. Dragga, Sr.

request the honour of your presence

at the marriage of their children

Linda and Sam

on Saturday, the third of September

nineteen hundred and seventy-seven

at two o'clock in the afternoon

United Methodist Church

Fayetteville, New York

Figure 7.1
Sam's wedding invitation.

Consider also the invitation to my wedding (see Figure 7.2). To my family, this invitation was a very important document. If our wedding invitation had not been a traditional Chinese one, my family's friends and relatives might have thought something was wrong—perhaps that my parents didn't approve of the marriage. Many messages can be read into a couple's wedding invitation. That's why they're so important to the family.

As a result, John and I chose to have our invitation printed in Chinese as well as in English, signalling our respect for my parents. Moreover, to read this invitation, guests would open it from left to right and begin reading the right-hand page, from top to bottom and right to left. To us, the positioning of the Chinese text on the right-hand page before the English text on the left-hand page was yet another way of showing our respect for my family and culture.

Like all American invitations, ours contained important information about the wedding ceremony, the American reception (wedding cake, hors d'oeuvres, champagne, and punch), and the Chinese banquet (a nine-course Chinese feast and champagne). However, our invitation was also adorned with traditional good luck colors and symbols. For example, gold and red are colors that suggest happiness, prosperity, and strength; note the gold foil lettering printed on bright red paper.

Two other key symbols appear on our wedding invitation: pairs of phoenixes and dragons, as well as the character for marriage, 囍. In Chinese culture, the phoenix represents the female or the bride, and the dragon the male or the groom; consequently, these animals are standard decorations for the borders of the invitation. Complementing the animals is the ceremonial character for marriage, designed in several different type styles. These characters appear in the corners and in the center of the invitation. The Chinese character for the feeling of happiness is 喜. However, it is always placed beside another character. When this character is combined to form 囍, the new character meaning "double happiness" is created, thus suggesting the wedding of two happy people. Interestingly, "double happiness" is not used in ordinary writing; it is reserved for artistic and ceremonial purposes, such as weddings.

As the design of our invitation illustrates, John and I never had any doubt that our wedding would strongly reflect my Chinese culture. (GG)

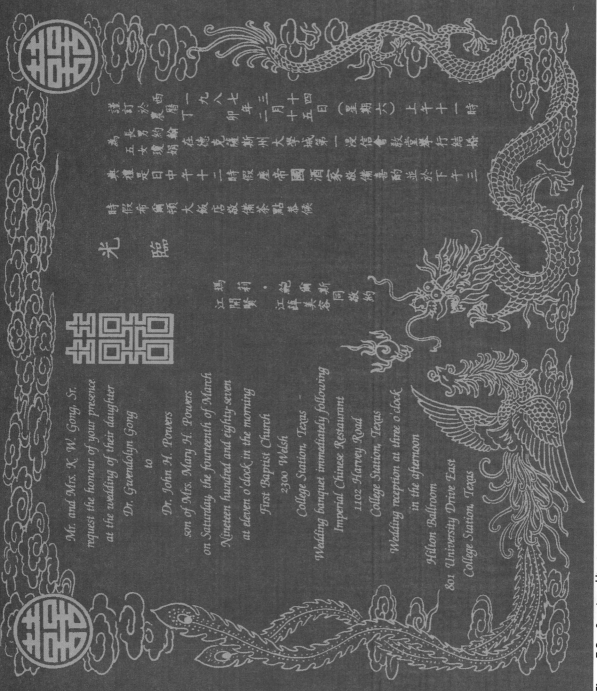

Figure 7.2 Gwen's wedding invitation.

1. In your journal, compose your own vignette for this chapter. Describe and explain a ritual or ceremony that you have participated in or witnessed. For example, if you are married, describe your wedding. What were your invitations like? How did you dress? How big was the wedding? Where was it? Who did you invite? Who aided your planning and who interfered?

2. Design the invitation for a coming celebration, such as a birthday, graduation, or holiday party. In your focus group, exchange invitations. Describe to your group the celebration you are planning and explain who will be invited. Review the invitations and decide how effectively each fits its purpose and audience. Which of the invitations do you consider superior? Why? How would you improve the remaining invitations?

Write More About It

In Chapter 16, we will ask you to take a position on a specific issue. Using your journal response, you might argue for or against the materialism and astronomical costs associated with weddings; or you might defend or attack the institution of marriage. You might take a stand on the symbolic importance of a specific ceremony or ritual, such as a graduation, family or school reunion, national holiday, birthday, and the like.

The way a piece of writing inscribes and displays a message integrates the canons of memory and delivery. Classical rhetoric emphasized oral communication: **memory** was the speaker's memorization of his or her message, and **delivery** was the speaker's vocalization of the message. In written communication, the writer inscribes the message instead of memorizing it. And the writer's choices regarding the visual display of the message substitute for oral delivery.

In the time before microcomputers and laser printing, the canons of memory and delivery were of little importance to written communication because the choices available to the writer for inscribing or displaying a message were limited. Professional printing services were available but expensive and thus reserved for particularly important documents or for mass publications. The individual writer composing a letter or essay was ordinarily deprived of this technology and its rhetorical power.

For example, a traditional typewriter offers only a single choice of type. To emphasize a specific word or phrase, you can either underline or capitalize it. Regardless of the type of document you are composing—essay, résumé, proposal, memo, poem, brochure, poster—you use the same type in the same size. Regardless of your audience—children, grandparents, friends, supervisors, clients, teachers—you use the same type in the same size. The only choices available to you are the size of your margins and single spacing versus double spacing.

Typewriters with removable typing balls allow additional choices: you can, for example, switch from plain type to italic type in the middle of your essay simply by changing typing balls. This process of changing typing balls while you are typing, however, can be slow and tedious, and extra typing balls are expensive.

The microcomputer brings a wider variety of type choices. Several are displayed in Table 7.1. The choices are easily accessed by clicking a mouse button or pressing a couple of keys on the keyboard. And the microcomputer allows you to integrate words and illustrations. You thus have access to the rhetorical power that comes with the canons of memory and delivery. You have the power to use typography and illustration to improve the readability of your writing and to reinforce your message.

Table 7.1 A Variety of Typographical Choices	
Typeface	Avante Garde
	Bookman
	Chancery
	Courier
	Helvetica
	Schoolbook
	Palatino
	Times
Style	Plain
	Bold
	Italic
	Outline
	Shadow
Size	9 point
	10 point
	12 point
	14 point
	18 point
	24 point

In addition, the microcomputer offers a new way of inscribing your message. Instead of composing and revising with a pen or pencil and typing a final copy, more and more writers are composing and revising at the keyboard, and their final copy is either a paper or disk version. Writing is thus more and more often a process of creating electronic images visible on a screen and possibly later transferring the images to paper.

If your type choices are to be effective for either paper or screen, you will need a basic understanding of typography. Some of this knowledge will come through participation; that is, you will experiment with different type choices as you design a résumé or create a brochure. Such experimentation, however, might easily lead to disaster. With the wide variety of new type choices available, for example, you might be tempted to exercise all your choices on a single page. This decision is likely to produce visual chaos (see Figure 7.3). Learning through observation, as a consequence, is also necessary.

The Society of Communicators

will hold a

MEETING

for the

election of officers

on

Sunday, April 2

8:00 p.m.

1500 Wilson Avenue

The Society of Communicators is a **non-profit organization** dedicated to the *effective communication* of information. Meetings are held monthly, featuring prominent communicators from business, government, and academia. Dues are $75.00 per year.

Officers serve for two years. To nominate a candidate for the position of **President, Vice President, Treasurer, or Secretary,** submit the candidate's name to the ***Chair of the Election Committee*** before the start of the meeting.

Figure 7.3
Multiple type choices displayed on a single page

GUIDELINES ON TYPOGRAPHY

In choosing type, keep in mind that the more words you use, the more important readability is. Several characteristics of type influence its readability.

Typeface

While a wide variety of designs are available, every **typeface** is either *serif* or *sans serif*. Serifs are the horizontal lines that finish off the major strokes of each letter. Sans serif is, literally, without serifs (see Figure 7.4).

This is serif type.

serif

This is sans serif type.

Figure 7.4
Serif versus sans serif type

Serif type gives a decorative or artistic impression. It is also considered more subjective, traditional, conservative, and formal. Conversely, **sans serif type** gives a clean or plain impression and is considered more objective, contemporary, progressive, and informal. More important, serif type is usually considered easier to read because its horizontal lines serve to guide the reader's eye from left to right across the page (Burt 8–9; Zachrisson 128–131). In addition, the serifs make each letter and word visually more distinct and thus easier for readers to identify and decipher (Craig 123).

Type Style

A variety of **type styles** are available for each type design (see Figure 7.5). Of all styles, plain (also called roman) is the easiest to read.

Each type style has appropriate uses. **Plain style** is effective for virtually all of your writing. Keep in mind that if you switch from plain style, you decrease readability. So if you switch, do it selectively. Also do it systematically so that the significance of the switch from plain to italic, for example, is obvious.

Italic style is often used for special words such as titles of books and magazines, foreign words, emphasized words, technical terminology, minor headings, and words specifically identified as words (e.g., "the word *italics* might. . . "). If italic style is unavailable, underlining is the traditional substitute.

Bold style is usually appropriate for the title of your essay and its major headings. Often bold is also used to emphasize key words and to identify technical terminology. (Check with your instructor on ways you might incorporate bold type.) Keep in mind, however, the importance of using each style systematically; if you are using italics to emphasize key words, reserve bold for a different purpose. Bold italic style is often effective for middle-level headings (i.e, inferior to bold major headings and superior to italic minor headings).

> Plain is the style of this type.
>
> **Bold is the style of this type.**
>
> *Italic is the style of this type.*
>
> ***Bold italic is the style of this type.***
>
> Outline is the style of this type.
>
> Bold outline is the style of this type.
>
> *Italic outline is the style of this type.*
>
> Shadow is the style of this type.
>
> Bold shadow is the style of this type.
>
> *Italic shadow is the style of this type.*

Figure 7.5
Various styles of type

Outline and shadow styles, as well as such variations as bold outline, bold italic outline, and bold italic outline shadow are ordinarily restricted to the titles and headings of promotional publications such as posters and brochures. All such fancy styles quite effectively solicit attention, but are difficult to read. Use such styles cautiously and selectively.

Type Size

Type size is determined according to **points,** each point equaling 1/72 of an inch. This point size identifies the size of the traditional metal piece on which the raised design of a letter sits (see Figure 7.6). In a typeface such as Schoolbook, each letter occupies the full space on the metal piece, whereas a typeface such as Times occupies less of the available space. Thus a 24-point Times letter is smaller than a 24-point Schoolbook letter, even though the metal pieces on which the letters sit are the same size (see Table 7.2). A full page of 12-point Schoolbook type, as a consequence, shrinks to 75 percent of the page if you switch the type to 12-point Times. Although we have generally stopped using metal pieces of type, we still use this traditional way of measuring type size.

Ordinarily, use type sizes of 10 points (elite type) or 12 points (pica type) for most of your writing. Readability decreases as type size does. Sizes such as 14, 18, and 24 points are appropriate for headings. The larger the type size, the more important the heading.

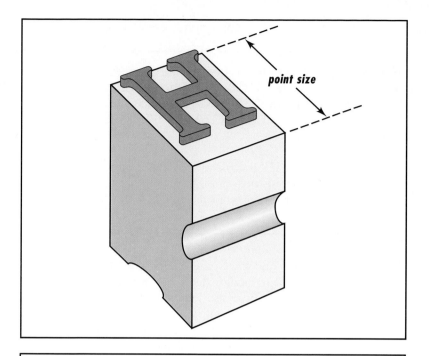

Figure 7.6
A traditional piece of type

Table 7.2 24-point Type of Two Typefaces

Schoolbook	Times
a	a
A	A
b	b
B	B
c	c
C	C

Upper- and Lowercase Letters

Type is easiest to read if it is displayed using upper- and lowercase letters. The uniform size of **uppercase letters** makes them more difficult for readers to identify (Carter, Day, and Meggs 85; Tinker 57–61). **Lowercase letters** are visually more varied and distinctive and thus easier to recognize.

In Figure 7.7, for example, which paragraph is easier to read?

TYPE IS EASIEST TO READ IF IT IS DISPLAYED USING UPPER- AND LOWERCASE LETTERS. THE UNIFORM SIZE OF UPPERCASE LETTERS MAKES THEM MORE DIFFICULT TO IDENTIFY. LOWERCASE LETTERS ARE VISUALLY MORE VARIED AND DISTINCTIVE AND THUS EASIER TO RECOGNIZE.

Type is easiest to read if it is displayed using upper- and lowercase letters. The uniform size of uppercase letters makes them more difficult to identify. Lowercase letters are visually more varied and distinctive and thus easier to recognize.

Figure 7.7
All uppercase versus upper- and lowercase type

Ordinarily, use upper- and lowercase letters. Use all uppercase letters selectively for emphasis or for major headings. Keep in mind, however, that writers started using all uppercase letters on typewriters before computers offered quick access to different type sizes and type styles. Instead of all uppercase letters, therefore, consider using a larger type size for headings or bold or italic type style for emphasis.

Leading

Leading (pronounced *ledding*) is the space between consecutive lines of type. It is called leading because of the traditional printing practice of using thin strips of lead to separate lines of type. If the readability of your type is low because of its design, style, or size, you might choose to compensate partially for this difficulty by using additional leading (Carter, Day, and Meggs 81; Craig 129). In Figure 7.8, for example, notice how the readability of the 9-point sans serif type improves when the paragraph is double spaced.

Line Length

The number of characters in each line of type also influences the readability of your writing. Your reader's eyes have to cross the page from left to right and again to the left to start the next line. Long lines of type interfere with your reader's ability to locate the next line of type (Carter, Day, and Meggs 86; Felker et al. 79–80). A typical **line length** is 50 to 75 characters. The longer the line of type the more difficult it is to read and the more important it is that you minimize this difficulty by using more leading (Tinker 129). In Figure 7.9, for example, notice how readability improves with the switch from single spacing to double spacing.

Leading (pronounced ledding) is the space between consecutive lines of type. It is called leading because of the traditional printing practices of using thin strips of lead to separate lines of type. Leading is measured in points, with one to two points of leading typical for 10-point and 12-point type. Oftentimes type and leading are described as 10 on 12 or 10/12: this signifies 10-point type occupying a 12-point space (i.e., 10-point type with 2 points of leading). If the readability of your type is low because of its design or style or size, you might choose to partially compensate for this difficulty by using additional leading (e.g., double spacing as opposed to single spacing).

Leading (pronounced ledding) is the space between consecutive lines of type. It

is called leading because of the traditional printing practices of using thin strips

of lead to separate lines of type. Leading is measured in points, with one to two

points of leading typical for 10-point and 12-point type. Oftentimes type and

leading are described as 10 on 12 or 10/12: this signifies 10-point type

occupying a 12-point space (i.e., 10-point type with 2 points of leading). If the

readability of your type is low because of its design or style or size, you might

choose to partially compensate for this difficulty by using additional leading

(e.g., double spacing as opposed to single spacing).

Figure 7.8
Single spacing versus double spacing of low-readability type

The number of characters in each line of type also influences the readability of your writing. If lines of type are long, as the reader's eyes cross the page from left to right and again to the left to start the next line, it is often difficult to identify which line of type is the next line. A typical line length is 50–75 characters. The longer the line of type, the more important it is that you minimize this difficulty by using more leading.

The number of characters in each line of type also influences the readability of your writing.

If lines of type are long, as the reader's eyes cross the page from left to right and again to

the left to start the next line, it is often difficult to identify which line of type is the next

line. A typical line length is 50–75 characters. The longer the line of type, the more

important it is that you minimize this difficulty by using more leading.

Figure 7.9
Single spacing versus double spacing of a long line of type

Alignment

You have four choices for aligning type on the page: *left aligned, right aligned, justified* (left and right aligned), and *centered* (see Figure 7.10).

Type that is **left aligned** has the highest readability (Carter, Day, and Meggs 88). The lines of type all start in a consistent position on the left, and the unequal line lengths constitute a visible difference between consecutive lines of type. This difference between one line and the next as well as the consistent starting position for each line leaves it easier for your readers to locate the beginning of each new line of type and to avoid either skipping a line or reading the same line again. Word spacing is also uniform, contributing to a high readability. Use left-aligned type for most of your writing.

Type that is aligned on the right margin is more difficult to read because each new line starts in a different location on the left. The word spacing, however, is uniform and consecutive lines are easily differentiated by their unequal length. Use type that is **right aligned** for brief and special passages only: for example, right-aligned type could be appropriate for a caption displayed on the left side of a photograph.

Type that is **justified** is also more difficult to read because line lengths are equal and word spacing is unequal (Carter, Day, and Meggs 88–89). Equally long lines are less visibly distinctive; as a consequence, your reader is more likely to read the same line twice or to skip a line. In addition, the simultaneous left and right aligning of type causes variable word spacing. Often, the variable spacing creates vertical rivers of white space that interfere with your reader's ability to cross the page horizontally from left to right. Use justified type whenever the design of the page is as important as the readability of the type, such as for promotional publications.

Type that is **centered** also has a low readability because each line starts in a different location on the left. The word spacing is uniform, however, and line lengths are unequal. Use centered type for major headings or for brief passages such as title pages or invitations.

Left Aligned
You have four choices for aligning type on the page: left aligned, right aligned, justified (i.e., left and right aligned), and centered. Of your four choices, left aligned has the highest readability. Use left-aligned type for most of your writing.

Right Aligned
You have four choices for aligning type on the page: left aligned, right aligned, justified (i.e., left and right aligned), and centered. Of your four choices, left aligned has the highest readability. Use left-aligned type for most of your writing.

Justified
You have four choices for aligning type on the page: left aligned, right aligned, justified (i.e., left and right aligned), and centered. Of your four choices, left aligned has the highest readability. Use left-aligned type for most of your writing.

Centered
You have four choices for aligning type on the page: left aligned, right aligned, justified (i.e., left and right aligned), and centered. Of your four choices, left aligned has the highest readability. Use left-aligned type for most of your writing.

Figure 7.10
Left-aligned, right-aligned,
justified, and centered type

Summary of Guidelines on Typography

1. Choose a serif type.
2. Choose plain style. Use bold and italic style selectively and systematically.
3. Choose 10-point or 12-point type. Use larger and smaller sizes selectively and systematically.
4. Choose upper- and lowercase type. Avoid using all uppercase type.
5. Use more leading (e.g., double spacing) if the readability of your type is low.
6. Choose a line length of 50 to 75 characters. For longer lines, use more leading.
7. Choose type that is left aligned with a ragged right margin.

1. Given the guidelines on typography here, how would you revise the typography of Figure 7.3, the poster announcing the annual meeting of the Society of Communicators?
2. Bring samples of effective and ineffective uses of typography to show to your focus group. Explain to your group why you consider each sample effective or ineffective. Who has the most effective and least effective samples? In your journal, record your conclusions regarding the use of typography.

Write More About It

In Chapter 15, we will ask you to evaluate a subject. This exercise could help you to generate ideas for this evaluation. The guidelines on typography in this chapter constitute your knowledge by observation. Use these guidelines as the basis for your evaluation of a sample of effective or ineffective typography.

GUIDELINES ON ILLUSTRATIONS

Illustrations will often improve your reader's understanding of your subject. A table of statistics or a photograph of your subject, for example, could clarify a difficult point. Or a diagram or line graph could emphasize a critical piece of information.

Before you decide to use illustrations, however, analyze your aim and your audience:

- *What are you trying to accomplish through your writing?* If you are writing instructions for repairing a bicycle, a diagram of the bicycle would be important. Similarly, if you are writing a persuasive essay on recycling, a graphic display of the energy savings achieved through recycling might emphasize a critical point. If you are analyzing a short story, however, a picture of the major character would be unnecessary.

- *How familiar is your audience with your subject?* If your readers have no previous knowledge of your subject, illustrations might be necessary. For example, if you are describing a gas compressor to business majors, a photograph or diagram would be essential. If you are addressing mechanical engineering majors, however, you could omit the illustrations.

- *How motivated is your audience to read about your subject?* If your audience is bored by, afraid of, or hostile to your subject, adding illustrations might improve their attitude by making your subject look easier to digest. For example, if you are explaining a new word processing program to students who dislike using computers, you could minimize their anxiety by including pictures of all the various display screens associated with the program. A couple of such pictures might do the job for more enthusiastic students.

Tables and Figures

If you decide to use illustrations, you have to distinguish between two basic types: tables and figures. A **table** is the display of numbers or words in columns and rows. All other illustrations are **figures.** This distinction is important because tables and figures are numbered separately, such as Table 1 and Figure 1. In a List of Illustrations, you would list the tables and figures separately: Table 1, Table 2, and so forth, then Figure 1, Figure 2, and so on.

In the paragraph or paragraphs immediately preceding each table and figure, specifically direct your reader to examine the illustration. By doing so, you identify the point in your discussion at which the reader should consult the table or figure for pertinent information. Use the table or figure number to give this instruction. The following are possible variations:

See Table 1. . . .

. . . (see Figure 1).

Table 2 shows that. . .

In Figure 2, the scores on. . .

Notice that Table 3 has. . .

. . . as displayed in Figure 3.

In the paragraphs preceding or following the illustration, it is important to explain its meaning because two people looking at a picture, for example, often arrive at two different impressions. If you explain how you interpret the illustration, you minimize the likelihood of misinterpretations. Ordinarily, you position the table or figure as close as possible to this explanation—on the same page as the explanation or on the page immediately following. (See the style manual of your academic field for specific directions regarding the location of tables and figures.)

In addition to numbering tables and figures, give each illustration a label that clearly and specifically describes the information displayed (e.g., Table 1. Bachelor's Degrees Conferred by Colleges and Universities in the United States, According to Field of Study, 1991–1992). See the style manual of your academic field for guidelines.

In order for your illustration choices to be effective, you will need to be familiar with several characteristics of tables and figures. You will acquire this knowledge partially through participation (i.e., by creating illustrations and by using borrowed illustrations) and partially through observation (i.e., by reviewing the following guidelines on the design of tables and figures).

Guidelines for Tables

Of all illustrations, tables are the least visually compelling. Columns and rows of words and numbers do little to make reading easier, with a single important exception. Instead of displaying information as a sequence of sentences, tables make it easier to locate specific information. Readers can start with the column or row of their choice, read only the columns or rows they consider necessary, and skip the remainder. By putting information in a table, you give readers the power to decide which information is important or interesting. Imagine, for example, if the tables of departure times at airports were given instead as a series of sentences:

> Flight 129 to Atlanta leaves from gate 26 at 8:05. Flight 735 to Boston leaves from gate 17 at 9:22. Flight 214 to Chicago leaves from gate 29 at 9:34. Flight 112 to Detroit leaves from gate 18 at 9:43. Flight 257 to Houston leaves from gate 23 at 9:52. Flight 173 to Los Angeles leaves from gate 36 at 10:08. Flight 163 to Memphis leaves from gate 40 at 10:17. Flight 219 to New York City leaves from gate 38 at 10:23. Flight 141 to Philadelphia leaves from gate 33 at 10:30. Flight 195 to Seattle leaves from gate 30 at 10:44. Flight 339 to Toronto leaves from gate 28 at 11:07.

If you are going to Philadelphia, for example, your boarding time could easily come and go before you located the sentence with information on your flight. Only people traveling to Philadelphia are interested in information on that flight, and that is the only flight that is of interest to them. It is much more efficient, therefore, to display all flight information in a table (see Table 7.3).

Table 7.3 Table Illustrating Efficient Display of Information

Time	Departing to	Flight	Gate
8:05	Atlanta	129	26
9:22	Boston	735	17
9:34	Chicago	214	29
9:43	Detroit	112	18
9:52	Houston	257	23
10:08	Los Angeles	173	36
10:17	Memphis	163	40
10:23	New York City	219	38
10:30	Philadelphia	141	33
10:44	Seattle	195	30
11:07	Toronto	339	28

If you have information that is of different importance to the different members of your audience, use a table to display that information. Or if you wish to give your readers the ability to retrieve specific pieces of information quickly, use a table to display that information.

Summary of Guidelines for Tables

1. Because the type in a table is often small (e.g., 9 points), choose a typeface of high readability (e.g., Schoolbook). If necessary, use additional leading.
2. To separate your tables from surrounding paragraphs, use boxes or horizontal lines. Also effective is a change of typeface. If you are using a serif type for your paragraphs, for example, switch to a sans serif type for your tables.
3. Give each column a heading that clearly and specifically identifies the information listed. For tables of numbers, include the unit of measurement (e.g., *gallons, median hourly wage, parking tickets per driver*). If numbers are large, add a designation such as "in thousands" or "in millions" to the column heading.
4. For tables of words, align the words on the left margin of each column. For tables of numbers, change fractions to decimals; within each column, align numbers on the decimal point.
5. If columns, rows, or individual cells require explanation or qualification, use alphabetized notes at the bottom of the table. Use superscript lowercase letters to designate each note.
6. Use thin horizontal lines to separate headings and notes from the rows of information. Use either white space or thin vertical lines to separate the columns and rows.

7. If your table is too wide for the page, orient it with the top of the table along the left margin. If your table is too long for the page, continue it on a second page. At the top of the continuation, give the table number and title with the word *continued* or the abbreviation *cont'd*. Repeat all column headings.

Guidelines for Figures

While tables are effective for displaying specific pieces of information, figures are designed to dramatize and emphasize, to offer approximations, to illustrate ideas, and to summarize impressions. If you want your reader to locate a particular quality or quantity, use a table. If you want to give your reader a quick overview, however, use a figure.

If you were trying to determine the success or failure of the recycling program at your school, for example, you could closely examine Table 7.4 and decipher that the program was flourishing or you could glance at Figure 7.11 and arrive immediately at the same conclusion. Because the specific recycling figures for a given year are unimportant to you—only their continuing rise—a table is here a less effective illustration.

Table 7.4 Table Offering Specific Detail

Table 4. Five-Year Profile of Recycling Programs

Year	Tons of Bottles and Cans	Tons of Paper
1990	1	2
1991	3	4
1992	8	6
1993	9	7
1994	12	11

Because figures emphasize and dramatize information, it is especially important that you consider the ethics of your visual display. Does your figure give a fair portrait of the information? Or does your figure disguise or distort? Your credibility as a writer hinges on the integrity with which you discuss and display information.

A wide variety of figures are available to illustrate your ideas. Your job as a writer is to choose the figure that is appropriate for your aim and audience.

Line Graphs

A **line graph** such as Figure 7.11 shows how a subject or how several subjects change according to two variables. Line graphs emphasize the degree of change (high or low) and the direction of change (positive or negative). A line graph comprises a vertical line (the y axis) intersecting a horizontal line (the x axis), with diagonal lines plotting the change to the subjects. Time is often one of the two variables and the line graph thus shows the degree and direction of change over time. If time is one of the variables, it is always displayed along the x axis, progressing chronologically from left to right.

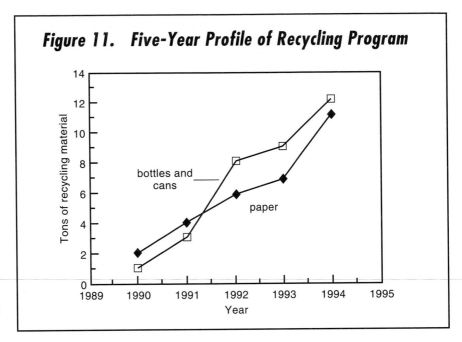

Figure 11. Five-Year Profile of Recycling Program

Figure 7.11
Figure offering emphasis and immediate understanding

Summary of Guidelines for Line Graphs

1. Start the vertical scale at zero. Use consistent intervals (e.g., 10, 20, 30) and equally space the intervals on the vertical and horizontal scales. To do otherwise is to distort the degree and direction of change.
2. Label the vertical and horizontal axes to identify each variable.
3. Keep the subjects you plot to a minimum. The more diagonal lines, the more difficult the line graph is to decipher, especially if the diagonals are close together or intersect each other.
4. Keep each diagonal line as distinctive as possible by using different colors or symbols (e.g., circles, squares, triangles).

5. Label each diagonal line to identify the subject that is plotted.
6. Separate your line graph from surrounding paragraphs by using a box or horizontal lines.

Column Graphs

A **column graph** shows the approximate quantity of a subject or of several subjects at consecutive points in time (see Figures 7.12 and 7.13). Quantity is displayed along the vertical axis, and time along the horizontal axis. The columns are arranged in chronological order from left to right along the horizontal axis. Such a horizontal series going from left to right is widely associated with progression through time.

Use a column graph instead of a line graph if you wish to emphasize the difference in the quantity of an item at two or more points in time as opposed to the degree and direction of change. If you were interested, for example, in displaying the difference between the low ratio of traffic tickets per driver in 1970 and the high ratio in 1975, a column graph would be the appropriate figure. The difference in the height of the columns would dramatically illustrate the quantitative difference.

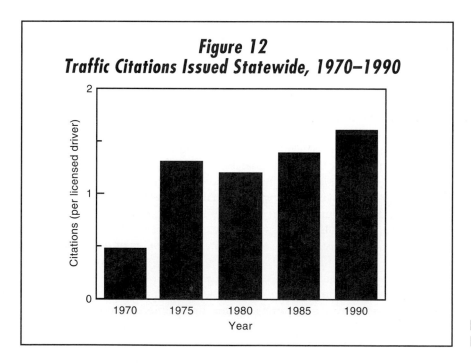

Figure 7.12
Example of a column graph

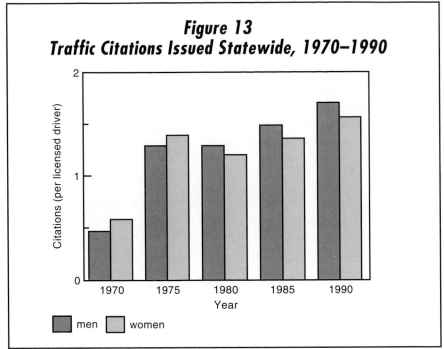

Figure 7.13
Example of a multiple-column graph

Summary of Guidelines for Column Graphs

1. Start the vertical scale at zero. Use consistent intervals (e.g., 10, 20, 30) and equally space the intervals on the vertical and horizontal scales.
2. Label the vertical and horizontal axes to identify each variable.
3. Keep the subjects you plot to a minimum. The more columns you group together at each interval of time, the more difficult it is to compare and contrast the same subject at different points of time.
4. Make all columns equal in width. Wider columns look bigger or more important; narrower columns look smaller or less important.
5. In a multiple-column graph, use a different color or type of shading for each subject. Use a consistent style of color or shading, however, to avoid visual distractions (e.g., different intensities of the same color, different colors of the same intensity, various densities of dots, various densities of vertical lines).
6. Label each column to identify the subject that is displayed.
7. Use two-dimensional columns. Using three-dimensional columns on a two-dimensional scale often leads readers to misinterpret the graph. If the two-dimensional column does the job, the third dimension is unnecessary and distracting.
8. Separate your column graph from surrounding paragraphs by using a box or horizontal lines.

Bar Graphs

A **bar graph** displays the approximate quantity of two or more subjects at a single point in time (see Figure 7.14). The different subjects are displayed along the vertical axis and quantity is displayed along the horizontal axis.

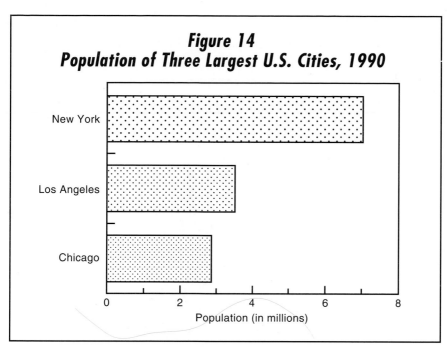

Figure 14
Population of Three Largest U.S. Cities, 1990

Population (in millions)

Figure 7.14
Example of a bar graph

Use a bar graph if you wish to emphasize the differences in quantity among your subjects. If you were interested, for example, in displaying the difference in the population of major American cities in 1990, you would use a bar graph. The differences in the length of the bars would dramatically illustrate the population differences.

Summary of Guidelines for Bar Graphs

1. Start the horizontal scale at 0. Use consistent intervals (e.g., 10, 20, 30) and equally space the intervals on the horizontal scale.
2. Label the horizontal axis to identify the variable.
3. Label each bar to identify the subject that is displayed.
4. Make all bars equal in width. A wider bar would look bigger or more important; a narrower bar would look smaller or less important.
5. Use a different color or shading for each subject. Use a consistent type of color or shading, however, to avoid visual distractions (e.g., different intensities of the same color, different colors of the same intensity, various densities of dots, various densities of vertical lines).

6. Use two-dimensional bars. Using three-dimensional bars on a two-dimensional scale often leads readers to misinterpret the graph.
7. Separate your bar graph from surrounding paragraphs by using a box or horizontal lines.

Pie Charts

A **pie chart** displays the divisions of a subject. It also emphasizes the relative size and proportion of each piece of the pie (see Figure 7.15).

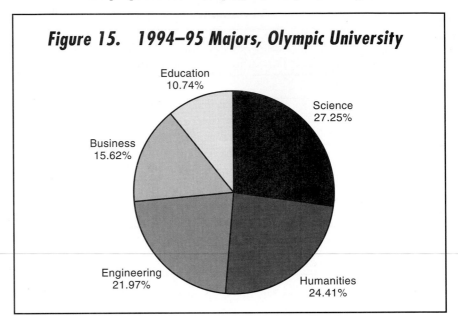

Figure 15. 1994–95 Majors, Olympic University

Education 10.74%

Science 27.25%

Business 15.62%

Engineering 21.97%

Humanities 24.41%

Figure 7.15
Example of a pie chart

Use a pie chart to show the number of pieces of the pie, to show the relative size of the pieces, and to emphasize the importance or influence of a particular piece or of particular pieces. For example, if you wished to illustrate the different brands of personal computers used by students at your college or university, you would create a pie chart, dividing the pie according to the computer brands. The pie chart would display the most widely used brand or brands at your college or university.

Summary of Guidelines for Pie Charts

1. Limit the number of pieces to seven or eight. The more pieces of the pie, the more difficult it is to determine their relative size.
2. Thinking of the circle as a clock, start dividing the circle at 12 o'clock. Progressing clockwise, start with the biggest piece and stop with the smallest.

3. Label each piece and identify its size.
4. Ordinarily, color or shading are unnecessary. If you use color or shading, do so cautiously and systematically to avoid visual distractions. Use a progressive color or shading (e.g., the smaller the piece, the lighter the color or shading). Use a uniform color or shading for all pieces of the pie (e.g., different intensities of the same color, different colors of the same intensity, various densities of dots, various densities of horizontal lines).
5. Separate your pie chart from surrounding paragraphs by using a box or horizontal lines.

Organizational Charts

Organizational charts display the divisions and hierarchical relationships within organizations such as companies, agencies, clubs, associations, and committees (see Figure 7.16). Each position of authority is identified within a box. The boxes are organized vertically and horizontally according to level of authority.

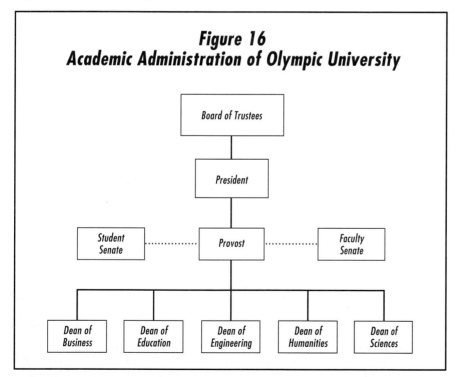

Figure 16
Academic Administration of Olympic University

Figure 7.16
Example of an organizational chart

Use an organizational chart if you wish to identify the managerial or administrative relationships within an organization. For example, if you are discussing the inefficiency of a city agency, it might be appropriate to illustrate the organization of the agency and display the several levels of minor officials through which information filters to the director. Such a dramatic visual display reinforces your message and effectively substitutes for several paragraphs describing the agency's organization.

Summary of Guidelines for Organizational Charts

1. Design boxes so that the higher the level of authority, the bigger the box. Give all positions on the same level of authority the same size box.
2. Use no color or shading to fill the boxes. Type fills each of the boxes and color or shading interferes with readability.
3. Choose a typeface of high readability for the titles that identify each position (e.g., Schoolbook). The size of the titles is often small (e.g., 8 points or less), and readability is thus critical.
4. Use solid lines or arrows to link positions having direct relationships. Use dots or dashes for special or indirect relationships (e.g., to lawyers, inspectors, advertisers).
5. Separate your organizational chart from surrounding paragraphs by using a box or horizontal lines.

Flow Charts

A **flow chart** displays the chronological sequence of steps in a process or procedure. In the traditional flow chart, a labeled box symbolizes each step, with lines or arrows identifying the chronological sequence (see Figure 7.17), p. 223. It is also possible to reinforce the subject by using pictorial images for each of the steps.

Use flow charts to summarize a series of instructions or a complicated process. For example, you might design a flow chart to explain the registration process at your school to a group of new students. The flow chart would serve as a capsule version of your explanation—a quick reference aid that each student could check periodically during the process of registering.

Summary of Guidelines for Flow Charts

1. Whenever possible, organize the flow chart to progress in a single direction, either horizontally, vertically, or diagonally (e.g., top to bottom, left to right). Flow charts that twist, circle, and zigzag are more difficult to decipher. The visual complexity also gives the impression that the process or procedure is equally complicated.
2. Use boxes of the same size for all steps. Boxes of equal size indicate that each step is equally important to the completion of the process or procedure.

3. Use no color or shading to fill the boxes. Type fills each of the boxes and color or shading interferes with readability.
4. Choose a typeface of high readability for the label of each step (e.g., Schoolbook). Since the size of the boxes often restricts you to a small type size (e.g., 8 points or less), readability is critical.
5. Use solid lines or arrows to link the boxes. Use dashes to link the boxes for special or optional steps.
6. Separate your flow chart from surrounding paragraphs by using a box or horizontal lines.

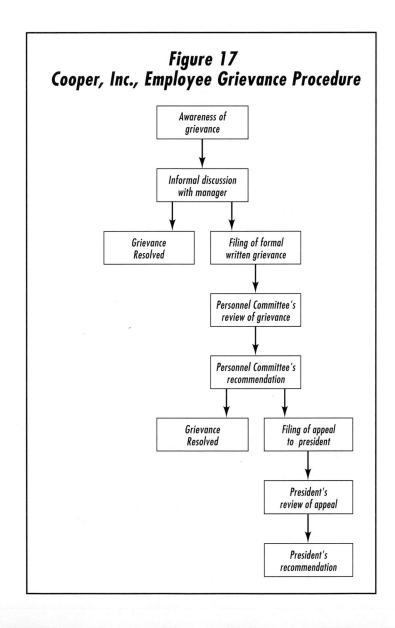

Figure 7.17
Example of a flow chart

Diagrams

A **diagram** is a labeled picture that identifies the important parts of a subject and displays their physical and spatial characteristics. Diagrams omit all unnecessary visual information in order to emphasize the details pertinent to the discussion (see Figure 7.18).

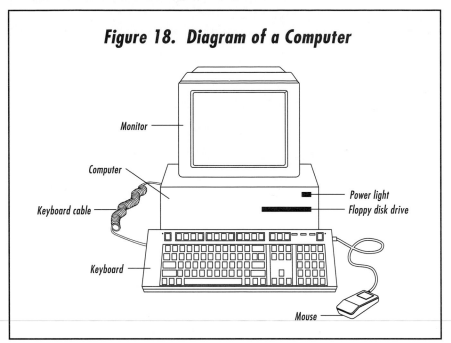

Figure 18.   Diagram of a Computer

Figure 7.18
Diagram of a computer

A map is a special type of diagram. Ordinarily, diagrams aim at a realistic representation of their subjects, but a map symbolizes the physical and spatial characteristics of its subject (e.g., city maps, wiring diagrams).

Use a diagram to identify, for example, the rooms of a building, the plumbing of a house, the circuitry of a computer, the muscles of a human leg. Imagine the difficulty of trying to describe such subjects without using a diagram.

Summary of Guidelines for Diagrams

1. Keep diagrams simple. Omit all unnecessary details and decorations.
2. Label each important part of your subject.
3. Choose a typeface of high readability (e.g., Schoolbook). The type size of the labels is often small (e.g., 8 points or less) and readability is thus critical.
4. Separate your diagram from surrounding paragraphs by using a box or horizontal lines.

Drawings

A **drawing** is a picture of the important physical characteristics of a sub-ject, displaying only the details of relevance to the discussion. A drawing is similar to a diagram, but without the labeling of parts. That is, a diagram focuses on picturing and identifying the parts of a subject, whereas a drawing emphasizes the subject as a whole. Consider, for example, a dia-gram of a computer versus a drawing of a computer (see Figures 7.18 and 7.19). The diagram calls your attention to the major parts of the computer (monitor, keyboard, disk drive), whereas the drawing asks you to look at the computer as a complete object.

Use a drawing to emphasize particular physical characteristics of your subject. For example, if you were on a campus committee that was solicit-ing contributions to build a new library, your advertising materials might include a drawing of the new library, including the surrounding trees and bushes, but possibly omitting surrounding buildings. Your objective would be to focus on the new building and show it as a fitting and attractive addition to the campus. If your drawing included bigger or more beautiful surrounding buildings, your visual message could be missed.

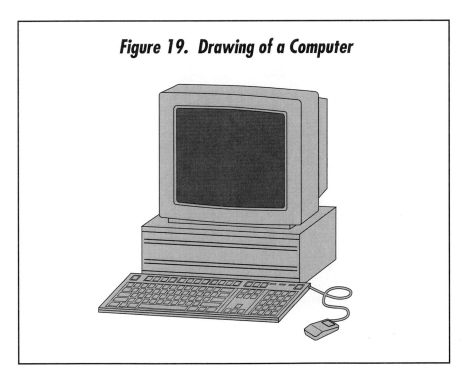

Figure 19. Drawing of a Computer

Figure 7.19
Drawing of a computer

Summary of Guidelines for Drawings

1. Keep your drawings simple. Eliminate unnecessary details or decorations.
2. Choose a style of drawing that is appropriate to your aim and audience (such as comic exaggeration or realistic representation).
3. Separate your drawing from surrounding paragraphs by using white space, a box, or horizontal lines.

Photographs

A **photograph** is the most realistic representation possible; therefore, if you see a photograph of a subject, it is usually easier for you to recognize the subject itself thereafter.

Photographs, however, often include visual information that is of little relevance to your discussion. For example, the subject of your essay might be bicycles; however, if your photograph shows a man riding a bicycle while wearing a Cleveland Indians T-shirt, readers are likely to notice the T-shirt and pay less attention to the bicycle.

If you want your readers to be able to recognize your subject, use a photograph. If the subject is unavailable for photographing (such as the new library that is still being built) or if you wish to emphasize particular characteristics of your subject, use a drawing or diagram.

Summary of Guidelines for Photographs

1. Consider the angle from which your readers will most likely view the subject (e.g., pedestrians view a building from the side, helicopter pilots view a building from above). Choose this angle for your photograph.
2. Keep your photographs simple. If possible, eliminate unnecessary or distracting details.
3. Use a clear and crisply focused photograph.
4. Separate your photograph from surrounding paragraphs by using white space, a box, or horizontal lines.

Creating or Borrowing Illustrations

If you decide to use illustrations, you have two choices: either create new illustrations or borrow existing ones. If you create new illustrations, you might consider using computerized graphics programs. Such programs give you the power to illustrate your ideas, even though you might have little artistic ability. A wide variety of such programs are available. A program such as Cricket Graph® or DeltaGraph®, for example, automatically designs tables, line graphs, column graphs, bar graphs, and pie charts. You supply the numerical information, identify the type of illustration you desire, and click a button. A program such as SuperPaint® or UltraPaint® is effective for organization charts, flow charts, and simple diagrams and drawings. And programs such as Adobe Illustrator® or Aldus Freehand® allow you to design sophisticated diagrams and drawings. Investigate the full variety of such programs to improve your ability to communicate visually.

If you borrow illustrations, you need to cite the source, just as you cite the sources of ideas and words that you borrow. By citing the source of an illustration, you give credit to its creator and add to its credibility because you identify it as published. For example, if you borrow a diagram from a journal article or a book to use in your essay, you would cite the source immediately below the diagram:

Reprinted from "The Ethics of Typographical Display" by T. Cooper and N. Cooper, 1990, *Journal of Composition Studies, 44,* p. 167.

or

Reprinted from *Typography* (p. 298) by D. Powers, 1988, New York: Variety Publishing Company. Copyright 1991 by Variety Publishing Company.

If the source is also listed in your bibliography, however, you might use a simple parenthetical citation:

(Cooper & Cooper, 1990, p. 167)

(Powers, 1991, p. 298)

If you change the illustration or create a new or different version of the illustration, you still have to cite the source. In this case, however, you would identify your illustration as an adaptation:

Adapted from "Creating Effective Illustrations" by Z. Green, 1991, *Journal of Pictorial Communication, 11,* p. 83.

If you borrow information from a source to create your illustration, cite the source of that information immediately following your illustration:

The data in columns 2 and 3 are from *Statistical Display* (pp. 11–14) by T. Hopper, 1994, Chicago: Creative Publishers.

If your essay is to be published and if the illustration is copyrighted, you are legally required to obtain written permission from the copyright holder to use the borrowed illustration. The copyright holder is the owner of the illustration—usually this is the author, illustrator, and/or publisher.

In this case, the citation identifies the copyright holder and your receipt of permission:

> From "The Ethics of Typographical Display" by T. Cooper and N. Cooper, 1990, *Journal of Composition Studies, 44,* p. 167. Copyright 1990 by T. Cooper and N. Cooper. Reprinted by permission.
>
> or
>
> From *Typography* (p. 298) by D. Powers, 1988, New York: Variety Books. Copyright 1988 by Variety Books, Inc. Reprinted by permission.

This legal requirement also applies to adaptations:

> From "Creating Effective Illustrations" by Z. Green, 1991, *Journal of Pictorial Communication, 11,* p. 83. Copyright 1991 by Iguana Publishing Company. Adapted by permission.

If the illustration has no copyright, no permission is required. Nevertheless, you need to cite the source of the illustration.

Your obligation to cite the source of borrowed illustrations has a single exception: **clip art.** Such special books or disks of available illustrations supply you with pictorial images, symbols, and decorative borders. Your ownership of the book or disk gives you the right to use the illustrations without identifying their source. You simply cut and paste, either manually or electronically, from the book or disk of clip art to the page you are designing. A variety of such books (e.g., Rudolf Modley and William R. Myers, *Handbook of Pictorial Symbols,* Dover Press, 1976) and disks (e.g., ClickArt®, Cliptures®) are available.

Summary of Guidelines on Citing Sources of Illustrations

1. If you borrow an illustration from a journal article or a book, cite the source immediately below the illustration.
2. If you change the illustration or create a new or different version of it, cite the source, identifying your illustration as an adaptation.
3. If you borrow information from a source to create your illustration, cite the source of that information immediately below your illustration.
4. If your essay is to be published and if the illustration is copyrighted, obtain written permission from the copyright holder to use the borrowed illustration or your adaptation of it. In this case, your citation identifies the copyright holder and your receipt of permission.

1. In your focus group, create a variety of appropriate illustrations to accompany a proposal. Choose among the following subjects for your proposal or develop a different subject:

   - to the board of trustees to build a parking garage on your campus
   - to your city council to prohibit the use of cigarette machines within the city limits
   - to the governor of your state to require recycling of newspapers
   - to the president of the United States to institute a national program of licensing handgun owners

2. In the periodicals section of your school library, examine journal articles that include tables and figures. Locate examples of each of the illustrations discussed in this chapter. How does each table and figure contribute to its article? Are the illustrations necessary? Which articles could use different or additional illustrations?

   Write More About It

   In Chapter 15, we will ask you to evaluate a subject. This exercise could help you to generate ideas for this evaluation. The guidelines on illustrations in this chapter constitute your knowledge by observation. Use these guidelines as the basis for your evaluation of tables and figures.

3. Which of the expressive essays from Part III, if any, would benefit from the addition of one or more tables or figures? Which of the referential essays from Part IV? Which of the persuasive essays from Part V? Explain your answers.

4. In your focus group, create a list of tables or figures that would be appropriate for one of the essays in Part VI, Readings. Compose a brief justification for your choice of illustrations.

GUIDELINES ON PAGE DESIGN

The appropriate display of words and illustrations on the page or screen is essential to the success of your writing. To achieve a lucid display, use white space and adopt or adapt a basic **page design.**

White Space

White space is neither a passive attribute of page design nor the simple absence of typography and illustrations (Felker et al. 81; White 59). White space is a positive and dynamic influence on readability.

The white space of margins, for example, serves a critical function. By framing the typography and illustrations, white space assures readers that your discussion of your subject is contained and controlled. In paper copies, the margins also invite interactive communication by offering readers a space for commenting on your message, taking notes, or asking questions.

By using white space to separate the discourse blocs on your page or screen, you visually emphasize the different categories of information that you are discussing. You also identify appropriate points at which readers might stop to digest the information. Without this white space separating your discourse blocs, you signal to readers that your discussion is a continuous sequence of ideas and that it is designed for uninterrupted reading.

If you use white space to separate your discourse blocs, you might also introduce labels or headings to identify the various subjects you discuss. Ordinarily, you align major headings on the center of the page and minor headings on the left margin. Triple space between the heading and the preceding discourse bloc and double or single space between the heading and its discourse bloc: this practice visually reinforces the separation of the blocs as well as the relationship of the heading to the following discourse bloc.

White space also offers easier and quicker access to information and retrieval of information. For example, by displaying a series of items as a list and surrounding it with white space, you call special attention to this information. Your readers will perceive immediately—before reading—that this information is a series of items. The length of the list and each item in the series will also be evident. Later, if your readers need to refer to this information again, they will have little or no difficulty again locating the list or specific items on the list. If a series of items is important for readers to notice or if they might need to refer to it more than once, display the series as a list. If the items are listed in no special order, introduce each item with a bullet (•); if the list is sequential (e.g., a series of steps in a process), alphabetize or number the items.

Basic Page Designs

Five basic designs are available: essay, book, letter, memo, and circular. Each design has several variations. Ordinarily, you will adopt the design specifications that your teacher or boss gives you.

Essay Design

Essays (see Figure 7.20) typically use letter-size paper (8.5 × 11 inches) with 1-inch margins on all sides. The type is usually double-spaced and aligned on the left. A five-space indentation signals the beginning of a new paragraph. Tables and figures occur immediately following the paragraph that mentions the illustration. Identifying information such as title, author's name, recipient, and date is displayed on a title page or at the top of the first page. The list of sources, if necessary, is given on the last page. The individual pages are either stapled or paper clipped together.

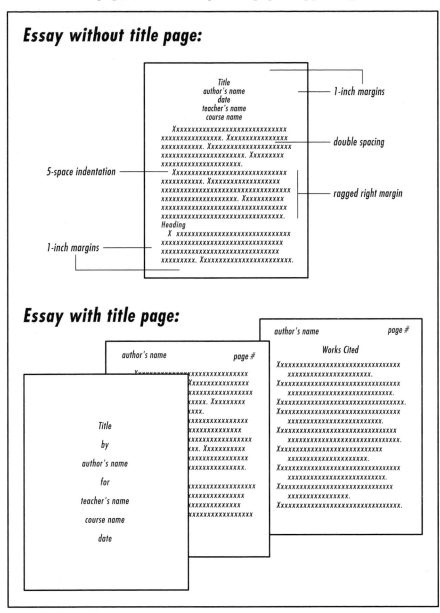

Figure 7.20
Samples of essay design

Book Design

Books (see Figure 7.21) ordinarily use letter-size paper (8.5 × 11 inches), with a 1.5-inch margin on the left side of the page and 1-inch margins on the remaining sides. The wider left margin leaves space for the binding (e.g., plastic, spiral, or three-ring). Type is usually displayed in a single column, though a double-column design is also possible. A single column of type is ordinarily double spaced and either aligned on the left or justified. A double-column design is usually single spaced and justified. A five-space indentation signals new paragraphs. Tables and figures occur immediately following the paragraph mentioning the illustration. A title page gives identifying information such as title, author's name, recipient, and date. The list of sources, if necessary, is given on the last page.

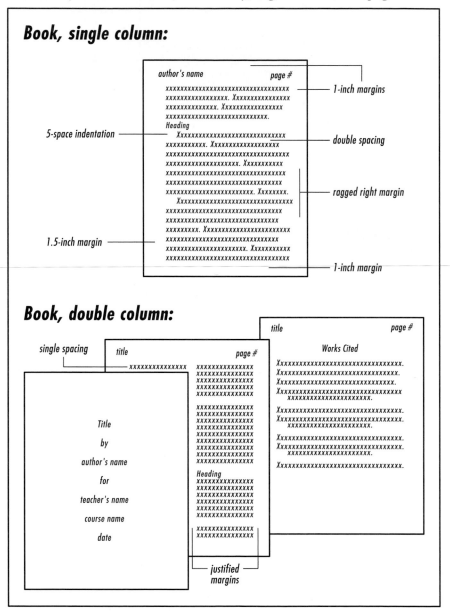

Figure 7.21
Samples of book design

Letter Design

Letters (see Figure 7.22) typically use letter-size paper (i.e., 8.5 × 11 inches), with margins of at least 1 inch on all sides. Type is displayed in a single column aligned on the left. Single spacing is used within paragraphs, double spacing between paragraphs. Ordinarily, if the closing and signature are aligned on the left margin (i.e., full block style), the five-space paragraph indentation is unnecessary; if the closing and signature are displayed on the right side of the letter (i.e., modified block style), paragraph indentations are appropriate. Tables and figures typically occur on accompanying pages. No title is given, but a subject line is possible. The recipient, recipient's address, and date are identified before the greeting; the author's name is displayed following his or her signature. Information sources, if necessary, are specified informally (e.g., "according to. . .") within the appropriate paragraph.

Memo Design

Memos (see Figure 7.23) are typically reserved for communication within organizations. The memo uses letter-size paper (8.5 × 11 inches), with 1-inch margins on all sides. Type is displayed in a single column aligned on the left. Paragraphs are single spaced, with double spacing between paragraphs. The five-space indentation to signal new paragraphs is optional. Tables and figures occur immediately following the paragraph mentioning the illustration. Date, recipient, author's name, and subject are labeled and listed at the beginning of the memo. If necessary, information sources are given informally (e.g., "according to. . .") within the appropriate paragraph. Computerized correspondence (e.g., e-mail) ordinarily adopts memo design.

Circular Design

Circulars (see Figure 7.24) cover miscellaneous news and advertising materials. In school or on the job, for example, you might be asked to compose fliers, brochures, résumés, and newsletters.

Fliers serve to advertise events, organizations, products, and services. A flier is typically a single side or both sides of a single page, either letter size (8.5 × 11 inches) or legal size (8.5 × 14 inches). Margins and typographical display are variable. Illustrations are usually pictorial figures. Ordinarily, fliers display a title and omit the date of composition, author's name, recipient, and information sources.

Brochures, similarly, advertise events, organizations, products, and services. A brochure is typically both sides of a single page, usually either letter size (8.5 × 11 inches) or legal size (8.5 × 14 inches). It is folded to create two, three, or four columns on each side of the page. Margins and typography are variable. Tables and figures are possible. Brochures usually display titles and headings, while omitting the date of composition, author's name, recipient, and information sources.

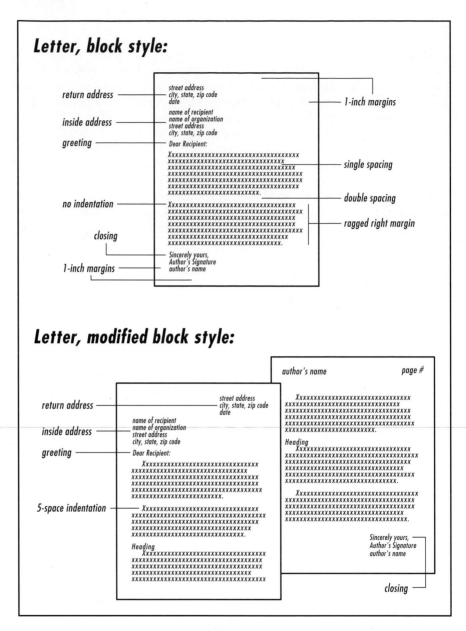

Figure 7.22
Samples of letter design

Résumés advertise individuals, specifically their job credentials. Ordinarily, résumés identify your name, address, telephone number, education, job experience, special skills, honors and awards, and campus or community activities. Often, you list the names of your references (if you have their permission and the space) and specify the date of composition. A résumé is one side of one or more pages, letter size only (8.5 × 11 inches). Margins are typically 1 inch on all sides. Type is displayed in one or two columns. Illustrations are avoided, with the possible exception of a professional photograph of you.

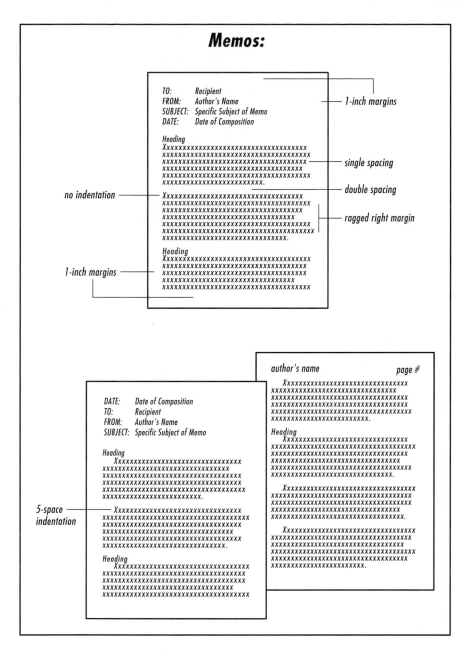

Figure 7.23
Samples of memo design

Newsletters are small and specialized newspapers for specific groups, such as a company's employees, a club's members, or a store's regular customers. A newsletter is typically both sides of two to sixteen pages, letter size (8.5 × 11 inches) or legal size (8.5 × 14 inches). It is aligned vertically, usually with two or three columns on each side of the page. Margins and typography are variable. Illustrations are likely, especially photographs. Ordinarily, newsletters display the date of composition and specify the group of recipients on the cover page. Often, a newsletter is composed collaboratively, with several writers contributing their articles to a single editor, who reviews the articles and designs the pages. In each article, titles and headings are typical. Information sources are identified informally (e.g., "according to. . . ") within the appropriate paragraph. Each author's name might also be displayed, either following the title or the article.

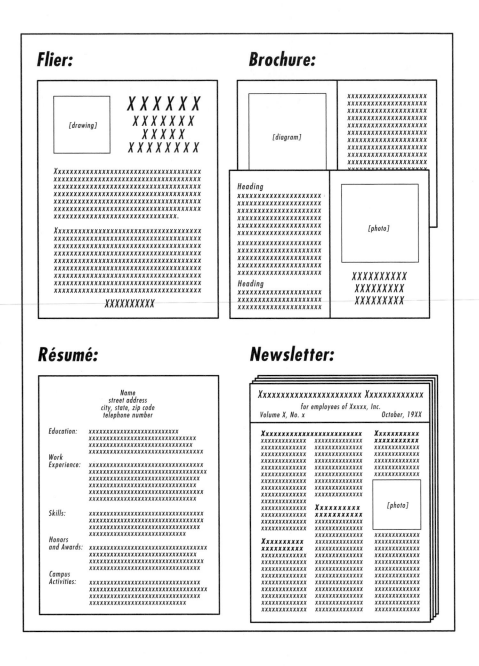

Figure 7.24
Samples of circulars

1. Locate examples of each of the five basic page designs (i.e., essays, books, letters, memos, and circulars). In your focus group, discuss the similarities and differences among your examples. Which variations of each design do you consider superior? Which do you consider inferior? Why?

Write More About It

In Chapter 15, we will ask you to evaluate a subject. This exercise could help you to generate ideas for this evaluation. The guidelines on page design in this chapter constitute your knowledge by observation. Use these guidelines as the basis for your evaluation of the page design samples.

2. Examine the style manual of your academic field. Does it include specifications on page design, especially of essays? If it does, what are those specifications? If it doesn't, ask a professor from your academic field for advice. How does he or she design essays? In your focus group, compare and contrast the design practices of the various academic fields?

Issues for Writing

In this chapter we have discussed the characteristics of typography, tables, and figures, as well as the integration of words and illustrations on the page or screen. In coming chapters, you will have a variety of opportunities to practice your individual and collaborative abilities regarding memory and delivery. Figure 7.25 offers a series of questions to guide you during the design of your writing.

Memory and Delivery Guide

1. Is your text handwritten, typewritten, or computerized? Why? If handwritten, is your handwriting legible? If typewritten, do you have typographical choices of design, style, and size? If computerized, are you designing a paper copy or a screen copy?
2. Does the typography aid reading? Consider your choices regarding

- typeface
- leading
- type size
- line length
- type style
- alignment
- upper- and lowercase letters

3. Are illustrations necessary? If so, are tables or figures appropriate? If you are using tables, does the typography aid their reading? If you are using figures, which of the following are appropriate:

- line graphs
- organization charts
- column graphs
- flow charts

Figure 7.25
Memory and delivery guide

Figure 7.25
Memory and delivery guide
(continued)

- bar graphs   • diagrams
- pie charts   • drawings
                  • photographs

Do the figures emphasize appropriate information? Is the visual display ethical?
4. Is white space used effectively?
5. What is the appropriate page design (essay, book, letter, memo, or circular)?

Index of Key Terms

Works Cited

Burt, Cyril. *A Psychological Study of Typography*. Cambridge: Cambridge UP, 1959.

Carter, Rob, Ben Day, and Philip Meggs. *Typographic Design: Form and Communication*. New York: Van Nostrand, 1985.

Craig, James. *Designing with Type*. 3rd ed. New York: Watson, 1992.

Felker, Daniel B. et al. *Guidelines for Document Designers*. Washington: American Institutes for Research, 1981.

Tinker, Miles A. *Legibility of Print*. Ames: Iowa State UP, 1963.

White, Jan V. *Editing by Design*. 2nd ed. New York: Bowker, 1982.

Zachrisson, Bror. *Studies in Legibility of Printed Text*. Stockholm: Almqvist, 1965.

PART III

Expanding Your Repertoire: Expressive Aim Writing

Expressive Aim Writing: An Overview

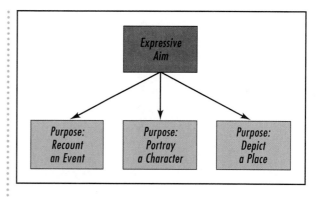

I arrived early for my interview. I presented extra copies of my cover letter and résumé to the receptionist and waited for my name to be called. Dressed in a blue suit and armed with a briefcase full of sample materials and letters to substantiate my teaching experience and educational background, I was confident about my chances of being selected. Summer teaching jobs were hard to come by, and summer teaching jobs in special programs for writing teachers were even harder to find and compete for. But here I was at the interview, certain of my qualifications to be just the kind of writing instructor this program was seeking.

The receptionist called my name, handing me a folder with my name typed in the upper tab. "You'll need to present this file for your interview. Go right in." His tone was matter-of-fact, shaking my confidence a bit. Reminding myself of my purpose and abilities, however, I regained my sense of self and stepped into the office.

Behind a large desk sat a portly man, engaged in a telephone conversation. As he turned and looked up at me, I handed my folder to him. The man grinned broadly. "I'll call you back later," he said excitedly to the person on the phone. "The answer to my problem has just walked in the door!"

"Come in and have a seat," invited my interviewer.

I was so relieved. Obviously, here was a person who had seen my file and knew a qualified candidate when he saw one. Both my self-confidence as well as my faith in this interviewer's judgment were growing. I sat down in a chair in front of the desk, pleased with the way things were going.

The interviewer held my folder and located my name, typed in capital letters across the tab label. "I am so happy to see you. I can tell you right now that you are the answer to our prayers. We have had lots of applicants for these positions, but this year we need additional teachers and tutors. I know you are qualified because you made the interview; my staff screens and verifies your experience and background, you know."

I was speechless. It seemed apparent that I was in: I had landed this job without saying a word about myself. My thoughts were interrupted by this warm job offer: "Welcome to our summer staff. You'll love teaching college algebra and trigonometry to our students."

"College algebra and trigonometry?" I asked. I could feel the blood rushing to my face. Surely he was joking.

Unfortunately, he was serious. He assumed that I taught mathematics—a subject area in which they obviously needed extra instructors. Realizing that something was amiss, he opened my folder, scanned my application, and immediately began to explain his confusion. "Rarely have we ever interviewed any English teachers who are Asian. In fact, you're a first, I believe. Of course, we've had numerous Asian math and science teachers. So, you see why I thought. . . ." (GG)

Put yourself in my place: you're a qualified English teacher, seeking summer employment. You also just happen to be Asian and female. Imagine that this incident happens to you. What significance can you glean from this interview? What lesson or revelation does this experience teach you? Why would this narrative and its meaning for you be of interest or value to others?

These are questions that I asked myself as I began to recall and informally write down details pertaining to that interview. In fact, this brief narrative functions much like a journal entry might—as a possible subject for a future essay. In its present form, the narrative reacquaints me with the incident so that I can revisit the story, characters, and place. I can also discern the significance of the experience, for without significance, my essay may lack purpose—a *raison d'être*. If a writer reconstructs a series of events just for the sake of telling a story, or describes a character or place just for the sake of describing it, then the writing may seem to be more an exercise in filling space on a page than an attempt to derive meaning from a rhetorical situation. Both the writer and audience will undoubtedly sense the missing ingredient: the insight or "truth" that we discover in our daily lives. Recalling an experience without also explaining its significance yields an incomplete text, as does recalling significance without including the experience that triggered it. Taken together, however, the experience and its significance enjoy a symbiotic and effective relationship.

So let's return to those questions, queries that would enable me to explore the potential of the incident and its meaning as a future essay subject. What significance did I glean from this interview? The lesson or revelation that this experience taught me pertained to ethnic stereotyping. In this case, the interviewer's assumption was that *all* Asians are "good" at math and science and, as a consequence, *all* Asians choose careers in those fields of study and work. I quickly discovered that despite the availability of my personal file, academic background, work experience, and recommendations, I was still subject to this prejudice. I also discovered that educated individuals and minorities could be guilty of stereotyping: ironically, my interviewer was African American. And I was painfully reminded that I am different; people cannot help seeing my ethnicity and gender before knowing anything else about me.

Of what value and interest is this insight to my audience? For those who are in any way different (such as racial or religious minorities), stereotyping is a reality. All of us, therefore, need to be aware of such prejudice and find ways to overcome it.

Expressive aim writing gives you the opportunity to remember events, portray people, and describe places so that you can experience your own insights about them and the ways they have edified or changed you. In Chapters 9 and 10, you'll be asked to write about subjects that have resulted in important personal revelations. Your ideas for writing don't have to be bizarre or momentous to be interesting. You will find that routine events or fairly common subjects often lead to significant perceptions: that is, through the ordinary comes the extraordinary.

This chapter is designed to aid your journey through the territory of expressive rhetoric. It is your guide to the recursive and dynamic processes of planning, translating, and reviewing expressive essays.

EXPRESSIVE AIM IN WRITING

In expressive aim writing, the focus is on the writer and his or her perceptions on a subject. Working individually or collaboratively, writers convey their insights regarding people, ideas, places, and things. Types of expressive aim writing include the following:

autobiographies	personal journals
personal letters	diaries
confessions	travelogs
personal essays	memoirs

The focus of expressive aim writing is always on you as the writer—your impressions, your perceptions, the impact of the experience on you.

In school, you will often have opportunities to develop and communicate your understanding of particular times in your life. In a history class, for example, you might be asked to discuss your impressions following a visit to a local historical site. Or your psychology teacher might ask you to describe your earliest realization that boys and girls are different.

Writing that you produce in your daily life will also reflect an expressive aim. As a college student applying for an academic scholarship, you may need to write a personal essay describing a particular high school teacher who influenced your choice of major. Or, as a foreign exchange student, you may keep a travelog of all the places you visit during your first year away from home. After you graduate from college, you may write similar kinds of texts. For example, you may compose an autobiographical essay for a local conservation magazine, in which you describe your participation in an archaeological dig in Ecuador. Or you may write a personal letter to a relative or friend, describing your new job.

On the job itself, you are likely to discover that expressive writing is unusual; ordinarily, writers in business and industry either explain subjects or try to influence decisions. Expressive writing is typically limited to educational experiences, such as a training session to develop your managerial skills or to develop your professional ethics. In such on-the-job training, the teacher might ask you to describe a leader you admire or to recall a situation that challenged your sense of morality. As with all expressive writing, the focus is on your perception of the experience—the impact of this leader or situation on your thinking.

Often, expressive aim writing also has subordinate aims. For example, you may write a narrative of your summer job as a salesclerk in a department store. This experience gave you insights about how complicated your job can become when company policy about customer service is pitted against your own sense of right and wrong. Your essay includes anecdotes about your interaction with difficult customers: here your aim is expressive. To clarify your narrative, however, you also include an overview of your job description and company policies: here your aim is referential. In your text, you also analyze and evaluate the company motto—"The customer is always right"—posing the following question: How can the customer always be right if that patron is shoplifting, damaging merchandise, swapping or altering sales tags, and so on? While you describe your personal experiences, you also provide compelling evidence that unscrupulous customers are often defended at the expense of salesclerks. As a consequence, you suggest that the store motto needs to be modified: here your aim is persuasive. While your dominant aim is thus expressive, you also introduce subordinate referential and persuasive aims.

EXPRESSIVE PURPOSES IN WRITING

Expressive aim writing always has a variety of possible purposes. Whenever you write, you are responding to a rhetorical situation by creating a text with the goal of producing some effect on your readers. The following are three key purposes common to expressive aim writing that we'll explore further in Chapters 9 and 10:

- to **recount an event** or series of events and its significance to the writer
- to **portray a character** and his or her significance to the writer
- to **depict a place** and its significance to the writer

These three purposes are characteristic of expressive writing across a wide variety of academic disciplines, as the following list of sample writing assignments demonstrates:

- For a sociology class, volunteer to be an aide in a nursing home for one week. Write an essay about your experience. What did it teach you about the residents, their lives, and yourself? Write a character sketch of one of the residents or one of the other aides. What did you learn from your interaction with this individual? Describe the nursing home itself. Is it more like a home or a hospital?

- For an engineering course, portray Galileo as a major contributor to the field of engineering. Recall your earliest memories of building a flying machine. Describe your vision of a space station.

- In a public relations course, view a videotape of the opening ceremonies of the 1994 Winter Olympics in Lillehammer, Norway. Discuss the emotional impact the ceremonies have on you as a typical viewer. Depict the city of Lillehammer during the Olympics. Describe your favorite athlete from the 1994 Olympics.

- In a history class, write a character sketch of Rosa Parks, the African-American woman who in 1955 refused to move to the back of the bus in Montgomery, Alabama. Depict the city of Montgomery as it was in 1955. Recall your earliest experience of racial prejudice.

- For an architecture course, describe a building on campus. Interview the architect and give your impressions of this man or woman. Record your experience of using this building.

- In a political science course, discuss your experience as a visitor to Tiananmen Square in Beijing, China. Describe Tiananmen Square and discuss the meaning that it has for you. Portray the man or woman who served as your guide.

- For a business administration class, recall your experience as a waiter or waitress at a local restaurant. Describe your boss, noting specifically his or her administrative abilities. Depict the restaurant itself, addressing such subjects as its size, number of employees, customer capacity, exterior and interior design, location, and atmosphere.

Often your expressive writing will have subordinate purposes. For example, you might write a narrative of your visit to a music studio. In remembering this event, you might also portray several of the singers or musicians you observed and depict the studio itself.

Realistically speaking, there may be times when you may not be certain about your dominant purpose for writing at the outset. You might start with the idea of remembering a series of events, but during your revising decide that a portrait of the characters involved or a depiction of the place itself is more important and meaningful.

Unless you are assigned a specific subject to discuss, one of the most difficult matters you'll confront is choosing a good subject, so be prepared to devote a day or two to coming up with writing ideas. This time will be a good investment. Start your search for a subject by analyzing and clarifying your rhetorical situation or task. For example, if your writing task asks you to write about a personal experience, generate a list of subjects concerning memorable incidents at home, school, or work. If your writing task requires you to write about a person or place, try listing people and locations you like or dislike.

To write a text that *you* can become involved in, you need to select a good subject. To write a text that *readers* can become involved in, however, you need to do even more. Try to select experiences, people, and places that are significant to you because, through them, you have somehow changed—gained insight or a new understanding of yourself in relation to the world around you. It's always a good idea to share your list with other writers (classmates, roommates, friends, teachers, family); be sure to explain who your readers may be, and then gauge their responses or interest level in your subjects. Your own gut feeling about good subjects will often be confirmed by others.

Expressive aim writing requires you to reflect on and derive personal insights from human experiences and the human condition. This is no small task. To fulfill these requirements, you may have to relive and reexamine times that open your eyes to revelations ranging from joyful to painful. And this process of careful consideration may understandably take time. Keep in mind, however, that all expressive writing has purpose and that your composing processes can help you to discover why, what, and how you write.

ASSESSING AND MAPPING THE EXPRESSIVE RHETORICAL SITUATION

In addition to determining your expressive aim and purpose, consider your knowledge of your subject and the people you are addressing. Use the knowledge continuum to identify key words regarding your subject and the sources of your knowledge, from knowledge by participation to knowledge by observation. On the audience continuum, illustrate your analysis of your readers. Use the narrow arcs positioned closer to the writer (you) to identify readers whose background, education, experience, or occupation is similar to yours; use the wider arcs to identify the readers who are different from you. On each arc, also identify your readers' level of motivation, from those likely to perceive your list of key words as worthwhile reading to those who might consider your ideas boring or trivial. By combining the two continua, you create a **map of the expressive rhetorical situation.**

Consider, for example, Figure 8.1. The student writer, Tamikka Jameson, is preparing to write an expressive essay about the experience of buying her first microcomputer. She wishes to explore the significance of owning a computer and to narrate how she came to purchase a Macintosh. On this map, Tamikka indicates that she has gained knowledge through both participation and observation.

Tamikka classifies her audience according to their attitudes toward computers—students who want to buy computers, students who already own computers, and students who neither own nor like computers. She believes that students who like computers will be interested in reading

Figure 8.1 Mapping
Tamikka's rhetorical situation

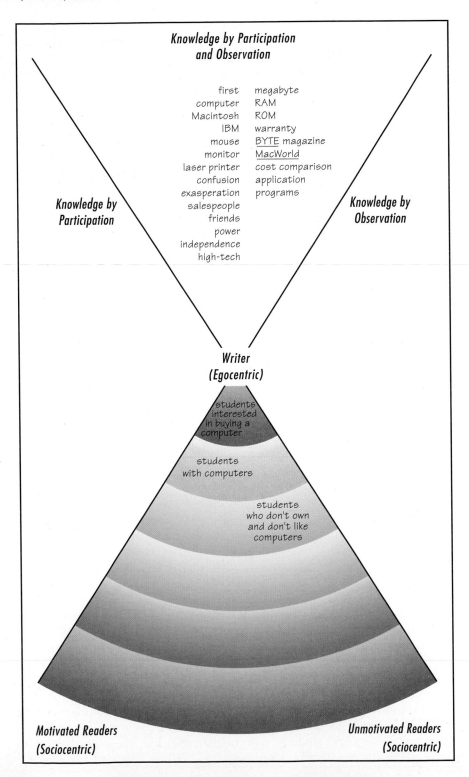

about her experience. Tamikka purchased her computer a couple of weeks ago and thus still identifies most closely with students who are interested in buying a computer. As a consequence, she maps this group closer to herself than students who already own computers. She anticipates that students who dislike computers will be unmotivated readers and maps them accordingly on the audience continuum.

Read More About It

See Chapter 4, pp. 85–93.

RESEARCHING AND DISCOVERING EXPRESSIVE INFORMATION

Expressive aim writing enables you to recreate a human experience so that your audience can live it with you. Moreover, your narrative and descriptive information serve to trigger a genuine **epiphany**—a personal moment of insight that allows you to understand some event, person, or place in a new light. This epiphany is the thesis of your expressive aim writing. To communicate your thesis effectively, you need to establish your credibility (ethos), provide specific and accurate details (logos and pathos), and emphasize the connection between your experience and its significance (ethos, logos, and pathos).

Invention Guide for Expressive Writing

Aim and Purpose

1. What is your writing task?
2. Are you writing individually or collaboratively?
3. Is the text's dominant aim expressive?
4. Are there subordinate aims? What are they and how do they affect the information in the text?
5. What is your purpose for writing? What specifically do you want your text to accomplish? Does your purpose satisfy the requirements of your writing task?
6. Are there subordinate purposes? What are they and how do they affect the information in the text?

Mapping the Rhetorical Situation: Subject and the Knowledge Continuum

1. What is your subject?

---

2. What is your relationship to the subject? That is, will the point of view in your essay be that of a participant, observer, or participant-observer?

3. Map your knowledge on the knowledge continuum by listing key words regarding your subject. Mapping is an ongoing process: continue to revise and refine your map as you learn more about your subject.

Mapping the Rhetorical Situation: Readers and the Audience Continuum

1. What is the demographic profile of your readers (age; gender; social, economic, and educational levels; personal and professional backgrounds and experiences; cultural and situational factors and contexts)? How will their profile affect their responses to the subject and text?

2. Select representative members of your audience, and role-play to determine the following:

   - readers' motives for reading your text
   - readers' enthusiasm about your subject
   - readers' sense that your subject is timely

3. How can you help readers to process and interpret your text more effectively (organization, memory cues, language, and visual signposts)?

4. Map your readers on the audience continuum. Mapping is an ongoing process: continue to revise and refine your map as you learn more about your audience.

Information: Research and Discovery

1. What kind of knowledge does your writing task require?

   Knowledge by participation (personal records, brainstorming, pentad, classical topics, visualizing, and computer-assisted invention)—documentation and bibliography usually unnecessary

   Knowledge by observation (interviews, questionnaires, and library resources)—documentation and bibliography usually necessary

   Knowledge by participation and observation (combination of sources identified above)—documentation and bibliography usually necessary

2. Which research strategies will you use to locate and generate information? Why?

3. How will you establish your credibility?

4. How will you provide specific and accurate details for the following distinctive features?

- narrative action
- characters
- description
- setting
- dialogue
- point of view
- narrative organization

5. How will you emphasize the connection between your experience and its significance?

Establishing Credibility

Because of its autobiographical nature, expressive aim writing gives special importance to the writer. The writer's credibility or ethos, as a consequence, is essential. Readers must appreciate the writer's reconstruction of his or her experience and must trust the writer's interpretation of its significance. If the details are inconsistent, sparse, or illogical, or if the meaning derived from experiences is tangential or inappropriate, the writing may sound superficial, contrived, and incoherent.

For instance, suppose you write an essay about winning first prize at a local science competition. You briefly describe the nature of your project investigating the effects of chemical carcinogens on harvest ants, the judges and the judging process, the competition, and so on. When you explain how this experience has affected you, you mention the prize money and the chance you had to advance to the district science competition in the state capital. But you omit key information: you're an entomology major, and because of the recognition you and your science project received, you were awarded a full scholarship at the local college. Without this scholarship, you would have been required to work full time at a pest control company, enrolling in college night classes as time permitted. The specific details make your experience realistic, logical, and important to your audience. Just telling the general story about the science competition won't give your audience a sense that this story is your authentic recollection. You need to value the experience you write about as a turning point in your life. If not, your readers may question or lose their confidence in you and your judgment, thus jeopardizing the possibility for effective communication.

Regardless of the expressive aim writing task that you as a writer undertake—be it chosen or assigned; a story about an event, person, or place; individually or collaboratively authored—the subject that you ultimately develop must be one you know well and can make both engaging and relevant to readers.

Providing Specific and Accurate Details

What type of information can you research and generate in order to write effective expressive texts? The answer to this question leads us to the distinctive features of expressive aim writing, including narrative action and organization, point of view, descriptive detail, character, dialogue, and setting.

Narrative Action

Expressive aim writing often involves the telling of a story. We all have memories that we would like to share with others. Often these memories are interwoven with other recollections and we must devote much energy to focusing on a single event and its significance to us. While the discovery of an epiphany or personal insight in a story is strategic, the narrative itself must be strong enough to support and justify that insight.

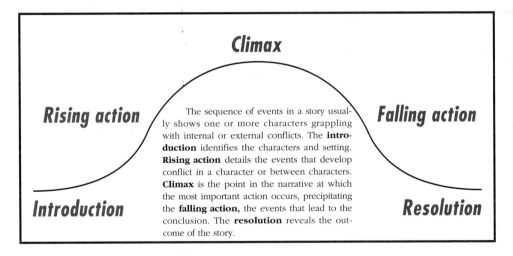

Figure 8.2 The "shape" of information in a story

Figure 8.2 illustrates the flow and effect of information in a typical story. Stories build tension to show conflict as a plausible and powerful catalyst for change and to draw readers into the drama of the story at an emotional and intellectual level. To engage your audience in reading your story, you don't need to write about superhuman events or exaggerate ordinary life experiences for the sake of narrative tension. We learn more about our human condition through daily life that may seem deceptively routine. You need not "spin a yarn" or resort to telling tall tales.

Neither should you introduce information that contributes little or nothing to the reader's understanding of the events, the characters, or the significance of the story. In remembering your visit to a hospital, for example, you might mention that you noticed a janitor repairing a wall and painting it white. But is it important to mention this episode? Does the repairing of the wall serve to explain your feelings regarding the practice of medicine? Does the white paint reinforce your impression of the hospital as a sterile institution? Are there more important details to mention regarding your visit? You will probably have to experiment through several versions of your story to achieve a delicate balance: enough specific information to help your reader comprehend the characters and events, but not so much information that the reader drowns in the details and fails to see the significance of your story.

To derive **significance** from an experience and convey your insight effectively, you need to be sure you understand that experience well. Scrutinize the movement of your story as if you were a detective checking the veracity of a murder suspect's alibi. Start by jotting down or typing into a computer all the incidents or actions in your story in chronological order. Once this list is complete, ask yourself the following questions:

- Which action contributes to the rising action in the narrative? to the complication? to the climax? to the falling action? to the resolution?

- How might you visualize this information in terms of its shape as a story?

- Does every action in your story seem appropriate and necessary? If not, which actions can you cut?

- Which sequences of action are the most important to the building of tension and meaning in your essay? Which sequences of action are less important and can be consolidated and summarized?

Narrative Organization

When you arrange the ideas in your essay according to a sequence of time, you are using **chronological organization.** Narratives that tell a story or present a series of steps in a process occur along a time line and thus benefit from this kind of sequential structure. Several possible chronological patterns appear below:

Simple Chronological Order: introduction, rising action, climax, falling action, resolution

Complex Chronological Order: resolution, introduction, rising action, climax, falling action *or*
resolution, introduction, rising action, climax, falling action, resolution *or*
climax, introduction, rising action, climax, falling action, resolution

These chronological patterns allow you to take the events in a story and alter their sequence for dramatic effect. As you can see, the simple chronological order reveals action exactly as it happened in time. With complex chronological order, however, the writer starts the narrative in the present time, then flashes back to the past, beginning the sequence of events at that point. Or the writer can start the narrative in the present time, flash back to the past to begin the sequence of events, and then bring the reader back to the present.

Arrangement Guide for Expressive Writing

Evidence: Establishing Unity

1. Has your research yielded sufficient, plausible, and pertinent information to support your thesis?

2. How do your research data reflect the three rhetorical appeals: ethos, logos, and pathos?

3. How does your research shape your thesis statement (significance)? Is your thesis statement specific and concrete? Focused and feasible? Interesting?

4. How do the patterns of organization in your text help readers see and follow the logic and approach to your subject? Have you chosen a simple sequential organizational pattern (chronological, spatial, hierarchical) or a complex combination of patterns? Why?

Discourse Blocs: Developing Ideas

1. What is the internal structure of your text? Identify and outline the discourse blocs in your essay that narrate the story line and the discourse blocs that summarize or describe.

2. What modes of development have you used within the discourse blocs? Why?

3. What functions do the various discourse blocs serve (title, introduction, transitional blocs, conclusion)?

Coherence and Cohesion: Making Connections

1. Have you connected sentences by using repetition, substitution, and transitions?

2. Do you use parallelism for coordinated and listed items? To reinforce ideas of equal importance or similar meaning?

Outlining: Tracing Your Path

1. Have you written an outline, either before or after you've drafted your text? Does it seem logical and clear?
2. How will you refine the design and development of your text in the next draft?

Point of View

Point of view is the perspective from which you write. It reveals how you have acquired knowledge of your subject. In first-person singular narration *(I)*, you participate in your story, interacting with other characters and experiencing personally the action of the narrative. If you write in first-person plural *(we)*, the voice that readers hear is a collective voice, such as the voices of collaborators. In third-person narration *(he, she, they)*, you observe the characters and events of your story without directly participating.

A writer or narrator can only reveal to readers information that he or she can learn from one of the three ways of knowing. For example, suppose you tell a story that you know by participation, perhaps a brush with death when you were six years old. In your first-person narrative, you might describe your thoughts and feelings while lying in a hospital bed and waiting for your parents to visit you. But if you report what the doctors and nurses wrote on your hospital chart, or what they said during whispered exchanges in the hospital halls while you lay in your bed unconscious, your point of view is incongruous with your details. There is no possible way, given your perspective in this story, for you to know what the doctors and nurses wrote or said. You therefore appear to be an unreliable narrator, losing your ethos and your readers' trust. In this case, as the narrator from a participant point of view, you are limited in your knowledge, especially your knowledge of the actions, thoughts, and feelings of others.

But let's say that you now know this information because, at age twenty, you have been told this story over and over again by relatives and your family physician. A solution to your point of view problem is to allow other characters to speak—to revise your purely participant point of view to reflect your participant-observer way of knowing. Identifying how you possess knowledge about a subject is strategic in determining which point of view and whose voices you employ in your writing.

To double-check the reliability and feasibility of your point of view, examine your map of the expressive rhetorical situation. What kind of knowing does your subject require of you? Check the sequence of action and comments by and about characters. Given your point of view in this story, is it feasible that the narrator knows this information? If you find you've included information that cannot logically be revealed from your point of view, consider revising your details. If that isn't workable, consider changing your point of view.

Descriptive Detail

Another way that your expressive aim writing can reflect real life is through the use of description. Expressive aim writing *shows* rather than *tells* readers about experience. So that your texts have a sense of realism and authenticity, incorporate vivid and accurate **descriptive details.** For example, refer to people, places, and things by name. Identify the color, make, model, and year of the truck in your story; does it have the look, smell, and comfort of a fancy vehicle or of a dilapidated pickup? Take your audience for a walking tour of the historical district in your hometown, but remember to provide readers the names of streets and key landmarks. Move your readers through space and time in a chronological or spatial order: north to south, east to west, clockwise or counterclockwise. Let readers hear the high-pitched sound of a passenger train in the distance and smell the sweet yeasty aroma of bread rising in a bakery next door. But choose only the details that genuinely contribute to your reader's ability to grasp your subject.

By offering these specifics, you instill readers with a feeling that they are there with you, experiencing the same conflict and resolution that you are. Writing descriptively is a way to involve your readers' senses of sight, hearing, touch, taste, and smell. In choosing descriptive details, keep in mind that your readers have five senses, not one or two. Creating sensory impressions makes shared or familiar experiences more immediate for your audience (thus establishing logos and pathos), but it can also introduce readers to new experiences.

Effective description requires you to use concrete and precise words that support a dominant impression. If, for example, you are describing a raccoon that visits your yard at night, you might decide to characterize it as adorable or destructive. If you describe how this animal noisily roots around your backyard in search of food, killing your flowers and eating vegetables from your garden, you build the impression that the raccoon is destructive. On the other hand, if you describe its beautiful fur, its amusing face, its delicate hands and feet, and the little babies it is trying to feed, you characterize it as adorable. Decide on the dominant impression you want to convey and select details that will clarify your perception and build a single, unified picture.

Here is a practical tip for generating vivid and specific description. Underline or boldface every character, location, time, act, or gesture in your chronological list. Make a master list of these names; then, beside each name, brainstorm for descriptive details. Be sure to include specific and sensory words and phrases, keeping in mind that your descriptions should convey a dominant impression to readers.

Style Guide for Expressive Writing

1. *Individuality.* How much of you is in this sample of expressive writing? What features of style indicate your personal likes and dislikes regarding wording, sentence structure, spelling, and punctuation?

2. *Time.* How does the time period during which you are writing influence your expressive style? Does your age or your audience's age influence your style? How?

3. *Dialect.* Are you using a local dialect or a universal dialect? Why? What features of style are characteristic of the dialect you are using?

4. *Collaboration.* Is your expressive writing collaborative? How have editors or coauthors influenced your style?

5. *Subject.* What is the subject of your expressive writing? What specialized wording or phrasing is typical of expressive writing on this subject? How does this subject influence the spelling and punctuation of your expressive writing?

6. *Type of document.* What type of expressive writing are you composing? What is its common function? How will your audience use this expressive writing? What features of style are characteristic of this type of expressive writing?

7. *Relationship to audience.* What is your relationship with your audience? Is a formal or informal style appropriate? What is the appropriate degree of formality or informality? How does this degree of formality or informality influence your expressive style?

Characters

The people who appear in your expressive writing can be thought of as **characters.** In novels, short stories, and plays, characters are often considered on a continuum from those who are flat to those who are round. **Flat characters** are one-dimensional, simple, and predictable, often slipping into stock representations or stereotypes: for example, the absent-minded professor, the kindly grandmother, the mad scientist. **Round characters,** on the other hand, are three-dimensional, complex, and dynamic. These characters are believable because they resemble real people, including people you may have met before. Consider, for example, the major characters on the classic television series *M*A*S*H:* each exhibits a wide variety of thoughts and feelings, attitudes and interests. Hawkeye is never just a doctor or just a rebellious officer; he is both and more. Hoolihan is never just a nurse or just a dedicated soldier; she is both and more.

To make the people who populate your expressive nonfiction "real" for your readers, you need to include specific and significant details about them. For example, breathe life into your characters by revealing their names, occupations, and relationship to you and others; describe their physical appearance, actions, thoughts, and emotions. Let your characters speak so that readers can hear their voices. Show us characters by comparing and contrasting them to others.

While developing characters is important, be selective about the attention you devote to them. Use adjectives, but avoid unnecessary embellishment. Consider the importance of your characters in your text. For major characters, you might include details regarding their dress, walk, and habits of speech. Conversely, for minor characters, a brief, functional description, such as their occupation, is often enough.

Here is an excerpt from "I'm So Hungry, I'm Starving to Death," an essay written by Lisa about Helena, who is an anorexic. Lisa paints a picture of Helena from the point of view of Helena's family members as they witnessed her wasting away.

> As Helena's food intake decreased, she displayed a number of symptoms that we gradually became aware of. For example, we noticed Helena's eating behavior, which ranged from her persistent need to diet to her complete starvation, one of the earliest signs of this disorder. She began to waste away, her eyes became sunken and glazed over, while her abdomen began to hollow out. At the same time, Helena denied her skeletal appearance and insisted that she was still overweight. She lamented that, when she looked in the mirror, she saw a fat, ugly person. Besides being blind to her physical condition, Helena often became hostile and irritable toward her family and friends. Problems between her and us worsened, and we all began to bicker constantly. In addition to this irritability and hostility, we witnessed Helena's bouts of depression and her preoccupation with doing strenuous physical exercise. Finally, the most detrimental behavior that Helena engaged in was self-induced vomiting, which usually occurred immediately after she ate any amount of food. Helena fled to the bathroom directly after each meal, often staying there for extended periods of time. We witnessed Helena's behavior, but we thought she was just "going through a phase." If we had recognized her behavior patterns in the early stages, we might have helped her get treatment and recover before her physical condition became life threatening. But we didn't. We saw her every day. We lived in the same house. We saw Helena change. But we didn't say or do anything about her or to her about this change.

As you can see, Lisa presents the character Helena in vivid and specific detail. However, we never actually hear Helena speak; she is present and her actions and words are recounted to us, but she is never "heard or seen." And so it was with Helena in daily life: she lived with her family, she spoke—even bickered—with her family, and she stopped eating and started vomiting and exercising strenuously. Yet no one in her family ever seemed to really hear or see that Helena was in trouble. This character perhaps is more moving to readers because of the quiet yet painful way in which Lisa portrays Helena and because of the deep love that Lisa and Helena—twin sisters—share. (If you would like to read the entire essay, see Chapter 12.)

Because expressive writing usually involves some kind of change in the way characters act or think, it is important to help your readers see and appreciate your characters—how they think and why they act the way they do. If you communicate this appreciation, your readers will be prepared for the changes that occur and will be genuinely concerned about your characters. Making readers empathize with the characters in your expressive writing is called establishing pathos. It is a significant accomplishment.

Here is a strategy that may help you to develop the characters in your expressive texts. Formulate a list of descriptive details for each of your characters. Once the list is complete, answer the following questions:

- Do the details create a dominant impression of each character?
- Can you draw a mental picture of each character based on the details you've assembled?
- Is each character adequately developed for the purposes of your story?

Dialogue

In addition to naming and describing characters, you can also use dialogue to give your characters dimension. **Dialogue** allows you to capture the language that characters actually use to express their ideas. Dialogue can also help you advance the action in a story. By conversing with one another, for example, characters can show readers the conflict, climax, or resolution.

Consider the following conversation excerpted from the narrative at the beginning of this chapter:

> The receptionist called my name, handing me a folder with my name typed in the upper tab. "You'll need to present this file for your interview. Go right in." His tone was matter-of-fact, shaking my confidence a bit. Reminding myself of my purpose and abilities, however, I regained my sense of self and stepped into the office.
>
> Behind a large desk sat a portly man, engaged in a telephone conversation. As he turned and looked up at me, I handed my folder to him. The man grinned broadly. "I'll call you back later," he said excitedly to the person on the phone. "The answer to my problem has just walked in the door!"
>
> "Come in and have a seat," invited my interviewer.
>
> I was so relieved. Obviously, here was a person who had seen my file and knew a qualified candidate when he saw one. Both my self-confidence as well as my faith in this interviewer's judgment were growing. I sat down in a chair in front of the desk, pleased with the way things were going.

The interviewer held my folder and located my name, typed in capital letters across the tab label. "I am so happy to see you. I can tell you right now that you are the answer to our prayers. We have had lots of applicants for these positions, but this year we need additional teachers and tutors. I know you are qualified because you made the interview; my staff screens and verifies your experience and background, you know."

I was speechless. It seemed apparent that I was in: I had landed this job without saying a word about myself. My thoughts were interrupted by this warm job offer: "Welcome to our summer staff. You'll love teaching college algebra and trigonometry to our students."

"College algebra and trigonometry?" I asked. I could feel the blood rushing to my face. Surely he was joking.

The dialogue is augmented by descriptions and explanations that help readers understand the conflict between the job Gwen applied for and the job the employer actually offered. The effect of the irony of both characters' expectations (English instructor versus math instructor) seems more immediate and real when you hear the characters speak and see them interact.

In order to clarify which speaker said which words, display your dialogue using two simple guidelines:

Read More About It

See Part X, p. 713.

1. Enclose each speakers' words and accompanying punctuation in quotation marks.
2. Start a new paragraph whenever you change speakers.

In addition, consider carefully how you describe each speaker's expression. For example, it's fine to say that Camille *replied,* Juanita *grimaced,* and Alice *pleaded.* But you don't have to shift to more and more elaborate words and phrases every time the speaker changes. To do so may give your readers the impression that the dialogue and characters are awkward, contrived, or comical. Consider, for example, the following dialogue:

"Who is it?" inquired my sister.

"It's Bill!" I announced emphatically.

"Where are you?" she hastily queried.

"I'm at the office," I immediately rejoined.

"What are you doing there?" she interrogated with urgency.

"I'm addressing envelopes," I retorted with rapidity.

If it is clear who is speaking, often no identification of the speaker is necessary:

"Who is it?" asked my sister.

"It's Bill!" I said.

"Where are you?"

"I'm at the office."

"What are you doing there?"

"I'm addressing envelopes."

How can you troubleshoot to ensure that your dialogue is believable? Decide which are your major characters. Whose voices definitely need to be heard? Read their dialogue aloud. Does it sound authentic and realistic? If you haven't captured their voices, call them on the telephone or brainstorm to recall how these people might phrase ideas. Keep in mind that if a character's speech sounds unnatural, readers are likely to doubt the reality of the character.

Setting

Setting indicates where and when something happens: the Empire State Building at noon, the Grand Canyon on a rainy day during the prime tourist season, a bus to St. Louis on New Year's Eve. In "The Wall," an essay featured in Chapter 10, the writer Krista highlights setting to engender in her readers a sense of beauty and awe for this national monument:

> In Constitution Gardens, Washington, D.C., stands The Wall, on which these words appear:
>
> > In honor of the men and women of the Armed Forces of the United States who served in the Vietnam War. The names of those who gave their lives and of those who remain missing are inscribed in the order they were taken from us. Our nation honors the courage, sacrifice, and devotion to duty and country of its Vietnam veterans. (Ashabranner 180)
>
> Inscribed on this monument are the names of 58,132 Americans, missing or killed in the Vietnam War (Lopes 15). Each name has been carefully etched into the lustrous black granite brought from Bangalore, India. Visitors from all over come to see The Wall and pay their respects. A visitor once described the experience by comparing it to walking down into an open grave. The analogy is eerie, but accurate. As you begin your descent along the 493.5 feet of black granite slabs, The Wall rises until it looms above you. According to Sal Lopes in *The Wall*, it rises gradually for 246.75 feet until it reaches a height of over 10 feet (15). As you continue your journey past this apex and along the second major segment of The Wall, each step takes you closer to the surface. The first set of slabs, the west wall, points to the Lincoln Memorial. The other, the east wall, points to the Washington Memorial. The mere sight of such a structure is apparently overwhelming. The craftsmanship, work, and expense alone are enough to astound most people; however, the impact of this Vietnam memorial on its visitors goes beyond these considerations.
>
> As Maya Ying Lin, the designer of The Wall, explains:
>
> > I didn't want a static object that people would just look at, but something they could relate to as a journey, or passage, that would bring each to his own conclusions. . . . I had an impulse to cut open the earth . . . an initial violence that in time would heal. . . . It was as if the black-brown

earth were polished and made into an interface between the sunny world and the quiet dark world beyond, that we can't enter. . . . The names would become the memorial. There was no need to embellish. (Lopes 16)

People who come to The Wall do interact with it and the names that appear on it. They are overcome at the sight of the memorial, not because of its tremendous physical stature, but its overwhelming emotional impact.

Krista gives us a physical description of The Wall in the first paragraph. Note the kinds of verbs (*inscribed, etched, rises, looms*), adjectives (*missing, killed, lustrous, eerie, black, sunny, quiet, dark, polished*), and nouns (*honor, courage, sacrifice, devotion, monument, veterans, lives, Americans, granite, grave, slabs, craftsmanship, journey, passage, earth, violence, names*) she uses to help readers draw a mental picture of this place.

Often the setting influences how readers interpret the characters and their actions. For example, in the narrative in Chapter 1, Uma can't read or write in English though she can speak four languages fluently. How would this 27-year-old woman be viewed if she were from Washington, D.C., instead of Kuala Lumpur, Malaysia? What if she were from Quebec? Mexico City? What if that incident happened in 1940 instead of 1988? Setting may seem a relatively straightforward concept, but its simplicity is often deceptive because setting superimposes a rich cultural context onto the physical aspects of time and location.

Because of the importance of setting, consider the following strategy when you write. Start by identifying specifically the time and place for every action in your narrative or description of a character or place. Make sure you've drawn a verbal picture of each setting: name streets, buildings, and businesses. Suggest the time of day by describing the position of the sun or moon. Identify the season of the year by revealing the type and color of leaves in the trees. Note the weather conditions by describing the still air or the humid sea breeze against your face. Once your descriptions of time and place are complete, review your choice of details:

- Are they vivid enough to make readers imagine that they are there?
- Do the details genuinely contribute to the readers' understanding and appreciation of the setting or serve only as unimportant distractions?
- How does the setting change as the story unfolds and the time frame shifts? Why?

As you might have noticed, the approaches that you can use to research and discover specific details are rooted in the knowledge continuum. For example, if you know about your subject because you have first-hand experience, try research strategies that help you tap your memory. Your journal entries, for example, can help you locate possible subjects to research. By remembering cultural, educational, and familial experiences, you often discover subjects for expressive writing with which readers easily identify and which yield remarkable personal insights. To explore these subjects further, you can brainstorm. Or you might use the pentad to discover specific details: who? what? when? where? how? and why? You can also use the classical topics (definition, classification and division, process, cause and effect, comparison and contrast) to help you recall pertinent information and possibly develop appropriate illustrations; for example, you might make flow charts of narrative action or tree diagrams of the relationships among characters.

To gain understanding of a subject by observation, you might conduct interviews, develop questionnaires, and find library materials. And if your knowledge about a subject is the result of both participation and observation, you could use a combination of research strategies. You might rely on your memories of an experience and then check them against outside sources, revising your recall as necessary. Or knowledge gained by observation could remind you of additional ideas that you know by participation.

Read More About It

See Chapter 4, pp. 94–115.

Realizing and Communicating Significance in Your Experience

Unless you include a thoughtful interpretation of your experience, your expressive writing may seem empty or pointless to readers. That is, readers rightfully expect a satisfactory answer to the question, "So what?"

Take, for example, the case of Seth, who wrote an essay about his recent car wreck. Seth describes how he borrows the family car without permission, goes to a party, and gets drunk. Rather than catching a ride with a sober driver, Seth drives home, smashing the car into a tree. The accident is quite serious, and Seth is lucky to be alive. What significance does Seth derive from this incident? He reports that he learned that "wearing seat belts does save lives" because the police say he never would have survived otherwise. Is the significance realized from this accident likely to satisfy Seth's audience? Are there other more important insights that Seth might have derived from this incident?

Of course, you need not be heavy-handed in your effort to reveal the lesson you learned from a particular occurrence. At the same time, remember that the fundamental fascination of expressive writing rests in its ability to tap the experience of your readers. If expressive writing is successful, readers will see something of their daily lives and themselves in your text; they will appreciate your experience and learn from it, too.

COMPOSING EXPRESSIVE AIM ESSAYS

In this chapter, we have described the major characteristics of expressive aim writing, offering you knowledge by observation. In the following chapters, you will develop your understanding of expressive aim writing by participation: you will compose essays in which you remember events, portray people, and depict places. While responding to these writing tasks, we encourage you to maintain a writing portfolio that contains all notes, drafts, and maps of the "territory of rhetoric" you travel.

Memory and Delivery Guide for Expressive Writing

1. Is your expressive writing handwritten, typewritten, or computerized? Why? If handwritten, is your handwriting legible? If typewritten, do you have typographical choices of design, style, and size? If computerized, are you designing a paper copy or a screen copy?

2. Does the typography aid reading? How do your typographical choices establish your credibility, clarify ideas, and motivate your audience? Consider your choices regarding

   - typeface
   - type style
   - type size
   - upper- and lowercase letters
   - leading
   - line length
   - alignment

3. Are illustrations necessary? If so, are tables or figures appropriate? If you include tables, does the typography of the tables aid their reading? If you include figures, which of the following are appropriate?

   - line graphs
   - column graphs
   - bar graphs
   - pie charts
   - organization charts
   - flow charts
   - drawings
   - diagrams
   - photographs

   Do the figures emphasize appropriate information? Is the visual display ethical? How do your illustrations establish your credibility, clarify details, and communicate the significance of your experience?

4. Is white space used effectively?

5. What is the appropriate page design (essay, book, letter, memo, or circular)?

Index of Key Terms

CHAPTER 9

Repertoire Focus: Recounting Events

Everyday experiences stamp us with indelible impressions. Upon examination, these impressions reveal to us special, sometimes even life-altering, meanings. Human experience shows us aspects of the human condition that we might never even have imagined. This chapter encourages you to relive experiences that may or may not have turned out as you anticipated, and explore what these experiences mean.

REPERTOIRE WRITING TASK: EVENTS

Select an event that will appeal to readers much like you; a general college audience; a general adult readership; or a specific campus, community, or professional group. Choose specific details and present them dramatically so that your audience can understand the relationship between your experience and its meaning to you.

Below are three variations of the writing task, originating from the different ways you may "know" about the experience you recount:

Knowledge by Participation

Write an essay about an event that has happened to you. How has this experience changed or affected you?

Knowledge by Observation

Write an essay about an event that you were not directly involved in, and explain its significance to you. This event may be one that you learned about indirectly (through interviews, reading, television, or another medium); it may be either a famous public event or a little-known private one. Nevertheless, your subject should be something that others have written about, yielding some form of published biographical, social, or historical information that you can integrate into your essay. How has this experience changed or affected you?

Knowledge by Participation and Observation

Write an essay about an event that you know about both through personal experience and from other sources (through interviews, reading, television, or another medium), and explain its significance to you. The event should be one that others have written about, either formally or informally, yielding some form of published biographical, social, or historical information that you can integrate into your essay. How has this experience changed or affected you?

REPERTORY COMPANY OF STUDENT WRITERS: THEIR RESPONSES TO THE TASK

Before you begin to address the writing task, you may find it helpful to meet other student writers in our repertory company and to read their essays, which were written in response to the same assignment. Often these responses began as journal entries, which the student writers developed into full essays. We encourage you to reread your journal to discover ideas to research and write about further.

To provide you with some additional context, we've included journal entries, a map of the rhetorical situation (the knowledge continuum and audience continuum), and research strategies for each essay. You'll also find some questions for discussion and analysis after each selection.

KNOWLEDGE BY PARTICIPATION

The first essay, "Twenty-five Steps Away," was written by Karen Phillips. Her knowledge of her subject comes from direct personal experience—knowledge by participation—and she tells her story from the perspective of the "writer as participant."

Reviewing Journal Entries

In the following excerpts from Karen's journal, written while she was composing "Twenty-five Steps," you'll discover Karen's honest remarks about her subject, the internal and external influences on her composing processes, and her impressions of her writing community. Do her comments sound familiar? Have you ever thought or felt this way when writing? How is Karen's experience different from past writing experiences you've had?

JOURNAL

This paper is supposed to be expressive aim writing. . . . As far as my subject goes, the statement that triggered an idea in my mind was that it should concern a significant event in my life. By far, the most traumatic incident in my past occurred my sophomore year in high school, and I think I can make it interesting by tying in my new philosophy on friendship—kind of like a moral. The only thing I'm worried about is sharing that experience with my peers and members of my focus group on paper. I've never talked about it much because it's embarrassing, and the only people I've told have been extremely close friends. It will be really weird telling it to strangers.

I really shouldn't worry about it too much because I like the members of my group a lot. I had an awful group experience last spring, and I'm hoping this will be better. Rosalinda's really quiet, but she seems very nice, and Tonya and especially Michelle are very receptive.

I decided to go with the sophomore year idea, and I worked on it this weekend. It was really strange to sit down at the kitchen table with pen and paper to write. It reminded me of research papers in the 7th grade. I was surprised, though, at how expressive I could be writing that way. Once I got started, the words just flowed out. The only problem was my hand got awfully tired! Out of practice, I suppose.

Anyway, I wrote four and a half pages. It consisted of the intro and the first half of the incident. I still need to write about my reactions to what happened and how it affected my attitudes about friendship.

I reread what I had written, and it's so painful to recall how I felt. I'm still worried about letting my group read it. I'm afraid they'll think I was the biggest nerd! Oh well, maybe it's going to be good for me to write about it—kind of like therapy. Maybe it will help me deal with my experience instead of bottling it up inside me. I'll try to think of it that way.

I let my group read my paper today. Before I handed it over, though, I made them promise not to think I was a nerd! I was really nervous while they read, but at least I had their papers to concentrate on.

After we read each other's papers, we gave them back to read the comments they wrote. I jotted a few notes to myself in the margins, and they agreed with them. They also had some great ideas of their own. I was really impressed and excited. Usually I'm not very receptive to criticism, but the mood is very supportive in our group and I agreed with their suggestions, so it was very beneficial.

Tonya had a super idea for my intro! She listened to my story about how Darla had called me one day out of the blue and suggested that I include our phone dialogue and then flashback to high school. The reason I really like this strategy is because I'm trying to incorporate more narration into my paper. Show, not tell.

On the whole, the members of my group were very positive, and the other changes in sentence structure and mechanics that they pointed out I recognized as ones that will improve the quality of my paper. Michelle's comments were especially interesting. I think she and I must write a lot alike, because she and I think on the same wavelength about papers. Every suggestion she made I might have made myself. Overall, I was very pleased with the experience. I feel that I can trust the members of my group and that our critiques will be very productive.

Well, I made the final set of changes my group suggested and finished writing the ending. I really hope I've developed my characters ok. I've tried to let them speak and do stuff—like the book tells us to. Remembering dialogue and how my "friends" said things was so hard. Brought back lots of funny feelings. That's when I knew I had made my characters sound pretty real. I could hear them and see them making me feel weird again. I was a kid again and wearing that school uniform.

Can't believe I have worked on this one paper for two weeks. In class on Friday, we were asked to record how many drafts we've written of our papers. Gee, I've made so many changes here and there at different times, I'm not sure how many times I've revised. I guess 3 times maybe. At least that's how many times I made copies for my focus group. Who knows? Got to stop now and work on my description. Michelle thinks I need more specific words. She told me to put in words like reprimand *and* hurled *and* grovel *and all. I like her ideas.*

———————————

I feel pretty good about my paper. It's been kind of a catharsis for me. I'm glad I picked this subject and followed through with it. Anyway, I turned it in so now I'll just have to wait and see.

Mapping Karen's Expressive Rhetorical Situation

The map of Karen's rhetorical situation for her essay is reproduced as Figure 9.1. Karen has gained knowledge of her subject by participation. Accordingly, on her map she lists her experiences on the "knowledge by participation" side of the continuum. Because her story and its significance are derived from direct personal experience, she researches her memory of this event by brainstorming and using the pentad.

Karen is writing for an audience of her peers. She knows that her readers will be male and female, of college age, some members of cliques, some loners, and so on. Although she is embarrassed about revealing that this incident happened to her, she thinks her readers will identify with it and empathize with her. Karen believes her peers will see themselves in her experience. As a result, she considers her audience to be fairly interested in her subject, and she maps them as "motivated readers."

Twenty-five Steps Away

Draft 3—Final Copy

1   "Karen, I just want you to know how sorry I am for what happened that spring. I knew it was wrong, and yet I didn't have the courage to stand up for you and risk my own position. I think about you a lot, about the kind of person you really are, and I feel ashamed.

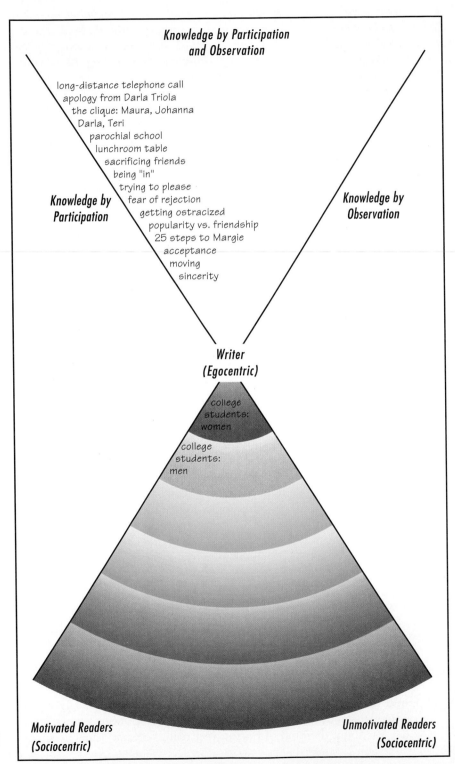

Knowledge by Participation
and Observation

long-distance telephone call
apology from Darla Triola
the clique: Maura, Johanna
Darla, Teri
parochial school
lunchroom table
sacrificing friends
being "in"
trying to please
fear of rejection
getting ostracized
popularity vs. friendship
25 steps to Margie
acceptance
moving
sincerity

Knowledge by Participation

Knowledge by Observation

Writer
(Egocentric)

college
students:
women

college
students:
men

Motivated Readers
(Sociocentric)

Unmotivated Readers
(Sociocentric)

Figure 9.1
Mapping Karen's rhetorical
situation

I hope you'll forgive me." I couldn't believe my ears. Here it was, five years after that miserable semester, and the renowned Darla Triola had actually called me long distance to apologize? Had she spent long hours agonizing over the experience, just as I had done, and come to the same realization of what true friendship really means? It was almost too good to be true, but the humble pleas and compliments kept coming. Never in my wildest dreams had I imagined this day would come.

2   I had devoted my energy during my first year in high school to acquiring a place among a select group of girls who defined the concept of *popular*. Athletic and confident, Maura led the clique. She was supported by Johanna, who was attractive, yet so self-conscious about her height that she had adopted a distinctive slouched walk. Darla and Teri, girls I had known since elementary school, completed the quartet. Darla was the token blonde and always managed to have a date. Even in eighth grade, when we basically didn't exist in the senior high realm, Darla went to Homecoming with Trevor, a popular red-headed senior. This foursome was the ultimate authority on the opposite sex and all matters of fashion. In our little world, style was limited to the accessories we could sneak by Mr. Kramer, the pear-shaped dean, to spice up our drab navy and gray uniforms.

3   I examined their every word and deed. I laughed at their jokes, learned to love their favorite songs, and could even quote lines from their favorite movie, *Sixteen Candles,* which I had never seen. The status they held in our parochial 3-A school was phenomenal, or so it seemed to me. I'm afraid to say I practically worshipped them. I became a groupie, so to speak, and my ultimate goal was to be accepted and bask in the popularity that would stem from this association.

4   The eventual result of this outpouring of energy was two-fold. On the one hand, I could say that my efforts paid off, for during my sophomore fall semester, I was "in." I even had my hair cut in the same style as theirs—a shoulder-length bob. Life was great. I had a junior boyfriend, Lowell, and after football games we all hung out at Chili's, where Maura even bought me a chocolate shake for my fifteenth birthday. At school, their reserved, prime-location table for four was even converted to five for my sake, much to the lunch monitor's chagrin and daily reprimands. However, being "in" had its sacrifices. Not only had I allowed my self-esteem to be contingent upon their whim, but my obsession had blinded me to friends that I'd made before I'd become a groupie. These friends seemed too shy, plain, or old-fashioned to associate with. My best friend in sixth and seventh grade had fallen by the wayside. Now the girl who welcomed me to a new school when I was eleven was merely a band member with stringy brown hair and an unfashionably large nose.

5   Although I considered myself "in," uncertainty tugged at my emotions. I still felt as if I stood on the fringes. I continued to grovel for acceptance, especially from Maura. While I was often the brunt of

jokes, I refused to accept the impending doom. To me, my connections were worth always being the scapegoat. The taunts became worse, however, and my feelings were hurt most of the time. The situation was a vicious circle; the more I strived to please, the more wretched I became. I walked on eggshells around Maura in constant fear of rejection. When she hurled stinging words at me, the others never stood up in my defense. I began to sense that it was all a show, that my friends were not completely genuine.

6   It all came to a head one day in the lunchroom, the site of my previous glory. I had stood in line with the four girls and had taken my tray to my regular spot. I realized I needed to go back for napkins, and when I returned, my lone tray appeared at the next table. Three guys at the next table were snickering, so I thought it was a joke. I picked up my tray and went back over to sit in my usual spot. A few minutes later, Darla and I decided to go buy nickel peppermint sticks. When I returned, I discovered that my tray had been moved again. I scowled at the neighboring table, but the boys pointed to Maura and Johanna and stated, "They did it." I didn't want to believe them. I looked at my so-called friends and then back at the three guys. The boys laughed and nodded. As the sickening feeling in my stomach rose, I glanced back at the girls one last time. They wouldn't even look me in the eye. Maura had her back to me, and she continued the conversation as if I weren't even there. In her mind, I wasn't. As an ostracized member of the group, I did not exist.

7   I wanted to dig a hole in the lunchroom tile and crawl in. I was paralyzed for a moment between the leers of the boys and the backs of the girls. I didn't know what to do. I couldn't move. Even the surrounding "popular" tables had noticed. I felt like everyone in the world was against me. My heart ached so badly I couldn't even cry. In an instant rush of emotion, all the jibes came back to me and the pieces fell into place. I had never truly been accepted. I had only been tolerated by a group of girls who, while they defined the concept of popularity, knew nothing of the meaning of true friendship.

8   Now what remained for me to do was to uproot my horror-stricken self and find a chair, anywhere, far away from my tormentors. Every eye in the lunchroom looked upon me with scorn, except two, those of a certain girl with a big nose. How I walked the twenty-five steps to Margie's table I will never know, but it took every ounce of courage I could muster to swallow what was left of my pride and quietly ask her, "Would you mind if I sat here?" When she smiled and replied, "Of course not," I could have hugged her on the spot. I had discovered what a true friend was. Although I had forsaken her, she accepted and forgave me, an acceptance that meant much more than the acceptance of four superficial goddesses ever could have. I sat at Margie's table for the rest of that year before my family moved away.

9   Once I arrived in a new town, the characteristic I demanded of my new friends was sincerity. I was no longer solely interested in

friends whose status would improve my image. The friendships I made my junior and senior years have been true and lasting ones because I had learned a very painful lesson. Never again would I allow my peers to reduce me to a sniveling heap for their attention. Instead of drawing strength from my weaknesses, my new-found friends reciprocated my concern for their happiness and security.

10   Now, as I listen to Darla elaborating on the qualities she admires most in me, it occurs to me that maybe it would have done her some good to have been rejected once in her life. Maybe if she had been lucky enough to have a dateless best friend, she wouldn't be turning to an old acquaintance for consolation.

Reading Critically: Questions for Discussion

1. Is the title clear and appropriate?
2. Karen's story starts in the present, flashes back to the past, and then returns to the present in the last paragraph. Why does Karen use this complex chronology to tell her story? Is it effective?
3. Is the significance that Karen sees in this story supported by the details of the narrative?
4. Do you identify with this story? Which details help you to identify with it or keep you from identifying with it?
5. If Karen were writing for a high school audience, how might she change the way she tells her story?

KNOWLEDGE BY OBSERVATION

Two different drafts of "Filthy Grins" appear next. "Filthy Grins" was written from the perspective of the writer as observer. The author, Christine Wilson, researched the information in this essay by conducting interviews with Child Protection Services personnel and reading a newspaper article on the subject.

Reviewing Journal Entries

Christine's journal entries for "Filthy Grins" are very different from Karen's. While Karen writes full sentences and seems to enjoy recording her thoughts in her journal, Christine uses her journal to jot down ideas and lists of things to do. Only after her paper is completed does she write in full sentences and paragraphs. In a sense, Christine's entries during her writing processes represent an extension of her invention and planning strategies; the entries written after she's finished her essay represent her evaluative and reflective commentary.

JOURNAL

My concerns about my paper:

   my characters need more development

   more action and description

   more interaction with the children—show contrast better between sad house, happy kids

   conclusion needs more

Anyone's paper should

   catch the reader in the beginning

   give some action

   develop characters so reader can identify with them

   Introduction—dialogue

   Middle of paper—description of the situation

   Conclusion—outcome of family, personal significance to me

Overall, I'm happy with the way it turned out. I tried to write this paper on the computer, but I couldn't do it because of the nuisance of the quotes. With pen and paper I could get my ideas out better. Also my creativity is highest in the evening when I don't have access to a computer.

The style is flowing but could use more coherence. There are no hangups for readers in the reading except the transition at the end.

The invention was hard at first but once I got my pen moving it came easier than I thought. I started writing about the family but wrote more about the house, the setting. Writing so many different drafts helped me to see more structural awkwardness and stumbling blocks for readers.

I would've liked to be able to talk more about the mother and the kids but I couldn't figure out how to ask the case worker at Child Protective Services. That would've been difficult and inconvenient for her. She already had helped me so much with my research for this observation paper. The newspaper article featured the Stewarts, but no one ever mentioned how to find them. Wouldn't have been right, either, I guess. What would I have asked them, face-to-face? Good that I'm not a social worker. Being somebody like a social worker is hard not because it takes work. It's hard because you have to be able to ask hard questions and find out ugly things sometimes.

Mapping Christine's Expressive Rhetorical Situation

Christine has gained knowledge of her subject by observation, so she lists details on the "knowledge by observation" side of the knowledge continuum (see Figure 9.2). How does she conduct her research without having actually been at the scene where the event takes place? Christine learns about this story by interviewing her roommate and her roommate's supervisor, both employees at Child Protective Services, and by reading a newspaper article that focused on the Stewart family.

"Filthy Grins" is written for an audience of general adult readers. Christine classifies her audience according to their educational levels, asserting that her readers will live in the community where her university is located. She divides her audience according to those with no high school education; some high school education; high school graduates; some college education; college graduates (graduate students, professors, and administrators). Christine gauges motivation in terms of schooling; she feels that the most interested readers will be those with lots of education or with no formal education. Professors and administrators seem to take on social causes in town and around campus, and people who have limited finances and schooling will be more likely to empathize with families that are having trouble staying together and making ends meet, according to Christine. She thinks that people who are high school graduates and college students have other worries and might find it difficult to identify with this family's situation; as a consequence, she maps these two groups as unmotivated readers.

Interestingly, Christine can be classified as a member of these two "unmotivated" audiences, signaling a potentially major problem. Could she be writing about a subject that she isn't interested in? If not, could she have analyzed and mapped her readers inaccurately? How could misjudging her audience affect the way she writes her essay? By studying her map, Christine should see the possible problems with her audience analysis.

Filthy Grins

Draft 2

1   I go to work with my roommate Kyra whenever we both can make the time. I am a new college student, majoring in teacher education, and she is a brand new social work graduate with her first job. She assists Glenda, a case worker at the Child Placement Service. She needed someone to split the rent and I needed a place to stay. All of the campus housing was full. Kyra is a good roommate.

2   A couple of weeks ago, I went to the office with Kyra. She told me about a case she and Glenda, her supervisor, have been investigating. The case had been featured in the local newspaper this week, so I was, of course, fascinated to learn more about it.

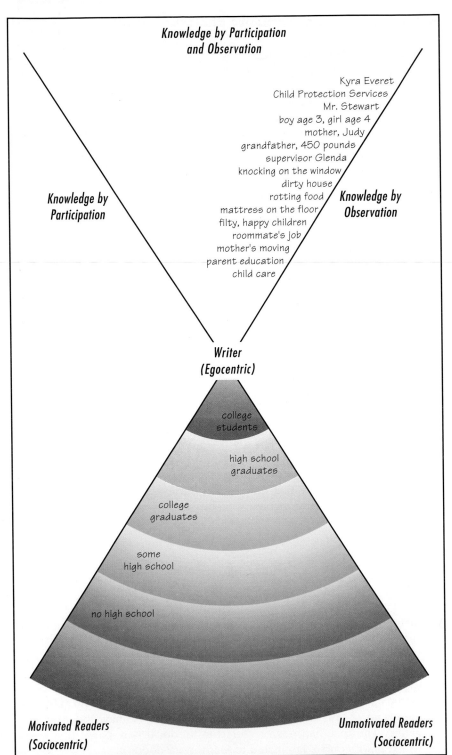

Figure 9.2
Mapping Christine's rhetorical situation

3   The case involves a 20-year-old woman who is getting a divorce and she has been granted temporary custody of her 3 and 4-year-old kids until the divorce is final, but the ex-husband is fighting to have the kids live with him. The woman is very poor, so she and the kids move in with the woman's father.

4   Before Kyra could tell me much more, Glenda comes in. She overhears Kyra telling me about this case and explains that usually cases are confidential. This case is an exception in lots of ways because a newspaper reporter decided to do a story about this family. Now everybody knows. Glenda says she thinks maybe it's for the best because people need to know the complexity of broken families, the pain kids feel, the love kids need, the helplessness social workers feel, the poverty out there. Everyone loses, she says. So that day in the office, the three of us sit and read the newspaper article. We talk about what the article says, and Glenda and Kyra confirm and question information in them, always careful to keep their comments brief and accurate. In the article, the reporter interviews Mr. Stewart, the father of the kids. He gives a full account of how he goes to Child Protective Services with his complaint. Glenda says that that's how it all got started, all right. They would never have known about the grandfather if Mr. Stewart hadn't reported him to Kyra. The grandfather was the major concern. "You have to see for yourself—he's 450 pounds," he said.

5   Kyra recalls that this is how she got involved in the case. She recalls that she had to go interview the grandfather and take pictures of the scene and all. Glenda told Kyra about the conditions to expect—lots of dirt and gross conditions. Kyra had tried to tell me about it when I asked her what it was like to be a social worker—maybe I'd change majors. She said it was not always fun or safe. I ought to understand that.

6   Then she went on to describe the place. She told about broken toys in the yard, dirt on the porch. She knocked on the door, but nobody answered so she drove to a pay phone to check in with Glenda at CPS. Talking on the phone, she saw a man waiting to use the phone. He explained that she'd need to knock on the window pane in the back where the old man's room is. That's how she met Mr. Stewart, the father of the children she was investigating. He had driven by the house to check on them and seen her car.

7   So Kyra went back to the house and knocked, as the father had said, on the bedroom window. She felt like she was sneaking around or like people thought she was breaking into the house. She dismissed the thought. A few minutes later, a large man appeared in the doorway. This must be grandpa, she thought, as she looked at the figure taking up the whole entry way. He welcomed her in and began to give her a tour of the house.

8   Grandpa had arthritis and didn't move around much. He

explained that his wife and eldest daughter both worked full time and don't have the time to clean up the house.

9   As she was preparing to leave, the 2 grandchildren came through the door. They ran to grandpa and waited to see who Kyra was. They were happy. Their faces were covered with dirt and grins. Now Kyra realized why people quit work with CPS after about two years. She felt sick at the thought of having to take away the children and glad to be out of that house.

10   Kyra's case is still going on. The newspaper report says that the father must be interviewed again and the house must be cleaned from top to bottom. Another interview with the mother and grandparents is also needed for more evidence of neglect.

11   What did I learn? How did this event change me? Kyra's story impressed upon me the importance of parental education. It also taught me about the importance of a family who loves you.

Christine makes substantial changes in her fifth and final draft of "Filthy Grins." In her earlier drafts, she uses no dialogue, summarizing instead what others have said. In this draft, she shows the characters engaged in conversation. As you read the final draft, notice how Christine also adds more descriptive details and elaborates on the significance of her experience. What effect do her revisions have on her readers? What other changes has Christine made in her final draft? Do you think the changes strengthen her essay? Why or why not?

Filthy Grins

Draft 5—Final Draft

1   Sitting in the brightly lit box of an office, Kyra, newly-employed as a Child Protective Specialist I, cradled a warm phone on her shoulder. She had worked for the Child Protection Services for a total of three months, of which two were spent in training. At the moment she restlessly listened to a disconcerted father talk about the quality of his children's care.

2   "You have to see for yourself," he grumbled.

3   "I will, Mr. Stewart," she assured him.

4   "They're my kids, Ms. Everet! Can't stand to see my flesh and blood living in that disease ridden hell hole. They should be living with their daddy."

5   "I understand, sir. We'll see what the situation is over there and . . ."

6   "I already know what the situation is. I just want you to fix it," Mr. Stewart demanded.

7   "There is a lot of paperwork involved. Sometimes it takes time, but I'm starting the process tomorrow."

8   "These are my kids we're talking about, not a couple of forms for the government."

9   "It's all I can do right now. We'll be in touch with you soon."

10   "Whatever," he resignedly replied.

11   When she came home from the office, Kyra was deep in thought. What have I gotten myself into? Kyra wondered, as she slipped into an old pair of jeans and a T-shirt. She had heard about this family through her supervisor at the Child Protection Services. The parents of a four-year-old girl and three-year-old boy were getting a divorce. The twenty-year-old mother, Judy, decided to move with her children back home with her parents and teenage sister. Mr. Stewart and Judy were in a custody battle, and Mr. Stewart was worried about his children's health. The grandfather was the focal point of the conversation with her supervisor.

12   "No person weighs that much," Kyra insisted.

13   "There are people who weigh even more than 450 pounds. He smokes as well—about three packs a day," continued her supervisor, Glenda. "You need to take pictures out there tomorrow."

14   Glenda had also told Kyra about the trash all over and the poor excuses for sleeping areas. In the morning while applying her make-up, Kyra tried to imagine the Stewart family. She soon found out that her images couldn't relate to the reality.

15   Only when she turned down the "second dirt road on the left, past the farm road" did Kyra begin to be sickened. She sat in her car, taken aback by the overall sadness of the sagging wooden white house.

16   After carefully stepping over broken toys in the yard and wading through the dirt on the porch, she knocked firmly on the front door, making it rattle on its hinges. She continued this endeavor until she grew uncomfortable with standing on a stranger's porch. She went to the pay phone at the local food mart and called to inform Glenda that there was no answer and that she would be returning to the office. As soon as she finished her sentence, a man waiting to use the phone (so she thought) said "You have to knock on the window. His bedroom is in the back and he can't hear you knock."

17   Caught off guard by this strange man, Kyra repeated this to her supervisor.

18   "Who is with you?" Glenda asked.

19   "I don't quite know, just a minute," replied Kyra.

20   The man identified himself as Mr. Stewart, the father of the children she was investigating. He had driven by the house to check on them and had seen her car.

21   Kyra went back to the house and knocked, as the father had said, on the bedroom window. A few minutes later, a large man appeared

in the doorway. This must be grandpa, Kyra thought, looking at the figure taking up the whole entry way. He welcomed her in and began a tour of the house, at her request.

22   Grandpa had arthritis and didn't move around much. He explained that his wife and eldest daughter both worked full time and didn't have the time to clean up the house.

23   Kyra found a path on the grimy rug, her white Keds standing out in their dingy surroundings. As she hopped over trash and dirty plates, Kyra paused to take snapshots. The kitchen made Kyra lose her already small appetite. The dishes were stacked high, items usually refrigerated were spoiling on the table, and food was rotting on the floor. The grandfather's room was full of trash: TV dinner trays and empty cigarette packs. One bare full mattress on the floor of another room provided the two children a humble place to sleep. The teen's room was just as bad with her bed sheets piled on her bed.

24   As she was preparing to leave, the two grandchildren bounded through the door. They ran to Grandpa, hugged him and waited to see who the stranger was before tearing off to their bedroom. They were obviously happy—a little dirty perhaps, but loved. Their tight faces were covered with dirt and smiles. Kyra realized why the average working period for this job with CPS was only two years. She felt that it was not her place to educate this family about personal hygiene and diseases among children that could be induced by such an environment. Kyra thought, me, the newly-graduated college student with the messy room, telling these people to keep their clothes off of the floor. She felt queasy at the thought of having to take away the children. Kyra thanked Grandpa on her way out the door. She couldn't wait to get out of this depressed area. She returned solemnly to her office to make her report.

25   It has been three months since my roommate first investigated this case. The mother has since taken her children and moved to the Dallas area. She is going to business school now to get a job that offers more than minimum wage. The local CPS will no longer have contact with her or her family unless another case is opened.

26   Kyra's experience impressed upon me the importance of parental education. In my future career endeavors, I would like to promote a greater number of parental skill classes where low income families are taught how best to provide care for their young children. Also as a teacher, I would understand that much help begins with teachers' increased awareness of different, withdrawn or angry personalities suggesting possible abuse or neglect. This story has had an everlasting hold on me. I have constantly been motivated to find ways to prevent and find future solutions to the recurring problems facing these lower income families. Night schools for parents or opportunities for affordable priced child care need to be implemented by business and neigh-

borhood communities. The cycle will not be broken if no solutions are given to these families.

Works Cited

Everet, Kyra. Personal interview. 6 Feb. 1992.

Thaxton, Brian. "A Family at the Crossroads." *The Daily Citizen* 4 Feb. 1992: B1.

Wexler, Glenda, Supervisor, Child Protective Services. Personal interview. 6 Feb. 1992.

Reading Critically: Questions for Discussion

1. Is the title of this essay clear and appropriate? Why do you think it is or isn't?
2. Is the writer's use of dialogue effective? Why does the writer not use dialogue to record Kyra's conversation with the grandfather?
3. Does the writer find appropriate significance in Kyra's experience?
4. Does the writer provide a vivid physical description of the grandfather's house? Which sensory details of the description are most important?
5. The writer lists three sources of information but never formally identifies which information comes from which source. Does this omission damage the writer's credibility? How might the writer integrate source citations? Or should she leave them out and call her bibliography "Works Consulted"? Are source citations necessary for this essay?

KNOWLEDGE BY PARTICIPATION AND OBSERVATION

The third essay is a collaboratively authored piece about Operation Desert Storm, "United We Stand, Separately We React." The three writers—Angela Jordan, Hector Longoria, and Stephanie Sellers—experiment with an approach to coauthorship that allows each person to recount his or her reaction to learning that the United States and its allies had begun bombing Iraq. They embed their individual stories within a conventional introduction and conclusion, attempting to tie their varied reactions to the war together coherently. The title of their essay reflects not only their perceptions about the Gulf War, but also their own strategy for writing.

Reviewing Journal Entries

The journal entries written by Angela, Hector, and Stephanie reveal as much about their group dynamics as their thoughts about writing. Here are some sample entries from each writer:

JOURNAL

WAR. I do not want to write about war. I remember when first meeting Angela we were deciding what to write about. I suggested sex—it was a joke. I thought it was humorous and would break the ice. I was told, "not funny, not appropriate." OK. We'll write about war. (HL)

I wrote my part of the paper tonight. I wrote about my feelings during the first week of the war. My memory wasn't real specific, but I do remember my feelings. After reading what I wrote, I think I did a good job of getting those across. I also picked up an article about the war today that I think will be helpful. It describes the first moments of the war in good detail. (AJ)

I wrote my part. Still needs work. It is sort of unemotional—I'm not exactly happy with it. Our group hasn't gelled yet. I'm not sure we like each other or ever will. Angela thinks we don't care, but that's very wrong. Hector is very creative. (SS)

I read their papers today. What do they really feel about war? This war? They don't have any emotion in their sections. How did the Gulf War change them? Make them think? Feel? Their emotions about the war, if there are any, are dry and dull. Wave the flag and do not question the authority of those in power. (HL)

We met at Stephanie's office this afternoon. Our paper really came together. Everyone offered a lot of suggestions that I think were very helpful. It took a lot longer than I expected, but it was worth it. Once we started working together, everything clicked. We didn't end up using as much research as we had, but what we included is effective. It actually ended up being kind of fun. I'm pleased with what we were able to accomplish considering we got off to such a shaky start. (AJ)

We met at my office and worked on our essay. It's coming together now. Angela is very inflexible about changing anything she writes. It's the "sacred cow" syndrome. Anyway, I believe it really looks good. Now, we're all going to proofread a copy and meet again on Monday night. (SS)

We met and it was very productive. I can understand that my paper was a little too strong, but I'm toning it down. I think that I need to consolidate all of the past reaction to a very concentrated thing. I used the shower because that's what I did after I found out about the war. I felt we were all going down the drain. I still do not like their little "oh, I was scared, what were you scared about" attitude in their papers. I guess I was too angry about the war to be scared. I am too concerned about the politics of knowing who is doing what and why. (HL)

I made my group mad today. I still do not know why "Steve on the front line" is there over and over again. I was like, so what, either give some significance or stop writing it. They think it creates an "effect." Well, it affected me by making me feel sick. . . . (HL)

Hector came by my office and brought some changes in. They were really good suggestions. I also added a few things I thought would make the paper "flow better." We're ready to print? (SS)

Angela called me and wanted to make more changes. Before she told me her ideas, I read to her the changes Hector and I made. Then I wrote down her changes. I went back to my office, changed stuff, and reprinted. (SS)

We turned in our essay. Angela was unhappy because she didn't agree with all of the changes Hector and I made without her consent. Hector and I agreed, though. Anyway, it's done now. (SS)

I'm very frustrated by the way this paper went. Communication, which is a vital part of any collaboration, was horrible. Our group started out on the wrong foot by not meeting when they were supposed to and then there was animosity in the air. I'm not very happy with a lot of the changes. The night before the paper was due I was told of some of the changes my group had made in my part of the paper. That was okay. The changes made sense. The day we were supposed to hand the paper in, I found many changes in my part that I was not told about. Changes that I feel were not okay. Changes that weren't my style and alterations that changed the meaning of what I felt, and what I was trying to say. I feel a loss of control over my own work and that disturbs me. (AJ)

The idea of a collaborative paper and working in groups is really not a bad idea. I felt that there were times when it was effective and served a useful purpose. I was really happy with our paper until I read the version to be handed in. When we got together to work on the paper earlier, things went well and I felt that suggestions were offered and accepted or rejected that were helpful, but I have to admit that my opinion has changed due to what I feel as group members going over the line. This was supposed to be a collaborative effort and I feel that it wasn't collaborative in an equal way. . . . I'm angry . . . (AJ)

The voices of these three group members indicate that their attitudes about the task and one another are formed early in their collaboration. Moreover, note their conflicting perceptions about how their meetings went and what they thought of each other. For example, Hector and Stephanie think Angela doesn't like them and is inflexible. Angela, on the other hand, thinks the group works okay—despite a shaky start. She likes the suggestions others make and views herself as very open to change.

Read More About It

See Chapter 3,
pp. 69–75.

Obviously, Angela's disposition takes a different turn as time goes on.

Researching and writing with others is becoming more and more common in academic and professional settings. Imagine that you are a member of this group. What strategies can you think of that might diffuse the tension and problems among your peers? Angela says that communication was lacking. Do you agree? How can you address this specific dilemma?

Mapping Angela, Hector, and Stephanie's Expressive Rhetorical Situation

Figure 9.3 illustrates the rhetorical situation as Angela, Hector, and Stephanie have analyzed it. The three writers have gained knowledge of the war by both participation and observation, as the knowledge continuum shows. Although they have experienced the start of the military conflict with Iraq from afar, their impressions are more immediate because of visual and print-based news reports. For each writer, where and how they learned of the military conflict was a personal and firsthand experience—knowledge by participation. Thus, their way of knowing about the Gulf War appears in the participation-observation part of the continuum.

This essay is intended for an audience of college readers. Like Christine, these writers basically classify their audience according to educational levels (i.e., those with no high school education; some high school education; high school graduates; some college education; college graduates; graduate students; advanced degree holders). Interestingly, Angela and Stephanie assume that their readership will naturally be interested in this subject; they see their audience as supportive of the troops and hence the war ("going to war to protect a vulnerable country"). Hector thinks the audience includes people more ambivalent about U.S. involvement in the war. Rather than viewing his readers as supporters of the war effort with relatives or friends in danger, Hector envisions part of the college audience as dissenters angry about "going to war for oil." He isn't enthusiastic to write about this war, and he modifies his collaborators' view that all readers will be motivated to read their paper. For this reason, he insists that the "significance" part of their narratives be strong—even emotional, if necessary.

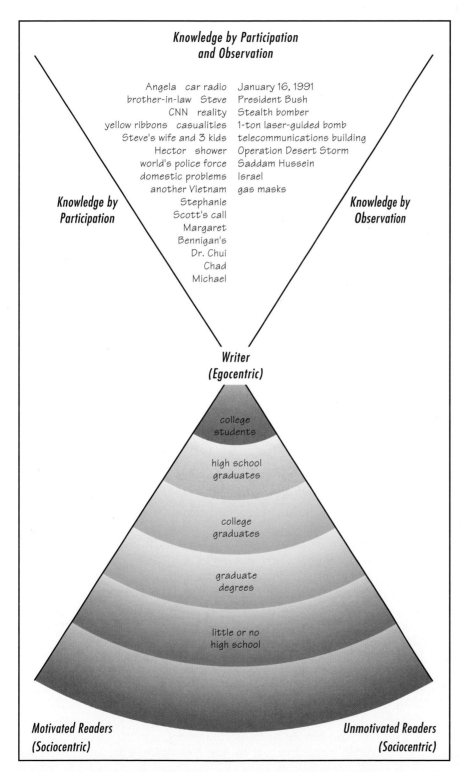

Figure 9.3
Mapping Angela, Hector, and
Stephanie's rhetorical situation

United We Stand, Separately We React

Draft 3—Final Draft

WAR!
War with Iraq?
War with Iraq over national interests.
War with Iraq over the petroleum interests in the Middle East.

1   On January 16, 1991, a U.S. Air Force Stealth bomber dropped a 2000 pound laser-guided bomb targeted precisely on the microwave dishes atop Baghdad's international telecommunications building, crippling the city (Kelly 21). Operation Desert Storm had begun.

2   War not only shatters the lives of soldiers but also the lives of their families. But, how about those Americans who are somewhat removed from it? The Persian Gulf War was only as close as the television. Americans could turn it on and off according to their moods. Those with personal interests could not get war off their minds. Others could become as involved as they wished. Many Americans did have strong emotional reactions to the war with Iraq; reactions were varied regardless of the geographical location in the United States. There is no right or wrong reaction to war—only individual perceptions. These perceptions, though diverse and often divergent, united America in its time of crisis. Looking at three students at Texas A&M University, we can begin to see that war affects people differently, yet there are common threads in their experiences.

Angela is a speech and English major and a medical records supervisor for a large clinic. She plans to teach elementary or middle school after graduation.

3   I first heard we had gone to war on the car radio as my husband and I were on our way to eat supper. A feeling of uncertainty came over me. I wasn't sure what this really meant.

4   For months, the media had been predicting that we might go to war, but I never thought that it would happen. Things became a little more real to me when my brother-in-law, Steve, who is in the Marines, was shipped to Saudi Arabia right after Christmas. I had never experienced anything like this before. The Vietnam War was going on when I was born, but I was too young when it ended to remember anything about it. All I knew about war was what I had learned in history class. But this was no longer history class; this was real, and Steve was there on the front line.

5   I didn't know what to think; things were transpiring so quickly. My uncertainty turned to fear for the Americans who were doing the

fighting. Going out to eat didn't seem to matter anymore. I remember going home and watching CNN to find out what was going on. They would have live telecasts from Baghdad, and at any moment I expected to see the television screen go blank because the area had been bombed. I felt fear, but I also felt a sort of morbid curiosity. It was almost like watching a soap opera to see what was going to happen on the next episode, but it wasn't a soap opera because it was real, here and now, with Steve on the front line.

6   It didn't seem important where I was or what I was doing. That's not what mattered. What mattered was that there were men and women losing their lives for a cause that they were obligated to believe in. These people had volunteered to serve and defend their country. No matter how I felt about what was wrong or right, I felt that I needed to support what they were doing. War had been declared, and our troops in the desert needed the support of every American. I wasn't going to let them down.

7   The overall response from the American public overwhelmed me. I had never experienced anything like this before. Although there were some protests, I felt there was much more support for the troops than protest against them and their actions. Everywhere I went—to the mall, to the grocery store, or down the street—I saw yellow ribbons as a symbol of support. There was a revival of the "Proud to be American" spirit. CNN reported that things were going very well for the United States, and the American public was right there to support them. Even though things appeared to be going well, there were still going to be casualties; the fact that Steve was on the front line made it so important for me to be a part of the support. I was still very frightened.

8   The first week of the war was a very emotional time for me, time filled with uncertainty. My thoughts were with Steve for much of the time, but they were also with his wife and three kids in North Carolina. The war affected all of us and made us come together as friends, students, families, and country because many people were like me and had a "Steve" in the sands of Desert Storm.

Hector is an economics major who is an editor of a student economics journal. He plans to enter law school after graduation.

9   I walk into my apartment and sling my backpack on the couch. I turn to my roommate, "Hey Tito, ¿Nadien me llamo?"

10   "No," Tito rips out with that twangy Puerto Rican accent.

11   The apartment door opens, and I can hear footsteps approaching. It's Enrique.

12   Enrique adds the customary handshake. "¿Cómo estás?"

13   "Bien."

14   "Did you hear that we began bombing Iraq?"

15   "What? Really?"

16   "Yeah! Go check it out next door on my TV."

17   I spring over to Enrique's apartment. He and Tito slowly follow as they jabber away in Spanish. The door is open. In the left corner of the room, the TV broadcasts CNN. I sit. I listen. I watch.

18   After the first thirty minute broadcast, I turn to Enrique and sigh. I get up and go back home. Tired from a long day at school, I want to take a shower.

19   I place my body in the warmth of the shower. It feels good to get the grime off. I begin to think of the events of the war and all of its consequences.

20   It was inevitable. Once we started sending troops I knew there was no turning back. We did it now; we have bitten off more than we can chew. I don't think people know that the Arabs have been fighting Jews for centuries. These people are religious fanatics. Unlike a political or economical belief in democracy or free trade, these people are willing to die for their religious beliefs. Our troops are over there defending Kuwait's freedom and our economic interests. Is that enough for their morale to win? God, I hope so. Everybody thinks that if we hit them hard, they'll just lie down and die? I don't think they will. They are going to get back up and try again and again, and heaven help us if we become vulnerable. They will be on us like vultures. I think we are just too damn shortsighted to see the effects of this war. But what do I know? There are experts out there that have advised our leaders of the ins and outs of war, and they are probably right. But what happens if we beat them? Do we think we're going to march in, defeat them, and march out? It didn't happen in World War II. If NATO troops in Europe are not enough, we're going to have to have a permanent presence in the Middle East as well. That does wonders for our country! While we decide to become the World's Police Force, other countries devote their resources on technological research and development, education, and economic growth. We should be concentrating on domestic issues such as education, drugs, technological development, competitiveness, and the environment. In the future, we are going to be too damned busy fighting wars because we are so overextended. In the long run, we're going to drain not only America's power and prestige, but also the American people.

21   My chest is red from the heat of the water. I scrubbed my body down; it feels good. It is better than what I think the American people are feeling.

22   People say, "But this war is bringing the American people together." Sure, this war is bringing the American people together, but it is making us lose sight of why the American people were not together in the first place. Nobody wants to answer these questions or better yet hear the solutions. Instead, they like to be unified and

blind. It amazes me to see how our politicians find it in "our" best interests to go to war. What are "our" best interests? It's more like the interest of the multinationals. If it wasn't for the dollar sign, they could not have cared less about Kuwait or entering a war with Iraq. But our politicians are so shortsighted, or should I say "concerned" about their own self-interests that they don't seem to care about the damage they are doing. I just hope they allow our troops to use everything they have. It would be a tragedy to have another Vietnam.

23   I turn off the water and open the curtain. The mirror is foggy. I grab my towel and dry myself. I wrap the towel around my waist and open the door. The air rushes in and cools my body. Ahh! I grab my glasses and walk next door to Enrique's.

———————

Stephanie is an English major and a secretary for a professor in the mathematics department. She plans to teach high school English when she graduates.

24   I can clearly remember when I found out that the United States had decided to bomb Iraq. My friend Scott and I were going out to eat with my boss' wife, Margaret. As I was heading for the door to leave for Bennigans restaurant, the telephone rang. Cursing to myself because the call would make me late, I answered it. It was Scott.

25   "Steph," Scott said, "do you know that we just went to war with Iraq? Do you think we should still go out and eat?"

26   Many questions came into my mind all at the same time. Was it appropriate to go out to eat and socialize when our country was at war? Should we stay at home and watch CNN? Shouldn't we have been considering the soldiers whose lives were in danger? I had never before experienced a wartime situation, unless I count Grenada, but I don't remember that at all. I was scared because I didn't know how to act. Scott's question demonstrates that many people in my generation don't know how to react to a wartime situation. On the phone, we decided to go on to Bennigans.

27   On the way across town to the restaurant, I began to think about the ramifications the Persian Gulf War would bring to my life. Would Saddam Hussein try to retaliate on the United States? Would American travellers be harmed? My boss, Dr. Chui, was in China. Would he make it home safely? I thought about my best friend's fiancé, Chad Carter, who was a Grunt in the Marines. Would he be transferred over to Saudi Arabia? Would my best friend's brother, Michael, also a Marine, have to go fight for Kuwait's freedom? I began to wonder how many Americans would lose their lives over a small country that housed a lot of oil. I knew that the President and his advisors knew best, and I knew that Kuwait was crucial to the United States' well-being. But what would the costs be to our country?

28   Walking into Bennigans, I noticed the solemn aura of the restaurant. Two televisions were broadcasting CNN. The news of the bomb-

ings reverberated into the room. We ordered our food and then noticed that President Bush was on the television making his address to the nation. Everyone in the room stared, scared to take their eyes off the television.

29   Over dinner, Margaret told us she was worried about Dr. Chui. He was supposed to fly out the next day. Would he still be able to make his flight? We discussed how long we thought the war would last, and we argued over whether we should be involved. The three of us understood why we were involved, yet we were truly scared. I was scared for Dr. Chui, for Chad, for Michael, and for myself. Was anything safe anymore? As we parted, we shared a timid look, apprehensive about the future.

30   When I arrived at my apartment, my roommate was watching CNN. We sat down and watched the live coverage into the night. We spent a lot of time in front of the TV that first week of the war. I can vividly remember one night I was watching the news when Saddam Hussein decided to retaliate against the U.S. by attacking Israel. When I saw the Israeli people wearing masks because of the fear of chemical warfare, chills went up and down my spine. The sight of newborn babies in "incubator-type" protective areas made me shudder. I knew that at any moment the journalists reporting the news in Israel could be harmed and the television screen could go black. I tried to imagine how I would feel if I was being forced to wear a gas mask to protect myself. Those images and that fear stay with me still.

31   Desert Storm made me think about how power-hungry people like Hussein can cause the entire world major problems. It frightened me to know that one domineering leader in a country so far away could try and succeed, at least temporarily, to take over another country and consequently give rise to a multi-national war. Life wasn't safe; war wasn't a remote event in history books. And peace in our time, among our people, is not guaranteed.

---

32   "This is an historic moment. . . . I am convinced not only that we will prevail, but that out of the horror of combat will come the recognition that no nation can stand against a world united," declared President Bush in his address to the nation on January 16, 1991. United we did stand; separately we did react. Whether Americans rally around the flag to burn it, to defend it, or to hide behind it, the freedom to express these individual reactions are the building blocks of the American nation. Three college students reacted quite differently to war; they reacted with uncertainty, anger, and fear. We should reflect on these reactions with the openness that will allow us to see the spectrum of perspectives and emotions that war brings.

Works Cited

Bush, George H. "Address to the Nation." CNN taped broadcast.
    Washington, D.C., 16 Jan. 1991.
Kelly, Michael. "Blitzed." *New Republic* 11 Feb. 1991: 21–22.

Reading Critically: Questions for Discussion

1. How is the writing style of the opening and closing paragraphs different from Angela's, Hector's, and Stephanie's individual narratives?
   How does the style of the individual narratives differ?
2. Why is the brief description of each student displayed in italics? What
   impact does this have on the reader's perception?
3. Which of the students offers the most vivid impression of his or her
   reaction to the start of the war? What details contribute to this vivid
   impression?
4. Does the concluding paragraph satisfactorily reconcile the different
   reactions—uncertainty, anger, fear—of the three students? Can it?
   Should it?
5. There are only two references to outside sources—almost as if they
   were added just so the paper would fulfill the task by including both
   kinds of knowledge. The essay contains the writers' feelings and
   memories of their experiences, but their ways of knowing are almost
   entirely knowledge by participation. What advice would you offer
   these writers? Would you encourage them to pursue this subject and
   do more research by observation? Would you suggest that they
   explore new subjects? Why?

CHAPTER 10

Repertoire Focus: Portraying Characters and Depicting Places

Our perceptions of ourselves and our world are shaped by familiar people and places. For example, we know about the roles and responsibilities of family members through our personal interaction with our own relatives. We may know about famous and not-so-famous landmarks—local, national, or foreign—because we actually visited those places. This knowledge may be augmented by understanding gained from sources such as other people, books, articles, films, television, radio, and newspapers.

It has been said that each person is the sum of his or her experiences. Whether or not your life experiences are direct, indirect, or some combination thereof, they surely contribute to making you who you are. One of the most effective ways to examine the significance that people and places have for you is to write about them. The writing task in this chapter asks you to discover or rediscover a particular character or place that has made such a contribution.

REPERTOIRE WRITING TASK: CHARACTERS AND PLACES

Describe a character or place using specific, vivid details to create a dominant impression, so that your audience can understand your subject and its importance to you. Your audience may be readers much like you; a general college audience; a general adult readership; or a specific campus, community, or professional group.

Below are three variations of this writing task, based upon the different ways you may "know" about the character or place that you focus on:

Knowledge by Participation

Write an essay about an individual or place that you know personally and explain his, her, or its impact on you. How has this person or location changed or affected you?

Knowledge by Observation

Write an essay about an individual or place that you know indirectly (through interviews, reading, television, or another medium) and explain his, her, or its impact on you. This person or location should be one that others have written about either formally or informally, yielding some form of published biographical, social, or historical information that you can integrate into your essay. How has this person or location changed or affected you?

Knowledge by Participation and Observation

Write an essay about an individual or place that you know about directly and indirectly (through interviews, reading, television, or another medium), and explain his, her, or its impact on you. This person or location should be one that others have written about either formally or informally, yielding some form of published biographical, social, or historical information that you can integrate into your essay. How has this individual or place changed or affected you?

REPERTORY COMPANY OF STUDENT WRITERS: THEIR RESPONSES TO THE TASK

The following essays have been written by student writers in our repertory company in response to the same writing tasks presented in this chapter. To research and write their texts, these student writers created their own writing communities or groups; these groups met regularly to talk, read, think, and write with one another. Interacting in their writing communities, these writers exchanged ideas and strengthened their sense of what writing and being a writer mean. As you write, take full advantage of your own writing communities. Remember: writing is a social act.

For each essay, we've included journal entries, a map of the rhetorical situation (the knowledge continuum and audience continuum), and research strategies. You'll also find some questions for discussion and analysis following each selection.

KNOWLEDGE BY PARTICIPATION

"Birds in the Tabernacle" was written by Jase Graves. Jase introduces his childhood friend "Little Matthew" to his readers, maintaining a participant, first-person point of view. Throughout the essay, notice how Jase uses descriptive detail to create a dominant impression of Matthew.

Reviewing Journal Entries

Jase's journal entries reflect his seriousness about writing—how and why he writes the way he does. While these are only a few of his thoughts about his writing processes, these excerpts give you a strong sense of how analytic and deliberate Jase is. His word choice is intentional: he wants every detail and action to serve a purpose, as these entries make clear.

JOURNAL

My purpose throughout this composition is to express my emotional development in my relationship with Matthew. To achieve this, I chose words and phrases to convey different levels of "psychological" depth. . . .

The development of the text:

death without realization

self-serving shallow indifference in the intro

well-meaning attempts—physical sympathy

*realization of love and acceptance and role-
reversal*

*physical disappointment; realization
of death*

*vindication through realization of purpose through death
in the conclusion*

loss; acceptance

———————————

*After group evaluation, I realized that in some instances, my complex
phrasing interrupted the progression of the piece in terms of meaning and
sentence structure. To correct this, I shortened sentences by dividing them
by clause and provided separate thoughts on which the reader could concentrate. Also, I modified certain descriptive elements in order to make
images clearer and personal rather than simply factual and academic. I
was pleased with group response and their constructive evaluations.*

———————————

*Following more group proofing, I redesigned my closing exposition to
provide more effective clarity and a better sense of closure. To achieve this,
I reread the work and evaluated my personal emotional reactions. Next, I
redeveloped my phrasing to express more accurately how I felt influenced
by my experience. I feel that in some cases I may have sacrificed compelling elements for the sake of clarity. However, I realize that this is necessary to provide understanding to my audience.*

———————————

*I pursued this task without a definite notion of how the subject had
truly influenced my life. I found that through the process of writing this
essay and of recollecting my relationship with this little boy, I came to a
realization of what Matthew's death had done to me. To this point, I wasn't
led to express these emotions in any way. Therefore, in developing this
essay, I was a bit hesitant to articulate my feelings and relive them in a
focused way. In doing this, I not only discovered what I really experienced
but also how I was affected. This writing experience was enlightening and
cathartic unlike any scholastic endeavor I have ever undertaken.*

Mapping Jase's Expressive Rhetorical Situation

Jase's map of his rhetorical situation is shown in Figure 10.1. In his essay,
Jase recounts the development of his friendship and respect for a little
boy, Matthew. We see Matthew through Jase's eyes only. And Jase's
understanding of the subject of this essay is by participation, as the knowledge continuum illustrates.

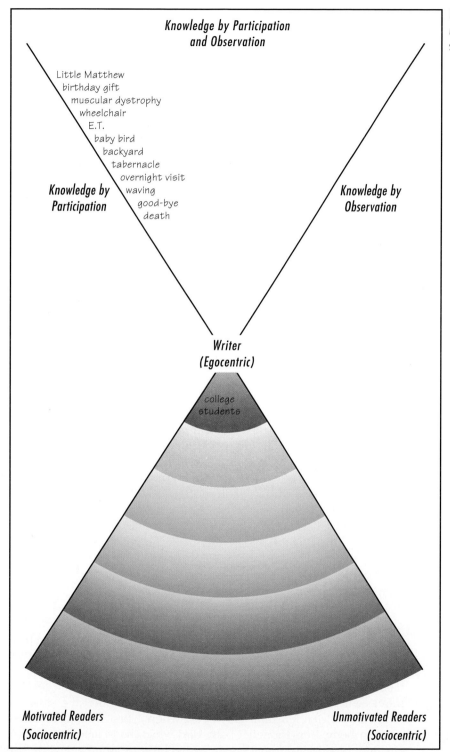

Figure 10.1
Mapping Jase's rhetorical situation

Because he is writing for his peers, Jase tries to select a subject that he believes is important to him as well as relevant to his readers. Friendship is a subject that interests almost everyone, and Jase thinks this is especially true of college students, who are now adults and may therefore view childhood relationships with more sensitivity and maturity. For example, friendships you took for granted as a child may now be reassessed; you may value your old friends more now that you're away from home and them. Your perspective changes. As Jase admits in his journal, had it not been for this opportunity to write about Matthew, he would never have realized how Matthew changed him or what he learned from this little boy and about himself. Jase considers his audience to be motivated and interested in this story and character, as his map of the audience continuum shows.

Birds in the Tabernacle

Draft 3—Final Draft

1   I didn't weep that crisp day two Decembers ago when I was informed by my mother that "Little Matthew" had died. I had done my weeping six years previously when I had peddled desperately down that bumpy tar road for the last time, away from the little white frame house and the little sick boy waving from the window.

2   Matthew entered my heart during my eighth grade year after my mother requested that I deliver a birthday gift to her fifth grade student with muscular dystrophy whom she had affectionately christened "Little Matthew." Realizing this opportunity to redeem my shaky honor from whatever domestic code I had violated on that particular day and, simultaneously to perform a shallow act of charity to use the next time I needed divine vindication, I took the card and the rolled-up poster of E.T. and headed over a few blocks to the lower middle-class neighborhood where Matthew lived. I was utterly oblivious to the notion that this brief bicycle ride was only the initial step on a journey that would transform my life forever.

3   On my arrival at his modest home, I stumbled up the curious ramp to the screen door where I heard the haunting mechanical whir of Matthew's wheelchair for the first time. Impersonally, I followed the chair inside, presented the gifts, and found myself indifferent to Matthew's cheerful gratitude as I dispassionately evaluated the physical curiosity seated across from me. Matthew always associated his appearance with that of the little alien on the poster I had brought. In fact, one of his favorite activities was to perform the scene from the movie where E.T. extends his healing finger to touch the small boy who had befriended him. However, when I first beheld Matthew's stricken body, I envisioned a baby bird which had fallen from its nest. His thin, blond hair was like soft feathers resting upon a slightly over-

sized head which leaned to one side due to the weakened muscles in his unsteady neck. His arms were like naked wings which awkwardly bent down at his wrists. I was almost unaware of the lifeless stems dangling from the chair until I recognized the new Nikes attached to the ends, which, I was later informed, had been given at last year's birthday. I was overcome with pity for Matthew's deformities and shame for my unappreciated health. However, when I saw his face, I experienced exonerating comfort from his magnificent smile, which was only enhanced by the crowded teeth protruding from his lips. What was I to do with this helpless baby bird I had stumbled upon, or what was he to do with me?

4   As I returned to Matthew regularly throughout that school year, my visits were initially for the sake of sympathy for this pitiful, sick child to whom I felt a duty to befriend. He always greeted me with his curious grin as if I were the highlight of his day. This gave me an unusual feeling of personal significance unlike anything anyone had given me before. Matthew pretended to need me, even if he truly didn't.

5   These early encounters with Matthew consisted of typical boyhood activities, including watching professional wrestling, playing video games, and discussing the female mind. In fact, I often found myself unaware of Matthew's physical shortcomings until I heard the whir of his mechanized legs or felt the fragile warmth of his weak body as he leaned on my side while we sat together for a game of video football. Matthew always won, and not because I let him.

6   As our relationship progressed and something more of a genuine friendship developed between us, I began to lose the helpless image of Matthew which I had contrived from physical influences. In fact, as the wind cooled and autumn littered his backyard with debris from the foliage above, Matthew introduced me to a world which transcended anatomical restraints and suggested that perhaps I was the invalid receiving charity.

7   Matthew's backyard had not been accessible to this point due to a viral infection of the lungs that had weakened his immune system. But now he had had time to recover.

8   Matthew became a new creature outside. Although his skin seemed even more fair, almost to the point of translucency, his respiration was smoother, and he could almost support his head in an erect position. As his body tottered with every lump or depression on the leafy earth in the yard, Matthew led me to the miniature wooden structure on the right side of the yard next to the fence. I recognized that this was a replica of a small church, as there was a tiny steeple attached to the roof in the shape of a cross. "This is my tabernacle," he proudly declared in an unfamiliarly steady voice. Matthew explained how the tabernacle was a homemade birthday gift from his father, who had crafted it especially for a small person in a wheelchair; however, I managed to squat down and follow him inside.

9   The tabernacle was strangely larger within, and I was able to sit up comfortably on the carpet floor while Matthew positioned his chair to the front of the room facing me. When he began to speak, I became amused at the notion that, in his church, Matthew was the preacher, and I was the heathen masses. I soon realized, however, that this was no game as Matthew was not presenting his typical jocular demeanor. Instead, he spoke with conviction and maintained an earnest presence. My astonishment and slight embarrassment prevented words, other than a few amens and hallelujahs, from reaching my attention until Matthew suggested that we should pray. As I bowed and listened, I didn't hear the pleas for health and healing that I expected. Rather than praying for his own well-being, Matthew asked for my blessing and thanked God for bringing me to him. Initially, I was unable to explain the tingling sensation coursing through my body, but as we silently left the tabernacle and made our way back to the house, I realized that Matthew loved me and that I loved him, too.

10   As the weeks passed, I continued to visit my friend almost daily until the night that I was to spend with Matthew and his family. The day progressed, as usual, with playing, talking, and visiting at the tabernacle. That evening, however, as Matthew's mother undressed him to reveal his bony frame, covered with braces and plastic and steel to bind him together where his muscles failed, I saw the baby bird again and almost wept. I was to sleep on the floor next to Matthew's tiny waterbed, as I feared that my restless tossing might injure him. However, I found myself unable to sleep as I lay in the hot sleeping bag listening to the deliberate breath wheezing from the bed beside me. After walking to the bathroom, I began to read an article in a magazine concerning the outlook for those suffering from muscular dystrophy. After I had read the passage suggesting that almost all victims die before their teens, I began to weep silently. The following morning revealed my red eyes and the salty deposits lining my cheeks, which I quickly washed when I saw them. After breakfast, I feigned a stomach ache and said goodbye. I knew that this was the last time that I would visit the house in front of the tabernacle, and I believe that Matthew was aware of this when he appeared at the front window with a wave of his little bent wing and his curiously confident smile.

11   I don't know why I so cowardly left that day or why I never visited with Matthew, other than a few short telephone conversations. Perhaps I was too sorry for his condition, or more likely, too sorry for mine. I rarely thought of Matthew after that year, but when his smile did enter my mind, cluttered with shallow, teenage concerns, I shivered and tried to forget again.

12   Matthew's death was no surprise or shock to me. I knew that he was aware of his fate and he accepted it fearlessly. However, with this death, I realized that the tiny wing waving goodbye was not that of a baby bird or even a little sick child about to die. Instead, it was the wing of an angel preparing to ascend to God and leave behind the

true baby bird who would now have to learn to fly by himself.

Reading Critically: Questions for Discussion

1. What illustrations, if any, might be appropriate for this story?
2. Do you trust the narrator? Explain why you do or don't.
3. With only one exception, the story has no dialogue. The exception is Matthew's explanation: "This is my tabernacle." Do you think this is a significant exception? Or would the story benefit from hearing the characters speak more often?
4. Members of Jase's writing group suggested that he shorten his sentences and use simpler words. Examine the writer's word choice. What do you think of his writing style? What revisions, if any, would you recommend?
5. Is the significance that the writer attributes to the story supported by the details of the narrative? What meaning would you derive from this experience?
6. What do you think of the ending? Is it overly sentimental or appropriately moving? Explain your answer.

KNOWLEDGE BY OBSERVATION: A PLACE

Krista Hierholtzer is the author of the next essay, "The Wall." So that you can see how her essay evolves, we have reproduced her second and fourth drafts. We suggest that you read both drafts at one sitting and consider how and why this writer revises her organization of information.

As her title suggests, Krista researches the Vietnam memorial, a place that she has "seen" through the eyes and words of others. As a result, she adopts the observer point of view. While Krista has never "been there," so to speak, her description of The Wall conveys the powerful effects that such an historic monument can have on us. Her words, images, and reactions help those who have never visited the memorial to experience this place, and they enable those who have been there to experience it again.

Reviewing Journal Entries

Krista's journal entries for "The Wall" are reminiscent of Christine's entries for "Filthy Grins" (see Chapter 9). Like Christine, Krista uses her journal to jot down ideas, take notes, and formulate a numbered list of ideas that pertain to this task and her progress; she too writes in phrases sometimes. After she submits her essay, Krista writes an entry containing mostly full sentences. In this entry, Krista discovers that by having to focus on and research her subject, she has in turn developed a deeper interest in the

Vietnam War and greater awareness of the American people's confusion about it. Here are a few entries from Krista's journal.

JOURNAL

I had a hard time choosing a subject. I'd like to write this essay from observation—get a little distance from my subject. I can't think of anybody who has been a major influence on me that I don't know personally. So I better choose a place.

The Vietnam Memorial was mentioned on the news tonight. The Wall will be a good subject—it is emotional and alive and important.

I located a book in the library today—The Wall by Sal Lopes. It has lots of photographs. I wish I could put pictures in this essay. I'm concerned about making the Wall come alive, bringing the pictures to life in the eye of my readers. It is difficult.

I need to be descriptive. I need to remember this! The Smithsonian has a book—Reflections on the Wall—that should be useful. But I think I need to find a couple more sources.

1st draft is pretty good, got ideas down, added sample letters and significance, but I need better images.

Had a difficult time doing draft 2. It's hard to take the idea already in your head and change it. A lot of frustration and paper wads. The group suggests I change my organization and start right off the bat with a description of the Wall. Maybe they're right. After all, this is supposed to be about a place.

After much struggle, I made the necessary changes. I like it much better. Need to do grammar and MLA check.

I am proud of the paper. I think it flows well and has a good impact. I produced good visual pictures for my readers, emotional pictures. I like working on the computer—so easy. Only problem is the first draft, hard to compose and think in that noisy cold computer lab. I am proud of my work and I love the subject. I loved learning more about The Wall. Maybe I'll go there someday.

Mapping Krista's Expressive Rhetorical Situation

Because Krista's knowledge of her subject is gained by observation, she lists details for her essay on the "knowledge by observation" side of the continuum. Figure 10.2 shows a full picture of her rhetorical situation.

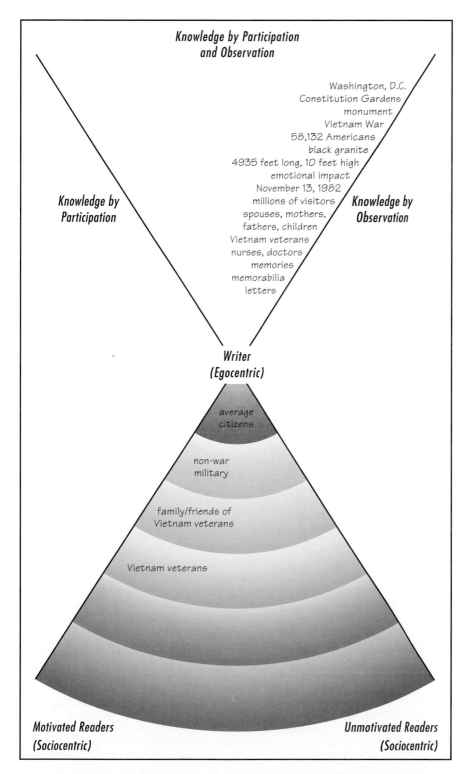

Figure 10.2 Mapping Krista's rhetorical situation

Krista's intended audience for this essay are general adult readers. Due to the nature of her subject, Krista divides her audience in terms of their relationship to the military and war: active duty war veterans; friends or relatives of active duty war veterans; non–war military (National Guard); citizens who never knew or lost anybody in the Vietnam War. Krista wanted to identify her readers according to their relationship to The Wall and the names on it. Classifying readers according to age (i.e., readers born before, during, after the war) or attitude (i.e., prowar versus antiwar) conflicted with her ideas about what this memorial represents to Americans. She views all her readers as very motivated and interested; however, she classifies those who have experienced Vietnam and those who have known or lost loved ones in the war as the most actively engaged members of her audience.

The Wall

Draft 2

1   The Vietnam War divided and disrupted America, and The Wall is helping America and her citizens to heal and deal with the emotional scars of that military conflict. Since its dedication on November 13, 1982, The Wall has become one of the most popular American monuments, with 4.5 million visitors reported in 1986 (Ashabranner 12). Visitors come to The Wall for many reasons. Some travel there to say goodbye to a relative: a mother or father, a husband or wife, a son or daughter, and so on. Some come to bid farewell to comrades who did not return from the war, missing or killed. Some visit to say they're sorry and ask for forgiveness for transgressions that their loved ones may never have even known. And some people come simply to learn and remember, knowing no particular name to search for in the granite. These visitors report that they need to be there to pay their respects. As Michael Norman says,

> To touch the wall is to touch the dead, to get close to them. And as they make this crossing—as those who never knew the war come close to those taken by it—they begin to understand Vietnam and thus honor the generation of veterans who survived the war. We have never asked for more than that. (Lopes 19)

2   The Wall stands in Constitution Gardens, Washington, D.C. It reads:

> In honor of the men and women of the Armed Forces of the United States who served in the Vietnam War. The names of those who gave their lives and of those who remain missing are inscribed in the order they were taken from us. Our nation honors the courage, sacrifice, and devotion to duty and country of its Vietnam veterans. (Ashabranner 180)

3   Inscribed on this monument are the names of 58,132 Americans, missing or killed in the Vietnam War (Lopes 15). Each name has been carefully etched into the lustrous black granite brought from Bangalore, India. Visitors from all over come to see The Wall and pay their respects. A visitor once described the experience by comparing it to walking down into an open grave. The analogy is eerie, but accurate. As you begin your descent along the 493.5 feet of black granite slabs, The Wall rises until it looms above you. According to Sal Lopes in *The Wall,* it rises gradually for 246.75 feet until it reaches a height of over 10 feet (15). As you continue your journey past this apex and along the second major segment of The Wall, each step takes you closer to the surface. The first set of slabs, the west wall, points to the Lincoln Memorial. The other, the east wall, points to the Washington Memorial. The mere sight of such a structure is apparently overwhelming. The craftsmanship, work, and expense alone are enough to astound most people; however, the impact of this Vietnam memorial on its visitors goes beyond these considerations.

4   As Maya Ying Lin, the designer of The Wall, explains:

> I didn't want a static object that people would just look at, but something they could relate to as a journey, or passage, that would bring each to his own conclusions. . . . I had an impulse to cut open the earth . . . an initial violence that in time would heal. . . . It was as if the black-brown earth were polished and made into an interface between the sunny world and the quiet dark world beyond, that we can't enter. . . . The names would become the memorial. There was no need to embellish. (Lopes 16)

5   People who come to The Wall do interact with it and the names that appear on it. They are overcome at the sight of the memorial, not because of its tremendous physical stature, but its overwhelming emotional impact.

6   If the sight and appeal of The Wall itself are overwhelming, the sight and appeal of the people who visit it are almost indescribable. Thumbing through *The Wall,* the images in the photographs come alive. Grown men, age showing hard on their faces, stand weeping and giving letters and teddy bears to their lost sons. Mothers, trembling on their wobbly knees, clutch pictures and trace the names with their fingers. Wives, children tugging on their skirts, say their tearful goodbyes and show the proud father his legacy. Young children clad in school clothes gaze in wonder over what it all means. All of these images are seen again and again in pictures from the memorial sight, but perhaps the most moving are those of the Vietnam veterans themselves (Lopes).

7   A lone veteran stands clenching his fists and trembling, as The Wall looms behind him. Tears slowly start to trickle down his cheeks. A flag is raised proudly on top of the memorial by another veteran. He can no longer stand, his legs were part of his sacrifice; but he

shows his strength and love. Another group of veterans huddles together in front of The Wall, each holding the other up as they seek comfort from those who understand. A veteran passes by. He carries a sign. It is a simple sign. The message is clear. It reads: "I am a Vietnam veteran and I like the memorial. And if it makes it difficult to send people into battle again I like it even more" (Lopes 110). Another man sees this veteran and embraces him with a smile. Nurses and doctors stand heads bowed at the massive numbers of names before them. These were the ones they could not save. The memories haunt them. They come here to try and bury those memories with the dead. The memorial is for the living as well as the dead.

8   People of all ages and all walks of life come and grieve for America's loss. Perhaps what they leave behind at the memorial itself is the biggest tribute to the impact of The Wall. Over the years, over 4900 artifacts have been left by visitors at the memorial (Lopes 18). An entire separate warehouse in Lanham, Maryland, has been established to preserve the memorabilia (Lopes 18). They range from letters and childhood toys to uniforms and purple hearts. Here are some examples of letters from the book *The Wall* by Sal Lopes that have been left at the monument over the years. They need no explanation, because they, like the names, speak for themselves.

> How angry I was to find you here, though I knew that you would be. I've wished so hard that I could have saved you. I would give my life if somehow it would bring you all back. It is only now on my second trip to this monument that I can admit that you, my friends, are gone forever, that I can say your names and speak of your deaths. I've carried the anguish of your deaths for so long, but I think I can stop looking for you now. I think I can start living without letting you die. (Lopes 93)

> This marks the second year I have come to the Wall. I have seen the names of those I know, and, yes I have cried. My problem is I don't know the names of those I tried to help only to have them die in my arms. . . . In Vietnam, at age 20, I was put in charge of a riverboat. Now every time I get on a boat, I only see blood running over the deck and into the water. I try to take my two sons fishing, but we never stay long. . . . They are too young to understand that their father does not like the reflections he sees in the water. For these reasons I write to say I'm sorry. . . . I did the best I could. . . . I wish I knew your names so I could touch your names in the black stone. But I don't and I'm sorry. . . . Attached to this letter are my service medals. These belong to you and your family and friends. I don't need them to show I was there. I have your faces to remind me in my sleep. . . . On the day we meet again please do one thing. "Tell me your name." (Lopes 58)

> Now I am grown and I look a lot like you. Who would have known I would grow up to look like someone I never even knew. (Lopes 80)

We did what we could but it was not enough because I found you here. You are not just a name on this wall. You are alive. You are blood on my hands. You are screams in my ears. You are eyes in my soul. I told you you'd be all right, but I lied, and please forgive me. I see your face in my son, I can't bear the thought. You told me about your wife, your kids, your girl, your mother. And then you died. Your pain is mine. I'll never forget your face. I can't. You are still alive. (Lopes 56)

Just wanted you to know I love you brother. Still talk to Cathy and your babies. They're grown and proud of you. You're me, and I'm you. I'll always watch over them for you. I'll see you soon. Just thought I'd let you know everything is O.K. (Lopes 103)

Damn you brother—why didn't you come back? I want you back, but not in a box. I still love you, and I'd love you if you came back in one piece, or your arms or legs or mind gone. I wasn't that young when you died because I cried too. God has you now but I want you too, so damn you for not coming back! (Lopes, back cover)

9   These letters show the raw emotion of The Wall. They show the interaction that the designer hoped would be there—the journey. They show how people do reach out and touch the dead. This memorial is so important. It is not only a tribute to those living and dead, but it is a place of healing for individuals and our nation. I have never experienced the emotion of visiting The Wall, but it is so vital to me. I am an American, and I feel an obligation and desire to respect and honor these people. I know the pain this conflict has caused in my country. I read and I see. I want the wounds to heal. I want my wounds and my sorrow for these Americans who gave their lives to be laid to rest with the dead. I also am a daughter, a sister, a lover, and a friend. I can't begin to imagine the pain, but I know the support, any support, must help. The emotion of the monument reaches far beyond the boundaries of those who see it and those who touch it. Someday I will touch it and I too will reach out for the dead.

Works Cited

Ashabranner, Brent. *Always to Remember*. New York: Putnam's, 1988.
Lopes, Sal. *The Wall*. New York: Collins, 1987.
Scruggs, Jan C. *To Heal a Nation*. New York: Harper, 1985.
Smithsonian Institute. *Reflections on The Wall*. New York: Stackpole, 1987.

_____

In expressive aim writing, the personal significance of an event, person, or place is very important. Expressive aim writing stresses the writer—how the writer's values, attitudes, and ideas are influenced by the world he or she lives in. Compare the significance of The Wall in the second and fourth drafts of this essay. Which do you prefer and why? What other changes do you notice? If you were a member of Krista's focus group, what comments and suggestions would you offer her regarding her revisions in draft 4?

The Wall

(Draft 4—Final Draft)

1   In Constitution Gardens, Washington, D.C., stands The Wall, on which these words appear:

> In honor of the men and women of the Armed Forces of the United States who served in the Vietnam War. The names of those who gave their lives and of those who remain missing are inscribed in the order they were taken from us. Our nation honors the courage, sacrifice, and devotion to duty and country of its Vietnam veterans. (Ashabranner 180)

2   Inscribed on this monument are the names of 58,132 Americans, missing or killed in the Vietnam War (Lopes 15). Each name has been carefully etched into the lustrous black granite brought from Bangalore, India. Visitors from all over come to see The Wall and pay their respects. A visitor once described the experience by comparing it to walking down into an open grave. The analogy is eerie, but accurate. As you begin your descent along the 493.5 feet of black granite slabs, The Wall rises until it looms above you. According to Sal Lopes in *The Wall*, it rises gradually for 246.75 feet until it reaches a height of over 10 feet (15). As you continue your journey past this apex and along the second major segment of The Wall, each step takes you closer to the surface. The first set of slabs, the west wall, points to the Lincoln Memorial. The other, the east wall, points to the Washington Memorial. The mere sight of such a structure is apparently overwhelming. The craftsmanship, work, and expense alone are enough to astound most people; however, the impact of this Vietnam memorial on its visitors goes beyond these considerations.

3   As Maya Ying Lin, the designer of The Wall, explains:

> I didn't want a static object that people would just look at, but something they could relate to as a journey, or passage, that would bring each to his own conclusions. . . . I had an impulse to cut open the earth . . . an initial violence that in time would heal. . . . It was as if the black-brown earth were polished and made into an interface between the sunny world and the quiet dark world beyond, that we can't enter. . . . The names would become the memorial. There was no need to embellish. (Lopes 16)

4   People who come to The Wall do interact with it and the names that appear on it. They are overcome at the sight of the memorial, not because of its tremendous physical stature, but its overwhelming emotional impact.

5   The Vietnam War divided and disrupted America, and The Wall is
helping America and her citizens to heal and deal with the emotional
scars of that military conflict. Since its dedication on November 13,
1982, The Wall has become one of the most popular American monuments, with 4.5 million visitors reported in 1986 (Ashabranner 12).
Visitors come to The Wall for many reasons. Some travel there to say
goodbye to a relative: a mother or father, a husband or wife, a son or
daughter, and so on. Some come to bid farewell to comrades who did
not return from the war, missing or killed. Some visit to say they're
sorry and ask for forgiveness for transgressions that their loved ones
may never have even known. And some people come simply to learn
and remember, knowing no particular name to search for in the granite. These visitors report that they need to be there to pay their
respects. As Michael Norman says, "To touch the wall is to touch the
dead, to get close to them" (Lopes 19).

6   If the sight and appeal of The Wall itself is overwhelming, the
sight and appeal of the people who visit it is almost indescribable.
The pages of *The Wall* are filled with photographs that come alive.
Grown men, age showing hard on their faces, stand weeping and giving letters and teddy bears to their lost sons. Mothers, trembling on
their wobbly knees, clutch pictures and trace the names with their fingers. Wives, children tugging on their skirts, say their tearful goodbyes
and show the proud father his legacy. Young children clad in school
clothes gaze in wonder over what it all means. All of these images are
seen again and again in pictures from the memorial sight, but perhaps
the most moving are those of the Vietnam veterans—the survivors
(Lopes).

7   What do these snapshots capture? One shows a lone veteran,
tears trickling down his cheeks, his clenched fists trembling, as The
Wall looms behind him (Lopes 110). A flag is raised proudly on top of
the memorial by another veteran. He can no longer stand, his legs
gone; yet his face seemed to reflect his strength and love, not bitterness or anger. Another group of veterans huddles together in front of
The Wall, each holding the other up as they seek comfort from those
who understand. A veteran passes by. He carries a sign. It is a simple
sign, and the message is clear. It reads: "I am a Vietnam veteran and I
like the memorial. And if it makes it difficult to send people into battle
again I like it even more" (Lopes 110). Another man sees this veteran
and embraces him with a smile. Nurses and doctors stand, heads
bowed at the massive numbers of names before them. These were the
ones they could not save. The memories haunt them, and this collage
of snapshots of visitors at The Wall are themselves haunting. These
visitors come to the wall to try and put those memories to rest with
the dead, clarifying that this memorial, like all memorials, is for the
living as well as the dead.

8   Over the years, over 4900 artifacts have been left by visitors,
themselves one of the biggest tributes of the impact of The Wall

(Lopes 18). An entire separate warehouse in Lanham, Maryland, has been established to preserve the memorabilia (Lopes 18). These remembrances range from letters and childhood toys to uniforms and purple hearts. Here are several excerpts from letters that indicate the powerful nature of The Wall and its effect on those who visit:

How angry I was to find you here, though I knew that you would be. I've wished so hard that I could have saved you. I would give my life if somehow it would bring you all back. It is only now on my second trip to this monument that I can admit that you, my friends, are gone forever, that I can say your names and speak of your deaths. I've carried the anguish of your deaths for so long, but I think I can stop looking for you now. I think I can start living without letting you die. (Lopes 93)

Now I am grown and I look a lot like you. Who would have known I would grow up to look like someone I never even knew. (Lopes 80)

This marks the second year I have come to the Wall. I have seen the names of those I know, and, yes I have cried. My problem is I don't know the names of those I tried to help only to have them die in my arms. . . . In Vietnam, at age 20, I was put in charge of a riverboat. Now every time I get on a boat, I only see blood running over the deck and into the water. I try to take my two sons fishing, but we never stay long. . . . They are too young to understand that their father does not like the reflections he sees in the water. For these reasons I write to say I'm sorry. . . . I did the best I could. . . . I wish I knew your names so I could touch your names in the black stone. But I don't and I'm sorry. . . . Attached to this letter are my service medals. These belong to you and your family and friends. I don't need them to show I was there. I have your faces to remind me in my sleep. . . . On the day we meet again please do one thing. "Tell me your name." (Lopes 58)

Damn you brother—why didn't you come back? I want you back, but not in a box. I still love you, and I'd love you if you came back in one piece, or your arms or legs or mind gone. I wasn't that young when you died because I cried too. God has you now but I want you too, so damn you for not coming back! (Lopes, back cover)

We did what we could but it was not enough because I found you here. You are not just a name on this wall. You are alive. You are blood on my hands. You are screams in my ears. You are eyes in my soul. I told you you'd be all right, but I lied, and please forgive me. I see your face in my son, I can't bear the thought. You told me about your wife, your kids, your girl, your mother. And then you died. Your pain is mine. I'll never forget your face. I can't. You are still alive. (Lopes 56)

Just wanted you to know I love you brother. Still talk to Cathy and your babies. They're grown and proud of you. You're me, and I'm you. I'll always watch over them for you. I'll see you soon. Just thought I'd let you know everything is O.K. (Lopes 103)

9   These letters show the raw emotion The Wall can help its visitors release. They show the interaction that the designer hoped would be there—the journey. They show how people do reach out and touch the dead.

10   This memorial is a significant landmark. It is not only a tribute to those Vietnam War missing and dead, but it is a place of healing for a country and her people. While I have never visited The Wall, I can sense its relevance to me, an American, for that is what it symbolizes: one people coming together at one place, striving to identify with the myriad of emotions that the war generated. I can understand its powerful effects by seeing snapshots, reading letters, and peering into the faces of those who have sojourned to The Wall. This memorial has touched those who have seen and touched the smooth, cold, black granite; from afar, however, I rub my thumb across my fingertips, to take the chill away.

Works Cited

Ashabranner, Brent. *Always to Remember*. New York: Putnam's, 1988.

Lopes, Sal. *The Wall*. New York: Collins, 1987.

Scruggs, Jan C. *To Heal a Nation*. New York: Harper, 1985.

Smithsonian Institute. *Reflections on The Wall*. New York: Stackpole, 1987.

Reading Critically: Questions for Discussion

1. As you were reading, did you realize Krista's knowledge of The Wall comes chiefly from a photographic essay on the subject? How might she explain or emphasize that she is looking at a book of photographs?

2. What sensory details does Krista provide of The Wall? Which senses does she appeal to? Which does she ignore? Why?

3. Is the physical description of The Wall's dimensions necessary? Why?

4. How does Krista's description of the visitors contribute to your understanding of The Wall?

5. What is the function of the quotations from various letters?

KNOWLEDGE BY OBSERVATION: A CHARACTER

Written by Suzanne Young, "In the Dark with Mary Shelley" is another expressive aim essay that is researched and written from an observer point of view. Just as Krista has never visited The Wall, Suzanne has never and, quite obviously, will never meet the subject of her essay: Mary Shelley, the author of *Frankenstein*. Suzanne can, however, present a sketch of this nineteenth-century author and explain how she—an aspiring writer—has been affected by Shelley.

Reviewing Journal Entries

For Suzanne, her journal is like a diary. She "talks" in it, and her entries contain advice, criticism, observations, and ideas that she, in effect, gives herself. This selected set of entries reveals Suzanne's relationship with her focus group and her thoughts about the internal and external influences on her writing. Her entries also suggest how Suzanne revised in response to comments from her group and writing teacher.

JOURNAL

Well, I've got a great idea for this paper. I want to write about the summer Mary Shelley decided to write Frankenstein. *I've always loved that story. And Mary Shelley. I'm not sure how I'm going to approach it, though.*

I've finished my first draft. I don't think it's good. I don't feel that I had enough time to absorb my main idea. Working on the computer for the first time was such an experience! I think I spent half of my time trying to figure out how to use the word processor. Maybe that's why my paper wasn't very good. Hope the second draft goes better.

Met with my group today. They had a lot of constructive criticism. I think I'll scrap the majority of the first draft. There was too much pure narration. It was more of a short story. I need to focus on Mary Shelley, the author. There are a few good points, though. We all like the long quote, but are concerned that it's too long. Don't know what to do. I'll see what I can do in 2nd draft.

Arrgh!! I had a systems failure and lost everything! I started again and got everything done in time. I didn't know what to do with the block quote. I didn't have time to worry about it. Things to look at in draft:

1. good transitions?
2. should characters be more developed? what about Mary?

3. do I show more significance this time?
4. is my conclusion adequate?
5. block quote?

_____

Everyone likes 2nd draft. A few changes only. They want me to keep the conclusion the same, but I think it needs more. Talked to my teacher; she suggested I use ellipses to shorten the block quote. I think it will work.

_____

I'm close to the finish line. I've marked up my 4th draft with corrections. I'll type them in tomorrow. The paper feels so much stronger to me.

_____

I'm done. I think my paper turned out well. My group really had some great criticisms and I really think they helped my paper.

I do wish that I had had more time to think about my first draft. I think it wasn't good because I didn't have the time to really digest my subject. I am happy with my final draft though. I really worked on it.

Working on the computer was pretty interesting. The one problem was that it took a while to learn how to use the computer. I did like using it because it made a lot of things easier. I still like writing by hand, though. When I compose I have a certain place I sit. I have to be very comfortable. I really didn't like sitting in the computer lab to write my paper. Maybe if I get my own computer . . . !

Reread your journal entries and analyze them. What purposes are they serving? Why? What are you learning about your writing processes and yourself as a writer? If you are part of a focus group, how does your impression of your group compare to Suzanne's? Why? Does your group need to try some strategies that might strengthen it? Which strategies? If possible, share these ideas with your group at your next meeting. How does technology influence your writing? Have you ever "lost" what you were writing on the computer?

Mapping Suzanne's Expressive Rhetorical Situation

Suzanne learns about the author of *Frankenstein* by reading Shelley's biography, her journal, and her introduction to the novel—gaining knowledge by observation. As a consequence, her essay contains numerous quotations and ideas from other people as well as appropriate documentation. Thus, Suzanne can easily identify her way of knowing on the knowledge continuum, as shown in Figure 10.3.

The part of the essay that discusses Mary Shelley's impact on Suzanne, however, should be typical expressive aim writing. That is, the descriptive details concerning the story and the character are important because they give Suzanne the opportunity to explain their significance or meaning to her.

Although her subject may be fascinating to her, Suzanne is well aware that Shelley may be boring and irrelevant to many in her audience: general adult readers. For that reason, she tries to inject some horror and humor in the introduction. But she can't maintain this tone throughout, for she has a serious message to deliver later on in her essay. She realistically analyzes her audience as a spectrum of adults who do or do not like to read and write. She considers those who like to read and write to be her most motivated and interested audience members; conversely, she views her least engaged readers to be those who rarely if ever read and write.

In the Dark with Mary Shelley

Draft 5—Final Draft

1   A long, jagged scar extended from his hairline to his eyebrow. He was much taller than any normal man, standing some seven or eight feet tall. A deathly blue pallor colored the skin which stretched across his frame. He was dim-witted and had eyes which contained a haunted look. Probably the most striking features of the Frankenstein of my youth, however, were the two huge, gray bolts that protruded from his neck.

2   I was cheated and lied to from a very early age, for I was led to believe Frankenstein was a monster. No Halloween was complete without seeing the monster's ugly visage decorating a wall or a trick-or-treater dressed as Frankenstein. Hollywood lied to me when they produced such movies as *The Bride of Frankenstein* which perpetuated the myth. Even the cereal manufacturers lied to me! I used to eat Frankenberry cereal with a cute little pink Frankenstein on the box.

3   Nobody told me the truth, and I feel cheated because it was not until I was well on my way to adolescence that I discovered the truth. How did I discover it? I read the book.

4   Picking up my paperback copy with the gruesome fiend on the cover, I fully expected to discover the nameless mad scientist and his assistant, Igor, who created the semi-human fiend, Frankenstein, who terrorized the countryside. I was dumbfounded when I began reading. None of the gruesome, disgusting details I expected to find in the book were true. There was no hump-backed Igor. There was no mad scientist out to destroy the world, and there was no monster named Frankenstein. What there was was a young genius science student named Victor Frankenstein who mistakenly used his skills to bring to life a misunderstood and lonely fiend. The story was terrifying, but only because of the possibility that some similar horror might occur in real life.

5   With the very first reading, this book came to mean something very important to me. It started my quest to know the truth. I had been led to believe in one reality throughout my childhood, and now that I knew the "monster myth" was false, I wanted to find the complete truth about the book and its author. As I began to research, I

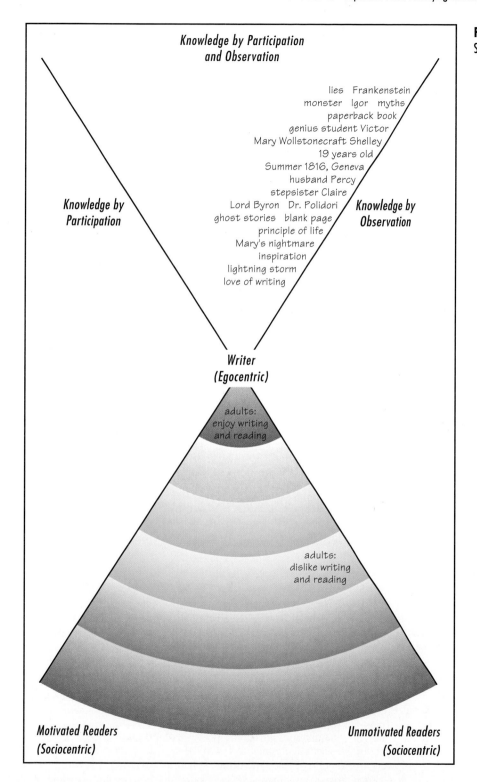

Figure 10.3 Mapping Suzanne's rhetorical situation

learned more about myself, as well as the book.

6   My first shocking revelation came when I discovered Frankenstein was written by a young woman who was only nineteen-years-old at the time. I was intrigued. What would cause a young woman to choose such a forbidding subject to write about?

7   The book was written by Mary Wollstonecraft Godwin in the summer of 1816, while she was living in Geneva, Switzerland, with Percy Bysshe Shelley, her lover and future husband; Claire Clairmont, her step-sister; Lord Byron; and Byron's physician, Dr. Polidori. The weather that summer was very forbidding and often kept the group indoors. One particularly stormy night, as the group warmed themselves by the fire, Byron made an entertaining proposition. "We will each write a ghost story," he said (Shelley viii).

8   While Mary was a very intelligent woman, she was slightly intimidated by this challenge. Mary was in the company of two of the greatest poets of her time, and she was driven by a desire to write a story that would equal theirs. In her own words, she wanted to write a story "which would speak to the mysterious fears of our nature, and awaken thrilling horror—one to make the reader dread to look round, to curdle the blood, and quicken the beatings of the heart" (Shelley ix). Even though she was caught by this desperate desire to write a blood curdling ghost story, the topic of her story was lost to her. Even when all of her comrades had begun their own stories, she was still lost, and each day she was greeted by the dreaded question from her fellow ghost story writers who asked, "Have you thought of a story?" (Shelley ix).

9   When I read of Mary's predicament, I immediately empathized. I have known the traumatic anxiety of wanting to write but having no idea of how to begin. I, too, have felt what Mary calls the "blank incapability of invention" (Shelley ix), those moments when you can only stare at a blank page with the desire to create, but as hard as you might try, the desire does not translate into words. I therefore shared in her elation when I read her account of the night she was inspired.

10   Her inspiration came several nights after Byron's initial proposition. The topic of ghost stories was still fresh on everyone's mind when Byron and Shelley began one of their many philosophical discussions. They took the ghost stories with which they were toying into another realm when they began to discuss philosophical doctrines pertaining to the nature of the principle of life (Shelley ix). Mary, who quietly sat listening, heard the debate over whether or not a corpse could be re-animated.

11   That night, as Mary slept, she was haunted by horrific visions. Later, when asked about her inspiration, she explained her nightmare:

> . . . My imagination, unbidden, possessed and guided me . . . I saw—with shut eyes, but acute mental vision,—I saw the pale student of unhallowed arts kneeling beside the thing he had put together. I saw the hideous phantasm of a man stretching out, and then, on the working of

some powerful engine, show signs of life, and stir with an uneasy, half vital motion. Frightful must it be; for supremely frightful would be the effect of any human endeavor to mock the stupendous mechanism of the Creator of the world. His success would terrify the artist. . . . He would hope . . . this thing . . . would subside into dead matter. . . . He sleeps; but he is awakened; he opens his eyes; behold the horrid thing that stands at his bedside, opening his curtains, and looking on him with yellow, watery, but speculative eyes. . . .

I opened mine in terror . . . and I wished to exchange the ghastly image of my fancy for the realities around . . . . I could not easily get rid of my hideous phantom; still it haunted me. I must try to think of something else. I recurred to my ghost story—my tiresome unlucky ghost story! O! if I could only contrive one which would frighten my reader as I myself had been frightened that night!

". . . I have found it! What terrified me will terrify others; and I need only describe the spectre which had haunted my midnight pillow."
(Shelley x)

12   The next morning, Mary immediately began her work. She was possessed with the tale and her desire to equal the talent of the company she was keeping. Eager to win approval, she often showed passages of her work to her lover, Percy Shelley. He was taken with Mary's ghost story and persuaded her to develop it further. What started as a short story ended as a novel.

13   Mary drew from many of that summer's events to flesh out her novel, and each page contains accounts of occurrences and places which inspired her. One fantastic lightning storm, which Mary witnessed, thrilled her so much that she included it in a passage of her novel. The climax of her novel, when the scientist, Frankenstein, and his creature meet for the first time since the moment of creation, takes place at the Mer de Glace, an ice-ridden valley, void of vegetation, where Mary and Percy Shelley visited during that summer (Dunn 141). It was not difficult for Mary to remember these moments, for her manuscript was her constant companion. During moments of inspiration, she wrote of those places and events that awed her.

14   Once I had finished reading about Mary and the summer of 1816, I knew my quest was completed, and because of it, I had discovered new qualities in myself. I saw myself in Mary. I saw a young woman who had a love of writing, but who was often intimidated by those around her. Mary made me proud to be a writer and a woman because she had faced her challenge and had conquered it. Byron had dared everyone present that summer to write a ghost story, but Mary had been the only one to complete an original, full-length work. She has inspired me to face any writing task with determination and courage, no matter how difficult I find it. She has also taught me to openly accept any source of inspiration, and finally, she has proven that gender should be no burden. My success will ultimately rely on my skill as a writer, as did her success.

15   Completing my research has brought me full circle. I began with the myth but ended where Mary Shelley had begun. My quest has become a bizarre rite of passage for me. I exchanged the beliefs I held as a child for the oftentimes more painful truths of adulthood. It has been a rude awakening, but I appreciate the truth more.

16   Now as I read through *Frankenstein* once again, I read with new appreciation for its contribution to literature and its impact on me. I can read this novel purely for the pleasure of the story, but at the same time, I envision the images of its creation. I can see Mary, Percy Shelley, and Lord Byron sitting by a blazing fire in a darkened room, the light reflecting off their faces. I can faintly hear the intense philosophical discussions, and I can understand Mary's fear as she lay awake that night haunted by visions of human re-animation.

17   I cannot help but crave a similar occurrence in my own life: to experience my own moment of inspiration and to devote my energy in an all consuming project—a book that can catch the imagination of the literary and generate a myth. At least now, I know it can be done.

Works Cited

Dunn, Jane. *Moon in Eclipse: A Life of Mary Shelley.* London: Weidenfeld, 1978.

Jones, Frederick L., ed. *Mary Shelley's Journal.* Norman: U of Oklahoma, 1947.

Shelley, Mary W. *Frankenstein.* Philadelphia: Running, 1990.

Strickland, Margot. *The Byron Women.* New York: St. Martin's, 1974.

Reading Critically: Questions for Discussion

1. Suzanne starts this story by describing the monster myths associated with Frankenstein. Why does she start this way? Is it effective?
2. Why does Suzanne narrate the circumstances leading to Shelley's writing of *Frankenstein?*
3. Why does Suzanne identify with Shelley? What details does Suzanne offer to explain or justify this identification?
4. Suzanne's story includes Shelley's explanation of her nightmare. What impact does this direct quotation have on the story? Would a summary of Shelley's nightmare be more or less effective? Why?

KNOWLEDGE BY PARTICIPATION AND OBSERVATION

The following essay was written by Matthew Coplen, Lisa Haley, and Kate Satterwhite. These three student writers decide to focus on Kyle Field from the perspective of those who have both direct and indirect knowledge of this football stadium. They gain their knowledge by participation by attending a football game at Kyle Field together; although they had all been to games there before and had all remembered attending campus tours of the football stadium, they wanted to experience being at this location at the same time. They also added to their knowledge about Kyle Field by researching written sources that describe it. When reading their essay, notice the participant-observer point of view ("we") that the coauthors use.

Reviewing Journal Entries

Matthew, Lisa, and Kate had never before written a collaborative essay; though they were accustomed to researching a subject with other people, they had never tried to coauthor anything. Their journal entries reveal their concern and uncertainty about collaboratively writing a text. Their apprehension is apparent throughout the process of writing. First, they all express only a modicum of enthusiasm for their subject, but stick with it rather than exploring other possible subjects. Second, all three group members were so amiable and cooperative that none of them really wanted to take the lead or offend anybody else. Hence, as time passed, they all agreed to always agree—at least in each other's presence. Here are some selected entries from their individual journals.

JOURNAL

We met as a group today for the first time. . . . We considered writing about the Alamo, but didn't feel very strongly about that subject. We brainstormed and thought of a place on campus since we all know these places best. Right now it seems that we're going to write about Kyle Field. We don't feel that strongly about it either, but so far it's the best idea we have come up with. (KS)

Today our group met in class. . . . We narrowed down to two choices: the university or Kyle Field. I wanted Texas A&M because it is where we all are and will receive our education; that's important to me. But, we finally decided on the football field. (LH)

I got some information on Kyle Field from the Sports Office. We, in our group in class, brainstormed awhile and came up with our feelings on Kyle Field; why it's special and why it's significant. We decided on the order of our discourse bloc or ideas and set the time and place for our next meeting. (LH)

We decided to all go to a game together and then each write our own version of the introduction for next time. In our intro, we wanted a vivid description of Kyle Field. (LH)

We met today in the library. My version of the intro describes what it was like when we came into Kyle Field. That's how I tried to describe it. I tried to use vivid, descriptive words. I tried to describe, without telling the reader what it was. Kate and Matthew did this also. We put it together in the library. We concentrated on the intro and the historical paragraph for the first draft. (LH)

In class, we decided that we have to use "we" in our paper throughout. When we write on our own, we use "I" then we meet and revise using "we." It's strange. I think of split personalities. We're going to write our significance sections for the next meeting. (KS)

Met in the library to work on collaborative paper. We had a real problem combining our thoughts. Each of us finds real different significance in what Kyle Field means. It is hard to make a paper sound real when we can not decide what we really want to say. (MC)

We all wrote the rough draft of our paper together. It took a long time to write because we collaborated on each sentence, one by one. When you write alone, you usually just write down the first things that come to mind and then go back to revise later. We kind of revised as we went along because we paid so much attention to each sentence. (KS)

We met to put together the "hellish" significance section. We decided to blend our voices, instead of having separate narratives and interpretations. It was hard, but we did it. We added some transitions here and there, too. "We." (LH)

Between class last week and today's revision, we did some more research and learned more facts, but the truth is we still cannot find the significance of the field.

How can we make this subject interesting for our audience? Don't they already know everything we're telling them? Sometimes, I'm not sure that even we would want to read anything more about this subject. We've really got our work cut out for us. Maybe we should look at our map again or try some different strategies to get people's attention—tell a story or give 'em some numbers. (MC)

Turned in our essay today. I feel very apprehensive about it. It was probably the hardest paper I've ever written because of trying to collaborate on what the central idea should be. It seemed to be almost impossible to put our thoughts together with any coherence. We all write so differently. (MC)

It was definitely challenging to write my first collaborative paper. I found that I had to restrain myself as far as making corrections on the paper. Before I did anything, I felt like it was necessary to discuss the mat-

ter with my teammates. However, considering that we don't know each other very well, I think we did a good job. We never had any big disagreements and everyone participated fully every time we got together.

The major problem we had was the subject. We never really were able to figure out what the field meant to us. We know, but we don't have words for it.

I'm also afraid that no one—except other A&M football fans—will think our subject is interesting. And those who are interested have probably already heard everything we're going to say about the field. If they know this stuff already, why should they read our essay? I don't have a good answer to this question, but it's too late to do anything about it. The paper is due this afternoon. (KS)

Mapping Matthew, Lisa, and Kate's Expressive Rhetorical Situation

Matthew, Lisa, and Kate map their rhetorical situation in Figure 10.4. As this map shows, Kyle Field is a subject that these writers know about from participation and observation. Their memories of campus tours and the legends or myths they have heard since arriving at the university will provide most of their information, despite the availability of written sources.

Matt, Lisa, and Kate see the readers of this essay as students, alumni, and other adults who may or may not have been college football fans. They speculate that the readers who are fans will be able to identify with them and become involved in their description of this location (close proximity to writers, motivated); on the other hand, those who may not care about college football will find this subject dull (far from writers, unmotivated). As their journal entries indicate, the writers realize that it may be difficult to keep their readers interested in this subject. As you read their essay, you will notice that they provide a variety of statistics to intrigue and impress their audience. Is this effective? Or does the abundance of objective information interfere with their expressive aim and make the communication of personal significance subordinate to the reporting of facts and figures?

Perhaps this group should have reviewed the map of their rhetorical situation and reevaluated the audience's level of interest in this subject. What do you think? In staying with this subject, have the members of this focus group rushed to consensus?

Read More About It

See Chapter 3, p. 72–74.

Kyle Field: Home of Dreams

Draft 5—Final Draft

1   The day is November 28, 1991; the place is Texas A&M University. Three excited students begin a trek. As we boldly walk toward our destination, clearly our minds are focused on one thing: football.

Figure 10.4 Mapping Matthew, Lisa, and Kate's rhetorical situation

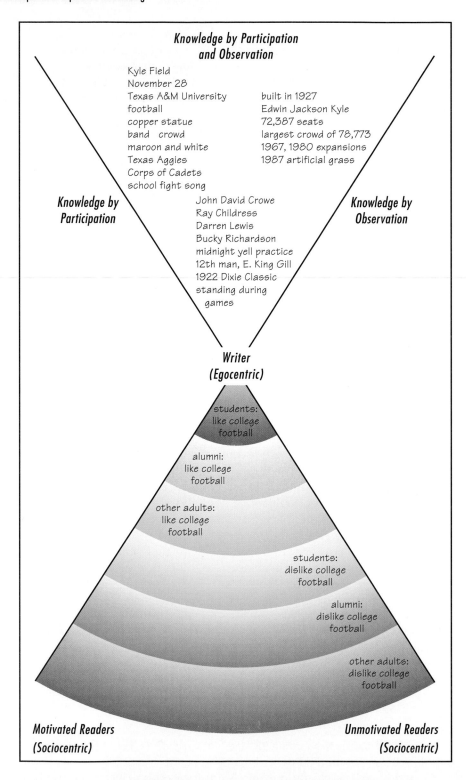

Keeping a brisk pace, we hear the reverberating roar of the crowd in the distance. We pass a copper statue of a uniformed man, and we think of the generations that have gone before us and those that are yet to come. As we move closer, we can hear the crowd chanting, urging the players on. The band plays merrily, loudly, triumphantly, engulfing the crowd with fanfare. Whistles blow, hands clap, and the commentators' voices echo over the loud-speaker system. We walk in quickly and enter the enormous concrete ramps that spiral up like an entrance to the sky. We are immersed in a colorful mass of people who push with impatience and anticipation. An excitement travels among us, tingling with electricity. With just few more steps, our journey is completed. We enter the magnificent, monstrous stadium and view our surroundings.

2   Down many feet below us, lies a lush field of green, and all around sweeps a sea of maroon and white. We head for our places. Shoulder to shoulder, we all stand, anxiously awaiting the commencement of play. Teams assemble along the sidelines of the field, and the captains gather at mid-field for the coin toss. As the starting players huddle on the field and the band plays the school fight song, we proudly consider why we are here: we are Texas Aggies, and this is Kyle Field. As we stand together, we remember the first time we learned about this place. We were on a campus tour, and our guides were two students: a Corps of Cadets unit commander and a student government officer. Here is what they told us and what we have since come to understand about this key campus landmark.

3   Kyle Field, built in 1927, is the home of the Texas Aggies and their football team. As numerous campus publications and members of the Corps of Cadets tell us, it was named after Edwin Jackson Kyle, former dean of agriculture and president of the Athletic Council. It has a seating capacity of 72,387, but can accommodate more than 78,000. The largest crowd in Kyle Field history was 78,773 in the game against the University of Texas in 1987. Kyle Field was expanded in 1967 and again in 1980. In 1987, an all-weather astroturf replaced the natural grass surface ("Kyle Field" 39).

4   The memories of football permeate the field. Many Aggie greats have made Kyle Field their home. John David Crowe, Ray Childress, Darren Lewis, Bucky Richardson, and many others have played here. The list goes on, but the spirit of the players remains the same. These players have come to Kyle Field with the hopes and dreams of Heisman trophies, Southwest Conference titles, and national championships. The field is the keeper of the drive, desires, and ambitions of past players and fans wanting their efforts to be recognized, wanting to be number one.

5   Yet, Kyle Field is more than just an arena where balls are thrown, fans scream, and bands play. It is also the scene of midnight yell practice where the night before a game, fans gather to exhibit the burning

spirit that resides within them for their team and university. This oval-shaped structure is the ultimate symbol of devotion and camaraderie that exists among the students and the former students of Texas A&M. This spirit has evolved since 1922, with the assistance of A&M's first 12th man, E. King Gill.

6   Outside the stadium stands the physical reminder of the Aggies' unrelenting support for their team. A copper statue of E. King Gill is erected at the north gates of Kyle Field, welcoming all Aggies to the game. This statue honors the memory of this man's readiness to support his team, and today he symbolizes the student body's involvement in the school and the team. In 1922, in the Dixie Classic, A&M coach Dana X. Bible became concerned about having enough players in the event of injuries. He called upon the basketball player, Gill. Without hesitation, Gill rushed down to the field and began to suit up. Although he was never put in the game, his willingness to help his team has come to mean something very special to all Aggies. It signified the true meaning of school spirit. E. King Gill set an important precedent. Because of him, Aggie fans stand up throughout entire football games. This gesture illustrates Aggies' willingness to support their team, in the tradition of Gill.

7   As we stand and cheer, we recall why this field is so significant to us. Kyle Field is a place on our university's campus where the spirit and support that Aggies have for their team, school, and most importantly, for each other is expressed boldly and proudly. The band is playing again, and we look down at the playing field, glad to know the history and meaning of Kyle Field. Would you like for us to give you a tour after the game?

Works Cited

Campus Tour. Texas A&M University. Summer 1989.

Dethloff, Henry C. *A Centennial History of Texas A&M: 1876–1976.* College Station: Texas A&M U, 1975.

"Kyle Field: Home of the Texas Aggies." *Texas A&M Football '91* Fall 1991: 39.

Reading Critically: Questions for Discussion

1. What sensory details do the writers provide to depict Kyle Field? Are the details sufficient to create a vivid picture of the football field? Explain your answer.
2. Is the title of the essay clear and appropriate? Why do you think it is or isn't?
3. How do the writers communicate the significance of their subject?
4. How do the writers convey enthusiasm for their subject?
5. Notice how the information sources have been cited. Can you determine which information comes from which of their sources? What revisions, if any, would you recommend?

PART IV

Expanding Your Repertoire: Referential Aim Writing

Referential Aim Writing: An Overview

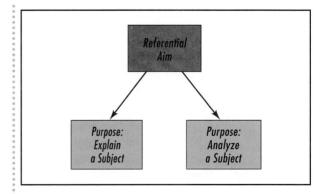

I was seven years old, standing in the kitchen, talking to my mother while she cooked dinner. I was holding a book and making my first effort at literary criticism.

"Do a lot of people like this Cinderella story?" I asked.

"Yes, I think so. Why?" she asked.

"Well, I've been thinking and I have two questions. First," I said, "the fairy godmother said that at midnight everything would turn back to the way it was and everything did except for the glass slipper that came off her foot and that Prince Charming found. Why didn't that glass slipper change back into one of her old shoes?"

"Maybe it's because the slipper came off her foot," my mother offered.

"No, the fairy godmother didn't say that Cinderella had to be wearing the stuff at midnight. She just said that Cinderella had until midnight to enjoy the ball and then everything would turn back to the way it was. But it didn't."

"What's your second question?"

"Second," I said, "I don't see why the prince doesn't know who Cinderella is until he puts the glass slipper on her foot. If he's so much in love with her, why doesn't he know who she is as soon as she enters the room?"

"Maybe it's because she's not wearing fancy clothes," suggested my mother.

"Yeah, but he said that he was in love with her, not with her clothes. Does he love her or does he love the way she looks? He should know right away that it's her. How are they going to live happily ever after if he can't tell who she is just because she's not wearing fancy clothes?"

"I can tell you've really thought about this."

"Yeah, I have. And I'm going to go think about some other stories," I said, leaving the kitchen. "I think there's something wrong with that Sleeping Beauty." (SD)

This episode is my earliest memory of using a referential aim. I was analyzing a story and explaining my interpretation. And I guess I never stopped explaining and analyzing. In school, I liked reading and discussing stories. As the editor of my high school newspaper, my job was to review stories that explained and analyzed school programs and policies. In college, my major was English because English majors were always reading stories and writing interpretations. Following graduation, I was editor of a company newspaper, writing and editing explanations and analyses of financial statistics, sales techniques, and security practices. In this book, I am still explaining and analyzing, but the subject here is writing itself.

In school and on the job, the writing that you do often has a referential aim. **Referential aim writing** is designed specifically to improve your reader's understanding of a subject. For example, you might report the results of your biology experiment, discuss the collapse of communism, determine the impact of industry consolidation on airline ticket prices, identify the relationship of higher speed limits to traffic fatalities, decipher the meaning of a novel, or summarize the available research on compressed natural gas refueling facilities. Or you might explain your company's vacation policy, review the regulations for ordering new equipment, discuss the causes of yesterday's mechanical failure, answer a letter asking for information on your company's hiring practices, or issue a news release announcing your promotion to division manager.

Your ability to communicate information on a subject is critical to your academic and professional success. The following chapters, therefore, offer opportunities to exercise and develop your referential writing abilities. This chapter describes the characteristics of referential writing. Keep in mind, however, that your referential composing processes are subject to various internal influences such as physical condition, emotional condition, and knowledge as well as external influences such as readers, task, time, environment, technology, and collaborators. No two writing experiences, as a consequence, are identical. No single, generic process of referential writing has the flexibility to address all the important variables of the composing situation.

REFERENTIAL AIM IN WRITING

In the communication triangle, referential aim writing emphasizes the subject. The writer's objective is to offer information that improves the reader's understanding of the subject. While composing and revising, the writer decides which information is likely to clarify the subject and considers how the organization of information, the words and illustrations, and the design of the pages might aid the reader's understanding.

A wide variety of referential aim writing is possible, including the following:

biographies	case histories
news reports	minutes of meetings
accident reports	court testimonies
research articles	historical analyses
medical diagnoses	laboratory or field experiments
investigative reports	literary and rhetorical analyses

textbooks   summaries

questionnaires   definitions

hypothesis-support essays   problem-solving alternatives

If your dominant aim is to offer information, your writing is chiefly referential, though subordinate expressive or persuasive aims are also possible. For example, you might be asked by the editor of your school's newspaper to investigate the causes of campus traffic accidents. Your investigative article is thus primarily referential. In writing the newspaper article, however, you might describe your experience of colliding with a truck while you were biking to your psychology class. Here your aim is expressive. You might also criticize campus police officers for failing to stop drivers who violate the speed limit. Here your aim is persuasive.

Your subordinate aims influence your choice of information as well as the way you organize, word, and display that information. For example, a photograph of you and your bike after the collision might be a particularly effective illustration for the narrative of your biking accident. In your criticism of campus police, you might choose several graphics to display various traffic accident statistics.

Keep in mind that your subordinate aims could change as you research, write, and revise. For example, after composing the narrative of your bicycle accident, you might decide that it contributes little to the reader's understanding of typical traffic accidents on campus. Or the process of composing your narrative might inspire you to interview several victims of campus traffic accidents and add their vivid stories to your newspaper article.

REFERENTIAL PURPOSES IN WRITING

If your dominant aim is referential, you also have to decide on the purpose of your referential writing. Ordinarily, the purpose of referential writing is to explain or analyze a subject.

You **explain a subject** in order to improve your reader's understanding of its meaning or characteristics. In a memo to your boss, for example, you might identify a specific job opening within your division of the company and summarize the qualifications of the candidate who has applied for the job.

You **analyze a subject** in order to improve your reader's understanding of its importance, composition, operation, causes, effects, similarities to or differences from associated subjects. In a flier to majors in your field, for example, you might discuss the origins and specifications of your school's new internship program or clarify the relationship of the internship program to the school's scholarship program.

Often, your referential aim writing will have subordinate purposes. You might be asked to write a medical article for a local magazine regarding the biological and psychological causes of alcohol addiction. Your primary objective would be to analyze your subject, but you would also have to explain certain aspects of alcohol addiction. You might consider it necessary to introduce and define a number of technical terms. Or you might decide to specify the typical personality traits of addicted individuals. In a different article, your primary objective might be to explain cerebral palsy to the families of afflicted children. In addition to identifying the characteristic behaviors (explanation), you might compare cerebral palsy and paralysis in order to distinguish the two neurological disorders (analysis).

It is important, however, that your integration of subordinate purposes be flexible. For example, you might start writing with the idea of introducing and defining the biological and psychological terminology regarding alcohol addiction. In revising, however, you could decide that this specialized vocabulary is itself difficult to explain: thus, if you simplified the language, you could focus on alcohol addiction, avoid unnecessary definitions, and aid the reader's understanding of your subject.

Each academic field offers you a variety of opportunities to explain or to analyze a subject. Consider, for example, the following possibilities:

- In a course on finance and accounting, identify the size of IBM by listing its operating revenues, net income, total assets, and number of employees. Specify and describe each of IBM's subsidiaries.

- For a biology class, explain the meaning of *polycythemia*. Compare and contrast this disease to leukemia.

- In a novels course, analyze the reliability of the narrators of Mary Shelley's *Frankenstein*. Identify the characteristics of a reliable narrator.

- In a political science class, report the findings of your political polling. Analyze why voters are supporting particular candidates.

- For a geography class, give a definition of *hypsography*. Discuss the importance of this field.

- For a film studies class, summarize the storyline of Spike Lee's *Do the Right Thing*. Discuss its similarities to his later films.

- In a business administration course, explain the meaning of *quality circles*. Describe how and why a company would adopt this practice.

- For a chemistry course, report the results of your experimentation with hydrochloric acid. Discuss the significance of your results.

By identifying the dominant and subordinate aims and purposes of your referential writing, you answer a critical question: Why am I writing? By asking this question and checking your answer to it periodically, you focus on your objective and compose more effectively and efficiently.

ANALYZING AND MAPPING THE REFERENTIAL RHETORICAL SITUATION

In addition to identifying why you are writing, you also have to consider the people you are addressing (using the audience continuum) and how you have acquired your information (using the knowledge continuum). By joining the audience continuum to the knowledge continuum, you develop a **map of the referential rhetorical situation.** This illustration serves as a visible reminder to you of your relationship to your audience and to your subject.

On the knowledge continuum, list key words regarding your subject and identify the sources of your knowledge, from knowledge by participation to knowledge by observation.

Use the audience continuum to indicate how close you are to your readers. On the narrow arcs positioned closer to the writer (you), identify the readers who are like you in background, education, experience, or occupation; on the wider arcs, identify the readers who are different from you. On each arc, also specify your readers' level of motivation, from those who might consider your list of key words important to those who might see nothing extraordinary or significant in the information you have to offer.

For example, Figure 11.1 presents Lisa Haley's map of the knowledge and audience continua. Lisa learns about the influence of cubism on the poetry of William Carlos Williams by observation, and therefore she lists facts uncovered through her research on the "knowledge by observation" side of the knowledge continuum. Lisa never actually reads any of Williams's poems on her own; instead, she reports other people's interpretations of his poetry and cites the same lines that her sources mention. How important would documentation be in her text? Why?

Her essay, "The Cubist Imagination," is intended for an audience of college students. Lisa classifies her readers according to their majors. While Lisa thinks that English and fine arts majors will be motivated and interested in this essay, she imagines that students in other majors will be indifferent to her subject, requiring her to find ways to engage these readers. What kinds of strategies do you think Lisa would use to interest her audience?

In college and on the job, typically you are assigned subjects for writing. In history class, your teacher might ask you to discuss the life of Martin Luther King, Jr. Your job is to decide how you have knowledge of this man, how much you already know, and how you might find out more about him. Do you have family or friends who were acquainted with Martin Luther King, who recall listening to his speeches, or who remember the day he was assassinated? Can you examine pertinent newspaper stories of the 1950s and 1960s? Are biographies of Martin Luther King available at the library? Similarly, on the job your boss might direct you to analyze the cause of yesterday's chemical spill. Again you have to decide how you have knowledge of this accident, how much you already know,

Read More About It

See Chapter 4, pp. 85–93.

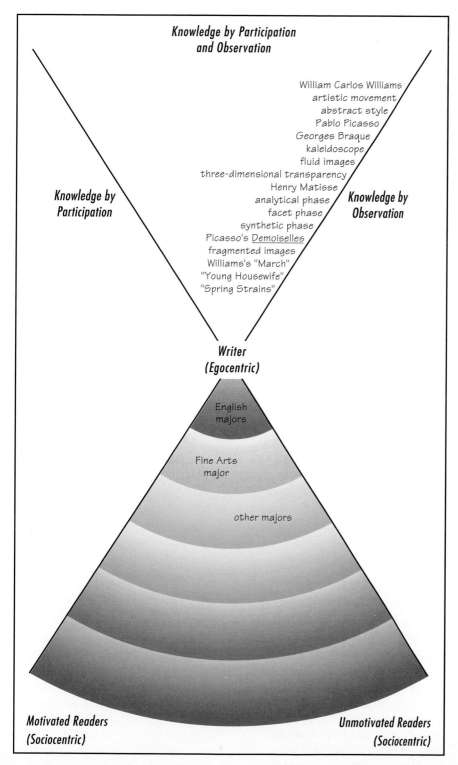

Figure 11.1
Mapping Lisa's rhetorical situation

and how you might acquire additional information. Did you witness the spill? Did you speak to people who did? Can you review company records to determine the frequency of chemical spills or the causes of earlier spills? What do police and fire investigators claim is the cause?

If you have a choice of subjects, however, you ordinarily choose a subject that is familiar to you, either through participation or observation. For example, because you have knowledge by participation, you might choose to explain the meaning of *driver's education* or analyze the operation of the internal combustion engine. If you have been reading magazine and newspaper articles on the subject of AIDS, you have knowledge of the disease through observation and might choose to explain or analyze this subject. Or given your knowledge by participation and observation, you might choose to explain standardized testing or analyze public schooling versus private schooling.

RESEARCHING AND DISCOVERING REFERENTIAL INFORMATION

Because the objective of referential writing is to improve your reader's understanding of your subject, you have to research and discover information that establishes your credibility, develops and clarifies your thesis, and motivates your audience.

Establishing Credibility

A writer establishes credibility by identifying his or her qualifications to discuss a subject or by displaying knowledge of the subject. For example, if you are composing a historical analysis of immigration laws, you could check family records or brainstorm to develop a list of your credentials:

- you are a history major
- you are a child of immigrants
- you have a part-time job as a law clerk
- you have interviewed clients regarding their immigration experiences
- you have studied several books on this subject

To display your knowledge of your subject, you might cite sources of information and thus prove your familiarity with the available research. Using and spelling technical terminology appropriately is also critical to your credibility. In this case, it would be important for you to distinguish between *immigration* and *emigration* and to check the spelling of these two words; otherwise, readers who know the difference might start to question your authority.

Invention Guide for Referential Writing

Aim and Purpose

1. What is your writing task?
2. Are you writing individually or collaboratively?
3. Is the text's dominant aim referential?
4. Are there subordinate aims? What are they and how do they affect the information in the text?
5. What is your purpose for writing? What specifically do you want your text to accomplish? Does your purpose satisfy the requirements of your writing task?
6. Are there subordinate purposes? What are they and how do they affect the information in the text?

Mapping the Rhetorical Situation: Subject and the Knowledge Continuum

1. What is your subject?
2. What is your relationship to the subject? That is, will your point of view in your essay be that of a participant, observer, or participant-observer?
3. Map your knowledge on the knowledge continuum by listing key words regarding your subject. Mapping is an ongoing process: continue to revise and refine your map as you learn more about your subject.

Mapping the Rhetorical Situation: Readers and the Audience Continuum

1. What is the demographic profile of your readers (age; gender; social, economic, and educational levels; personal and professional backgrounds and experiences; cultural and situational factors and contexts)? How will their profile affect their responses to the subject and text?
2. Select representative members of your audience, and role-play to determine the following:

   - readers' motives for reading your text
   - readers' enthusiasm about your subject
   - readers' sense that your subject is timely

3. How can you help readers to process and interpret your text more effectively (organization, memory cues, language, and visual signposts)?

4. Map your readers on the audience continuum. Mapping is an ongoing process: continue to revise and refine your map as you learn more about your audience.

Information: Research and Discovery

1. What kind of knowledge does your writing task require?

   Knowledge by participation (personal records, brainstorming, pentad, classical topics, visualizing, and computer-assisted invention)—documentation and bibliography usually unnecessary

   Knowledge by observation (interviews, questionnaires, and library resources)—documentation and bibliography usually necessary

   Knowledge by participation and observation (combination of those identified above)—documentation and bibliography usually necessary

2. Which research strategies will you use to locate and generate information? Why?

3. How will you establish your credibility?

4. How will you develop and clarify your thesis?

   - What is your thesis or major assertion?
   - What is the information that supports your thesis? Is it sufficient? Plausible? Pertinent?

5. How will you motivate your audience to digest or use your explanation or analysis? How will you communicate that this information is easy to read and important to know?

Developing and Clarifying Your Thesis

In referential writing, the thesis is the writer's major assertion regarding the subject. If you were composing a literary analysis of a novel, for example, you might focus your discussion and discover your thesis by asking and answering specific questions (see Table 11.1). If you asked "What is the significance of the setting?" you might answer that the setting symbolizes a decaying society. This answer emphasizes your key idea or insight and unifies the supporting details of your interpretation.

Table 11.1 Questions for a Literary Analysis

Meaning

What does the story reveal about its subject? What insights or impressions does it offer? Does the story have a specific message? If so, how would you summarize it?

Type of Story

How might you categorize this story? Is it the story of a journey, coming of age, romance, individual versus society, good versus evil? How is this story similar to other stories of this type? How is this story different from other stories of this type?

Title

What is the significance of the title? Does it have several meanings? How does the title contribute to the reader's understanding of the plot, characterization, setting, or meaning of the story?

Point of View

Who is the narrator? Is the narrator third person omniscient (a godlike observer who sees and knows all)? Why is this type of narrator used? Is the narrator third person limited (a human observer)? If so, is the narrator reliable? Is he or she biased? How do you know? Why is this type of narrator used? Is the narrator first person (a human participant)? If so, is the narrator reliable? Is he or she biased? How do you know? Why is this type of narrator used?

Plot

Which sections of the story constitute the major stages of plot (introduction, rising action, climax, falling action, resolution)? Which stages of plot are elaborated? Which are abbreviated? Why? How is the plot developed? Through the narrator's description and commentary? Through dialogue? Through the actions of the characters? What is the significance of a specific occurrence or episode? How does this occurrence or episode contribute to the reader's understanding of the plot, characterization, setting, or meaning of the story?

Table 11.1 Questions for a Literary Analysis *(continued)*

Narrative Organization	How is the narrative organized? Is it a simple chronological series or a complex organization? Why is the narrative organized the way it is? How does the narrative organization contribute to the plot, characterization, setting, or meaning of the story?
Characterization	How are characters developed? Through the narrator's description and commentary? Through dialogue? Through the actions of the characters? Which characters are flat or one-dimensional? Which characters are round or three-dimensional? Which characters are static? Which characters are dynamic? How do the dynamic characters change? Who or what causes them to change? What is the significance of a specific descriptive detail regarding a character? How does it contribute to the reader's understanding of the character?
Setting	When and where does the story occur? What is the significance of this setting? What is the significance of a specific descriptive detail? How does it contribute to the reader's understanding of the setting? How does the setting contribute to the plot, characterization, or meaning of the story?
Images	Does the story utilize a repetition of images (such as specific colors, noises, or objects)? If so, which images occur? How do the images contribute to the reader's understanding of the plot, characters, setting, or meaning of the story?
Influences	What are the social, political, historical, economic, or biographical circumstances surrounding the writing or the reading of the story? How might the writer's attitudes regarding such issues as sex, race, religion, liberty, or violence influence the plot, characterization, setting, or meaning of the story? How might a reader's attitudes influence his or her interpretation of the story?

You develop and clarify your thesis by offering supporting information. If you were explaining your school's registration process, for example, personal records and brainstorming might give you insights on this subject. Or you could analyze the process according to the five questions (who? what? when and where? how? why?). The classical topics of definition, classification and division, process, cause and effect, and comparison and contrast might lead you to important ideas. A diagram of the registration process is also a possibility. In addition to knowledge by participation, you might integrate knowledge by observation; for example, you could interview school officials, distribute a questionnaire to students, or locate appropriate newspaper articles. Your job here is to research and discover information that is sufficient, plausible, and pertinent.

Your information is **sufficient** if you answer all the questions your audience is likely to have regarding your subject. Analyze your audience to determine how much they need to know about your subject and how much they already know. You want to avoid boring or intimidating your audience with too much information or confusing them with too little. Whenever you are in doubt, however, choose to include the information. If you do, your explanation or analysis might be dull, but at least you have improved or reinforced your audience's knowledge of your subject. If you omit the information and it proves necessary to their understanding, you essentially paralyze your readers and leave them incapable of digesting or using the information you have given.

For example, if you were the manager of a clothing store, you might compose a memo to your salesclerks regarding the store's upcoming sales of men's and women's swimsuits. In your memo, you might mention the importance of strictly following the store's policy on the sale of swimsuits. Inexperienced salesclerks might have no knowledge of this policy and might be paralyzed without a thorough explanation of it. You could pause to explain the policy, but experienced salesclerks will consider your explanation unnecessary and boring; they already know that sales of swimsuits are final and that refunds or exchanges are prohibited. Nevertheless, if you are unfamiliar with the level of experience of the salesclerks, or if different clerks have different levels of experience, the wise choice is to offer the explanation.

Your information is **plausible** if you identify reliable sources of information and avoid inconsistent or contradictory ideas. Reliable sources of information such as rigorous experiments, prestigious newspapers, professional journals, and interviews with subject specialists improve the believability of your referential writing. If it is your experience that a source typically supplies correct information or if the source has a reputation for accuracy and integrity, it is likely that the information is correct. Conversely, inconsistent or contradictory ideas raise questions regarding the accuracy of your explanation or analysis. For example, if a news release declares that a company's new recycling program is exhaustive and comprehensive, but proceeds to explain that the program covers only the recycling of paper, the news release loses believability.

Read More About It

See Chapter 4,
pp. 94–115.

Your information is **pertinent** if you focus the audience's attention on your thesis and avoid unnecessary details or digressions. Once again, you need to be sensitive to your audience as you decide which information is essential and which is distracting, which information clarifies your explanation or analysis and which interferes with your audience's understanding. If you were explaining wireless telegraphy to engineering majors, you might briefly identify its inventor, Guglielmo Marconi. You probably would not need to mention his receipt of the 1909 Nobel Peace Prize, however, because this information does little to improve your audience's understanding of wireless telegraphy.

Motivating Your Audience

In addition to establishing credibility and developing a thesis, you also have to solicit the audience's attention to your explanation or analysis. Readers will not automatically examine every piece of referential writing that is offered to them. Your job is to motivate your audience to read your explanation or analysis and add it to their previous knowledge of the subject. You motivate your audience to do so by emphasizing the simplicity and the significance of your information; that is, you have to show that your explanation or analysis is easy to read and important to know.

To emphasize the simplicity of your explanation or analysis, offer examples and illustrations. By making your ideas vivid and easily accessible, examples and illustrations improve the clarity and memorability of your explanation or analysis. **Examples** identify practical applications or specific occurrences. **Illustrations** display vital characteristics of your subject. For example, if you were analyzing your company's economic situation, you might give examples of this year's major successes and failures and design tables and figures to display appropriate statistics. If you were explaining the meaning of the word *acronym* (a word derived by combining the initial letters of a series of words), you might give examples such as *scuba* or *radar* and illustrate their derivation by highlighting the pertinent letters (*self-contained **u**nderwater **b**reathing **a**pparatus; **ra**dio detecting **a**nd **r**anging*).

Similarly, **narratives** dramatize and personalize your information, making your explanation or analysis easier to understand and remember. If you were describing the operation of a commercial printing company, for example, you might describe how a particular book was printed, guiding your readers through each stage of the printing process.

You might also **compare and contrast** your subject to one that is more familiar to your audience, thus simplifying your discussion and easing understanding. You could, for example, explain how a color photocopier is similar to and different from a black-and-white photocopier.

Or you might consider **division** of the subject to allow your audience to digest it more easily. For example, if you discussed the printing

Arrangement Guide for Referential Writing

Evidence: Establishing Unity

1. Has your research yielded sufficient, plausible, and pertinent information to support your thesis?
2. How do your research data reflect the three rhetorical appeals: ethos, logos, and pathos?
3. How does your research shape your thesis statement (major assertion)? Is your thesis statement specific and concrete? Focused and feasible? Interesting?
4. How do the patterns of organization in your text help readers see and follow the logic and approach to your subject? Have you chosen sequential organization (chronological, spatial, hierarchical), categorical organization, or a combination of the two? Why?

Discourse Blocs: Developing Ideas

1. What is the internal structure of your text? Identify and outline the discourse blocs in your essay.
2. What modes of development have you used within the discourse blocs? Why?
3. What functions do the various discourse blocs serve (title, introduction, transitional blocs, conclusion)?

Coherence and Cohesion: Making Connections

1. Have you connected sentences by using repetition, substitution, and transitions?
2. Do you use parallelism for coordinated and listed items? To reinforce ideas of equal importance or similar meaning?

Outlining: Tracing Your Path

1. Have you written an outline, either before or after you've drafted your text? Does it seem logical and clear?
2. How will you refine the design and development of your text in the next draft?

process, your analysis would have sections for typesetting, graphic design, page proofs, printing, and folding and binding.

The easier your explanation or analysis is, the more likely your audience is to incorporate it. The more difficult your explanation or analysis, however, the more you need to emphasize the importance of your information. Audiences will tolerate difficult reading, but only if it is justified. If you believe your writing will be difficult to read, therefore, you have several choices:

- Discuss why your audience needs the information you are offering.
- Describe how your audience will benefit from reading your writing.
- Show how your audience can use your explanation or analysis.
- Integrate quotations or statistics that emphasize the importance of your subject.

To discover the information necessary to motivate your audience, consider brainstorming to develop a list of examples. Analyze your subject according to the five questions (who? what? when and where? how? and why?) to develop appropriate narratives. Examine the classical topics (definition, classification and division, process, cause and effect, comparison and contrast) to determine appropriate divisions of your topic or similarities and differences. Visualize your subject to discover effective illustrations. Interview sources for provocative statistics or quotations. Check books, newspapers, and magazines for additional examples, illustrations, statistics, and quotations.

COMPOSING REFERENTIAL AIM WRITING

In this chapter, we have explained two basic purposes of referential writing—explaining and analyzing—and the characteristics of the referential rhetorical situation. By reading this chapter, you have gained knowledge through observation. A clear understanding of referential writing, however, comes through participation also. The following chapters, therefore, give you opportunities to explain and analyze. As you practice referential writing, keep a portfolio of the maps of your rhetorical situations and the various versions of your essays. This portfolio is a log of your journey through the territory of referential rhetoric, identifying the types of audiences you have addressed and the sources of knowledge that you have investigated.

Style Guide for Referential Writing

1. *Individuality*. How much of you is in this sample of referential writing? What features of style indicate your personal likes and dislikes regarding wording, sentence structure, spelling, and punctuation?

2. *Time*. How does the time period during which you are writing influence your referential style? Does your age or your audience's age influence your style? How?

3. *Dialect*. Are you using a local dialect or a universal dialect? Why? What features of style are characteristic of the dialect you are using?

4. *Collaboration*. Is your referential writing collaborative? How have editors or coauthors influenced your style?

5. *Subject*. What is the subject of your referential writing? What specialized wording or phrasing is typical of referential writing on this subject? How does this subject influence the spelling and punctuation of your referential writing?

6. *Type of document*. What type of referential writing are you composing? What is its common function? How will your audience use this referential writing? What features of style are characteristic of this type of referential writing?

7. *Relationship to audience*. What is your relationship with your audience? Is a formal or informal style appropriate? What is the appropriate degree of formality or informality? How does this degree of formality or informality influence your referential style?

Memory and Delivery Guide for Referential Writing

1. Is your referential writing handwritten, typewritten, or computerized? Why? If handwritten, is your handwriting legible? If typewritten, do you have typographical choices of design, style, and size? If computerized, are you designing a paper copy or a screen copy?

2. Does the typography aid reading? How do your typographical choices establish your credibility, clarify your thesis, and motivate your audience? Consider your choices regarding

   - typeface
   - type style
   - type size
   - upper- and lowercase letters
   - leading
   - line length
   - alignment

3. Are illustrations necessary? If so, are tables or figures appropriate? If you include tables, does the typography of the tables aid their reading? If you include figures, which of the following are appropriate?

   - line graphs
   - column graphs
   - bar graphs
   - pie charts
   - organization charts
   - flow charts
   - diagrams
   - drawings
   - photographs

   Do the figures emphasize appropriate information? Is the visual display ethical? How do your illustrations establish your credibility, clarify your thesis, and motivate your audience?

4. Is white space used effectively?

5. What is the appropriate page design (essay, book, letter, memo, or circular)?

Repertoire Focus: Explaining a Subject

In any type of writing, you will often explain key ideas or objects, to develop not only a shared vocabulary but also shared meanings with your readers. When your purpose is to explain a subject, you present information about an idea or object so that readers gain further understanding of your subject and its importance, so that they begin to know it as you know it.

REPERTOIRE WRITING TASK: EXPLANATION

Select a subject that interests you and that will appeal to either readers much like you; a general college audience; a general adult readership; or a specific campus, community, professional group. Consider carefully what your readers already know about this idea or object and how your essay might further their understanding of its relevance or importance.

Three variations of this writing task follow, based upon the different ways you can "know" about your subject.

Knowledge by Participation

Write an essay that explains the meaning, influence, and significance of a key idea or object that you came to know about through direct experience.

Knowledge by Observation

Write an essay that explains the meaning, influence, and significance of a key idea or object that you came to know about through indirect means (through interviews, reading, television, or another medium). Your subject should be one that others have written about, yielding some form of published biographical, social, or historical information that you can integrate into your essay.

Knowledge by Participation and Observation

Write an essay that explains the meaning, influence, and significance of a key idea or object that you came to know about through direct experience as well as through indirect means (through interviews, reading, television, or another medium). Your subject should be one that others have written about, yielding some form of published biographical, social, or historical information that you can integrate into your essay.

REPERTORY COMPANY OF STUDENT WRITERS: THEIR RESPONSES TO THE TASK

As you begin thinking about this writing task, you may find it helpful to meet other student writers and read their essays, written in response to the same assignment. All of these student writers worked within their own writing communities or groups; their groups met regularly to talk, read, think, and write with one another. They also reviewed their journal responses to assignments in Chapters 1–7—responses that may have reminded them of writing ideas. Interacting within their writing communities, these writers exchanged ideas and strengthened their sense of what being a writer means.

To provide you with some additional context, we've included journal entries, a map of the rhetorical situation—the knowledge continuum and audience continuum—and research strategies for each essay. You'll also find some questions for discussion and analysis after each selection.

KNOWLEDGE BY PARTICIPATION

The first essay, "I'm So Hungry, I'm Starving to Death," written by Lisa Niels, is about anorexia nervosa. Lisa learned about this condition through her sister, Helena, who almost died of self-starvation. Despite the fact that Lisa writes about her sister and explains what anorexia is and what it can do to its victims from the perspective of the writer as participant (i.e., family member), she keeps her emotions in check. Why does she seem so cool, even when Helena is in the hospital? Lisa realizes that the voice in the paper is "we," Helena's family, and so she knows that she cannot mask her personal emotional involvement in this subject; however, she wants her readers to understand the need to recognize anorexics and help them seek help, which is what her family failed to do. In order to gain credibility and ensure that readers will follow her advice, Lisa tries to maintain a more informational, less emotional tone in her essay. Do you think her strategy works? Why or why not?

Reviewing Journal Entries

Accounts of how people write are usually noteworthy for what they say. Lisa's journal entries for her essay are interesting because of what they don't say, however. Instead of commenting on her strategies or the members of her focus group, she mentions what a positive experience writing about her sister was. Lisa didn't write many entries regarding this essay, and the following samples are typical:

JOURNAL

I have been so interested in this subject. It feels good to write about something I know personally even if the subject makes me write about Helena. I know Helena and the disorder. I can write this paper.

I feel very confident about my knowledge in this area. On paper, I can talk about anorexia in this paper very comfortably. Although I thoroughly enjoyed writing the expressive paper, this one was much easier for me to write. It came very natural to me—probably because I had knowledge of what Helena went through first-hand.

———————————

I feel that writing this essay was a good experience because it helped me understand anorexia and my sister better. Maybe I can deal with them a little more each time. Or write or talk about them a little more.

Lisa was extremely reluctant to talk about Helena in her group or to her teacher. Thinking that this subject was too painful or awkward for her to write about, some group members suggested she switch to another subject. But Lisa refused, saying that although she might not be able to talk aloud about her sister's condition, she found it much easier to write an academic paper about it. Her greatest difficulty was in getting started—in writing the introduction.

Throughout the development of her essay, Lisa reminded her focus group that she wanted to write this essay, and she wanted it written in this way. Have you ever felt this way about a subject you've written about? Why? How did this feeling influence your writing processes?

Mapping Lisa's Referential Rhetorical Situation

Lisa's map of her rhetorical situation for this essay appears in Figure 12.1. Lisa learns about anorexia nervosa through her firsthand knowledge of someone who suffers from the condition: her sister Helena. Accordingly, she lists the details of her experience on the "knowledge by participation" side on the knowledge continuum. Lisa relies on her memories and personal experiences to serve as her research and sources.

Lisa's audience consists of other college students who may have an anorexic friend or relative. She imagines that her readers are 18 to 25 years old and much like most college students. While she is reticent about revealing her sister's illness, she thinks her readers need to know how to identify and deal with this all-too-common problem. In this way, Lisa's essay is a referential text that has a subordinate persuasive aim. She wants readers to feel compassion for the victim as well as her family and friends. Lisa thinks that half of her audience—women college students—will be highly motivated and interested in her subject, whereas the other half—male college students—will be somewhat less motivated and interested. Her map of the audience continuum reflects her audience analysis.

Anorexia Nervosa

(Draft 1)

1   Past researchers and scientists have agreed upon five basic stages that all individuals pass through in life. These five stages include birth,

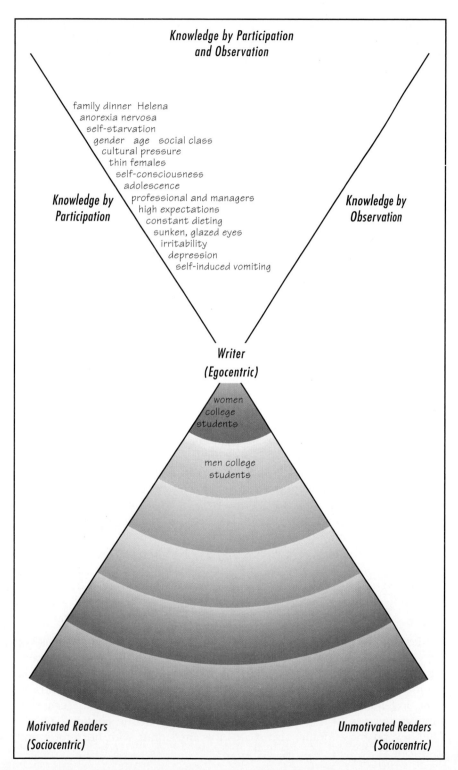

Figure 12.1
Mapping Lisa's rhetorical situation

growth, maturation, decline, and death. Although I agree that these are five of the most important stages of the human life, I feel that these researchers and scientists have failed to include one very important phase of life. This important stage that has been overlooked is adolescence.

2   As I recall, this is a very difficult period of life in which teenagers are faced with various different pressures. Because the stress and peer pressure associated with this stage of life is so tremendous, many adolescents resort to dysfunctional means of coping with this pressure.

3   One of the most dysfunctional means that adolescents use as a means of coping with this pressure is an eating disorder known as anorexia nervosa.

Lisa stops writing at this point and prints the following words in large letters at the bottom of the page: "Too much emphasis on adolescence→Needs to get more to point." She comments that she has not found a way to introduce Helena, and that she is worried that her essay sounds dry and boring. She refuses to go beyond the introductory discourse bloc until the beginning feels "right." With her group's encouragement, Lisa composes another introduction.

Untitled

(Draft 2)

1   As another Wednesday evening wound to a close, my family and I flocked around the kitchen table like a pack of hungry wolves. We hurriedly passed the plates back and forth among each other until everyone had received a heaping portion of everything on the table. After filling our plates, a quiet hush fell upon the table as we commenced filling our stomachs. Everyone except Helena. She nervously chattered with only the smallest portion of food on her plate.

2   As the meal ended, everyone made room for the last bite, leaving our plates spotless. Helena was busy forcing down her third bite. After dessert was served, she was in the bathroom throwing up the three bites of food she had reluctantly consumed earlier.

Lisa shows her introduction to her focus group, explaining her use of the intentional fragment "Everyone except Helena." She asks her group members what they think of using the fragment throughout the opening paragraph, expressing concern that the repetition might lull readers to sleep instead of creating a meaningful emphasis and rhythm. Her group supports her use of this tactic and recommends that she continue with it. After several more drafts, Lisa shares this final draft with her group and instructor:

I'm So Hungry, I'm Starving to Death

(Draft 5—Final Draft)

1   As another Wednesday evening wound to a close, my family and I gathered around the kitchen table like a pack of hungry wolves. Everyone except Helena. She was always last to arrive at the table. We hurriedly shuffled plates back and forth among each other until everyone had received a heaping portion from each dish. Everyone except Helena. After filling our plates, a quiet hush fell over the table as we filled our stomachs. Everyone except Helena. She nervously chattered with only the smallest serving of food on her plate. As the meal ended, everyone savored the last bite, leaving our plates relatively spotless. Everyone except Helena. She was busy forcing down her third bite. After dessert was served, everyone helped clean the kitchen. Everyone except Helena. She was in the bathroom throwing up the three bites of food she had reluctantly consumed earlier.

2   Helena's behavior is characteristic of anorexia nervosa, a psychological eating disorder in which a person achieves self-satisfaction through self-starvation. The term *anorexia* means loss of appetite; however, this is not necessarily typical of the disorder. In fact, most anorexics do have an appetite, but they suppress it to the point of starvation. It seems to me that the most common factors contributing to the onset of anorexia are gender and age.

3   I have noticed myself an increased incidence of anorexia among females. This high occurrence among females is probably highly related to the fact that females are more apt to diet because of cultural pressures to be thin. In addition, the earlier onset of puberty in females causes the adolescent female to be more aware of her weight and more self-conscious, which can later lead to eating disorders such as anorexia. This fact can be illustrated by Helena's case. As an adolescent female, she too faced these cultural pressures to be thin, which led to her increasing degree of self-consciousness concerning her weight. As a result of this self-consciousness and other stressing factors of being fifteen, Helena developed anorexia just as many other teenaged females do.

4   As can also be seen from Helena's case, age is an important variable contributing to the onset of this particular disorder. Adolescence is a very difficult period for most young people. As many of us know from experience, adolescents are faced with a host of pressures including personal insecurities, social influences, and family tensions. When these pressures are combined with any major change or problem over which the teen has little or no control, she feels as if every aspect of her life is out of control. Within two months, Helena lost her grandmother, and her boyfriend of three years broke up with her. Because Helena had no control over these traumatic events, she began to feel as if her whole life was out of control. Unfortunately, she came to feel that her weight was the only aspect of her life that she had power over. Like many other teenaged females who

encounter changes and problems, Helena became obsessed with controlling her weight, and this obsessive pattern of behavior eventually developed into anorexia.

5   As Helena's food intake decreased, she displayed a number of symptoms that we gradually became aware of. For example, we noticed Helena's eating behavior, which ranged from her persistent need to diet to her complete starvation, one of the earliest signs of this disorder. She began to waste away, her eyes became sunken and glazed over, while her abdomen began to hollow out. At the same time, Helena denied her skeletal appearance and insisted that she was still overweight. She lamented that, when she looked in the mirror, she saw a fat, ugly person. Besides being blind to her physical condition, Helena often became hostile and irritable toward her family and friends. Problems between her and us worsened, and we all began to bicker constantly. In addition to this irritability and hostility, we witnessed Helena's bouts of depression and her preoccupation with doing strenuous physical exercise. Finally, the most detrimental behavior that Helena engaged in was self-induced vomiting, which usually occurred immediately after she ate any amount of food. Helena fled to the bathroom directly after each meal, often staying there for extended periods of time. We witnessed Helena's behavior, but we thought she was just "going through a phase." If we had recognized her behavior patterns in the early stages, we might have helped her get treatment and recover before her physical condition became life threatening. But we didn't. We saw her every day. We lived in the same house. We saw Helena change. But we didn't say or do anything about her or to her about this change.

6   As yet another Wednesday evening came to a close, my family and I assembled in the kitchen to prepare supper. Everyone except Helena. When the bread was done, we all seated ourselves around the table to enjoy a hearty meal. Everyone except Helena. After we ate and cleaned the dishes, we all sat around the table discussing the day's events. Everyone except Helena. As we carried on with the daily routine of our lives, Helena was in the hospital, slowly recovering from the advanced stages of anorexia because we, her loving family, failed to recognize the symptoms and characteristics of this disorder.

7   Do you know Helena? Does she live at your house or down the street? Does she go to school or work with you? Talk to her. Encourage her to seek help. Go with her to counseling or to a doctor's office if accompanying her will assure she gets there. She doesn't know it, but she needs help—before it's too late.

Reading Critically: Questions for Discussion

1. Does Lisa satisfactorily explain the meaning of *anorexia nervosa?*
2. How does Lisa establish her credibility to write on this subject?

3. How does Lisa motivate her audience to read her explanation of this subject?

4. Is the last paragraph necessary? Does Lisa's essay have more impact without it? Does the essay do a better job of explaining the subject without that last paragraph? Explain your answers.

KNOWLEDGE BY OBSERVATION

Wendy Greener researches the Myers-Briggs Type Indicator, a test that indicates an individual's personality type (e.g., introvert or extrovert), in order to write the next essay, "Discovering Yourself with Myers-Briggs." This test is used widely in companies like AT&T, Exxon, General Electric, and Honeywell to give employees a greater awareness of their personality traits and to help them use this awareness to strengthen their decision making and team efforts. In this essay, Wendy adopts the observer point of view and uses the APA system of documentation to cite her sources.

Reviewing Journal Entries

Wendy's journal entries show how she selects her subject, one that she likes and finds lots of research materials about. In these entries, she also reveals how she researches and thinks about organizing her essay. Here are some excerpts from Wendy's journal:

JOURNAL

I'm going to write an explanation of a concept, but I want to really learn something that I can apply in some other classes. Maybe I should try to select a subject that I will have to research then. What is something that I want and need to learn about? My professor says I should think about finding topics this way: If you could learn about any three things, what would they be? Imagine that there is no time limit or anything. What would I want to know about?

I've got to brainstorm to find a potential concept to write my paper on. I am a speech major, and in the past, one of my profs has deemed me "very sanguine." I never understood this term until I inquired about it and I found out that it was a personality type. For my paper, I think I'd like to further research the four different personality types. I'd like to know how they were thought up and how they're used in different settings, especially in business and government.

After today's class, I really feel confident about my topic for this referential essay. Tonight, I went out and purchased a book by Francis Littauer called Personality Plus. *It contains the personality profile test, too—I'm anxious to get started reading it.*

I discussed my topic with my group. They seemed to think it would be a unique and interesting subject to research. I told them about this quote I found: "We are born with our own set of temperament traits, and these traits show up very early in our lives." We must have spent half of our time talking about experiences and sources that showed how this quote applies to us. I'm excited about this research!

Wendy, you've got to narrow your focus. What's your thesis? First, I need to define personality. . . . I need an attention-getter. Four types: sanguine, melancholy, phlegmatic, choleric.

Personality Plus: Sanguine, melancholy, phlegmatic, choleric—What do these words mean? They sound like diseases or no, maybe they are new kinds of cars which are coming out in 1994? These are the first thoughts that came to my mind when I heard these terms.
The concept of the four different personality types is not a new issue. Socrates derived the four humors of the body, I think.

Organizational notes:
Opening scenario: how I came to know of the concept, history of the four temperaments, explanation of them. Why it is important to know about them? Learn to know yourself and work with others better. Conclusion? The four personality types derived by Socrates have their own unique characteristics. Is this a good thesis? I'll ask my group at the next class.

Talked with my group and my teacher about my ideas, and everybody nixed them. They say they didn't, but I think they did. They said I needed to do more research and not just focus on Socrates. Wasn't there more I could do with personality than look at "pop psychology" books?
My teacher had a good idea, even if I didn't appreciate it at the time. She said I might think about applications of personality types—like how they are used and all. Then maybe I'd find my focus. I'm very frustrated, but I've got to put that behind me.
I guess I should be glad everybody told me what they honestly thought before I did anymore research on "pop psych" and tried to write that paper. I'd rather know the painful truth now and have time to do something better. I'm going to sit down and really plan out my strategy for tackling this essay. I know I can do it.

Myers-Briggs. I went to the library and did a key word search. I got lots of help from a student worker at the computer reference desk. He asked me to make out a list of descriptors or key words related to my subject, so I gave him a few words: personality, types, sanguine, measures of personality, and so on. He gave me a print-out. Wow. I'm surprised at the number of sources on the list.

I've done some research on personality types and psychology, and I've got gobs of information. I've found out about a test called the Myers-Briggs Type Indicator. It's now my real subject—my main focus. I never realized how much information is out on this subject, especially on one test. I will have to thumb through my sources this week and decide which ones to take notes on!

After meeting with my teacher, I feel a little more reassured about this subject. I've been taking notes for days now, and I'm feeling like I can start explaining this Myers-Briggs test to someone else. Guess I should start thinking about who my audience for this essay really is.

I should write for my peers. But who else would I want or would possibly be asked to read this explanation? People who are in government or business or counseling or education? Why would they want to know about this test? What can I tell them? What tone should I have in the essay? Serious, funny, scholarly? Nope.

My group read my draft, and I got lots of helpful advice. As far as structure, I have a well-organized piece. I need to find a closing idea which will tie my topic together. After this my paper will be done. The main body of my paper is the best part of my paper because it is factual and informative. My peers' papers are going well, but everybody is at a different stage of writing. We all work at different rates.

I've polished and revised my essay. I added a few more transitions and added a conclusion that I think is a real clincher to the piece. My group read my paper. I made a few changes in mechanics. Kristi said I needed to check my documentation style, but I'm not sure what she means—something about APA or MLA being confused. I'll type up the final draft with these changes and it will be ready.

Mapping Wendy's Referential Rhetorical Situation

Because Wendy's knowledge of her subject is gained by observation, she lists her details on the "knowledge by observation" side of the continuum. Figure 12.2 shows her map of her rhetorical situation.

Wendy intends her essay for an audience of college students, business managers, career counselors, and people in other occupations. She thinks that college students will be highly motivated and interested in her

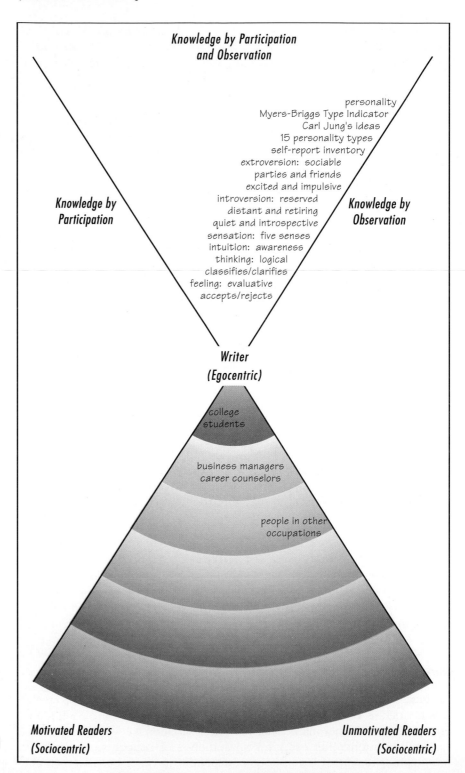

Figure 12.2
Mapping Wendy's rhetorical situation

subject: after all, she is. Wendy considers that business managers and career counselors will also be interested in this personality test because of its widespread application in corporate settings and in job placement decision making. She believes that readers in other occupations, however, will show little interest in the Myers-Briggs Type Indicator.

Discovering Yourself with Myers-Briggs

(Draft 3—Final Draft)

1   You've just been handed a questionnaire asking you to identify which answer comes closer to telling how you usually feel or act. Here are three of the questions:

  1. Are you usually
      a. a "good mixer" or
      b. rather quiet and reserved?

  2. Would you rather be considered
      a. a practical person, or
      b. an ingenious person?

  3. Do you usually
      a. show your feelings freely, or
      b. keep your feelings to yourself?

These are interesting questions, but what are they attempting to measure? The answer, simply stated, is your personality. Personality, as defined by Larry A. Hjelle, Professor of Psychology at Villanova University, is a "stable set of characteristics and tendencies that determine those commonalties and differences in the psychological behavior (thoughts, feelings, and actions) of people that have continuity in time" (Ziegler, 1978, p. 4).

2   The method of determining one's personality has been debated for years. A reliable guide to discovering personality types is the Myers-Briggs Type Indicator, a test that identifies an individual's personality based on three dimensions: extroversion versus introversion, sensation versus intuition, and thinking versus feeling.

3   This personality profile test was designed by Katherine Briggs and Isabel Briggs Myers. In general terms, it seeks to explain the central aspects of people's personalities, both to individuals themselves and to their co-workers. It also describes a variety of talents and emphasizes the ways in which some people are not just different from each other, but opposite or complementary. The test has been in existence for several years and has proven to be highly effective.

4   The purpose of the test is to identify the basic preferences of people in regard to perception and judgment, so that the effects of each preference, singly and in combination, can be established by research and put to practical use. Although this is its main purpose, the test also has very specific uses, primarily through counseling, for team-building, career planning, time management, communication, and organization development.

5   The Myers-Briggs Type Indicator is closely linked to Jung's theory of psychological types. The structure of the test itself is a paper and pencil self-report inventory. It is non-threatening and easy to follow. For example, the directions at the beginning of the test read as follows:

> There are no "right" or "wrong" answers to these questions. Your answers will help to show how you like to look at things and how you like to go about deciding things. Knowing your own preferences and learning about other people's can help you understand what kinds of work you might enjoy and be successful doing, and how people with different preferences can relate to each other and be valuable to society. (Briggs & Myers, 1977)

6   The test is divided into three separate parts containing a total of 126 questions. On the average it is completed in about one hour. The Myers-Briggs Type Indicator relies on choices between two attitudes—extroversion or introversion—and two pairs of functions—sensation or intuition and feeling or thinking—to describe and differentiate categories of people according to the way they prefer to use their minds. These three components are the basis of the test.

7   The first of these dimensions is the degree of extroversion versus introversion within an individual. According to Raymond Corsini, author of *Current Personality Theories,* for the extrovert "psychic energy flows outward to the object; objective facts or external happenings are the most important factors of life" (Corsini, 1977, p. 105). Typical extroverts are sociable, like parties, have many friends, need to have people to talk to, and do not like reading or studying by themselves. They crave excitement, take chances, often stick their necks out, act on the spur of the moment, and are generally impulsive.

8   On the opposite end of the spectrum is the introvert. For this type of person, according to Corsini, "the significance of the internal object lies not in itself, but in how it relates to his own psychology. It is not the situation objectively considered, but the situation as he reacts to it that is the dominating factor" (Corsini, 1977, p. 106). Typical introverts are quiet, retiring sorts of people, introspective, fond of books rather than other people; they are reserved and distant except to intimate friends. They also tend to plan ahead and distrust the impulse of the moment (Corsini, 1977).

9   These descriptions may sound almost like caricatures because they portray "perfect" extroverts and introverts. In fact, however, most people are mixtures who fall in the middle rather than at the extremes of the dimensions (Corsini, 1977).

10   The second dimension which is measured by the Myers-Briggs Type Indicator are two modes of perception—sensation and intuition. According to Salvatore Maddi, a psychology professor at the University of Akron, "these two alternatives are nonrational functions, not because they are contrary to reason but because they are outside the province of reason

and therefore not established by it" (1980, p. 500). The term *sensation* refers to perception through the five senses. This type of personality perceives mostly through the senses; spontaneously sensed convictions constitute reality for such individuals. They perceive reality as it currently exists and are therefore occupied with the present moment (Maddi, 1980).

11   Intuition, on the other hand, is an immediate awareness of the whole, without a real comprehension of the details. Intuition concerns itself with possibilities, perceiving things as they might be or might have been. The intuitive individual, as a consequence tends to be concerned with the future or the past (Maddi, 1980).

12   The third dimension measured by the Myers-Briggs Type Indicator is thinking versus feeling. Used in judging, these two are considered rational functions. Jung considered the thinking individual as one whose every important action proceeds from intellectually considered motives (1971). This type of person meets a situation with logical thought and determines appropriate actions by arriving at logical conclusions. Thinkers classify, clarify, and name: oftentimes, as a result, they are considered impersonal (Corsini, 1977).

13   Feeling involves the appreciation or depreciation of experience. According to Walter Mischel, a professor at Stanford University, the feeling function is personal and represents the individual's acceptance or rejection of something based on his or her own values and the perception of an object's intrinsic worth. Overall, the feeling function of the Myers-Briggs Type Indicator is chiefly concerned with values and morality, although it is not necessarily related to conventional attitudes (Mischel, 1985).

14   The Myers-Briggs Type Indicator, reflecting patterns of Jungian psychological types, relies on choices between the three dimensions to describe and differentiate categories of people according to the way they prefer to use their minds. It should be stressed, however, that every individual experiences extroversion and introversion and utilizes sensation, intuition, thinking, and feeling. One or more of these dimensions, however, will generally dominate and characterize a person's typical way of relating to others. By taking this test, you might achieve a better understanding of your personality and a fuller appreciation for the different perspectives from which people view the world.

References

Briggs, K.C., & Myers, I. (1977). *Myers-Briggs type indicator: Form G*. Palo Alto, CA: Consulting Psychologists Press.

Corsini, R. (1977). *Current personality theories*. Itasca, IL: Peacock Publishers.

Jung, C. (1971). *Psychological types* (H.G. Baynes, Trans.). Princeton, NJ: Princeton University Press. (Original work published 1921).

Maddi, S. (1980). *Personality theories*. Homewood, IL: Dorsey Press.

Mischel, W. (1985). *Introduction to personality*. New York: Holt, Rinehart, and Winston.

Ziegler, D. (1978). *Personality*. New York: McGraw-Hill.

Reading Critically: Questions for Discussion

1. Is Wendy a credible writer on this subject? Why do you think she is or isn't? How does Wendy's writing style contribute to your impression?
2. What is Wendy's thesis?
3. Is Wendy's explanation of the Myers-Briggs Type Indicator clear? Why do you think it is or isn't?
4. How does Wendy motivate her audience? Does she emphasize the importance of her subject? Does she make her explanation easy to read? Cite appropriate passages to support your answers.

KNOWLEDGE BY PARTICIPATION AND OBSERVATION

"Stress and the College Student" is the collaborative product of K. E. Bratz, Betsy Branan, and LaRae Fisher. They refer directly to their intended audience of college students as "you." As college students, these three writers know about stress both by participation and observation; furthermore, they warn their fellow college students about how this phenomenon can affect their college experiences.

Reviewing Journal Entries

This collaborative writing experience was a first for K. E., Betsy, and LaRae. Their journal entries reveal the system they developed for completing their task:

JOURNAL

I like working with my group on this paper. Our subject is stress. It's a good subject because we know it's something everybody has—and we can do observation (research) and participation (tons of 1st hand experience!) that we can refer to. Meetings will be at my house. They will gather research at library. I'm typing it all on the computer after each group meeting. Cool. (BB)

Met with LaRae and Betsy at Betsy's apartment to narrow down a subject. We decided to do stress because it is something that everybody experiences. I like my group and am curious to see how this collaborative paper turns out since I've never done one before. Wonder why Betsy hasn't done any research? (KEB)

It's interesting that our group picked stress to write about. I've had lots of practical experience to draw upon. (LF)

We looked over research materials. I had a hard time thinking about this task; just received my grade on another essay and I'm blue. (KEB)

I feel like we have a really good subject and paper. However, I hate meeting outside of class. It is so hard to find a convenient time and place to meet. We met tonight again and I have two tests tomorrow. Oh well. (KEB)

We haven't gotten too far on the paper; it's slow. But we know where we're going, I think. It helps so much to have 3 heads instead of one. I like collaborative writing. (BB)

I think the paper is getting stronger, but I'm so sick of it. We've got to write the conclusion and check our research. We have lots of material that we packed into the essay—and more we could add if we needed to. (KEB)

We've cut out a lot of what we were going to cover. It's best to keep it short, factual, and to the point. We are spending a lot of time checking for consistency and grammatical correctness. Maybe too much time. But at least the paper will be good even if it does take forever to complete. (BB)

I'm sick of stress. I wish we could just turn in this paper. Our system of working together has worked out well. We get together for about 1½ hours to write. Then I type it all in. Next class, I have a clean copy for each member. There, we sit and revise our own copy. Then we share our revision ideas and make a joint new copy, which I then type. . . . (BB)

We met at least six times for no less than 1½ hours each time. It was very slow-moving. We first produced an outline which we followed pretty much. We changed the direction of our essay about midway through because we felt as if we were rambling on towards nowhere. So we refined the direction a bit. We started with the intro and slowly moved forward. Unlike individual papers (where you can use stream of consciousness, omit words and even paragraphs temporarily in a draft). We inched forward word by word, sentence by sentence. We would get only 1–2 paragraphs done at each meeting, and always at the next meeting we would spend a large amount of time editing the previous paragraph. There the intro seemed to get the most attention, the conclusion the least. (LF)

What did this collaborative authorship teach me? OK. I've noticed what a difference writing ahead and editing and proofreading can make. I've always been a one-time writer. I wouldn't necessarily write the night before—it could be a week in advance. But I seldom made any grandiose changes. Co-authoring makes that practice impossible. I've learned that others' advice is good, but it doesn't have to be used. Take that advice, weigh it carefully, and if it doesn't apply, throw it out. (LF)

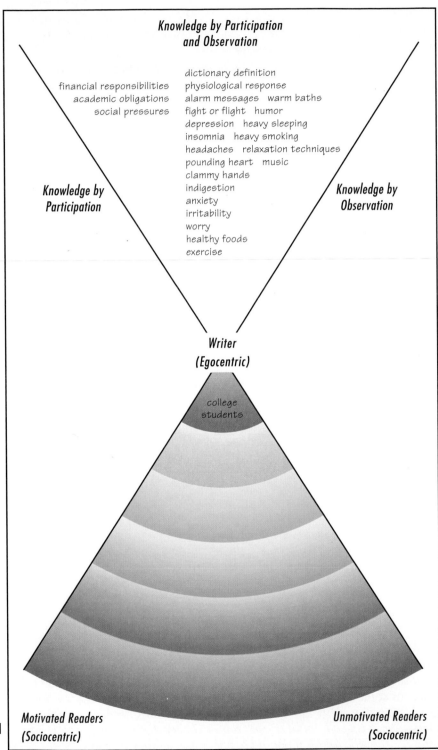

Figure 12.3

Mapping K. E., Betsy, and LaRae's rhetorical situation

Mapping K. E., Betsy, and LaRae's Referential Rhetorical Situation

Figure 12.3 illustrates the focus group's analysis of their rhetorical situation. K. E., Betsy, and LaRae understand the concept of stress both by participation and through observation. Therefore, they list their details in the "participation-observation" part of the knowledge continuum.

As their journal entries have shown, the students selected their subject because of its relevance to college readers. Often college readers are classified in different ways, and writers analyze them to try to appeal to every type or segment of audience possible. In this case, however, the writers view their readers as being basically all alike: the experience of being in college unifies them and may naturally engage them in the text. The audience continuum reflects this audience analysis. The writers believe that their audience will want to understand stress and its influence on them as college students.

Stress and the College Student

(Draft 4—Final Draft)

1   *The American Heritage Dictionary* defines stress as "a mentally or emotionally disruptive or disquieting influence" (1205). Although this is a good definition, it is too vague to adequately describe what students experience as they deal with the many factors that cause stress during college. Stress is more simply defined as a "physiological response to a perceived demand" (*Stress Management,* 1989, p. 6). And college students certainly understand demands. Faced with financial responsibilities, academic obligations, and social pressures, college students are frequently affected negatively by these often overwhelming demands. Negative effects range from psychological problems such as depression and physiological problems such as insomnia to social problems such as withdrawal. Any combination of these problems may lead to academic burnout which, in turn, can result in dropping out of school. However, it is possible to avoid these extremes. By understanding what stress is and how it affects you, you will be able to recognize its symptoms and apply simple measures to reduce its harmful effects.

2   As stated before, stress is a physiological response. It is the result of the body's autonomic nervous system's reacting automatically to certain stimuli in our environment. When you are threatened, frightened, or tense, such as before an exam or during a speech, your brain sends messages to organs in your body. The alarm messages prepare the body for "fight or flight," another term for stress. The senses become keener: your muscles tighten for action; your heart rate increases so that more blood and oxygen can reach the muscles, brain, and vital organs; stored sugar and fat are released and enter the bloodstream to build energy; and your hands begin to perspire as the body prepares to cool itself. Normally

these changes are good for equipping your body for physical activity and allowing your body to function at peak efficiency during emergencies (Rosenthal, 1991). However, our bodies may not be able to accommodate the fight or flight message.

3   Often, before our stress is resolved, another source of stress, or stressor, may arise. For example, you may be in the process of writing a research paper when you find that you must tackle another assignment that has come up in another class. Therefore, the problem with stress occurs when it becomes prolonged and built up. Or, as Rosenthal, author of "How to Win the Burn-Out Game" explains, stress occurs "when our alarm system gets triggered so indiscriminately that we no longer can recognize when our bodies are reacting to important issues or are just in tune with a stressful environment" (p. 7). Without physical release or a break, stress can result in physical or emotional illness.

4   There are many symptoms which may indicate that you are encountering too much stress. Several physical symptoms are the most obvious indicators of stress: headaches, a pounding heart, clammy hands, and indigestion. Other symptoms may be mental or emotional such as anxiety, irritability, worry, and depression. Behavioral symptoms of stress, such as the tendency to sleep a lot and increased smoking, drinking, or eating, often go unnoticed as indicators of a problem. It is a common misconception among students that these activities are stress relievers. Whether or not these symptoms are recognized as harmful, if they are not dealt with, they may result in more serious health difficulties: high blood pressure, ulcers, arthritis, and diabetes (*Facts to Relax By*, 1982).

5   There are several ways of responding to stress that can immediately reduce its detrimental effects. First, deal with the stress so that you can relax enough to gain perspective on your situation. Immediate relief of stress can be gained by simple methods of relaxation. According to the U.S. Government document *Stress Management*, "relaxation calms the body and mind, but without clouding the senses" (1989, p. 12). In fact, people who practice relaxation techniques on a daily basis actually react quicker to stressors and recover more quickly than those who do not practice relaxation (*Facts to Relax By*, 1982). Relaxation can be any activity which calms the mind and refreshes and restores the body.

6   One method of relaxation is the evening soak. Warm baths relieve stress by relaxing tense muscles. However, this can be counterproductive if the water is too hot and thereby causes muscles to constrict (Shimer, 1990). Another stress reliever is finding humor in tense situations. For example, if giving speeches makes you nervous, try to imagine the people in the audience in their underwear. Or try this technique: simply blow a situation out of proportion. The next time you believe that you cannot pay your utility bill on time, imagine the possible consequences that begin with an eviction notice and end with your having to live in your car for the remainder of the semester. Shimer, in his two-part series "Unwind and Destress," recognizes the benefits of this technique and points out, "When

your scenario reaches a point of absurdity, you begin to smile at yourself" (1990, p. 76). Finally, music, which is readily accessible, momentarily soothes you during a stressful time. Classical music, such as that by Bach or Debussy, is a popular choice to relax by. However, if Led Zeppelin or Garth Brooks is your preferred music, then listen to it. Forcing yourself to listen to music that you do not like may create stress rather than relieve it. Although these methods are good for temporary relief, you can take more permanent measures to reduce the negative effects of stress.

7   A healthy lifestyle is essential for managing stress. This includes eating right and exercising. When you are stressed, you may feel that you do not have time for three well-balanced meals; however, if you take the time to eat healthy meals, you will actually feel and perform better. College students frequently skip breakfast. As studies indicate in *Facts to Relax By,* "Breakfast skippers work less efficiently, suffer mid-afternoon fatigue and are most prone to obesity" (1982, p. 62). Therefore, those of you who regularly skip breakfast are doing yourselves a disservice. Another belief that you may have is that caffeine can be substituted for sleep; this is not true. Few of you may realize that the caffeine in one or two cups of coffee can cause irritability, muscle tension, headaches, nervousness and high blood pressure. Therefore, by minimizing caffeine intake, eating three well-balanced meals daily, and in particular, beginning the day by eating breakfast, you will increase your ability to respond to stress.

8   But good nutrition alone is not sufficient for successfully combatting stress. Exercise, combined with good nutrition, can greatly improve your ability to deal with stress. Researchers agree that exercise alters the way the body handles stress. "The exercised heart does not beat as fast in response to stress hormones, and it returns to resting levels quicker" (*Facts to Relax By,* 1982, p. 66). In addition, exercise will increase your energy level, confidence, work performance, concentration, optimism, and self-esteem. All of these results work together to provide you with a less stressful and more enjoyable college experience.

9   The effects of stress do not have to cripple college students' health, happiness, and productivity. Although every college student encounters different stressors and reacts differently to them, easy methods can successfully help reduce their negative effects. Relaxation, however it is achieved, is one alternative for immediate and short-term relief. Perhaps more successful is the combination of eating right and exercising, the best alternative for relieving stress on a long-term or permanent basis. Most important, learning to deal with stress as a college student can only improve your ability to cope with the problems of life after graduation.

References

American Heritage Dictionary. (1982). 2nd ed. Boston: Houghton Mifflin.

Facts to Relax By. (1982). Logan: Utah Valley Hospital.

Rosenthal, M. H. (1991, January 7). How to win the burn-out game. *USA Today,* pp. 70–72.

Shimer, P. (1990, July). Unwind and destress: First part in a two-part series. *Prevention,* pp. 101–115.

Shimer, P. (1990, August). Unwind and destress: Second part in a two-part series. *Prevention,* pp. 76–89.

Stress Management. (1989). Washington, DC: U.S. Government Printing Office.

Reading Critically: Questions for Discussion

1. How do the writers try to establish their credibility? Is this effective?
2. What do the writers do to motivate the audience? What might the writers do in addition?
3. Does the explanation improve your understanding of stress? Which questions does it answer? Which questions does it leave unanswered?
4. The writers focus a lot of attention on stress-reduction techniques and offer less information on the causes and symptoms of stress. Is this appropriate for their aim and audience?

CHAPTER 13

Repertoire Focus: Analyzing a Subject

In this chapter, you will be asked to analyze a historical event, a social or cultural trend, a technological innovation, or an artistic work in order to improve your reader's understanding. When you explain a subject, you present information that furthers your audience's understanding of it; in doing so, you provide readers with shared ways of referring to and thinking about an idea or object. Analyzing a subject, however, requires you to go beyond explanation. For example, you might analyze your subject in terms of the following perspectives:

- importance
- composition
- development
- operation
- advantages
- disadvantages
- causes
- effects
- similarity to associated subjects
- difference from associated subjects

Analyses are among the most common texts you will compose during and after college.

REPERTOIRE WRITING TASK: ANALYSIS

Select a subject that interests you and that will appeal to either readers much like you; a general college readership; a general adult readership; or a specific campus, community, or professional group. Consider carefully what your readers already know about your subject and how your essay might add to their understanding of its relevance or importance.

Below are three variations of the analysis writing task, based upon the different ways you may "know" about subjects:

Knowledge by Participation

Write an essay that explicates and analyzes a historical event, a social or cultural trend, a technological innovation, or an artistic work (poem, short story, novel, essay, play, painting, sculpture, architectural structure, musical composition, movie) that you came to know through direct experience.

Knowledge by Observation

Write an essay that explicates and analyzes a historical event, a social or cultural trend, or a technological innovation that you came to know through an indirect means (through interviews, reading, television, or another medium). Your subject should be one that has been written about by others, yielding some form of published biographical, social, or historical information that you can integrate into your essay.

Knowledge by Participation and Observation

Write an essay that explicates and analyzes a historical event, a social or cultural trend, a technological innovation, or an artistic work (poem, short story, novel, essay, play, painting, sculpture, architectural structure, musical composition, movie) that you came to know through direct experience as well as through indirect means (through others, by reading, by watching television or another medium). Your subject should be one that has been written about by others, yielding some form of published biographical, social, or historical information that you can integrate into your essay.

REPERTORY COMPANY OF STUDENT WRITERS: THEIR RESPONSES TO THE TASK

Before you begin your writing task, you may find it helpful to read the following essays, written by other student writers in response to the same writing tasks presented in this chapter. To research and write their texts, these student writers worked within their own writing communities or focus groups; the groups met regularly to talk, read, think, and write with one another. Interacting within their writing communities, these writers exchanged ideas and strengthened their sense of what it means to be a writer. As you write, ask those around you—your classmates and room-mates, for example—for feedback about your ideas and your writing. Remember: writing is a social act.

For each essay in this chapter, we've included journal entries, a map of the rhetorical situation (the knowledge continuum and audience contin-uum), and research strategies. You'll also find some questions for discus-sion and analysis following each selection.

KNOWLEDGE BY PARTICIPATION

"The Unique Relationship of Elizabeth Bennet and Her Father" was written by Tamara Jones. For this writing task, Tamara decides to reread Jane Austen's *Pride and Prejudice,* a novel that she read when she was a junior high school student. She has never read any published analyses of this work and does not conduct library research to support her ideas; instead, she uses quotations from *Pride and Prejudice* to substantiate her points. In this way, Tamara interacts directly with the novel, and her analysis pre-sents her understanding gained by participation.

Read More About It

See Table 11.1, pp. 339–340.

Reviewing Journal Entries

Tamara's journal entries focus on how she does research to support her analysis without going to the library. At first, she just wants to make her points about the relationship between Elizabeth and Mr. Bennet; as she begins to read and write, however, she realizes that she must also bolster her assertions with some type of support. In this case, she decides that she can substantiate her ideas by integrating direct quotations from *Pride and Prejudice.*

JOURNAL

I haven't read Austen's book in years. I always liked it, so I'm hoping it will be fun to reread and write about. At least I don't have to read any articles about it—I can say what I think.

My main problem with the referential paper is tied to the book. I need to cite exact pages in the novel, and it's been so long since I've had to do this kind of thing. Obviously, it is a better way to prove my point, but I would rather just tell my point. It is more effective, however, to let Mr. Bennet and Elizabeth prove the point for me. Working closer to the text is a new experience for me but it is the better way.

This essay is better than ones I've written before. I used the correct internal documentation, and I have more than enough examples to back up my thesis. I now know how important it is to write a thesis and support it. I hope to be an English teacher one day, and I want my students to leave my class knowing how to write this kind of analysis essay well.

I am excited about this essay because it deals with something I care about and know I can defend. Using examples from the novel really made me see how to make a point and support it. Now readers know how and why I think what I do about Elizabeth and her father. And now I know how to analyze characters and relationships in a book. Funny I never really understood this before.

Mapping Tamara's Referential Rhetorical Situation

Figure 13.1 shows Tamara's analysis of her rhetorical situation. Tamara analyzes the father-daughter relationship in *Pride and Prejudice* and shows how Mr. Bennet encourages Elizabeth to have her own opinions about women's roles and place in society. Readers learn about these characters from Tamara's perspective; she presents her interpretation and substantiates it by weaving Austen's words into the analysis essay. Tamara gains her understanding of the subject of this essay by participation—reading Austen's novel—as the knowledge continuum illustrates.

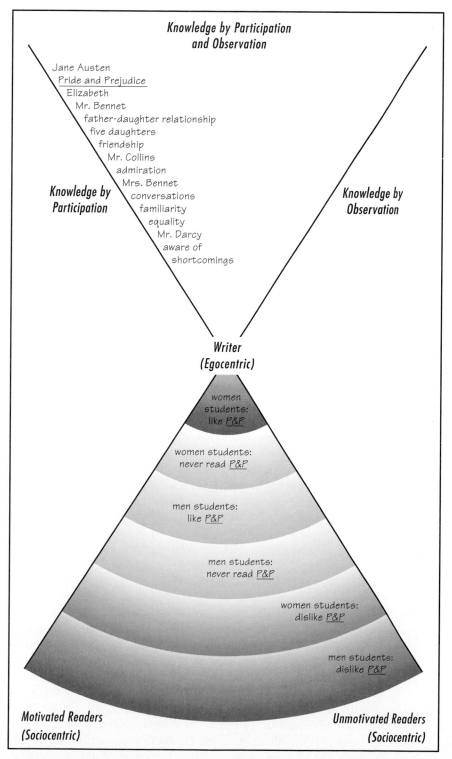

Figure 13.1
Mapping Tamara's rhetorical situation

In writing for her peers, Tamara chooses a subject that is interesting to her and is relevant to her readers as well. She thinks that women's roles in society is a subject that almost everyone will find compelling, especially women students who have read *Pride and Prejudice* and enjoyed it as much as she has. In fact, Tamara believes that even women who haven't read the novel could be highly motivated and interested in this story and characters; college-age men, she realizes, may be less concerned about her analysis of this father-daughter relationship. She also expects that some readers, both women and men, may dislike this novel. Her map of the audience continuum reflects her assessment of her readership.

The Unique Relationship of Elizabeth Bennet and Her Father

(Draft 3—Final Draft)

1   Jane Austen's literary works are imitations of life, giving the reader an insight into how relationships can shape the nature of the characters in her novels. In *Pride and Prejudice*, the heroine, Elizabeth, has a unique relationship with her father, Mr. Bennet. The relationship is not one that can be explained by the fact that they are father and daughter; it goes much deeper than that dimension. Elizabeth and Mr. Bennet have a relationship that stems from the mutual love and respect they have for each other. Elizabeth's extraordinary personality is partly a product of the relationship that she has with her father.

2   Mr. Bennet has five daughters, but his second daughter, Elizabeth, is his friend as well as his daughter. In the first chapter, Mrs. Bennet is very direct in her disapproval of his strong partiality to Elizabeth. She tells him, "Lizzy is not a bit better than the others. . . . But you are always giving her the preference" (52). His relationship with Elizabeth is an unusually close one. He prefers her because of her intelligence and her companionship. He misses his conversations with her when she goes to visit her friend, Charlotte, and he writes for her to return. He misses her as his friend more than as his daughter, and he tells her "I'm glad you are come back, Lizzy" (248). The oldest daughter, Jane, has been gone, but her absence is not felt by him as much as the absence of Elizabeth. In Chapter 14, while Mr. Collins is amusing Mr. Bennet with his obvious absurdities he knows that Elizabeth feels the same way. He only has to glance at her because they share an understanding that allows them to both laugh at Mr. Collins. The narrator says, "His cousin was as absurd as he had hoped, and he listened to him with the keenest enjoyment, maintaining at the same time the most resolute composure of countenance, and except in an occasional glance at Elizabeth, requiring no partner in his pleasure" (113). Also, when he expresses his disapproval of her marrying Mr. Collins, his preference to her is exposed. Because of his lack of money, his daughters need to be married, but he is unwilling to allow Elizabeth to sacrifice her happiness for economic reasons. He encourages her sense of independence.

3   Elizabeth's admiration for her father is not automatic because he is her parent. Mrs. Bennet is definitely not admired by Elizabeth. Her mother embarrasses Elizabeth at every opportunity. At the Netherfield Ball, for example, "In vain did Elizabeth endeavor to check the rapidity of her mother's words. . . . Her mother only scolded her for being nonsensical" (141). Elizabeth is ashamed of her mother at this point in the book. Mrs. Bennet does not inspire any of the same kind of feelings in Elizabeth that her father produces. Elizabeth shows her mother outward respect, but their relationship stops with this superficial respect. The nurturing that Elizabeth needs to feed her character does not come from Mrs. Bennet.

4   The discussions between Elizabeth and her father are some of the few two-sided conversations or arguments between males and females in the novel. They discuss Jane's relationship with her suitor, Mr. Bingley. Mr. Bennet says, "So, Lizzy, your sister is crossed in love I find" (176). Mr. Bennet does not hesitate to discuss this romantic topic with Elizabeth. He also asks Elizabeth about her prospects for an interesting suitor, "When is your turn to come? You will hardly bear to be long outdone by Jane" (176). The conversation is comfortable. Mr. Bennet does not embarrass Elizabeth, nor is Elizabeth hesitant to answer him. Later in the novel, Elizabeth advises him not to allow her younger sister, Lydia, to go on a vacation with a military family, the Forsters. Elizabeth is extremely candid in her reasoning.

> "Excuse me—for I must speak plainly. If you, my dear father, will not take the trouble of checking her exuberant spirits, and of teaching her that her present pursuits are not to be the business of her life, she will soon be beyond reach of amendment. Her character will be fixed, and she will, at sixteen, be the most determined flirt that ever made herself and her family look ridiculous. . . . Vain, ignorant, idle, and absolutely uncontrolled! Oh! my dear father, can you suppose it possible that they will not be censured and despised wherever they are known, and that their sister will not be often involved in the disgrace?" (258)

5   Her father does not disagree with her assessment of Lydia, but he does not take her advice. Elizabeth is very serious in her grievances against Lydia and feels perfectly at ease in voicing them to her father. Elizabeth speaks from a position of familiarity and equality with her father that none of her other sisters possess.

6   Elizabeth is not blinded by love and affection for her father. She is aware of his faults as a husband and a father. In Chapter 42 of the novel, her feelings toward this subject are expressed. The narrator explains, "Elizabeth, however, had never been blind to the impropriety of her father's behavior as a husband. She had always seen it with pain; respecting his abilities, and grateful for his affectionate treatment of herself" (262). It hurts her to see how he responds to his role as a father and a husband, but she understands how he came to be this way. It is a sign of friendship to be painfully aware of someone's

faults and to respect that individual in spite of his or her shortcomings. She has witnessed the disadvantages of an unsuccessful marriage, and she is determined not to condemn herself to one. Mr. Bennet's main concern about Elizabeth's marrying Mr. Darcy is that he will not be an equal match for her, and she will be unhappy. He asks her, "Lizzy, what are you doing? Are you out of your senses to be accepting this man?" (384). Elizabeth's happiness is as important to him as it is to her. After she tells him that she loves Mr. Darcy he tells her, ". . . I have no more to say. . . . I could not have parted with you, my Lizzy, to any one less worthy" (385). Mr. Darcy is an extremely wealthy man and will be able to provide a good life for Elizabeth, but this is not Mr. Bennet's concern. He has to know that Mr. Darcy is worthy of Elizabeth's love.

7   Elizabeth's relationship with her father has helped her become the person she is at the beginning of the novel. Elizabeth and her father have an understanding that has allowed her to have her opinions about love and life. She certainly did not receive encouragement for them from her mother. Her father repeatedly encourages her to speak her mind and to listen to what her heart tells her. Mr. Darcy's aunt, Lady Catherine, comments that "[d]aughters are never so much consequence to a father" (240). She was wrong when she applied this statement to Elizabeth and Mr. Bennet. Elizabeth is of very much consequence to her father. She is also Jane Austen's aspiration for women, and Mr. Bennet is needed to help shape Elizabeth's character. Mr. Bennet can't be the perfect 19th-century father because Elizabeth could not have evolved from him in that situation. Their relationship is essential to the believability of Austen's premise that marrying for love can exist without starvation or social alienation. Women can be intelligent and independent while at the same time being beautiful.

Works Cited

Austen, Jane. *Pride and Prejudice*. New York: Penguin, 1988.

Reading Critically: Questions for Discussion

1. Do you have to be familiar with Austen's *Pride and Prejudice* in order to understand Tamara's analysis of the father-daughter relationship? Is this appropriate? Should Tamara devote more time to identifying and introducing the characters she discusses?
2. What is Tamara's thesis? Is her thesis adequately supported?
3. Whenever she quotes a passage from the book, Tamara consistently cites the page on which the quoted passage occurs. Does this practice help to establish her credibility? Why do you think it does or doesn't?
4. Does Tamara do a good job of getting her readers interested in her analysis? What more could she do to motivate her audience?

KNOWLEDGE BY OBSERVATION

Hayley Hamby researched the status of physical education in public schools today in order to write the next essay. This subject appeals to Hayley because she is thinking about majoring in physical education. Hayley tells her focus group that she has profited from researching the various ways that physical education has been used in different school curricula. She believes she now knows enough about the area to make it her major. In this essay, Hayley adopts the observer point of view.

Reviewing Journal Entries

Hayley writes very short journal entries for "Why Can't We Just Play Ball?" Her comments reveal that she likes this subject and finds lots of research materials for this essay. However, she also displays her uncertainty about how to weave these research materials into her own writing. Here are a few entries from Hayley's journal.

JOURNAL

I am worried about this paper. I want to write about something that is important to me and that I need to learn about. I need to find a subject that is new, exciting for me.

Here I am in college and what's my major? Everyone always asks. I say, "I'm not sure yet." What do I want to do with my life? OK. Maybe I can do the Sherlock Holmes thing about this. Research a possible major for yourself. Good idea. This will make me research something that I need to learn about NOW. I like this.

I want to be a teacher, but what kind? I mean, math, science, English, etc. My roommate says I might be a good P.E. teacher. That doesn't sound so bad. Kids running and all. I could keep in shape and be around kids. I love them. I never had much P.E. in school, though. Our school district sometimes had the money to have classes and sometimes didn't. Just what is it and how has it changed in schools over the years? An analysis of this trend. That's it.

I talked to two professors today and got lots of information on the status of elementary P.E. in America today. I can do this.

My big problem will be trying to conglomerate all of the information so that it will flow well together. I'm not sure what tagging means, but I'm trying.

Mapping Hayley's Referential Rhetorical Situation

Because Hayley's knowledge of her subject is gained by observation, she lists her details on the "knowledge by observation" side of the continuum. Figure 13.2 shows her map of her rhetorical situation.

Hayley intends her essay for an audience of general adult readers. She thinks that parents of schoolchildren, school board members, counselors, teachers, as well as local health professionals will be highly motivated and interested in her subject. Other readers, however, might respond to this subject with indifference.

Untitled

(Draft 1)

1   There are many changes being made in physical education classes in America. Over the past two and a half decades numerous significant innovations have occurred. Because of these changes, teaching physical education to children has gained recognition as an integral and irreplaceable part of the total school curriculum and child-development process (Gabbard 1). The traditional trends of "skill related" fitness was becoming less and less popular as new certified physical educators enter the elementary schools (Gabbard 2). "Educators generally agree that the primary purpose of education is to help each child develop to his or her fullest potential" (Gabbard 5).

2   The Chrysler Fund/AAU Physical Fitness program tests measure four basic skills: endurance run, pull-ups (for boys) and flexed arm hang (for girls), sit and reach (testing flexibility) and sit-ups. The program encompasses some 42,000 schools and agencies representing 9.7 million students in the 50 states and the District of Columbia (Vejnoska 1A). During the last decade, participants achieving satisfactory levels in the test's four components dropped from 43 percent to 32 percent (Vejoska 1A).

3   Even though massive changes are being made in many physical education programs, there are still many school districts that do not place emphasis on providing their children with quality programs that promote lifetime fitness (Walker 12B). Professionals now say, "Physical education is more than recess, more than simply a time to play" (Graham 5).

4   The Council on Physical Education for Children has developed criteria that states what is developmentally appropriate in physical education in schools. The curriculum has an obvious scope and sequence based on goals and objectives that are beneficial for youngsters. Fitness activities are used to help children increase their physical fitness

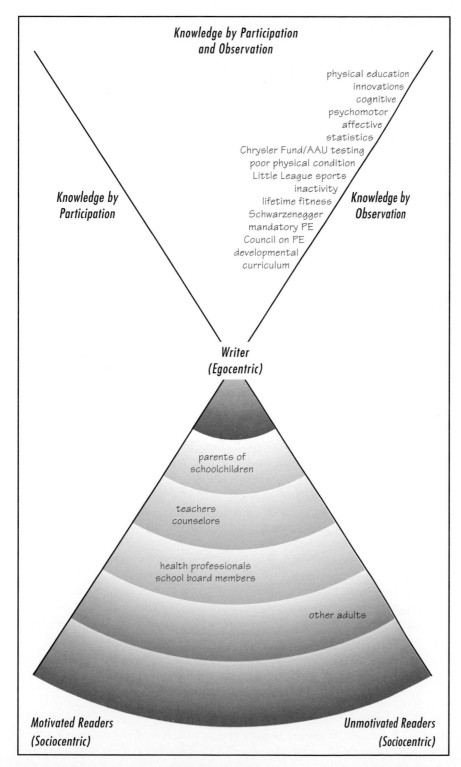

*Knowledge by Participation
and Observation*

physical education
innovations
cognitive
psychomotor
affective
statistics
Chrysler Fund/AAU testing
poor physical condition
Little League sports
inactivity
lifetime fitness
Schwarzenegger
mandatory PE
Council on PE
developmental
curriculum

*Knowledge by
Participation*

*Knowledge by
Observation*

*Writer
(Egocentric)*

parents of
schoolchildren

teachers
counselors

health professionals
school board members

other adults

*Motivated Readers
(Sociocentric)*

*Unmotivated Readers
(Sociocentric)*

Figure 13.2
Mapping Hayley's rhetorical
situation

levels in a supportive, motivating and progressive manner which promotes positive lifetime fitness attitudes and habits (Wikgren 4).

In her first draft, Hayley reports a lot of facts about her subject. As she continues writing, she will need to tie together these isolated bits of information for her readers by defining and interpreting the facts. As her journal reveals, Hayley recognizes that she needs to learn more about what tagging is and how to tag sources within her sentences. In draft 1, she only uses in-text parenthetical references. In addition, her focus group suggests that Hayley try to involve her readers in her essay with a more interesting introduction and a compelling conclusion.

As you read draft 3 of Hayley's essay, consider the changes she has made. How has she improved the essay? What additional changes would you recommend?

Why Can't We Just Play Ball?

(Draft 3—Final Copy)

1   Is it no longer appropriate to get out a box of balls, have the kids choose teams, and play supervised dodge ball every day in physical education classes? There are many changes being made in physical education classes in America. Over the past two and a half decades numerous significant innovations have occurred. Because of these changes, teaching physical education to children has gained recognition as an integral and irreplaceable part of the total school curriculum and child-development process (Gabbard 1). The traditional trends of "skill related" fitness are becoming less and less popular as new certified physical educators enter the elementary schools (Gabbard 2). "Educators generally agree that the primary purpose of education is to help each child develop to his or her fullest potential" (Gabbard 5). Quality physical fitness curricula strive to meet this goal by implementing cognitive, psychomotor and affective activities into each lesson. The cognitive domain encompasses inquiry, creativity, perceptual abilities, movement awareness and academic reinforcement. Self-concepts, socialization, positive attitudes and joy are all affective benefits gained by children who participate in quality physical education programs. Psychomotor development is the most obvious of the three domains. This domain includes biological growth, health and skill related fitness, efficiency in movement and repertoire of motor skills (Gabbard 5). Although this is the ideal situation, not all schools are providing this for their children, which leads to problems (Gabbard 5).

2   Numerous statistics convey the poor physical condition of American children. The Chrysler Fund/AAU Physical Fitness program tests measure four basic skills: endurance run, pull-ups (for boys) and

flexed arm hang (for girls), sit and reach (testing flexibility), and sit-ups. The program encompasses some 42,000 schools and agencies representing 9.7 million students in the 50 states and the District of Columbia (Vejnoska 1A). The results of these tests are unflattering to today's youth. During the last decade, participants achieving satisfactory levels in the test's four components dropped from 43 percent to 32 percent (Vejoska 1A). "You can have as much fun with Nintendo (computer games) as you can with kick-the-can or stickball. But when the technological games receive more emphasis, it's going to have an effect, for instance, on weight gain" (Vejnoska 1A).

3   More kids than ever before participate in little league sports, but this does not result in higher fitness levels. Many parents believe that these activities provide sufficient fitness aspects to the lives of their children. Most of these programs are very good for the children, but they do not promote lifetime fitness. Many "non-athletes" fall between the cracks and develop a strong dislike for any type of physical activities because of these unpleasant experiences. Ten years ago, recreational activities for children included all the neighborhood kids playing kickball, soccer, and chase. Children were more physically active in their free time in the summer and after school. In her article in *USA Today,* Vejnoska refers to the phenomenon as "youth suffering from a too-peaceful lifestyle, which results in a loss of cardiovascular endurance" (1A). If inactivity continues through adulthood, these individuals will later increase the risk of heart problems.

4   Even though massive changes are being made in many physical education programs, there are still many school districts that do not place emphasis on providing their children with quality programs that promote lifetime fitness (Walker 12B). Arnold Schwarzenegger has made it his mission to get mandatory physical education in all 50 states (Brown 10C). Professionals now say, "Physical education is more than recess, more than simply a time to play" (Graham 5). Children who participate in quality physical education programs should feel good about themselves as movers and learn the importance of fitness and how to take part in lifetime health and fitness activities. These programs should give children a good foundation of skill development and cognitive physical activity. If these qualities are implemented, children will be on their way to becoming adults who derive the benefits of physically active and healthy lives (Graham 5).

5   The Council on Physical Education for Children has developed criteria that states what is developmentally appropriate in physical education in schools. The curriculum has an obvious scope and sequence based on goals and objectives that are beneficial for youngsters. The cognitive, motor, affective and physical fitness development of every child is enhanced through skills, concepts, games and educational gymnastics, rhythms and dance experiences. A curriculum which consists solely of large group games would not provide students with the individual experiences they need. Appropriate physical

fitness tests do not serve the purpose of qualifying students for awards, but they are used as ongoing processes to help children understand, enjoy and improve their physical health and well-being. As stated previously, the curriculum should not consist solely of large group games; although, when they are selected, designed, sequenced and modified by teacher and/or students to maximize the learning and enjoyment of the students, they can be appropriate. Two of the popular forms of past punishment in physical education classes were running and push-ups. This is not at all appropriate in physical education classes. Fitness activities are used to help children increase their physical fitness levels in a supportive, motivating and progressive manner which promotes positive lifetime fitness attitudes and habits (Wikgren 4).

6   Hopefully the question, "Why can't we just play ball?" has been answered. American children do not engage in daily activities which insure adequate physical exercise. Therefore, it is up to the school curricula and parents to make sure the needs of the children are met. It is important that the cognitive, psychomotor and affective domains are all addressed within each physical education lesson. The ultimate goal of a well-rounded class is to promote lifetime fitness by helping children develop to their fullest potential.

Works Cited

Brown, Ben. "P.E. Should Teach Lifelong Skills." *USA Today* 13 Sept. 1990: 10C.

Gabbard, Carl, Elizabeth LeBlanc, and Susan Lowy. *Physical Education for Children: Building the Foundation.* Englewood Cliffs: Prentice Hall, 1987.

Graham, George, Shirley Ann Holt-Hale, and Melissa Parker. *Children Moving.* Chicago: Mayfield, 1987.

Vejnoska, Jill. "Youngsters Are Getting FATTER, Not Fitter." *USA Today* 13 Sept. 1990: 10C.

Walker, Herschel. "Children's P.E. Classes Sadly Underemphasized." *The Dallas Morning News* 21 Sept. 1990: 12B.

Wikgren, Scott. "Developmentally Appropriate P.E." *Teaching Elementary Physical Education* 24 (Sept. 1991): 4.

Reading Critically: Questions for Discussion

1. Consider the title of Hayley's essay. Does it effectively identify the subject or thesis of the analysis?
2. What is the subordinate aim of Hayley's essay? Is this aim appropriate for her audience?
3. If Hayley were writing to schoolchildren, how would this essay differ? Which information would she keep? Which would she omit? What

new information would she offer? How would the writing style change? Would she still cite sources of information? How would she establish her credibility?

KNOWLEDGE BY PARTICIPATION AND OBSERVATION

In the following essay, Elaine Barton and Kenneth Fontenot analyze *Citizen Kane,* a film that they both have seen and liked. Because their analysis also includes the result of library research, these two student writers gain knowledge of this classic film through both participation and observation.

Reviewing Journal Entries

Elaine's and Ken's journals contain a record of how two completely different kinds of writers produced a coauthored essay. Elaine is an "outline-and-draft" writer; sometimes she revises after writing her draft, and sometimes she doesn't. Ken, on the other hand, never uses outlines. He gathers his research materials and begins drafting, editing and revising as he writes. Here are some entries that illustrate how two writers' composing processes clash.

JOURNAL

We talked in class and thought we'd like to analyze a subject we all really liked but didn't really always understand. Ken thought of movies. He loves movies—so do I. Godfather *trilogy,* Exorcist, Raging Bull, Citizen Kane. *Wow. Then, we were thinking of two separate papers, two different subjects. Decided to try writing together. Coauthors. Sounds kinda impressive, eh? (EB)*

Citizen Kane. *We viewed the film together at Elizabeth's (a mutual friend). I really love this movie. We took notes as we watched. Next, we're supposed to meet at the library to search the stacks. (EB)*

Went to the library. One of my professors suggested a couple of articles we might check. We found these and their bibliographies led us to 12 other sources. I'm delighted. (EB)

Since we're writing a coauthored paper now, I am anticipating difficulties. How are we gonna do this? We came up with the idea of examining Citizen Kane *as an Aristotelian tragedy. Since I took a drama writing course last semester and studied the structure of ancient Greek drama, this seems like a natural. It looks like we will take a look at how* CK *meets Aris-*

totle's six elements of tragedy. That should simplify it somewhat, I think. I really like the subject, not necessarily the tragedy part. It's a great movie and it should be interesting. But how will we write it? (KF)

The movie truly is one of the best films I have seen. Very much enjoyed it and plan to re-watch it Friday with Ken and his girlfriend. Am looking forward to it. (EB)

My notes from 3 nights working at Ken's apartment:
Aristotle's Poetics:
Decide to use object, media, and mode—that Aristotle describes. We set up a broad outline (Ken doesn't like to write from an outline).
Writing is so slow. Mostly, Ken directs the paper and I help phrase some of the ideas. We both contribute to word choice and take turns being "dictionary person" or "thesaurus person."
This is not the way I'm used to writing. Generally, I would just put down the ideas, and then go back and edit. But I find that this may be better and since you get it "right" the first time (or at least have something you're satisfied with) you don't run the risk that is possible the way I write, of not ever going back to revise at all. (EB)

Man, oh, man. That was rough. I am not looking forward to writing a collaborative paper again any time soon. It's so hard to get two people to agree on anything—especially an act of creation. And the time! I thought we'd never finish! That was partly my fault though because I didn't want to pinpoint what research we would use before we started. I just wanted to get going with it because I knew it would take a long time. We spent a lot of time reading the research. Also, we decided we would edit it as we went because we figured we wouldn't go back and do a very good job editing it later. This is, in fact, the way I normally write, but it was new to my collaborator. I'm not so sure how the essay turned out. It seems like it might be confusing to a reader who didn't know about Aristotle's teachings concerning tragedy beforehand. I'm glad we thought to put in a diagram to help explain it. I'm worried about the subject. It seems like our paper would have to be 30 pages long to really do it right. I'm just glad it's over. (KF)

By coauthoring their essay, what do you think Elaine and Ken have learned about the processes of writing? How will this experience help them in other classes as well as possible work situations after they graduate from college?

Mapping Elaine and Ken's Referential Rhetorical Situation

Elaine and Ken come to understand *Citizen Kane* directly by watching the film and indirectly by researching library sources. In Figure 13.3, the two writers map information about their subject on the participation and observation sides of the knowledge continuum.

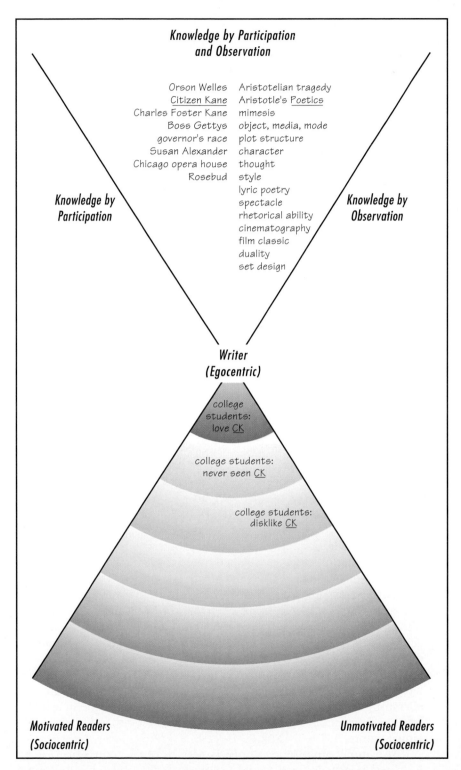

Figure 13.3
Mapping Elaine and Ken's rhetorical situation

While *Citizen Kane* may be a fascinating film, an Aristotelian analysis of it may not be. Elaine and Ken imagine that their readers will be college students. They classify their audience very simply: those who love *Citizen Kane* (highly motivated), those who have never seen the movie (indifferent), and those who dislike the movie (unmotivated). They map their readership knowing that this subject will be more academic than entertaining. According to these writers, researched writing ought to be academic. What do you think?

Elements of an Aristotelian Tragedy as Exhibited in *Citizen Kane*

(Draft 3—Final Draft)

Before *Citizen Kane,* it's as if the motion picture was a slumbering monster, a mighty force stupidly sleeping, lying there sleek, torpid, complacent—awaiting a fierce young man to come kick it to life, to rouse it, shake it, awaken it to its potentialities, to show it what it's got. Seeing it, it's as if you never really saw a movie before; no movie has ever grabbed you, pummeled you, socked you on the button with the vitality, the accuracy, the impact, the professional aim, that this one does.

Cecelia Ager

1   From Ingmar Bergman to Francis Ford Coppola to Martin Scorsese, the familiar pattern of the Aristotelian tragedy has been used to depict the dialectical nature of human kind in film. Widely regarded as the greatest motion picture of all time, Orson Welles' *Citizen Kane* was one of the first films to use Aristotle's formula.

2   In his *Poetics,* Aristotle views tragic drama as a mimesis of real life. He explicates what he believes to be the basic form of tragedy. Specifically, he outlines three component parts—object, media, and mode—and among these further distributes six basic elements—plot structure, character, thought, style, lyric poetry, and spectacle (see Figure 1).

3   The most important of Aristotle's subgroups is object. Object is composed of plot structure, character, and thought. The first and most essential element is plot structure. Aristotle considered the structure of events to be of utmost importance because he saw tragedy as a "representation not of people as such but of actions and life" (37). Although the character of Charles Foster Kane is important, it is his actions which are the focus of the drama. Kane himself is aware of this fact as is evident in his statement to Thatcher as he signs over control of his newspaper empire: "If I hadn't been very rich, I might have been a really great man" (Mankiewicz and Welles 340). In fact, all throughout *Citizen Kane* the actions of Kane and the actions of other characters have greater impact on Kane's life than his own individual nature.

4   The most obvious example is Mrs. Kane's acquisition of an indebted boarder's deed to the Colorado Lode, and her subsequent

---

Figure 1:   Aristotle's Elements of Tragedy

Objects

1. plot structure
2. character
3. thought

Media

4. style
5. lyric poetry

Mode

6. spectacle

---

decision to place Charles under Thatcher's charge, in order to keep Charles away from his abusive father. Charles' own character had nothing to do with this crucial turning point in his life. Rather, he was a victim of the actions of others. Another instance of a character's control over Kane's life is Boss Gettys' attempted blackmail which led to Kane's defeat in the governor's race. Once again Kane is victimized by events that had nothing to do with his individual character. In the words of biographer Joseph McBride, "Our heroic conception of Kane as a tragically flawed character marching through time to his doom is tempered with an understanding that he was not in complete control of the events of his life, that some force has ordered them" (45).

5   There are even occasions when Kane's own actions have greater consequence on his life than his character. Although Kane's search for love is part of his personal premise, it is the actions that he takes to receive love that have a greater impact on his life. Kane demands love from others on his terms instead of letting others come to love him for who he is. After Kane loses the election to Boss Gettys, a drunken Leland confronts Kane and reveals to the audience Kane's tragic flaw. "You don't care about anything except you. You just want to persuade people that you love them so much that they ought to love you back. Only you want love on your own terms" (Mankiewicz and Welles 388). Kane expects that his constituents will vote for him based on his character and not his actions, specifically his affair with Susan Alexander. But, in fact, it is his actions, not his character, which lead to his defeat at the polls.

6   Another instance when Kane's actions are more consequential is exemplified by his behavior during his marriage to Susan Alexander. Not only does Kane build Susan a huge opera house in Chicago, but he also forces her to continue her singing career after her dreadful

debut. Although it seems Kane truly loves Susan, his domination of her is more significant. It is not the fact that he is angry with her, but the fact that he slaps her which causes her to leave him. Once again, it is Kane's action, rather than his persona, that is most essential in mimicking real life.

7   The second element of the object subgroup is character. F. L. Lucas describes Aristotle's conception of character in this way:

> . . . Aristotle demanded that the character of tragedy shall be good, [but] he has also demanded . . . that the character of the tragic hero should not be too good. . . . So he is left with a hero, not specially outstanding in goodness, nor yet guilty of depravity and wickedness, but only of a tragic error. (128)

8   Kane exemplified just this type of duality. His longing for the simplicity of his childhood that Rosebud represents is contrasted with the complexity of his desire for greatness. Concurrently, Kane's ideals for his newspaper as set out in his "Declaration of Principles" are contrasted with the actuality that his newspapers engaged in yellow journalism under his direction. As Aristotle prescribes, Kane's duality mimics the duality of human nature. Elaborating on this point, James Naremore says, "Nearly everything in the story is based on this sort of duality or ambiguity, so that we are constantly made aware of the two sides of Kane" (67).

9   The last element of object is thought. By thought, Aristotle means the choice of words in the production of rhetoric (53). Kane demonstrates his rhetorical ability in his campaign speech as he vilifies Boss Gettys while he glorifies himself. "I made no campaign promises because until a few weeks ago I had no hope of being elected. Now, however, I have something more than a hope. And Jim Gettys . . . Jim Gettys has something less than a chance" (Mankiewicz and Welles 376). Kane's use of parallelism, repetition, and humor reveals his effectiveness as a rhetorical speaker. Shortly thereafter, Kane does make promises: "The working man . . . and the slum child may expect my best efforts in their interest. The decent, ordinary citizens know I'll do everything in my power to protect the underprivileged, the underpaid, and the underfed" (377). Kane now deftly shifts from the humorous appeal to the emotional appeal, effectively eliciting the commiseration of his audience.

10   The second subgroup that Aristotle delineates is media, which is comprised of style and lyric poetry. According to Aristotle, style is "the verbal expression achieved through the choice of words, which has the same force whether in verse or in prose" (38). The best example of this is Kane's last word: "Rosebud." James Maxfield explains the symbolic meaning of Rosebud:

> The name itself, Rosebud, refers to an early stage of a flower, a stage full of potential for growth and expansion of beauty. Kane's murmuring of

the word on his deathbed perhaps expresses his sense that his original potential as a human being was never realized. (200)

11   Herman J. Mankiewicz and Orson Welles' use of the word *Rosebud* in the screenplay is only one of many instances when style is used effectively.

12   The second element of media is lyric poetry. This is the one area where *Citizen Kane* fails to meet the criteria for a dramatic tragedy set forth by Aristotle. However, modern drama rarely, if ever, uses verse.

13   The final subgroup as delineated by Aristotle is mode, which is composed of only one element—spectacle. Although Aristotle places least importance on spectacle for the writer, Welles—the director—is able to fully employ this element. In fact, the spectacle of *Citizen Kane* is one of the most phenomenal aspects of the film. From the opening to the closing scene, the cinematography is years ahead of its time in depicting the mood and character of the film (see Figure 2). Bosley Crowther says that "Mr. Welles and Mr. Toland have used the camera not only to record a story but to comment on it, to compose by visual contrasts and sharp glimpses caught from unusual points an over-powering suggestive film" ("The Ambiguous *Citizen Kane*" 5).

14   James Naremore states that the "technique of the opening segment establishes the camera as a restless, ghostly observer, more silent and discrete than the journalists who poke about among Kane's belongings, but linked to them in certain ways" (71).

15   The set design was also innovative. Designer Perry Ferguson used ceilings on his sets with more frequency and variety than Holly-

Figure 2
Camera angle heightens the dramatic impact of Kanes's election rally (Lebo 53).

wood was used to. According to Harlan Lebo, "The ceilings were not merely flat surfaces over the drama below. Ferguson varied them with every manner of texture and treatment—beams, filigree, stained glass, even skylights. . ." (68). The combination of the set design and cinematography gives the spectacle element of *Citizen Kane* an added significance.

16   Despite the fact that *Citizen Kane* is one of the most innovative films ever produced, it still follows Aristotle's archetype of tragic drama. Although the element of lyric poetry is not employed, the film conforms to Aristotle's remaining five elements: plot structure, character, thought, style, and spectacle. These five elements are classified into the three components of object, media, and mode, which Welles uses to mimic humanity. Welles' use of Aristotle's prescription for tragedy is one reason why *Citizen Kane* has become a classic film.

Works Cited

Aristotle. *Poetics*. Trans. Stephen Halliwell. Chapel Hill: U of North Carolina, 1987.

Crowther, Bosley. "The Ambiguous *Citizen Kane*." *New York Times* 4 May 1941, sec. 9:5.

Lebo, Harlan. *Citizen Kane: The Fiftieth-Anniversary Album*. New York: Doubleday, 1990.

Lucas, F. L. *Tragedy: Serious Drama in Relation to Aristotle's Poetics*. London: Hogarth, 1957.

Mankiewicz, Herman J., and Orson Welles. *The* Citizen Kane *Book*. Boston: Little, Brown, 1971.

Maxfield, James. "'A Man Like Ourselves': *Citizen Kane* as an Aristotelian Tragedy." *Literature and Film Quarterly* 14 (1986): 195–203.

McBride, Joseph. *Orson Welles*. New York: Viking, 1972.

Naremore, James. *The Magic World of Orson Welles*. New York: Oxford UP, 1978.

Reading Critically: Questions for Discussion

1. What is the function of the opening quotation?
2. How do the writers establish their credibility?
3. Do the illustrations serve to clarify the analysis? What other illustrations might be included to improve your understanding?
4. If you haven't seen *Citizen Kane,* does this analysis make you want to see it? If you have seen the film, does this analysis make you want to see it again? That is, does this Aristotelian analysis improve your appreciation of the film?

PART V

Expanding Your Repertoire: Persuasive Aim Writing

Persuasive Aim Writing: An Overview

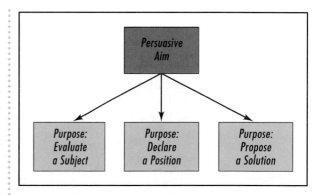

*T**he old car was sitting in the driveway. I was sitting in the old car. I was
sixteen.*

*"So you see," I explained to my father, "I'm having trouble with this
stick shift because I'm left-handed and I simply don't have the sensitivity in
my right hand to move the stick shift to the right spot at the same time that
I'm pressing on the clutch with my left foot. Why can't I just drive the new
car with the automatic transmission?"*

*"You're getting impatient," he answered, smiling at my explanation,
"but if you keep practicing, I'm sure you'll get it."*

I was discouraged. He was unconvinced.

*My father was a gifted automotive mechanic. This was his occupation.
It was also his vocation. In the diagnosis and repair of engines, he was
sensitive to the slightest noise or vibrations. He could always determine
how a car ought to sound and how it ought to drive. To my father, using a
manual transmission was essential to developing this sensitivity to a car's
operation. If you were using a manual transmission, you were communicating with your car.*

*"But," he added, "even if you don't drive this car, remember that
sometime—maybe in an emergency—you might have to drive a car that
has a manual transmission and you'll be sorry if you don't know how."*

"Okay," I said. "I'll keep trying."

*I hadn't convinced him that I couldn't drive the old car. But he had
also implied that I wouldn't have to, thus reminding me that his sensitivity
wasn't limited to the mechanical intricacies of engines and transmissions.
(SD)*

Persuasion is the ability to influence people's opinions. We all have this
ability, and we exercise it daily. We tell friends why we like classical
music and why we dislike opera, why we have majored in engineering,
why we believe wind power is the answer to the energy crisis, why butter
is superior to margarine, and why we think the Cleveland Indians keep
losing. Simultaneously, advertising tries to influence us to choose this
toothpaste or that toilet paper, friends give us their opinions of their
teachers, teachers explain why their classes are important, political candidates justify their voting records, and coaches motivate us with promises
of a winning season.

In short, you have developed your persuasive abilities through daily
practice, achieving through trial and error a basic understanding of effective and ineffective persuasion techniques within different rhetorical situations. Similarly, the ability to write persuasively comes with a great deal of
practice, and the following chapters give you opportunities to exercise
your persuasive writing abilities. This chapter, however, is designed to
minimize your trial and error by describing the characteristics of persua-

sive writing and strategies for composing a persuasive essay.

Like expressive and referential aim writing, persuasive writing is achieved by planning, translating, and reviewing your decisions regarding invention, arrangement, style, memory, and delivery.

PERSUASIVE AIM IN WRITING

In **persuasive aim writing,** the communication triangle emphasizes the reader. The writer's job is to influence the reader's attitude or actions on a subject. Thus the writer gives special attention to the reader's knowledge and opinion of the subject as well as the reader's opinion of the writer. The writer chooses the information likely to have the desired impact on the reader's attitude or actions, always considering how word choice, organization, and the visual display of information might influence the reader's opinion.

The following are examples of persuasive aim writing:

advertisements	political messages
religious sermons	editorials
proposals	fundraising appeals
sales letters	legislative debates
position papers	reviews of products or services
job evaluations	letters of recommendation

Adversarial and Conciliatory Persuasion

Persuasive aim writing also has two basic orientations: adversarial persuasion and conciliatory persuasion. In **adversarial persuasion,** your objective is to prove that your opinion is the only appropriate opinion on the subject. No compromise is possible. This is a rhetorical situation of winners and losers. Political candidates on the campaign trail, for example, exercise adversarial persuasion. The voters have to choose among the available candidates, rivals for a single elective office. Each candidate's objective is to identify his or her differences from the opposing candidates and prove the superiority of his or her experience, ability, and positions on major issues.

In **conciliatory persuasion,** however, compromise is possible. Your objective is to bring together opposing sides to decide a given issue. All sides are partial winners and partial losers. Political officials discussing legislation typically use conciliatory persuasion, trying to build a coalition that will support a proposed law.

Adversarial persuasion and conciliatory persuasion are opposite points on a continuum as opposed to two different types of persuasion. Often, for example, the closer that candidates come to election day, the more adversarial is their political persuasion.

You communicate your persuasive orientation through the information you cover, the way you organize that information, the words and illustrations you choose, and the way you display your words and illustrations on the page or screen. For example, if you were creating a brochure for a political candidate, you might list his or her legislative successes, starting that list with his or her major victories. You might describe your candidate with adjectives such as *effective, industrious, courageous, responsible,* and *honest,* and you might include several photographs of the candidate looking as effective, industrious, courageous, responsible, and honest as possible. You might also display this information on the page using red, white, and blue. This uncompromising characterization of your candidate as the ideal political official is adversarial persuasion. To emphasize that your candidate is a simple man or woman of the people, however, you might develop a less adversarial campaign. You might give a chronological listing of the candidate's service to the community, minimize the glorifying adjectives, stick to a single photograph, and design the brochure on white paper with black ink.

Subordinate Aims

Virtually all writing is at least partially persuasive. If the writer's primary focus is to influence the reader's opinion, the writing is primarily persuasive. Nevertheless, it is possible to have subordinate referential or expressive aims. If you write a letter of recommendation for a friend, your dominant aim is persuasive because you are trying to influence the prospective employer's hiring decision. To prove your case, however, you might discuss your friend's specific qualifications, such as job experience and education. Here your aim is referential. You might also include a personal narrative that illustrates your friend's perseverance, generosity, or integrity. Here your aim is expressive. Thus, though your letter of recommendation is primarily persuasive, it also has subordinate referential and expressive aims.

Subordinate aims influence your choice of information as well as how you organize, word, and display that information. In discussing your friend's qualifications, for example, you might display the pertinent credentials as a numbered list, from most important to least important, using specialized terminology to describe the various job skills. In the narrative, however, a chronologically organized paragraph and simple wording might be your choice.

Your decisions regarding aim, however, have to be flexible. As you research, write, and revise, your subordinate aims especially might change. After writing the personal narrative for your friend's letter of recommendation, you might notice that your letter is getting quite long and decide that the narrative is unnecessary.

PERSUASIVE PURPOSES IN WRITING

If you decide that your dominant aim is persuasive, you also have to determine the purpose of your persuasive writing. Persuasive writing typically serves to evaluate a subject, declare a position on a given issue, or propose a solution to a problem.

You **evaluate a subject** in order to convince your readers that the subject is either satisfactory or unsatisfactory. For example, as a columnist for the school newspaper, you might write a review of a new word processing program, assessing its various operations and judging its merits relative to its cost. Your objective would be to give a qualified or unqualified recommendation of the program or to advise against it.

You **declare a position** on a given issue in order to convince your reader to adopt your position. For example, you might write a newspaper editorial that endorses a political candidate, offering all the reasons why you think this candidate is right for the office. Your objective is to persuade the voters to support this candidate also.

You **propose a solution** to a problem in order to convince your reader that your solution is appropriate. For example, you might serve on a campus committee that proposes banning tobacco on campus as a way of minimizing the maintenance and repair costs associated with its usage. Your objective is to convince the campus community and especially the administration that your proposed solution is fair and effective.

In each situation, the persuasion might be more or less conciliatory, more or less adversarial. In your review, for example, you could be conciliatory, praising as well as criticizing the word processing program, rejecting this version of the program, but anxiously anticipating a new and improved version. In your editorial, you could be adversarial, praising your candidate and repudiating the opposing candidate. In your proposal, you might balance the adversarial and the conciliatory, explaining that though your committee objects to tobacco usage on campus, its objection is strictly a question of economics. Your proposal could emphasize the savings to smokers as well as nonsmokers if lower maintenance and repair costs serve to stabilize tuition.

Your persuasive writing might also have subordinate purposes. For example, your primary objective might be to evaluate the parking situation on campus. In doing so, you determine that the number of parking spaces available for handicapped drivers is insufficient. You assess a variety of proposals addressing the situation and determine which of the available alternatives is the appropriate solution. This evaluation leads you to propose adding 100 new spaces for handicapped drivers. As you explain your proposal, you also declare your opposition to the administration's proposal of adding only 25 new parking spaces for handicapped drivers.

Your integration of subordinate purposes, however, has to be flexible. You might start writing with the intention of denouncing the administration's proposal. While revising, however, you might decide that because you are writing to administration officials, it would be more effective for you to be conciliatory and emphasize the superior merits of your solution.

Each academic field offers you opportunities to evaluate a subject, declare a position, or propose a solution. Consider, for example, the following writing situations:

- For a public administration course, evaluate the ability of your city officials to recruit new companies and create new jobs. Voice your opinion of the city's decision to build a new prison. Develop a proposal to improve the local economy.

- In a biology course, write a proposal to research genetic causes of chemical dependency. Evaluate previous studies of this subject. Declare your position on the funding for this type of research: Are we spending enough money?

- In a literary studies class, declare your position on Mark Twain's *The Adventures of Huckleberry Finn*. Do you believe this book is racist? Review the different interpretations of this book. Which interpretation do you consider superior? Propose adding more women writers and a wider variety of international writers to the reading list of your literary studies class.

- For a chemistry class, develop industrial guidelines for the disposal of toxic chemicals. Evaluate the effectiveness of the guidelines. Discuss your opinion of violators.

- In a physical therapy course, propose a program of exercises for a victim of a bicycle accident. Evaluate the victim's progress. Declare your position on the wearing of bicycle helmets.

- For a marketing course, review the job opportunities for marketing majors. Propose the creation of a résumé writing service for local marketing majors. Voice your opinion of single-page versus multipage résumés.

- In a political science course, declare your position on the creation of biological weapons. Write a proposal to investigate their worldwide proliferation. Determine which biological weapons are the deadliest.

- For an engineering class, evaluate existing designs for a solar-powered vehicle. Which designs look promising for city driving? Which look promising for highway driving? Propose a design for a family-size solar-powered vehicle. Voice your position on designing for energy efficiency versus human comfort and safety.

ANALYZING AND MAPPING THE PERSUASIVE RHETORICAL SITUATION

In addition to deciding on your dominant and subordinate aims and purposes, you also have to consider your relationship to your subject and to your audience. **Mapping your persuasive rhetorical situation** gives you a visible reminder of your audience's level of motivation and similarity to you as well as a list of key words regarding your subject. Use the knowledge continuum to identify your relationship to your subject. List key words regarding the subject and specify how you acquired this information—through participation or through observation.

Use the audience continuum to specify your proximity to your readers. On the narrow arcs closer to the writer (you), identify the readers who share with you a common background, perspective, or occupation; on the wider arcs, identify the readers who are different from you. Also specify your readers' level of motivation, from those who are likely to consider your list of key words interesting and important to those who might judge it boring and insignificant.

Figure 14.1 illustrates how one student, LaRae Fischer, has mapped her persuasive rhetorical situation.

In this map, LaRae lists key words regarding her subject—global warming. As a campus activist, she is familiar with this issue and identifies her general knowledge on the "participation" side of the continuum. LaRae is also a biology major and has read widely on the impact of global warming. She lists this information on the "observation" side.

LaRae analyzes her audience according to their attitudes about environmental issues. She thinks that students and other adults who share her concern for the environment will be interested in the position she takes on this subject. As a consequence, she positions these readers on the "motivated" side of the audience continuum. She maps all other readers on the "unmotivated" side—a reminder that she must work hard to convince these members of her audience.

In college and on the job, you will ordinarily be assigned subjects to investigate. Given a subject, you have to decide three things:

1. What, if anything, do you already know about this subject?
2. How did you acquire this knowledge?
3. How might you add to your knowledge?

Your psychology teacher, for example, might ask you to review several new studies of schizoid behavior. In your investigation, you might consider your sources of knowledge on this subject. Do you have family, friends, or neighbors who have been diagnosed as exhibiting schizoid behavior? Could you interview psychologists on this subject? Does the library have books or articles on schizoid behavior? Similarly, your boss

Read More About It

See Chapter 4, pp. 85–93.

Figure 14.1 Mapping LaRae's persuasive rhetorical situation

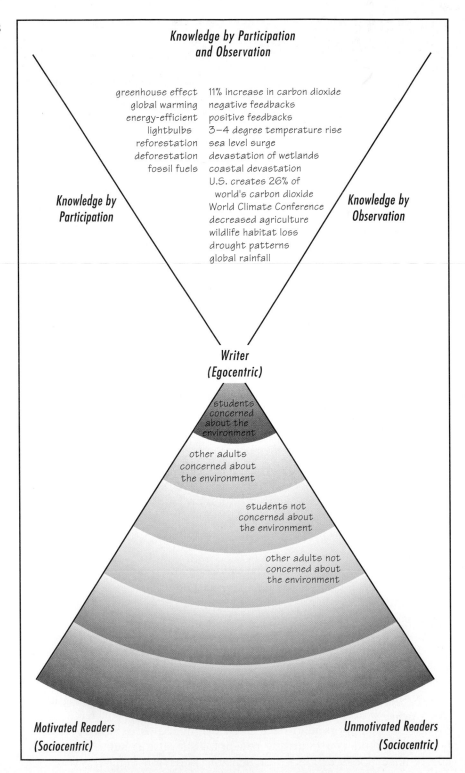

might direct you to write a proposal for a restaurant's new advertising campaign. Have you been to this restaurant? Could you interview the owners to determine their attitudes and ideas? Are the materials from the restaurant's previous advertising campaigns available for you to examine? What do empirical studies of restaurant advertising recommend?

If you have the opportunity to choose your subject, however, you will ordinarily pick a subject that is familiar to you, either through participation or through observation. Because you have knowledge by participation, for example, you might choose to evaluate the foreign language classes at your local high school, give your opinion of a proposal to raise tuition, or propose a campus-wide Halloween Festival. Or your previous reading on a subject—knowledge by observation—might lead you to evaluate the architecture of Frank Lloyd Wright, declare your position on the theory of evolution, or propose a way to stimulate the economy of Haiti. Or using your knowledge by participation and observation, you might choose to evaluate different methods of birth control, voice your opinion on the colorization of black-and-white films, or propose raising the legal driving age to 18.

RESEARCHING AND DISCOVERING PERSUASIVE INFORMATION

In order to write persuasively, you need to discover information that will influence your reader's opinion. If you are evaluating a subject, declaring a position, or proposing a solution, you are making a claim. This **claim** is the thesis of your persuasive writing. You might claim that the local newspaper is biased, that teachers deserve higher salaries, or that installing streetlights at specific locations will stop crime on campus. If you wish your audience to approve your claim, however, you will need to establish your credibility (using ethos), prove your claim is logical (using logos), and motivate your audience (using ethos, logos, and pathos). Persuasive information is necessary to accomplish your objectives. You discover this persuasive information through participation and through observation.

Establishing Credibility

While establishing credibility (ethos) is always important, it is essential to effective persuasion. By exhibiting your knowledge of your subject and your basic integrity, you characterize yourself as both authoritative and ethical. To establish your credibility, brainstorm to develop a list of your qualifications to write on a given subject. If you are evaluating a book on biodiversity, for example, you might mention your previous studies of this subject, your biology degree, and your World Wildlife Organization membership.

Invention Guide for Persuasive Writing

Aim and Purpose

1. What is your writing task?
2. Are you writing individually or collaboratively?
3. Is the text's dominant aim persuasive?
4. Are there subordinate aims? What are they and how do they affect the information in the text?
5. What is your purpose for writing? What specifically do you want your text to accomplish? Does your purpose satisfy the requirements of your writing task?
6. Are there subordinate purposes? What are they and how do they affect the information in the text?

Mapping the Rhetorical Situation: Subject and the Knowledge Continuum

1. What is your relationship to the subject? That is, will your point of view in your essay be that of a participant, observer, or participant-observer?
2. Map your knowledge on the knowledge continuum by listing key words regarding your subject. Mapping is an ongoing process: continue to revise and refine your map as you learn more about your subject.

Mapping the Rhetorical Situation: Readers and the Audience Continuum

1. What is the demographic profile of your readers (age; gender; social, economic, and educational levels; personal and professional backgrounds and experiences; cultural and situational factors and contexts)? How will their profile affect their responses to the subject and text?
2. Select representative members of your audience, and role-play to determine the following:

   - readers' motives for reading your text
   - readers' enthusiasm about your subject
   - readers' sense that your subject is timely

3. How can you help readers to process and interpret your text more effectively (organization, memory cues, language, and visual signposts)?

4. Map your readers on the audience continuum. Mapping is an ongoing process: continue to revise and refine your map as you learn more about your audience.

Information: Research and Discovery

1. What kind of knowledge does your writing task require?

   Knowledge by participation (personal records, brainstorming, pentad, classical topics, visualizing, and computer-assisted invention)—documentation or bibliography usually unnecessary

   Knowledge by observation (interviews, questionnaires, and library resources)—documentation and bibliography usually necessary

   Knowledge by participation and observation (combination of sources identified above)—documentation and bibliography usually necessary

2. Which research strategies will you use to locate and generate information? Why?

3. How will you establish your credibility?

4. How will you prove your claim?

   - What is your claim?
   - What is your evidence? Is your evidence sufficient? Plausible? pertinent?
   - Do you have supporting claims? What is the evidence for your supporting claims?
   - Does your evidence have a valid relationship to your claim?
   - What are possible objections to your claim? What are possible objections to your supporting claims? How will you answer these objections?

5. How will you motivate your audience to approve your claim? What kinds of evidence or techniques will you use (statistics, examples, narratives, illustrations, quotations, similes and metaphors, questions and directions)?

6. Is your persuasive writing ethical?

Identifying with your audience is also a way to establish your credibility. By emphasizing that you and your audience have similar views on a given subject or on a variety of subjects, you show that you deserve to be trusted. If you and your audience often think alike, your readers are unlikely to consider you either irrational or irresponsible. For example, if you are supporting a special tax on guns, you might explain that, like your audience, you typically oppose new taxes.

Self-deprecation might also be appropriate, especially if your audience is hostile or suspicious. By demonstrating your ability to criticize or ridicule yourself, you reveal a capacity for objectivity on virtually all subjects. You might, for example, acknowledge that you don't know everything about your subject or admit that you've changed your mind on the issue.

Occasionally, it is necessary to show that you have no ulterior or selfish motivations. Caution is important here, however: if you simply declare the purity of your motives, you might arouse cynicism instead of trust. Give evidence of your sincerity. For example, you might propose that your school build a bigger library. If you declare that your only objective is to improve the school's academic services, your audience could be suspicious. It would be more convincing to explain that you will probably graduate before the new library is completed and, therefore, it will not benefit you but the students who come after you and the school itself.

Proving Your Claim Is Logical

Proving your claim is logical (logos) is often difficult. In addition to using personal records and brainstorming to discover evidence, you might analyze your subject according to the five questions (who? what? when and where? how? why?) or according to the classical topics (definition, classification and division, process, cause and effect, comparison and contrast). Or you might visualize your subject, using notations and diagrams to discover ideas. You might also interview sources, develop and distribute a questionnaire, and visit the library to locate appropriate books and articles. Your job here is to discover all the information necessary to justify your claim.

To prove your claim is logical, the evidence you discover has to be sufficient, plausible, and pertinent. In addition, the relationship of the evidence to the claim has to be **valid**: that is, your claim has to be a direct consequence of the evidence. And you have to consider and answer possible objections to your claim. If you discover that your supporting evidence is unsatisfactory, consider modifying your claim according to the available evidence. For example, you might offer the following claim:

Steven Spielberg is the world's greatest film director.

In order to prove your claim is logical, you brainstorm, consider the classical topics, compose a questionnaire, and locate appropriate film reviews and magazine articles at the library. Through brainstorming, you identify the various Steven Spielberg films that you have enjoyed seeing: *Jaws, E.T., Raiders of the Lost Ark, Close Encounters of the Third Kind, The Color Purple, Jurassic Park, Schindler's List*. Using the classical topics, you determine that a definition of the word *greatest* is critical: Does *greatest* signify the director of the most popular films, the most critically acclaimed films, or the most award-winning films? You realize that only once has a Steven Spielberg film received the Academy Award for Best Picture and that only once has he received the Academy Award for Best Director. You decide this unexceptional record is a possible objection to your claim.

In your questionnaire, you ask 1000 people to identify their favorite film director from a list of 25. You also ask people to identify their ten favorite films from a list of 100. You discover that Steven Spielberg is always among the top five directors and is listed most often as the favorite. You also discover that only Steven Spielberg films are always listed among people's ten favorite films and that Steven Spielberg is the only director who has two or more films listed among people's ten favorites.

It occurs to you, however, that your questionnaire offered people a list of 25 *American* film directors and a list of 100 *American* films. You decide, as a consequence, to modify your claim:

> Steven Spielberg is the greatest American film director.

Your library research uncovers film review after film review praising various Steven Spielberg films. The only exception is the film *1941*, which is widely criticized. You also locate a list of the 50 top money-making films, which includes five Steven Spielberg films. And you come across several articles that explain why so often the greatest actors, actresses, directors, and films have never received Academy Awards.

With this information, you have sufficient, plausible, and pertinent evidence to justify your claim. Your evidence is substantial and has clear relevance to your claim. You establish that Steven Spielberg's films are consistently among the most popular and critically acclaimed. You also show that winning awards is often a poor indicator of excellence, thus answering a possible objection to your claim. Your evidence is believable because you cite credible sources of information. The findings of your questionnaire are similarly plausible, especially because you asked the opinions of 1000 people. Your evidence also has a valid relationship to your claim: if Steven Spielberg's record for directing popular and critically acclaimed films is without equal, a direct consequence is that Steven Spielberg is likely to be judged the greatest American film director.

In the process of proving that your claim is logical, you offer supporting evidence. Often, this evidence is itself a claim and you have to prove that this supporting claim is also logical. Proving a supporting claim is especially important if it is a likely source of objections. To prove that your evaluation of Steven Spielberg is logical, you also have to claim that your definition of *greatest* is a logical definition. You also have to prove that your questionnaire is a reliable and valid indicator of people's opinions and that you have credible sources of information. To prove your supporting claims, again you give evidence and again this evidence is often itself a claim. Persuasive writing is thus a pyramid: you establish a claim on the basis of evidence and supporting claims, which you establish on the basis of evidence and supporting claims, which you establish on the basis of evidence and supporting claims to which no objections are likely.

Read More About It

See Part VII.

Ordinarily, the way to distinguish evidence from claims is fairly simple. Evidence is often introduced by the word *because* or by words with the meaning of *because,* such as *since, for, as, inasmuch as,* and *due to.* Claims are often introduced by the word *therefore* or by words with the meaning of *therefore,* such as *thus, hence, so, consequently, as a consequence,* and *as a result.* If the evidence has a word introducing it, the claim usually has none, and vice versa:

> I propose that the city establish a science museum *because* such a facility would support the education of local children and bring tourists to the city.

> A science museum would support the education of local children and bring tourists to the city; *therefore,* I propose that the city establish such a facility.

Motivating Your Audience

In addition to establishing your credibility and proving that your claim is logical, you also have to motivate your audience to approve your claim by citing authorities (ethos), using logic (logos), and arousing emotions (pathos). If all your audience does is acknowledge that you are credible and that your claim is logical, your persuasive writing is ineffective—a victim of inertia. The more difficult it is for your audience to adopt your evaluation, position, or proposal, the more inertia you are likely to notice.

This **inertia** has three chief causes: either readers underestimate the need for action, underestimate their ability to act, or overestimate the cost of action. No persuasion is possible, therefore, unless you show the audience that approval of your claim is essential because of the size, severity, or urgency of the issue you discuss. In order to emphasize size or severity, discuss the likely impact of the issue either on the audience itself or on groups or individuals important to the audience. That is, appeal either to the audience's self-interest or to its sense of altruism. If you oppose your city council's banning of controversial books from the city library, you could show that the city council is banning a lot of books or that the book banning is stifling important ideas. Your objective is to identify the damage that the city council's action does to the audience itself or to the people using the library. In order to emphasize urgency, demonstrate either that the situation is deteriorating quickly or that the opportunity to address

Arrangement Guide for Persuasive Writing

Evidence: Establishing Unity

1. Has your research yielded sufficient, plausible, and pertinent information to support your thesis?
2. How do your research data reflect the three rhetorical appeals: ethos, logos, and pathos?
3. How does your research shape your thesis statement (claim)? Is your thesis statement specific and concrete? Focused and feasible? Interesting?
4. How do the patterns of organization in your text help readers see and follow the logic and approach to your subject? Have you chosen sequential organization (chronological, spatial, hierarchical), categorical organization, or a combination of the two? Why?

Discourse Blocs: Developing Ideas

1. What is the internal structure of your text? Identify and outline the discourse blocs in your essay.
2. What modes of development have you used within the discourse blocs? Why?
3. What functions do the various discourse blocs serve (title, introduction, transitional blocs, conclusion)?

Coherence and Cohesion: Making Connections

1. Have you connected sentences by using repetition, substitution, and transitions?
2. Do you use parallelism for coordinated and listed items? To reinforce ideas of equal importance or similar meaning?

Outlining: Tracing Your Path

1. Have you written an outline, either before or after you've drafted your text? Does it seem logical and clear?
2. How will you you refine the design and development of your text in the next draft?

the issue is immediate and limited. You might emphasize that the city council is banning more and more books with each passing day or that unless the book banning is stopped immediately, the damage to the library and the community's reputation will be impossible to repair.

It is equally important for you to assure your audience of its ability to approve your claim. Often, readers believe themselves to be the wrong people to approve a claim. They imagine that the people likely to adopt a given evaluation, position, or proposal have more (or less) education, experience, money, political power, social status, athletic skill, or artistic ability. Your job is to prove otherwise. For example, if you are proposing that your readers vote for a particular candidate, you have to demonstrate that this candidate's supporters are like the people of your audience.

You also have to show that the cost of approving your claim is justified, again appealing either to the audience's self-interest or to its sense of altruism. For example, if you are soliciting contributions to a charity, you might mention the satisfied feeling that comes from making a donation or the impact that each donation has on the lives of the recipients.

Different types of evidence and techniques (ethos, logos, and pathos) are available for motivating your audience, including statistics, examples, narratives, illustrations, quotations, similes and metaphors, and questions and directions.

Statistics have substantial persuasive power, possibly because numerical information is decisive and unambiguous. If you are proposing a city-wide recycling program, for example, you might cite statistics regarding the tons of items disposed of daily that could be recycled, thus emphasizing the size or severity of the issue. To show urgency, you could specify the capacity of the city's landfill, the quantity of garbage the city landfill receives each week, and the time remaining before the landfill reaches its capacity. You also could cite the number of cities that have established recycling programs, thus emphasizing your city's ability to do so. Statistics on the minor cost to tax-paying citizens of your recycling proposal versus the major cost of building a new city landfill would also be persuasive evidence.

Examples make your ideas easier to understand and easier to remember by linking a specific object to your generalized claim. In proposing a city-wide recycling program, give examples of numerous items that are often discarded instead of recycled, thus emphasizing the size of the issue. Mention the years and years required for various items such as newspapers and plastic bottles to decay in the city landfill, thereby showing the severity of the issue.

Narratives serve to dramatize and personalize your ideas, making your evaluation, position, or proposal easier to understand and easier to remember. By linking your claim to a specific story, you emphasize the human dimension to your ideas. To show the size, severity, or urgency of the recycling issue, record the dire experiences of a city that never instituted a recycling program. Chronicle the lives of ordinary people who recycle daily, thus implying your audience's ability to recycle as well. To establish the relatively minor cost of approving your claim, include stories that describe how easily people acquire the recycling habit.

Illustrations improve understanding by making your ideas vivid and easily accessible. To emphasize the size, severity, and urgency of your recycling program, you might design a line graph showing that the city landfill has been receiving more and more garbage each year for 25 years. Or to emphasize your audience's ability to approve your proposal, you might display a regional map identifying the neighboring cities that have established a recycling program.

Quotations associate your ideas with the words of important, famous, or credible people. A quotation from the mayor of your city on the desirability of a recycling program might serve to emphasize the size, severity, or urgency of the issue. Quotations from a variety of citizens of different educational backgrounds and economic levels voicing their approval of your proposal could show your audience that it has a similar ability to act on this issue. Or you might incorporate quotations from the mayors of cities with recycling programs, testifying to the merits of their programs.

Similes and metaphors allow you to associate your claim with objects or ideas that are more familiar to your audience. (Similes are explicit comparisons, using the words *like* or *as;* metaphors are implicit comparisons.) To emphasize the necessity of your recycling proposal, you might describe the city's landfill as being "like a ticking time bomb" (simile) and discuss the tragic consequences of ignoring this peril. To emphasize your audience's ability to approve your proposal, you might describe people who start to recycle as "the pioneers of the city's recycling program" (metaphor) thus encouraging all citizens to imitate their behavior. Or you might describe the higher taxes associated with your proposed recycling program as "each citizen's contribution to a better environment" (metaphor) thus comparing the costs to a charitable donation.

Questions and directions encourage audiences to collaborate with you as you compose your claim. Audiences who thus participate in the composition of a claim are often more willing to approve it. To emphasize the size, severity, or urgency of your recycling proposal, you might ask audiences a question such as *How many cans and bottles do you normally throw in the garbage each week?* Or you could give a direction such as *Count the number of cans and bottles you throw in the garbage this week.* To minimize the costs of approving your proposal, you might give directions such as *Consider that this recycling program will cost you only fifty cents a week in higher taxes. Make a list of all the things you could buy each week for fifty cents. Then cross off your list everything less important than a cleaner environment.*

To discover the information necessary to motivate your audience, brainstorm to develop a list of effective questions and directions. Analyze your subject according to the five questions (who? what? when and where? how? and why?) to develop a provocative narrative. Explore the classical topics (definition, classification and division, process, cause and effect, comparison and contrast) to discover appropriate similes and metaphors. Visualize your subject, using notations and diagrams to discover inspiring illustrations. Interview sources for perceptive quotations. Identify books and articles that might give you statistics, examples, narratives, quotations, and illustrations.

Style Guide for Persuasive Writing

1. *Individuality.* How much of you is in this sample of persuasive writing? What features of style indicate your personal likes and dislikes regarding wording, sentence structure, spelling, and punctuation?

2. *Time.* How does the time period during which you are writing influence your persuasive style? Does your age or your audience's age influence your style? How?

3. *Dialect.* Are you using a local dialect or a universal dialect? Why? What features of style are characteristic of the dialect you are using?

4. *Collaboration.* Is your persuasive writing collaborative? How have editors or coauthors influenced your style?

5. *Subject.* What is the subject of your persuasive writing? What specialized wording or phrasing is typical of persuasive writing on this subject? How does this subject influence the spelling and punctuation of your persuasive writing?

6. *Type of document.* What type of persuasive writing are you composing? What is its common function? How will your audience use this persuasive writing? What features of style are characteristic of this type of persuasive writing?

7. *Relationship to audience.* What is your relationship with your audience? Is a formal or informal style appropriate? What is the appropriate degree of formality or informality? How does this degree of formality or informality influence your persuasive style?

Using Persuasive Information Ethically

It is possible to motivate your audience without proving the logic of your claim, but such a rhetorical practice is considered unethical. It is deception instead of persuasion. Whenever you motivate your audience, you necessarily arouse emotions. You liberate your readers from the chains of inertia by substituting pity, love, fear, anger, hope, and so on. Arousing emotions to motivate your audience is appropriate and ethical. Substituting emotions for logical evidence to prove your claim, however, is inappropriate and unethical.

Each time you write a persuasive essay, you assume a series of **ethical obligations,** corresponding to the sides of the communication triangle. You have a vital obligation to yourself to preserve a reputation for integrity. If you damage or lose your credibility, you jeopardize all the persuasive writing you might do thereafter. Your second obligation is to your subject: You have to communicate your knowledge as clearly and logically as possible. By trying to establish the logic of your evaluation, position, or proposal, you contribute to human knowledge regarding your subject. Your third obligation is to your audience: You have to motivate your audience to approve only logical claims. If you encourage approval of illogical or unproven claims, you trick your audience. You also diminish human knowledge of your subject and possibly damage your credibility.

COMPOSING PERSUASIVE AIM WRITING

This chapter has identified the major characteristics of persuasive writing and the persuasive rhetorical situation. Reading this chapter has supplied you knowledge through observation. The ability to write persuasively, however, also comes through participation—by writing persuasive essays, editorials, letters of recommendation, critical reviews, and so on. The following chapters, therefore, offer opportunities for you to evaluate subjects, declare positions, and propose solutions. Keep a portfolio of all the maps and evolving versions of your writing as a chronicle of your journey through the territory of persuasive rhetoric.

Memory and Delivery Guide for Persuasive Writing

1. Is your persuasive writing handwritten, typewritten, or computerized? Why? If handwritten, is your handwriting legible? If type-written, do you have typographical choices of design, style, and size? If computerized, are you designing a paper copy or a screen copy?

2. Does the typography aid reading? How do your typographical choices establish your credibility, clarify the logic of your claim, and motivate your audience? Consider your choices regarding

   - typeface
   - type style
   - type size
   - upper- and lowercase letters
   - leading
   - line length
   - alignment

3. Are illustrations necessary? If so, are tables or figures appropriate? If you include tables, does the typography of the tables aid their reading? If you include figures, which of the following are appropriate:

   - line graphs
   - column graphs
   - bar graphs
   - pie charts
   - organization charts
   - flow charts
   - diagrams
   - drawings
   - photographs

   Do the figures emphasize appropriate information? Is the visual display ethical? How do your illustrations establish your credibility, clarify the logic of your claim, and motivate your audience?

4. Is white space used effectively?

5. What is the appropriate page design (essay, book, letter, memo, or circular)?

Repertoire Focus: Evaluating a Subject

As human beings, we constantly evaluate our surroundings. We judge the merits of clothing styles, cars, restaurants, movies, television shows, songs, people's opinions, political candidates, friends, neighbors, teachers, drivers, sales clerks, and so on. For our evaluations to be fair, however, our praise or criticism should be based on satisfactory supporting evidence.

In college and on the job, you will be asked to compose written evaluations of a variety of subjects. You might review theories or procedures, assess research methods or findings, weigh information sources, judge proposals or complaints, and evaluate materials or equipment. In each case, supporting evidence is essential to establish your credibility, to prove the logic of your opinion, and to motivate your audience to adopt your evaluation. Your ability to compose rigorous and systematic evaluations is thus crucial to your academic and professional success.

REPERTOIRE WRITING TASK: CRITERIA-EVALUATION

Select a subject to evaluate. Before you begin your assessment, you will first have to define and explain your subject, giving readers the background information, reasons, and evidence (arguments and counterarguments) they will need to know to trust your judgment and recommendation. Your principal goal is to convince your audience that your critical assessment is informed and reasonable, based on criteria that are generally accepted as appropriate for judging this kind of subject. Because this is persuasive aim writing, consider fully what your readers already know about this subject, what their perceptions and attitudes may be about it, and why. Your audience for this essay may be readers much like you; a general college audience; a general adult readership; or a specific campus, community, or professional group.

Below are three variations of this writing task, originating from the different ways you may "know" about the subject you assess.

Knowledge by Participation

Write an essay assessing a subject (media, fine arts, literary works, education, government, campus, leisure) that you know of through direct experience.

Knowledge by Observation

Write an essay assessing a subject (media, fine arts, literary works, education, government, campus, leisure) that you learned about indirectly (through interviews, reading, television, or another medium). Your subject should be one that others have written about, yielding some form of published biographical, social, or historical information that you can integrate into your essay.

Knowledge by Participation and Observation

Write an essay assessing a subject (media, fine arts, literary works, education, government, campus, leisure) that you know about both from personal experience as well as from other people (through interviews, reading, television, or another medium). Your subject should be one that others have written about, yielding some form of published biographical, social, or historical information that you can integrate into your essay.

REPERTORY COMPANY OF STUDENT WRITERS: THEIR RESPONSES TO THE TASK

As you begin to address your writing task, you may wish to meet other student writers in our repertory company and read and discuss their essays, which were written in response to the same assignment. These student writers interacted in their own writing communities or focus groups to develop multiple drafts of their essays.

The three essays in this chapter focus on the subject of education: types of educational systems, the process of selecting textbooks, and the development of programs for at-risk students. In each case, the student writers in our repertory company expressed a deep commitment to learning about and assessing these aspects of education. These student writers scanned their journals to help them recall interesting subjects to pursue. You may find it helpful to reread your journal to discover ideas to research and evaluate for this writing task.

To provide you with some additional context for the essays that follow, we've included journal entries, a map of the rhetorical situation (the knowledge continuum and audience continuum), and research strategies for each essay. You'll also find some questions for discussion and analysis after each selection.

KNOWLEDGE BY PARTICIPATION

The first essay, "Means and Values of Education," was written by Matthew Coplen. He evaluates three different educational systems from the perspective of the "writer as participant." Although Matthew discusses homeschooling in this essay, he does not quote from library sources or use the ideas of others to assess that particular system.

Reviewing Journal Entries

Here are some excerpts from Matthew's journal written while he was composing "Means and Values of Education."

JOURNAL

Talked to my instructor about my persuasive essay today. The hardest thing for me now is finding a subject. Writing persuasively is hard; I want to write from what I know. The general subject area I am interested in is education. Why? I really liked writing the homeschooling paper. When I think of how many people are turning from public school to other systems, I'm amazed. But can I write about homeschooling again? My teacher wants me to talk to my focus group about it.

My group says that what I know about homeschooling is now kind of mine. My common knowledge, especially if I don't actually cite particular ideas from those books and articles I have read specifically. This is hard for me. I like to use sources, but I want to evaluate current systems and I don't think I necessarily should have to research them all to support what I believe to be important. I know lots about these systems without using experts. What I have to say is valid, and everyday people—parents, school kids, and teachers—all can trust me to be honest and fair. I can speak from experience about so many aspects of education.

I'm convinced educational systems ought to be evaluated. I can do a good job on this subject. My group is not as confident as I am. But that's good. I want them to keep me on my toes.

Wrote another draft—my third—and I feel good about it. My teacher suggests that I explain important aspects of education. I'll do it next time and I bet it'll help. This comment gave me a focal point to base my assessment on. I'm getting there, I think.

I feel confident about my writing. I know this subject and, as a freshman, I know that public education can be good. Until you go away to a new school or college, you never know how good your background is. I'm here in college and I believe I'm competitive with other students from the "elite" special schools. I can make it just as well as any of those guys. I'm proof that public schools, even the small ones that don't have a lot of fancy equipment, are doing a good job. As I've been writing drafts of my essay, I realize more and more how maybe we don't even need homeschooling and private schools. Guess the options need to be there, but I'm glad I went to my high school.

When I started writing notes about my subject, I thought maybe homeschooling was the best system for kids to learn. Then I started thinking that private schools were tops because they're so strict and have prestige. But I began to evaluate myself and my background. I'm not so bad. I'm able to make it just as well as those guys from other systems. If my success is a criterion, then the public schools would be winners. Hope my essay can say this without seeming biased. I really believe in my message here.

Mapping Matthew's Persuasive Rhetorical Situation

Matthew's rhetorical situation for this essay is mapped in Figure 15.1. Matthew draws on his own knowledge of educational systems; he uses no outside references to make his case. Accordingly, on the knowledge continuum, he lists the details he will use to make his case on the "knowledge by participation" side of the continuum.

Matthew writes for readers interested in education: parents, students, teachers, administrators. He considers this subject to be important to most people, so he spends little time "hooking" his audience. In other words, Matthew is a young college student who is passionate about the quality of education currently available; he believes his readers will share his interest. What do you think?

Means and Values of Education

Draft 4—Final Copy

1   Education means many different things to many different people in today's society. Some people simply concern themselves with teaching that comes from inside the classroom, others concern themselves with learning from experience, and still others seek to educate using classroom learning as well as practical experience. For these reasons, education in this essay will refer to teaching through the use of previous experience and classroom learning. This is important because it allows education to be viewed from different perspectives. Not only does education refer to scholastic achievement, but also to social maturity.

2   Based on the previous definition, three different avenues can be explored in order to determine the best location for providing an education: the home, a private school, and a public school. All three of these will be evaluated for their ability to provide an education socially as well as scholastically.

3   Homeschooling is a growing educational trend that provides a solid scholastic background, but most people find that it cannot help students in their social development. Parents provide one-on-one teaching that guarantees individual attention as well as genuine concern. Homeschoolers are also able to use computers and other technological advantages when they are available or affordable. However, children who have been homeschooled may lack social maturity. They usually have little outside contact with their peers, they do not have as many opportunities to compete and interact with others, and they do not seem to have the communication skills necessary to develop friendships. Another potential problem with homeschooled children is that most parents cannot provide a complete or diverse education when compared to a public or private school. This problem is magnified by older students as parents have problems with

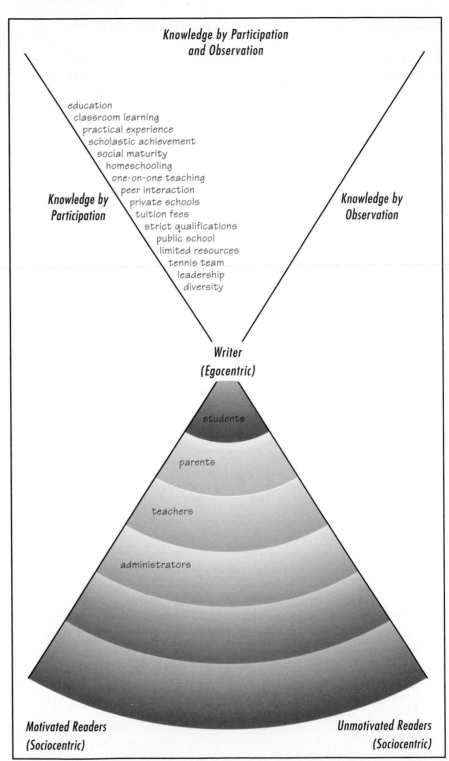

Figure 15.1
Mapping Matthew's rhetorical situation

advanced math and science courses, as well as foreign languages. It seems that a homeschool, on the whole, is not able to provide a very complete education.

4   Private schools are usually associated with a church or non-government organization, but their main feature is that a tuition fee is often required in order to attend. This in itself is one of the problems with private schools. Many students cannot afford a private school, and therefore, miss out on this educational opportunity. In an evaluation of private schools, it appears that they provide the best scholastic education of the three alternatives. Private schools sometimes require strict qualifications to be met in order to attend, and therefore, they simply have a higher quality of student. Also, private schools can afford to hire the best teachers, provide better student-to-teacher ratios than public schools, and provide better and newer learning facilities. Because of these reasons, private schools would provide the best education if education were simply a scholastic concern. However, since education also deals with social development, problems arise in the area of private schools. These schools, unlike the home, do provide daily interaction with peers, but too many times these peers are all cut out of the same cloth. A rich private school student may be unable to relate or sympathize with students who are different racially, economically, culturally, linguistically, and so on. Because a private school is unable to provide a complete and balanced social education, it also does not seem to be the best educational alternative.

5   The third and final educational alternative discussed here is the public school. Like the first two alternatives, public schools do not provide as strong an education as a private school. They have the worst student-to-teacher ratio of these three methods, they have less money to hire teachers, and they have fewer resources available. At this time, however, people see these problems and are striving to deal with them. Socially, public schools provide the most complete education. Students have the opportunity to participate in athletics and other extra-curricular activities sponsored by the school. They also are able to interact with students of different races and backgrounds. Also, they learn to deal with peer pressure as they are forced to make tough decisions.

6   Based on these evaluations, it is easy to see that a complete education is difficult to furnish. All three methods have their strong points and their weak points. In order to determine which method is best, we must decide which criteria are the most important in a school. To begin with, schools must provide a strong scholastic education. This is the normal function of schools. This scholastic education also needs to be diverse and well-rounded. Society today forces us to know foreign languages and history of other countries in order to compete in the job market. The second criterion that a school must meet is the social educational needs of students. This includes athletic teams, bands, and clubs, but it also includes teaching students to interact

with others, learn to make difficult decisions, and appreciate difference in others. With these two criteria in mind, we can now determine which school provides the best and most complete education.

7   As stated earlier, a homeschool does not seem to provide a complete education. While it does promise attention and understanding, it cannot provide a solid scholastic background, and students are unable to develop emotional maturity simply due to lack of social contact. Because of this, the homeschool has been dropped from the list of viable methods.

8   While a homeschool seems to lack strength in both aspects of education, public and private schools seem to meet both requirements in most ways. Both schools have strong scholastic programs with a private school probably providing a slightly better one. Also, both schools seek to provide for its students socially. There are athletic teams, clubs, and other extracurricular activities available to all students. Based on this, it appears public and private schools would both suffice, but I would like to offer some evidence to show that a public school is the best educational method.

9   Three years ago, I graduated from a public high school. My years as a student taught me many things about life. One of the most valuable lessons I learned was the value of leadership. In a world where society pulls us in many directions, we have to learn when to follow and when to lead. Athletics were invaluable in teaching me this. I competed three years for the tennis team and learned from all of them. My first year I gained respect by being myself, and by the third year, I was the one who was teaching the lessons. I also greatly appreciated the many people I met at a public school. My hometown is sixty percent Hispanic and learning how to live with our cultural differences was very important to me. Also, college has shown me that I did receive a good scholastic education in my high school, but more importantly, I learned to respect people of all different walks.

10   As I sit and wonder where I am headed after college, I wonder if someday I will have children, and I wonder where they will get their education. I fear for them as they walk into a classroom, but I know I cannot provide every scholastic need, and I certainly cannot provide for their social growth in relation to their peers. Students need to see the reality of life. Every problem does not have an easy solution, and every question does not have an easy answer, but public school will teach them how to search for the answers. Education should not be teaching students how to answer a question; education should teach a student how to look for the answer.

Reading Critically: Questions for Discussion

1. What does the title of this essay tell you? Can you predict the subject of this essay from the title?

2. If you were Matthew's group member, what comments and suggestions would you offer him regarding the introduction? For example, is his opening sentence effective?

3. While Matthew identifies the criteria for evaluation late in his essay, he alludes to them earlier when he describes homeschooling, private schools, and public schools. What do you think of this organization of the information? Why? What other possible arrangement might Matthew try, if he were to revise this draft?

4. What is Matthew's claim and how does he support it?

5. Matthew establishes his ethos in his conclusion, explaining his own public school background. How well does he establish his credibility? How does the placement of this information help or hinder his ethos? Do you trust his evaluation? Why or why not?

6. Discuss the relevance and effectiveness of the last sentence in this essay. If Matthew were to revise this draft, would you encourage him to change this closing line? Why?

KNOWLEDGE BY OBSERVATION

Like Matthew, Michelle Mauldin, the author of the next essay, decides to write about something that has affected or will affect her. In the end, she chooses to research the textbook selection process used in Texas public schools. Michelle's knowledge of this process comes exclusively from an interview and published research. Her perspective in this essay is therefore from the observer point of view.

Reviewing Journal Entries

The journal entries for "Oh, The Choices We Make" reveal how difficult it was for Michelle to decide on a subject to write about. She also gives us some insight into how she views evaluation; she thinks that her opinion of the textbook selection process will be fair only if she offers readers both criticism and suggestions to improve the process. Do you agree with Michelle? Could she have assessed the effectiveness of the process without offering additional information? What effect does her approach have? Does it influence your perception of her ethos? Why or why not?

JOURNAL

I have no idea what I want to write about. My group members are considering evaluating the concert series here and maybe the academic programs. But I'm not sure what to do.

Another group meeting and class, and still no subject. I am so frustrated but nothing comes to mind. Tonya's going with the concert subject and Karen's doing adolescent literature. I thought about textbook censorship in the schools, but I'm afraid that's overdone. My teacher suggested something about the media, but that doesn't excite me much. Tomorrow I'm going to sort through some different research. Go back through my journal again. I know there's something in there that I care about and want to do external research on. I keep going back to the field of education. All of my life I've been in school. Something must click.

My teacher and group think textbook selection in public schools might be interesting. I don't know anything about it really. I hear on the news that textbooks have been subject to banning and many are full of really outrageous errors. How are these books chosen? Maybe I shouldn't rule out this subject.

I have a subject! Finally! Today I was browsing through the curriculum section and I stumbled upon 3 different books on the textbook selection process. I got interested in them so I went to the electronic card catalog to find out more—nothing. I ended up going through ERIC and I'm sitting here looking at about 30 different article possibilities. Some can be immediately ruled out, but I have a lot of sorting out to do.

I took part of my paper to my teacher today. She said I'm on the right track, but I need more information on the actual process. She suggested I talk with a Dr. Wiseman, which I'm going to try to do tomorrow. I just wrote the rest of my body and I'm realizing that this is the paper I've most enjoyed putting together, and it's also the one I was dreading the most at the beginning. I'm a little stumped about whether or not to include information about improvements. I don't want to criticize the process without offering some suggestions, but I don't want to overburden my readers. How much is too much? I guess that's at my disposal.

I interviewed Dr. Wiseman and finished up my essay this afternoon. The interview went well and I found out a lot of information. After I incorporated everything she told me into the paper, I found out that the rest of the paper had to be altered. A couple of my suggestions suddenly seemed unreasonable given the procedures involved in the actual selection of texts. So I went back through the research and rethought my position and came up with two new suggestions for improvement. I like my evaluation.

I really enjoyed this paper. I feel like I've learned a lot. And I'm finding that once you have all your information and ideas placed in front of you, the writing practically does itself. I'm going to re-edit my essay in the morning before I turn it in.

Mapping Michelle's Persuasive Rhetorical Situation

Figure 15.2 illustrates Michelle's rhetorical situation. Michelle lists her information on the "knowledge by observation" side of the knowledge continuum. As you study her map and read her essay, consider the following questions: How does she research this selection process without ever having participated in it? Is her assessment believable, if she has never selected texts before? What can Michelle do to gain credibility and to foster trust in this essay? Why are credibility and trust important? How do the key words in the knowledge continuum indicate Michelle's understanding of her subject?

Michelle writes "Oh, The Choices We Make" for an audience of local community members interested in education: parents, students, school teachers and administrators. She classifies her audience according to their level of activity in public schools, dividing her audience into those with direct involvement in schools (teachers, administrators, students); some involvement (parents, local politicians or community leaders and groups); and little or no involvement (high school graduates who don't have family or friends in school now, but who may someday). Michelle assumes that motivation will vary depending upon her audience's relationship to the school system; she contends that even those readers who are uninvolved in the schools will be somewhat interested in this subject.

Oh, The Choices We Make

(Draft 3—Final Copy)

1   A close examination into the teaching and learning in public classrooms of today reveals a sad and unfortunate fact: the majority of school textbooks are inadequate. Because textbooks play such an important role in classroom organization and instruction, this is particularly detrimental to both students and teachers. So what can be done? An evaluation of the selection process as well as some common criteria for textbook selection reveals many interesting aspects involved in text adoption in public schools.

2   First of all, it is important to understand the process of textbook selection. In Texas, the State Board of Education disperses a list of acceptable texts for the classroom. According to Dr. Donna Wiseman, Professor of Education and Curriculum Instruction at Texas A&M University, the procedure for obtaining this list is a complicated and lengthy one. To begin, a Textbook Adoption Committee, made up of mostly teachers and other school system educators, is formed at the state level. This committee is then divided up into particular subject areas, and each one is given a list of *all* the available books for that subject. Obviously this is a very extensive list, and the process of going through it takes much time, which is why it is begun a year in advance. Dr. Wiseman is also careful to point out the political ramifications involved. Publishers are aware of committee members and do everything in their power to influence them in order to make sure that

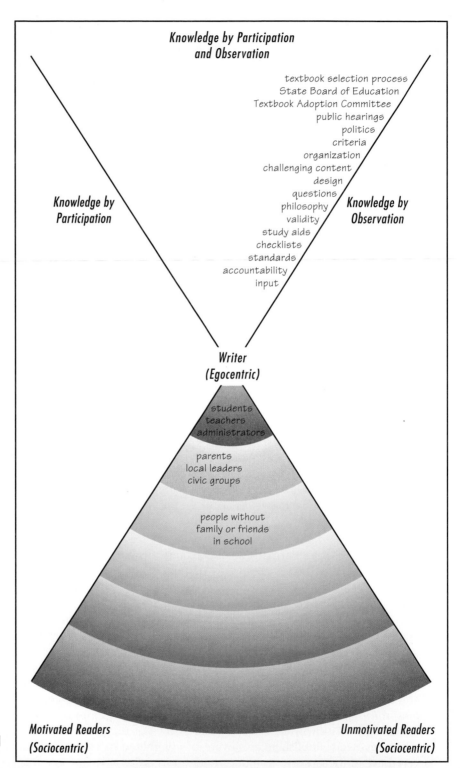

Figure 15.2
Mapping Michelle's rhetorical situation

their texts will be chosen. Therefore it is possible that some texts may not be selected for their content alone.

3   Once the committee members have sorted through the lists and made their selections, the chosen texts are then subject to hearings. During the hearings, others in the educational system are allowed to make suggestions or throw out undesirable texts. Dr. Wiseman again states that politically active participants have quite a large voice in this part of the adoption procedure. This has been evidenced by the Gablers, a conservative, older couple from Longview, Texas. They have devoted their whole lives to raising money and staying politically active enough to insure that certain texts stay out of the public class-room. According to Dr. Wiseman, the Gablers are extremely opposed to student-centered activities and open-ended questions and discus-sion that allow children freedom of expression and thought. Their conservative beliefs have prohibited many of the newer theories and trends in education from being implemented in the classroom through the use of textbooks, according to Dr. Wiseman. It is alarming to note the influential role that politics plays in this part of the adoption process, but it is important to recognize.

4   After the texts pass inspection at the hearings, the Board of Edu-cation compiles this list of State Adopted Texts to be dispersed in each individual school district. Dr. Wiseman states that there are usu-ally five or six text choices for each subject, and local school boards and committees then pick and choose from this list. Local textbook selection committees have only this list to make their choices from, for if they decide upon a text that is not on the list, they will have to pur-chase the classroom books without state support. Thus textbook selection at the state level is a process involving many players and steps.

5   Many different criteria are involved in the selection of appropriate texts. Though each school district has a different set of standards for selection, there are some universal criteria common to almost every school district. For example, committees usually look at the organiza-tion and content of a text to see if it is easily accessible and readable (Conn 31). In addition to this, the instructional design of the text is examined for the sequence of units and the balance of presentation and reinforcement. Equally important are the questions present within the text. Are they meaningfully and directly related to the selections? Also, the outside reading and resource suggestions in both the students' and teachers' editions of texts are examined for validity (Conn 31).

6   These general guidelines are only a basis for selection, and most districts look at much more specific aspects of texts. The Education Research Service (ERS) Report *Procedures for Textbook and Instruc-tional Materials Selection* outlines several more criteria considered by text selection committees. For example, does the textbook meet the basic philosophy of the American democratic society? Does the con-tent challenge the students? Does the text reflect valid scholarship?

Does it support and complement the basic educational objective within a specific subject area and classroom? Does the text include adequate and relevant study aids (Conn 35–36)? Though these criteria are fairly thorough and intended to be helpful, there are often obstacles in the selection process that might prohibit their implementation.

7   Often the selection committees are unaware of how to select or create a selection criteria checklist. And once a checklist is created, it can be too lengthy or complicated to be used efficiently (Bailey 87). For example, many criteria call for an analysis of the content that is too specific to be considered in the time allowed. It is unrealistic to believe that a committee is going to consider every piece of literature in each of the books on the lists. Though this is certainly a desirable procedure, there is simply not enough time or energy. Another problem is that exemplary textbook checklists are in short supply, which explains why incomplete and irrelevant criteria are often found in many district checklists (Bailey 87). Some committees are unsure of exactly what to look for in the texts, and thus might spend too much time focusing on minor details. Thus educators are left making difficult decisions about instructional materials without the proper guidelines or guidance. And, as a result, classrooms are sometimes inundated with textbooks that are inefficient and inadequate. To combat this problem, several considerations are in order.

8   First, the process for identifying leaders and members of subject area curriculum committees should be an explicitly stated policy. Once a committee is formed, members should meet on a regular basis to consider the success or failure of chosen texts (Bailey 88). Too often committees meet three or four times before a school year begins and fail to follow up on the success of the texts they decide upon. Progress must be checked in order to see what changes must be implemented to improve the success of instructional materials. Also, explicit directions for developing the textbook criteria checklist should be established (Bailey 88). Standards should include an easily understandable and workable checklist that contains items the whole group feels are relevant and important to any instructional material. Once this checklist is established, it should be used as a guideline for all potential selections.

9   Also, opportunity for input into the textbook/material adoption process should be offered to all people who are affected by it (Bailey 88). In his article in the *English Journal,* James Squire states that eighty percent of all final adoption decisions today are made by classroom teachers (20). However, the students are rarely given any input into the process. Granted, they are not properly trained or skilled in the selection procedure, but surely they should be allowed to provide input on their opinion of texts and other instructional materials. After all, who can better determine the effectiveness of the texts than those who are expected to learn from them?

10   Another important consideration is the accountability of the text. Who are the authors? What do they stand for, and what are their credentials (Guth 15)? A good way to eliminate anthologies with poor selections and errors is to investigate the people responsible for their existence. And since most anthologies are created by well-known and credible educators, committees should be familiar with them and other works that they have authored. This in turn would guarantee the validity and appropriateness of the text.

11   Though these are just a few considerations for upgrading the quality of textbooks present in classrooms, there are endless possibilities for improvement. However, it is painfully obvious that without some changes in the state adoption process of textbook selection, teachers and students will remain limited in their choice of instructional materials. The role of politics in this process is a disconcerting and unpleasant realization, but with the values and standards of society today, it is also inevitable and unchangeable. Educators and selection committees can only hold fast to the belief that the choices they make will benefit the greatest number of students possible, cognizant that the current selection is inadequate and flawed.

Works Cited

Bailey, Gerald D. "Guidelines for Improving the Textbook/Materials Selections Process." *NASSP Bulletin* 72.505 (1988): 87–92.

Conn, Sandra. "Textbooks: Defining the New Criteria." *Media & Methods* 24.4 (1988): 30–31, 64.

Educational Research Service Report. *Procedures for Textbook and Instructional Materials Selection.* Arlington: ERS, 1976.

Guth, Hans P. "A Plea for Better Books." In "The Textbook Gap: A Teacher-Author-Publisher Dialogue." *English Journal* 78.6 (1989): 14–21.

Squire, James. "For Better Textbooks." In "The Textbook Gap: A Teacher-Author-Publisher Dialogue." *English Journal* 78.6 (1989): 14–21.

Wiseman, Donna. Professor, Education and Curriculum Instruction, Texas A&M University. Personal interview. 4 Dec. 1991.

Reading Critically: Questions for Discussion

1. Who do you think "we" in the title of this essay refers to? Who is the audience that Michelle's essay tries to reach?
2. Michelle knows of her subject because she has used outside sources to research it. How has she integrated the ideas of her sources into her text? How effectively does she use tagging to introduce her sources and their information?
3. Review the map of Michelle's rhetorical situation. What is the relationship between the subject and audience? How do you imagine her

readers will respond to the key words in the knowledge continuum? Has Michelle used rhetorical appeals to motivate her audience regarding the state textbook selection process? Identify and discuss them.

4. How effectively has Michelle explained the criteria and process that she is evaluating? Do you agree with her assessment? Why or why not? Could she have used an illustration to help readers follow the process (i.e., a flowchart)? If she did use a figure, where would she introduce and place it in the text?

5. One of the most important sources in this essay is the interview of Dr. Wiseman. Is the interview information as credible as the published articles cited at the end of the essay? Have you ever used your interview notes (or questionnaire data) in an essay? Why or why not?

KNOWLEDGE BY PARTICIPATION AND OBSERVATION

The third essay is "Ridersville ISD: Is It at Risk?" Written by Tonya Armstrong, this essay reflects both direct and indirect knowledge. Tonya has gained a personal understanding of the at-risk programs in this school district as a program volunteer; in addition, she has learned about the program from others: the director of the at-risk programs and the Texas Education Agency. Do you think her research has been extensive enough?

So that you can get a glimpse of Tonya's essay as it takes shape, we've included drafts 1 and 3 of this text.

Reviewing Journal Entries

Tonya's journal entries are very abbreviated. Sometimes, when a writer has little to record, it may indicate that he or she is not interested in the subject. Do you think this is what Tonya's brief entries reveal? Review some entries in your journal. Do you have a string of short comments? If so, why do you think those entries are so brief?

JOURNAL

I feel lazy. I'm not sure about this essay. The teacher postponed our due date on the syllabus, and I really suppose I'll just waste time because I have extra time. I feel real lazy.

My subject is okay because I have already done the research and know something about at-risk programs here. I needed to volunteer to help in these activities for my service duties in several clubs. I even had interviewed the director here before so that I could make a report to my sorority about this as a service project. So, my research was almost done before I knew it. The TEA stuff is new. Needed it to do the criteria.

———————

I need to talk to my prof. I feel like something's missing in my paper. Did I do enough research? What is missing? The paper is so ordinary. I explain the programs and tell how they meet the TEA criteria. The paper still sounds so flat. Wonder if I'm persuading readers of my evaluation. I just don't know and I feel lazy.

———————

How is it I can be interested in this subject but talk about it in such an ordinary, blah way? My enthusiasm for this doesn't show in my paper, and I'm upset. I can't get the energy to do justice to this subject. Can a person like a subject but not be able to feel excited about writing about it? Does this mean I'm really not motivated about at-risk programs? Wish I could call someone from class to talk this out. It's really late so that's out of the question.

Does Tonya sound tired to you? Her condition could be associated with her lack of interest in this subject or to her own physical and mental fatigue. Have you ever felt tired and lazy when you've tried to complete an assignment? What strategies have you used to alter your internal and external influences and to rejuvenate yourself as you complete the task?

Imagine that you are a member of Tonya's group or that the two of you are enrolled in the same writing class. What cues might you notice that would signal Tonya's fatigue? Generally speaking, do group members have a responsibility to help each other get through a task? Why or why not? What criteria would you establish to determine when a peer or focus group should intervene to "revive" another student in a class like this one?

Mapping Tonya's Persuasive Rhetorical Situation

Figure 15.3 is a map of Tonya's rhetorical situation. She has gained knowledge of local at-risk programs by both participation and observation, as the knowledge continuum shows.

Tonya addresses her essay to general adult readers in the local Ridersville community. In her view, this community consists of administrators, teachers, parents, and students; these readers will be the ones most interested in this subject because they are most likely to be directly affected by the program. She also thinks the community consists of civic or social groups that might tackle education issues.

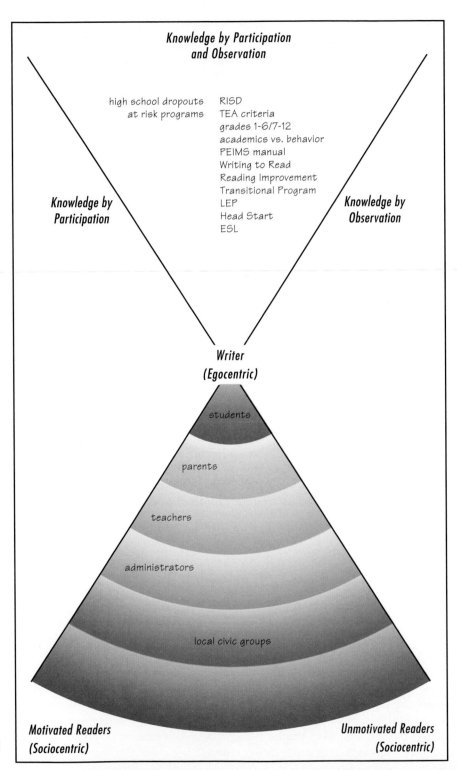

Figure 15.3
Mapping Tonya's rhetorical situation

Untitled

Draft 1

1   To most American students, high school is a goal that is obtainable as long as they apply themselves and put forth effort. However, due to poverty, drugs, and divorce, more and more students are finding that it is becoming difficult to concentrate on school because their attentions are on these other problems rather than academics. Due to these distractions, many students are dropping out of high school. The numbers of dropouts are increasing at an astonishing rate, and this state is realizing that this is a major problem. To combat the situation, "at-risk" programs have been developed. "At-risk" refers to any student from K–12 who has been labeled as a possible candidate for dropping out of school without some kind of intervention. The criteria brought forth by TEA in the 1987–88 school year gives all districts in Texas a general guideline for how to set up an at-risk program, and the individual details are left up to each district. After evaluating the at-risk program at Ridersville Independent School District (RISD) by the criteria brought forth by TEA, I have discovered that overall the district does a very good job providing help for students who really need it.

2   The At-risk Student Information section of the *Public Education Information Management Systems (PEIMS) Manual* outlines criteria for K–6. This document states that a student is designated as at-risk if he "did not perform satisfactorily on a beginning-of-school year readiness or achievement test; failed at least one reading, writing, or math section of the more recent third through fifth grade TAAS; is a student of limited English proficiency; has been a victim of abuse as confirmed by the Texas Department of Human Services; engages in delinquent conduct as described by the Texas Family Code #51.03(a); or was retained in a grade level in grades 1–6." For grades 7–12, a student will be classified as at-risk if he or she "was retained at least once in grades 1–6 and is still unable to master the essential elements in the 7th grade or higher; has fallen behind at least two years below grade level in reading or math; has failed at least two courses and is not expected to graduate within four years of 9th grade entrance; has failed at least one reading, writing, or math section of the most recent 7th through 12 TAAS exam; is a homeless student or non-handicapped student who resides in a residential placement facility outside the district of parent/guardian residence."

3   The districts in Texas were given these criteria to create an at-risk program, and to be an excellent program, the school should provide activities designed especially for the at-risk group represented by each criteria. Dr. Richard Burnett provided an extensive outline of the district's program.

4   According to Dr. Burnett, on the prekindergarten through 6, three of the criteria deal with academics, either actually in the classroom or on achievement tests. To meet the needs of these students, RISD offers a number of programs—some are federally funded and some are state funded. For those students whose problems are in reading, help for them comes from a federally funded program, when Lyndon B. Johnson was building his "Great Society." The student in this program is taken out of a regular class during reading time and goes to a small, hands-on reading lab to receive instruction from a reading specialist. Using the same idea, the state funds a resource math program to help students who are falling behind in math or failed the math section on the TAAS test. Also, for those students who are "at-risk" academically, the school requires on-campus tutoring if the student falls below a 70 in any class. An interesting program in RISD for at-risk reading students is called "Writing to Read." This is a whole language-based program in which students strive to improve both reading and writing. This uses sight words and repetitive words, studying literature, and engaging in creative writing. This program has become so successful that the district includes all students in it as a preventative measure.

Tonya stops writing here. Her second version of this essay resembles the third and final draft reprinted below. From her journal entries and her comments in her focus group, it is apparent that Tonya was less motivated to complete multiple drafts on this subject. Her focus group discusses her seeming lack of interest and energy when she is writing this essay, but Tonya is certain this subject is good for her because she had done most of the research and knew about the subject from her volunteer work in the schools in that community. Do you think Tonya should have changed her subject? Why or why not? Compare the introductory discourse bloc in drafts 1 and 3. Are the changes Tonya makes effective?

Ridersville ISD: Is It at Risk?

Draft 3—Final Copy

1   To most American students, graduation from high school is a goal that is obtainable as long as they apply themselves and put forth effort. However, due to several different reasons like poverty, drugs, and divorce, more and more students are finding that it is becoming difficult to concentrate on school because their attentions are being focused on these other problems rather than academics. Due to these distractions, many students are dropping out of high school. The numbers of dropouts are increasing at an astonishing rate, and the state of Texas is realizing that this is a major problem. To combat the situation, "at-risk" programs have been developed. "At-risk" refers to any student from prekindergarten through twelfth grade who has been

labeled as a possible candidate for dropping out of school without some kind of intervention (TEA). The criteria brought forth by the Texas Education Agency (TEA) in the 1987–88 school year gives all districts in Texas a general guideline for how to set up an at-risk program, but the individual details are left up to each district. After evaluating the at-risk program at Ridersville Independent School District (RISD) by the criteria brought forth by TEA, I, a former high school graduate who has volunteer experience in at-risk programs, discovered that overall the district does a very good job providing help for students who really need it.

2   The At-risk Student Information section of the *Public Education Information Management Systems (PEIMS) Manual* outlines at-risk criteria for prekindergarten through sixth grades. This document states that a student is designated as "at-risk" if he or she "did not perform satisfactorily on a beginning-of-school year readiness or achievement test; failed at least one reading, writing, or math section of the more recent third through fifth grade Texas Assessment of Academic Skills (TAAS); is a student of limited English proficiency; has been a victim of abuse as confirmed by the Texas Department of Human Services; engages in delinquent conduct as described by the Texas Family Code #51.03(a); or was retained in a grade level in grades 1–6." For grades 7–12, a student will be classified as "at-risk" if he or she "was retained at least once in grades 1–6 and is still unable to master the essential elements in the 7th grade or higher; has fallen behind at least two years below grade level in reading or math; has failed at least two courses and is not expected to graduate within four years of 9th grade entrance; has failed at least one reading, writing, or math section of the most recent 7th through 12 TAAS exam; is a homeless student or non-handicapped student who resides in a residential placement facility outside the district of parent/guardian residence."

3   The districts in Texas were given these criteria to create an at-risk program, and to be an excellent program, the school should provide activities designed especially for the at-risk group represented by each criteria. Dr. Richard Burnett, the at-risk coordinator in RISD, provided an extensive outline of the district's at-risk program. The program he described is explained and evaluated below.

4   According to Dr. Burnett, on the prekindergarten through sixth grade level, three of the criteria deal with academics, either actually in the classroom or on achievement tests. To meet the needs of these students, RISD offers a number of programs. Some of these are federally funded and some are state funded. For those students whose problems are in reading, help for them comes from a federally funded program, Chapter One, that was started in 1965, when Lyndon B. Johnson was building his "Great Society." The student in this program is taken out of his or her regular class during reading time and goes to a small, hands-on reading lab to receive instruction from a reading specialist. Using the same concept, the state funds a resource math

program to help those students who are falling behind in math or failed the math section on the TAAS test. Also, for those students who are at-risk academically, the school requires on-campus tutoring if the student falls below a 70 in any class. An interesting program in RISD for at-risk reading students is called "Writing to Read." This is a whole language-based program in which students strive to improve both reading and writing by using sight words and repetitive words, studying quality literature, and engaging in creative writing. This program has become so successful that the district is trying to include all students as a preventative measure.

5   The state has one criteria that deals with a student of limited English proficiency (LEP). Dr. Burnett reports that Ridersville has two different programs for this type of at-risk student: Head Start and English as a Second Language (ESL). Head Start is a federally funded program for prekindergarten children who are language-deficient or whose family meets strict economic guidelines. This is a full day program where these LEP students are fed breakfast and lunch and get instruction in basic life skills and manners such as teethbrushing and saying "please" and "thank you." They also receive an introduction to the English language before they have to go to school. The ESL program in the elementary schools has the LEP student mainstreamed for the majority of the day to get interaction with his or her peers and teacher. However, this LEP student also spends about two hours a day in a special classroom to learn English and also receive extra help in the academic subjects where he or she has problems.

6   For those students at the elementary level who have been classified as at-risk due to abuse or delinquent behavior, the district provides counselors and nurses on every campus and will call in specialists whenever necessary (Burnett).

7   In grades 7 through 12, all four criteria for at-risk students deal with academics. In the junior highs, tutoring before or after school is mandatory for any student who fails any class for a six-week period. If in the next semester his or her grade improves to passing, the student no longer has to stay in tutoring. Also in junior high, a program called "Reading Improvement" is offered for students who have been retained in a grade or score below 40% on an achievement test. This is a special reading elective for these students to improve reading skills and comprehension. If a student was retained in either sixth or seventh grade, he or she is placed in what is called a "Transitional Program." This student is placed in a self-contained classroom for all subjects. He or she is taught the basic skills and is prepared to go on to high school with his or her peers.

8   Upon reaching high school, the academically at-risk student may be put in correlated math, science, or English classes. These classes are typically smaller and the goal is to catch the student up with his or her peers. There are also mandatory tutoring programs for when the student falls below a 70 in any subject for a six-week grading period

like in junior high. In high school there are programs to teach basic job skills to those students who are not college bound, so that they will be better prepared to compete in the business world.

9   All in all, the Ridersville Independent School District has a fully developed series of programs for at-risk students. Dr. Richard Burnett, the at-risk coordinator, has carefully established programs on all levels to help at-risk students in all categories as designated by the state. Students in this school district are given many avenues from which to receive help, from mandatory tutoring to special classes. Yet even with a program as outstanding as this, high school dropouts are still a big problem. Therefore, RISD has complied with the state's criteria but nevertheless continues to look for more ways to help at-risk students because one dropout is too many.

Works Cited

Burnett, Richard. Coordinator, At-risk Program, Ridersville Independent School District. Personal interview. 1 Nov. 1993.

Texas Education Agency (TEA). "At Risk Information: Mandatory State Defined Criteria." *Public Education Information Management Systems (PEIMS) Manual.* Austin: Author, 1991. 3.139A.

Reading Critically: Questions for Discussion

1. All of the information for this essay comes from two sources. Do you think Tonya's research needs to be expanded? Who else could she have interviewed? What would be the impact of additional interviews on her logos and ethos?

2. Would Tonya's essay be strengthened if she included figures that showed Dr. Burnett's outline of at-risk programs as well as TEA's criteria? Where would you suggest that she introduce these figures? How would these figures be represented (e.g., bulleted listing, organizational chart)?

3. This essay contains no opposing arguments. Does this omission seem fitting to you, or is it inappropriate? Why?

4. Does Tonya satisfactorily establish her credibility regarding this subject? Explain your answer.

5. Do you agree with Tonya's assessment of RISD's at-risk program? Why or why not?

CHAPTER 16

Repertoire Focus: Declaring a Position

Sooner or later, in class or on the job, you will have the opportunity or the obligation to declare your position on a variety of important issues. For example, you might decide to write a letter to the editor of your campus newspaper supporting your school's new admission policy. In your physics class, you might compose a research report that supports or opposes continued funding of the space shuttle. Or your boss might ask you to write a memo voicing your position on whether or not the company should establish a toll-free telephone line for the customer service division. In each case, you write in order to convince your readers to adopt your position. To accomplish your objective, you will need to supply evidence to establish your credibility, prove the logic of your position, and address your audience's self-interest, sense of altruism, or both.

REPERTOIRE WRITING TASK: THESIS-SUPPORT

Examine an issue critically, take a position, and develop a reasoned argument for your stance. In order to make your argument convincing, analyze your audience carefully, use rhetorical appeals judiciously, and provide sound, sufficient evidence and counterarguments. Because this is persuasive aim writing, consider fully what your readers already know about this subject. What are their perceptions and attitudes about it, and why do they hold such beliefs? Your audience may be readers much like you; a general college audience; a general adult readership; or a specific campus, community, or professional group.

Below are three variations of this writing task, based on the different ways you may "know" about the subject that you focus on.

Knowledge by Participation

Write an essay that argues a particular position on a controversial or vital issue that you know of through direct experience.

Knowledge by Observation

Write an essay that argues a particular position on a controversial or vital issue that you know of indirectly (through interviews, reading, television, or another medium). This issue should be one that others have written about formally or informally, yielding some form of published biographical, social, or historical information that you can integrate into your essay.

Knowledge by Participation and Observation

Write an essay that argues a particular position on a controversial issue that you know of both directly through personal experience and indirectly (through interviews, reading, television, or another medium). This issue should be one that others have written about formally or informally, yielding some form of published biographical, social, or historical information that you can integrate into your essay.

REPERTORY COMPANY OF STUDENT WRITERS: THEIR RESPONSES TO THE TASKS

The following essays are responses by other student writers in our repertory company to the writing tasks presented in this chapter. To research and write their texts, these student writers created their own writing communities or groups. By interacting with their classmates and exchanging ideas, they strengthened their writing processes and their identities as writers. As you compose, take full advantage of the feedback that your classmates—members of your own writing community—offer.

For each essay, we've included journal entries, a map of the rhetorical situation (the knowledge continuum and audience continuum), and research strategies. You'll also find some questions for discussion and analysis following each selection.

KNOWLEDGE BY PARTICIPATION

In "Dream a Little Dream for Me," Kristi Koenig tries to convince her readers to take time to pursue their dreams. To make her case, she narrates her experience as a student volunteer in the Conservation Internship Program for the National Parks Service. Kristi has written this essay in first person, clearly revealing that she has gained her understanding of this experience through participation. As you read this essay, notice how Kristi uses some expressive aim strategies such as narration, description, dialogue, and chronological order to accomplish her persuasive aim purpose. "Dream a Little Dream for Me" is a good example of a text whose primary aim is persuasive and subordinate aim is expressive.

We've included three different drafts in order to show you how Kristi's essay develops. As you can see, Kristi is so fluent and enthusiastic about her experience at Big Bend that she has difficulty deciding what and how much to write. Her sentences are long and occasionally unwieldy, yet always packed with details. Kristi's fifth draft is more concise than her earlier ones; however, she still needs to work on her organization and selection of information.

Have you ever written about a subject that you knew so well and were so passionate about that you bombarded your readers with too much information? How did you discover you were "overwriting"? What did you do to address the problem?

Reviewing Journal Entries

Kristi's journal entries indicate her interest in her subject and her sensitivity to her audience's needs. Instead of using statistics and other objective data to make the case that her readers should pursue "a lifelong dream," Kristi recounts her personal experience, using it to establish ethos and to provide logos for her persuasive purpose. Here are some of her thoughts as she writes this essay.

JOURNAL

What do I want to say in this paper? I want to share my internship experience. I was thinking about writing about my canoe venture, my guided tour, and my solo backpack trip—to focus on these instead of rambling blow by blow about every minor incident. I need to evaluate the experience, the benefits, and I need to convince my audience that my assessment is informed and reasonable. What are my readers' attitudes about internships and about the park service? People I have shared my experience with always ask why? Or are you a "parks" major? Maybe I should claim that this was beneficial even though I was out of the field— not a parks major—because I became compelled to spend time in nature, to get away and absorb the tranquility. I got used to no people for miles and miles, no traffic, no modernity. It became an outing to travel 200 miles (?) to the grocery store. I want to share the love I now have for the land, the atmosphere, the way of life—the rustic natural attitude that shapes life there. I want my readers to know that I lay under the stars feeling engulfed in the black night that knew no street lights. So much to say and so little time.

I am worried about this paper, and my group hasn't met lately. We need to because I need someone to read my latest drafts of this essay. I love the subject; there's so much to tell about. I am typing my drafts into the computer, and I'm trying to decide how to proceed. After my conference with my teacher today, I think pros/cons will be a beneficial addition, but until it is in the computer, it is hard to know what else I need to add. I need to work on transitions; it follows in a very chronological order, so that is fine, but I need to tie in how this relates to the reader and I need a conclusion.

I don't know whether to list pros and cons or whether to blend them in the same paragraph. I am still working on the connection between my paper and the reader—it may be interesting, but I need a clear reason— evident to the reader—for writing this paper. I need to persuade the reader in some way, and if nothing else I need/want to make him or her think about pursuing his/her dream or a dream that he/she has never really confronted head on.

———————

I am still worried about not having enough reader input. My roomie finally relented and read my paper—helped with my commas! Overall she said she enjoyed it.

———————

I am pleased with this paper—really. I have wanted to write about this experience for a long time and now I finally have. I went back and read my journal from when I was in the park each time before I wrote my drafts and it really helped pull me back, and it started the memories and love for the park flowing again. Hope my readers will feel their need to get the same kind of experience.

———————

Tonight I am working hands on with my printed copy to make changes and clarifications and then I will move to the computer. Sometimes I just really need a "tangible" paper to be able to see the needs, strengths, weaknesses of the essay. I am hoping I can find areas for revision.

———————

I returned to the computer today just to reread, and I found some other areas for revision—a transition added clarification—and some cosmetic amendments. I really like this essay.

Mapping Kristi's Persuasive Rhetorical Situation

Kristi's rhetorical situation for this essay can be mapped as shown in Figure 16.1. Writing this essay gives Kristi the opportunity to record her positive experience working in Big Bend National Park and to convince readers to consider such an adventure as well. As they read the essay, readers will interpret such public service through Kristi's eyes, those of a college student who takes a semester off to fulfill a dream. And Kristi's understanding of her dream is by participation, as the knowledge continuum shows.

In writing for college students in general, Kristi tries to select a subject that she believes is important to her and relevant to them. When she discusses this essay with her focus group, Kristi becomes animated and excited. She welcomes any chance to recall her "dream semester," a time when she had the courage to do the unexpected: to leave college and be a part of the National Park Service (she refers to her action as "leaving the rat race"). Kristi considers her audience to be motivated and interested in her story and challenge; in fact, she contends that many young people would volunteer to do some type of national service if they had more information about such opportunities. Her map of the audience continuum reflects her belief.

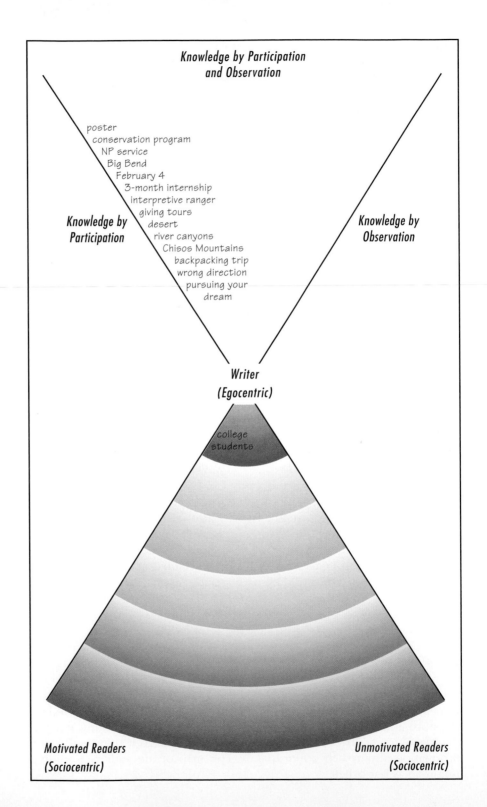

Figure 16.1
Mapping Kristi's rhetorical situation

Dream

Draft 1

1   Have you ever considered setting all aside and following a dream?

2   The dream I had was to do something that no one I knew had done. I wanted a challenge and an adventure, yet it had to be worthwhile. My opportunity arrived in the form of a small poster advertising a conservation program. I glanced at it but didn't give it much thought, but my mom said, "That sure sounds interesting. Why don't you get some information or an address?"

3   Well, I hung onto the address for four months before I finally wrote a brief letter requesting information. The next thing I knew I was pouring over leaflets of information and scenarios of other students who had interned for the NP Service. I was tantalized and challenged to say the least. On a whim, truly never expecting to drop my college lifestyle and trek out to the great unknown, I applied and requested Big Bend, Texas. Several weeks later, I got a note that I was being considered for 3 places, one of which was Big Bend. I waited around—no news, so I registered for spring classes, took final exams, packed a suitcase, and never mentioned to my friends the possibility of not returning for the spring.

4   Ring . . . ring . . . ring. Startled, I answered the phone and heard a faraway voice offer me the chance of a lifetime.

5   "Hello, Ms. Koenig. This is Clyde Stonaker from Big Bend National Park, and I am sorry to disturb you, but I'm calling in regards to the Conservation program. Are you still interested in working in the Park? We would need you here by February 4th."

6   One month later with "Big Bend or Bust" plastered on the back of my '73 VW, and the controversy of leaving college settled with my mother, I was en route to Big Bend. At first I tried to comprehend/ believe that a desert, mountains, and only 13 people existed outside my door. I couldn't believe that I had chosen to live all alone without companionship, television, radio, or a grocery store for 200 miles.

7   You may wonder what this means for you, but what I am going to share with you changed my outlook on life and on other cultures. This experience which lasted 3 short months still fills my thoughts and draws me back, to remember and to explore places of the country which I haven't ventured to yet, or which I can never see enough of, still captivate my spirit for adventure that resides within all of us. My reason for sharing my internship with you is so that you too can believe wholeheartedly in their educational worth, and in their ability to build a stronger more dynamic/versatile person.

8   I want to share with you a desert where the land is cut by a river that is now contained by canyons 1000s of feet high, where the sky-blue touches/reaches the dusty windswept earth, where bluebonnets

grow knee-deep but only after a good soaking rain. This is the land where cowboys from Mexico still cross the Rio Grande on horseback to buy a few groceries at the (tourist trap) "general store." Sometimes I rose in the morning to walk to work and I listened to the silence, or gazed at the full moon descending lazily behind the mountains of Mexico. It was in this place that I watched masons from Mexico reconstruct an historic home of a settler gone 100 years since. Upon my arrival, I consumed the surrounding beauty with my eyes, all the information with my mind, then one day it was my turn to give the answers, smiles, maps, and directions. The position of Park Ranger was now mine, too. As an interpretive ranger, each day I led visitors on a guided walk from desert bush and bird to an historic military compound, all the while supplying them with narrative, tall tales, and bits of trivia. I felt as if I had lived in Big Bend all along—my whole life. I felt the unity and a sense of belonging to humankind and nature. I found my dream and never wanted to leave. And still the experience only got better.

9   Just as I settled into my routine, I discovered that I was to go on a solo backpacking trip that would entail my spending one night out and traveling over 20 miles on foot. I raised my eyebrows and wondered, "Can they be serious?"

10   Two weeks later on a cool Saturday morning in March, as the sun was rising over the Chisos Mountains, I slipped out of the ranger's truck and hoisted my pack upon my back. With a topographic map, compass, and a charged up park radio, I glanced around and meandered off—unbeknownst to me, in the wrong direction. Five hours later, while hiking out of a creek bed, I ran into the major park highway, and I knew that I was in the wrong place. After contacting my sponsor over the radio, I was transported to the ending point of my route to hike it backwards. I had lots of miles to make up before sundown, yet as I hiked I had work to do: I took a people-animal count of all those I saw, collected water samples and trash, and made a general overview of the trails I was traveling. All of the work was minor in comparison with the reliance and confidence that I gained in myself. I learned to trust my intuition and decisions about paths, directions, and the cairns (small, man-made directional rock piles) to follow. I firmly believed in my ability to complete this challenge, if not by might but by sheer faith and determination. That night, my body ached with fatigue, yet my spirit soared with the majesty of the land that surrounded my every turn and with the knowledge that I was brave enough to try this alone. I had traveled about 17 miles, and I unpacked and spread out on the side of a sloping rock, just in time to watch the setting sun paint the rocks, hillsides, and mountains a flaming burnt orange, and then the world turned a dusky purple. I awoke with the moon directly overhead blasting out the stars and my watch read 11 pm, a long time until morning.

11   Packing up I noticed my left ankle was tender and swollen, yet not having much choice but to continue, I massaged it, put on several pairs of socks and carried on. As the day wore on, I began having difficulty walking and stopped more frequently to rest. The cairns faded in and out never allowing me to fully rely on them to lead the path. Yet as I reached a low in my stamina, I stumbled across an old foundation of a settler's house and water well, a mile further ahead I found a park directory sign and felt home free, the rest had to be down hill, instead it was long hill, windy and an incredibly hot day, in which I was rationing my water supply. . . .

Notice that in the third draft, Kristi expands her introduction, including a definition of the word *dream*. She also adds a conclusion, but still has difficulty in controlling the details of her narrative to support her persuasive purpose. What advice would you offer Kristi?

Dream a Little Dream for Me

Draft 3

1   Have you ever considered setting your job or schooling, organizations or obligations aside, to actually jump out of the rat race for a period of time, to follow a dream? A dream, by definition, is anything that we imagine or believe possible, yet many individuals never imagine, grasp, or pursue their dream or the opportunity for fulfillment.

2   High school graduates often have dreams of attending college; once in school, the dream moves on to graduation, yet for some it may entail completing a co-op experience in their career field. Even though I was planning to become a teacher, the dream I had was to do something involving nature; I didn't know quite what, but it had to be something that no one I knew had done. I wanted a challenge and an adventure, yet it had to be worthwhile. My opportunity arrived in the form of a small poster advertising a Conservation Internship program. I glanced at it but didn't give it much thought. Then my mom said, "That sure sounds interesting. Why don't you get some information or an address?"

3   Well, I hung onto the address for four months before I finally wrote a brief letter requesting information. The next thing I knew I was pouring over leaflets of information and scenarios from others who had interned for the National Park Service. I was tantalized and challenged to say the least. On a whim, not really expecting to postpone my college and lifestyle to trek out to the great unknown, I applied for a position in Big Bend National Park for the coming spring. I mailed my application in mid-October, and around the first part of November, I received a note that I was being considered for three locations, one of which was Big Bend. I had never been to Big Bend or even heard of it; I knew only that it was in Texas and that

my folks were moving back to Texas in December, so whether I stayed in college or interned, I would be in the same state as my family. Several weeks passed and still no news about the position, so I registered for spring classes, took fall final exams, packed a suitcase, and never mentioned to my friends the possibility of my not returning in the spring semester.

4   Ring . . . ring . . . ring. "Hello?" I answered the phone on New Year's Eve, hearing a faraway voice offer me the chance of a lifetime.

5   "Hello, Ms. Koenig. This is Clyde Stonaker from Big Bend National Park, and I am sorry to disturb you, but I'm calling in regards to the Conservation program. Are you still interested in working in the Park? We would need you here by February 4th."

6   Stunned, I tried to gather my thoughts and asked for a day or two to talk this over with my family.

7   One month later with "Big Bend or Bust" plastered on the back of my '73 VW, I was en route to Big Bend. At first I tried to believe that I had chosen to do this and that I was actually following through with a dream that was my very own. I wanted to pick up and leave college and society and to do something brave and challenging. And a semester in the Texas desert as a Park Ranger was all that and more. Yet as reality set in and the desert opened up before me, I had to think through why I had chosen to do this, and I had to decide this was going to work and be one of the best experiences of my life. At first I had to comprehend a mosaic of realities: that only 13 people lived within 75 miles of my doorstep, that the grocery store was about 150 miles away, that I would have no telephone, radio or television for 3 months, and amazingly that mountains and a desert were mere footsteps beyond my little home. These "everyday basics" were drastically different from anything I had grown up with or really considered when jumping at the chance to live in the great outdoors, and I did have to adjust to the change.

8   You may wonder what this means or can mean for you, yet what I am going to share with you changed my life and my decisions for my future. My outlook toward what is important in life, toward different cultures, and about where I will live after I finish college all expanded and changed to some extent because of my internship. I hope that by reading this you can fully realize the possibilities available for you—no matter what age you may be—and that you can come to understand more about pursuing your dreams and the development of self that takes place during one of these experiences. This internship, which lasted three short months, still fills my thoughts and draws me back to explore and remember the beauties and aura of the park. I believe there is a sense of adventure that resides within us all, and I call on you to seek within yourself and act upon it. In addition, I want to share key moments of my internship to illustrate the educational, physical, emotional, and mental growth of such a worthwhile program.

9   Think if you will of a desert, where the land is cut by a river that is now contained by steep, rocky canyons, where sky-blue reaches the dusty windswept earth, where bluebonnets grow knee-deep but only after a good soaking rain. This is a place where cowboys from Mexico still cross the Rio Grande on horseback to buy a few groceries at the "general store" or to use the only pay phone within a 75 mile radius. Often I found myself listening to the beauty of silence, and early in the morning I loved to see the lazy full moon hang over the mountains of Mexico. It was in this place that I watched Adobe masons from Mexico reconstruct an historic home of a settler gone 100 years since. Upon my arrival, I consumed the surrounding beauty with my eyes, all the information with my mind, and the various trails with my strength, then one day it was my turn to give the answers, smiles, maps, and directions. The position of Park Ranger was now mine, too. As an interpretive ranger, each day I led visitors on a guided walk from desert bush and bird to an historic military compound, all the while supplying them with narrative, tall tales, and bits of trivia. Curiously, I felt as if I had lived in Big Bend all along—my whole life. For the first time, I encountered a sense of unity with nature and the people around me. I knew almost at the start of my internship that I had found my dream and I was living it! Yet, the experience only got better.

10   Just as I settled into my routine of leading the historic walks and working the Visitors' Center, I discovered that I was to go on a solo backpacking trip that would entail my spending one night out and traveling over 20 miles on foot. I raised my eyebrows and wondered, "Can they be serious?" Two weeks later on a cool Saturday morning in March, as the sun was rising over the Chisos Mountains, I slipped out of the ranger's truck and hoisted my pack upon my back. With a topographic map, compass, and a charged up park radio, I glanced around and meandered off—unbeknownst to me, in the wrong direction. Five hours later, while hiking out of a creek bed, I ran into the major park highway, and I knew that I was in the wrong place. After contacting my sponsor over the radio, I was transported to the ending point of my route to hike it backwards. I had lots of miles to make up before sundown, yet as I hiked I had work to do: I took a people-animal count of all those I saw, collected water samples and trash, and made a general overview of the trails I was traveling. All of the necessary work was minor in comparison with the reliance and confidence that I gained in myself. I learned to trust my intuition and decisions about paths, directions, and the cairns (small, man-made directional rock piles) to follow. I firmly believed in my ability to complete this challenge, if not by might but by sheer faith and determination. When I stopped that night, my body ached with fatigue, yet my spirit soared with the majesty of the land that surrounded my every turn and with the knowledge that I was a survivor. I had traveled about 17 miles, including my miscue off on the wrong trail. I unpacked and spread

out on the side of a sloping rock, just in time to watch the setting sun paint the rocks, hillsides, and mountains a flaming burnt orange. Then the world turned a dusky purple and grew quiet for nightfall.

11   Now that you are familiar specifically with one of the significant events of my internship and with the personal fulfillment of my dream, I would like to share the pros and cons of pursuing one's dreams in an effort to persuade you to follow your own dreams. You may wonder why I take time to worry that you are just living the rat race day-to-day existence, but I know first-hand the glories of working as a volunteer, away from the confines of society, in a place centered around the land and the environment.

12   Benefits outweigh the disadvantages of any experience, yet every experience is bound to have both pros and cons. When pursuing a personal, lifelong dream each of us will have different needs and reasons for seeking out one particular experience. Any experience you choose: Teachers' Corp, Candy Striper, Peace Corp, or Park Service will force you to leave behind your present lifestyle as a means of moving beyond the ordinary that you already know, in an effort to understand others and develop into a stronger individual. Often family members and co-workers won't understand your need to challenge yourself in such a dramatic fashion, yet we must know and believe for ourselves that the opportunity is worthy and valid. The most difficult aspect of fulfilling my dream was returning when the three months were over. Others may have the chance to remain indefinitely, but college and family called me back long before I was ready to return— at least for a while. The benefits of such an experience are limitless, and any that you choose will provide you with practical skills to use and memories to value for the rest of your life. Not only do you venture to new surroundings and find personal satisfaction, but you also gain friends, close ties, and insight into the inner workings of this environment, such as how the Park Service handles rescue missions or natural fires. Most importantly, you gain the fulfillment of your dream and the knowledge that you pursued it and succeeded.

13   The memories that shape and compel my future prompt me to speak out to others, and to call you to fulfill your dream and perhaps have never acted on. Everyone can imagine at least one reason, if not hundreds, for not fully pursuing their dreams: "I can't leave work" or "I don't think I would qualify." Yet I challenge these responses and ask, Can you afford not to pursue the dream and adventure that you have always wanted yet never sought after?

_____

After draft 4, Kristi's group urges her to condense her narrative. They are worried that her story is too long and that some of her details are extraneous. They suggest that the story seems more important than her claim: readers could get caught up in the story and forget why she is telling the story. Nevertheless, Kristi remains convinced that her testimony is the most persuasive evidence she has to offer. She therefore has difficulty cutting any of the narrative material. In her final draft, Kristi tries to negotiate these competing demands. As you read, identify the changes she has made. Do you think these changes make her essay more or less persuasive?

Dream a Little Dream for Me

Draft 5—Final Draft

1.   Have you ever considered setting your job or schooling, organizations or obligations aside, to actually jump out of the rat race for a period of time, to follow a dream? A dream, by definition, is anything that we imagine or believe possible, yet many individuals never imagine, grasp, or pursue their dream or the opportunity for fulfillment.

2.   High school graduates often have dreams of attending college; once in school, the dream moves on to graduation, yet for some it may entail completing a co-op experience in their career field. Even though I was planning to become a teacher, the dream I had was to do something involving nature; I didn't know quite what, but it had to be something that no one I knew had done. I wanted a challenge and an adventure; and it had to be worthwhile. My opportunity arrived in the middle of May 1990 in the form of a small poster advertising a Conservation Internship program. I glanced at it but didn't give it much thought. Then my mom said, "That sure sounds interesting. Why don't you get some information or an address?"

3.   Well, I hung on to the address for four months before I finally wrote a brief letter requesting information. As I pored over leaflets of information and scenarios about others who had interned for the National Park Service, the opportunity for this challenge to become a reality began to tickle my desires. The longer I considered applying for an internship, the more I was compelled to live an adventure and not just dream one. On a whim, not really expecting to postpone my college and lifestyle to trek out to the great unknown, I applied for a position in Big Bend National Park for the coming spring. I mailed my application in mid-October, and around the first part of November, I received a note that I was being considered for three locations, one of which was Big Bend.

4.   I had never been to Big Bend or even heard of it; I knew only that it was in Texas and that my folks were moving back to Texas in December, so whether I stayed in college or interned, I would be in the same state as my family. Several weeks passed and still no news about the job, so I registered for spring classes, took fall final exams, packed a suitcase, and never mentioned to my friends the possibility of my not returning in the spring semester.

5.   Ring . . . ring . . . ring. "Hello?" I answered the phone on New Year's Eve, hearing a faraway voice offer me the chance of a lifetime.

6.   "Hello, Ms. Koenig. This is Clyde Stonaker from Big Bend National Park, and I am sorry to disturb you, but I'm calling in regards

to the Conservation program. Are you still interested in working in the Park? We would need you here by February 4th."

7   Stunned, I tried to gather my thoughts and asked for a day or two to talk this over with my family.

8   One month later with "Big Bend or Bust" plastered on the back of my '73 VW, and the controversy of leaving college settled with my mother, I was en route to Big Bend. At first I tried to believe that I had chosen to do this and that I was actually following through with a dream that was my very own. I wanted to pick up and leave college and society and to do something brave and challenging. And a semester in the Texas desert as a Park Ranger was all that and more. Yet as reality set in and the desert opened up before me, I had to think through why I had chosen to do this, and I had to decide this was going to work and be one of the best experiences of my life. It is only natural to have initial misgivings when leaving your family, friends, and career preparation to live in an isolated area, yet the difficulties at the onset of my experience only worked to strengthen my inner spirit and later my love for the Park.

9   While settling into Big Bend, I first had to comprehend a mosaic of realities: that only 13 people lived within 75 miles of my doorstep, that the grocery store was about 150 miles away, that I would have no telephone, radio or television for 3 months, and amazingly that mountains and a desert were mere footsteps beyond my little home. These "everyday basics" were drastically different from anything I had grown up with or really considered when jumping at the chance to live in the great outdoors, and I had to adjust to the change.

10   As my time in Big Bend slipped by, I experienced many adventures, from canoeing the Rio Grande to hiking to find "reported" dinosaur bones. Yet I would like to share one of the most important events that occurred during my stay in the Park. My outlook concerning what is important in life and where I will live after I finish college all expanded and changed to some extent because of my internship. I am going to share with you what changed my life and my decisions for my future, and you may wonder what this means or can mean for you. I hope that by reading this, you can fully realize the possibilities available to you—no matter what age you may be—and that you can understand more about pursuing your dreams and the development of self that takes place during one of these experiences.

11   My internship, which lasted three short months, still fills my thoughts and draws me back to explore and remember the beauties and aura of the park. I believe there is a sense of adventure that resides within us all, and I call on you to seek within yourself and act upon it. In addition, I want to share key moments of my internship to illustrate the educational, physical, emotional, and mental growth of such a worthwhile program.

12   Think of a desert, where the land is cut by a river that is now contained by steep, rocky canyons, where sky-blue reaches the dusty

windswept earth, where bluebonnets grow knee-deep but only after a good soaking rain. This is a place where cowboys from Mexico still cross the Rio Grande on horseback to buy a few groceries at the "general store" or to use the only pay phone within a 75 mile radius. Often I found myself listening to the beauty of silence, and early in the morning I loved to see the lazy full moon hang over the mountains of Mexico. It was in this place that I watched adobe masons from Mexico reconstruct an historic home of a settler gone 100 years ago. Upon my arrival, I consumed the surrounding beauty with my eyes, all the information with my mind, and the various trails with my strength.

13   Then one day it was my turn to give the answers, smiles, maps, and directions. The position of Park Ranger was now mine, too. As an interpretive ranger, each day I led visitors on a guided walk from desert bush and bird to an historic military compound, all the while supplying them with narrative, tall tales, and bits of trivia. Curiously, I felt as if I had lived in Big Bend all along—my whole life. For the first time, I encountered a sense of unity with nature and the people around me. I knew almost at the start of my internship that I had found my dream and I was living it! Yet, the experience only got better.

14   Just as I settled into my routine of leading the historic walks and working the Visitors' Center, I discovered that I was to go on a solo backpacking trip that would entail my spending one night out and traveling over 20 miles on foot. I raised my eyebrows and wondered, "Can they be serious?"

15   Two weeks later on a cool Saturday morning in March, as the sun was rising over the Chisos Mountains, I slipped out of the ranger's truck and hoisted my pack upon my back. With a topographic map, compass, and a charged up park radio, I glanced around and meandered off—unbeknownst to me, in the wrong direction. Five hours later, while hiking out of a creek bed, I ran into the major park highway, and I knew that I was in the wrong place. After contacting my sponsor over the radio, I was transported to the ending point of my route to hike it backwards. I had lots of miles to make up before sundown, yet as I hiked I had work to do: I took a people-animal count of all those I saw, collected water samples and trash, and made a general overview of the trails I was traveling.

16   All of the necessary work was minor in comparison with the reliance and confidence that I gained in myself. I learned to trust my intuition and decisions about paths, directions, and the cairns (small, man-made directional rock piles) to follow. I firmly believed in my ability to complete this challenge, not by might but by sheer faith and determination. When I stopped that night, my body ached with fatigue, yet my spirit soared with the majesty of the land that surrounded my every turn and with the knowledge that I was a survivor. I had traveled about 17 miles, including my miscue off on the wrong trail. I unpacked and spread out on the side of a sloping rock, just in

time to watch the setting sun paint the rocks, hillsides, and mountains a flaming burnt orange. Then the world turned a dusky purple and grew quiet for nightfall.

17   Now that you are familiar specifically with one of the significant events of my internship and with the personal fulfillment on one of my dreams, I would like to share the pros and cons of pursuing one's dreams in an effort to persuade you to follow your own dreams. You may wonder why I take time to worry that you are just living the rat race day-to-day existence, but I know first-hand the glories of working as a volunteer, away from the confines of society, in a place centered around the land and the environment.

18   Every experience is bound to have both pros and cons, whether they are emotional, physical, or personal. As my experience shows, the benefits outweigh the disadvantages. When pursuing a personal, lifelong dream each of us will have different needs and reasons for seeking out one particular experience. Any experience you choose: Teachers' Corps, Candy Striper, Peace Corps, or Park Service will force you to leave behind your present assumptions and conveniences as a means of moving beyond the ordinary that you already know, in an effort to prompt you to understand others and develop into a stronger individual. Often family members and co-workers won't understand your need to challenge yourself in such a dramatic fashion, yet we must know and believe for ourselves that the opportunity is worthy and valid. The most difficult aspect of fulfilling my dream was returning when the three months were over. Others may have the chance to remain indefinitely, but college and family called me back long before I was ready to return—at least for a while. The benefits of such an experience are limitless, and any that you choose will provide you with practical skills to use and memories to value for the rest of your life. Not only do you venture to new surroundings and find personal satisfaction, but you also gain friends, close ties, possible job connections, and insight into the inner workings of this environment, such as how the Park Service handles rescue missions or natural fires. (There's no time to tell you more about these benefits now.) Most importantly, you gain the fulfillment of your dream and the knowledge that you pursued it and succeeded.

19   The memories that shape and compel my future prompt me to speak out to others, and to call you to fulfill your dream—one perhaps you have never acted on. Everyone can imagine at least one reason, if not hundreds, for not fully pursuing their dreams: "I can't leave work" or "I don't think I would qualify." Yet I challenge these responses and ask, Can you afford not to pursue the dream and adventure that you have always wanted yet never sought?

Reading Critically: Questions for Discussion

1. Is the title clear and appropriate? Why do you think it is or isn't?

2. Kristi defines the word *cairns* as "small, man-made directional rock piles." How could Kristi revise this definition to avoid using biased language?

3. Most of Kristi's essay is devoted to establishing her credibility: that is, because of this 3-month internship, she believes she has the authority to advise you to try to fulfill your dreams. Is Kristi credible?

4. What evidence does Kristi offer to prove the logic of her position? Is this evidence sufficient, plausible, and pertinent?

5. How does Kristi try to motivate her audience? Does she succeed? Does she address the audience's self-interest? Sense of altruism? Both? After reading Kristi's essay, would you consider joining the Teachers' Corp, Candy Stripers, Peace Corps, or Park Service?

KNOWLEDGE BY OBSERVATION

Elaine Barton is the author of the next essay on Ella's Place, a shelter for abused women and children in her community. Elaine gains her knowledge about this home, as well as about domestic violence, from interviews and library research. As a result, she writes her essay from an observer point of view.

Reviewing Journal Entries

Elaine's journal entries for "Shelter Is Available" reveal how involved she became in this research. Elaine could have reported on her subject in a clinical manner; however, she decides to use more ethical and emotional appeals. Her entries help us see why.

JOURNAL

My first subject choice was about protective services procedures and child sexual abuse cases. After thinking over the problems I would have in gathering data about confidential cases, I decided to move to something else. But still related, of course. I ended up researching women's shelters. I want to appeal to abused women (and anyone who knows them) of all ages in this community to seek shelter and protection at Ella's Place.

I interviewed Lucinda Couch, director of Ella's Place. The location of the home is confidential to keep irate spouses and others from coming after family members at the shelter, so I really had to convince Ms. Couch to see me there. I began my arrangements by contacting Gwen at Child

Protective Services. I made up my interview questions—notes and major subjects, really—that I wanted to be sure to ask about. I felt nervous but really motivated to learn about this shelter and let others know it's out there.

As I wrote my drafts, I had to be careful not to sound like a documentary. I did not use many of the statistics I had planned on because I thought this essay should have a personal appeal to the reader. When women are scared and hurt, they don't need to hear a "machine" voice, telling them about a place to go for help; they need a human, caring voice. So, I decided to play down "hard" evidence, yet give these readers accurate and ample information. In writing, I tried to use the method of slowly and carefully writing the early drafts so that I'd have less major editing to do in the later drafts.

If abuse is the problem, women can look to Ella's Place to help them get some answers. I hope my essay makes my readers understand this. Learning about how unable abused women and children can be to take control of their situations is so frightening. Now, whenever I hear women and kids talk about things or see their faces as they talk, I try to detect signs of their being in trouble. They may look "normal." They try to stare in another direction, anything not to have eye contact. But I think to myself, Do they blame themselves? Are they scared? You can see signs of this, I believe, by looking in these people's eyes—making them look into my eyes. Writing this essay has changed me and the way I see the world of women and children.

Mapping Elaine's Persuasive Rhetorical Situation

Because Elaine's knowledge of her subject is gained by observation, she lists her details on the "knowledge by observation" side of the continuum. Figure 16.2 illustrates her persuasive rhetorical situation.

Elaine intends her essay for an audience of general adult readers in her local and university community. Due to the nature of her subject, Elaine divides her audience into the following groups: victims of physical or verbal abuse; friends and relatives of victims; and all the people who are potential victims or friends and relatives of potential victims. Elaine identifies her readers according to their relationship to the victims of domestic violence. Consequently, she views all readers as very motivated and interested; however, she sees those who have experienced abuse and those who have known victims as the most actively engaged members of her audience.

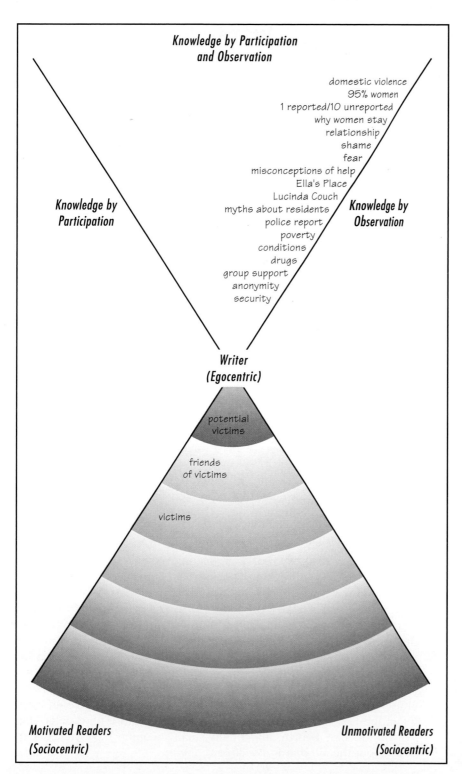

Knowledge by Participation and Observation

domestic violence
95% women
1 reported/10 unreported
why women stay
relationship
shame
fear
misconceptions of help
Ella's Place
Lucinda Couch
myths about residents
police report
poverty
conditions
drugs
group support
anonymity
security

Knowledge by Participation

Knowledge by Observation

Writer (Egocentric)

potential victims

friends of victims

victims

Motivated Readers (Sociocentric)

Unmotivated Readers (Sociocentric)

Figure 16.2
Mapping Elaine's rhetorical situation

Shelter Is Available

Draft 3—Final Draft

1   Domestic violence is one of America's most serious crimes, an outrage that has gained widespread attention only since the 1970s. The term *domestic violence* may refer to abuse of a man, woman, or child within a family setting—but, typically, women and children are the ones who suffer at the hands of aggressive males. Among spouse abuse, "95% of the victims are women" (*Domestic Violence* 1). Two disturbing characteristics of this shocking offense are the frequency of its occurrence and the low frequency of reporting by the victims. The National Woman Abuse Prevention Project reports that "[a]ttacks by husbands on wives result in more injuries that require medical treatment than rape, auto accidents and muggings *combined*" (3). Additionally, 10 cases of abuse go unreported for every call made by a battered woman to the police, according to the United States Department of Justice's Crime in the United States (14). The public, according to sociologists Donileen Loseke and Spencer Cahill, often has difficulty comprehending why someone would not report these personal assaults that go on behind closed doors to the police, or at least leave the abusive situation (304). Children, completely dependent on their parent or care-giver, are quickly forgiven for not taking punitive action, whereas wives and girlfriends may be secondarily victimized by a society too quick to judge and with too little compassion (305).

2   Several explanations are plausible for a woman to remain in such a dreadful situation. First, it is hard for people to abandon a relationship with someone they love, especially if they feel they have much invested in it. "The reluctance of battered women to leave can be adequately and commonsensically expressed in the lyrics of a popular song: 'Breaking up is hard to do.'" (Loseke and Cahill 304). To add to the woman's confusion, the abuser is likely to beg her forgiveness and promise that it will never happen again—after each occurrence. Because of her tangible and intangible investments in the relationship, she will want to believe him. Second, a woman may feel ashamed of the situation, as if she is somehow to blame. This feeling is often enforced by the verbal abuse that so often accompanies physical attacks (*Domestic Violence* 45). The abuser may try to convince her that she is worthless and therefore deserves the beatings he subjects her to. Third, women who are victims of domestic violence often live with a very real fear for their safety, and even their lives—a fear that is not easily empathized with by those not subjected to the physical abuse and accompanying threats battered women may have endured. Often the abusing mate will inform his victim that if she seeks help, he will kill her. Fourth, and finally, many women have misconceptions about the aid that is available to them.

3   These misconceptions that are held by women in abusive situations many times keep them from seeking any help at all, thereby perpetuating the exploitation. Using Ella's Place, a women's shelter, as a case in point, the facts of accessible assistance to victims will refute these false beliefs. In a recent interview, Lucinda Couch, director of Ella's Place, provided information regarding the services available through the shelter. One common myth held by battered women is that in order to benefit from social services, one must make an official police report; however, a police report is *not* required to receive counseling or shelter. The only prerequisite essential to becoming an Ella's Place client is that abuse must have taken place. Another misconception dispelled by Couch is that women who employ the services of such shelters are impoverished, destitute people who can't afford a hotel. Actually, shelters such as Ella's Place are the refuge to abused women and children of all socio-economic statuses. Any woman who is a victim of domestic violence is welcome at Ella's Place, regardless of her income. Even if a woman could afford to rent a hotel room to escape her abusive situation, the women's shelter is a better alternative: anonymity, security, and group support and counseling are the advantages over a hotel. Finally, women may worry about the conditions of a public shelter. Some common concerns, according to Couch, are overcrowded, run-down accommodations and drug use of fellow clients. One visit to Ella's Place, however, would eliminate such worries. The home can accommodate 50 clients at a time, and the occupancy is held to 50 or fewer women and children. The house is comfortable and clean. In fact, after a 24-hour adjustment period, each client is required to perform various household duties. Regarding the drug use issue, prospective clients are screened for drug use and no "using" is allowed during a stay at Ella's Place. Only if a woman who admits to drug use is in a documented program for treatment will she be allowed. Restrictions apply to street drugs and alcohol as well.

4   Women's shelters such as Ella's Place are reported by sociologists to be "the most important resource for women caught up in a violent relationship" (Berk, Newton, and Berk 787). If women could overcome the anxiety involved in seeking help and refuge at such a shelter, they would discover a community resource capable of helping them to recover from an abusive situation.

Works Cited

Berk, Richard A., Phyllis S. Newton, and Suzanne F. Berk. "What a Difference a Day Makes: An Empirical Study of the Impacts of Shelters for Battered Women." *Journal of Marriage and the Family* 48 (1988): 780–788.

Couch, Lucinda. Director of Ella's Place. Personal Interview. 2 December 1993.

Domestic Violence: Understanding a Community Problem. National Women Abuse Prevention Project. Washington: United States Department of Justice, 1988.

Loseke, Donileen, and Spencer Cahill. "The Social Construction of Deviance: Experts on Battered Women." *Social Problems* 31 (1984): 296–310.

United States Department of Justice. *Crime in the United States*. Washington: GPO, 1982.

Reading Critically: Questions for Discussion

1. How does Elaine try to establish her credibility? Does she succeed?
2. What is Elaine's claim? Is it explicit or implicit? Does she offer sufficient and appropriate evidence to support it?
3. Why doesn't Elaine interview victims of domestic violence? Would interviews with several residents of Ella's Place, for example, improve this essay? Explain your answer.
4. Elaine briefly mentions the advantages of a women's shelter over a hotel: anonymity, security, group support, and counseling. Should she elaborate on these advantages? Or is more explanation unnecessary?

KNOWLEDGE BY OBSERVATION

"Who'll Decide for You What's Art and What's Obscenity?" by Kenneth Fontenot was written from the perspective of the "writer as observer." Kenneth has researched the information in this essay exclusively from newspaper articles. Notice that Kenneth didn't have time to go back and research the full citations. What do you think of this method? Is it complete or adequate? Should Kenneth have recorded all of the bibliographic information when he conducted his initial research? What do you do? Why?

Reviewing Journal Entries

Kenneth's journal entries might well be titled "the confessions of a procrastinating essayist." He admits that he has changed his subject at the last minute, assuming that he would write about a subject that he'd already researched. Consequently, he put off exploring his research materials for this essay until days before the paper was due. When he really sat down to begin considering the aim and purpose for this essay, he discovered that he didn't really feel like writing about the subject—multiculturalism in education. Multiculturalism is a controversial subject, yet Kenneth isn't motivated to tackle it, so he wisely changes his focus. But, as he says in one of his entries, "Time's a killer."

JOURNAL

This is not going to be pretty. Here it is three days before the essay is due, and I just changed my subject. I wanted to do something on multicultural education because I had already had the research for it. But I couldn't find anything really controversial that I wanted to follow up on now. So I decided to change my subject to the NEA.

I just got back from the library where I got more research than I'll ever need, but it's all from newspapers. I need to go back tomorrow and try to get some articles from journals.

I had an argument today with one of my conservative friends about the NEA. This should be an interesting paper.

Well, I must admit—I'm a little disappointed in myself. I don't think this paper is really up to par. I've already thought of two counterarguments I didn't discuss. And I think I should have argued just one thing (the NEA should not be restricted) instead of two (and the NEA should not be abolished) because the paper is really too long for a persuasive paper, especially considering I didn't talk about two points that I should have. Since I changed my subject, I only had one day to write it and nobody to read it. Too late to meet with my group. I think it is well written in the sense that it flows, but I don't think it was very well conceived. I don't think that I would want my conservative friend to read it simply because it is not as strong an argument as it should be. Time's a killer.

Mapping Kenneth's Persuasive Rhetorical Situation

Kenneth's knowledge of the NEA is gained by observation, so he lists his details on the "knowledge by observation" side of the continuum (see Figure 16.3).

"Who'll Decide for You What's Art and What's Obscenity?" is written for an audience of general adult readers. Kenneth divides his audience according to two major camps: conservatives and liberals. For Kenneth, his audience's motivation will be high, regardless of political ideology. Is this a satisfactory division of the audience?

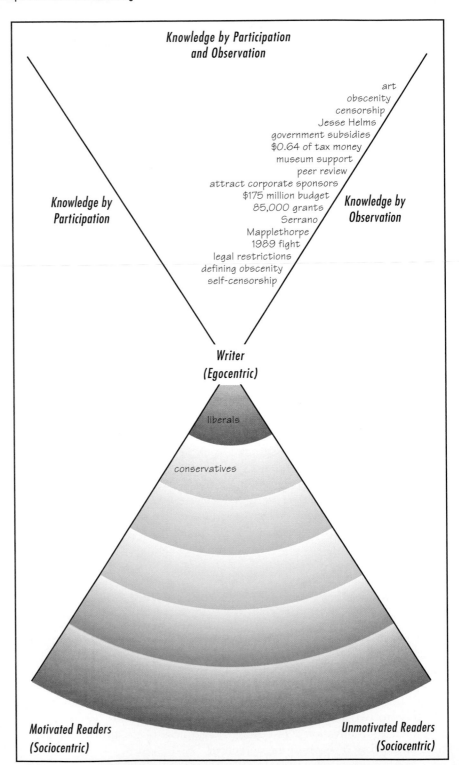

Figure 16.3
Mapping Kenneth's rhetorical situation

Who'll Decide for You What's Art and What's Obscenity?

Draft 2—Final Draft

1   What is art? It's a difficult question to answer, isn't it? Despite the trouble people have defining it, a handful of representatives in Congress think they know what art is. They may not be able to give you a definition of it, but they know it when they see it. Not only do they know what it is, but they also know what it is not. Moreover, they know what's obscene. At least, this is what they would have you believe. In fact, they'd like to decide for the whole country what's art and what's obscenity.

2   With communism collapsing around the world, it is truly ironic that, in the so-called land of the free, artists can be subjected to censorship by the U.S. government. However, this has happened thanks to Jesse Helms and other members of Congress. Reacting to two National Endowments for the Arts (NEA) funded projects that they deemed obscene, Helms led the charge to place restrictions on the NEA in 1989. And what's more, if certain people have their way, the NEA will be abolished altogether. It is vital to America that the NEA not only remain in existence, but also be able to operate without Congressional content restrictions on prospective project grants.

3   There are some who believe that it's not the job of the government to patronize the arts, but that it's up to the private sector. Their simple reasoning is that they shouldn't have to pay for endowments to the arts through the government because they don't want to. The arts, they contend, are not a necessity like the military, and therefore, government has no business taxing people for it. It is up to individual citizens and corporations to support it.

4   Perhaps those against involuntary patronage of the arts don't realize how minimal the NEA's budget is. The approved budget for 1991 is $175 million, less than one-tenth of 1 percent of the national budget ("Uncle Sam"). With this budget, only 64 cents of the average taxpayers' money goes to the NEA (Steele). Surely most Americans would be willing to continue paying this minimal amount to support such a noble cause as the development and appreciation of artistic talent.

5   Yet, even presented with these facts, there are still some who resent funding the NEA with their taxes. Even 64 cents a year— roughly the cost of a canned soft drink—is too much to pay to the government for support of the arts. This kind of philosophical belief is hard to argue against with fact, but there is still much to be said against it.

6   Yes, it is true that there are many people who, feeling an overburden of taxes, believe that mandatory support of the arts should not be governmental policy. But as many people believe similar things about other areas of the budget. There are those who don't believe we

should spend anything on foreign aid, others who think we should spend much less on defense, and still others who think we should spend more on education. There are probably very few Americans who would be satisfied if they knew exactly how their tax money is spent.

7   Some of those against government patronage of the arts would also be surprised to learn that the NEA does much more than just give grants to artists. Its rigid peer review of artistic quality is held in high esteem. Cynthia Mayeda, head of the Dayton Hudson Foundation, the second largest corporate supporter of the arts, says that, because many foundations don't have art specialists, the panel of the NEA is needed to ascertain which artists are most worthy of patronage (Steele). Much of the agency's funds go to museums and places of historical and architectural value. In New Mexico alone, the NEA's presence is felt in many diverse areas. For example, in Santa Fe the Museum of New Mexico is operating on 16 grants from the NEA that help pay for publications, exhibits, and various artist-in-residence programs. The agency also helps the New Mexico Community Foundation in the restoration of churches. Steve Rogers, curator of the Wheelwright Museum of the American Indian, stressed that the NEA is as important to cultural history as it is to supporting new artistic minds (Hickox).

8   Besides its diversity in distribution of funds, the NEA has great power as a governmental agency to attract corporate sponsors. In fact, with only $171 million in funds in 1990, the agency generated over $1 billion in support of the arts from corporations ("Uncle Sam"). With so much money from the private sector, some abolitionists would contend that the endowment is not needed. But the fact is that the NEA's primary purpose is to support the obscure, the marginal, the avant-garde of the art world rather than established symphonies, theaters, and museums that have an easier time attracting corporate sponsorship. So far, of the 85,000 grants the agency has given, 90 percent have been for $50,000 or less ("Uncle Sam"). It is the NEA's leadership role, in addition to its grants, that has made it so essential.

9   Along with those who want to abolish the NEA, there are those who want to restrict it. Much of this current controversy is due to two photography exhibits in 1989 that were funded by the NEA and that many considered obscene. The first was a work by Andres Serrano in which a crucifix was submerged in the artist's urine. The second was a photo exhibit by Robert Mapplethorpe that included homoerotic photos, nude photos of children, along with noncontroversial photos of flowers and art objects (Gadberry).

10   The reaction to these shocking photos was predictable. Senator Alphonse D'Amato denounced Serrano's work on the Senate floor. Over 20 senators rushed to join him in writing an angry letter to Hugh Southern, acting chair of the NEA, demanding to know what steps it would take to revise its grant procedures. The senators said the work

was "shocking, abhorrent, and completely undeserving of any recognition whatsoever" (Vance 39). Senator Helms quickly joined in the fray saying that, although he does not know him, Serrano is "not an artist, he is a jerk. Let him be a jerk on his own time and with his own resources. Do not dishonor our Lord" (Vance 39).

11   Helms led a campaign to restrict the NEA from funding anything that smacked of indecency, obscenity, or a slur on religious beliefs (Fields). After a long battle, a compromise was finally reached in the fall of 1989. The bill barred the NEA from using its funds to "promote, disseminate, or produce obscene material, including, but not limited to, depictions of sado-masochism, homoeroticism, the sexual exploitation of children, or individuals engaged in sex acts and that taken as a whole do not have serious literary, artistic, political, or scientific value" (Fields 10).

12   The following fall, Congress overwhelmingly dropped the restrictions and agreed to fund the NEA for three more years instead of one year that was agreed upon earlier. Congress was essentially leaving it up to the courts once again to decide what was obscene and what wasn't. One restriction was left in, however. If a grant recipient's work was later judged to be obscene by a court, the artist would be required to repay the funds. Congress also decreased the amount of the NEA's money that went to the states from 29 percent to 27.5 percent ("NEA Funded").

13   Because Congress passed the restrictions in 1989, we don't have to guess what would happen if restrictions were placed on the NEA; we already know. By looking closely at the compromise restrictions of 1989, it is evident that the framers of the bill believed it would have little effect on the NEA. In fact, neither Serrano's or Mapplethorpe's work could be considered obscene under the wording of the restrictions. Serrano's work failed to meet the requirement of sexual content and it certainly had serious artistic and political value. And Mapplethorpe's work, taken as a whole, clearly has serious artistic and political value as well.

14   Given these assertions, the pro-restrictionist would ask what all the fuss concerning the restrictions was for if they had no real effect anyway. But if the situation is diagnosed closely, certain unplanned yet still dangerous effects are evident. Carole Vance points out several problems with restrictions. The first is that it forces the NEA panel members, who are not from the legal world but the art world, to make technical decisions about what is obscene (49). The clear intent of the restrictions is to apply the same test for obscenity that was spelled out in Miller v. California, a 1973 supreme court case. According to the Miller ruling, a work was considered obscene if it met *all three* of the following criteria:

(1) the average person, applying contemporary community standards, would find that the work, taken as a whole, appeals to prurient interest,

(2) the work depicts or describes, in a patently offensive way, sexual conduct specified by statute, and (3) the work, taken as a whole, lacks serious literary, artistic, political, or scientific value. (Vance 49)

15   There are enough problems in that definition to tax a team of lawyers let alone a panel of artists. For instance, what constitutes an average person? Who defines contemporary community standards? And who decides what's serious and what's not? It's difficult to think of anything that would meet the standard, and if you tried to create something that did meet all the requirements, you would undoubtedly fail because your work would, by definition, have political value.

16   So once again, the pro-restrictionist would ask, "So, what's all the fuss about?" The problem with this, as Vance points out, is that the panel, acting without expertise in legalese, will "worry what obscenity *might* mean and perhaps decide to play it safe and fund landscapes this year. . . . The injunction to avoid funding art that '*may* be considered' obscene . . . can suggest that panelists reject any work that *might* offend any group, no matter how small" (49).

17   This is a very serious problem. If artists are going to create works of art, they cannot be worrying about how their works will be received. Vance tells of an artist she knows who expressed concern that she will not be able to tell what's obscene when she serves on an upcoming panel for the NEA, "apparently anticipating difficult and wrenching deliberations over what is in fact a null set" (50). For example, the chair of the NEA, John Frohnmayer, rejected grants to four performance artists who were recommended for full funding by the panel. All four deal with political and sexual issues, and at least two of them do so graphically (Salisbury).

18   This self-censorship by the arts community is perhaps more dangerous than actual censorship by the government because it often goes unchecked. It is the formal kinds of censorship that often encourage self-censorship among artists and institutions. For example, when formal censorship is highly publicized, it serves to create a "witch-hunt" atmosphere within the art world. Artists reacting to this are much more likely to censor their own works. When these restrictions were in place, many artists did not even apply for grants from the NEA, fearing that they would be turned down. Others decided sexual topics were too risky to attempt (Vance 51). A situation such as this in America is simply intolerable.

19   No matter what evidence is offered concerning the harmful effects of restrictions on the NEA or the need for government endowment of the arts, there will still be many people who look at certain works of art and say, "There's no way we should be paying for this." Perhaps the experience of Cynthia Gehrig, head of the Jerome Foundation, may shed some light on this subject. She finally decided to see performance artist Karen Finley, whose work concerns sexual identity, sexual power, the oppression of women, and violence. Finley sometimes

uses her body to depict what she is saying including pouring chocolate on herself to reinforce her message. Gehrig describes her experience in these words:

> I almost didn't go because I thought it would be disturbing, and I wasn't
> sure I wanted to be put through that. But it was such a moving experi-
> ence. She forces you, as a woman, to see the lies and compromises
> women live in their lives, how we deal with men, with our children. I'm
> so glad I went and so glad I had the choice to go or not to go. (Steele)

20   The need for the NEA is clear. Art is one of the noblest pursuits of
humankind, and any government would be foolish not to support its
development and appreciation among its citizens. The need for an
unrestricted NEA is also clear. Artists cannot be at their best if they are
constantly worrying about perceptions of their work. We owe it to
them not to make the extremely difficult work of creation any harder
than it already is. The oppression of women and minorities in this
country has destroyed the chances of countless potentially great
artists. America should not compound this atrocity by censoring artists
today or at any time in the future. All representatives of Congress
should be notified that the American people will not tolerate its intru-
sion into the art world any longer.

Works Cited

Fields, Howard. "Congress Passes Compromise NEA Bill." Publishers
    Weekly 20 Oct. 1989: 10.
Gadberry, Greg. "Outrage Over Arts Is Aimed at NEA." *Maine Sunday
    Telegram* 17 Dec. 1989.
Hickox, Katie. "Imperiled Funds Support a Variety of Projects." *New
    Mexican* 15 Jan. 1990.
"NEA Funded for Three Years With Less Restrictive Language." *Pub-
    lishers Weekly* 9 Nov. 1990.
Salisbury, Stephen. "NEA Chairman Rejects Grant to Four Artists."
    Philadelphia Inquirer 30 June 1990.
Steele, Mike. "Should Politicians Decide What Audiences See?" *Min-
    neapolis Star and Tribune* 27 July 1990.
"Uncle Sam, an Embattled Patron of the Arts." *Insight/Washington
    Times* 2 July 1990.
Vance, Carole S. "Misunderstanding Obscenity." *Arts in America* May
    1990: 49–52.

Reading Critically: Questions for Discussion

1. Is the title clear and appropriate? Does it serve to motivate the audience?
2. In the opening paragraph, Kenneth ridicules conservative representa-

tives. What impact do you think this ridicule will have on the liberals and conservatives who compose his audience? Does it help or hurt his credibility? Are his readers more or less likely to adopt his position?

3. Kenneth offers his claim in the second paragraph: "It is vital to America that the NEA not only remain in existence, but also be able to operate without Congressional content restrictions on prospective project grants." What evidence does Kenneth supply to prove his claim is logical?

4. In the third through fifth paragraphs, Kenneth anticipates and answers possible objections to his claim. Do you consider his answers persuasive? What other persuasive strategies do you find in Kenneth's essay?

5. Notice that Kenneth's citations and list of sources omit specific page numbers. Does this omission damage his credibility?

KNOWLEDGE BY PARTICIPATION AND OBSERVATION

The following essay was written by Rochelle Davis, Melissa Smith, and Mel Walton. "Scholastic In-Aptitude Test" argues against the widespread use of the SAT by college and high school administrators. As these three writers know about this test both directly and indirectly, they share a participant-observer perspective.

Reviewing Journal Entries

Rochelle, Melissa, and Mel had never before written a collaborative essay; though they were accustomed to researching subjects with other people, they had never tried to coauthor anything. From their comments, you'll notice that they enjoyed writing collaboratively, stating at times that they thought the experience of writing together actually improved their own styles. To make it easier to consolidate their work, they tried to produce this essay on the computer. Melissa and Mel express their new-found love for composing at a terminal rather than writing everything by hand first.

Interestingly, these writers might have chosen to compose separate mini-position papers, combining them in the way that the authors of "United We Stand, Separately We React" do in Chapter 9. Instead, Rochelle, Melissa, and Mel approach their task by dividing up discourse blocs within the essay. Notice how the groups' writing approaches influence arrangement in these two essays.

JOURNAL

We picked our subject for our paper today—observation and participation. We decided on a real hot subject for us: the SAT. We are going to try and persuade our readers against the test. We believe it is an inaccurate test which is too limited. (MS)

I will prepare the introduction and background of the SAT. I began writing the intro and have acquired a test packet to help in explaining the uses and explanations for the test. (RD)

I went to the library to get some articles on the SAT. I'm looking specifically for articles against the SAT. I found a couple—most of the ones were missing. I'm writing my section arguing against the test. Rochelle did the intro and Mel's arguing for the SAT. (MS)

Am finding it difficult to present an unbiased opinion due to my deep seated aversion to the SAT and its unreliability. Have finished the draft on the intro and we are meeting to collaborate on putting the parts together. (RD)

I went to the library to find articles about the SAT—I have to write the "for" arguments and it is going to be extremely difficult because I don't agree with the reasons it is used or the validity and reliability of the test itself. It is limited, biased, and relied upon too heavily. No, no, no, no, no— FOR SAT! (MW)

There are no articles in support of the SAT in the library. I checked WILS and ERIC. My teacher suggested that I check the pamphlet put out by ETS to get a starting point. We'll see. (MW)

Today I went to the undergraduate office in Bizzell and got SAT info. I think I can do most of my part from this—yeah!

I also went back to the library to look up some of the articles I had bibs on yesterday. Since Melissa was sick, I figured it would help if we had some sources already in hand on Sunday. That way we can establish the tone and pertinent points to bring up and then go write. 6 out of 10 articles are not even on the shelves—I'm so frustrated. I'm leaving this library. (MW)

I called Melissa to tell her about the library dilemma. (MW)

We met tonight and worked on what to do. Rochelle had done an intro and we went from there. I wrote about 2 paragraphs just to record our ideas and now I can go hit the computer. (MW)

Man, I went to town today on that computer. I couldn't believe how easily the words come to me. We meet again tonight to put it all together. (MW)

I met with Rochelle and Mel at McDonald's to go over our drafts. Our paper seems to be coming together. We're going to meet tomorrow night at the library to compose on the computer together in order to bring a draft to our teacher. I think we might need to work on our transitions. Our sections seem to end abruptly and start quickly. (MS)

My group met at the library. We put all of our information on one disk.

The computer makes it a lot easier to revise and edit our paper. There are still some things about the computer that frustrate me, but it really does make composing a lot easier. (MS)

We met with our teacher this afternoon. She read our first draft and said that it was taking shape. She wanted to talk about our discourse blocs. I am definitely beginning to see an improvement in my writing and thinking about writing. I am more aware of developing an idea—a bloc—more now. I never understood that till now. The credit goes to my teacher and Rochelle and Mel for their constructive criticism. Through their comments, I have learned to evaluate my essays better. My writing is getting better the more I write.

My group is meeting at 8:30 to work on our next draft. We are going to add some information as well as revise areas that our teacher asked about. I have direction. (MS)

We have worked so well together. It seems that when one of us can't think of the right thing to say the others can. We are all so exhausted this week: I have 5 papers due this week. Rochelle has two and a mandatory holiday party to attend where she works. Melissa has 2 tests and a paper. I'm so glad we're finishing this one. (MW)

This was my last draft to prepare with Rochelle and Mel. I divided our subject up into three separate parts and started to work on it that way. Rochelle was responsible for the introduction bloc of the paper. Mel took care of the section "for" the SAT and I was responsible for the arguments against it. What we did after we wrote our sections was we met and combined the three. We did this on the computer. The computer made it easy for us to view all of our work (after we put it on disk) at one time. We took each section and read it, making the necessary changes. We also had to add and delete certain parts so our paper would flow from one section to the next. After we felt comfortable with the body of the paper, we wrote the conclusion together. Writing collaboratively was fun and using the computer made writing and revising together feasible. (MS)

We all three are happy with this paper. I'm not saying that it is perfect. But we said what we wanted. I will compose on the computer at every possible moment now that I've tried it. I couldn't believe how easily the words come to me and it is so much quicker to just type and erase on the screen than to write and then type.

This class has helped me so much. I am no longer intimidated by word limits on papers—actually I now have to be careful about writing longer papers, rather than ones that are too short. Working in a group has helped that, I think, because we can talk about what we are thinking and planning. We also get exposed to two other writing styles that we can try and improve and incorporate into our own style. (MW)

After the hectic time getting this paper completed to a point that we are comfortable with, I can now look back and sigh with relief. . . .

Additionally, the collaboration helped each of us realize our individual strengths and weaknesses. Fortunately, as a group each weakness in one was matched with a strength in another. It was apparent that the practice in writing we have had made the actual creation of this piece second-nature. We didn't need to think extensively about what we were doing because the practice has allowed us the freedom to write and the practice "fixes" itself. (RD)

Mapping Rochelle, Melissa, and Mel's Persuasive Rhetorical Situation

Rochelle, Melissa, and Mel map their rhetorical situation in Figure 16.4. As the map shows, the SAT is a subject that these writers know about from personal experience as well as through outside sources. They have all taken the SAT and do not support its widespread use. From their journals, we can tell that these writers will have to make conscious efforts to balance their arguments and maintain fairness in their essay. They appear to know that they will probably need to turn to outside studies to present "pro" arguments. The knowledge continuum contains a list of the information these writers have gathered by participation and observation.

Rochelle, Melissa, and Mel expect that their readers will be from their university and local community. They divide these readers into their first-year college peers as well as high school seniors and juniors; high school administrators, counselors, and teachers; college administrators, counselors, and teachers; parents; other adults who took the SAT; other adults who never took the SAT. The members of the focus group think that the interest level will be highest among those who are in their first year of college or are high school seniors and juniors, with the least interest shown by those who have never taken the SAT. Rochelle, Melissa, and Mel recognize that there may be older readers who never took the SAT, yet have grandchildren or friends who are subject to this test; however, they see these readers as perhaps less interested in the subject than others.

Scholastic In-Aptitude Test

Draft 4—Final Draft

1   The three-week wait was over. The seal was ripped on the envelope containing the SAT results. A sweat begins to break as nervous tension sets in. Her head begins to swim as she questions how the scores can be so low. She is graduating in the top quarter of her class with an 87.5 average, yet her scores reflect less than 900. The score of 880 reveals at least 150 to 200 points lower than her previous scholastic performance would predict. What could possibly have caused this severe failure?

2   This type of scenario is not rare. Thousands of students each semester take this exam that is designed to test the probability of a

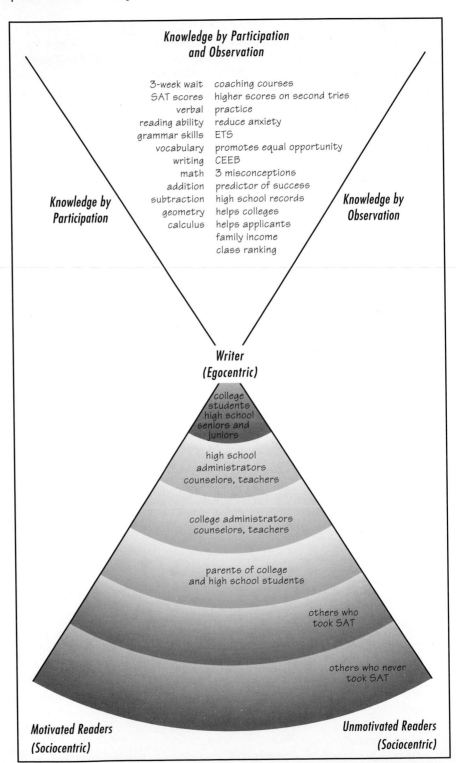

Figure 16.4
Mapping Rochelle, Melissa, and Mel's rhetorical situation

student's success in college. Whether questionable results are attributable to factors such as test stress, the inaccuracy of basing an education on simple factors such as the two this measures, or simple unpreparedness on the part of the test-taker is difficult to determine. However, the statistics and arguments lean heavily toward the general failure of this device in determining the success rate of college prospects.

3   The Scholastic Aptitude Test, or SAT, is a standardized exam used nationwide. The exam consists of two parts, one verbal and one math. The verbal portion includes writing excerpts to test reading ability, grammar skills in recognizing improper usage, a quite challenging vocabulary section and a writing exercise used to provide a sample of composition ability. The math section covers basics such as addition and subtraction, ranging to geometry and calculus. This test coupled with high school class standing are the two main factors used to determine performance capabilities of prospective college freshmen.

4   Considering the test only encompasses two categories of the educational process, we will argue that it is an inaccurate indicator of an individual's potential for success in the pursuit of higher education.

5   The SAT provides college admissions officers with a basis for comparison of students who come from widely varied high school backgrounds. High school academic records are used in conjunction with SAT scores as a means to predict which prospective students will be most likely to perform satisfactorily in the college environment. Because school course offerings and grading standards vary widely across the U.S., some means of placing students on the same scale must be enacted. The SAT is used to rank students on a national scale so that the same variables are used when evaluating each student for possible admission to college.

6   The SAT questions students on information they have been exposed to throughout their academic careers. A publication by The College Board entitled *Taking the SAT 1991–92* gives suggestions for preparing to take the exam. The SAT Committee, which is the publisher of this informational publication, prescribes that "doing well on the SAT is a natural result of hard work in academic courses in school and a strong interest in reading and other mentally challenging activities" (*Taking,* 1991, p. 4). According to this precept, a student who has completed a wide selection of strong academic courses, has read a wide selection of materials, and has consistently worked hard on studies should have the best strategy already worked out in order to do well on the SAT. Nevertheless, special assistance, such as pre-tests and courses designed to "coach" the student to successful scores, is available.

7   With regard to coaching courses and ways to prepare for the exam, a familiarity with the exam's organization, the types of questions presented, the terms and concepts explored, and the methods of timing and scoring the exam should provide students with the neces-

sary information to help them perform well. The publication previously mentioned, *Taking the SAT 1991–92,* supplies these types of information along with practice tests that allow the students to test himself or herself and become familiar with personal strategies to consider before going to take the actual exam. The amount of practice a student may want to have prior to taking the test is a subjective decision that must be made personally by the student. For those students who feel they need more practice, there are several books of practice tests available; however, it should be noted that practice is not likely to dramatically improve their scores. The College Board asserts that "if you are nervous about taking tests, [practice] can help you relax. But simply drilling on hundreds of questions cannot do much to help you develop the skills in verbal and mathematical reasoning that the test measures" (*Taking,* 1991, p. 4). The College Board does not recommend for every student to take coaching courses to aid in preparation for the SAT. It has not been statistically proven how much these courses may improve students' scores.

8   One other important point to recognize is that SAT scores usually improve after a second attempt at the exam. An average increase of 15 to 20 points on each of the two sections is reported and out of 100 students, five will show an improvement of 100 points or more on one or the other of the sections, whereas only 1 of 100 shows a drop of that magnitude. However, that same research has shown that short-duration familiarization courses (20 hours) improve scores on the average about 10 points on the verbal section and about 15 points on the math section. Some longer-duration courses (40 hours) that specifically stress working to enhance the underlying skills measured by the test show average increases of 15 to 20 points on the verbal section and 20 to 30 points on the math section. The coaching courses may or may not show improvements to a degree that warrants the time, effort, and resources required by them.

9   The College Board stresses that the best way to do well on the SAT is to study hard and take demanding courses in school. Students are urged to do more in regular schoolwork, leisure time on one's own, and working with other students or adults to prepare for the SAT. This information seems to suggest that a major factor responsible for under-achievement on the SAT stems from test anxiety and from not having a strong enough academic background rather than from any fault on the part of the exam.

10   Arguments placing blame on the dependence on exam scores can be found in an article entitled "Academic Course Grades as Better Predictors of Graduation from a Commuter-Type College than SAT Scores." In this article, the authors rate the SAT last as a predictor of college success. The number and types of academic courses taken in high school rank ahead of SAT scores when determining potential success, and the foremost indicator is related to high school standing. The SAT is a one-time overview of the academic abilities of a student

and is inherently limited. External factors such as anxieties or environmental forces can (and usually do) have immense effects on test scores, yet these factors are not considered during the grading or evaluation of the final results.

11   "The SAT is constructed, administered, scored, and explained to the public by the Educational Testing Service (ETS), the nation's largest non-profit educational-research organization, with over 2400 employees" (Crouse & Trusheim, 1988, p. 97). They claim that the SAT measures important abilities that are related to educational success. However, Crouse and Trusheim argue in their article, "The Case Against the SAT," that the test is unnecessary. Their study reveals how ETS has violated the public confidence placed in it. According to Crouse and Trusheim, "The ETS and the College Entrance Examination Board have behaved more like corporations bent on defending their products at all costs than like non-profit institutions working for the public good" (1988, p. 98). In other words, these organizations have failed to gather serious evidence for their claims, or have often ignored or denounced evidence that undermines their positions. A possible basis for the inadequacy of their arguments could be the numerous and arguable fallacies usually attributed to the exam.

12   The three most prevalent misconceptions surrounding the SAT stem from ETS' belief in the importance of the test. Their conviction relates to the notions that the SAT: (1) helps colleges with admissions criteria; (2) helps applicants make choices that correspond to their abilities; and (3) promotes equal opportunity by standardizing all students. With regard to helping colleges, ETS believes that the scores are used as a supplement to the student's secondary school records in determining his or her college success. This argument is insufficient in that studies have shown that school records are a better indicator of potential success than any exam could be; records present a chronological context and profile of a student, taking into account factors that the SAT cannot (White, Nylin, & Esser, 1985). As an aid to students as they choose colleges, the SAT ranks last; preceding it on the list are family income, personal preferences, family influences, and academic prowess. The decision as to which college to attend is more strongly influenced by the other factors because typically by the time the SAT is taken (late in high school), the other considerations have already determined students' choices. Finally, the belief that the SAT promotes equal opportunity for all races was assumed to be inherent in the exam because of its standardization. The flaw in this theory lies in the fact that the same criteria are not used for all applicants, and the only way to truly provide equal opportunity is through the implementation of affirmative action measures.

13   In light of the information presented here, use of the SAT as the sole indicator of a prospective student's possible success in college should be strongly discouraged. There are several variables that influence performance that are more accurate predictors than the SAT. As

mentioned, class rank, secondary school records, and other types of sequential data more accurately suggest the future performance of a student in college.

Works Cited

Crouse, J., & Trusheim, D. (1988, November). The case against the SAT. *Public Interest,* pp. 97–102.

Taking the SAT 1991–92: *SAT Study Guide.* (1991). Princeton, NJ: Educational Testing Service.

White, W. F., Nylin, W. C., & Esser, P. R. (1985, February). Academic course grades as better predictors of graduation from a commuter-type college than SAT scores. *Psychological Reports,* pp. 375–378.

Reading Critically: Questions for Discussion

1. What is the function of the opening scenario? Is it effective?
2. How do the writers try to establish their credibility?
3. The writers discuss the Educational Testing Service's claims regarding the SAT. Is their refutation of this position satisfactory?
4. This persuasive essay was a collaborative exercise. Is the multiple authorship obvious? Why do you think it is or isn't?
5. Which piece of evidence do you consider especially persuasive? Is this information sufficiently emphasized?

Repertoire Focus: Proposing a Solution

Quite possibly the most important skill you'll need to develop during your college years is the ability to propose solutions to problems. As a student, as a citizen, and later as a professional, you will often have opportunities to propose solutions, and your proposals will cover a variety of issues. You might serve on a campus committee that proposes more effective ways of distributing information on job opportunities to graduating students. In your engineering class, you could propose a design for refrigerators that heightens their energy efficiency. In your community organization, you might propose additional legislation on drunk driving to your local representative. On the job, you might propose to your boss that the company adopt a new vacation policy for part-time sales clerks.

In writing proposals, you will try to prove to your audience that your solution is appropriate. It is especially important, therefore, that you discuss and answer possible objections to your solution.

REPERTOIRE WRITING TASK: PROBLEM-SOLUTION

Define and explain the problem clearly, and propose your solution as the most feasible, developing a reasoned argument for it. Be certain to make your argument convincing by analyzing your audience carefully, using rhetorical appeals judiciously, as well as providing sound, sufficient evidence and counterarguments. Because this is persuasive aim writing, consider carefully what your readers already know about this subject; what are their perceptions and attitudes about it, and why do they hold these beliefs?

Here are three variations of this writing task, based upon the different ways you may "know" about your subject.

Knowledge by Participation

Write an essay proposing a solution to a problem faced by your community or by a group to which you belong, and address your proposal to one or more members of the community or group. The problem you select should be one that you know about through personal experience.

Knowledge by Observation

Write an essay proposing a solution to a problem that your community or group is coping with and that you came to know of through indirect means (through interviews, reading, television, or another medium). Your subject should be one that others have written about informally or formally, yielding some form of published biographical, social, or historical information that you can integrate into your essay. Address your proposal to one or more members of the community or group.

Knowledge by Participation and Observation

Write an essay proposing a solution to a problem that your community or group is coping with and that you came to know of through direct experience and indirect means (through interviews, reading, television, or another medium). Your subject should be one that others have written about informally or formally, yielding some form of published biographical, social, or historical information that you can integrate into your essay. Address your proposal to one or more members of the community or group.

REPERTORY COMPANY OF STUDENT WRITERS: THEIR RESPONSES TO THE TASK

To address the writing task, you may find it helpful to read essays that were written in response to the same assignment by other student writers in our repertory company. All of these student writers created their own writing communities or groups, meeting regularly to serve as editors of each other's multiple drafts. They also reviewed their journal responses to remind themselves of possible writing ideas.

To provide you some additional context, read and discuss the following journal entries, maps of rhetorical situations (the knowledge continuum and audience continuum), and research strategies for these essays. You'll also find some questions after each selection.

KNOWLEDGE BY PARTICIPATION

The first essay, "Children and Poverty in Inner City Houston," was written by Ursula Houston. Ursula grew up in Houston, Texas, went to school in the inner city, and holds strong views about the need for quality educational opportunities for all schoolchildren in the city. Obviously, then, this writer bases her essay on her knowledge by participation and reveals her description of the problem and its solution from her personal perspective. We have included two drafts of this essay for you to analyze.

Reviewing Journal Entries

In Ursula's journal entries, we see a contrast between the way she approaches this writing task as opposed to the way her group members do. Her group members set agendas for every meeting and require everyone to participate. Ursula perceives her group members to be driven; in fact, in one entry, she refers to them as "workaholics." Ursula, on the other hand, would prefer a more "laid-back group." Consider these selected journal excerpts.

JOURNAL

I met with the group to talk about subjects for the writing task. To be honest, I had nothing ready to present to the group, so I didn't really participate. When the group finished with business for the day, I stayed to talk about my social life. I need some advice about personal matters, so why not ask these people?

The group objective for today was draft 2. Each of us should have a reworked paper to let others read. We're talking about invention still. But I just didn't have time to mess with this for class. My life is in turmoil. I think my group is mad at me.

I skipped my class and our group meeting. Sorry.

Draft 3 was due in our group and I haven't even started the first draft. My group members like to push hard and do lots of drafting and reading and responding. They make it fun, but I'm just not into it. They've said they understand if I don't do stuff as long as I understand that they have invited me to be in on everything and get their advice. They call themselves student editors, but I think they're workaholics in this class.

I met with the group. They're on draft 4, can you believe it? I'm still finishing my first write through. I like my subject, and I know I'll be able to pump it out in a snap. Inner-city schools are my deal. I know them so well. No sweat, Jeannette.

Since I don't have my work done today, I'm reading everyone else's papers. They said I had to participate if I was going to be in the group. So, I read and commented on their papers. They plan to revise another time. Blows my mind.

I finished my draft but left it at home. So, I did the exact same thing I did at the last class and group meeting. I read other people's papers and commented. It's weird. I show up to give them editorial advice. I get nothing back from them because this is our last formal meeting to discuss drafts. Our next meeting is about comparing retrospectives. Who's got time to write retrospectives? I should have gotten into a more laid-back group. These guys drive me nuts. To make everyone happy, though, I will revise and write a new draft 2. On my own time.

If you were a member of Ursula's group, what advice would you give her? What strategies would you suggest to encourage Ursula to participate in the group more effectively? What would you do if those strategies failed?

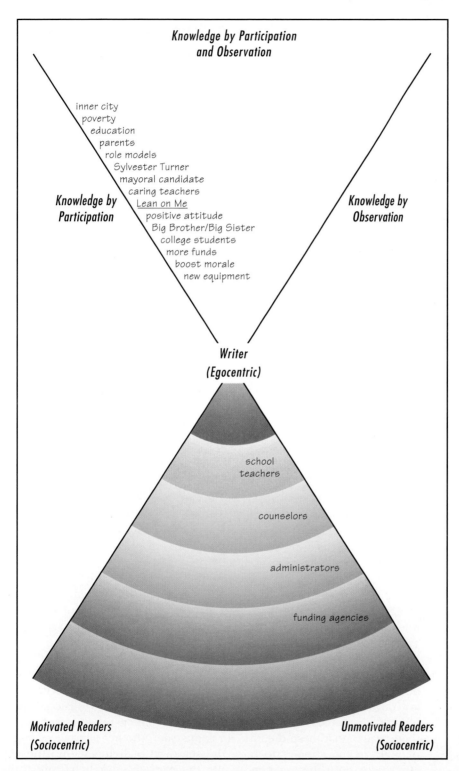

Figure 17.1
Mapping Ursula's rhetorical situation

Mapping Ursula's Persuasive Rhetorical Situation

Ursula's rhetorical situation for this essay appears in Figure 17.1. Ursula's knowledge of poverty and inner-city education is gained through participation. Accordingly, the knowledge continuum reflects her relationship to this subject.

Ursula is writing for an audience of Houston schoolteachers, counselors, and administrators, as well as local and state funding agencies. She knows that while citizens in Houston may be concerned about inner-city education, it may be a situation that people have come to simply accept. Her readers may feel that inner-city problems are so insurmountable that maybe they're not worth tackling. As a consequence, Ursula knows she will not have motivated readers, for the most part. The groups she wishes to convince are tough to rally. Her map of the audience continuum reflects her audience analysis.

Poverty in the Inner City

Draft 1

1   I am tired of driving down the streets of inner-city neighborhoods observing poverty. Many children are left hungry at night. Many adults are without homes. Why must people live like this? After analyzing the situation, I have found that the root of the problem to be based on education. Many of these impoverished children do not realize its importance.

2   If no one takes a sincere concern and becomes involved in the problem, the cycle will continue. There are various ways to attack this situation to allow the populous to better themselves. The basis of the problem resides in education, but it can be solved through parents, teachers, programs, and funding. Parents must realize that they need to teach their children the importance of an education. They need to explain to their children that the only way out of subsidized housing is to obtain a quality education.

3   Some people feel that educating these children will be a waste of time because the goals may seem unrealistic and unattainable. But to bring the dreams closer to home, parents should point out various role models from the local community. One such example is Sylvester Turner. He grew up in Acres Homes, an inner-city neighborhood in Houston. His father was a painter and his mother was a maid. He graduated valedictorian of his high school. He went on to obtain a degree from the University of Houston and even further to receive a law degree from Harvard. Recently, he ran for mayor of Houston. This type of success story should be told to the children because it makes them realize that these dreams can come true. Another alternative that may aid in the attempt to raise the standard of living within these areas is to train the teachers within the various schools to care for

these students. I have been enrolled in some of these schools and observed a large percentage of teachers who do not care about the students. Sure, there are teachers who stay after school everyday to hold extra tutorials sessions to insure that their students comprehend the material. But we still have teachers who are simply there to pick up a paycheck. They sense the fact that these teachers are not genuinely concerned about their welfare. They feel that if the teacher does not care whether or not they learn, then why should they care? This leads to an even more depressing situation because many of these young people are eager to learn, but they don't have anyone who is willing to spend time with them.

4   Some may feel as if this solution is a bit far-fetched because it is difficult to change the morale of adults; however, this is not true. The movie *Lean on Me,* based on a true story, illustrates that it can be done. In that film, the principal went through the school and fired all of the teachers who were not doing their jobs. He motivated the remaining staff and this positive attitude spilled over to the students. With lots of hard work and dedication, all things are possible.

5   Big Brother-Sister programs, if properly implemented, can also be effective. The public schools should implement a program, in congruity with the local universities, and ask for enthusiastic volunteers to come into the schools to explain the importance of an education. These college students could also educate schoolchildren about the various professional fields that they could enter after obtaining a degree from college. This will enable the students to choose from a wide range of professions. This may, in turn, give them something to look forward to. The mere presence of someone's taking interest in them is positive.

6   Often it is difficult to convince college students to participate in the program. But all it takes is one public school official to go the neighboring universities and explain the situation. Once they realize how much the children need them, they will be more than willing to help. The types of bonds that can be formed from a relationship established in this manner are strong and lasting.

7   Infiltrating more funds to the inner-city schools will also help boost the morale and possibilities for positive change for these youths. More money will, in turn, change the way kids perceive school. I have attended poor and wealthy schools within the same school district, and the differences between the two are profound. The poor schools had old band instruments and old athletic equipment, and they rarely went on educational field trips.

8   The wealthy school was always receiving new equipment and taking trips. The students are able to observe this type of treatment, and it makes them feel inferior.

9   The argument most often heard with reference to this solution is that the money is not in the budget. This is not true because I have attended schools in predominantly white areas and these schools

were never at a loss for money. The schools received new band uniforms and a few instruments every other year.

10   Between teaching the children the importance of education, to encouraging parents to be more supportive, to infiltrating more funds into the schools, to setting up Big Brother-Big Sister programs, there has to be a way for all of these inner-city children to raise themselves out of poverty. They are not there because they lack the intelligence. They are living there because they lack the initiative. My solutions are formulated to boost their morale and to educate them to the fact that there is another way of life. Giving them control over their own destiny and giving them the option to improve their lives is all that needs to be done.

Children and Poverty in Inner-City Houston

Draft 2—Final Draft

1   I am tired of driving down the streets of inner-city Houston observing poverty. Many children of this once oil-rich city go hungry at night. Many live in temporary homes or places that their parents will never own. Why must our children live like this? After analyzing the situation in Houston, I have found that the root of the problem lies in the educational system. Many of these impoverished children do not realize its importance.

2   If no one takes a sincere concern and becomes involved in the problem of children and poverty in Houston, the cycle will continue. There are various ways to attack this situation to allow young Houstonians to better themselves. The basis of the problem resides in education, but it can be solved through parents, teachers, programs, and funding. Parents must realize that they need to teach their children the importance of schooling. They need to explain to young people that the only way out of subsidized housing or homelessness is through quality education.

3   Some people view educating these children as a waste of time because the goals may seem unrealistic and unattainable. But to bring the dreams closer to home, parents should point out various role models from the local community. One such example is Sylvester Turner. He grew up in Acres Homes, an inner-city neighborhood in Houston. His father was a painter and his mother was a maid. He graduated valedictorian of his high school. He went on to obtain a degree from the University of Houston and even further to receive a law degree from Harvard. Recently, he ran for mayor of Houston. This type of success story should be told to the children in the inner-city of Houston because it makes them realize that, through education, they can make promising futures for themselves.

4   Another alternative that may aid in the attempt to raise the standard of living for Houston children is to train the teachers within the

various schools to care for these students. I have been enrolled in some of these schools and observed a large percentage of teachers who do not care about these particular schoolchildren. Sure, there are teachers who stay after school everyday to hold extra tutorials sessions to insure that their students comprehend the material. But we still have teachers who are simply there to pick up a paycheck. The students sense the fact that these teachers are not genuinely concerned about their welfare. They figure if the teacher does not care whether or not they learn, then why should they care? This leads to an even more depressing situation because many of these young people are eager to learn, but they don't have anyone who is willing to give them the nurturing and encouragement to excel. All too often, many teachers go through the motions that their jobs require, but action without commitment is empty.

5   This solution is often considered a bit far fetched because it is difficult to change the morale of adults; however, this is not true. The movie *Lean on Me,* based on a true story, illustrates that it can be done. In that film, the principal went through the school and fired all of the teachers who were not doing their jobs. He motivated the remaining staff and this positive attitude spilled over to the students. Through hard work and dedication, everything is possible—even in Houston.

6   Big Brother-Big Sister programs, if properly implemented, can also be effective. The public schools should implement a program, in congruity with the local universities, and ask for enthusiastic volunteers to come into the schools to explain the importance of an education. These college students could also educate schoolchildren about the various professional fields that they could enter after obtaining a degree from college. This type of program gives youngsters in the inner city something to look forward to, something to aspire to. The mere presence of ambitious college students' taking interest in kids in poverty is positive and can change lives.

7   Oftentimes it is difficult to convince college students in the public arena to participate in such programs. I realize this drawback. However, all it takes is one public school official to go to the neighboring universities and explain the problem and need to college students; if college students are asked, they will come. Once they realize how much these "city kids" need them, they will be more than willing to help, and the types of bonds that can be formed from a relationship established in this manner are strong and lasting.

8   Infiltrating more funds to the inner-city schools will also help boost the morale and possibilities for positive change for these youths. More money will, in turn, change the way kids perceive school. I have attended poor and wealthy schools within the same school district, and the differences between the two are profound. The poor schools had old band instruments and old athletic equipment, and they rarely went on educational field trips. On the other hand, the

wealthy school was always receiving new equipment and taking trips. The students can observe this type of difference in money and treatment. If a school gets little funding, then it is not valued; it and its mission are not seen as important. But if a school gets lots of funding, then it and its mission are viewed as important and valuable. So, which school do you think kids in inner-city Houston attend? How do you think they perceive education in their neighborhood is valued or is worth?

9   The argument most often heard against the matter of funding is that there is no money in the Houston school budget. This is not true because I have attended schools in predominantly white areas and these schools were never at a loss for money. The schools received new band uniforms and a few instruments every other year. The problem does not rest in the fact that the money is not there. It is simply misallocated. Lamar, an elite school in Houston, recently received renovations totaling two million dollars. This money could have been used for the betterment of the schools in impoverished neighborhoods. True, it is important to conduct school in an attractive building, but it is more important to have enough teachers and books allocated to each school. That is not the case right now in Houston: currently, Houston schools are of two types: the haves and the have nots. This distinction must end if Houston's inner-city children are to have a chance to beat poverty by looking to education.

10   Between teaching the children the importance of education, to encouraging parents to be more supportive, to infiltrating more funds into the schools, to setting up Big Brother-Big Sister programs, there has to be a way for all of these inner-city children to raise themselves out of poverty. They are not there because they lack the intelligence. They are living there because they lack the initiative. My solutions are formulated to boost their morale and to educate them to the fact that there is another way of life. Giving students control over their own destiny and giving them the option and hope to improve their lives is a must.

11   I propose that we implement a plan that will incorporate all of the alternatives I've described above. The educational system within the Houston's inner-city will not be able to operate at its maximum potential with an absence of any one of these aspects. Many view the situation as hopeless, but it's not. It's a situation that can be accomplished, for if we cannot see hope for these inner-city children, then how can they?

Reading Critically: Questions for Discussion

1. Does Ursula establish her credibility to write on this subject?
2. Ursula proposes several different solutions to the problem of inner-

city poverty. Would this essay be more effective if she focused on a single solution? Explain your answer.

3. Ursula offers a specific example of a man who escaped inner-city poverty—Sylvester Turner. Would more such examples be persuasive? Would a more detailed examination of Turner's story be persuasive? How did he escape poverty? Did he, for example, have supportive parents, caring teachers, a Big Brother, or other kinds of help?

4. How does Ursula motivate the audience? Does she address the audience's self-interest? Sense of altruism? Both?

KNOWLEDGE BY PARTICIPATION

The next essay, "A Solution to the Problem," was written by Michelle Harris. Michelle knows about her subject—family planning programs in high schools—from personal experience. As you read through the essay, consider how this writer knows about her subject and compare her knowledge to your own. Using only knowledge by participation, could you have written this essay? Which subjects could you write about using first-hand knowledge?

Reviewing Journal Entries

The following entries are rarely about writing or Michelle's subject; rather, they are comments directed at her teacher—comments that reveal how disgruntled Michelle is about the class, the writing, and the teacher.

JOURNAL

Today the first draft of our essay was due in our group. I didn't have much done, and it's a good thing. Once again, I learned that I did not understand the task. Just like last time. I started only to find out that I was doing something wrong. My group gets it, but I just never seem to. Is it me or them or the teacher?

I am discouraged about this class. I thought I'd do bad in your class. After my conference with you the first day, I was determined to prove something to you. But then you began to think I was trying to pull something over on you. Yes, I did miss class and didn't always do what the group set up as goals, but that doesn't mean I'm trying to get by without working.

I haven't gotten a really good start yet and some groups have already started their third drafts. My group may be doing that, but I'm not sure. I haven't called them or heard much from them lately. I've stopped going to class. I'll write more on this paper during the holidays.

I finished my first draft and let my boyfriend look over it. I really worked hard on this paper.

————————————

I called my group members to ask for a meeting on revisions for the latest drafts. Ursula can't meet. Wendy is out of town. Miller said he'd come but never showed up. I went and talked to you and you gave me a lot of help on my paper. However, I have continued to make other revisions beside yours on the paper.

————————————

Once again we are turning in essays. One of my classmates added some revisions to my paper when we read them in class before submitting them.

I was glad the paper was finished. It has been a hard semester of writing. It's almost over, thank God.

I feel that my writing skills have improved some; however, I don't think I will ever feel natural and comfortable about writing again. You've made me too aware. Should I thank you?

Mapping Michelle's Persuasive Rhetorical Situation

The map of the rhetorical situation for this essay appears in Figure 17.2. Michelle's knowledge about unplanned pregnancy and family planning programs in inner-city schools comes from knowing young women who became pregnant in high school and from her volunteer work. The knowledge continuum reflects her relationship to this subject; her details are listed on the "knowledge by participation" side of the continuum.

Generally speaking, Michelle is writing for taxpayers. She breaks down this broad group into educators, legislators, parents, and high school students. Michelle believes that, although her audience ought to be motivated about this subject, readers will undoubtedly be skeptical and indifferent. Her goal is to try not to become adversarial, but instead to project a no-nonsense yet caring tone. Michelle must therefore present her readers with accurate information in an engaging manner in order to convince them to consider her solution. The map of the audience continuum reflects her audience analysis.

A Solution to the Problem

Draft 3—Final Draft

1   Who do you blame when a teenager becomes pregnant? Who do you blame when her educational goals are impeded because an unborn child has become her primary focus?

2   Those were the questions that I asked myself when one of my best friends from high school told me that she was pregnant. She was an honor student with a 3.98 grade point average. She was salutatorian of our senior class. In addition, she excelled in many student

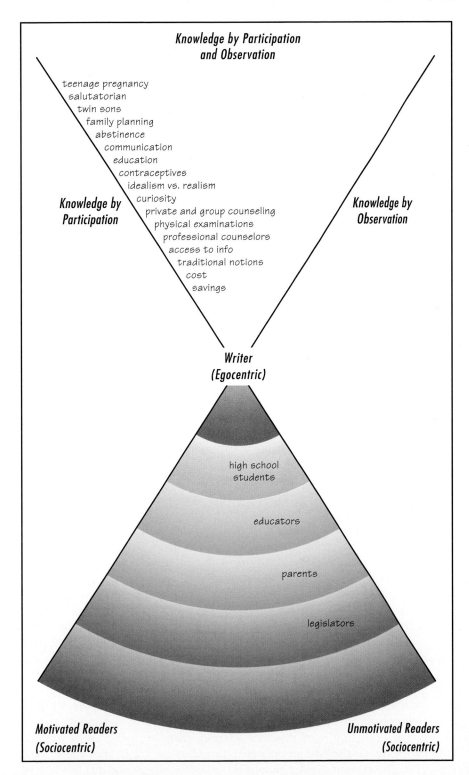

Figure 17.2
Mapping Michelle's rhetorical situation

organizations. However, upon graduation, college was not in her immediate plans; instead her plans were devoted to how she would provide for her twin sons.

3   Teen pregnancy is a major social problem in inner-city schools. In fact, it is compared with such problems as teen drug abuse and gangs. Unlike drugs and gangs, there are many feasible solutions to the problem of teen pregnancy. As a former member of a family planning program and a former student in an inner-city school, I propose that a family planning program be implemented in inner-city secondary schools. Family planning is the process of educating, counseling, and distributing contraceptives to high school students in a unified program.

4   Numerous studies and educational research have been conducted to explore approaches to combat the problem of teen pregnancy. Contrary to the solution of family planning, other solutions such as abstinence, increased communication, and education have been proposed. All three are good ideas and do address the problem; however, they all have flaws.

5   A narrow view of alleviating this increasing problem is the idea of abstinence. Abstinence is defined as the voluntary refrain of sexual activity. Moreover, abstinence is the only foolproof way to avoid pregnancy. In the decades prior to the 70s, it was considered a disgrace for a young girl to become pregnant before she was married. If this occurred, the student was often forbidden to continue her education in a public school. For many teens, this public shame was all the reinforcement they needed to overcome sexual desires.

6   As idealistic as the above argument may seem, it is not realistic at all today. Telling a person not to participate in sexual activities because it is morally wrong is not dissuading. Prohibiting a person from an education hurts us all in this society, not only the young girl. Today's teens are less affected by the impressions that adults have of them. The fact that teens succumb to peer pressure and yield to sexual temptations supports the notion that abstinence is not an attainable solution to teen pregnancy.

7   A more acceptable solution to the increased rate of teen pregnancy is communication. When teens and their parents have a close relationship, all are more likely to be relaxed when discussing sexual information. Communication helps parents and the teen talk about sexuality more comfortably. And, if the teenager is sexually active, the parents can assist the teen in making an informed decision about contraceptives and sexually transmitted diseases. Communication enables everyone to have some responsibility for everyone else in the home; in the end, that's what really counts.

8   On the other hand, once the teen has made the decision to have sex and use birth control, the communication process has little or no effect. From my own visits to a family planning program, I noticed that many of the patients never returned to the clinic after their initial visit. The patient's name would be called by the attendant, but few of

them answered. The fact that teens do not continue family planning programs is true despite their parents' knowledge of their using contraceptives. Motivation decreases because the teen does not want to go through the extra effort of visiting a clinic on a regular basis to get contraceptives. As a result, the teen is left unprotected. Inner-city schools need solutions that will not only get sexually active teens to use birth control, but a system to promote its continued use.

9   Education, by far, has contributed the most to the decrease in teen pregnancy. It has done so by instituting sex education classes in schools, by showing documentaries on television, and by placing sexual information articles in popular teen magazines. These tactics of providing information to teens have cleared some of the false ideas about sexuality that teenagers may have been told by other uninformed, impressionable young people. However, education alone is not enough. The amount of information presently supplied to teenagers about sexuality is hardly significant. For most teens, their curiosity will not be satisfied until they experience the act for themselves. Though many teens are educated on sexuality, they fail to realize the consequences of pregnancy.

10   As stated earlier, there are many solutions to the problem of teen pregnancy. However, a family planning program instituted in secondary schools is clearly the best. If the program were implemented in schools, it would have two objectives. First of all, it would give counseling to both male and female teens on safe sex. The counseling process would be private; group sessions would also be available, however. Information would be distributed on abstinence, sex, safety, and contraceptives. Documents and pamphlets would also be provided to address any questions that teens feel they need to know about. Secondly, the program would assist teens in getting contraceptives if these young people were sexually active. Of course, certain guidelines would be required. They would include a physical examination and regular check-ups.

11   The program also would require professional sex counselors. These counselors must be educated in teen behavior and knowledgeable about the various methods of birth control. The program would encourage parent-teen communication about sex, assure access to contraceptives to sexually active teens, increase teens' knowledge in sex education, and balance the information about sexuality and responsibility in the school atmosphere. Family planning is a more concrete solution than the ones I discussed earlier. My program incorporates all the solutions.

12   Family planning in secondary schools would give teens an easier access to the benefits of its program. In an attempt to do this, the program would be open before and after school. It would also be open on Saturdays, according to each school's individual needs. Furthermore, the teen would not be required to have a parent's permission to be a patient in the program; anyone seeking assistance would be ser-

viced. The program is not by any means promoting sexual activity. It simply realizes that teens have vulnerable moments just as adults do. If Americans truly want to alleviate the problem of teen pregnancy, they must realize that only a combination of the other solutions will work. A family planning program is an attempt to provide teens with every advantage possible to avoid unwanted and unplanned pregnancies.

13   There will be some opposition to the family planning program. Some of the more conservative members of the community might be advocates against the program. Many of these residents tend to honor traditional values about sexuality. They contend that sex education is a matter that should be discussed between parents and their teenager, not the school and the student. And some fear that a family planning program would increase teens' desires to become sexually active.

14   Contrary to these fears and beliefs, family planning programs only wish to offer accurate information that teens can benefit from in a positive way. First of all, it must be noted that contraceptives would only be given to teens as a last resort to ensure the teen won't get pregnant and won't get sexually transmitted diseases. Second, the teen would receive contraceptives only after she has been counseled by a professional counselor in the program. Third, some of this information would be made available to parents who would like to know more about how to communicate factual and necessary information to their teenager.

15   Another argument against the program I propose might be cost. Yes, it would require a substantial amount of funding to implement. Presently the government is spending billions of dollars on teen pregnancy each year. A family planning program in schools would only spend more of America's tax dollars. Furthermore, there is at least one family planning clinic in every county, and most of them are free. Instead of spending more tax dollars on family planning programs in schools which will eventually result in higher taxes, the government should promote the family planning centers that are already available to the public. Or so defenders of this solution say.

16   Indeed, it would cost a great deal of money to pay for my proposed program. The money spent on welfare programs needs to be shifted into family planning program. According to the League of Women Voters, more than half of all women on welfare are teenagers. However, once the family planning program begins to succeed and prevent unplanned pregnancies, the government would actually spend less on teen welfare. Governor James R. Thompson of Illinois set up a program similar to the one I'm proposing, saving $14,000 for every pregnancy it prevented. In fact, the program would decrease governmental spending on welfare because the demand for it would be lower: that is, fewer pregnancies means less support for new mothers and their unplanned babies.

17   Clearly, a family planning program in secondary schools is the optimal solution to deal with the unyielding rates of teen pregnancy. It is the only solution that offers the teen every method of birth control available, whether it be through the concept of abstinence or through contraceptive use. Family planning is also more practical than any of the other solutions because it realizes that the program cannot stop the problem of teen pregnancy, only hinder it enormously. Parents, educators, and the government must attend to this growing epidemic of unplanned births. They must realize that the problem will not go away by itself. Talking will no longer suffice; we must act now.

Reading Critically: Questions for Discussion

1. Is the title of this essay effective? Why do you think it is or isn't?
2. In discussing this issue, Michelle tries to avoid adversarial language. Is she right to try? Does she succeed?
3. How does Michelle establish her credibility? Does she offer sufficient evidence?
4. Does Michelle do a satisfactory job of discussing and answering objections to her solution? What other objections might her audience have?

KNOWLEDGE BY OBSERVATION

"Changing the Future with Preventive Discipline," by Robin Moore, focuses on the concept of punishment in schools. As someone who plans to be a schoolteacher, Robin acknowledges in her journal that this subject is related to her future career and is one that she can research. Robin thus researches preventive discipline using external sources, taking an observer point of view.

Reviewing Journal Entries

Robin's journal entries are very short. They are written partly for the teacher, who Robin knows will read them; however, they are mainly written for herself. Robin writes them as a way of articulating to herself all of the different things she has done to meet the writing task.

JOURNAL

I finally managed to pick a subject that I like and that I could find some information on in the library. This subject also applies to my future. Discipline. I'm supporting the use of preventive discipline in my paper.

I've tried to organize my notes and my essay, and it sounds pretty organized. I plan to make many revisions and edit much more thoroughly this time. I know that realistically I just don't see the things my group and teacher see when they read. I hope I can overcome this, though.

I am working harder on this essay than all of the others together. I have more thoroughly edited the final copy. I tried to simplify what I wanted to say and be concise. I don't think this is the best essay I've ever written, but I think it definitely is a major improvement.

Mapping Robin's Persuasive Rhetorical Situation

Figure 17.3 illustrates Robin's rhetorical situation. Robin's relationship to her subject is pictured on the observation side of the knowledge continuum.

The readers that Robin is addressing in this essay are teachers. Starting with her first sentence—"As teachers . . . , we. . . "—Robin presents herself as a teacher talking with other teachers. What do you think of Robin's analysis of her audience? Do all teachers think alike? How do you think this particular conceptualization of her readers will help or hinder Robin's ability to select and marshall appropriate evidence?

Changing the Future with Preventive Discipline

Draft 5—Final Draft

1   As teachers, one of the biggest challenges we are faced with in the classroom is maintaining discipline. Obtaining a universal model for discipline that would work in every instance would be ideal. However, administrators, teachers, and parents sometimes have conflicting ideas about the meaning of discipline. This diversity may stem from different definitions assigned to the word: 1) "training that corrects, molds, or perfects the mental facilities or moral character," 2) "control gained by enforcing obedience or order," and 3) "a rule or system of rules governing conduct" (Webster's). Between these definitions plus various others defined by educators, parents, and psychologists, it is apparent why teachers have divergent views about their expectations and responsibilities toward classroom discipline. Because of this, students receive mixed signals about what is considered acceptable behavior. Three alternatives commonly used as solutions are corporal punishment, behavior modification, and preventive discipline. Although the first two types provide immediate reform, their long term effects are negative, and in some cases damaging. Preventative discipline is the most appropriate solution to the discipline problem because it teaches appropriate behavior while providing long term positive effects on the students.

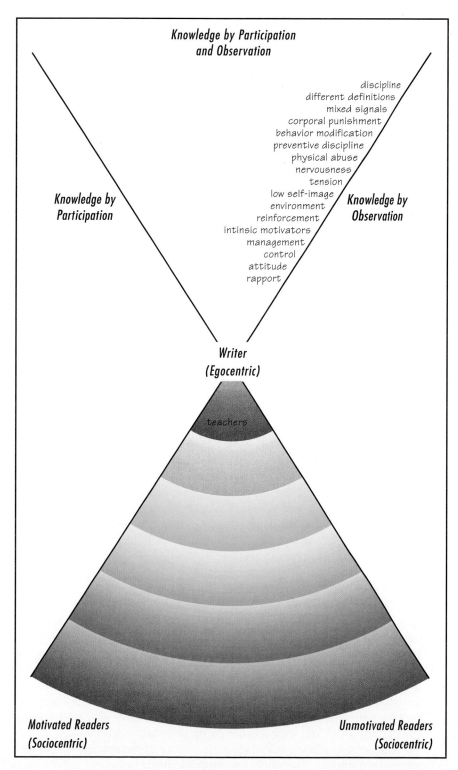

Figure 17.3
Mapping Robin's rhetorical situation

2   Many schools use a discipline system which includes corporal punishment, or punishment in the form of physical abuse, such as swats with a paddle. The main argument for the use of corporal punishment is that it has an immediate effect, temporarily stopping the misbehavior. Also, it is easy to use, it does not require any special training or knowledge, and it does not require any investment of time (Silverman 3). However, punishment in the form of physical abuse has no positive effects. Research has shown that corporal punishment creates nervousness and tension, which in turn causes slower learning. Marvin Silverman notes that physical punishment does not teach children constructive ways to deal with conflict; but, it teaches children that violence is an acceptable way to resolve conflicts. The adult is modeling violence for the child. According to Silverman, before people can have a positive influence on each other, people must first interact in a constructive way; corporal punishment does not allow for any type of positive interaction. Finally, the use of corporal punishment is strongly associated with the development of a low self-image in children (Silverman 4). With all of these negative outcomes of corporal punishment, it is amazing how many schools insist that it is an appropriate form of discipline.

3   Another type of discipline, which is the most widely known and researched, is behavior shaping. Advocates of this notion believe that misbehavior occurs because it is reinforced by the environment. In order to reverse misbehavior, the child's environment is manipulated to produce new standards of "good" behavior. This shaping process is implemented through rewarding students for gradual improvements in behavior that come closer to a desired outcome (Curwin and Mendler 107). Reinforcement can be given every time a desired behavior occurs or given periodically, which may be on a set schedule. In the initial phase of behavior shaping, it is best to give continual reinforcement until the student gradually progresses to one of the variable schedules, which is the most effective (Curwin and Mendler 107). Even though rewards are given, which is positive, they are given after the behavior occurs, leaving the student able to behave in either a positive or negative way. This also suggests that punishment must be given if the behavior is not moving toward the desired outcome, producing too much time and attention spent on discipline in the classroom, thereby producing a negative atmosphere. Rewards and punishments are perceived differently between students and teachers; therefore, the teacher must know what each student perceives as reward and punishment. For instance, one student may be punished by removal from the class, whereas another student may act up especially to be removed from the class. This traditional form of discipline is outdated and ineffective for the number of discipline problems there are today. Children are no longer motivated primarily by teacher appraisal, but they are driven by peer appraisal; because of this we have to stop placing ourselves at the center of the reward system and incorporate intrinsic motivators for our students to behave.

4   As teachers, we all want our students to have a positive attitude toward us, to be enthusiastic about coming to our classrooms, and to be excited about what we are teaching; therefore, we are responsible for setting the stage for a positive learning environment. If our class time consists of mostly discipline problems, then it is obviously impossible for students to benefit from this type of environment. This is why we must find a way to reduce behavioral problems at the beginning of the school year and to prevent them from happening throughout the semester, a problem that may be remedied through preventive discipline.

5   Preventive discipline techniques are most effective when used in collaboration with each other. French, Lavay, and Henderson outline these techniques in their article "Take a Lap," and they may be broken down into three categories: teacher's management in the classroom, teacher's control over the environment, and teacher's attitude and rapport toward students. The teacher's management in the classroom category contains three techniques. First, a teacher must have "with-it-ness," or know what is going on in the classroom at all times. If the students know that the teacher is always aware of what they are doing, they will be less likely to misbehave. Second, the teacher must have a strong class structure in which all students are engaged in maximum participation, all know what they will be held accountable for, and all pay attention. And then, the teacher must provide movement management, or smooth transitions. If the teacher's lesson is highly structured with high participation and smooth transitions, then students will not have the opportunity to misbehave. Also, the authors state that students are often interested when presented with challenging and fun lessons; therefore, many of the offenders will not want to misbehave.

6   In the next category, there are five techniques which involve the teacher's control over the environment. First, the teacher must present classroom rules at the beginning of the school year and give consequences for disobeying them. "Once the student knows what behaviors are not acceptable and the consequences of those behaviors the probability of those misbehaviors will decrease" (French, Lavay, and Henderson 181). For example, posting rules and consequences in the classroom may serve as a visual reminder of what is expected of the students. According to Stefanich, most students prefer firm teachers over permissive ones. Effective teachers are very explicit about their own desired behaviors in the classroom, and use these standards when giving feedback to their students (Stefanich 13). In a second example, the student and teacher design a contract together which outlines acceptable behaviors and future expectations for performance in the class. When the student misbehaves, the teacher may refer back to the terms of the contract, displaying a sound basis for his or her disapproval. Second, the teacher must have control over the physical environment of the classroom or gym. Extreme temperatures, lack of

ventilation, excessive lack of equipment, and inappropriate space are just a few factors that can cause behavioral problems. These factors can usually be controlled by the teacher. Third, the teacher's proximity to the students may help control disruptive behavior, since the teacher is a "source of protection, strength, and identification" (French, Lavay, and Henderson 181). Fourth, the teacher must have competence in the knowledge and skills of his or her field. According to the authors of "Take a Lap," students are much more likely to respect and want to learn from a teacher whom they realize is competent in the subject area. Relating to teacher competence is self-sufficiency, the fifth teacher control technique. It is important for the teacher to be able to take care of discipline problems on his or her own, because if outside sources are always used, such as the principal, then the student knows that the teacher cannot handle misbehavior, and therefore problems will likely continue.

7   The final group of preventative techniques relate to the teacher's attitude and rapport towards his or her students. First, the teacher must maintain a high degree of enthusiasm. Students can read a teacher's attitude very distinctly; therefore, a positive and enthusiastic attitude or a negative and apathetic attitude can be read and modeled very easily. The teacher may also try a technique called interest boosting. According to the authors, if the teacher takes a special interest in a student who may be a potential behavior problem, the student will probably be more willing to cooperate with the teacher (French, Lavay, and Henderson 181). Also, if the teacher takes time to give each student special attention some of the time, then all of the students will know that the teacher is genuinely interested in all students. The teacher will gain more respect and cut down on behavior difficulties. A third technique is signal interference in which teachers have set signals used to control the class. For example, in elementary school, a teacher might put his finger over his mouth as a signal to "stop talking." This technique is more effective when administered consistently and with consequences. Finally, and most importantly, is the ability of the teacher to create a learning environment. If the teacher generates a challenge and interest in every student, as well as provides motivating and instructionally sound activities, then discipline problems will be minimal in the classroom.

8   Although there are few arguments against preventive discipline, supporters of corporal punishment and behavior modification still use these types of punishment because they're immediate in their effects and fairly easy to administer. Preventive discipline techniques take time to learn and implement; while they may hold this drawback, the positive learning effects on the students are more what we as educators want to accomplish: students who are responsible for their actions and who have been taught to respect others through respecting themselves.

9   The nature of behavior problems is changing in our society. Today's youth have entirely different problems in their lives and different motives for misbehaving than did former generations. Teachers, administrators, and parents need to reach a common definition of discipline and become consistent in reinforcing their ideas of appropriate behavior. We as teachers need to encourage students to succeed, to be creative, and to display a sense of humor while having a positive effect on their self-esteem. In order for this to occur, negative aspects of our teaching philosophies should be erased, such as modes of discipline that contain an ineffective or negative effect on our students. Perhaps experienced teachers are afraid to try new methods, or they may even be too lazy to exert the effort that goes into preventive discipline. For whatever reason, the majority of teachers do not utilize preventive discipline techniques. In order to adjust to the modern problems facing our students, and to produce positive and motivated individuals who are capable of being productive in society, we must practice and support the use of preventive discipline in our classrooms.

Works Cited

Curwin, Richard, and Allen Mendler. *The Discipline Book: A Complete Guide to School and Classroom Management*. Reston: Reston Publishing, 1980.

French, Ron, Barry Lavay, and Hester Henderson. "Take a Lap." *The Physical Educator* 54 (1985): 180–185.

Silverman, Marvin. *How to Handle Problem Behaviors in School*. Kansas City: H&H Enterprises, 1980.

Stefanich, Greg. *The Cascade Model: A Dynamic Approach to Classroom Discipline*. Dubuque: Kendall/Hunt, 1987.

Reading Critically: Questions for Discussion

1. Does Robin do a satisfactory job of discussing and answering objections to preventive discipline?
2. Robin addresses the audience as a teacher speaking to teachers. In doing so, she tries to establish credibility with the audience. Are additional information sources also necessary to establish Robin's credibility?
3. Even though she addresses the audience as a teacher speaking to teachers, Robin's knowledge source is observation of the subject—readings from three books and a journal article. Would this proposal be more persuasive if Robin described personal experiences of classroom discipline?
4. Does Robin appropriately cite sources of information? Do you always know which source supplied which information?

5. In the final paragraph, how does Robin try to motivate the audience?

KNOWLEDGE BY PARTICIPATION AND OBSERVATION

"But I *Have* to Graduate" is the collaborative work of Tricia Goodwin and Chris Griffith. This essay is written from the point of view of two participant-observers. Can you think of subjects that you know of both directly and indirectly? Make a list of these writing ideas in your journal.

Reviewing Journal Entries

In the following notes from their journals, Tricia and Chris reveal how they collaborated on their research and writing responsibilities. Have you tried coauthoring a text? If so, how did you and your coauthors divide responsibilities? How did your process compare with that of Tricia and Chris?

JOURNAL

This paper is a collaborative one. Chris and I have decided to write about the registration process here. We plan to propose a solution to the scheduling problems that graduating seniors face. We are going to interview several advisors to obtain data. (TG)

At our meeting, we discussed the subject and then talked about:

solution to make sure both of us were clear on possibilities

the different groups who preregister with seniors

dividing the work load—interviews, sections to write

We also collaborated on questions for interviews so we both knew what info we're looking for.

We agree that this is fun! (CG)

Met with Chris at my apartment to discuss our paper. Divided work: I'm going to explain and evaluate the existing process and Chris will discuss our proposal. Set next meeting time. (TG)

Having problems with the Honors program. People there don't want to answer my interview questions. Chris was able to get info from the Athletic department. (TG)

Discussed how we felt when our interviewees were evasive in answering. Looked at the arrangement of our essay in terms of the kinds of info we're getting. (CG)

———————

We met with our teacher to get her feedback about the subject and our research. Guess we're doing okay. It's hard for us to get together to work on this paper. I'm afraid our different styles are going to clash when we finally put everything together. Maybe this won't happen because this paper is certainly about facts and not just emotions. (TG)

———————

Chris came over. We were able to read typed portion of our paper. Styles seem to work okay together. We need to work on some structure problems and mechanics. (TG)

———————

We proofed a typed copy. We felt the essay was maybe B material, but no more. Tricia and I plan to go the library computing center to proofread and type our final copy.
I'm still worried about the student worker argument—is this informational enough? (CG)

———————

I enjoyed working on this task collaboratively. Chris and I worked well together. It was not easy to meet because our schedules conflicted, but we did well—considering. Each of us wrote different sections of the paper. Then we put them all together, and they flowed pretty well. We made copies of the typed draft and made the changes we thought needed to be made. Then we got together and battled it out until we had composed a draft that we were both satisfied with. (TG)

Mapping Tricia and Chris's Persuasive Rhetorical Situation

Figure 17.4 shows how Tricia and Chris map the knowledge continuum for their essay. Their understanding of preregistration for graduating seniors comes from witnessing the difficulties that these students encounter as they try to enroll (participation); in addition, their knowledge also comes from outside sources (observation). What kinds of research strategies would you expect Tricia and Chris to use? How important would documentation be in a text such as this one? Why?

The authors intend their essay for an audience of university administrators, academic advisors, and students. Tricia and Chris reason that all three of these groups on campus will be motivated to explore this problem and the proposed solutions, adding that students—especially graduating seniors—will show the greatest amount of interest in this subject. Look at the audience continuum; do you agree with the two writers' analysis of their readers? Why or why not?

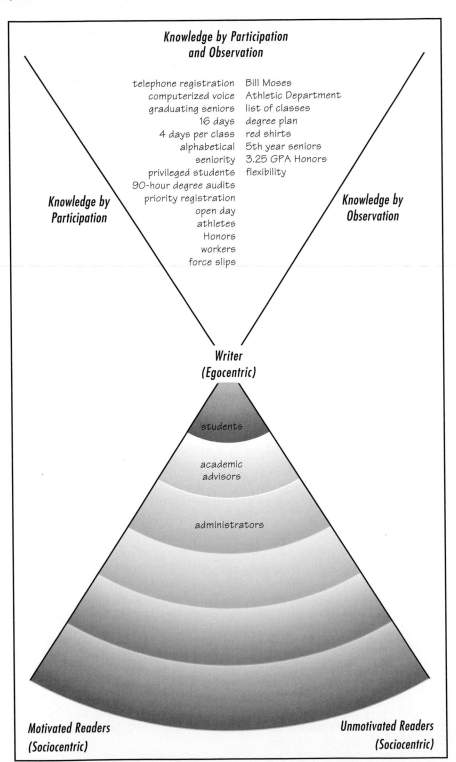

Figure 17.4
Mapping Tricia and Chris's rhetorical situation

"But I *Have* to Graduate"

Draft 3—Final Draft

1   As the alarm clock sounded on Monday morning, Mary Lou, a senior in college who will be graduating next semester, slowly dragged herself out of bed only to spend the next few hours on the telephone trying to preregister for her final fifteen hours of courses. The computerized voice answered, for the third time, "Sorry, the class you have requested is full. No other sections are available at this time." Mary Lou angrily slammed the phone down and began to wonder how she would graduate next semester if she couldn't even enroll in the courses required for her degree. At the same time, Jane Doe, an academic advisor, dragged herself out of bed only to sit behind a desk for hours, listening to hundreds of screaming seniors complaining about preregistration and enrollment problems. Every semester Jane dreads the four-day period when seniors preregister because she knows she will be faced with a number of graduating seniors who share the same problem Mary Lou encountered. In most cases, Jane can only listen. She can do nothing to solve the problems of these students because the classes required for them to graduate have already been filled with students who have preregistered before these graduating seniors.

2   In many smaller colleges, preregistration may be done in person by each student and involves standing in one endless line after another. However, at our college, preregistration for the next semester is done by means of touch tone telephone approximately six weeks before the current semester ends. Here, preregistration elapses over a period of sixteen days, and these sixteen days are divided equally among the four levels of classification (freshman, sophomore, junior, senior). Therefore, each individual class has a period of four days in which the students of that particular class are to preregister. Because of the vast numbers of students attending our institution, students cannot be allowed to preregister at random during their particular four-day period. This four-day period assigned to each class must be very organized and structured. Thus, each class is broken down into groups of three according to the first letter of their last name. Each letter group is assigned a certain day on which it is eligible to preregister. For example, seniors with a last name beginning with A-G may be scheduled to preregister on Monday, H-O on Tuesday, and P-Z on Wednesday. Although the manner in which the letters are grouped remains fairly constant from one semester to the next, the order in which these groups preregister alternates each semester. This brings us to the fourth and final day allotted for preregistration of each class. This final day reserved for each class is known as open day: any member of that particular class is eligible to preregister. This open day

offers students a last chance to add, drop, rearrange, or adjust their schedules; however, this last chance is provided only after all other members of that class have been given the opportunity to register.

3   As would be expected, each level of classification is ranked according to seniority, with seniors registering first, then juniors, sophomore, and freshmen, respectively. However, there are several groups of students who have the privilege of preregistering even before seniors. These students include student athletes, student workers, and Honors students. What is so special about these students that they have special privileges? In discussing the answers to this question, we will take each group and explain their preregistration procedures as well as the rationale behind allowing these students to register early.

4   Student athletes preregister the day before registration opens, according to Bill Moses, the Athletic Department Academic Advisor. These students are required to go to their academic advisor and get a list of their classes to ensure that they are following their degree plan. Then, they take the list of courses for which they wish to enroll to Mr. Moses. He simply enters their requests into his computer, and their registration for the following semester is finalized. The reasoning behind allowing student athletes to preregister early is based primarily upon the need to schedule their classes around practice. This practice time varies from sport to sport. All students who participate in athletic teams—football, baseball, basketball, tennis, swimming, track, golf, and so on—have to arrange their classes so they don't conflict. Two interesting factors concerning student athlete pre-preregistration that warrant examination are "red shirts," those students who are not actually on the travelling team and fifth-year seniors, who have played out their eligibility, but are still on scholarship and allowed to register early. Although red shirts do practice with the team, their need to enroll in the classes of their choice does not appear as imperative as those who actually play. In discussing fifth-year seniors, we must emphasize: these students no longer place at all or practice. They simply carry their preregistration privileges from their "playing days" over to their days as "ex-players." Essentially, they become just like the regular students on campus; however, when it comes to registration, they still receive special treatment and benefits. In an interview, Mr. Moses explained that not only is it important for student athletes to schedule their classes around practice, but it is important for them to get the professors they want. What about the graduating seniors who also want "good" professors?

5   The second group of students with "pre-preregistration" privileges is student workers. This group includes both on and off campus job holders. These students begin requesting their classes on the same day as senior registration starts. Prior to this day, each student is required to drop by the Registrar's Office and pick up a form for his or her employer to fill out and sign. The student has to present this

form on the day assigned for student worker preregistration. Upon presenting this form, the student's class schedule for the next semester is entered into one of the terminals at the Registrar's Office. The rationale in allowing student workers to register early is fairly obvious: these students must schedule their classes around their job schedules. But don't the majority of employers realize the importance of education and attempt to offer students more flexible schedules?

6   The last group of students allowed early preregistration are the Honors students. Registration for these students usually begins three days prior to senior registration. To be eligible for Honors preregistration, a student must meet several criteria; however, this differs depending upon the student's classification. Those who are currently enrolled must have a 3.25 cumulative grade point in course work taken at this institution, and they must either be enrolled in at least one Honors course during the coming semester, or have completed at least six hours of Honors courses. Freshmen who have recently entered the university, but have not yet taken an Honors course, are allowed to register early if they "have at least an 1150 SAT or 28 ACT score and have ranked in the top 15% of their high school graduating class" (Spring Schedule—1992, 42). A freshman who is currently enrolled in at least one Honors course can also preregister. All students planning to preregister as an Honors student must be registering for one or more Honors courses to be taken the next semester. Again, referring to the Spring Schedule—1992, "credentials of each student are automatically checked by the telephone registration system" to ensure that only those eligible get preregistration privileges. Those students who initially preregister with Honors students, but then drop the Honors courses after registration will encounter a permanent block from Honors preregistration in the future.

7   The rationale for allowing Honors students to preregister early is based primarily on a need for maximum flexibility when scheduling their classes. There are very few Honors courses compared to the regular courses; therefore, those students who need these Honors classes need to build their entire schedule around these particular courses. Honors students must register for regular classes as well, but their main concern is arranging these courses around the Honors offerings. "If such flexibility were not available through Honors preregistration, few students, if any, would be able to accumulate the number and distribution of Honors courses required for Honors graduation" (Noble).

8   Our proposed solution to this preregistration problem for graduating seniors consists of three steps. The first step is mandatory 90-hour degree audits for all majors. A successful example to follow is the College of Arts & Sciences. The undergraduates are required to pick up their 90-hour degree audits from their academic advisors' offices within a month's time frame following their publication or be blocked from preregistration. These audits highlight the hours still required, transfer hours accepted, and grade point averages. The student should

know, at this point, if he or she is eligible to graduate at the end of the following semester.

9   Next, if the student is eligible to graduate, he or she will apply for graduation at this time before preregistration for the final semester. After signing his or her name and identification number on the list for application, the name would then be entered into the Registrar's computer data base and "tagged" as a "graduating senior." This tag would simply differentiate this senior from other seniors who will not be eligible to graduate next semester. These tags will be added much like the blocks put into the system, the library, and the health center. Four days will be added to the registration schedule. These four days are to be added *prior to* the first day of senior registration. Those seniors who have applied to graduate at the end of the following semester will have priority over the student athletes, student workers, and Honors students.

10   In a final attempt to accommodate the graduating seniors, advisors will not be allowed to "force" any students into courses during preregistration. Two days will be reserved following the freshman open registration for raising limits in classes (forcing). No force slips will be presented to advisors until this time. For two consecutive days, students will have the opportunity to take their completed force slip with their classification clearly indicated and plead their cases to their advisors. The two consecutive days will accommodate all class schedules: Monday, Wednesday, Friday classes and Tuesday-Thursday classes. At the end of these two days, the advisors will prioritize these force slips according to seniority: graduating seniors, seniors, juniors, sophomores, and freshmen.

11   This proposal is not advocating a total revision of the registration process that exists. On the contrary, we are proposing an amendment that will lessen the number of anxious graduating seniors outside advisors' offices. And we are proposing a fair system, based on the current sense of seniority and privilege. We hope that by implementing our plan, graduating seniors will not find themselves in Mary Lou's situation. Such problems will be eliminated. In addition, implementation of this plan would ease the jobs of academic advisors such as Jane Doe because they won't have to deal with frustrated graduating seniors for whom they can provide no help.

Works Cited

Moses, Bill. Athletic Department Academic Advisor, Iroquois University. Personal interview. 4 December 1992.

Noble, David. Coordinator of the Honors Program, Iroquois University. Personal interview. 2 December 1992.

Spring Schedule—1992. Oneida City: Iroquois University, 1992.

Reading Critically: Questions for Discussion

1. How do Tricia and Chris try to establish their credibility to write on this subject?
2. What is the function of the opening discourse bloc? Could it be omitted?
3. Do Tricia and Chris answer all possible objections to their proposal?
4. Do you consider this proposal persuasive? Explain why you do or don't.
5. Is this proposal conciliatory or adversarial? Cite specific passages to support your opinion.

PART VI

Readings

Expressive Aim Writing

Knowledge by Participation: Event

So Tsi-fai

Sophronia Liu

Sophronia Liu came to America from Hong Kong when she was twenty years old. She received a B.A. and M.A. from the University of South Dakota. For the past ten years, she has been living and working in the Twin Cities, Minnesota. She continues to write and perform as an actress, and she is an active organizer in the local Asian American community. This essay, written in response to a writing assignment in a graduate course, tells of the suicide of Liu's sixth-grade classmate, So Tsi-fai, an experience that helps Liu understand the effects of social and educational classifications. Liu recounts her story and its personal significance to her by recalling details gained from knowledge by participation.

1   Voices, images, scenes from the past—twenty-three years ago, when I was in sixth grade:

2   "Let us bow our heads in silent prayer for the soul of So Tsi-fai. Let us pray for God's forgiveness for this boy's rash taking of his own life. . . " Sister Marie (Mung Gu-liang). My sixth-grade English teacher. Missionary nun from Paris. Principal of The Little Flower's School. Disciplinarian, perfectionist, authority figure: awesome and awful in my ten-year-old eyes.

3   "I don't need any supper. I have drunk enough insecticide." So Tsi-fai. My fourteen-year-old classmate. Daredevil; good-for-nothing lazybones (according to Mung Gu-liang). Bright black eyes, disheveled hair, defiant sneer, creased and greasy uniform, dirty hands, careless walk, shuffling feet. Standing in the corner for being late, for forgetting his homework, for talking in class, for using foul language. ("Shame on you! Go wash your mouth with soap!" Mung Gu-liang's sharp command. He did, and came back with a grin.) So Tsi-fai: Sticking his tongue out behind Mung Gu-liang's back, passing secret notes to his friends, kept behind after school, sent to the Principal's office for repeated offense. So Tsi-fai: incorrigible, hopeless, and without hope.

4   It was a Monday in late November when we heard of his death, returning to school after the weekend with our parents' signatures on our midterm reports. So Tsi-fai also showed his report to his father, we were told later. He flunked three out of the fourteen subjects: Eng-

lish Grammar, Arithmetic, and Chinese Dictation. He missed each one by one to three marks. That wasn't so bad. But he was a hopeless case. Overaged, stubborn, and uncooperative; a repeated offender of school rules, scourge of all teachers; who was going to give him a lenient passing grade? Besides, being a few months over the maximum age—fourteen—for sixth graders, he wasn't even allowed to sit for the Secondary School Entrance Exam.

5   All sixth graders in Hong Kong had to pass the SSE before they could obtain a seat in secondary school. In 1964 when I took the exam, there were more than twenty thousand candidates. About seven thousand of us passed: four thousand were sent to government and subsidized schools, the other three thousand to private and grant-in-aid schools. I came in around no. 2000; I was lucky. Without the public exam, there would be no secondary school for So Tsi-fai. His future was sealed.

6   Looking at the report card with three red marks on it, his father was furious. So Tsi-fai was the oldest son. There were three younger children. His father was a vegetable farmer with a few plots of land in Wong Juk-hang, by the sea. His mother worked in a local factory. So Tsi-fai helped in the fields, cooked for the family, and washed his own clothes. ("Filthy, dirty boy!" gasped Mung Gu-liang. "Grime behind the ears, black rims on the fingernails, dirty collar, crumpled shirt. Why doesn't your mother iron your shirt?") Both his parents were illiterate. So Tsi-fai was their biggest hope: He made it to the sixth grade.

7   Who woke him up for school every morning and had breakfast waiting for him? Nobody. ("Time for school! Get up! Eat your rice!" Ma nagged and screamed. The aroma of steamed rice and Chinese sausages spread all over the house. "Drink your tea! Eat your oranges! Wash your face! And remember to wash behind your ears!") And who helped So Tsi-fai do his homework? Nobody. Did he have older brothers like mine who knew all about the arithmetic of rowing a boat against the currents or with the currents, how to count the feet of chickens and rabbits in the same cage, the present perfect continuous tense of "to live" and the future perfect tense of "to succeed"? None. Nil. So Tsi-fai was a lost cause.

8   I came first in both terms that year, the star pupil. So Tsi-fai was one of the last in the class: He was lazy; he didn't care. Or did he?

9   When his father scolded him, So Tsi-fai left the house. When he showed up again, late for supper, he announced, "I don't need any supper. I have drunk enough insecticide." Just like another one of his practical jokes. The insecticide was stored in the field for his father's vegetables. He was rushed to the hospital; dead upon arrival.

10   "He gulped for a last breath and was gone," an uncle told us at the funeral. "But his eyes wouldn't shut. So I said in his ear, 'You go now and rest in peace.' And I smoothed my hand over his eyelids. His face was all purple."

11   His face was still purple when we saw him in his coffin. Eyes shut tight, nostrils dilated and white as if fire and anger might shoot out, any minute.

12   In class that Monday morning, Sister Marie led us in prayer. "Let us pray that God will forgive him for his sins." We said the Lord's Prayer and the Hail Mary. We bowed our heads. I sat in my chair, frozen and dazed, thinking of the deadly chill in the morgue, the smell of disinfectant, ether, and dead flesh.

13   "Bang!" went a gust of wind, forcing open a leaf of the double door leading to the back balcony. "Flap, flap, flap." The door swung in the wind. We could see the treetops by the hillside rustling to and fro against a pale blue sky. An imperceptible presence had drifted in with the wind. The same careless walk and shuffling feet, the same daredevil air—except that the eyes were lusterless, dripping blood; the tongue hanging out, gasping for air. As usual, he was late. But he had come back to claim his place.

14   "I died a tragic death," his voice said. "I have as much right as you to be here. This is my seat." We heard him; we knew he was back.

15   . . . So Tsi-fai: Standing in the corner for being late, for forgetting his homework, for talking in class, for using foul language. So Tsi-fai: Palm outstretched, chest sticking out, holding his breath: "Tat. Tat. Tat." Down came the teacher's wooden ruler, twenty times on each hand. Never batting an eyelash: then back to facing the wall in the corner by the door. So Tsi-fai: grimy shirt, disheveled hair, defiant sneer. So Tsi-fai. Incorrigible, hopeless, and without hope.

16   The girls in front gasped and shrank back in their chairs. Mung Gu-liang went to the door, held the doorknob in one hand, poked her head out, and peered into the empty balcony. Then, with a determined jerk, she pulled the door shut. Quickly crossing herself, she returned to the teacher's desk. Her black cross swung upon the front of her gray habit as she hurried across the room. "Don't be silly!" she scolded the frightened girls in the front row.

17   What really happened? After all these years, my mind is still haunted by this scene. What happened to So Tsi-fai? What happened to me? What happened to all of us that year in sixth grade, when we were green and young and ready to fling our arms out for the world? All of a sudden, death claimed one of us and he was gone.

18   Who arbitrates between life and death? Who decides which life is worth preserving and prospering, and which to nip in its bud? How did it happen that I, at ten, turned out to be the star pupil, the lucky one, while my friend, a peasant's son, was shoveled under the heap and lost forever? How could it happen that this world would close off a young boy's life at fourteen just because he was poor, undisciplined, and lacked the training and support to pass his exams? What really happened?

19   Today, twenty-three years later, So Tsi-fai's ghost still haunts me. "I died a tragic death. I have as much right as you to be here. This is my seat." The voice I heard twenty-three years ago in my sixth-grade classroom follows me in my dreams. Is there anything I can do to lay it to rest?

Reading Critically: Questions for Discussion

1. The writer starts this essay with a series of incomplete sentences. Do you consider this technique effective? Why do you think it is or isn't?
2. This expressive essay has a complex chronology. Trace the organization of the narrative. Why does the writer choose to tell the story this way? How would the story be different if the writer used a simple chronology?
3. What are other possible titles for this essay? Explain and justify your suggestions.
4. What descriptive details does the writer offer to characterize So Tsi-fai?
5. The writer includes two quotations from So Tsi-fai: "I don't need any supper. I have drunk enough insecticide." and "I died a tragic death. I have as much right as you to be here. This is my seat." Discuss the significance of these two quotations. Notice also that both quotations are repeated twice in the essay. What is the purpose of this repetition?
6. Why does the writer include the uncle's description of how So Tsi-fai died and how So Tsi-fai looked lying in his coffin? Are these descriptive details necessary or unnecessary?
7. What significance does the writer derive from this experience? How does the writer communicate this significance?

Knowledge by Observation: Character

Herman Hollerith:

Inventor, Manager, Entrepreneur — A Centennial Remembrance

George E. Biles, Alfred A. Bolton, and Bernadette M. DiRe

George E. Biles, Alfred A. Bolton, and Bernadette M. DiRe were at The American University when this essay was published in the Journal of Management. *Their profile of Herman Hollerith, the inventor of the first electronic tabulating machine eventually used to automate the 1890 census, was first presented at the 48th Annual Meeting of the Academy of Management in Anaheim, California, in 1988. The authors write this tribute to Hollerith, who died in 1929, using information gained from interviews, letters, newspapers, journals, government documents, and biographies. Following the manuscript requirements for the* Journal of Management, *the authors use the APA documentation style.*

Introduction

1   The American founding fathers wrote into the Constitution that a census should be conducted every 10 years. For 100 years (10 censuses by the Bureau of the Census' clock), a census that determined citizens' tax obligations and apportioned elected representation was tabulated laboriously by hand.

2   The Bureau of the Census, now part of the U.S. Commerce Department, was created to conduct each decennial census. For many years, the Bureau of the Census attempted to streamline the process of counting American citizens and sorting the accumulated data. In 1890, the first *automated* census was conducted—an event that can be attributed to one man: Dr. Herman Hollerith.

3   This essay is about Herman Hollerith. Hollerith's legacy of automating the U.S. census process is profound. The continuous growth of the American population has always demanded careful and timely counting of citizens. In 1890—the 11th decennial census—approximately 63 million citizens were counted. To conduct this 11th census, Hollerith invented and used electric tabulating machines that permitted a complete tally to be determined in $2\frac{1}{2}$ years. In the upcoming 21st census to be conducted in 1990, Hollerith's electric tabulating machines seem minuscule in comparison. For example, Bureau of the Census mainframe computers currently permit some one million data items to be tabulated *per minute*. Compare this figure with the 10,000 to 20,000 data cards the Bureau of the Census could process *per day* on each of the 56 Hollerith electric tabulating machines during the 1890 census. 1990 will be the 200th anniversary of the first census. 1990 will also be the 100th anniversary of the first automated census. Hollerith's contributions in automating the census process and the resulting legacy he left to the modern world bear reexamination and retelling.

Background

4   The process of counting American citizens has changed considerably in our history. The first census, taken in 1790, counted only free white males over and under 16 years old, free white females, all other free persons (including any Indians who paid taxes), and slaves. The government provided no printed forms. Enumerators had to provide their own paper to record information. This census took 18 months to complete.

5   The census of 1880, the 10th census, took almost 10 years to complete. Because of the explosive growth of the American population, it was obvious that techniques had to be developed to record data faster. Although information was collected, practical limitations of time and analytical capabilities made it virtually impossible to use much of it. Totals were tallied for numbers of citizens in particular categories. However, categories were neither combined nor cross-referenced.

6   During the decade of the 1880s, the census superintendent, General Francis A. Walker, encouraged inventions to streamline the analytical process. One special agent in the Census Bureau, Herman Hollerith, was intrigued by the notion of developing an automated machine to assist in census enumerating. Hollerith began working for the Census Bureau in 1879, after graduating from Columbia University (Austrian, 1982). In addition to working as a Census Bureau special agent, Hollerith also compiled life tables for Dr. John Billings, head of the Census Bureau's Division of Vital Statistics. Dr. Billings apparently provided the catalyst that prompted Hollerith to invent his electric tabulating machine (Hollerith, V., 1971). At a dinner party one evening, Billings commented that the Census Bureau needed to automate the census process. His remarks seemed to stimulate Hollerith's creative genius.

7   A competition to automate the 11th census of 1890 was announced. A committee was appointed by the Superintendent of the 1890 Census to evaluate the competition. The results were conclusive. Herman Hollerith had developed an electric tabulating machine system that counted the sample schedules in slightly under 186 hours. Another competitor, the Pidgin Automatic Mechanical System, was stopped after 452 hours and before completing the test. The third system was eliminated after 163 hours with less than 3 out of 12 tables completed (Austrian, 1982; Hollerith, V., 1971; Rex, 1981). The Census Bureau Superintendent declared, "by the use of electric tabulating machines it has become possible . . . for the first time in the history of statistical work, to aggregate from the schedules all the information which appears in any way desirable" (Hollerith, V., 1971, p. 73).

8   The 1880 census costs were almost 5.8 million dollars (Hollerith, H., 1888). For this price, the census included data on the following subjects:

> Race or color, sex, age, relationship of each person to head of family, civil or conjugal condition, whether married during the census year, occupation, number of months unemployed, whether sick or otherwise temporarily disabled, whether the person attended school during the census year, cannot read, cannot write, place of birth, place of birth of father and mother. (Hollerith, H., 1888, p. 242)

9   The 1890 census, using Hollerith's electric tabulating machine system, saved more than 2 years' time over the 1880 Census and $5 million in taxpayer's money (Austrian, 1982).

Herman Hollerith: The Man and the Inventor

10   Born on February 29, 1860 in Buffalo, New York, Herman Hollerith was the son of a German immigrant couple. In 1879, at the age of 19, he graduated from Columbia University School of Mines with the degree Engineer of Mines. That fall, one of his former professors requested that Hollerith come to the Census Bureau to work as a Special Agent. Hollerith decided to go and remained at the Census Bureau for 3 years—until 1882. He left Census and went to the Massachusetts Institute of Technology as an instructor in the Department of Mechanical Engineering. Hollerith was invited to MIT by the former superintendent of the 1880 census, General Francis Walker. Walker was then MIT's president. While at MIT, Hollerith began experimenting with an electric tabulating machine.

11   Then 22, Hollerith was younger than many of his students. After a year at MIT, the idea of reteaching the same material appalled him. He left MIT to spend a year in St. Louis experimenting with electromagnetically operated air brakes for railroads. After his year in St. Louis, which shaped many of his subsequent ideas regarding enumerating railroad car shipment information, Hollerith returned to Washington as an assistant examiner in the U.S. Patent Office. Less than a year later, Hollerith departed the Patent Office and opened his own office as "Expert and Solicitor of Patents." His experience with patents benefitted him immensely in succeeding years.

12   Hollerith adopted a concept of using punched holes in cards to record facts for census-taking. His inspiration allegedly came from observing a train conductor punching holes in passenger tickets to identify travelers. Identifying features such as male, female, tall, short, bald, bearded, wearing glasses, and so on stimulated Hollerith's imagination so that the notion of punched holes in paper became the centerpiece of his electric tabulating machines.

13   Of course, the use of punched cards as a control and modeling technique was not unique to Hollerith. Perforated paper rolls had been used as early as 1725 to guide mechanical looms. Various perforated paper and card guided looms had been designed and were in use at that time to create intricate weave patterns. The Jacquard loom, named after Joseph Marie Jacquard in 1801, uses up to 50,000 oblong punched cards to control the raising of loom warps. Some Jacquard looms are still in use today (Peake, 1925; Wingate, 1964).

14   Charles Babbage's "analytical engine" used punched cards to guide and direct its calculations. Babbage adapted Jacquard's punched card system as a control device. The Babbage analytical engine is generally considered to be the forerunner of the modern computer and Babbage is generally credited as being the father of the modern computer (Moseley, 1964; Spencer, 1985).

15   Whether Herman Hollerith connected the Jacquard or Babbage inventions with his own electric tabulating machines is speculative. As

an Engineer of Mines degree holder and a former MIT instructor, Hollerith, one could assume, had some awareness of these inventors. Indeed, Hollerith's older sister, Bertha, married a man in the silk-weaving business. That industry made wide use of the Jacquard loom. However, no direct evidence exists that Hollerith had anything to do with the weaving industry at all. The idea of using punched paper rolls and ultimately manila stock cards to control his electric tabulating machines seems to have been an offshoot of Hollerith's railroad experience.

Hollerith's Electric Tabulating Machine

16   The Hollerith electric tabulating machines tallied items by causing an electrical current to trigger simple clock-like counting devices. When an electrical current flowed through a hole punched into non-conducting paper strips, a counter was actuated by an electromagnet. In the first versions of the electric tabulating machine, rolled strips of paper were used as a nonconductive material. Later manila stock cards were used. Holes were punched in the cards using a hand operated pantograph punch. These cards were then read by a hand-operated card reader. The card reader permitted current to be sent to appropriate electromagnets that then triggered the counters.

17   The size of the Hollerith cards was determined, oddly enough, by the size of the U.S. dollar bill at that time. Hollerith found that to store the cards that were to be processed, he needed a large supply of containers. He was able to obtain such containers from the U.S. Treasury Department for free—containers that held cut dollar bills.

18   To organize the cards, Hollerith designed a "sorting box." Because the early census card had a maximum of 24 classifications in any one field, the sorter was designed with 24 compartments. The first sorter was semi-automatic. A compartment cover was electrically unlatched according to the classification and the operator would then remove the card from the card reader and insert it by hand into the appropriate compartment.

19   The first model of Hollerith's electric tabulating machine was designed to analyze statistical data. Its first public use was by the City of Baltimore in 1887 for tabulating mortality statistics. The state of New Jersey and the New York City Health Department soon followed, offering Hollerith practical tests for the prototype that he used in the 11th (1890) census.

20   Enumeration counting was often interrupted because of poor quality rolled paper. The edges of the paper would flake off, collect in the mercury cups that provided conductivity, and clog the machines. After replacing rolled paper with cards, Hollerith found that clerks placed cards in the machines incorrectly for processing. He made a simple correction. To control the quality of the materials, Hollerith

used heavy stock manila paper. He insisted that all cards for use with his machines be purchased from his company, an example of vertical integration. In addition, he cut off the upper left hand corner of each card to indicate proper placement and positioning.

21   The electric tabulating machine became the centerpiece for all Hollerith's future business endeavors (J. Case, personal communication, September 21, 1987; B. Chevis, personal communication, October 26, 1987; Hollerith, V., 1971; Rex, 1981).

Herman Hollerith, The Business Person

22   Hollerith's alma mater, Columbia School of Mines, awarded him an honorary doctorate in 1890 because of the success of the 11th (1890) census. He received the Franklin Institute of Philadelphia's highest award—the Elliott Cresson Medal—in 1890 as the most distinguished inventor of the year.

23   Hollerith then went to Austria to use his electric tabulating machine in the Austrian National Census of 1890 (Zemanek, 1974). He received an unsolicited request from Canada to use his machines in their 1891 census.

24   In 1892, Hollerith exhibited his electric tabulating machine at the Columbian Exposition of the World Fair. That same year, he demonstrated the machine at the American Association for the Advancement of Science. His reputation as an inventor of a useful and usable counting device was rising rapidly.

25   However, there were setbacks to this pattern of success. Hollerith submitted a bid to Czar Alexander III of Russia to conduct that country's decennial census. At about the time of this bid, a small group of Austrian inventors broke some of Hollerith's technical patents on the electric tabulating machine. The Austrians commenced building and marketing their own version of an electric tabulating machine. Russia concluded it would be cheaper to buy Austrian machines yet spent considerable time dithering over the decision. Hollerith then pulled a colossal bluff. He advised the Russians that because they had not decided upon his machines, they should buy the Austrian machines. Hollerith privately hoped that the Russians would decide against buying Austrian machines that had no track record. He banked upon the Russians contracting for Hollerith's improved, although as of then yet to be built, new electric tabulating machines. While he waited for the Russians to decide between the Hollerith and Austrian machines, he became increasingly uneasy about his personal financial situation. He moved his family into his mother-in-law's home and virtually had to shut down his Washington D.C. factory to cut costs.

26   Hollerith had negotiated with Western Electric to provide the investment capital necessary to manufacture the improved machines for the Russian census. This agreement, however, was contingent

upon a signed contract with the Russians. Troubled by the delays he was experiencing with the Russians choosing between his and the Austrian machines, Hollerith considered selling out to Western Electric altogether. To complicate matters further, a request came in March, 1896 from France, asking Hollerith to take their decennial census of occupations.

27   Hollerith was in a classic cash-flow dilemma. He had neither the cash nor the new machines to bid for the French occupations census job. He needed the infusion of capital he would receive from Russia if he were awarded their census contract. In some desperation, Hollerith borrowed $20 from his mother-in-law to go to the Library Bureau in Boston to seek an income-producing contract. The Library Bureau, a branch of the American Library Association, was one of the first consulting firms ever in existence in the United States. The Library Bureau provided consulting services to its clients by studying "the unproductive side of . . . expense account[s]. . . . " As consultants, the Library Bureau would examine client organizations and develop plans to reduce organizational expenses. Hollerith was particularly interested in the Library Bureau's services because their operations included offices in London and Paris. Hollerith negotiated a 10-year agreement with the Library Bureau. He agreed to provide them a service that today would be viewed as a decentralized remote data processing network (Austrian, 1982; J. Case, personal communication, September 21, 1987; Rex, 1981).

28   As part of their contractual relationship, the Library Bureau provided financing for Hollerith's work on the French census. Stipulated in the contract was permission for the Library Bureau to use Hollerith's patents for "Improvements in Tabulating and Other Machines and Apparatus" in England, France, Germany, and Italy. This contract succeeded in giving Hollerith some short-term financial relief. The contract, however, was terminated 2 years later when the Library Bureau failed to send Hollerith statements and payments due from rentals of his electric tabulating machines abroad (Austrian, 1982).

29   Almost concurrent with the Library Bureau contract, the Russians, after almost 6 years of indecision, decided to purchase Hollerith electric tabulating machines for their census instead of the Austrian machines. The Russian contract gave Hollerith financial security. He concluded it was time to expand his business horizons.

30   Until 1896, Hollerith had conducted all of his business under the names "Hollerith Electric Tabulating System" or "Hollerith Machines." In 1896, he incorporated a New York corporation called the Tabulating Machine Company.

31   With a capital base of $100,000, 1,000 shares of $100 par value stock were issued. Hollerith owned 502 shares of the Tabulating Machine Company. The remaining shares were held by people whom he held in high regard: his attorney, Samuel Metcalf; George Bond, a Pratt & Whitney engineer; Bond's friend, Charles Tyler; Ferdinand

Roebling, whose father and brother had designed and built the Brooklyn Bridge; Henry Adams, subsequently chief statistician for the Interstate Commerce Commission; J. Shirley Eaton, who later became the auditor of the Southern Railroad; Professor George Swain, Hollerith's closest friend from the census days; Harry Thayer, the manager of Western Electric's New York City operation; and Albert Salt, Thayer's assistant manager and protege. Thayer advised Hollerith on all aspects of the business. Besides having the business acumen that Hollerith lacked, Thayer provided a diplomatic manner to balance the inventor's mercurial and abrupt demeanor.

32   Officers of the new Tabulating Machine Company were elected at its first meeting, December 16, 1896. The election of the officers was pre-arranged as both Thayer and Hollerith were abroad on that date. Roebling became the first president; Salt, vice president; Thayer, treasurer; and Metcalf, secretary. Thayer and Hollerith were the only salaried officers in the corporation. In addition to holding a controlling amount of stock, Hollerith received $500 per month. The shareholders had agreed that no dividends would be declared until all loans to the company had been paid. As evidence of the company's initial success, 6 months after that first meeting a 4% dividend was paid to shareholders.

33   The Tabulating Machine Company's training program consisted of completely breaking down electric tabulating machines and rebuilding them. All parts had been designed by Hollerith to fit together comfortably without forcing. This was one of the early examples of interchangeable parts among machines being used in manufacturing. Yet the responsibilities of the company's employees did not stop with the inner workings of the machine. According to a director of the company, "[Employees] needed not only a good knowledge of the Hollerith Punched Card System and the construction of the machines, but also to understand commercial and other organizations in order to be able to apply the system to any kind of work. [Employees] had to be versed to some extent in Accountancy, Engineering (electrical and mechanical), Organization, etc., procedures, so as not to offend principles" (Austrian, 1982, p. 132).

34   Relinquishing, even slightly, manufacturing and operating control of the Tabulating Machine Company was difficult for Hollerith. He believed no one was as knowledgeable about his machines as he. As a result, Hollerith was often prickly and irritable. His irritability caused relatively high employee turnover. He was excitable and demanding in his home life as well (B. Chevis, personal communication, October 26, 1987).

35   Hollerith continued to develop and improve the operating capabilities of his machines. Shortly after the 12th census of 1900, the Tabulating Machine Company purchased the Taft-Price Manufacturing Company of Woonsocket, Rhode Island. Acquiring this New England firm was attractive for two reasons: (a) available engineering skills of

the Taft-Pierce employees, and (b) the Taft-Pierce focus on interchangeable parts. Hollerith's newly expanded company was able to provide a wider variety of services to commercial clients. The Tabulating Machine Company was able to concentrate more on commercial applications with its expanded capability. Among the companies to employ the electric tabulating machine system were Marshall Field, Eastman Kodak, National Tube Company, American Sheet and Tin Plate Company, Pennsylvania Steel, Union Pacific Railroad, Pennsylvania Railroad, Western Electric, and Yale & Towne Manufacturing Company. The Tabulating Machine Company was well on its way to commercial success.

36   The Census Bureau had served as the proving ground for Hollerith's electric tabulating machines for many years. From the introduction of his machine in the 11th census of 1890, hundreds of census clerks had tested the design and abilities of his machines. The inventor, based on this extensive usage, continuously upgraded and improved upon the machine's original design. Indeed, the electric tabulating machines had become an indispensable component of the census enumeration process. This indispensability spawned a series of events that challenged a fundamental principle of free enterprise—the right of an inventor to own the intellectual property rights of his or her invention. This challenge, exacerbated by Hollerith's moody and prickly temperament, ultimately drove Hollerith and the Tabulating Machine Company out of the Census Bureau.

37   The rift had its beginnings in 1903. That year, Simon North became the Director of the U. S. Census. North had served in a variety of governmental posts, including being the chief statistician for manufacturers for the 12th census (1900). Upon assuming the Directorship of the U.S. Census, North found himself in virtually a supplicant's role to Hollerith's Tabulating Machine Company. To make North's role more difficult, his predecessor as Director of the Census Bureau was William Merriam, a former governor of Minnesota, who was then serving as President of the Tabulating Machine Company. "Doctor Hollerith's Workshop" at the Census Bureau had evolved into an integral component of the constitutionally mandated decennial enumeration process. A "revolving door" relationship had developed between the Census Bureau and the Tabulating Machine Company that gave Hollerith a decided competitive advantage over would-be challengers.

38   About the time that North assumed his role as Director, the Census Bureau had become a permanent bureau of the government. It had been moved from the Department of the Interior to the new Department of Commerce and Labor. Many new statistical analyses were being required that had not ever been performed by the Census Bureau. Moreover, the new President of the U.S., Theodore Roosevelt, wanted statistical facts as a foundation for social legislation he intended to introduce. The Census Bureau had rapidly evolved into a government-wide statistical clearinghouse. The Tabulating Machine

Company, as the prime contractor for tabulating statistical data for the government, was positioned to reap many of the benefits of the Census Bureau's new importance and stature.

39   North was increasingly uncomfortable with Hollerith's company's monopolistic position. In a nutshell, North believed the Tabulating Machine Company was charging the government exorbitant rates for its processing services and thereby earning excessive profits. North undertook steps he believed would break Hollerith's stranglehold on the Census Bureau. North wrote a letter to the President of the Tabulating Machine Company, Governor Merriam, stating he would use other mechanical means to process the census if Hollerith failed to reduce his royalty requirements (personal communication to Governor W. R. Merriam, September 17, 1904). Even when the Tabulating Machine Company reduced its rates, North continued to describe them as being excessive and exorbitant.

40   North requested a $40,000 appropriation from Congress to conduct experimental work in developing the government's own tabulating machinery. This appropriation was ultimately awarded and North hired a brilliant Russian-born inventor, James Powers, to develop tabulating equipment. Powers worked for 4 years at the Census Bureau to develop improved tabulating machinery. Powers' efforts were devoted to improving Hollerith's electric tabulating machines. Because Hollerith held the patents on these machines, he believed Powers and the government were infringing upon his patent rights. Therefore, a critical issue emerged as to whether the federal government was excused from existing patent infringement legislation. Hollerith warned North that if the government carried out any experimental work on any apparatus covered under Hollerith's patents, the Tabulating Machine Company would withdraw all of its electric tabulating machines from the Census Bureau. Hollerith was confident that North was so dependent upon Hollerith's electric tabulating machines, he would not run this risk.

41   Hollerith guessed wrong. Both of these two inflexible men stood upon their principles. As a result, on July 1, 1905, all of the Tabulating Machine Company electric tabulating machines were withdrawn from the Census Bureau. The impasse took its toll on both men. During this period, Hollerith became suspicious of his own fellow Tabulating Machine Company officers. For example, Hollerith complained bitterly about some of Governor Merriam's (the Tabulating Machine Company President and former director of the Census Bureau) financial activities with company money. Finally, Hollerith's friend, company treasurer, and primary adviser on company matters, Harry Thayer, gently chided Hollerith about his attitude toward Governor Merriam. Thayer told Hollerith that Merriam had been hired to attend to the financial side of the business and Hollerith was supposed to run the technical and scientific end. As Thayer said in a letter to Hollerith: "[Y]ou commenced to look for trouble and . . . have resented everything the Governor has

done. . . . It was to relieve you that he was hired. If he had to run to you with every question, where would the relief have been?" (Thayer, 1904).

42   Hollerith, more of a temperamental engineer than entrepreneur, was personally offended by what was happening at the Census Bureau. He wrote to President Theodore Roosevelt, highlighting what he perceived as shortcomings and inadequacies in North's steward-ship of the Census Bureau (personal communication to President T. Roosevelt, February 4, 1905). Hollerith also raised the issue of North hiring Powers to develop improved government machines. The ques-tions he asked in his letter centered around whether the government should be immune from patent protection laws. He questioned whether the Hollerith electric tabulating machines were protected from patent infringement by the federal government. He asked if the government was engaged in a proper activity in hiring James Powers.

43   Hollerith unleashed a continuing flurry of letters to everyone from both Presidents Roosevelt and Taft, to members of Congress, cabinet members, and the press. These letters stated, in essence, the govern-ment was trying to put a private citizen out of business. None of the letters, however, elicited any substantive redress. If Hollerith tasted any victory, it was the ultimate removal of North as Director of the Census Bureau. The furor over removing Hollerith's machines from the Census Bureau and the attempts to replace them with what turned out to be expensive and underperforming substitutes prompted North to say, "I am convinced that circumstances which now exist and which are likely to continue render it difficult, if not impossible, for me to conduct the [1910] 13th census of the United States" ("North resigns," 1909).

44   Frustrated, and with no other perceived course of action available, the Tabulating Machine Company filed for injunctive relief against the government on January 10, 1910, three months before the commence-ment of the 13th (1910) census (Tabulating Machine Company v. Durand, 1910). (Durand was North's successor as Director of the Cen-sus Bureau.) The broad issue of whether an inventor had recourse against the government had not been resolved despite the years of acrimonious exchanges and debate that had taken place between Hol-lerith and two branches of the federal government. The court found on March 14, 1910 that the changes made by Powers and the Census Bureau did not destroy the identity of the Hollerith electric tabulating machines ("Court rules," 1910). Hollerith decided not to pursue the case any further.

45   For the 13th census of 1910, the government used the tabulating machines developed by James Powers. These new machines were gener-ally not as successful in performing their functions as Hollerith's machines had been. For instance, the Powers sorting boxes ran only about two thirds as fast as the Hollerith sorting boxes. Quirks of newly designed and engineered machinery also slowed the process considerably.

46   Austrian cites an unidentified 1913 newspaper clipping: "We are now so far on the road to the fourteenth census [1920] that the details of the thirteenth, still unfinished in tabulation, might as well be abandoned" (Austrian, 1982, p. 304).

47   After 4 years working as a government employee to develop rival tabulating machines, Powers left the Census Bureau and established his own company. The Powers Company manufactured tabulating equipment that had been patented under Powers' name while he was an employee of the federal government. To the Tabulating Machine Company, the Powers Company became a formidable rival. The Powers Company ultimately changed its name to Remington Rand Corporation.

48   The census issue was no longer a paramount concern to Hollerith. He had decided to sell his company. The first decade of 1900 had taken its toll on him. To summarize what had transpired during that decade, Hollerith no longer did census work. Hollerith had been responsible for the ultimate ouster of the Director of the Census Bureau. Hollerith had sued the government on its right to infringe with impunity upon intellectual property rights and patents already granted. Although no clear-cut victory could be declared, the government, partially as a result of Hollerith's efforts, was no longer immune from its own patent laws. During this decade, the government realized it could not conduct a census unless electric tabulating machines were used. The automated census had become a necessity rather than merely an improved and more efficient way of enumerating data. Additionally, Hollerith during this decade redesigned his machines to perform different tasks through the use of pluggable wires. Up to then, changing a machine's capabilities entailed reengineering it by resoldering connectors. Hollerith simply transferred the concept of rerouting telephone calls on a switchboard to hardwire reprogramming the controller of his electric tabulating machines. In all, it had been an eventful decade. The stage was set for Hollerith to withdraw from his entrepreneurial activities.

49   As early as 1907, an offer was extended to buy the Tabulating Machine Company for $100,000. The Board of Directors turned it down. Yet, some of the members of the board were finding it difficult to devote the necessary time to monitor the business. For example, Harry Thayer, Hollerith's closest adviser, had advanced from Manager of Western Electric's New York operations to the Vice President of AT&T and was being groomed for the AT&T presidency. Also, Hollerith's health had become a matter of concern to his doctor. Hollerith, with his explosive temperament, was then approaching 50. He had high blood pressure and a penchant for working very hard. He never had been very good at delegating work to his subordinates or others in the company. He liked rich food and smoked expensive cigars. Hollerith's doctor urged him to slow down.

50   In 1911, Hollerith met Charles Flint, who believed that competition among small firms in the same industry was wasteful. Flint, called the "Father of Trusts," believed in consolidation and centralizing both manufacturing and distribution (Austrian, 1982). Flint believed that the Tabulating Machine Company would be a wise investment and spent much time convincing the inventor to sell the company. After much haggling, Flint offered the stockholders of the Tabulating Machine Company $450 per share for all outstanding stock. The offer was accepted and Hollerith received $1,210,500 for the 2,690 shares he then held. Hollerith invested $100,000 of his proceeds in the shares of the new company, which had the new name of the Computing-Tabulating-Recording Company. This new company was formed by merging three companies: Hollerith's Tabulating Machine Company, the International Time-Recording Company, and the Computing Scale Company.

51   Upon sale of the Tabulating Machine Company, Hollerith stepped down as General Manager. His "golden parachute" called for his staying on with the Tabulating Machine Division as Consulting Engineer at an annual salary of $20,000. A passive role in managing the Tabulating Machine Division of the Computing-Tabulating-Recording Company did not suit him at all. Shortly after the sale, Hollerith obtained the new board's agreement that all changes to the design of his electric tabulating machines must have his personal approval. It seemed that Hollerith was emotionally unable to loosen his hold on the Tabulating Machine Division. Hollerith also was a director of the new company, the Computing-Tabulating-Recording Company. That year, he relinquished this post to assume a position as consulting engineer. He resigned his board seat in 1914, citing health reasons and the difficulty of traveling to board meetings in New York.

52   1914 was also the year that the Computing-Tabulating-Recording Company hired a new general manager. The new manager, although enjoying a good reputation as a marketer, had just been fired as sales manager of a Dayton, Ohio firm—National Cash Register Company. The resulting cloud over his reputation precluded the Computing-Tabulating-Recording Company from considering him for the post of president, although he ultimately assumed that role. The new general manager was Thomas J. Watson, Sr.

53   Even though Hollerith still served as a consulting engineer with the Computing-Tabulating-Recording Company, he found himself less involved with its daily operations. As the Computing-Tabulating-Recording Company grew, relations between Hollerith and Thomas Watson, Sr., although cordial, grew increasingly strained. Hollerith viewed Watson as his replacement and resented him in that role, even though Hollerith had decided on the sale of his company only a few years earlier. Indeed, when Hollerith thought he was being ignored or otherwise cut out of an information loop, he would cry "The King is

Dead!" At board meetings, he was reluctant to sit anywhere but at the head of the table (Austrian, 1982, p. 308).

54   As time went on, more and more functions of the Tabulating Machine Division were transferred away from Washington to New York. In 1915, the general books were transferred. In 1917, customer records followed. Hollerith's once-familiar world was being replaced and he was less in demand and less involved. In 1918, he wrote "I am entirely out of touch with the Tabulating Machine Company affairs and really do not do anything but putter around with my own little personal affairs" (personal communication to G. Smith, December 5, 1918).

55   Hollerith was awarded his 31st and final patent in 1919. He remained as a consulting engineer with the Computing-Tabulating-Recording Company until 1921. In 1924, the Computing-Tabulating-Recording Company changed its name to International Business Machines Corporation.

56   Hollerith died of heart failure in his sleep in 1929 at his home in Georgetown, Washington, D.C. He was 69.

Conclusion

57   The 10th (1880) census took over 7 years to tabulate. At that time of massive immigration to American shores, genuine fears existed that the time taken to hand tally census information for the 11th (1890) census would render the data obsolete before it could ever be used for apportioning taxes and political representation. Herman Hollerith's electric tabulating machine revolutionized the ability to record accurately and in a timely fashion the demographic data for the 1890 census. Using the Hollerith machines, over 62 million citizens were recorded during that census in $2\frac{1}{2}$ years. Savings of about 5 years of effort and over 5 million dollars were realized. This was genuine progress and an improved productivity capability directly attributable to Hollerith's genius.

58   The 21st census (1990) will be held next year. When one compares and contrasts the innovative, albeit crude, equipment Hollerith developed 100 years ago to today's Census Bureau's computer capabilities, a deep appreciation emerges of the empowering legacy he left behind. The Census Bureau has its computing facilities and associated offices located in the Suitland, Maryland Federal Center. Two major computer systems (Sperry 1100/84A and 1100/84D) along with some lesser capacity systems are used by Census to tabulate decennial and non-decennial work. As a glimpse of Suitland's capabilities, one mainframe possesses four central processing units with 8 million 36 bit words of main memory and 32,000 words of high speed buffer storage. The machine has 32 tape drives, two 150 page per minute high speed laser printers, and 100 disk drives rated at 600 megabytes each. Approximately one million data items *per minute* can be recorded. At the

beginning of this essay, it was pointed out that one Hollerith electric tabulating machine could process 10,000 to 20,000 data items *per day,* depending upon the skill of the operator and the strength of his or her arms. Hollerith's electric tabulating machines paved the way for today's census capabilities.

59   Herman Hollerith left a major legacy for successive generations. He operationalized the use of electric tabulating machines in compiling, aggregating, and totaling data items. He built on the concept of vertical integration. His machines were able to transcend public sector and private business venture boundaries. He, as an inventor, stood his ground against the government being able to take or modify, with impunity, the intellectual property rights and patents of creative people such as himself. He developed interchangeable parts and plug-in wires that changed the purposes and applications of his machines. He also validated a widely held premise that technical genius, entrepreneurial ability, and management acumen are mutually exclusive attributes among most human beings.

60   We should pause to honor Herman Hollerith's myriad contributions to American society, to business and management history, and to the development of management information systems as we approach the 100th anniversary of his creative achievements.

References

Austrian, G. D. (1982). *Herman Hollerith: Forgotten giant of information processing.* New York: Columbia University Press.

Court rules Durand may alter machines. (1910, March 15). *Washington Evening Star,* p. 24.

Hollerith, H. (1888). An electric tabulating machine. *The Columbia University School of Mines Quarterly, A Journal of Applied Science, 10(3),* 239–256.

Hollerith, V. (1971). Biographical sketch of Herman Hollerith. *ISIS, 62(1),* 69–78.

Moseley, M. (1964). *Irascible genius: The life of Charles Babbage.* Chicago: H. Regner & Company.

North resigns office. (1909, May 27). *Washington Post,* p. 4.

Peake, R. I. (1925). *Common commodities and industries: Cotton.* (2nd ed.) London: Pitman Press.

Rex, F. J. (1981). Herman Hollerith: The first "statistical engineer." *Computers and Automation, 10,* 10–13.

Spencer, D. D. (1985). *Computers and information processing.* Columbus, OH: Charles E. Merrill Publishing Company.

The Tabulating Machine Company v. Edward Dana Durand, 64 Equity Docket S. Ct. D.C. 29065 (1910).

Thayer, H. B. (1904). [Letter to Herman Hollerith, September 23, 1904.] *In The papers of Herman Hollerith* (Containers 1–29). Washington, DC: Library of Congress. Manuscript Division.

Truesdell, L. E. (1965). *The development of punch card tabulation in the Bureau of the Census, 1890–1940, with outlines of actual tabulation programs*. Washington, DC: U.S. Department of Commerce, Bureau of the Census.

Wingate, I. B. (1964). *Textile fabrics and their selection*. (5th ed.). New York: Prentice-Hall.

Zemanek, H. (1974). *Otto Schaffler (1838–1928): Ein vergessener österreicher*. Wien: Technische Hochscule Wien und IBM-Laboratorium Wien.

Reading Critically: Questions for Discussion

1. What is the attitude of the writers toward Herman Hollerith? Cite specific passages to support your answer.
2. What is the primary purpose of this essay? What is the subordinate purpose?
3. How do the headings influence your reading of this essay?
4. The writers of this essay could easily have included illustrations, such as photographs of Hollerith and his tabulating machines. Would it be appropriate to include such illustrations? What would be the impact on the essay? Is the essay effective without such illustrations? Explain your answers.
5. In the narrative of Hollerith's life, identify the rising action, climax, and falling action.
6. Which narrative and descriptive details are crucial to the characterization of Hollerith? Which, if any, do you consider unnecessary?
7. Do the writers derive appropriate significance from their narrative of Hollerith's life?

Knowledge by Participation and Observation: Character

Coretta King: Revisited

Alice Walker

Alice Walker was born in Eatonton, Georgia, and is regarded as one of the most widely read American writers today. A graduate of Sarah Lawrence College, Walker has taught at numerous universities and colleges; she is currently on the faculty at the University of California at Berkeley. Walker's works include The Third Life of Grange Copeland *(1970),* The Color Purple *(1982),* In Search of Our Mother's Gardens *(1983),* Living by the Word *(1988),* To Hell with Dying *(1988),* The Temple of My Familiar *(1989), and* Possessing the Secret of Joy *(1992). Originally published in* Redbook *under the title "The Growing Strength of Coretta King," this essay develops out of her two meetings with Coretta King and thus two ways of knowing. The first meeting occurred in 1962, when Walker was a first-year college student at Spelman College in Atlanta (participation), and the second was her interview of Coretta King in 1971, three years after Dr. King's assassination (observation).*

1   I met Coretta Scott King for the first time in 1962 when I was a freshman at Spelman College in Atlanta and lived a few blocks from the neat but rather worn neighborhood where Coretta and Martin Luther King, Jr., lived. A group of us from Spelman were going to the World Youth Peace Festival in Helsinki that summer, and our adviser, a white peace activist from California, thought we should meet Mrs. King, who seemed, at that time, the only black woman in Atlanta actively and publicly engaged in the pursuit of peace.

2   I recall vividly our few minutes in the King home, a modest, almost bare-looking house with exceedingly nondescript furniture. I was delighted that the furniture was so plain, because it was the same kind of stuff most black people had and not the stylish plastic-covered French provincial that sat unused in many black middle-class homes. I felt quite comfortable on the sofa. Coretta that day was quick, bright-eyed, slim, and actually bubbly; and very girlish looking with her face free of make-up, shining a little, and her long hair tied back in a simple, slightly curly, ponytail. She herself was on her way to a peace conference in Geneva and, in addition, she was aglow with thoughts of an upcoming musical recital.

3   As she talked briefly to us, I sat on the sofa and stared at her, much too shy myself to speak. I was satisfied just to witness her exuberance, her brightness, her sparkle and smiles, as she talked about the peace movement, her music, and all her plans. She gave us several words of encouragement about our journey, the first trip abroad for all of us, but I don't recall what they were. She did not, and we did not, mention her husband. But she was so clearly a happy woman I couldn't help wishing I could sneak out of the living room and through the rest of the house, because I was positive he was there.

4   I have often thought that if it had not been for her husband, Dr. King, I would have come of age believing in nothing and no one. As it was, my life, like that of millions of black young Southerners, seemed to find its beginning and its purpose at the precise moment I first heard him speak. Through the years, like thousands of others, I followed him, unquestioningly, for my belief in him overcame even my disbelief in America. When he was assassinated in 1968 it was as if the last light in my world had gone out. But in 1962 people of eighteen, as I was then, felt at the beginning of things. The future looked difficult but bright. We had a tough, young, fearless friend and brother

who stood with us and for us. We hoped bluntly, as eighteen-year olds will that his wife was good enough for him. How lucky you are that he belongs to you! I had thought, looking at Coretta then, beginning to admit grudgingly that my hero had married a person, and not just a wife.

5   When I saw Coretta again it was at Dr. King's funeral, when my husband and I marched behind her husband's body in anger and despair. We could only see her from a distance, as she sat on a platform on the Morehouse campus. In my heart I said good-bye to the nonviolence she still professed. I was far less calm than she appeared to be. The week after that long, four mile walk across Atlanta, and after the tears and anger and the feeling of turning gradually to stone, I lost the child I had been carrying. I did not even care. It seemed to me, at the time, that if "he" (it was weeks before my tongue could form his name) must die no one deserved to live, not even my own child. I thought, as I lay on my bed listening to the rude Mississippi accents around me, that with any luck I could lose myself. I do not recall wanting very much to live. A week later, however, I saw Coretta's face again, on television, and perhaps it was my imagination, but she sounded so much like her husband that for a minute I thought I was hearing his voice. . . . "I come to New York today with a strong feeling that my dearly beloved husband, who was snatched suddenly from our midst slightly more than three weeks ago now, would have wanted me to be present today. Though my heart is heavy with grief from having suffered an irreparable loss, my faith in the redemptive will of God is stronger today than ever before."

6   I knew then that my grief was really self-pity, something I don't believe either Martin or Coretta had time to feel. I was still angry, confused, and, unlike Coretta, I have wandered very far, I think, from my belief in God if not from my faith in humanity, but she pulled me to my feet, as her husband had done in a different way, and forced me to acknowledge the debt I owed, not only to her husband's memory but also to the living continuation of his work.

7   Coretta was surprised, when I arrived to interview her for this article, that I remembered so well our first meeting in her home, for she had long since forgotten it. The first thing I noticed was that her eyes have changed. They are reserved, almost cool and she is tense; perhaps because she has been written about so often and because she is bored with it. She is not as slim as she was in 1962, but then, neither am I. Her hair this time falls down against her cheeks and is held back by a magenta-colored headband. Her dress is colorfully striped and her lipstick is very red.

8   I am embarrassed because I have dared to list among my interview questions things like "Do you enjoy dancing?" "Can you bougaloo?" "Do you save trading stamps?" I also want to know her favorite color and her horoscope sign. She rightly comments that even though people who are curious about her might like to know these things the

questions themselves are "not important." I feel rather foolish when she says this and hasten to explain that what I am most concerned about is what direction her music career—Mrs. King studied at the New England Conservatory of Music and often sings in concert—is taking. After that, I add, beginning to brighten a bit for her look now is much less severe, I would like to know whether she thinks a woman can maintain her art—in her case, her singing—without having to sacrifice it to her husband's ambitions, her children's needs, or society's expectations. I want to know her opinion of why black women have been antagonistic toward women's liberation. As a black woman myself, I say, I do not understand this because black women among all women have been oppressed almost beyond recognition—oppressed by *everyone*. Until recently, I comment, black women didn't even know what a real black woman looked like, because most black women were lightening their skin and straightening their hair. Ticking off another item on my shamefully long list—her assistant, Mrs. Bennet, had made it quite clear to me when I arrived that an hour of interviewing was the limit—I ask about the role she feels she has in the world, in the country, in her family, and in her immediate community.

9   Coretta's voice in conversation is quite different from the way it sounds when she gives speeches. It is softer and not as flatly Southern. When she talks she seems very calm and sure, though not relaxed, and she is cautious and careful that her precise meaning is expressed and understood. I have the feeling that she is far more fragile than she seems and the oddly eerie suggestion enters my head that the Coretta I am speaking with is not at all the one her children and family know. It strikes me that perhaps the reaction to overwhelming publicity must be a vigilant guarding of the private person. I try hard not to stare while Coretta talks, but I find I can't help it. I would have stared at Mary McLeod Bethune the same way. Coretta has changed a lot since 1962 but she continues to believe in and carry on her husband's work along with her own. I am trying to see where so much strength is coming from.

10   She leans back in her camel-colored swivel chair underneath the large oil portrait of her husband and pauses briefly to touch one of the many piles of correspondence on her desk. She begins at a mutual point of reference: the day we first met, nearly ten years ago. "I was on my way then," she recalls, "to the Seventeen-Nation Disarmament Conference in Geneva. Fifty American women had been invited and I was going as a delegate. I was also scheduled, the following Sunday, to give a recital in Cincinnati. Of course this presented something of a problem, because I would be away from the children for a week, but I thought it was important that I go. However, I wouldn't have gone had my husband not encouraged me to go." She smiles, slightly, and explains. "Periodically Martin and I would have these discussions about my being so involved in my singing and speaking and being away from home so much. We always agreed that when both of us

were under a lot of pressure to be away from home I would be the one to curtail my activities. I wasn't too unhappy about this. It was really a question of knowing what our priorities were. And since my top priority has always been my family there was never any conflict."

11   "Of course Martin had a problem throughout his career because he couldn't be with his family more. He never felt comfortable about being away so much. I don't think anybody who must be away from home a lot can really resolve this. But what you have to do is spend as much time with your family as you can and make the time that you spend meaningful. When Martin spent time with the children he gave himself so completely that they had a great feeling of love and security. I think this can best be done by individuals who feel secure within themselves and who are committed to what they are doing. People who have a sense of direction and who feel that what they're doing is the most important thing they *can* be doing. There was never a question in our minds that we were not doing the most important thing we could be doing for ourselves and for a better society for our children, all children, to grow up in."

12   At this point something goes wrong with my tape recorder and I lean forward to fix it, explaining with some vexation that I am the world's worst manipulator of simple gadgetry. Coretta charitably admits she's no genius with mechanical things either.

13   While waiting for the tape to rewind I tell her that her husband often crops up in my work and is very often in my thoughts. I tell her that in my novel, a copy of which I just gave her, one of the characters mentions that although Dr. King was constantly harassed and oppressed by the white world he was always gentle with his wife and children. I tell her how important I feel this is: that black men not take out their anger and frustration on their wives and children. A temptation that is all too obvious.

14   Coretta's face is thoughtful as she says, "Maybe I shouldn't say this, because I don't *know* it, it's just a feeling I have . . . but few black men seem to feel secure enough as men that they can make women feel like women. It was such a good feeling that Martin gave me, since the first time I met him. He was such a strong man that I felt like a woman, I could *be* a woman, and let him be a man. Yet he too was affected by the system, as a black man; but in spite of everything he always came through as a man, a person of dignity. . . . I miss this now, very much. Since my husband's death I've had to struggle on alone, and I can appreciate now, more than ever, how important it is to have somebody to share things with, to have someone who cares, someone who is concerned."

15   A rather ardent feminist myself I would like to spend a lot of time on the subjects of black woman and women's liberation. But Coretta only states that she understands the black woman's reluctance to be involved in liberating herself when all black people are still not free. Of course, she says, and laughs with humor and exasperation, "it is

annoying to have men constantly saying things like 'I know that must be a woman driver!'" She also believes that if women become irrevocably involved in social issues they will find themselves powerful as activists and as women. She thinks that women will liberate themselves to the extent of their involvement in the struggle for change and social justice. To me this sounds very logical, but I am stuck with the suspicion that, as with black people, there must be for women a new and self-given definition. I fear that many people, including many women, do not know, in fact, what Woman is.

16   We do, however, share a vast appreciation for the black woman, liberated or not. I think we both realize that in the majority of black women in the South we have been seeing women whose souls have been liberated for generations. In fact, it is when Coretta mentions some words of gentle courage from some old woman she has met somewhere that her eyes fill with tears. "The black woman," she says, "has a special role to play. Our heritage of suffering and our experience in having to struggle against all odds to raise our children gives us a greater capacity for understanding both suffering and the need and meaning of compassion. We have, I think, a kind of stamina, a determination, which makes us strong." Then she says something that I feel is particularly true: "Women, in general, are not a part of the corruption of the past, so they can give a new kind of leadership, a new image for mankind. But if they are going to be bitter or vindictive they are not going to be able to do this. But they're capable of tremendous compassion, love, and forgiveness, which, if they use it, can make this a better world. When you think of what some black women have gone through, and then look at how beautiful they still are! It is incredible that they still believe in the values of the race, that they have retained a love of justice, that they can still feel the deepest compassion, not only for themselves but for anybody who is oppressed; this is a kind of miracle, something we have that we must preserve and must pass on."

17   Coretta was born and raised in Marion, Alabama, a small town not far from the larger one of Selma, which her husband was later to make infamous. When she speaks of her upbringing in the "heart of Dixie" there is no bitterness in her voice. Like many blacks from the South she is able to dismiss or feel pity for white racists because she realizes they are sick. Instead, her voice warms with pride and respect for her father, who survived against fantastic odds. Not only did Obidiah Scott survive; he prevailed.

18   The Scotts owned a farm in Marion, and Coretta's father raised thousands of chickens. When his sawmill was mysteriously burned out only days after he purchased it he bought himself a truck and began a small pulpwood business. Recently, at seventy-one, Obie Scott ran for highway commissioner in his home town, something he wouldn't have dreamed of doing as short a time as six or seven years ago. He lost in the election, and Coretta thinks losing "got to him" but

the important thing, she says, is that he still has the courage to try to change things in the South so that all people can live there in harmony and peace.

19 "My father is a most industrious man," says Coretta. "If he'd been white he'd be the mayor of Marion, Alabama." From what she has told me about him I think she underestimates Obidiah Scott: if he had been white I doubt if he'd have stopped with the Alabama governorship.

20 Although active in several political campaigns, Coretta appears to have enjoyed her swing through her home state, in support of local black candidates, including her father, most. She explains that she gave a number of "Freedom Concerts" which her children helped her sing, and that they enjoyed campaigning as much as she. What emerges about Coretta is that the fabric of her life is finely knit. Each part is woven firmly into another part. Her office, which is in the basement of her house, is where she directs the business of the Martin Luther King, Jr. Memorial Center. When her children come home from school they troop downstairs to see her. She will usually stop whatever she is doing to talk to them. Her music is a skill that she uses for a variety of good causes: her Freedom Concerts bring out the crowds at local elections for black candidates; her other concerts are given to raise money for the memorial to her husband that she insists he must have. Her singing is also her means of reaching other peoples who can understand the beauty of her voice if not the words she sings.

21 The hour I was allotted for the interview has long since ended. But Coretta, much more relaxed now, is willing to discuss a few other topics that seemed to grow, organically, from answers she has given to my questions. About black people in power and the whites who work with them she says: "I don't believe that black people are going to misuse power in the way it has been misused. I think they've learned from their experiences. And we've seen instances where black and white work together very effectively. This is true even in places where you have a black majority, in Hancock County, Georgia, for example, or Fayette, Mississippi, where Charles Evers is mayor." About nonviolence she says, "It is very difficult to get people beyond the point of seeing nonviolence as something you do on marches and in demonstrations. It is harder to get people to the point of organizing to bring pressure to bear on changing society. People who think nonviolence is easy don't realize that it's a spiritual discipline that requires a great deal of strength, growth, and purging of the self so that one can overcome almost any obstacle for the good of all without being concerned about one's own welfare."

22 I am glad, while we're talking, to hear Coretta, the mother, talking to her oldest son, Marty, fourteen, who calls her on the phone. It seems he has been left at his school several miles away, it is pouring rain, and he wants somebody to come immediately to pick him up. Coretta is concerned but firm. She tells him that since he has missed the ride home that was arranged for him he will just have to wait until she can

send someone for him. He protests. She restates her solution; he will have to wait. Period.

23   We spend a few minutes discussing her role in life as she sees it. I am not surprised that what she would like to do is inspire other women to take a more active role in the peace movement, in the election of acceptable candidates, and in being involved in making the decisions that will affect their lives and the lives of their children. She says that she and Martin used to talk a lot about trying to organize women and she regrets that he never had time to get around to addressing women as women. "We have never used," she says, "the womanpower that we had."

24   While I am gathering up my paraphernalia to leave, Coretta comes from behind her desk and we chat a few moments about the pictures of her family that line the walls of her office. There is one that is especially charming, of her and her husband and the children on an outing in the park. Coretta's face in the photograph is radiant, although she ruefully comments that it was a hassle that day getting everybody dressed so they could have the picture made. Outside her office she introduces me to Dr. King's sister, Mrs. Farris, whom I had known slightly at Spelman. Mrs. Farris brings the presence of her brother strongly to mind; she has both his dignity and his calm. She is a woman of few words but they are pertinent ones. She assists Mrs. King with the bookkeeping.

25   When I leave the red-brick house on Sunset Avenue, the rain that had been beating down heavily all day has let up. And, though there is no promise of sun, there is a feeling that spring has already come to the winter-colored slopes of Atlanta. "You *Southern* black people," some- one had said to me several weeks before, "are very protective of Martin King and Coretta." I think about this as I leave the place where Martin King no longer lives except in the hearts of all the people who work there in his name.

26   As my plane takes off, I think of all the ways Martin and Coretta King's lives have touched mine. I think of that spring day so few, so many, years ago, and of Coretta's willingness to encourage a group of young women who were about to become involved in an exciting but somewhat frightening experience. I think of the years when I and most black Georgians, including atheists and agnostics, went to bed praying for Martin King's safety, and how we awoke each morning stronger because he was still with us. It was Martin, more than anyone, who exposed the hidden beauty of black people in the South, and caused us to look again at the land our fathers and mothers knew. The North is not for us. We will not be forced away from what is ours. Martin King, with Coretta at his side, gave the South to black people, and reduced the North to an option. And, though I realize the South belonged to me all the time, it has a newness in my eyes. I gaze down from the plane on the blood-red hills of Georgia and Alabama and finally, home, Mis- sissippi, knowing that when I arrive the very ground may tremble and convulse but I will walk upright, forever.

Reading Critically: Questions for Discussion

1. Why does the writer start this essay by remembering her first meeting with Coretta Scott King?
2. Why does the writer mention Mrs. Bennett, Obidiah Scott, Mrs. Farris? Why does she describe the difficulty she has with the tape recorder? Is this information necessary? Why do you think it is or isn't?
3. How does the writer establish credibility?
4. The writer describes Coretta Scott King on three occasions—at her first meeting, after the assassination of Martin Luther King, and at her interview. Which descriptive details do you consider essential? Why? What similarities and differences do you notice in the three descriptions?
5. Why does the writer interview Coretta Scott King? What insight does the writer achieve from the interview?
6. The writer includes several quotations from her interview with Coretta Scott King. Which quotation do you consider most important? Why?
7. How does this essay influence your impression of Coretta Scott King? Do you think the writer wishes you to have a better impression or a worse impression? How do you know? Cite specific passages to support your answer.

Knowledge by Participation and Observation: Place

Wyoming: The Solace of Open Spaces
Gretel Ehrlich

Gretel Ehrlich was educated at Bennington and the New School for Social Research. A native Californian who has moved to Wyoming, Ehrlich prefers life on the range over the city life in Southern California, as her writings illustrate. Her publications include The Solace of Open Spaces *(1985) and* Islands, Universe, and Home *(1988), both essay collections. The following essay captures Wyoming—the land and the residents—from both participation and observation.*

1   It's May, and I've just awakened from a nap, curled against sagebrush the way my dog taught me to sleep—sheltered from wind. A front is pulling the huge sky over me, and from the dark a hailstone has hit me on the head. I'm trailing a band of 2000 sheep across a stretch of Wyoming badland, a fifty-mile trip that takes five days because sheep

shade up in hot sun and won't budge until it cools. Bunched together now, and excited into a run by the storm, they drift across dry land, tumbling into draws like water and surging out again onto the rugged, choppy plateaus that are the building blocks of this state.

2   The name Wyoming comes from an Indian word meaning, "at the great plains," but the plains are really valleys, great arid valleys, 1600 square miles, with the horizon bending up on all sides into mountain ranges. This gives the vastness a sheltering look.

3   Winter lasts six months here. Prevailing winds spill snowdrifts to the east, and new storms from the northwest replenish them. This white bulk is sometimes dizzying, even nauseating, to look at. At twenty, thirty, and forty degrees below zero, not only does your car not work but neither do your mind and body. The landscape hardens into a dungeon of space. During the winter, while I was riding to find a new calf, my legs froze to the saddle, and in the silence that such cold creates I felt like the first person on earth, or the last.

4   Today the sun is out—only a few clouds billowing. In the east, where the sheep have started off without me, the benchland tilts up in a series of red-earthed, eroded mesas, planed flat on top by a million years of water; behind them, a bold line of muscular scarps rears up 10,000 feet to become the Big Horn Mountains. A tidal pattern is engraved into the ground, as if left by the sea that once covered this state. Canyons curve down like galaxies to meet the oncoming rush of flat land.

5   To live and work in this kind of open country, with its hundred mile views, is to lose the distinction between background and foreground. When I asked an older ranch hand to describe Wyoming's openness, he said, "It's all a bunch of nothing—wind and rattlesnakes—and so much of it you can't tell where you're going or where you've been and it don't make much difference." John, a sheepman I know, is tall and handsome and has an explosive temperament. He has a perfect intuition about people and sheep. They call him "Highpockets," because he's so long-legged; his graceful stride matches the distances he has to cover. He says, "Open space hasn't affected me at all. It's all the people moving in on it." The huge ranch he was born on takes up much of one county and spreads into another state; to put 100,000 miles on his pickup in three years and never leave home is not unusual. A friend of mine has an aunt who ranched on Powder River and didn't go off her place for eleven years. When her husband died, she quickly moved to town, bought a car, and drove around the States to see what she'd been missing.

6   Most people tell me they've simply driven through Wyoming, as if there were nothing to stop for. Or else they've skied in Jackson Hole, a place Wyomingites acknowledge uncomfortably, because its green beauty and chic affluence are mismatched with the rest of the state. Most of Wyoming has a "lean-to" look. Instead of big, roomy barns and Victorian houses, there are dugouts, low sheds, log cabins, sheep

camps, and fence lines that look like driftwood blown haphazardly into place. People here still feel pride because they live in such a harsh place, part of the glamorous cowboy past, and they are determined not to be the victims of a mining-dominated future.

7   Most characteristic of the state's landscape is what a developer euphemistically describes as "indigenous growth right up to your front door"—a reference to waterless stands of salt sage, snakes, jackrabbits, deerflies, red dust, a brief respite of wildflowers, dry washes, and no trees. In the Great Plains, the vistas look like music, like kyries of grass, but Wyoming seems to be the doing of a mad architect—tumbled and twisted, ribboned with faded, deathbed colors, thrust up and pulled down as if the place had been startled out of a deep sleep and thrown into a pure light.

8   I came here four years ago. I had not planned to stay, but I couldn't make myself leave. John, the sheepman, put me to work immediately. It was spring, and shearing time. For fourteen days of fourteen hours each, we moved thousands of sheep through sorting corrals to be sheared, branded, and deloused. I suspect that my original motive for coming here was to "lose myself" in new and unpopulated territory. Instead of producing the numbness I thought I wanted, life on the sheep ranch woke me up. The vitality of the people I was working with flushed out what had become a hallucinatory rawness inside me. I threw away my clothes and bought new ones; I cut my hair. The arid country was a clean slate. Its absolute indifference steadied me.

9   Sagebrush covers 58,000 square miles of Wyoming. The biggest city has a population of 50,000, and there are only five settlements that could be called cities in the whole state. The rest are towns, scattered across the expanse with as much as sixty miles between them, their populations 2000, fifty, or ten. They are fugitive-looking, perched on a barren, windblown bench, or tagged onto a river or a railroad, or laid out straight in a farming valley with implement stores and a block-long Mormon church. In the eastern part of the state, which slides down into the Great Plains, the new mining settlements are boomtowns, trailer cities, metal knots on flat land.

10   Despite the desolate look, there's a coziness to living in this state. There are so few people (only 470,000) that ranchers who buy and sell cattle know each other statewide; the kids who choose to go to college usually go to the state's one university, in Laramie; hired hands work their way around Wyoming in a lifetime of hirings and firings. And, despite the physical separation, people stay in touch, often driving two or three hours to another ranch for dinner.

11   Seventy-five years ago, when travel was by buckboard or horseback, cowboys who were temporarily out of work rode the grub line—drifting from ranch to ranch, mending fences or milking cows, and receiving in exchange a bed and meals. Gossip and messages traveled this slow circuit with them, creating an intimacy between ranchers who were three and four weeks' ride apart. One old-time

couple I know, whose turn-of-the-century homestead was used by an outlaw gang as a relay station for stolen horses, recall that if you were traveling, desperado or not, any lighted ranch house was a welcome sign. Even now, for someone who lives in a remote spot, arriving at a ranch or coming to town for supplies is cause for celebration. To emerge from isolation can be disorienting. Every thing looks bright, new, vivid. After I had been herding sheep for only three days, the sound of the camp-tender's pickup flustered me. Longing for human company, I felt a foolish grin take over my face, yet I had to resist an urgent temptation to run and hide.

12   Things happen suddenly in Wyoming: the change of seasons and weather; for people, the violent swings in and out of isolation. But goodnaturedness is concomitant with severity. Friendliness is a tradition. Strangers passing on the road wave hello. A common sight is two pickups stopped side by side far out on a range, on a dirt track winding through the sage. The drivers will share a cigarette, uncap their thermos bottles, and pass a battered cup, steaming with coffee, between windows. These meetings summon up the details of several generations, because in Wyoming, private histories are largely public knowledge.

13   Because ranch work is a physical and, these days, economic strain, being "at home on the range" is a matter of vigor, self-reliance, and common sense. A person's life is not a series of dramatic events for which he or she is applauded or exiled but a slow accumulation of days, seasons, years, fleshed out by the generational weight of one's family and anchored by a land-bound sense of place.

14   In most parts of Wyoming the human population is visibly out numbered by the animal. Not far from my town of fifty, I rode into a narrow valley and startled a herd of 200 elk. Eagles look like small people as they eat car-killed deer by the road. Antelope, moving in small, graceful bands, travel at 60 miles an hour, their mouths open as if drinking in the space.

15   The solitude in which westerners live makes them quiet. They telegraph thoughts and feelings by the way they tilt their heads and listen; pulling their Stetsons into a steep dive over their eyes, or pigeon-toeing one boot over the other, they lean against a fence with a fat wedge of snoose beneath their lower lips and take the whole scene in. These detached looks of quiet amusement are sometimes cynical, but they can also come from a dry-eyed humility as lucid as the air is clear.

16   Conversation goes on in what sounds like a private code: a few phrases imply a complex of meanings. Asking directions, you get a curious list of details. While trailing sheep, I was told to "ride up to the kinda upturned rock, follow the pink wash, turn left at the dump, and then you'll see the waterhole." One friend told his wife on roundup to "turn at the salt lick and the dead cow," which turned out to be a scattering of bones and no salt lick at all.

17   Sentence structure is shortened to the skin and bones of a thought. Descriptive words are dropped, even verbs; a cowboy looking over a corral full of horses will say to a wrangler, "Which one needs rode?" People hold back their thoughts in what seems to he a dumbfounded silence, then erupt with an excoriating, perceptive remark. Language, so compressed, becomes metaphorical. A rancher ended a relationship with one remark: "You're a bad check," meaning bouncing in and out was intolerable, and even coming back would be no good.

18   What's behind this laconic style is shyness. There is no vocabulary for the subject of feelings. It's not a hangdog shyness, or anything coy—always there's a robust spirit in evidence behind the restraint, as if the earthdredging wind that pulls across Wyoming had carried its people's voices away but everything else in them had shouldered confidently into the breeze.

19   I've spent hours riding to sheep camp at dawn in a pickup when nothing was said; eaten meals in the cookhouse when the only words spoken were a mumbled "Thank you, ma'am" at the end of dinner. The silence is profound. Instead of talking, we seem to share one eye. Keenly observed, the world is transformed. The landscape is engorged with detail, every movement on it chillingly sharp. The air between people is charged. Days unfold, bathed in their own music. Nights become hallucinatory; dreams, prescient.

20   Spring weather is capricious and mean. It snows, then blisters with heat. There have been tornadoes. They lay their elephant trunks out in the sage until they find houses, then slurp everything up and leave. I've noticed that melting snowbanks hiss and rot, viperous, then drip into calm pools where ducklings hatch and livestock, being trailed to summer range, drink. With the ice cover gone, rivers churn a milkshake brown, taking culverts and small bridges with them. Water in such an arid place (the average annual rainfall where I live is less than eight inches) is like blood. It festoons drab land with green veins: a line of cottonwoods following a stream; a strip of alfalfa; and on ditchbanks, wild asparagus growing.

21   I've moved to a small cattle ranch owned by friends. It's at the foot of the Big Horn Mountains. A few weeks ago, I helped them deliver a calf who was stuck halfway out of his mother's body. By the time he was freed, we could see a heartbeat, but he was straining against a swollen tongue for air. Mary and I held him upside down by his back feet, while Stan, on his hands and knees in the blood, gave the calf mouth-to-mouth resuscitation. I have a vague memory of being pneumonia-choked as a child, my mother giving me her air, which may account for my romance with this windswept state.

22   If anything is endemic to Wyoming, it is wind. This big room of space is swept out daily, leaving a boneyard of fossils, agates, and carcasses in every state of decay. Though it was water that initially

shaped the state, wind is the meticulous gardener, raising dust and pruning the sage.

23   I try to imagine a world of uncharted land, in which one could look over an uncompleted map and ride a horse past where all the lines have stopped. There is no wilderness left; wildness, yes, but true wilderness has been gone on this continent since the time of Lewis and Clark's overland journey.

24   Two hundred years ago, the Crow, Shoshone, Arapaho, Cheyenne, and Sioux roamed the intermountains West, orchestrating their movements according to hunger, season, and warfare. Once they acquired horses, they traversed the spines of all the big Wyoming ranges—the Absarokas, the Wind Rivers, the Tetons, the Big Horns—and wintered on the unprotected plains that fan out from them. Space was life. The world was their home.

25   What was life-giving to native Americans was often nightmarish to sodbusters who arrived encumbered with families and ethnic pasts to be transplanted in nearly uninhabitable land. The great distances, the shortage of water and trees, and the loneliness created unexpected hardships for them. In her book O *Pioneers!*, Willa Cather gives a set-tler's version of the bleak landscape:

> The little town behind them had vanished as if it had never been, had fall-en behind the swell of the prairie, and the stern frozen country received them into its bosom. The homesteads were few and far apart; here and there a windmill gaunt against the sky, a sod house crouching in a hollow.

26   The emptiness of the West was for others a geography of possibil-ity. Men and women who amassed great chunks of land and struggled to preserve unfenced empires were, despite their self-serving motives, unwitting geographers. They understood the lay of the land. But by the 1850s, the Oregon and Mormon trails sported bumper-to-bumper traffic. Wealthy landowners, many of them aristocratic absentee land-lords, known as remittance men because they were paid to come West and get out of their families' hair, overstocked the range with more than a million head of cattle. By 1885, the feed and water were desperately short, and the winter of 1886 laid out the gaunt bodies of dead animals so closely together that when the thaw came, one rancher from Kaycee claimed to have walked on cowhide all the way to Crazy Woman Creek, twenty miles away.

27   Territorial Wyoming was a boy's world. The land was generous with everything but water. At first there was room enough, food enough, for everyone. And, as with all beginnings, an expansive mood set in. The young cowboys, drifters, shopkeepers, school teach-ers, were heroic, lawless, generous, rowdy, and tenacious. The indi-vidualism and optimism generated during those times have endured.

28   John Tisdale rode north with the trail herds from Texas. He was a college-educated man with enough money to buy a small outfit near

the Powder River. While driving home from the town of Buffalo with a buckboard full of Christmas toys for his family and a winter's supply of food, he was shot in the back by an agent of the cattle barons who resented the encroachment of small-time stock men like him. The wealthy cattlemen tried to control all the public grazing land by restricting membership in the Wyoming Stock Growers Association, as if it were a country club. They ostracized from roundups and brandings cowboys and ranchers who were not members, then denounced them as rustlers. Tisdale's death, the second such cold-blooded murder, kicked off the Johnson County cattle war, which was no simple good-guy-bad-guy shoot-out but a complicated class struggle between landed gentry and less affluent settlers—a shocking reminder that the West was not an egalitarian sanctuary after all.

29   Fencing ultimately enforced boundaries, but barbed wire abrogated space. It was stretched across the beautiful valleys, into the mountains, over desert badlands, through buffalo grass. The "anything is possible" fever—the lure of any new place—was constricted. The integrity of the land as a geographical body, and the freedom to ride anywhere on it, was lost.

30   I punched cows with a young man named Martin, who is the great-grandson of John Tisdale. His inheritance is not the open land that Tisdale knew and prematurely lost but a rage against restraint.

31   Wyoming tips down as you head northeast; the highest ground—the Laramie Plains—is on the Colorado border. Up where I live, the Big Horn River leaks into difficult, arid terrain. In the basin where it's dammed, sandhill cranes gather and, with delicate leg-work, slice through the stilled water. I was driving by with a rancher one morning when he commented that cranes are "old-fashioned." When I asked why, he said, "Because they mate for life." Then he looked at me with a twinkle in his eyes, as if to say he really did believe in such things but also understood why we break our own rules.

32   In all this open space, values crystallize quickly. People are strong on scruples but tenderhearted about quirky behavior. A friend and I found one ranch hand, who's "not quite right in the head," sitting in front of the badly decayed carcass of a cow, shaking his finger and saying, "Now, I don't want you to do this ever again!" When I asked what was wrong with him, I was told, "He's goofier than hell, just like the rest of us." Perhaps because the West is historically new, conventional morality is still felt to be less important than rock-bottom truths. Though there's always a lot of teasing and sparring around, people are blunt with each other, sometimes even cruel, believing honesty is stronger medicine than sympathy, which may console but often conceals.

33   The formality that goes hand in hand with the rowdiness is known as "the Western Code." It's a list of practical dos and don'ts, faithfully observed. A friend, Cliff, who runs a trapline in the winter, cut off half his foot while axing a hole in the ice. Alone, he dragged

himself to his pickup and headed for town, stopping to open the ranch gate as he left, and getting out to close it again, thus losing, in his observance of rules, precious time and blood. Later, he commented, "How would it look, them having to come to the hospital to tell me their cows had gotten out?"

34   Accustomed to emergencies, my friends doctor each other from the vet's bag with relish. When one old-timer suffered a heart attack in hunting camp, his partner quickly stirred up a brew of red horse liniment and hot water and made the half-conscious victim drink it, then tied him onto a horse and led him twenty miles to town. He regained consciousness and lived.

35   The roominess of the state has affected political attitudes as well. Ranchers keep up with world politics and the convulsions of the economy but are basically isolationists. Being used to running their own small empires of land and livestock, they're suspicious of big government. It's a "don't fence me in" holdover from a century ago. They still want the elbow room their grandfathers had, so they're strongly conservative, but with a populist twist.

36   Summer is the season when we get our "cowboy tans"—on the lower parts of our faces and on three fourths of our arms. Excessive heat, in the nineties and higher, sends us outside with the mosquitoes. In winter, we're tucked inside our houses, and the white wasteland outside appears to be expanding, but in summer, all the greenery abridges space. Summer is a go-ahead season. Every living thing is off the block and in the race: battalions of bugs in flight and biting; bats swinging around my log cabin as if the bases were loaded and someone had hit a home run. Some of summer's high speed growth is ominous: larspur, death camas, and green greasewood can kill sheep—an ironic idea, dying in this desert from eating what is too verdant. With sixteen hours of daylight, farmers and ranchers irrigate feverishly. There are first, second, and third cuttings of hay, some crews averaging only four hours of sleep a night for weeks. And, like the cowboys who in summer ride the night rodeo circuit, nighthawks make daredevil dives at dusk with an eerie whirring that sounds like a plane going down on the shimmering horizon.

37   In the town where I live, they've had to board up the dance-hall windows because there have been so many fights. There's so little to do except work that people wind up in a state of idle agitation that becomes fatalistic, as if there were nothing to be done about all this untapped energy. So the dark side to the grandeur of these spaces is the small-mindedness that seals people in. Men become hermits; women go mad. Cabin fever explodes into suicides, or into grudges and lifelong family feuds. Two sisters in my area inherited a ranch but found they couldn't get along. They fenced the place in half. When one's cows got out and mixed with the other's the women went at each other with shovels. They ended up in the same hospital room, but never spoke a word to each other for the rest of their lives.

38   Eccentricity ritualizes behavior. It's a shortcut through unmanage-able emotions and strict social conventions. I knew a sheep herder named Fred who, at seventy-eight, still had a handsome face, which he kept smooth by plastering it each day with bag balm and Vaseline. He was curious, well-read, and had a fact-keeping mind to go along with his penchant for hoarding. His reliquary of gunnysacks, fence wire, wood, canned food, unopened Christmas presents, and maga-zines matched his odd collages of meals: sardines with maple syrup; vegetable soup garnished with Fig Newtons. His wagon was so over-loaded that he had to sleep sitting up because there was no room on the bed. Despite his love of up-to-date information, Fred died from gangrene when an old-timer's remedy of fresh sheep manure, applied as a poultice to a bad cut, failed to save him.

39   After the brief lushness of summer, the sun moves south. The range grass is brown. Livestock has been trailed back down from the mountains. Waterholes begin to frost over at night. Last fall Martin asked me to accompany him on a pack trip. With five horses, we fol-lowed a river into the mountains behind the tiny Wyoming town of Meeteetse. Groves of aspen, red and orange, gave off a light that made us look toasted. Our hunting camp was so high that clouds skidded across our foreheads, then slowed to sail out across the warm valleys. Except for a bull moose who wandered into our camp and mistook our black gelding for a rival, we shot at nothing.

40   One of our evening entertainments was to watch the night sky. My dog, who also came on the trip, a dingo bred to herd sheep, is so used to the silence and empty skies that when an airplane flies over he always looks up and eyes the distant intruder quizzically. The sky, lately, seems to be much more crowded than it used to be. Satellites make their silent passes in the dark with great regularity. We counted eighteen in one hour's viewing. How odd to think that while they cir-cumnavigated the planet, Martin and I had moved only six miles into our local wilderness, and had seen no other human for the two weeks we stayed there.

41   At night, by moonlight, the land is whittled to slivers—a ridge, a river, a strip of grassland stretching to the mountains, then the huge sky. One morning a full moon was setting in the west just as the sun was rising. I felt precariously balanced between the two as I loped across a meadow. For a moment, I could believe that the stars, which were still visible, work like cooper's bands, holding every thing about Wyoming together.

42   Space has a spiritual equivalent, and can heal what is divided and burdensome in us. My grandchildren will probably use space shuttles for a honeymoon trip or to recover from heart attacks, but closer to home we might also learn how to carry space inside ourselves in the effortless way we carry our skins. Space represents sanity, not a life purified, dull or "spaced out" but one that might accommodate intelli-gently any idea or situation.

43   From the clayey soil of northern Wyoming is mined bentonite, which is used as a filler in candy, gum, and lipstick. We Americans are great on fillers, as if what we have, what we are, is not enough. We have a cultural tendency toward denial, but, being affluent, we strangle ourselves with what we can buy. We have only to look at the houses we build to see how we build against space, the way we drink against pain and loneliness. We fill up space as if it were a pie shell, with things whose opacity further obstructs our ability to see what is already there.

Reading Critically: Questions for Discussion

1. Explain the significance of the title.
2. The writer offers several statistics regarding Wyoming (e.g., 58,000 square miles, population 470,000) without citing the sources of this information. Does this omission damage the writer's credibility? Why do you think it does or doesn't?
3. Why does the writer explain the origin of the name "Wyoming"? Is this a significant or unnecessary detail?
4. How is the essay organized? Why does the writer choose this way to organize the information?
5. Identify the discourse blocs of this essay. Compose appropriate headings to label the discourse blocs. Is the essay more effective with or without the headings? Is it easier to read?
6. The writer offers a series of brief narrative episodes to build a vivid impression of Wyoming. Identify the different episodes. How does each contribute to your impression of Wyoming? Which of the episodes do you consider most important?

Referential Aim Writing

Knowledge by Participation: Explanation

Toward Something American

Peter Marin

Peter Marin, a contributing editor at Harper's Magazine, *adapted this essay from his introduction to* The New Americans *(1988), a book of photographs. In "Toward Something American," Marin explains how America is a nation of immigrants who want both the "freedom from the past" and the "safety of the past." For this essay, Marin draws exclusively from his direct experience.*

1   It is a commonplace, I know, to say we are a "nation of immigrants." But that means far more than that we are all descended from foreigners. It also means that the very tenor and nature of American life—its underlying resonance, its deep currents—have been defined in large part by the immigrant experience and, in particular, by the immigrant's experience of displacement and loss. You can find writ small, in individual immigrant lives, the same tensions, ambiguities of desire, contradictions, and struggles that are writ large across almost all of American life and in most American lives.

2   I am thinking, specifically, about what happens to the traditions and values that previously gave order and meaning to immigrants' lives—the crisis that occurs in terms of *culture*. It is that crisis, I think, that is in an important sense our own, enveloping and involving all Americans—even those of us whose ancestors arrived here long ago.

3   Culture, after all, is more than the way immigrants (or, for that matter, the rest of us) do things, dress, or eat. It is also more than art, ritual, or language. It is, beyond all that, the internalized and overarching beliefs and systems of meaning that create community, dignify individual lives, and make action significant. It provides a way not only of organizing the world but also of realizing the full dimensions and dignity of one's own existence and the moral relation it bears to the full scheme of earthly and unearthly things.

4   And it is all of that which is called into question and threatened when immigrants leave one place for another. To put it as simply as I can: immigrants find themselves dislocated not only in terms of space but also in terms of meaning, time, and value, caught between a past no longer fully accessible and a future not yet of use. Inevitably, a sort of inner oscillation is set up, a tension between the old world and the new. The subsequent drama is in some ways more profound, more decisive than the material struggle to survive. It involves the immigrant soul, if by soul one simply means the deepest part of the self, the source of human connectedness and joy. The great tidal pulls of past and future, of one world and another, create a third and inner world, *the condition of exile*—one in which the sense of separateness and loss, of in-betweenness, of suspension and even orphanhood, become more of a home for the immigrant, more of a homeland, than either the nation left behind or America newly entered.

5   Perhaps it is easiest to understand all this by looking at the schisms that appear within immigrant and refugee families, the gaps that open up between generations. The parents are for the most part pulled backward toward the values of the past, often struggling to create, in the new world, simulacra of the cultures they left behind. But the children are pulled forward into the vortex of American life with its promise of new sensations, pleasures, experiences, risks, and material goods—most of which have more to do with fashion than with values, and few of which, in the end, can touch the soul, deepen the self, or lead someone to wisdom.

6   You will note that I said American "life" rather than American "culture." I want to make that distinction clear. For I am not absolutely sure that there really is an American culture—not, at least, in the ordinary sense of the word or in the form of anything that might replace in the heart or moral imagination what immigrant parents left behind. What we like to think of as the "melting pot" often seems more like a superheated furnace that must be fed continuously with imported values and lives, whose destruction creates the energy and heat of American life. And as interesting as that life is, and as liberating or addictive as it can become, in terms of values, America remains even now much what it was when the first Europeans arrived: a raw open space, a wilderness, though today it is a moral and spiritual wilderness rather than a geographical one.

7   I do not say that mournfully or deploringly. A wilderness, after all, is not empty. It has its own wonders and virtues. It is simply wild, untamed, essentially unknowable and directionless: open to all possibilities and also full of dangers. If you think about it, what one is really talking about here is freedom: the forms it takes in America, and what it costs as well as confers upon us. The ideas of wilderness and freedom have always been intertwined in America. It was the moral neutrality of the wilderness, the absence of preexisting institutions, of culture, if you will, which conferred upon the settlers the freedom they sought. Even while still on their ships, the Puritans claimed to be in "a state of nature" and therefore free of all sovereignty save their own. And now, 300 years later, freedom in America still means essentially *being left alone:* the chance to pursue, undeterred by others, the dictates (or absence) of appetite, will, faith, or conscience.

8   But that same idea of freedom, which is the real hallmark of American life and perhaps its greatest attraction, also causes immense difficulties for us. For one thing, it intensifies the fragmentary nature of our society, undermining for many Americans the sense of safety or order to be found in more coherent cultures. For another, it makes inevitable social complexity, competition between values, and rapidity of change, which often make the world seem threatening or out of control, inimical to any system of value.

9   Hence the nostalgia of so many Americans for the past, a nostalgia which exists side by side with perpetual change and amounts, in moral terms, to a longing for "the old country." The fact is that the values and traditions fed to the furnace of American life never disappear altogether—at least not quite. There remains always, in every ethnic tradition, in the generational legacy of every individual family, a certain residue, a kind of ash, what I would call "ghost values": the tag ends and shreds and echoes of the past calling to us generations after their real force has been spent, tantalizing us with idealized visions of a stability or order or certainty of meaning that we seem never to have known, and that we imagine can somehow be restored.

10   You can detect the pull of these ghost-values in our political debates about public issues such as abortion, pornography, and "law and order," and in the vast swings in American mores between the adventurous and the conservative. But equally significant and far more interesting are the ways in which these schizoid tendencies are at work in so many of us as individuals—as if we ourselves were (and indeed we *are*) miniaturized Americas.

11   Let me give two examples. Recently a friend of mine attended a wedding in New England at which two gay women were married in a traditional Jewish ceremony. And I have another friend, an Englishman, who decided after fifteen years in America and a marriage and three children and a divorce, to become a woman. After surgery he turned out to be a carbon copy of the conservative matrons he had seen, as a child, taking tea in his mother's drawing room. When I asked about the children, he said, "I just want to be a mother to them."

12   There you have it—America! I have not chosen these examples idly, extreme as they may seem. Both are, in essence, attempts to solve the immigrant's dilemma. Both reveal something that seems to me particularly and poignantly American: a combined hunger and innocence in which we ache for both freedom *from* the past and the safety *of* the past at the same time. We are apparently unwilling to sacrifice one for the other. It is as if we are—each one of us, each American—both the immigrant child straining to escape the past and the immigrant parent struggling to preserve it.

13   The end result, of course, is that we end up much the way our immigrant ancestors did: without a world in which we feel at home. The present itself seems continually to escape us. The good and the true always lie behind us or ahead. Always in transit, usually distracted, we are rarely satisfied or sustained by the world as it is, things as they are, or the facticity of the given, to use a fancy but accurate phrase. We tend to lack the deep joy or the gravid resignation engendered in other cultures by a sense of ease in time: the long shadow cast by lives lived for generations in a loved mode or place. "Home" is for us, as it is for all immigrants, something to be regained, created, discovered, or mourned—not where we are in time or space, but where we dream of being.

Reading Critically: Questions for Discussion

1. What is the subject of this essay? What is the writer trying to explain? What are his subordinate aims and purposes?
2. Is this title appropriate? Why do you think it is or isn't?
3. What is the writer's thesis? How does he support the thesis?
4. How does the writer establish his credibility? Cite specific passages that establish the writer's authority to address this subject.

5. How often does the writer emphasize the importance of the subject? Where in the essay does he do this? How often does he emphasize the clarity and simplicity of his explanation? Where does he do this?

6. How has the writer organized this explanation? Why does he organize it the way he does? Is a different organization possible? Is a different organization necessary?

7. The original version of this essay served as the introduction to a book of photographs. Do you think the essay is effective without the accompanying photographs? Explain your answer.

Knowledge by Observation: Analysis

Television Commercials and Food Orientations Among Teenagers in Puerto Rico

Wanda Del Toro and Bradley S. Greenberg

Wanda Del Toro wrote this essay when she was a doctoral student in communication at Michigan State University. Having completed her degree, she now is vice president of Danny Velez & Del Toro Strategy Consultants, Inc., located in Puerto Rico. Bradley S. Greenberg is the chair of the Department of Telecommunication at Michigan State University. This study appeared in the Hispanic Journal of Behavioral Sciences *and follows the APA style. For this essay, researchers Del Toro and Greenberg analyze the data that they collected on 225 high school students in San Juan, and thus their report is an example of knowledge by observation.*

Public and private ninth to twelfth grade high school students (n = 225) in San Juan were surveyed. The Spanish-language questionnaire assessed television behaviors, particularly those related to television commercials in conjunction with food preferences, consumption, and buying behaviors. Amount of television viewing was found to be consistently correlated with the amount of snacking that was done and with the belief that more eating in general was good for you. Girls expressed more desire than boys for TV-advertised foods and had more positive attitudes toward television commercials. TV viewing was not related to the number of meals eaten, number of meals skipped, or the frequency of eating out.

1　　Society is more nutrition conscious today than a decade ago. That this new interest has been fostered by the mass media is a paradox—television commercials that once pushed junk food for its social merits now promote the idea of balanced meals, citing the vitamin, mineral, and fiber content of the same foods. Fast-food chains have modified their commercials to boost nutritional aspects. How does this change impress television-conscious and food-conscious adolescents? This study probes the linkage between television advertising and food orientations among Puerto Rican adolescents.

2   Puerto Rico, a territory of the United States since 1898, is of particular concern because its television system airs both U.S. and local food advertising. Teenagers exposed to these commercials receive a dual dose of messages about the appropriateness of specific foods and eating behaviors. Furthermore, franchises in Puerto Rico for fast-food chains have been on the increase (Wagner, 1985b). The foods and eating behaviors endorsed by TV commercials can be enacted easily in terms of finding available eating sites.

3   Nutrition studies undertaken on the island by the Department of Health and other agencies have not examined the role of mass media behaviors. This exploratory study relates exposure to and attitudes/opinions about TV and its commercials to eating patterns, food consumption opinions, and buying behaviors of adolescents.

4   Commercial television communicates what is in vogue, what is appropriate or inappropriate behavior, and what is good or bad to eat and drink. Thus the nutritional messages conveyed through this medium ought to influence its adolescent audience. Gussow (1972, p. 50) argues that television's most powerful messages are its implicit ones, "the things it sells us when we don't even know we are being sold."

5   Given the transitional nature of adolescence, teenagers are exposed to both child and adult TV programming and commercials. Using market segmentation strategies to increase their revenues, advertisers are beginning to target ads to different sectors of the audience including adolescents. These strategies have been applied in Puerto Rico (Wagner, 1985a, 1985c). Local advertising strategies have incorporated cultural factors to increase their effectiveness (Wagner, 1985b)—for example, the use of local actors, local background, local music, and the portrayal of traditions in commercials.

6   Extensive research on children's advertising (Liebert, Sprafkin, & Davidson, 1982) shows that TV can serve as an important source of social learning; children learn about foods and different beverages from the media. Food advertising not only influences food preferences, but it can shape children's nutritional beliefs, attitudes, and behavior (Atkin, 1980). Research on children's ads shows that they "encourage poor eating habits . . . and are misleading" (Gussow, 1972, p. 51).

7   Kaufman (1980) studied the American prime time television diet and found that it emphasizes the consumption of nonnutritious foods as well as eating behaviors that are inconsistent with guidelines agreed upon by nutritionists. Thus there appears to be a strong resemblance between the diet television presents and the eating patterns of adolescents.

8   Within this social context of a heavy dose of food advertising, errat-
ic eating behaviors of adolescents, and the omnipresence of TV, the
intersection of these variable sets is studied. Given a first opportunity to
do so in Puerto Rico, the basic approach has been to compare these
behaviors among adolescent males and females of high school age.

Methods

9   The sample was 225 high school students from a public (n = 109) and
a private (n = 116) school in the Hato Rey metropolitan area. The metropolitan area was chosen because of its access to the cable system. A
class from grade levels 9–12 at each school was surveyed; ninth
(n = 60), tenth (n = 53), eleventh (n = 60), and twelfth (n = 50). Two
grade categories were produced by combining ninth and tenth
graders, separately from eleventh and twelfth graders. Because there
were twice as many females (n = 145) as males (n = 76), a weighting
process balanced gender across the grade levels. In age, 14–17-year-
olds accounted for 96% of the sample. The sample was 89% Puerto
Rican with no other country of origin exceeding 5%. The median
number of persons living in each household was 4.7, very similar to
the 1980 census results of 4.3 (National Puerto Rican Coalition, 1985).
In 97% of the cases, the mother lived at home, and in 81% the father
lived at home.

Variables

10   The Spanish questionnaire administered in the sampled school classes
assessed television behaviors particularly related to television commercials in conjunction with food consumption and buying behaviors.

11   *TV Exposure.* Respondents were asked how many hours they usually
watch TV on a school day and on Saturday and Sunday. They were
also asked how frequently (never, sometimes, always) they watch TV
while eating breakfast, lunch, and dinner.

12   *Exposure to TV Commercials.* Respondents were asked how many TV
commercials are watched when they come on: a few, some, most of
them.

13   *Eating Patterns.* Respondents identified the number of meals they eat
each day, and how many meals they skip each week. They also were
asked for the frequency of their snacking and of eating out (not at all,
not very often, often, very often). They were asked which daily meal
they most frequently eat outside the home.

14   *Food Consumption Opinions.* Eleven items measured opinions about
food consumption on a four-point scale from strongly agree to strong-

ly disagree. Two factors of four items each emerged and were labeled, *How Much I Eat* and *What Is Good to Eat*.

15 *Food Consumption Behavior*. To assess food consumption behavior, respondents were asked how many servings, per day, from zero to more than five, they eat from the four basic groups: meats/poultry/fish, dairy, fruits and vegetables, breads and cereals.

16 *Buying Behavior*. Respondents were asked how often they buy products or ask their parents to buy products after seeing them on TV commercials, given the responses "never, sometimes, and often" as options. They were asked if they receive an allowance and if they use that allowance to buy food. An open-ended question assessed what types of food they buy. For comparison, these food types were categorized as *good, bad,* and *fast* foods. *Good foods* include fruits and vegetables, *criolla* referring to local good foods, and ice cream, which nutritionists consider as a good source of calcium for teenagers (Kreutler, 1980). *Bad foods* include candies, chocolates, chips, and soft drinks that contain many calories but are low in important nutrients. *Fast foods* include respondents' self-report of fast foods, plus hamburgers, pizza, and local fast foods such as *empanadillas* and *alcapurrias*. Fast foods were separate from bad foods because the fast foods mentioned are high in important nutrients such as protein although saturated with fats and sodium (Kreutler, 1980).

17 *Attitudes and Opinions About TV Commercials*. These were assessed first by asking if they think TV commercials do or do not tell the truth. Then they were asked how much they trust TV commercials: no trust, a little, somewhat, a lot of trust. They were also asked the degree to which they think commercials can influence people: no influence, a little, some, a lot of influence.

18   In total, 16 items measured opinions about commercials on this scale: strongly disagree, disagree, agree, strongly agree. These 16 items were factor analyzed, using varimax rotation and selecting factors with a minimum eigenvalue of 1.0. Acceptable factor loadings were those above .4 and the factor score coefficient matrix was used to create indices for each factor. The four factors were identified as measures of *Usefulness* (6 items), *Desire for TV Food* (4 items), *Positive Attitude Toward TV Commercials* (3 items), and *Negative Attitude Toward TV Commercials* (3 items). Item content is in Table 1.

Results

19 The results have been organized to link television experiences to the nutritional attitudes and behaviors of these young people.

TABLE I Factor Indices for Opinions About TV Commercials by Gender and Grade Level

| | Gender | | Grade Level | |
	Boys	Girls	9–10th	11–12th
Usefulness	10.7	10.6	10.9	10.4
Desire for TV Foods	9.9	10.8*	10.5	10.3
Positive Attitudes	7.0	7.6*	7.5	7.1
Negative Attitudes	8.2	7.7*	8.0	7.9

Usefulness items:

TV commercials show me how I can make my friends find me more pleasant.

I know how to be more influential because of what I watch on TV commercials.

TV commercials have shown me how to watch my weight effectively.

I like to try products advertised on TV commercials to be more like my friends.

I learn to make myself more attractive from TV commercials about hygiene products.

Foods advertised on TV are usually good for me.

Desire for TV foods:

I like TV commercials about foods.

I want many of the foods that I see advertised on TV.

I learn about new foods from TV commercials.

TV commercials often give me ideas about foods I would like to try.

Positive attitude toward TV commercials:

I believe that sometimes it is fun to watch TV commercials.

I believe that TV commercials provide useful information.

TV commercials help me to learn about nutrition.

Negative attitude toward TV commercials:

I believe that commercials are too long.

I believe that TV commercials are boring.

I believe that TV commercials are a waste of time.

*p < .05 by t-test.

20 *Television Commercials.* The four factors that emerged from the 16 opinion items about TV commercials were their perceived usefulness, the desire for foods advertised on television, and dimensions of positive and negative attitudes toward TV commercials. Three factors systematically differentiated the boys' from the girls' responses, and none was different by age group. Table 1 presents the results and the specific items.

21   As for perceived usefulness, there were neither age nor gender differences. Moreover, the absolute level of perceived usefulness for commercials was quite low, with the average scores at about 11.0, on a scale of which its midpoint was 15.0. Therefore, Puerto Rican teenagers generally found television commercials less than useful.

22   For the other three opinion factors, results were systematically different. First, in terms of the desire for foods advertised on TV, the girls desired them significantly more and were more positive toward the content of the commercials than the boys; the girls were above the midpoint of 10.0 on this scale. The girls also expressed more positive attitudes toward the commercials (e.g., commercials are fun to watch) and less negative attitudes (e.g., commercials are too long, boring) than the boys. On both the positive and negative attitude scales, the average scores for all groups were below the scale's midpoint.

23   *Eating Patterns, Food Consumption Types, and Purchases.* Boys and girls did not differ in terms of claimed eating patterns. As reported in Table 2-a, they ate the same number of meals each day, snacked and skipped meals equally often, and ate outside the home at the same rates. For eating patterns, however, age made a difference; the older adolescents sampled here ate fewer meals (2.8) each day, snacked more often (3.0), and skipped more meals (4.5) each week.

24   Food consumption was assessed in terms of daily servings from the four basic food groups (Table 2-b). Boys claimed more daily consumption from the dairy food group (about 3 servings per day) than the girls, but were equal in three other food groups. Age groups did not differ on these measures.

25   Opinions about food consumption factored into two areas—how much is eaten and what is good to eat. On the first of these, girls believed more so than boys that they needed to eat less to remain healthy. There were no gender differences in terms of what was considered good to eat, and age did not differentiate either variable.

26   Items tapping the food purchase behavior of these adolescents are in Table 2-c. Boys and girls were equally likely to request their parents to buy food after watching commercials (with the modal response as "never"), equally likely to buy the items themselves after seeing them advertised (modal response was "sometimes"), and to use their allowance to buy food (mode was "no"). But the boys were more than twice as likely to buy what were categorized as "fast foods" and the girls were twice as likely to buy food poor in nutritional value. The younger adolescents were more likely to ask their parents for advertised products, more likely to buy "bad" foods, and less likely to buy "fast" foods.

27   *Television and Nutrition.* The final analyses related the youngsters' television habits with their nutritional behaviors, looking for linkages

TABLE 2 Food Orientations by Gender and Grade Level

	Gender		Grade Level	
	Boys	Girls	9–10th	11–12th
a. Eating Patterns				
Meals each day	2.99	2.89	3.05	2.82*
# of snacks	2.92	2.78	2.74	2.97*
Meals skipped/week	3.85	3.70	3.08	4.48*
Eating out	2.63	2.58	2.53	2.69
b. Food Consumption				
Servings per day of:				
Meats/poultry/fish	2.05	1.89	1.93	2.01
Dairy	2.90	2.21*	2.74	2.38
Fruits/vegetables	1.75	1.99	1.94	1.79
Breads and cereals	2.38	2.36	2.43	2.32
Index:				
How much I should eat	8.40	7.72*	8.25	7.85
c. Purchase Behaviors				
Requests to parents after watching ads				
Never	64%	51%	47%	68%**
Sometimes	35	48	52	31
Often	1	1	1	1
Types of foods bought				
Fast foods	73	34**	38	65**
"Bad" foods	24	56	55	28
"Good" foods	3	10	7	7

How much I should eat items

I need more than three meals a day.

I should eat every time I feel like it.

The more I eat, the healthier I will be.

If I am gaining weight, this means that I am eating correctly.

*$p < .05$ by t-test.

**$p < .05$ by chi-square.

between how and what one eats and their television diet. Partial correlations were computed between the set of TV exposure measures and the measures of eating patterns, food consumption types and opinions, and purchase behaviors, controlling for age, gender, and social class of the sampled teenagers. All correlations reported are significant at $p < .05$.

28   These are the principal findings:

29   The amount of television viewing was consistently correlated with the amount of snacking that was done, whether it was television watched during the week ($r = .21$), on weekends (.17), or during meals (.19). Thus the more television, the more snacking, without implying causality.

30   Television viewing was also consistently related to the opinion that more total eating was good for you, inclusive of television on weekdays ($r = .18$), weekends (.16), and with (.19) or without (.21) meals going on at the same time. Thus the more television the more eating in general was favored.

31   Television exposure on weekdays ($r = .14$), Sunday (.22), and across the week (.25) was related to how often the adolescents used their own allowance to buy foods. Saturday television viewing had a special relationship (.25) with using their own money to buy chocolate candy, pop, and potato chips, within the "bad" food category, and this relationship was similar to one for eating while watching Saturday television and the same bad food purchases.

32   Eating meals while watching TV was negatively correlated with the consumption of dairy products ($r = -14$), but not with the consumption of foods from any other major food group, nor did total TV viewing relate to food group consumption practices.

33   As for nonsignificant relationships, television exposure was not related to the number of meals eaten, to the number of meals skipped, to the frequency of eating out, to the consumption of foods from any major food grouping, to judgments of what is good to eat, or to making purchase requests of parents.

Discussion

34   One basic assumption in this study is that the more television watched, the more food commercials one is exposed to. It is possible to probe the TV schedule and determine if some kinds of show types, or some specific series, are most likely to have food advertising, for example, beer commercials within sporting events, and to link viewing of those specific shows and/or program types to the consequent food related behaviors. This would be an alternative approach, short of manipulating experimental exposure to specific ads and the individual responses to those ads.

35   The age range here was restricted. Would the results differ if the age groups had been considerably younger, in early elementary school, at a time when attitudes and behaviors related to food are perhaps more amenable to formative change? Then the linkage between TV viewing and food habits (which has not been studied in any age group in Puerto Rico) might be even stronger. It was age and not gender that separated these young people in terms of snacking behaviors, skipped meals, and meals per day. Thus an elaborated study involving a broader age range could be more sensitive to the notion that the linkage between TV and nutrition experiences should be examined within age/gender subgroups.

36   There is also reason to note several anomalous findings. For example, TV was related to snacking, but not to skipping meals or eating out; one could have predicted the relationships with snacking (that is what the product ads promote), and the lack of a relationship with skipping meals (no ads tell you to do that). But eating out also would have been an expected relationship; business magazines suggest that fast-food franchises are pervasive on the island, advertising has increased, and fast-food consumption is rising. Perhaps the fact that eating-out advertising is pervasive across media minimized any direct influence from amount of television exposure.

37   Television is related to what children spend their own money on; why is it not related to what they ask their parents to buy? U.S. research repeatedly has demonstrated that point-of-purchase requests by children of their parents are directly linked to TV commercials. We were not dealing with a point-of-purchase situation here, but it remains curious why these young people did not associate their TV viewing with what they asked their parents to buy. In this case, the answer may be that this age group is beyond the age of pestering parents for TV-related food purchases. Again, then, a younger sample could be expected to show a stronger relationship between what they see and what they ask their parents for—with toys and games and dolls as likely purchase targets as are food items. A younger group, however, may have little or no allowance and thus show a nil relationship between TV exposure and self-directed spending.

38   This study provides initial evidence about the nurturance of food habits and opinions from young people's collective experiences with television in Puerto Rico. To expand the study issues, collated studies of the content of food commercials, the content of food scenes during TV programs, including eating habits as well as the nature of foods consumed, should become part of the data base.

References

Atkin, C. (1980). Effects of television advertising on children. In E. Palmer & A. Dorr (Eds.), *Children and the faces of television* (pp. 287–303). New York: Academic Press.

Gussow, J. (1972, Spring). Counternutritional messages of TV ads aimed at children. *Journal of Nutrition Education, 4,* 48–52.

Kaufman, L. (1980). Prime-time nutrition. *Journal of Communication, 30,* 37–46.

Kreutler, P. A. (1980). *Nutrition in perspective.* Englewood Cliffs, NJ: Prentice-Hall.

Liebert, R. M., Sprafkin, J. N., & Davidson, E. S. (1982). *The early window: Effects of television on children and youth* (2nd ed.). New York: Pergamon.

National Puerto Rican Coalition. (1985). *Puerto Ricans in the mid '80s: An American challenge.* Alexandria, VA: Author.

Wagner, J. (1985a, August 28). Cable TV ads offer segmented markets. *Caribbean Business,* pp. 60–61.

Wagner, J. (1985b, October 18). From blind rivalry to collegiality, advertising learns about self, media. *Caribbean Business,* pp. 35–36.

Wagner, J. (1985c, October 30). Bynum talks to SME about coming marketing changes. *Caribbean Business,* pp. 48–49.

Reading Critically: Questions for Discussion

1. What is the primary purpose of this essay? What is its subordinate purpose?
2. What is your opinion of the title? Is it effective? Is it appropriate? What other titles for this article are possible?
3. How do the writers establish their credibility? How do the writers motivate their audience?
4. The writers display their numerical findings using two tables. What is your opinion of the tables? Do the tables effectively display the findings? What other illustrations might the writers have used?
5. Notice that the writers use major and minor headings to identify the discourse blocs of the essay. How effective are the headings in clarifying the organization of this analysis?
6. What is the essay's thesis? Do the writers offer sufficient evidence to support their thesis? Explain your answer.

Knowledge by Participation and Observation: Explanation

Producing a Video on a Technical Subject: A Guide

Danny Dowhal, Gary Bist, Peter Kohlmann, Stan Musker, and Heather Rogers

Danny Z. Dowhal is president of Imagineering Computer Animation and multimedia director for its parent company, The Learning Edge Corporation. He has been a programmer, writer, illustrator, and cartoonist. Gary Bist, Peter Kohlman, Stan Musker, and Heather Rogers are all technical writers at the IBM Canada Laboratory. Bist writes technical manuals for database and image software as well as word-processing software for non-English languages. Kohlmann also writes manuals, using his bachelor's degree in electrical engineering to decipher technical information. Musker writes and designs graphics for software running on mainframe computers. Rogers is a multimedia specialist who has written on-line interactive tutorials for computer software. Each of the writers brings his or her unique perspective and training to the design of videos, composing this referential aim text from the perspective of both participation and observation. Appearing in the IEEE Transactions on Professional Communication, this essay follows the IEEE style of documentation and is written primarily for professional writers.

Abstract—New media create new opportunities for the presentation of technical subjects, and video is one such form that is gaining in popularity. This article details how technical writers can team up to make a video on a technical subject. Based on experiences gained by the authors, it describes how to plan a video; how to write a script using visual and aural metaphors to represent technical concepts; the production process; and tips and techniques to enhance the presentation.

Introduction

1   New media have broadened the range of presentation options for the technical writer. When creating an overview of a sophisticated product, such as a complex computer system, one medium that many writers are considering is video.[1] Why choose video either to replace or

---

[1]For further reading please refer to Ron S. Blicq, "Lights! Camera! Action! Reporting by Video," in *Proc. IEEE Prof. Commun. Conf.*, Seattle, WA, Oct. 1988.

complement a manual? VCR's have gained wide acceptance in the business environment: many corporations have one in the office and routinely use it to show information of interest in the fields of technology and business [1]. Many employees also have VCR's at home, and increasingly use them to watch videos of educational value [2]. Since one goal of a technical product such as a computer system is to reach a large audience and explain the system in conceptual terms as quickly as possible, this accessibility makes video as suitable as a manual as a presentation vehicle, if not preferable.

2   In addition to its accessibility, video offers a wider set of presentation options than a manual, because it is a dynamic medium that can use several channels to communicate. For example, sound, moving and still visual images, animation, a full palette of colors, and text can be integrated into an effective and memorable presentation that differs substantially from one based on the static medium of the printed page. Such multisensory or multimedia forms of information presentation have been shown to improve understanding at a faster rate, thus meeting one of a writer's goals: to increase the rate of the audience's information processing, or, in other words, to build a shorter and more efficient path to the brain [3]. The writer who wishes to get a message across quickly to a diverse audience should consider these observations by Roy Pea of the Institute for Learning [4].

1. Multimedia communication is similar to face-to-face communication.
2. Multimedia is less restricted than written text. Many people come to understand text better with broader media support for its interpretation.
3. Multimedia can place abstract concepts in a specific context (for example, refraction in physics might be depicted in a film on lens and light behavior).
4. Multimedia allows for individual differences in preferred sensory channels for learning.
5. Multimedia lets you coordinate diverse external representations (with distinctive strengths) for different perspectives.

3   Finally, when one considers the future of multimedia as it extends to the personal computer market, it appears that videos created today can see extensive reuse later in interactive presentations for personal computer users or as extended online help. Video, therefore, may be considered a good long term investment in communication strategy.

Our Own Video Project: The Basis for This Paper

4   A small group of technical writers in our corporation met a year ago to consider producing a video. Our corporation had begun working on a complex software product that managed a set of computers, dividing up and assigning tasks to all the computer resources it controlled, so

that the entire set of computers was harnessed to work as a team. Our challenge as technical writers was to create an overview of this system that could be shown to a technically and culturally diverse international audience. Video seemed the appropriate medium; however, we had almost no experience in video production. The purpose of this paper is to act as a guide (based on our lessons) to those who are in a similar situation: technical writers familiar with the print medium who are considering the option of using video to give an overview of a technical subject. In this paper, when we refer to you, we refer to a small group of individuals like ourselves, who might come together in a corporation to produce videos similar to the one we created.

How Much Is It Going to Cost?

5   Once you have made the decision to produce a video, start by preparing a budget. Just as full-color books printed on high-quality paper will cost considerably more than black-and-white editions, so videos range in price depending on how spectacular you wish to make them. Simply stated, it is necessary to balance costs against returns, and preparing a budget creates a picture of that cost. Our budget costs, as originally estimated, are shown in Table I. (The video was targeted to run 40 minutes, and we used outside sources for creating the animation, videotaping the presenters, editing the video, duplicating it, and packaging it.)

6   If you must justify the expense of producing a video, consider evaluating the costs of not doing so. Often, the marketing of a new technology will require many presentations by skilled personnel,

TABLE I Typical Costs of Producing a 40-Minute Video

Activity	Time	Cost
Structure the video	6 weeks	$18.7K
Write the script	3 weeks	10.0K
Review the script	4 weeks	12.5K
Create the animation		
Create the artwork	3 weeks	9.0K
Record the narrator		
Record the music	2 weeks	19.0K
Videotape the presenters		
Arrange the packaging	1 week	3.7K
Edit the video	1 week	15.0K
Duplicate the video	1 week	0.9K
Distribute the video	2 weeks	5.0K
Total	7 months	93.8K

Note: Total time does not represent time from start to finish, as tasks can run in parallel. Rather, it is an estimation of the effort required for a person.

involving numerous trips. A further drawback is that, while traveling, these experts are not actually working on project deliverables, and so incur a double cost to the corporation. Moreover, live presentations reach at best a fraction of the desired audience, whereas video is available to large numbers of customers, and at their convenience. This ability to capture the experts and their expertise once and then distribute it to many people greatly reduces the overall costs in the long run [5]. It must be stated that a presentation by a speaker does have one advantage that no video can match: the chance for an audience to interact with a speaker. Also, the viewer of a video may not watch the entire video, and may be less convinced, since he knows that the video is showing the product under ideal, controlled circumstances. Nevertheless, a long-term cost analysis favors the video medium over presentations by speakers. A good video will supplant the limitations that do exist with dynamic and memorable display techniques.

The Variables Affecting Video Costs

7   How much work you can do in-house and how much you will need to contract out to experts will be a major factor in your costs. The two main factors are:

1. **People:** Do you have individuals in your organization with some degree of skill in scripting, creating graphics and animation sequences, narrating, and recording, and who have some familiarity with the packaging of videos?
2. **Equipment:** Do you have professional quality equipment to record and edit the video?

8   As you work through your project, you will learn what you can and cannot do with the people and equipment you have. If you find yourself producing many videos, you may choose to invest in more and better equipment and allocate more of your own time and your colleagues' time to the production work, which will increase your capital equipment costs but decrease your production costs. However, cost is dependent on priorities: if your colleagues' regular work is critical to the corporation's profits, then taking them off their projects so that you can produce a lower-cost video would not make economic sense, and a better choice would be to utilize them just to organize and write the script.

Selecting a Video Work Group from a Writers' Group

9   Producing a video is a complex operation that can be costly. When putting together the group of people who will create it, begin by analyzing the strengths you have within your own personnel. There are usually a number of talented people within a technical writing group: individuals with theatrical experience, recording experience, graphics and animation skills, or organizational skills. Many times, these same

people have contacts with others outside the corporation who can bring the missing elements to complete the set of skills required. We found we had most of these skills within an eight-person team, and knew whom to see and where to go to obtain the skills and services that were missing.

10   Look for the following skills within your group [6]:

11   *Business Skill:* Managing a video is similar to managing any project: it requires defining objectives, establishing a schedule, estimating and controlling expenses, monitoring progress, and adjusting to changes in personnel and plans as the video is developed. Business skills are necessary to see the video is planned, funded, and completed on time and within budget.

12   *Artistic Skill:* The artist's contribution is knowing how to use the medium of video to best convey the message about the product. One valuable artistic skill is the ability to visualize: to see a completed event in the mind's eye, and thereby guide its development [7]. Visualizing is helpful when creating the original script, and later, as the video is being produced, this skill ensures that the script is conveyed effectively through narration, graphics, animation, and live presentations. Other artistic skills include the ability to blend appropriate sounds and background settings to enhance the script, and coaching presenters and narrators to elucidate the storyline.

13   *Technical Skill:* Operating the cameras and microphones, setting the recording switches to the optimal levels, and advising on capital equipment purchases based on the latest developments in the video industry require strong technical knowledge. Technically skilled people are also helpful in knowing the limitations of the equipment; that is, what effects can and cannot be done with certain equipment.

Dividing Up the Tasks

14   Divide up the workload according to talent and interest. Start with the most important position: the director. Some experience in working in video and some training in theatre are recommended; look for your director in the group of people with artistic skills. He or she will be the final authority when several alternatives are possible as to how an idea might be presented, and will oversee the live presentations as they are videotaped.

15   The director can quickly identify many of the other tasks and will know what is needed and when. It will then be up to the rest of the people in the group to pick up these other tasks, which include:

- Reviewing and revising the script
- Getting and taping music if required

- Finding and recording a narrator
- Producing graphics
- Creating animation sequences
- Finding and rehearsing presenters
- Operating video cameras
- Arranging the packaging and distribution.

16   Make one key decision: how many of these tasks should be done in-house? This question is discussed later in this paper, but in practice, the decision becomes self-evident when the script is reviewed. At this point the video group determines what they want to achieve, and then has to consider whether they can do it themselves. If not, they must either change plans or buy the expertise from outside the corporation.

Managing the Video Production

17   Once group members have been chosen and the work divided, draw up a production schedule and choose a manager to ensure that the schedule is met. This is a job for a person with business skills, who can firmly yet diplomatically check that work is progressing [8]. (The director may also be the manager, or two people may share the responsibilities.) The manager would be likely to deal with some or all of the components and timelines shown in Fig. 1. Note that a number of tasks can be done in parallel once the script has been written and reviewed. By having different people work at different tasks, it is possible to speed up completion of the video in the latter half of the production cycle.

Who Has Final Control?

18   Once the work begins, it is important that artistic control remain firmly in the hands of the director. Just as product managers make final decisions on the products they are responsible for, so the director makes decisions on how the video will be made. Status meetings permit discussions on how various aspects might be handled and provide input from other team members, but final decisions should always rest in the hands of one person. In particular, the group must be careful about letting people from outside take control of the direction of the video. We notified others in our corporation who had a vested interest in the video of our progress; however, they were given no voice in the group, permitting us to continue working undisturbed.

Status Meetings

19   Status meetings are critical to the development of a video, acting as a forum both where ideas can surface as the video is planned and pro-

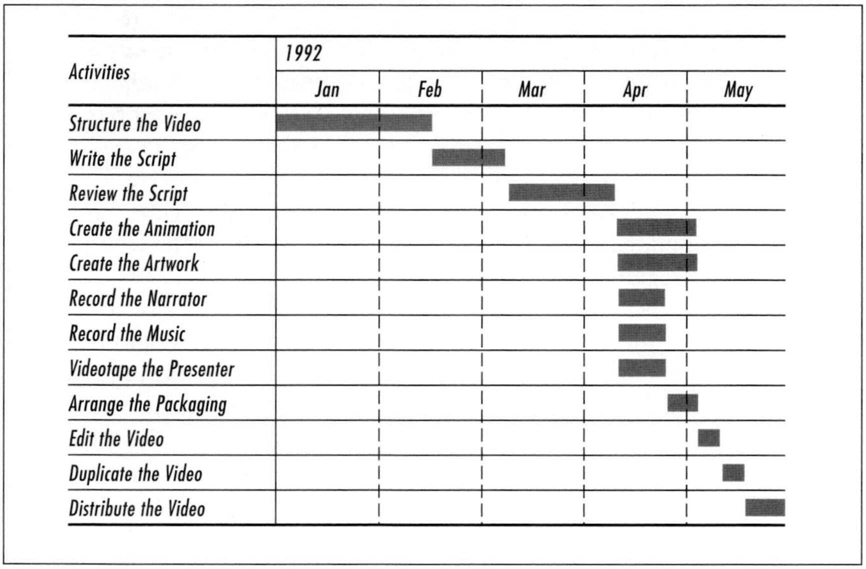

Activities	1992				
	Jan	Feb	Mar	Apr	May
Structure the Video	███	██			
Write the Script		██			
Review the Script			██		
Create the Animation				██	
Create the Artwork				██	
Record the Narrator				█	
Record the Music				█	
Videotape the Presenter				█	
Arrange the Packaging				█	
Edit the Video					█
Duplicate the Video					█
Distribute the Video					██

Figure 1 Timeline

duced, and where adjustments can be made to the schedule depending on recent events and resources. We used our status meetings to do the following:

- Brainstorm
- Watch, learn from, and critique other technical and business videos
- Develop and review our script
- Refine our original ideas
- Delegate work items
- Track our progress.

20   We met once every two weeks for an hour, which we found to be sufficient time to address all issues.

Writing a Script

21   Though video may be a new medium for technical writers, the main activity of creating one is very familiar: writing. The script is the key component to a video and a good indicator of its future success. Writing a script, however, differs from writing a book. Writers must have visual and aural sensitivity, so that their ideas can be translated into a dynamic (as opposed to static) presentation. Before you actually start to write the script, you should have a structure in place for the entire video. Imagine different modules that cover the basic ideas you wish to convey. The structure is the framework for the video.

22   Once you have the structure, the writing begins. A video script is a composite of several distinct scripts for a variety of experts working on the production. Different experts have their own vocabularies and concerns. For example, videographers use terms such as wipes, fades, scenes, and storylines; graphic artists refer to drop shadows, pixels, and animated sprites; actors focus on lines and diction. Three interrelated scripts emerge from the original structure: the technical script, for the cameraman and editor; the video storyboard, for the graphic artist; and the audio script, for the narrator.

23   The technical script provides information for the cameraman and editor. It is written with the video directions on one side and the associated audio segments on the other. Include the time (in minutes and seconds) that you intend to spend on each idea being covered in the video. Table II shows an example.

24   The video storyboard translates the technical script into a visual and aural format. A team member with artistic talent creates a sketch for each video scene. Like the technical script, each sketch is associated with the appropriate audio segments. This more visual format provides the graphic artist with a frame of reference for each graphic or animation sequence to be created. We found that the storyboard helped us to describe the video to interested individuals from outside

---

TABLE II
Example of a Technical Script

Video	Audio
CUT to medium shot of two circles of workstations around databases (cylinders resembling disk packs).	NARRATOR: Pieces of the network can serve as backups, should parts of the environment become unavailable. MUSIC fades out.

Sound Bite #1 0:20

Video	Audio
CUT to close up (head and shoulders) of interviewee, looking off camera, talking about the product. Text superimposed at the bottom of the screen identifies the speaker and gives his/her title	SPEAKER emphasizes the synergism of our product, how pieces join together.

Sound Bite #2 0:20

Video	Audio
CUT to close up (head and shoulders) of interviewee, looking off camera, talking about the product. Text superimposed at the bottom of the screen identifies the speaker and gives his/her title.	SPEAKER focuses on how our product provides enterprises with choices.

our team, in addition to providing our own group with a common visual representation of it prior to actual production. An example is shown in Fig. 2 [p. 566].

25 The audio script contains the dialog for the narrator, and can also contain stage directions if you are employing actors. While writing it, it is advisable to read it aloud, as the written word and the spoken word are different. We discovered that we modified our audio script as we read it aloud to others at our status meetings.

Using Metaphors

26 One of video's strengths as a medium is that it can effectively use metaphors to represent technical concepts. Consider using a metaphor whenever trying to explain a complex idea. For example, in our video, we wanted to show how large main frame computers are isolated from one another and require a special encoded message to exchange information. We created a picture of a computer system within an ancient fortress. The picture turned into an animation sequence enhanced with sound as the fortress lowered its drawbridge following a special knock on its door.

Special Effects

27 Special effects can be an important part of a video, but they must be used carefully. If overdone or implemented poorly, they will lower the quality of the production and evoke a negative reaction from the viewing audience. However, when used tastefully and implemented well, they can make your video more appealing. One of the special effects we used was a simulated touch screen found on some personal computers. At several points in a live presentation, the presenter would touch an icon on the screen. The special effect to show how the screen was touch-sensitive was done in the editing process, by cutting from a shot of the presenter touching the screen to graphics that simulated what would happen on the screen as a consequence. This transition gave the impression that it was a real touch screen. An electronic beep was added each time the presenter touched the screen, to make the sequence more realistic.

28 There were several advantages to using this special effect. It provided a visual break for the audience during a long presentation. It gave visual clues about the length of the presentation remaining: five icons were shown, so the audience knew at any time what topics were still to be covered. And it added a "high tech" dimension to the video, which can be an important psychological factor when marketing a product to a technically sophisticated audience.

Animation

29 The cost of high-quality two- and three-dimensional animation has been reduced significantly in the past few years. While traditional ink-

Figure 2
Video storyboard

3h

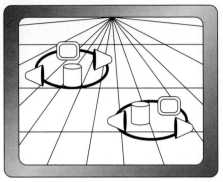

MUSIC fades out

Groups of computers stop turning

3i

SPEAKER emphasizes the synergism of our project, how pieces join together.

sound bite #1

3j

SPEAKER focuses on how our product provides enterprises with choices.

sound bite #2

and-paint character animation can cost over $50,000 per minute, depending on the quality, video animation produced on a personal computer is often under $5000 per minute without a noticeable difference in quality. Since animation is a very effective presentation technique, consider adding some to any video. If used sparingly, it can be accommodated by most budgets.

30   Animation is well suited to explain and describe conceptual topics, such as those associated with computers. For example, it can be used to present the flow of information in a network system or show how a new paging system works. The best candidates for animated sequences are often those most difficult to document on paper. Look for a process where several events are occurring simultaneously, or that includes abstract objects, such as virtual machines. The key is action: do not waste money on animation describing a static object. For example, use a diagram to illustrate the detailed layout of a disk for storing data in a computer system, but use animation to illustrate how the disk becomes filled with data and then fragmented over time.

Producing a Video with in House Resources

31   Video production is divided into three phases, as shown in Table III.

TABLE III

Phase	Action
Pre-Production	Planning, script writing, casting, and location selection.
Production	Assembling the technical experts on location and recording.
Post-Production	Editing the tapes into one master tape; then copying the tape for distribution.

---

32   The production phase comprises the shortest part of the schedule, but consumes the largest part of the budget, requiring many people with special skills and an assortment of expensive equipment. To achieve the right balance between controlling costs and achieving quality, determine which key roles can be done in-house, and buy only the technical expertise necessary for the other tasks [9]. To many people, this phase, for example, contains much of the fun and excitement of creating a video, but do not be tempted to do it yourself if the necessary skills are not there: remember that the recorded material is permanent, and changing it later will be expensive or impossible. In our first video production, we used our own skills to plan, manage, and write the script, but assigned most of the tasks in the production and post-production phases to the video pros.

33   Based on our experience, the following roles can be done with in-house personnel with limited knowledge of video technology:

Pre-Production Phase

34   Have someone in your video work group assume the role of managing producer, which means being responsible for the budget, schedules, and finished product. The producer should ensure that all variations of the script (technical, storyboard, and audio) are written; then plan the shooting schedule with times, locations, and characters. Once the script and schedule are ready, your group should cast the talent required. In-house technical experts can best describe your product, as the enthusiasm they feel for it can seldom be portrayed authentically by actors. When casting, observe your candidates and select those who will appear most natural on camera.

35   Also use in-house talent for the role of the narrator, as someone familiar with your product will prove more convincing than an actor reading from a script. Issue a casting call and select the narrator from within your own set of technical writers. (It will also save you an actor's fee.)

Production Phase

36   A member of your work group should assume the role of director, since the group knows what needs to be said and how to say it. As stated earlier, this is the most important role. If it seems too ambitious for your chosen director to assume this role, remember that your production crew will usually provide him or her with many helpful suggestions, and translate instructions into the hoped-for wizardry.

Post-Production Phase

37   Direct your own on-line editing session, but have a professional video editor actually make the cuts amongst the set of tapes. Guide the editor when creating the master tape by keeping your video storyboard on hand as a point of reference. Editing time is very expensive, so know exactly what you want to see in the final tape before entering the editing studio.

What Services Should be Contracted?

38   There are aspects of video production that should be left in the hands of professionals, especially if this is your first video experience [10]. Camera work, lighting, and editing are skills acquired over time and through apprenticeship. In the early planning stage of our video, we realized that we had neither the time to develop these skills nor the budget to purchase the necessary sophisticated equipment, so we decided to assign these tasks outside. For example, we planned our 40-minute video to include 10 minutes of animation, as we believed that this medium could explain a complex topic and provide some

mild entertainment (sometimes referred to as "edutainment"). We contracted this portion of the video to a professional animator, as we lacked the necessary hardware, software, and experience to create suitable three-dimensional animation.

39   We also contracted professional musicians to make the soundtrack. Our computer product is designed to harmonize a company's computing environment, and we chose to use a music metaphor to show this harmony. Synthesized computer sound did not achieve the effect we were looking for, so we had music arranged and recorded by professionals. In addition to creating the right sound, this gave us a piece of signature music that we now own and that will always be associated with our product. The arrangement and recording took only two days. By getting our own original music, we avoided paying the costly copyrights and royalties associated with a previously published song.

40   The final service we contracted was the copying or dubbing of the master tape into VHS format (for our North American customers) and PAL format (for our European customers).

Videotaping Live Presentations

41   Particular technical aspects are often best expressed by experts in your own corporation, as usually these people have already presented their particular field of knowledge several times and are well prepared to be recorded. They should be taped in a professional environment like the one where they would present their material to live audiences, such as a well-appointed conference. Before taping, carefully consider the background view. For example, we placed some diagrams on flip charts, which reinforced the message of one speaker and were used by him to emphasize points. Since presentations are performed before audiences, we added spectators to the scene and occasionally showed short clips of them as a group or individually to give a sense of audience involvement. It is also possible to have the audience participate; however, this tends to break the flow of the presentation, so in most cases is not advisable.

42   Once your background is set up, have your presenter go through a dry run. The purpose is to enable the video crew to make any final camera adjustments, for the rest of the group to make suggestions to improve the presentation, and for the presenter to adapt his or her message to the video medium. It must be remembered that presenting material to a camera is quite different from presenting it to a live audience because there is no feedback. We found that one dry run was sufficient for our presenter to adjust himself to the medium.

43   Then it's time to record. Two recording sessions are recommended. Set your camera slightly differently on each session; then later,

when you edit, this will allow you to mix a number of different shots of the same presentation for some variety. It also allows the presenter to make some small changes in the second session and permits a few errors in delivery, since in editing you can simply use the alternate recording of the same section.

44   The best tool for assessing a live presentation is the line monitor, as it shows the same picture that is being recorded on tape—the camera view. The acceptability of a take should be based on the presentation on the line monitor, as it is free from any external distractions and is exactly what will appear in the final video. We based all our evaluations on this view.

Managing Live Presentations

45   The director must be in charge of shooting any live presentation: the video crew shooting the scene will expect their instructions to come from one person, and will be confused by orders or comments from other members of the team, even if the remarks are intended to help. Whenever members of our video work group had suggestions, we consulted privately with the director.

46   Including members during the recording does have some advantages, however, as they can assist the technicians move equipment around and can provide constructive feedback to the director at the end of each scene. The following questions should be considered:

- Is the scene meeting the objectives?
- Is the content correct?
- Are the important parts of the picture being filmed?
- Does the set look like the one described in the script?
- Are the lines read with proper pronunciation and natural presentation [10]?

47   As each scene is recorded, comments to the director can provide a valuable perspective on the scene's success. If problems are pointed out, the director may choose to immediately record one more time, since reshooting at a later date will be expensive.

Encourage Analogies

48   Technical subjects can often be quickly explained to a diverse audience by using analogies to the everyday world. One good analogy is worth a thousand words of detail, and we encouraged their use during our recording sessions. In one presentation in our video, for example, a presenter effectively used the following analogy to explain how his software product could be likened to playing golf:

Like a game of golf, you could play it with one golf club; but you bring a set of clubs so that you can select the best club for the particular situation faced at the moment, such as a putter for the putting green and a driver for the fairways. Similarly, this software selects the best type of computer among a set of different types that it is managing to solve the particular problem faced at the moment. For example, a problem requiring floating-point arithmetic, which requires large computer resources, would be sent to a mainframe computer, and a problem which might be enhanced by a better visual display would be sent to a personal computer.

Details to Remember

49 By employing a professional video production crew, we were able to benefit from their experience and learn some tips and techniques. Here are some lessons we learned:

* *Keep a shot log.* You should maintain a record of every scene shot and take recorded. This record includes the scene name or number, the tape number, the scene start time, and the scene end time. This log will prove invaluable when it comes to locating items during the editing phase, since scenes are rarely filmed in order.

* *Record some cutaway shots.* For example, if demonstrating an activity on the computer, get shots of the hands on the keyboard and using the mouse. Or if employing an audience, take a set of individual reactions such as nodding, writing, smiling, and so on. These cutaways can be used in editing if material needs to be cut out, or if two scenes need to be joined. They provide a smoother transition than a simple cut.

* *Try to minimize background noise.* Before shooting a scene, check the noise levels by putting on a headset. In one scene we detected the hum from an overhead projector which had not been turned off. To further ensure clarity of sound when recording, place a separate microphone on the presenter to make certain you get a clear voice recording.

* *Check out the visual background.* See that the background harmonizes rather than clashes with the presentation. Use the line monitor, since what your eye sees might not be the same as the camera's view.

* *Record some room noise.* This allows for audio edits later, when you mix voice and room noise for smooth transitions. Note that you cannot go back and do this at a later time because the exact background noise in the room can never be reconstructed.

* *Get direct video output from computer screens.* If shooting a demonstration on a computer, get video output from the computer screen itself and record it at the same time as the live presentation. This technique gives a clear computer screen image, whereas you will get one with lines and reflections if you videotape the screen

itself. In addition, you will be able to focus the camera on the presenter. Later, during editing, you can cut between the computer screen and the presenter. Also remember to check the screen colors and the font size so that the lettering on the screen will be legible.

Post Production Editing, Packaging and Distribution

50   Once you have your tapes with all the live presentations, graphics, animation, and narration soundtrack, it is time for the final steps: editing the set of tapes into one master tape, and packaging and distributing copies of it.

Editing

51   Editing is an essential part of what makes a video interesting: it helps make smooth transitions from one topic to the next, associates ideas by placing scenes next to each other, and tightens the video by removing unwanted material. However, it costs money. The time of a film editor and equipment can easily exceed several hundred dollars per hour, so planning is important. Come prepared with your script, storyboard, and shot log, to make it easier to manage the hours of videotape you will have accumulated during shooting. Look through the "raw" (unedited) tape before editing begins, and choose the pieces you want to keep. Often the most difficult part of editing is deciding what to include and what to exclude from the final product. For example, if your script requires a 20-second clip of expert opinion on a topic, that 20 seconds may be hidden in ten minutes of tape which contains remarks about the topic. Making these decisions can take a long time. Unless you have your own editing suite, make as many of these decisions as possible before you start paying by the hour for your time with a professional editor. If you create a VHS dub of all the shots with time marks on them, this pre-editing can be done at home.

52   After you have made your editing decisions, choose the type of editing transition for each scene. There are many transitions available. Three of the most common are found in Table IV.

TABLE IV

Transition	Action
Cut	The switch from one image to the next is made instantly.
Fade	The visibility of the first image is reduced while that of the second image is increased. until the first image disappears.
Wipe	The first image is pushed off the screen by the second image.

53   While modern video editing suites are capable of an almost infinite number of variations of transitions, be careful that they do not become the center of attention. Reserve the more elaborate transitions for breaks between significant portions of the video. Editing, as a rule, should be transparent to the viewer.

Packaging and Distribution

54   Editing results in a Betacam master tape, which can then be copied or dubbed into VHS and PAL formats suitable for North American and European video machines, respectively. There are many packages available for the copied videotapes, from the simple black cases common in video rentals to leather boxes with cloth interiors. We selected a colored plastic case with a two-color label that included the video title, stock number, company logo, and a colored graphic that matched a scene from the tape. Distribution can usually be arranged through your present distribution channels. For example, we used our corporation's existing warehouse and ordering facilities to stock and distribute our video, in the same manner as we would stock and distribute a technical manual.

Conclusion

55   Prior to video, we in the technical writing field seemed better at collecting information than disseminating it. Manuals are very good as a comprehensive collection of details, but they are not the optimal means for presenting a fast overview to an audience of more than one. Video, with its multisensory appeal, makes information readily accessible and quickly transferable, and can filter out many of the low-level details by substituting metaphors that explain them conceptually. As such, it has a role to play in modeling information to make it more useful—a major demand of modern users [11]. We found we were able to convey a great deal of such useful information in 40 minutes, suggesting that video may be one answer to Edward Tufte's challenge of finding ways to increase information resolution [12].

56   Just as a brush and canvas do not make an artist, so buying a camcorder does not make one a videographer. Prior to creating our own project, we watched many existing industrial videos, and we felt that most were visually dull, lacked editing, and selected cast poorly, and that sometimes the topics did not suit the video medium. Our hope is that we learned what not to do from our exposure to these.

57   Our experience as writers, combined with our role as video critics, taught us the value of planning. We assessed the skills we had and those we lacked, then focused our activities on what we could do, and contracted the rest out to the pros. The positive feedback we have had to date indicates we made the right choices. In challenging

ourselves to broaden our planning, managing, and writing skills beyond the computer manual and into the world of multimedia, after one video we are more versed in this new medium and look forward to tackling more productions in the future.

Acknowledgment

58   The authors would like to thank Anne Stilman of IBM Canada Ltd. for her editorial assistance. They are also grateful to Imagineering Computer Animation Inc. and Videoframe Productions Ltd. for their contributions to the finished video. They exceeded the bounds of their contracts and showed infinite patience with us, the video novices.

References

[1] P. Drucker, "The new society of organizations," *Harvard Business Review,* p. 97, Sept.–Oct. 1992.

[2] T. Yager, "Information's human dimension," *Byte,* p. 154, Dec. 1991.

[3] R. D. Pea, "Learning through multimedia," *IEEE Computer Graphics Appl.,* p. 59, July 1991.

[4] E.J. Garrity and J.C. Sipior. "Multimedia: A vehicle for embedding expertise," in *Proc. IEEE/ACM Int. Conf. Developing Managing,* p. 314, July 1992.

[5] D. Hon, "Butcher, baker, candlestick maker: Skills required for effective multimedia projects." *Educ. Technol.,* vol. 32, no. 5, pp. 14–19, May 1992.

[6] R. Bergman and T. V. Moore, "Managing interactive video/multimedia projects," *Educ. Technol. Pub.,* p. 15, 1990.

[7] R. I. Stevens, "Implementation: The key to a successful project," *J. Systems Management,* p. 21, June 1992.

[8] R. Bergman and T. V. Moore, "Managing interactive video/multimedia projects," *Educ. Technol. Pub.,* p. 86. 1990.

[9] N. Purdom, "Making video work for the company," *Audio Visual.,* pp. 12–14, Apr. 1992.

[10] R. Bergman and T. V. Moore, "Managing interactive video/multimedia projects, *Educ. Technol. Pub.,* p. 93, 1990.

[11] R. Benjamin and J. Blunt, "Critical IT issues: The next ten years, *Sloan Management Review,* p. 14, Summer 1992.

[12] E. Tufte, "User interface: The point of competition." *American Soc. Inform. Science,* p. 15, June–July 1992.

Reading Critically: Questions for Discussion

1. In the introduction, the writers emphasize the superiority of multimedia communication. What is the purpose of including this information? Is it necessary?
2. Locate and summarize the writers' thesis.

3. How do the writers establish their credibility?

4. How is the essay organized? Why do the writers organize the information this way? Would a different organization be more effective?

5. The writers address their audience using *you* and *your* (e.g., "As you work through your project, you will learn what you can and cannot do with the people and equipment you have.") Do you consider this style appropriate to their aim and audience?

6. In explaining their subject, the writers incorporate a number of illustrations. Evaluate the merits of each table and figure. What do the illustrations contribute to the article? Which, if any, do you think are essential? Which, if any, do you consider unnecessary? What other illustrations, if any, would you like the writers to add?

7. Do you think the conclusion is effective? Why do you think it is or isn't?

Knowledge by Participation and Observation: Analysis

Teaching Maya Angelou's *I Know Why the Caged Bird Sings:*

A Thematic Approach

Carolyn Kallsen Pate

Carolyn Kallsen Pate teaches at Southwest Texas State University in San Marcos, Texas. Her essay appeared in English in Texas*, a journal sponsored by the Texas Council of Teachers of English. When explaining how instructors can teach Angelou's book thematically, Pate draws from her classroom experience (participation). When analyzing the autobiography, however, Pate relies on her own interpretation and refers to published scholarship (participation and observation). This essay follows the MLA style.*

1   High school students can learn much from studying Maya Angelou's first autobiographical text, *I Know Why the Caged Bird Sings*. Writing in a tradition that began with the black slave narratives and continued in black autobiographies of the twentieth century, Angelou challenges stereotypical images of blacks, particularly women. Like most contemporary American black women writers, she sees exploding these stereotypes as one of her missions. In *I Know Why the Caged Bird Sings* (hereafter called *Caged Bird*), Angelou is no exception; the themes she addresses are common in the writing of other black American women writers: the intimidation of color, racism, double jeopardy, and the importance of religion to the black community.

2   A thematic study of the work, then, is one of the most effective ways for students to learn not only about Angelou's book but also about matters important to other Afro-American women writers. For such a study, teachers could examine each theme individually. However, a more effective method would be to show how a larger theme of survival pervades and controls these issues so that they become subthemes. Teachers should begin by telling their students that Angelou herself declares the chief theme of her works to be survival: "All my work, my life," she says, "everything is about survival. All my work is meant to say, 'You may encounter many defeats, but you must not be defeated'" (qtd. in Tate 7). Angelou's words, then, are a sound basis for the study of *Caged Bird;* such an examination will show that in that text she has addressed the survival theme effectively. Throughout the book, she, her family, and her friends encounter many defeats, but they are not defeated; they survive. Out of such a study, a more important lesson will emerge: students will learn what it means to be black and female in America.

3   The intimidation of color is one of the most familiar themes of black women writers. As Mary Helen Washington says, black women "have been deeply affected by the discrimination against the shade of their skin and the texture of their hair" (xv). Therefore, the black girl grows up feeling that the ideal of physical beauty is to be blonde, straight-haired, blue-eyed, and fair. Conversely, she believes that anything else—especially having dark, kinky hair, brown eyes, and brown or black skin—is ugly. Angelou emphasizes the importance of this issue by presenting it on the first page of the prelude: "I was going to look like one of the sweet little white girls who were everybody's dream of what was right with the world" (1). With this prelude, Angelou shows that the black girl growing up must cope with and survive the white world's concept of beauty. References to this idea of beauty abound. For example, the young Maya explains her mother's light-skinned beauty by saying, "My mother's beauty literally assailed me. . . . her fresh-butter color looked see-through clean" (49). Later, when she tells about her mother's new husband, Angelou again pictures her mother's beauty: "Even if Mother hadn't been such a pretty woman, light skinned with straight hair, he was lucky to get her" (58). Maya sees a similar beauty in her Grandmother Baxter who was "a quadroon or an octoroon, or in any case she was nearly white" (50). Her grandmother's light skin "brought her a great deal of respect" (51). Later, Maya goes to work for Mrs. Cullinan, whose "kitchen became [Maya's] finishing school." Maya describes Mrs. Cullinan's girls as "beautiful. They didn't have to straighten their hair" (89). Obviously, Maya is intimidated by the white world's concept of beauty; so are other young black girls. Yet the fortunate ones manage to overcome the prejudice and to develop a sturdy self-esteem. Teachers might point out that Angelou herself, however, does not overcome her nega-

tive self-image until late in life; in the fourth volume of her life study, she reveals that she is still struggling with a negative self-image.

4   Her negative self-image is an internalization of the racism that she suffers at the hands of whites. A larger theme of the book, then, is the theme of racism. Again, Angelou suggests the importance of this theme by addressing it early—in the first chapter. She describes the cotton pickers who work on "the remains of slavery's plantations" (5). As the pickers ready themselves for the day's labor, they gather at her grandmother's store, "laughing, joking, boasting, and bragging" (6) about how much they will pick that day. However, by evening their mood has changed:

> If the morning sounds and smells were touched with the super-natural, the late afternoon had all the features of the normal Arkansas life. . . . Brought back to the Store, the pickers would step out of the backs of trucks and fold down, dirt-disappointed, to the ground. No matter how much they picked, it wasn't enough. . . . The sounds of the new morning had been replaced with grumbles . . . In too few hours they would . . . face another day of trying to earn enough for the whole year with the heavy knowledge that they were going to end the season as they started it. Without the money or credit necessary to sustain a family for three months. . . . In cotton-picking time the late afternoons revealed the harshness of Black Southern life, which in the early morning had been softened by nature's blessing of grogginess, forgetfulness and the soft lamplight. (7)

5   A few pages later, Angelou relates another episode of racism. She recalls the terror she felt the day the "used-to-be-sheriff" rode into the yard, warning her family that the Klan would ride that night: "A crazy nigger messed with a white lady today. Some of the boys'll be coming over here later" (14). She remembers, even after many years, "the sense of fear which filled my mouth with hot, dry air, and made my body light" (14). But she is more than afraid; she is humiliated: "His confidence that my uncle and every other Black man who heard of the Klan's coming ride would scurry under their houses to hide in chicken droppings was too humiliating to hear" (14).

6   The oppression of the black race by the white is so clearly shown in episodes like these that students will have little problem identifying similar passages by themselves. Teachers may, however, need to point out that blacks daily must overcome similar humiliations. Angelou suggests several techniques used by blacks to survive and overcome the oppression. These, too, teachers may have to point out to their students.

7   For instance, blacks survive such oppression, at least in part, because they can see humor in their situation. Angelou has that ability. In fact, Stephen Butterfield goes so far as to say that Angelou "has the power of joking at herself, of recreating the past in a comic spirit

without belittling the other people involved"; it is Angelou's "ability to laugh at her insecurities, [sic] that we remember most—the caged bird's mastery of her song" (209). Several times in *Caged Bird*, Angelou exhibits this ability. It is obvious when she recalls that in the Southern town of Stamps, Arkansas, the segregation was "so complete that most Black children didn't really, absolutely know what whites looked like. . . . I remember never believing that whites were really real" (20). She goes on to say that "people" were those who lived on her side of town; "the strange pale creatures . . . weren't considered folks. They were whitefolks" (51). Another time, Angelou humorously recalls that in Stamps, the whites "were so prejudiced that a Negro couldn't buy vanilla ice cream. Except on July Fourth. Other days he had to be satisfied with chocolate" (40). Angelou's account of her training in Mrs. Cullinan's kitchen again reveals her sense of humor. Maya learns that the doctor had taken out all of Mrs. Cullinan's "lady organs." Maya reasons that "a pig's organs included the lungs, heart and liver." Therefore, Mrs. Cullinan needed to drink alcohol in order to keep herself embalmed (89). With such recollections, the mature Angelou demonstrates that a sense of humor aids in surviving.

8   The young Maya, on the other hand, learns to survive racism by emulating Momma (her grandmother), an example of the Southern black woman's ability to triumph over oppression and humiliation. For Angelou, the "most painful and confusing experience I had ever had with my grandmother" occurs when Momma deals with the "powhitetrash" children who "throw their orders [to Momma] around the Store like lashes from a cat-o'-nine-tails" (23). Through the entire ordeal, however, Momma maintains her dignity, calmly singing and humming hymns. After the "powhitetrash" girls leave, Momma quietly walks back into her store and sings another hymn. The young Maya does not grasp the meaning of the scene she has just witnessed; she says, "Something had happened out there, which I couldn't completely understand, but I could see that [Momma] was happy" (26). "Whatever the contest had been out front, I knew Momma had won" (27). What she does not understand as a child, but appreciates as an adult, is the dignity and inner strength of her grandmother.

9   Later, on the night of graduation, both Maya and her friends triumph over racism. At their eighth-grade graduation ceremony, Donleavy, a white man who comes from Texarkana to deliver the commencement address, delineates "the wonderful changes [the] children in Stamps had in store" (151). As he speaks, however, the black children learn that only the white children will be the beneficiaries of the academic enrichment programs that Donleavy describes. "The white kids were going to have a chance to be Galileos and Madame Curies and Edisons and Gaugins," says Angelou, "and our boys (the girls weren't even in on it) would try to be Jesse Owenses and Joe

Louises" (151). These words show how little the white men expect of the black boys and suggest the even lower status of the black girls. Maya feels defeat before her name is called. "The accomplishment was nothing . . . Donleavy had exposed us," Angelou relates. "We were maids and farmers, handymen and washerwomen, and anything higher that we aspired to was farcical and presumptuous" (152). She continues, "It was awful to be Negro and have no control over my life. . . . As a species, we were an abomination. All of us" (153). It is remarkable that anyone could rise above such self-hatred, yet Maya and the others in the audience do just that, singing the Negro national anthem, "Lift Ev'ry Voice and Sing," by James Weldon Johnson and J. Rosamond Johnson, a song Angelou describes as "the hymn of encouragement." She recalls, "The tears that slipped down many faces were not wiped away in shame. . . . We were on top again. As always, again. We survived. The depths had been icy and dark, but now a bright sun spoke to our souls" (156). In this episode, Angelou acknowledges the central role that language and music play in the survival of black Americans. She says, "It may be enough, however, to have it said that we survive in exact relationship to the dedication of our poets (include preachers, musicians, and blues singers)" (156). With this parenthetical aside, Angelou again exhibits her sense of humor, a key factor in her survival; teachers may have to point out this bit of humor to their students.

10   All of the above episodes reveal the effects of white dominance over both sexes of blacks. Black women, however, endure another type of oppression, one not experienced by black men—sexual exploitation by both white and black men. This topic may be the most difficult for high school teachers to present because they may be embarrassed to discuss Angelou's rape; however, this chapter can be sensitively handled by careful selection of the details presented in the classroom. The issue is too important to the writings of Afro-American women to be ignored. One of the first points that teachers should make is that Angelou's exploitation is particularly traumatic because she is an innocent child when her stepfather, Mr. Freeman, rapes her. Students will easily identify with her physical pain. She says, "my hips seemed to be coming out of their sockets," "my legs throbbed," "the pit of my stomach was on fire," "my belly and behind were as heavy as cold iron" (66–67). Students will, however, less easily identify the complexity of Maya's emotional pain. Teachers should be careful to point out that her emotional problems are rendered so terrible because of her innocence. In her innocence, Maya does not understand why she is hurt. She cannot seek comfort for her pain because Mr. Freeman threatens her; therefore, she must remain silent. She imagines herself to be evil because what she allowed Mr. Freeman to do "must have been very bad if already God let me hurt so much"

(68). As if all this torment were not enough, young Maya faces another kind of violation from black men. As Butterfield notes, "Freeman's defense lawyers act as though she had raped him; and even her uncles, who later kick Freeman to death, make her feel responsible for having killed him" (212).

11   In this episode, Angelou "speaks of the special problems encountered by black women and affirms life in a way that no male author could duplicate" (Butterfield 212). With such affirmations, Angelou highlights the survival strategies of black Americans. But she also, time and again, reveals the importance of religion in surviving racism; students will be able to find examples of this theme with little help.

12   Momma provides the chief example, often showing her deep religious convictions. For instance, when the "powhitetrash" girls insult Momma, she maintains her dignity by singing hymns. She also deems it an honor to have the minister to dinner. Later, she reveals her strict Christian beliefs when Maya makes an innocent mistake by saying, "By the way, Bailey." Momma first prays with the children for God will forgive them; then she spanks them with a switch. Not until later that evening does Maya learn what she had done wrong. Momma explains that "'Jesus was the Way, the Truth and the Light' and that anyone who says 'by the way' is really saying 'by Jesus,' or 'by God' and the Lord's name would not be taken in vain in her house" (86). Teachers should again make sure that students see Angelou's humor demonstrated when she recalls another instance of Momma's strict adherence to proper words. Momma says she "bound" that was true because, according to Angelou, she wouldn't say "bet" (127).

13   By following Momma's example, young Maya comes to believe in God and learns the importance of telling the truth, not swearing, and relying on God in times of despair. As a young child, however, she does not always fully comprehend her grandmother's faith. Therefore, her own lack of comprehension hurts her as much as she was hurt after Mr. Freeman raped her. Teachers should probably make this comparison for their students. The episode which most poignantly illustrates this innocence occurs when Maya promises not to tell what Mr. Freeman has done to her. Because she has been taught not to break a promise, she is tormented by having made it:

> Could I tell her now? The terrible pain assured me that I couldn't. What he did to me, and what I allowed, must have been very bad if already God let me hurt so much. If Mr. Freeman was gone, did that mean Bailey was out of danger? And if so, if I told him, would he still love me? (68)

14   The same torment follows her into the courtroom where she lies on the witness stand, again because she had promised Mr. Freeman that she wouldn't tell. Later, at home, a policeman arrives. Maya thinks, "Maybe the policeman was coming to put me in jail because I had sworn on the Bible that everything I said would be the truth, the

whole truth, so help me God" (71). She believes that she has sold herself to the devil and has no escape. Not until a year later does Maya's recovery from this trauma begin, when she meets Mrs. Flowers, who throws Angelou her "first life line" and teaches her the power of words (77). Thus, for Maya, the deep religious faith she experiences as a child causes her trauma as she deals with her terrible rape. Students should spend some time discussing the somewhat paradoxical nature of this situation.

15   Students should also be led to see how, as Maya matures, she begins to understand why religion is an integral part of life in the black community. Angelou devotes chapter eighteen to that explanation. Early in the chapter she says, "People whose history and future were threatened each day by extinction considered that it was only by divine intervention that they were able to live at all" (101). Their belief in God gives them the strength to survive. At the revival service they are told that in Heaven "the mean whitefolks was going to get their comeuppance" (107). Angelou says, "They had been refreshed with the hope of revenge and the promise of justice" (107). They are assured of their place in Heaven: "Even if they were society's pariahs," Angelou relates somewhat sarcastically, "they were going to be angels in a marble white heaven and sit on the right hand of Jesus, the Son of God. The Lord loved the poor" (108).

16   Perhaps faith in God is the most important of the survival techniques; perhaps it's the sense of humor, the inner strength and dignity of Momma, or the dedication of the poets—or a combination. In any case, students should enjoy, as a culminating activity, debating the issues. As another culminating activity, students could show, in classroom discussion or in a written composition, the black women Angelou celebrates (Momma Henderson, Grandmother Baxter, Vivian Baxter, and Mrs. Flowers) embody the will to survive that sustains the black community in the face of tremendous hardships. Students could also debate or write about whether *Caged Bird* fulfills Angelou's self-proclaimed purpose—to write about survival. They could also comment on what Angelou says about the ability to survive in a world of oppression governed by white values: "You may encounter many defeats, but you cannot be defeated. . . . In fact, the encountering may be the very experience which creates the vitality and the power to endure" (Tate 7).

17   Regardless of the final activities a teacher chooses, students will begin to learn what it is to be black and female in America. They will have a beginner's understanding of the themes other Afro-American women writers use to destroy the stereotypes and myths about black women. Perhaps, with some encouragement, a few students will be inspired to read other volumes of Angelou's life story or books by other black women writers that give voice to the millions of black American women who struggle to survive in a racist and sexist society.

Works Cited

Angelou, Maya. *I Know Why the Caged Bird Sings.* New York: Bantam, 1970.

Butterfield, Stephen. *Black Autobiography in America.* Amherst: U of Massachusetts P, 1974.

Smith, Sidonie. *Where I'm Bound: Patterns of Slavery and Freedom in Black American Autobiography.* Westport: Greenwood, 1974.

Tate, Claudia, ed. *Black Women Writers at Work.* New York: Continuum, 1983.

Washington, Mary Helen, ed. Introduction. *Black Eyed Susans.* Garden City: Anchor, 1975.

Reading Critically: Questions for Discussion

1. Is the writer credible? How does the writer's style contribute to your impression? Explain.
2. In this analysis, the writer includes several quotations from the novel. Why? Would the essay be effective without the quotations?
3. Locate the writer's thesis. Identify the crucial pieces of evidence supporting the thesis. Is this essay effective? Why do you think it is or isn't?
4. How does the writer motivate her audience? Does she emphasize the importance of the subject? Does she make her analysis easy to read? Does she do enough? What other strategies could she employ?
5. How would this essay be different if the writer were addressing high school students instead of high school teachers?
6. If you have already read Maya Angelou's book, does this analysis improve your understanding and appreciation of it? If you haven't read it, does this analysis arouse your curiosity? Explain your answer.

Knowledge by Participation: Problem-Solution

The Phenomenon of Phantom Students:
Diagnosis and Treatment

Patricia Nelson Limerick

Patricia Nelson Limerick was educated at the University of California at Santa Cruz and Yale University. She has been on the faculty at Yale, Harvard, and the University of Colorado, where she has taught courses on Native American history, Western history, and environmental history. Limerick is the author of The Legacy of Conquest: The Unbroken Past of the American West *(1987) and* Desert Passages: Encounters with the American Deserts *(1989) and has coedited* A Society to Match the Scenery *(1991) and* Trails: Towards a New Western History *(1991). "The Phenomenon of Phantom Students: Diagnosis and Treatment" was published in* The Harvard Gazette, *a weekly university newsletter. This essay examines why college students typically don't converse with their professors outside of class and offers faculty members some possible solutions to the problem of "phantom students." A professor who refers to herself as a "reformed phantom," Limerick writes from personal experience.*

1   On any number of occasions, students have told me that I am the first and only professor they have spoken to. This was, at first, flattering. Then curiosity began to replace vanity. How had conversation between teacher and student become, for many students, a novelty? These students conducted themselves as if the University were a museum: the professors on display, the students at a distance, directing any questions to the museum's guides and guards—the graduate students.

2   The museum model is not University policy. No "guide for instructors" tells professors to cultivate aloofness and keep students in their place. No "guide for undergraduates" tells them to speak to graduate students, and only approach professors on extremely solemn and serious business.

3   This is not University policy, and it is by no means the experience of all Harvard students. Many confidently talk to their professors; in occasional cases, introducing a measure of shyness and humility would not be altogether unfortunate. I have no notion what the actual statistics are, but it is my impression that the disengaged are no insignificant minority. Harvard has an abundance of factors creating

phantoms—my term for the radically disengaged, those staying res-
olutely on the academic periphery, taking large lecture classes, writing
survivalist papers and exams. Phantomhood—even in its milder versions—is a significant problem and deserves the University's attention.

4   What creates phantoms? They tell remarkably similar stories. In
the basic narrative, the freshman arrives with the familiar doubt: did
Admissions make a mistake? Paradoxically, the doubt coexists with
vanity; high school was easy, and Harvard won't be much worse for
an individual of such certified achievement. Then, in the basic phantom story, a paper comes back with a devastating grade. Since a direct
nerve connects the student's prose to his self-respect and dignity, and
since the Expository Writing Program stands as the Ellis Island of Harvard, many of these initial injuries involve Expos.

Crucial Fork

5   The crucial fork in the road comes here: the paper, more than likely
produced in good faith, is a disaster; the student has been judged by
standards he doesn't understand. The split outcome really cannot be
overdramatized: one route goes direct to defeat, resignation, and cynicism; the other offers a struggle, rewriting, and very probably, the
learning of new skills.

6   Some of those new skills involve writing, but for this subject, the
significant skill involves conversation—direct, productive—in which
the grader of the paper says precisely and clearly how the paper went
wrong, and how the author can make it better. (On the instructor's
side, if there is any more intellectually demanding exercise in the academic world than this, I don't know what it is.) One successful round
of this kind of dialogue has, I think, an immunizing effect; on the
occasion of the next disastrous paper, the precedent set makes another collapse unlikely.

7   For the representative phantom, though, any number of things go
wrong. Even if the instructor clearly explains the paper's problems,
panic keeps the phantom from hearing. Conversation with instructors
becomes an unhappy experience, avoided by anyone with any sense,
in which papers are picked on to no particular result.

8   The essential groundwork completed, the phantom can become a
part of a community in which groups of the radically disengaged
make their unfortunate academic status a mater of pride or, alternatively, the phantom can think of himself as uniquely and distinctively
cut off from the University. In either case, the crucial transition is complete: from thinking, "I *may* be the fluke in Admissions," the student
has moved on to certainty: "I *am* the fluke." From here on, the
prospect for positive student/faculty contact meets the unpassable
obstacle: the student's own fatalism.

9   I draw here a portrait of extreme cases—with academic underper-
formance part of the package. There are a substantial number of indi-

viduals doing perfectly competent academic work who still would choose a visit to the dentist over a visit to a professor. Usually, no particular unhappy event explains their shyness, and one could certainly argue that their situation is not particularly unfortunate. They are doing the reading, and writing their papers, and getting solid educations. But they are missing something. Recently, my course assistant arranged for me to have lunch with a recently graduated student who had been in my class; four years of a good academic performance, and she had never spoken to a professor. She was a remarkable person, involved over a long time in volunteer work for the homeless. I think both she and Harvard would have profited had she been comfortable talking with professors.

Student/Faculty Contact

10   I address myself here to the problem of student/faculty contact in the ease of students both with and without academic problems. Reading and writing with both ease and intensity are fundamental goals; speaking with ease and intensity should be in the package.

11   How are students to be persuaded to talk to professors? This encouragement should not offer false advertising. One simply cannot say that all professors are at heart accessible and friendly. Some of them are certifiably grumpy, and many of them are shy. They are still worth talking to.

12   With a major interest in Indian/White relations, I cannot resist thinking anthropologically. White people and Indian people still confront each other through a fog of stereotypes (all Indians are noble and in touch with nature, or, alternatively, all Indians are demoralized and in touch with alcohol), and the impulse to provide a comparable analysis for student/professor relations is irresistible. Images have equal powers in both situations.

Commonly Held Student Myths about Professors

1a. *Professors Must Be Asked Specific, Better Yet, Bibliographic Questions.* Professors do not converse like ordinary people. To speak their language, you must address them in this fashion: "Professor X, I was very interested in your remarks about the unification of the Northwest Company and the Hudson's Bay Company in 1821, and I wondered if you might direct me to further reading." If you do not have a specific question like this, then you have no business troubling a professor.

1b. *Professors Only Like to Talk about Senior Theses.* This proposition was brought home to me at a Quincy House gathering. A number of students and I were speaking on a general, humane topic (sports?) when they discovered my hidden identity. The truth out, they began to tell me about their senior theses. The evening, I felt, became something of a busman's holiday.

2. *Professors Only Want to Talk with Other Elegant, Learned and Brilliant Conversationalists.* (Numbers 1 and 2 may appear to be contradictory, but they often coexist.) Living in the intellectual equivalent of Mt. McKinley or Mt. Whitney, professors do not like to descend the mountain to talk to the lowlanders. They are used to sophisticated, erudite conversation, in contrast to which normal speech sounds embarrassingly flat and pedestrian. Even if they seem to tolerate the speech of mortals, professors are inwardly thinking how stupid it sounds. They have, in their distinguished careers, heard nearly every insight there is. If a new idea seems to occur to a student in 1983, it can be assumed that the professor first heard that idea some time in the 1950s. Having a memory built on the order of a steel trap, the professor does not need to hear it again.

3. *If I Speak to a Professor, He Will Probably (and Maybe Rightly) Assume That I am a Grade-grubbing Toady.* (The students, of course, use a more vivid term.) This belief actually concerns attitudes to other students: dependent, hypocritical drudges hang around professors, asking insincere questions, and seeking recommendation letters; students with integrity keep their distance and avoid the dishonor of visibly trying to make an impression.

13   Countering these three assumptions does not require a debasing of professional status; respect for achievement and authority, and excessive deference and fear are two different matters. Number 1 and #2 are both extremely widespread, and #3 has, I think, the greatest power over phantoms. In the further reaches of phantomhood, these assumptions rest on considerable hostility toward the institution, a basic act of self-defense in which the individual reasons (if that's the word): "Harvard has ignored and injured me; well, Harvard is stupid any way." We are dealing here, in other words, with wounded dignity, a condition not known for bringing out the finest in human behavior.

14   In the last eight years, I have seen many phantoms emerge from hiding; I have enormous faith in their potential for recovery. Nothing encouraged me more than the Committee on College Life meeting last spring. I had promised to bring expert witnesses—verifiable phantoms. Having made the promise, I began to regret it. If these individuals barely had the courage to talk to me, how would they face a panel of five professors, two deans and five students? Would any consent to appear? The first five I called said yes—without reluctance. At the committee, they spoke with frankness and energy. To be equally frank, that amazed me—I evidently expected that I would have to act as their interpreter. They were, instead, perfectly capable of speaking for themselves.

15   There is a fairly reliable personal solution to the problem of phantomhood for faculty to follow:

1. *Discover the phantoms* (midterm grade sheets locate the ones with academic problems; reports from course assistants and from professorial visits to sections identify the others).

2. *Contact them.*

3. *Get an acknowledgment of the condition of phantomhood, directly and briefly.* (Don't milk it for its misery, which is often at a pretty high level.)

4. *Engage them in a specific project—ideally, rewriting a paper.* Here, the instructor is most productive when she uses her own enthusiasm for the subject to launch a discussion of the ideas in the paper, so that the student slides, without perceiving it, into what was hitherto unimaginable—"an intellectual conversation with a professor."

5. *Keep a careful eye out for achievement on the part of the student, during the conversation, and comment on it.* This is only in part "encouragement—the primary goal is to help the individual penetrate the mysterious standards of what constitutes "insight" or "a solid point."

6. *Hold out for concrete evidence of recovery—a successfully rewritten paper, for instance.* These second drafts are almost without exception much better papers primarily because the student now has what was wholly lacking before—faith in a living, actual audience.

7. *Encourage a wide application of the new principles.* The student's logical next step is to say to the instructor, "I can work with you because you are different from the others." Resist this. The sports analogy is the best: you may need a coach at the start of learning a sport, but you do not need a coach at your elbow for the rest of your career in that sport. Professors, like most other individuals, like snowflakes, are all different. That, surely, is part of their charm.

16   Phantoms are not beyond understanding, and certainly not beyond recovery. But there is another, equally complex party to the basic transactions of student/faculty contact. We might now take up the question of the genesis of shyness, harriedness and grumpiness in professors.

17   How nice to lead a leisured life in a book-lined office, I used to think, chatting, reading and (if *real* work meant actually teaching classes) working only a few hours a week. Cross the line into professorhood, and the plot thickens considerably. Those few minutes a week in class rest on hours of preparation. Reading exams and papers closely eats up time. Then, of course, there is "one's own work"—research and writing for promised articles and books. Add to this, participation in professional organizations and department and University committees, and one's leisured time in the book-lined office often comes down to checking the datebook to see where one is due next.

18   That is in part why professors can seem grumpy and aloof, even when they are genuinely committed to teaching. Phantoms, and prospective phantoms, should be advised not to take personal injury when cut short by an individual who will have to stay up most of the night revising the next day's lecture and writing recommendation letters. Schedule a meeting for a time when the universe at least gives the illusion of being a bit more in the professor's control, and try not to resent any accidental rudeness.

19   More important, phantoms should be encouraged to use empathy in understanding the professors. Phantoms are, after all, experts in shyness; shyness, while not universal in the professorial population, is no stranger. Consider the pattern: the individual is initially drawn to the world of books and private contemplation, communicating more often through writing than through speech. How nice, the susceptible individual thinks, that there is a profession that encourages and supports this retreat to private intellectual exertion. And that promise seems to hold for the initial years of graduate school, and then, abruptly, the treachery stands exposed. One has to walk into a classroom, cause everyone else to fall silent, and become the center of attention. It is a shy person's nightmare, and individuals evolve the best mechanisms for dealing with it that they can. Once the mechanisms are in place, the individual holds on to them. It is undeniably more dignified to seem aloof and uncaring than to seem scared and shy.

20   I write as a reformed phantom myself—one, happily, in the category in which academic problems did not play a part. My papers carried me through college and graduate school; I was a veritable sphinx in classes. Occupying—initially to my horror—the teacher's chair, phantomhood became a luxury I could not afford.

21   A few years ago, when I had just started teaching, an old professor of mine from Santa Cruz came to Yale for the year. "We're so fragmented at Santa Cruz," he said, "I am really looking forward to having hard-hitting intellectual conversations again."

22   "Hard-hitting intellectual conversations?" I didn't seem to have ever had one. It was a concept beyond the reach of an only partially recovered phantom.

23   Seven or eight years later, I am thoroughly addicted to the kind of conversations I thought I would never have. They provide the core of vitality for the university, the only real cement that makes such a collection of disparate individuals into a community. I want the phantoms included in the community.

Reading Critically: Questions for Discussion

1. How does the writer establish her credibility to write on this subject? Why does she wait until the end of the essay to admit that she was

once a phantom student? Does this admission amplify or diminish her credibility?

2. How does the writer motivate the audience? Does she address the audience's self-interest or its sense of altruism? Is she effective?

3. How does the writer explain the problem? Does she utilize narration? Definition? Description? Comparison and contrast? Analysis of causes? Classification and division? Cite specific passages.

4. What solution does the writer propose? Does she offer sufficient, plausible, and pertinent evidence to justify the proposal?

5. Does the writer anticipate and answer objections to the proposal? Is it necessary to do so?

6. This essay is addressed to college professors. How would you revise it for an audience of college students? Would you change the title? Would you modify the solution?

Knowledge by Observation: Position

Six Pawnee Crania:
Historical and Contemporary Issues Associated with the Massacre and Decapitation of Pawnee Indians in 1869

James Riding In

James Riding In teaches in the School of Justice Studies at Arizona State University in Tempe, Arizona, where he is an assistant professor. Published in the American Indian Culture and Research Journal, *this essay examines the practice of removing remains and property from Native American ancestral cemeteries for scholarly study and museum display. To make his point, Riding In focuses on one case in 1869, when six Pawnee scouts were shot and later decapitated, and he advocates that these six Pawnee crania—as well as other Native American remains and grave items—be returned to their appropriate tribes for burial. Riding In gains his knowledge of the historical development of this case by observation and uses a notes system when he refers to his sources.*

Introduction

1   Gaining equal burial protection under the law is a great concern of American Indians. The loss of this fundamental human right and the theft of tens of thousands, if not millions, of native bodies comprise only one segment of a larger pattern of mistreatment that has occurred simultaneously with forced removals, coercive assimilation, and genocide. While depriving Indians of burial rights, white society has jeal-

ously guarded its own dead through the statutory process. Until the 1970s, when growing opposition among Indians and other concerned individuals began to curb grave desecrations through the enactment of laws, many non-Indians saw nothing wrong with the practice of taking bodies and burial offerings from Indian cemeteries for scholarly study and museum display. This attitude was deeply rooted in the American past, a residual from an era of racial arrogance and ruthless territorial expansion.[1] Yet a life story—complete with birth, kinship ties, societal roles, individual aspirations, and death—is connected with each Indian remain, regardless of whether it has been disinterred or lies within the earth. This is one of the reasons why most Indians view deceased bodies as representing human life, not as scientific data to be exploited for profit and professional development.

2   This study emanates from the Pawnee reburial movement, a very successful grass-roots initiative aimed at retrieving the remains of hundreds of tribal ancestors taken without permission. Its intentions are several and varied but closely interrelated. It takes a broad look at the nature of Indian-white relations in the late 1860s in the Central Plains and the nation as a whole in an attempt to understand why United States soldiers and Kansas settlers attacked, killed, and decapitated six Pawnee in 1869 near Mulberry Creek. It also probes the changing intellectual and racial temperament of the country, showing that a correlation exists between public perception and social policy. Rather than focusing narrowly on just the six crania and specific points of ethics, morality, and law, it strives to show what the deaths of these individuals mean to the Pawnee, both then and now. Finally, it introduces some of the historical and contemporary actors in the unfolding chain of events related to the Mulberry Creek Massacre and other infringements against deceased Pawnee Indians. Although the information presented here pertains primarily to one tribe, this paper illuminates further the nature of Indian-white relations from the 1860s to the present.

Nineteenth-Century Indian-White Relations

Racism

3   To understand the milieu in which the killings and decapitations occurred, we need to discuss the context of nineteenth-century Indian-white relations. The issues that precipitated the attack—land, native rights, and cultural diversity—first surfaced during the mid-1850s, shortly after white settlers moved into the Central Plains, a geographical region that encompassed the ancestral Pawnee homeland. On 29 January 1869, a party of fourteen Pawnee men were attacked and slaughtered while traveling through Ellsworth County, an area that had formerly belonged to their people. Animosity, bigotry, and racism

toward Indians thrived among the incoming white settlers who were occupying Indian land. Kansas newspaper editors, politicians, and settlers viewed Indians as subhuman creatures who not only deterred larger numbers of homesteaders from entering the state but endangered the lives of those who were already there as well. Most Kansans wanted to create an environment free of Indians. To achieve this objective, they developed two fundamental strategies. They launched a massive propaganda campaign in newspapers and public addresses depicting Indians as murderous, barbaric, and untrustworthy savages. They also acted out their aggression, using violence to drive Indians from the state.[2]

4   Some Kansans endorsed removal as a means of resolving the "Indian problem," while others advocated a military solution. In August 1868, the *Kansas State Record* expressed this latter sentiment: "We only hope that Governor [Samuel] Crawford will put himself at the head of a band of our western men, follow the Indians to their homes, and do his work *á la Chivington*."[3] Several years earlier, the *Junction City Union,* seeing extermination as a viable option to ending the "Indian problem," had advised Major General [W. F.] Cloud, the commander of the state militia, not to fear criticism for giving "wild" Indians in the state a "Sand Creek whipping."[4]

5   State politicians generally shared the attitudes and opinions of their constituents. Crawford's Indian policy from 1865 to 1868 reflected elements of both perspectives. He advocated the suppression of Indian uprisings with military force, the creation of a state militia to fight Indians, the driving of "wild" Indians from the state, and the removal of reservation tribes in eastern Kansas (who had been located there with the promise that the land would be theirs forever). The Republican state convention issued a similar proclamation in 1868: "We demand in the name of our frontier settlers, that the uncivilized Indians be driven from the state, and the civilized tribes be speedily removed to the Indian country."[5] Not only did state legislators memorialize Congress for the removal of Indians and more military protection, but Kansas delegates in both houses of Congress also introduced measures calling for the same ends.[6]

6   White Kansans did have a need for protection. Indians fought defensive wars to preserve their way of life and territorial holdings, but whites generally distorted the picture, casting themselves as the innocent victims of uncontrollable native aggression. Numerous clashes between them and the Cheyenne, Kiowa, Comanche, Sioux, and Pawnee had erupted in the 1860s. Some bloody interracial encounters had occurred in 1868 near the site of the Mulberry Creek Massacre, in Ellsworth County, where the six Pawnee crania were obtained. In 1869, the Kansas legislature awarded several citizens a total of $58,944.34 in damages perpetrated by Indians in 1867-68. During this period, the Pawnee allegedly committed at least fifteen acts of aggres-

sion against white property. This violence heightened white anxiety, fear, and hatred of Indians.[7]

Blending Scientific Racism and the Frontier Mentality

7   Convinced of the correctness of their position, some settlers applauded the findings of research in human intelligence. During the early 1800s, phrenologists and craniologists conducted studies using human crania. After pouring sand into skulls, taking measurements, and noting the angle of facial bone structures, they offered conclusions grounded in racist stereotypes that Indians were mentally and culturally inferior to whites. These assertions had profound implications affecting federal and state Indian policy. In 1854, J. C. Nott used political terms to summarize the latest theories advanced by his colleagues: "Certain savage types can neither be civilized or domesticated. The *Barbarous* races of America (excluding the Toltecs) although nearly as low in intellect as the Negro races, are essentially untameable. Not merely have all attempts to civilize them failed, but also every endeavor to enslave them. Our Indian tribes submit to extermination, rather than wear the yoke under which our Negro slaves fatten and multiply."[8]

8   It should not come as a surprise that contemporaneous newspapers echoed identical themes.[9] An 1873 edition of the *Omaha Republican* reported to its readers that "[i]t is this savage, beastly spirit that always remains in an Indian's breast that so discourages the influence of civilization and Christianity."[10] Several weeks later, a published letter proclaimed that "[i]nstances are recorded where the most careful attention had been paid to the education of both males and females, and a single day's contact with the wild tribes seemed to destroy the whole influence as dew before the sun. The best educated Indians, as a rule, are the lowest, dirtiest, filthiest of the band. There may be, and are, exceptions, but this is the established rule."[11]

9   In this intellectual and social atmosphere, the surgeon general's office issued, in 1868, a memorandum ordering army field surgeons to collect Indian crania for scientific study. It noted that "a craniological collection was commenced last year at the Army Medical Museum, and that it already has 143 specimens of skulls . . . to aid the progress of anthropological science by obtaining measurements of a large number of skulls of the aboriginal races of North America." The memorandum particularly urged "medical officers stationed in the Indian country or in the vicinity of ancient Indian mounds or cemeteries in the Mississippi Valley or the Atlantic region" to become involved in gathering human remains.[12] In the past, such noted civilian phrenologists as Samuel G. Morton, regarded as the father of physical anthropology in America, had used military personnel to acquire Indian remains because of the geographic proximity of army posts to Indian battle sites and cemeteries. In fact, army skull collecting had begun in 1864 at the Sand Creek Massacre, when soldiers beheaded a number

of Cheyenne, Arapaho, and Kiowa corpses. The 1868 memorandum led to the decapitation of six of the men killed at Mulberry Creek.[13]

10   Although craniometry ultimately failed to achieve its objective, studies of this type stimulated and gave rise to the development of physical anthropology, a discipline that has thrived on accumulating and retaining large inventories of human remains.[14] Since white society had deemed that burial protection laws excluded natives, scholars soon perceived Indian bodies as empirical data belonging exclusively to the realm of science, rather than to the tribes and next of kin.[15]

The Mulberry Creek Killings and Decapitations

The Massacre

11   If the Mulberry Creek Massacre victims followed the usual Pawnee route, they probably departed their Nebraska reservation on foot about 20 January, entered Kansas in Jewel County, and proceeded southward. Pawnee parties of this nature customarily traveled light, carrying bows and arrows, light rifles, extra moccasins, lariats, and packs containing dried meat. Besides eating provisions brought from home, they hunted game or asked white homesteaders along the way for food.[16] The attack occurred nine days later, during a visitation at a farm near Mulberry Creek in Ellsworth County.

12   Pawnee and white representatives offered conflicting versions of the massacre. While the latter claimed that the deaths were justifiable, the former charged that the men had been attacked without provocation. The Pawnee asserted that a party of fourteen Pawnee had set out from the Nebraska reservation to trade with southern tribes. The army and settlers said that the Pawnee had entered Kansas to raid, loot, and plunder. The Indians claimed that the soldiers opened fire on them without provocation; the army countered that the victims had shot the first rounds. About the only thing that is certain is that two soldiers were wounded and eight or nine Pawnee died in a hail of bullets on that cold January day, including one who had been captured by the settlers and killed while "trying to escape." Settlers transported another wounded Pawnee to Fort Harker, where he was placed under the medical care of surgeon B. E. Fryer, an active procurer of Indian crania. The wounded man recovered, but, for fear that local settlers would kill him, army authorities recommended that he be transferred to and freed from another post. When and where this release occurred remains uncertain.[17]

Ethics, Decapitations, and Skull Doctors

13   Five men apparently survived the carnage and escaped, losing their winter clothing in the process. Traveling about for several days in freezing temperatures to protect and hide the bodies of their fallen

friends from the soldiers, they received severe cases of frostbite. After burying all but one of their dead over a wide area in central Kansas, the survivors returned home and told their leaders about the massacre. Three of them apparently died from the effects of exposure within a short period of time.[18] Counting these deaths, possibly twelve Pawnee men died as a result of the attack.

14   Fryer dispatched a civilian from Fort Harker to the massacre scene on 30 January to sever the victims' heads. He found only one of the corpses and took its cranium, but Pawnee survivors in the area prevented him from obtaining the others. A blizzard set in that day, enabling the survivors to scatter the other remains over a wide area. As temperatures warmed, Fryer resumed the search. Fryer's apologetic correspondence of 12 February to Brevet Lieutenant Colonel George A. Otis, an Army Medical Museum (AMM) curator, explains the reasons for the delay in procuring the Pawnee skulls:

> I had already obtained for the [Army Medical] museum the skull of one of the Pawnees killed in the fight you speak of, [and] would have had all had it not been that immediately after the engagement, the Indians lurked about their dead [and] watched them so closely that the guide I sent out was unable to secure but the one. Until within a day or two the snow has prevented a further attempt. Yesterday I sent a scout who knows the spot and [I] think I can get at least two more crania—that number being reported to me as left unburied by the Pawnees, and it may be that if the remaining five (eight not seven were killed) are buried or have been hid near where the fight took place about twenty miles from here, I can, after a time, obtain all. I shall certainly use every effort.[19]

15   Either Fryer or civilian surrogates scoured the countryside over the next several weeks looking for the hidden bodies. On 11 March, Fryer shipped twenty-six Indian crania to Washington, including six Pawnee from the Mulberry Creek Massacre, three Cheyenne, one Towantkeys [sic], two Kechi [sic], one Seneca, one unknown, one Kaw, three Caddo, six Wichita, and two Osage. Gloating over his contributions to science, he praised the condition of the skulls: "[S]ix [are] Pawnees four of them excellent specimens, two were injured a good deal by the soldiers, who shot into the bodies and heads several times after the fight in which these Indians were killed, was ended."[20]

16   Processing "fresh" Indian remains for shipment to Washington required a considerable amount of expertise and work. One contributor described his method of treating the head of a recently slain Kiowa Indian: "[H]is scalp and the soft parts of the face and neck were carefully dissected up from the skull, atlas and axis, and these were subsequently boiled and cleaned for the Army Medical Museum. The skull was carefully cleaned and then steeped in solution of lime for 36 hours."[21] Fryer must have used a similar technique to prepare the six Pawnee crania.

17   Evidence shows no sign of collusion between Fryer and the soldiers. Rather, Fryer simply functioned as an independent conduit of
Indian heads; apparently, he followed the surgeon general's order for
professional reasons. That is, promotion in the post–Civil War era
came slowly for most officers. His self-congratulatory correspondence
draws a portrait of him as an indefatigable and fearless collector of
Indian remains. About a year before the Mulberry Creek Massacre, on
5 February 1868, Fryer reported to Otis that he had spent six weeks
searching for a Kaw (Kansa) Indian grave. In another letter, Fryer
presented himself as a man who was willing to risk instigating an
Indian war if it would benefit scientific inquiry:

> A good deal of caution is required in obtaining anything from the graves
> of Indians, and it will have to be managed very carefully to prevent the
> Indians from finding out that the graves of their people have been dis-
> turbed—as this might be offered as an excuse (of course, a trifling one)
> for taking the "War Path" again—which is always *walked* each year, how-
> ever, as soon as the grass is high enough for the ponies.[22]

Nonetheless, Fryer hired a scout to go among the Cheyenne and Arapaho for the purpose of acquiring "the cranium—possibly the whole
skeleton of one of the greatest Indian Warriors of the Plains, who died
last Fall."[23] This was apparently a reference to Roman Nose, a famous
Cheyenne war leader who was killed at Beecher's Island on 25 September 1868.[24] In Fryer's way of thinking, uncovering the remains of
an important Indian figure, or at least promising to do so, might give
him a competitive edge over others vying for rank.

18   Operating under military authority and without moral or ethical
constraints, Fryer and many of his competitors aggressively collected
Indian crania. From 1868 to 1872, Fryer shipped Otis at least forty-two
human remains belonging to the Cheyenne, Wichita, Caddo, Osage,
and Kansa tribes, among others.[25] Fryer obtained two more Pawnee
skulls, sending the last one, a warrior killed on the Solomon River by
local citizens, to the AMM in April 1872. Overall, AMM curators
received several thousand Indian skulls.[26]

19   By the early 1870s, Otis had measured over eight hundred Indian
crania. Reporting his findings to the National Academy of Sciences, he
stated "[t]hat, judging from the capacity of the cranium, the American
Indians must be assigned a lower position in the human scale than
has been believed heretofore."[27] Subsequent craneometric research by
other AMM curators, however, challenged Otis's work, placing Indians
once again above African Americans on the intelligence ladder.[28]

The Victims, Their Families, Their Tribe

20 Very little is known about the six Pawnee men whose lifeless bodies
were beheaded in 1869. Apparently, no one recorded their names.

Treating the remains as specimens of a lower life form, AMM personnel assigned each cranium an identification number—529, 530, 531, 550, 5550, and 555—and estimated their ages at 25, 20, 30, 35, 25, and 45, respectively. When the AMM transferred the first four remains to the Smithsonian Institution in 1898, Smithsonian curators gave them new numbers.[29]

21   AMM accession records, Pawnee agency correspondence, and Fort Harker reports contain the key for establishing the tribal affiliation of the deceased, but ethnohistorical sources provide a means for understanding the ramifications of the massacre in a Pawnee context. Unlike the whites, who saw the deaths of the men as a benefit to humankind, the chiefs expressed grief and outrage at the loss of their friends and relatives, who probably belonged to the Pitahawirata band, one of the four Pawnee subdivisions.[30]

22   We can assume that immediate family members and friends of the deceased expressed sorrow through mourning. Each family had lost a key provider, a young man at the prime of his life. This means that the victims' dependents—including widows, grandparents, children, and other relatives—suffered economic hardship, possibly becoming the objects of charity. With white hunters on the brink of exterminating the buffalo and grasshoppers destroying crops periodically, the Pawnee suffered many economic hardships during the 1870s.[31] Tribal values stressed sharing and giving to the needy, but those families without male providers were especially at risk to deprivation.

23   These concerns prompted the chiefs to demand justice. They wanted compensation for the victims and punishment for the killers. Had other Indians committed the act, the Pawnee would have retaliated, but since the crime had been committed by United States soldiers, they refrained from seeking retribution. Given the racial climate of the time, the Pawnee could not risk killing whites, for fear of giving the settlers an excuse to start a racial war. Such an act could have resulted

---

TABLE 1 B. E. Fryer's Record of Sites Where Army Personnel Found and Decapitated Six Pawnee Bodies in the Winter of 1869

Fryer's Number	Site of Decapitation
21	Ascher Creek, near Solomon River
22	Bank of Salina River, 21 miles northwest of Fort Harker
23	Near Fort Harker
24	From same place (near Fort Harker)
25	Mulberry Creek, Kansas, 20 miles northwest of Fort Harker
26	Killed in same action (20 miles northwest of Fort Harker)

Source: SI, NMNH. NAA, AMM, B2, F509–31, Fryer to Otis, 11 February 1869.

in the indiscriminate slaughter of Pawnee men, women, and children by soldiers and settlers.[32]

24   To understand the impact of these deaths on the Pawnee as a whole in social, political, and economic terms, we need briefly to consider the customary role of adult males. Pawnee culture held men in high esteem. As sons, brothers, fathers, uncles, and friends, they had a responsibility to provide for the welfare of family members, relatives, and the poor. Individuals who lived up to these ideals were elevated to the status of warriors. Some of the older victims of the massacre may have achieved this rank, meaning that through acts of bravery, wisdom, piety, and generosity, they had earned a right to participate in tribal council meetings. Within Pawnee culture, only men of proven ability, experience, and wisdom commanded enough respect to lead others. The forty-five-year-old man killed at Mulberry Creek may have served as the *kahiki,* or the leader of the expedition.[33]

25   Not only did Pawnee men have an obligation to protect their homeland, but they also had a spiritual mandate to risk their lives in defense of the Pawnee way of life. Statements given by the chiefs after the attack indicate that the Mulberry Creek victims previously had gone to war against their most troublesome enemies, the Sioux, in alliance with the United States government. Shortly before the attack, the Pawnee victims had shown a soldier some papers indicating that they had been discharged from the United States Army on 1 January, less than a month before.[34]

26   The Mulberry Creek Massacre is indicative of the peculiar relationship the Pawnee had with the United States. The tribe was trapped between Sioux, Cheyenne, and Arapaho raiders on one side and a tide of white American settlement on the other. In fact, by the late

---

TABLE 2 Numbers Used by B. E. Fryer, the AMM, and the NMNH to Identify the Six Pawnee Crania Severed by Army Personnel in the Winter of 1869

Fryer	Army Medical Museum/ National Museum of Health and Medicine	National Museum of Natural History (Smithsonian)
21	529	225092
22	5550	—
23	530	243537
24	531	225292
25	550	225291
26	5551	—

Sources: Column 1: SI, NAA, NMNH, AMM, B2, F509–31, Fryer to Otis, 11 March 1869. Column 2: George A. Otis, List of the Specimens in the Anatomical Section of the United States Army Medical Museum (Washington, DC: Army Medical Museum, 1880), p.122. Column 3: Douglas H. Ubelaker to Roger Echo-Hawk and James Riding In, 5 December 1989.

1860s, homesteads surrounded their remaining lands, a small reservation situated on the Loup River. Unable to resolve the intertribal conflicts with diplomacy, they linked up militarily with the whites to fight foes who had disrupted their lives since the 1830s. Organized under white officers in special units called Pawnee Scouts, Pawnee men performed a variety of invaluable military duties, including guarding Union Pacific track layers, tracking enemy forces, and serving in combat.[35] George B. Grinnell, a student of Plains Indian warfare and culture, summed up the scouts' contributions: "They saved hundreds of lives and millions of dollars' worth of property, and in their campaigns wiped out in blood the memory of many an injury done to their race by the Sioux, the Cheyennes, the Arapahoes, and the Kiowas."[36] After white authorities refused to compensate the Pawnee for the Mulberry Creek victims and to punish the killers, the chiefs had to weigh the benefits of the alliance. As a result, they stopped plans to recruit a company of scouts that summer. However, the chiefs allowed men to join in 1870 and 1876.[37]

The Legacy of Scientific Racism

27   Racist research, government-sponsored headhunting operations, and other acts of arrogance fostered a climate that encouraged many white citizens to commit inhumane acts against dead Indians, including grave robbing and body snatching. With Indians viewed as subhumans, whites rarely considered issues of ethics and fairness when it came to Indian rights. In the eyes of many whites, the desecration of Indian graves was not considered a legal or moral wrong. After the Pawnee fled Nebraska in the mid-1870s to escape growing white pressure, relic hunters, followed by amateur and professional archaeologists, descended on every Pawnee grave they could find, removing highly prized physical remains and burial objects, especially skulls and peace medals.[38]

28   In one instance occurring several years after removal, Art Jewell, from Wheaton College at Wheaton, Illinois, offered John Williamson ten dollars to show him the location of former head chief Pita Resaru's grave. Williamson refused, because Pita Resaru had been his friend. Jewel returned in a wagon several days later and told Williamson that he had located the burial site and taken a body, along with a Buchanan peace medal. Some fifty years later, however, another grave looter found a peace medal and other burial objects that Williamson identified as having been buried with the chief.[39]

29   Grave desecrations and body thefts continued into the present century. B. E. Bengston, an amateur archaeologist, reported an incident involving the desecration of a Pawnee cemetery:

One farmer told about a party of men who had opened some of the graves, that, on leaving in an automobile, they had exhibited an Indian skull on a stick at the same time yelling at the top of their voices so that they might be noticed at the places they passed. This must have been a party of "Smart Alecks" as no archaeologist would have acted in such a rude and undignified manner.[40]

Despite this assertion about respectability, grave desecrations, by Pawnee standards, were never dignified affairs. For the Pawnee, a grave could be opened only for "compelling religious purposes."[41] Asa T. Hill, a noted amateur archaeologist who excavated several Pawnee burial sites, once boasted that digging up Indian bodies on Sunday was his form of golf. In another incident, a Kansas farmer satisfied the public's morbid curiosity by charging tourists a fee to see the unearthed bodies of 146 Indians who were ancestral to the Pawnee, Wichita, and Arikara.[42]

30   From the 1930s to the 1960s, federally funded work relief programs and archaeological salvage expeditions disinterred more Pawnee bodies and innumerable burial objects. During the Great Depression, Work Projects Administration funds put thousands of unemployed Americans to work, including some who helped archaeologists dig up Indian village and burial sites in Nebraska. The River Basin Survey, a massive federally funded "salvage" operation, disrupted other Pawnee graves.[43]

The Present

Changing Racial Attitudes and Repatriation

31 Today, many Americans have become more attuned to living in a culturally diverse society, meaning that some of the old racial attitudes have been supplanted with more enlightened ideals and values. The shift from racist dogma proclaiming the innate superiority of Anglo-Saxon people to increased sensitivity has enabled Indians to seek redress within the American political structure for some past wrongs. Equal burial protection under the law for Indians has been one area in which public perspectives have changed. Utilizing the mass media for communication, Indians have begun to educate the public about the abuses committed against Indians in the name of science. Newspapers demonstrate the transformation that has occurred in the public consciousness concerning the dead. Once a force used to mobilize opposition to native interests, editorialists more recently have written many position statements supporting Indian views regarding reburial and grave desecration. A Nebraska survey in 1989 shows the impact of these efforts. In that year, 69 percent of the people polled supported Pawnee efforts to recover tribal remains held by the Nebraska State Historical Society.[44]

32   Overwhelming public support encouraged the Nebraska legislature to enact Legislative Bill 340 (1989), enabling the Pawnee to recover and rebury nearly five hundred remains, along with associated

burial objects, dug up by Asa Hill and others. In Kansas, state legislators assisted the Pawnee, Arikara, and Wichita tribes in closing down a burial pit that had become a tourist attraction.[45]

Contemporary Significance of the Six Crania

33 The six crania in Washington are important spiritual and historical symbols to the Pawnee. At the time of these men's deaths, they belonged to a cadre of men—Pawnee Scouts—who have emerged as important cultural figures for modern-day tribal members. Virtually every living Pawnee traces his or her ancestry back to at least one of the hundreds of men who served as scouts from 1864 to 1876. Drum groups sing specially composed songs at tribal war dances that honor the memory of the scouts. Many editions of the brochure that is published about the Pawnee Indian Homecoming, an annual gathering of the Pawnee and their friends during the first week in July, contain pictures of scouts and accounts of their deeds. During the 1970s, tribal veterans organized a heritage organization to carry out social and civic functions in the spirit of the scouts.

34 Furthermore, the scouts established a tradition of military service that continues today. Hundreds of Pawnee men and women, following in the footsteps of their ancestors, have served during the United States' times of need. Proudly wearing army, navy, air force, coast guard, and marine uniforms, they have fought bravely in the Gulf War, Vietnam, Korea, World War II, World War I, and the Spanish-American War. Some never returned. Chief Petty Officer Martin Moshier, Jr. perished at sea on 4 November 1970 during the Vietnam conflict, while on a secret mission for the United States Navy. Marine PFC Thomas E. Littlesun died on 6 December 1968 in Vietnam. Five were fatally wounded during World War II. Others suffered grievously: Army sergeant Philip Gover lost an arm in Europe, and Alexander Mathews endured the Bataan Death March and several years of captivity. One Pawnee died during World War I. In all, Pawnee warriors have received numerous combat awards, including purple hearts, bronze stars, and distinguished service medals. A war mothers' association honors sons who served in the military.[46]

Status of the Six Remains

35 Ongoing attempts to secure the remains of military personnel left in Vietnam attests to the value American society places on recovering its fallen warriors. Persons involved in this effort only want to give the dead a proper burial and the families peace of mind. The same situation is true for the Pawnee. They want to bury the six crania, which have been in Washington since 1869, in the ancestral tribal homeland. Four of them now are at the Smithsonian Institution, while the other two are at the National Museum of Health and Medicine (NMHM), for-

merly the Army Medical Museum. In 1989, Congress passed the National Museum of the American Indian Act, enabling tribes such as the Pawnee to reclaim those remains in cases where a "preponderance of available evidence" exists.[47]

36   When tribal representatives and researchers asked for information regarding the Pawnee remains stored at the Smithsonian, Douglas H. Ubelaker, the head of the National Museum of Natural History's physical anthropology division, provided a listing but called into question the reliability of AMM documentation. Referring to the AMM records as sketchy, ambiguous, and leaving many questions unanswered, Ubelaker stated, "The remains sent in by B. E. Fryer are from south-central Kansas and were obtained in 1869. They are inferred to be Pawnee, but according to historic documents, the Arapaho, Cheyenne, Kiowa, and Sioux were also raiding in the area."[48] The part about Indian activities in Kansas is true, but Ubelaker in this instance took a stance that seems to violate the spirit of the 1989 federal legislation. Essentially, by dismissing records left by the person responsible for the decapitations or disinterments and for the identification of the deceased, Ubelaker makes it extremely difficult for the Pawnee and other tribes to reclaim their dead without expending large amounts of money for research. However, subsequent inquiry conducted on behalf of the Pawnee tribe by Native American Rights Fund (NARF) researchers found a substantial amount of evidence demonstrating that the Pawnee chiefs, army officials, Fryer, and others knew that soldiers and settlers had massacred a party of Pawnee in January 1869.[49]

37   Unlike the Smithsonian's stonewalling, NMHM personnel have taken a forthright position. Readily accepting the validity of AMM accession records and the right of the Pawnee to reclaim their dead, curators Gloria y Edynak and Paul S. Sledzik agreed to repatriate the two remains stored at the NMHM to the Pawnee tribe upon official request and to coordinate activities with the Smithsonian so that the other four scout remains, along with two others acquired by Fryer, would be returned together.[50] Although the six crania have not been returned yet, NMHM's cooperation is indicative of growing receptiveness among some elements of the scientific community to the notion that Indians should have the final say in the disposition of their dead. This is all that the Pawnee want.

Conclusion

38   Racial attitudes in the Central and Southern Plains and in academic circles have changed since the six Pawnee Scouts were gunned down and decapitated in 1869. Today, public opinion supports the Pawnee efforts to recover and properly rebury all remains, along with associated grave items, taken from them without permission. When the six Pawnee crania are put to rest in the ancestral Pawnee homeland, a

sordid chapter in the history of Pawnee-white relations will come to a close. Unburied, these crania are powerful icons of the violent interracial history of this country and the abuses committed for the sake of national expansion and research. Buried, they will show that the people of this country have accepted responsibility for their past wrongs.

Notes

1. See James Riding In, "Without Ethics and Morality: A Historical Overview of Imperial Archaeology and American Indians," *Arizona State Law Journal* 24 (Spring 1992):11–34.

2. Marvin H. Garfield, "The Indian Question in Congress and Kansas," *Kansas Historical Quarterly* 2 (February 1932): 37, 40–4.

3. Quoted in Garfield, "The Indian Question," 43.

4. Ibid., 10.

5. Ibid., 44.

6. Ibid., 42–44.

7. Idem, "The Military Posts as a Factor in the Frontier Defense of Kansas 1865–1869," *Kansas Historical Quarterly* 1 (November 1931): 50–62.

8. Quoted in Robert F. Berkhofer, Jr., *The White Man's Indian: Images of the American Indian from Columbus to the Present* (New York: Vintage Books, 1979), 58.

9. Alvin Josephy, *Now That the Buffalo Are Gone: A Study of Today's American Indians* (Norman, OK: University of Oklahoma Press, 1984), 31–34.

10. *Omaha Daily Republican,* 23 April 1873.

11. Ibid., 8 May 1873.

12. Memorandum for the information of medical office, 1 September 1868, quoted in D. S. Lamb, *The Army Medical Museum in American Anthropology* (Washington, DC: n.p., 1917), 626.

13. Robert E. Bieder, "A Brief Historical Survey of the Expropriation of American Indian Remains" (Unpublished ms., n.d.), 7–8.

14. See Reginald Horsman, *Race and Manifest Destiny: The Origins of American Racial Anglo-Saxonism* (Cambridge, MA: Harvard University Press, 1981).

15. Riding In, "Without Ethics and Morality."

16. J. R. Mead, "The Pawnee As I Knew Them," *Transactions of the Kansas State Historical Society* 9 (1906): 107–109.

17. National Archives, M617, Returns of Military Posts, reel 453, Fort Harker, January Returns, 1869; National Archives, Letters Received by the Office of the Adjutant General, 1861–70, reel 718, B. E. Fryer to post adjutant, Fort Harker, 25 February 1869; National Archives, McKeever to headquarters, Division of the Missouri, 6 March 1869.

18. National Archives, Smithsonian Institution, Office of Indian Affairs, microcopy 234, letters received, Pawnee agency, reel 660, Charles Whaley to H. Denman, 22 March 1869; Denman to N. B. Tay-

lor, 1 April 1869. For non-Pawnee accounts of the Mulberry Creek Massacre, see NA, OIA, M234, LR, R660, Edward Byrne to post adjutant, Fort Harker, KS, 31 January 1869, and sworn statement of Charles Martin, state of Kansas, Ellsworth County, 30 January 1869; *Annual Report of the Commissioner of Indian Affairs to the Secretary of Interior for the Year 1872* (Washington, DC: U. S. Government Printing Office, 1872), 223.

19. Smithsonian Institution, National Museum of Natural History, National Anthropological Archives, Army Medical Museum, box 2, file 509–531, B. E. Fryer to Bvt. Lt. Col. George Otis, 12 February 1869.

20. SI, NAA, B2, F509–531, Fryer to Otis, 11 March 1869.

21. Bieder, "A Brief Historical Survey," 38–39.

22. Ibid.

23. National Museum of Health and Medicine, AFIP 1002447, MM 573, PSS, Fryer to Otis, 5 February 1868.

24. Donald J. Berthrong, *The Southern Cheyenne* (Norman, OK: University of Oklahoma Press, 1963), 313–14.

25. SI, NAA, B2, F509–531, Fryer to Otis, 11 March 1869.

26. SI, NAA, Army Medical Museum Accession Records, "Master List."

27. Quoted in Paul S. Sledzik and Sean P. Murphy, "Research Opportunities in Osteopathology at the Armed Forces Medical Museum" (Unpublished ms., 1987), 3.

28. Ibid.

29. SI, NMNH, NAA, AMM, B2, F509–531, "List of Crania for Army Medical Museum," B. E. Fryer to Bvt. Lt. Col. George A. Otis, 11 March 1869; George A. Otis, *List of the Specimens in the Anatomical Section of the United States Army Medical Museum* (Washington, DC: Army Medical Museum, 1880), 122.

30. NA, SI, OIA, M234, LR, PA, R660, Samuel M. Janney to Ely S. Parker, 4 July 1869.

31. For discussions of the roles of Pawnee men, see Gene Weltfish, *The Lost Universe: Pawnee Life and Culture* (1965, reprinted Lincoln, NE: University of Nebraska Press, 1977) and Martha Royce Blaine, *Pawnee Passage: 1870–1875* (Norman, OK: University of Oklahoma Press, 1990).

32. NA, SI, OIA, M234, LR, PA, R660, Janney to Parker, 4 July 1869.

33. John B. Dunbar, "The Pawnee Indians: Their History and Ethnography," *Magazine of American History* 4 (April 1880): 262; George A. Dorsey and James R. Murie, *Notes on Skidi Pawnee Society,* ed. Alexander Spoehr (Field Museum of Natural History Anthropological Series 27, 1940), 87.

34. Blaine, *The Pawnee: A Critical Bibliography* (Bloomington, IN: Indiana University Press, 1980), 21–22; George Bird Grinnell, *Two Great Scouts and Their Pawnee Battalion* (1928; reprinted Lincoln, NE: University of Nebraska Press, 1973), 6.

35. NA, SI, OIA, M234, LR, PA, R660, Whaley to Denman, 22 March 1869. For works on the Pawnee Scouts, see George B. Grinnell,

Pawnee Hero Stories and Folk Tales (1889; reprinted Lincoln, NE: University of Nebraska Press, 1961), 323–24; Grinnell, *Two Great Scouts;* Thomas W. Dunlay, *Wolves for the Blue Soldiers: Indian Scouts and Auxiliaries with the United States Army, 1860–90* (Lincoln, NE: University of Nebraska Press, 1982); Donald F. Danker, *Man of the Plains: Recollections of Luther North, 1856–1882* (Lincoln, NE: University of Nebraska Press, 1961); Robert J. Bruce, *The Fighting Norths and the Pawnee Scouts: Narratives of Military Service on the Old Frontier* (Lincoln, NE: Nebraska Historical Society, 1932).

36. Grinnell, *Pawnee Hero Stories,* 323.

37. NA, SI, OIA, M234, LR, PA, R660, Janney to Parker, 1 August 1869, 2 February 1870; R661, Barclay White to F. A. Walker, 29 March 1872; White to E. P. Smith, 4 May 1874; Grinnell, *Two Great Scouts* 213, 245ff.

38. Orlan J. Svingen, "History of the Expropriation of Pawnee Indian Graves in the Control of the Nebraska State Historical Society" (Prepared for Native American Rights Fund, 1989), 9–14.

39. Nebraska State Historical Society, MS 504, Clarence Reckmeyer, Pawnee Indians, series 2, file 2, "Copied from the Unpublished History of the Pawnee Indians as Written by A. M. Brookings."

40. NSHS, Berndt Emil Bengston, "Two Pawnee Indian Villages and Burial Grounds," 25–26.

41. Svingen, "History of the Expropriation of Pawnee Indian Graves," 20.

42. Ibid., 12.

43. Ibid., 9–21.

44. *Omaha World-Herald,* 16 February 1989; *Lincoln Journal,* 18 October 1988. 2 March 1989; *Lincoln Star,* 16 December 1988, 1 January 1989; *Fremont Tribune,* 24 February 1989.

45. Walter R. Echo-Hawk, "Tribal Efforts to Protect against Mistreatment of Indian Dead: The Quest for Equal Protection of the Laws," *NARF Legal Review* 14 (Winter 1988): 1–4; H. Marcus Price III, *Disputing the Dead: U.S. Law on Aboriginal* Remains and Grave Goods (Columbia, MO: University of Missouri Press, 1991), 83–85; *Kansas City Star,* 25 November 1988; *The Pawnee (Oklahoma) Chief,* 5 September 1990.

46. This information was provided by Philip Mathews, Jr., of the Pawnee Tribal Business Council.

47. Price, *Disputing the Dead,* 31.

48. Correspondence from Douglas H. Ubelaker to Roger Echo-Hawk and James Riding In, 5 December 1989.

49. James Riding In, "Report Verifying the Identity of Six Pawnee Scout Crania at the Smithsonian Institution and the National Museum of Health and Medicine" (Prepared for the Native American Rights Fund, 1990).

50. Correspondence from Sledzik to Robert Chapman, Pawnee Tribal Chairman, 11 March 1991; Sledzik to Riding In, 18 October 1989, 3 January 1990.

Reading Critically: Questions for Discussion

1. This essay has a long and detailed title. Is a better title possible? If you think so, what title would you recommend? If you like the title, explain why.

2. Identify and locate the writer's claim. Does the writer offer sufficient, pertinent, and plausible evidence to prove the logic of his claim? Cite specific passages to justify your answer.

3. What is the writer's subordinate aim and purpose?

4. In declaring his position, the writer utilizes grisly descriptions of killings, mutilations, and dissections. Is this technique effective? Does it prove the logic of his claim or motivate the audience?

5. How does the writer establish his credibility? Does the citation of 50 information sources contribute to the writer's credibility? Why?

6. This essay includes two tables. Why does the writer choose to display this information in tables? Are additional illustrations desirable? Are additional illustrations necessary?

7. Do you consider this essay to be adversarial persuasion or conciliatory persuasion? Why? Which do you think is more likely to influence the reader's opinion? Why?

Knowledge by Participation and Observation: Evaluation

An Image of Africa: Racism in Conrad's *Heart of Darkness*
Chinua Achebe

Chinua Achebe was born in Ogidi, Eastern Nigeria. One of the first graduates of University College, Ibadan, Achebe has been on the faculty at the University of Nigeria, Nsukka, the University of Massachusetts, the University of Connecticut, and the University of Guelph in Ontario, Canada. He has also been awarded honorary doctorates from the University of Stirling, the University of Kent, and the University of Guelph. Although he is known chiefly as a novelist, Achebee has written essays, poetry, short stories, and children's literature. Among his publications are Things Fall Apart *(1958),* No Longer at Ease *(1960),* Arrow of God *(1964),* A Man of the People *(1966), and* Anthills of the Savannah *(1988). "An Image of Africa" was originally delivered as a public lecture at the University of Massachusetts, Amherst, and later published in the* Massachusetts Review. *A revised version appears in Achebe's* Hopes and Impediments *(1988). A scholar, teacher, and professional writer, Achebee's knowledge of his subject comes from both personal experience and library sources. Achebee uses a notes system of documentation in this essay.*

1   It was a fine autumn morning at the beginning of this academic year such as encouraged friendliness to passing strangers. Brisk youngsters were hurrying in all directions, many of them obviously freshmen in their first flush of enthusiasm. An older man, going the same way as I, turned and remarked to me how very young they came these days. I agreed. Then he asked me if I was a student too. I said no, I was a teacher. What did I teach? African literature. Now that was funny, he said, because he never had thought of Africa as having that kind of stuff, you know. By this time I was walking much faster. "Oh well," I heard him say finally, behind me, "I guess I have to take your course to find out."

2   A few weeks later I received two very touching letters from high school children in Yonkers, New York, who—bless their teacher—had just read *Things Fall Apart*. One of them was particularly happy to learn about the customs and superstitions of an African tribe.

3   I propose to draw from these rather trivial encounters rather heavy conclusions which at first sight might seem somewhat out of proportion to them: But only at first sight.

4   The young fellow from Yonkers, perhaps partly on account of his age but I believe also for much deeper and more serious reasons, is obviously unaware that the life of his own tribesmen in Yonkers, New York, is full of odd customs and superstitions and, like everybody else in his culture, imagines that he needs a trip to Africa to encounter those things.

5   The other person being fully my own age could not be excused on the grounds of his years. Ignorance might be a more likely reason; but here again I believe that something more willful than a mere lack of information was at work. For did not that erudite British historian and Regius Professor at Oxford, Hugh Trevor Roper, pronounce a few years ago that African history did not exist?

6   If there is something in these utterances more than youthful experience, more than a lack of factual knowledge, what is it? Quite simply it is the desire—one might indeed say the need—in Western psychology to set up Africa as a foil to Europe, a place of negations at once remote and vaguely familiar in comparison with which Europe's own state of spiritual grace will be manifest.

7   This need is not new: which should relieve us of considerable responsibility and perhaps make us even willing to look at this phenomenon dispassionately. I have neither the desire nor, indeed, the competence to do so with the tools of the social and biological sciences. But, I can respond, as a novelist, to one famous book of European fiction, Joseph Conrad's *Heart of Darkness,* which better than any other work I know displays that Western desire and need which I have just spoken about. Of course, there are whole libraries of books devoted to the same purpose, but most of them are so obvious and so crude that few people worry about them today. Conrad, on the other hand, is undoubtedly one of the great stylists of modern fiction and a

good storyteller into the bargain. His contribution therefore falls automatically into a different class—permanent literature—read and taught and constantly evaluated by serious academics. *Heart of Darkness* is indeed so secure today that a leading Conrad scholar has numbered it "among the half-dozen greatest short novels in the English language."[1] I will return to this critical opinion in due course because it may seriously modify my earlier suppositions about who may or may not be guilty in the things of which I will now speak.

8   *Heart of Darkness* projects the image of Africa as "the other world," the antithesis of Europe and therefore of civilization, a place where a man's vaunted intelligence and refinement are finally mocked by triumphant bestiality. The book opens on the River Thames, tranquil, resting peacefully "at the decline of day after ages of good service done to the race that peopled its banks." But the actual story takes place on the River Congo, the very antithesis of the Thames. The River Congo is quite decidedly not a River Emeritus. It has rendered no service and enjoys no old-age pension. We are told that "going up that river was like travelling back to the earliest beginning of the world."

9   Is Conrad saying then that these two rivers are very different, one good, the other bad? Yes, but that is not the real point. What actually worries Conrad is the lurking hint of kinship, of common ancestry. For the Thames, too, "has been one of the dark places of the earth." It conquered its darkness, of course, and is now at peace. But if it were to visit its primordial relative, the Congo, it would run the terrible risk of hearing grotesque, suggestive echoes of its own forgotten darkness, and of falling victim to an avenging recrudescence of the mindless frenzy of the first beginnings.

10   I am not going to waste your time with examples of Conrad's famed evocation of the African atmosphere. In the final consideration it amounts to no more than a steady, ponderous, fake-ritualistic repetition of two sentences, one about silence and the other about frenzy. An example of the former is "It was the stillness of an implacable force brooding over an inscrutable intention" and of the latter, "The steamer toiled along slowly on the edge of a black and incomprehensible frenzy." Of course, there is a judicious change of adjective from time to time so that instead of "inscrutable," for example, you might have "unspeakable," etc., etc.

11   The eagle-eyed English critic, F. R. Leavis, drew attention nearly thirty years ago to Conrad's "adjectival insistence upon inexpressible and incomprehensible mystery." That insistence must not be dismissed lightly, as many Conrad critics have tended to do, as a mere stylistic flaw. For it raises serious questions of artistic good faith. When a writer, while pretending to record scenes, incidents and their impact, is in reality engaged in inducing hypnotic stupor in his readers through a bombardment of emotive words and other forms of trickery, much more has to be at stake than stylistic felicity. Generally, nor-

mal readers are well armed to detect and resist such underhand activity. But Conrad chose his subject well—one which was guaranteed not to put him in conflict with the psychological predisposition of his readers or raise the need for him to contend with their resistance. He chose the role of purveyor of comforting myths.

12   The most interesting and revealing passages in *Heart of Darkness* are, however, about people. I must quote a long passage from the middle of the story in which representatives of Europe in a steamer going down the Congo encounter the denizens of Africa:

> We were wanderers on a prehistoric earth, on an earth that wore the aspect of an unknown planet. We could have fancied ourselves the first of men taking possession of an accursed inheritance, to be subdued at the cost of profound anguish and of excessive toil. But suddenly, as we struggled round a bend, there would be a glimpse of rush walls, of peaked grass-roofs, a burst of yells, a whirl of black limbs, a mass of hands clapping, of feet stamping of bodies swaying, of eyes rolling, under the droop of heavy and motionless foliage. The steamer toiled along slowly on the edge of a black and incomprehensible frenzy. The prehistoric man was cursing us, praying to us, welcoming us—who could tell? We were cut off from the comprehension of our surroundings; we glided past like phantoms, wondering and secretly appalled as sane men would be before an enthusiastic outbreak in a madhouse. We could not remember because we were travelling in the night of first ages, of those ages that are gone, leaving hardly a sign—and no memories.
>
> The earth seemed unearthly. We are accustomed to look upon the shackled form of a conquered monster, but there—there you could look at a thing monstrous and free. It was unearthly, and the men were—No, they were not inhuman. Well, you know, that was the worst of it—this suspicion of their not being inhuman. It would come slowly to one. They howled and leaped, and spun, and made horrid faces; but what thrilled you was just the thought of your remote kinship with this wild and passionate uproar. Ugly. Yes, it was ugly enough; but if you were man enough you would admit to yourself that there was in you just the faintest trace of a response to the terrible frankness of that noise, a dim suspicion of there being a meaning in it which you—you so remote from the night of first ages—could comprehend.

Herein lies the meaning of *Heart of Darkness* and the fascination it holds over the Western mind: "What thrilled you was just the thought of their humanity—like yours. . . . Ugly."

13   Having shown us Africa in the mass, Conrad then zeros in on a specific example, giving us one of his rare descriptions of an African who is not just limbs or rolling eyes:

> And between whiles I had to look after the savage who was fireman. He was an improved specimen; he could fire up a vertical boiler. He was there below me, and, upon my word, to look at him was as edifying as seeing a dog in a parody of breeches and a feather hat, walking on his hind legs. A few months of training had done for that really fine chap. He

squinted at the steam gauge and at the water gauge with an evident effort of intrepidity—and he had filed his teeth, too, the poor devil, and the wool of his pate shaved into queer patterns, and three ornamental scars on each of his cheeks. He ought to have been clapping his hands and stamping his feet on the bank, instead of which he was hard at work, a thrall to strange witchcraft, full of improving knowledge.

As everybody knows, Conrad is a romantic on the side. He might not exactly admire savages clapping their hands and stamping their feet but they have at least the merit of being in their place, unlike this dog in a parody of breeches. For Conrad, things (and persons) being in their place is of the utmost importance.

14   Towards the end of the story, Conrad lavishes great attention quite unexpectedly on an African woman who has obviously been some kind of mistress to Mr. Kurtz and now presides (if I may be permitted a little imitation of Conrad) like a formidable mystery over the inexorable imminence of his departure:

> She was savage and superb, wild-eyed and magnificent . . . She stood looking at us without a stir and like the wilderness itself, with an air of brooding over an inscrutable purpose.

This Amazon is drawn in considerable detail, albeit of a predictable nature, for two reasons. First, she is in her place and so can win Conrad's special brand of approval; and second, she fulfills a structural requirement of the story; she is a savage counterpart to the refined, European woman with whom the story will end:

> She came forward, all in black with a pale head, floating towards me in the dusk. She was in mourning. . . . She took both my hands in hers and murmured, "I had heard you were coming" . . . She had a mature capacity for fidelity, for belief, for suffering.

15   The difference in the attitude of the novelist to these two women is conveyed in too many direct and subtle ways to need elaboration. But perhaps the most significant difference is the one implied in the author's bestowal of human expression to the one and the withholding of it from the other. It is clearly not part of Conrad's purpose to confer language on the "rudimentary souls" of Africa. They only "exchanged short grunting phrases" even among themselves but mostly they were too busy with their frenzy. There are two occasions in the book, however, when Conrad departs somewhat from his practice and confers speech, even English speech, on the savages. The first occurs when cannibalism gets the better of them:

> "Catch 'im," he snapped, with a bloodshot widening of his eyes and a flash of sharp white teeth—"catch 'im. Give 'im to us." "To you, eh?" I asked. "What would you do with them?" "Eat 'im!" he said curtly . . .

The other occasion is the famous announcement:

> Mistah Kurtz—he dead.

At first sight, these instances might be mistaken for unexpected acts of generosity from Conrad. In reality, they constitute some of his best assaults. In the case of the cannibals, the incomprehensible grunts that had thus far served them for speech suddenly proved inadequate for Conrad's purpose of letting the European glimpse the unspeakable craving in their hearts. Weighing the necessity for consistency in the portrayal of the dumb brutes against the sensational advantages of securing their conviction by clear, unambiguous evidence issuing out of their own mouth, Conrad chose the latter. As for the announcement of Mr. Kurtz's death by the "insolent black head in the doorway," what better or more appropriate *finis* could be written to the horror story of that wayward child of civilization who willfully had given his soul to the powers of darkness and "taken a high seat amongst the devils of the land" than the proclamation of his physical death by the forces he had joined?

16   It might be contended, of course, that the attitude to the African in *Heart of Darkness* is not Conrad's but that of his fictional narrator, Marlow, and that far from endorsing it Conrad might indeed be holding it up to irony and criticism. Certainly, Conrad appears to go to considerable pains to set up layers of insulation between himself and the moral universe of his story. He has, for example, a narrator behind a narrator. The primary narrator is Marlow but his account is given to us through the filter of a second, shadowy person. But if Conrad's intention is to draw a *cordon sanitaire* between himself and the moral and psychological malaise of his narrator, his care seems to me totally wasted because he neglects to hint however subtly or tentatively at an alternative frame of reference by which we may judge the actions and opinions of his characters. It would not have been beyond Conrad's power to make that provision if he had thought it necessary. Marlow seems to me to enjoy Conrad's complete confidence—a feeling reinforced by the close similarities between their careers.

17   Marlow comes through to us not only as a witness of truth, but one holding those advanced and humane views appropriate to the English liberal tradition which required all Englishmen of decency to be deeply shocked by atrocities in Bulgaria or the Congo of King Leopold of the Belgians or wherever. Thus Marlow is able to toss out such bleeding-heart sentiments as these:

> They were all dying slowly—it was very clear. They were not enemies, they were not criminals, they were nothing earthly now—nothing but black shadows of disease and starvation, lying confusedly in the greenish gloom. Brought from all the recesses of the coast in all the legality of time contracts lost in uncongenial surroundings, fed on unfamiliar food, they sickened, became inefficient, and were then allowed to crawl away and rest.

The kind of liberalism espoused here by Marlow/Conrad touched all the best minds of the age in England, Europe, and America. It took different forms in the minds of different people but almost always managed to sidestep the ultimate question of equality between white people and black people. That extraordinary missionary, Albert Schweitzer, who sacrificed brilliant careers in music and theology in Europe for a life of service to Africans in much the same area as Conrad writes about, epitomizes the ambivalence. In a comment which I have often quoted but must quote one last time Schweitzer says: "The African is indeed my brother but my junior brother." And so he proceeded to build a hospital appropriate to the needs of junior brothers with standards of hygiene reminiscent of medical practice in the days before the germ theory of disease came into being. Naturally, he became a sensation in Europe and America. Pilgrims flocked, and I believe still flock even after he has passed on, to witness the prodigious miracle in Lamberene, on the edge of the primeval forest.

18   Conrad's liberalism would not take him quite as far as Schweitzer's, though. He would not use the word "brother" however qualified; the farthest he would go was "kinship." When Marlow's African helmsman falls down with a spear in his heart he gives his white master one final disquieting look.

> And the intimate profundity of that look he gave me when he received his hurt remains to this day in my memory—like a claim of distant kinship affirmed in a supreme moment.

It is important to note that Conrad, careful as ever with his words, is not talking so much about *distant kinship* as about someone *laying a claim* on it. The black man lays a claim on the white man which is well-nigh intolerable. It is the laying of this claim which frightens and at the same time fascinates Conrad, ". . . the thought of their humanity—like yours . . . Ugly."

19   The point of my observations should be quite clear by now, namely, that Conrad was a bloody racist. That this simple truth is glossed over in criticism of his work is due to the fact that white racism against Africa is such a normal way of thinking that its manifestations go completely undetected. Students of *Heart of Darkness* will often tell you that Conrad is concerned not so much with Africa as with the deterioration of one European mind caused by solitude and sickness. They will point out to you that Conrad is, if anything, less charitable to the Europeans in the story than he is to the natives. A Conrad student told me in Scotland last year that Africa is merely a setting for the disintegration of the mind of Mr. Kurtz.

20   Which is partly the point: Africa as setting and backdrop which eliminates the African as human factor. Africa as a metaphysical battlefield devoid of all recognizable humanity, into which the wandering European enters at his peril. Of course, there is a preposterous and perverse kind of arrogance in thus reducing Africa to the role of props

for the breakup of one petty European mind. But that is not even the point. The real question is the dehumanization of Africa and Africans which this age-long attitude has fostered and continues to foster in the world. And the question is whether a novel which celebrates this dehumanization, which depersonalizes a portion of the human race, can be called a great work of art. My answer is: No, it cannot. I would not call that man an artist, for example, who composes an eloquent instigation to one people to fall upon another and destroy them. No matter how striking his imagery or how beautifully his cadences fall, such a man is no more a great artist than another may be called a priest who reads the mass backwards or a physician who poisons his patients. All those men in Nazi Germany who lent their talent to the service of virulent racism whether in science, philosophy or the arts have generally and rightly been condemned for their perversions. The time is long overdue for taking a hard look at the work of creative artists who apply their talents, alas often considerable as in the case of Conrad, to set people against people. This, I take it, is what Yevtushenko is after when he tells us that a poet cannot be a slave trader at the same time, and gives the striking examples of Arthur Rimbaud, who was fortunately honest enough to give up any pretenses to poetry when he opted for slave trading. For poetry surely can only be on the side of man's deliverance and not his enslavement; for the brotherhood and unity of all mankind and against the doctrines of Hitler's master races or Conrad's "rudimentary souls."

21   Last year was the 50th anniversary of Conrad's death. He was born in 1857, the very year in which the first Anglican missionaries were arriving among my own people in Nigeria. It was certainly not his fault that he lived his life at a time when the reputation of the black man was at a particularly low level. But even after due allowances have been made for all the influences of contemporary prejudice on his sensibility, there remains still in Conrad's attitude a residue of antipathy to black people which his peculiar psychology alone can explain. His own account of his first encounter with a black man is very revealing:

> A certain enormous buck nigger encountered in Haiti fixed my conception of blind, furious, unreasoning rage, as manifested in the human animal to the end of my days. Of the nigger I used to dream for years afterwards.

Certainly, Conrad had a problem with niggers. His inordinate love of that word itself should be of interest to psychoanalysts. Sometimes his fixation on blackness is equally interesting as when he gives us this brief description:

> A black figure stood up, strode on long black legs, waving long black arms.[2]

As though we might expect a black figure striding along on black legs to wave *white* arms! But so unrelenting is Conrad's obsession.

22   As a matter of interest Conrad gives us in *A Personal Record* what amounts to a companion piece to the buck nigger of Haiti. At the age of sixteen Conrad encountered his first Englishman in Europe. He calls him "my unforgettable Englishman" and describes him in the following manner:

> [his] calves exposed to the public gaze . . . dazzled the beholder by the splendor of their marble-like condition and their rich tone of young ivory . . . The light of a headlong, exalted satisfaction with the world of men . . . illumined his face . . . and triumphant eyes. In passing he cast a glance of kindly curiosity and a friendly gleam of big, sound, shiny teeth . . . his white calves twinkled sturdily.[3]

Irrational love and irrational hate jostling together in the heart of that tormented man. But whereas irrational love may at worst engender foolish acts of indiscretion, irrational hate can endanger the life of the community. Naturally, Conrad is a dream for psychoanalytic critics. Perhaps the most detailed study of him in this direction is by Bernard C. Meyer, M.D. In this lengthy book, Dr. Meyer follows every conceivable lead (and sometimes inconceivable ones) to explain Conrad. As an example, he gives us long disquisitions on the significance of hair and hair-cutting in Conrad. And yet not even one word is spared for his attitude to black people. Not even the discussion of Conrad's anti-Semitism was enough to spark off in Dr. Meyer's mind those other dark and explosive thoughts. Which only leads one to surmise that Western psychoanalysts must regard the kind of racism displayed by Conrad as absolutely normal despite the profoundly important work done by Frantz Fanon in the psychiatric hospitals of French Algeria.

23   Whatever Conrad's problems were, you might say he is now safely dead. Quite true. Unfortunately, his heart of darkness plagues us still. Which is why an offensive and totally deplorable book can be described by a serious scholar as "among the half dozen greatest short novels in the English language," and why it is today perhaps the most commonly prescribed novel in the twentieth-century literature courses in our own English Department here. Indeed the time is long overdue for a hard look at things.

24   There are two probable grounds on which what I have said so far may be contested. The first is that it is no concern of fiction to please people about whom it is written. I will go along with that. But I am not talking about pleasing people. I am talking about a book which parades in the most vulgar fashion prejudices and insults from which a section of mankind has suffered untold agonies and atrocities in the past and continues to do so in many ways and many places today. I am talking about a story in which the very humanity of black people is called in question. It seems to me totally inconceivable that great art or even good art could possibly reside in such unwholesome surroundings.

25   Secondly, I may be challenged on the grounds of actuality. Conrad, after all, sailed down the Congo in 1890 when my own father was

still a babe in arms, and recorded what he saw. How could I stand up in 1975, fifty years after his death and purport to contradict him? My answer is that as a sensible man I will not accept just any traveller's tales solely on the grounds that I have not made the journey myself. I will not trust the evidence even of a man's very eyes when I suspect them to be as jaundiced as Conrad's. And we also happen to know that Conrad was, in the words of his biographer, Bernard C. Meyer, "notoriously inaccurate in the rendering of his own history."4

26   But more important by far is the abundant testimony about Conrad's savages which we could gather if we were so inclined from other sources and which might lead us to think that these people must have had other occupations besides merging into the evil forest or materializing out of it simply to plague Marlow and his dispirited band. For as it happened, soon after Conrad had written his book an event of far greater consequence was taking place in the art world of Europe. This is how Frank Willett, a British art historian, describes it:

> Gauguin had gone to Tahiti, the most extravagant individual act of turn-ing to a non-European culture in the decades immediately before and after 1900, when European artists were avid for new artistic experiences, but it was only about 1904–5 that African art began to make its distinctive impact. One piece is still identifiable; it is a mask that had been given to Maurice Vlaminck in 1905. He records that Derain was "speechless" and "stunned" when he saw it, bought it from Vlaminck and in turn showed it to Picasso and Matisse, who were also greatly affected by it. Ambroise Vollard then borrowed it and had it cast in bronze . . . The revolution of twentieth century art was under way!5

The mask in question was made by other savages living just north of Conrad's River Congo. They have a name, the Fang people, and are without a doubt among the world's greatest masters of the sculptured form. As you might have guessed, the event to which Frank Willett refers marked the beginning of cubism and the infusion of new life into European art that had run completely out of strength.

27   The point of all this is to suggest that Conrad's picture of the peo-ple of the Congo seems grossly inadequate even at the height of their subjection to the ravages of King Leopold's International Association for the Civilization of Central Africa.

28   Travellers with closed minds can tell us little except about them-selves. But even those not blinkered, like Conrad, with xenophobia, can be astonishingly blind. Let me digress a little here. One of the greatest and most intrepid travellers of all time, Marco Polo, journeyed to the Far East from the Mediterranean in the thirteenth century and spent twenty years in the court of Kublai Khan in China. On his return to Venice he set down in his book entitled *Description of the World* his impressions of the peoples and places and customs he had seen. There are at least two extraordinary omissions in his account. He says

nothing about the art of printing unknown as yet in Europe but in full flower in China. He either did not notice it at all or if he did, failed to see what use Europe could possibly have for it. Whatever reason, Europe had to wait another hundred years for Gutenberg. But even more spectacular was Marco Polo's omission of any reference to the Great Wall of China nearly 4000 miles long and already more than 1000 years old at the time of his visit. Again, he may not have seen it; but the Great Wall of China is the only structure built by man which is visible from the moon![6] Indeed, travellers can be blind.

29   As I said earlier, Conrad did not originate the image of Africa which we find in his book. It was and is the dominant image of Africa in the Western imagination and Conrad merely brought the peculiar gifts of his own mind to bear on it. For reasons which can certainly use close psychological inquiry, the West seems to suffer deep anxieties about the precariousness of its civilization and to have a need for constant reassurance by comparing itself to Africa. If Europe, advancing in civilization, could cast a backward glance periodically at Africa trapped in primordial barbarity, it could say with faith and feeling: There, but for the grace of God, go I. Africa is to Europe as the picture is to Dorian Gray—a carrier onto whom the master unloads his physical and moral deformities so that he may go forward, erect and immaculate. Consequently, Africa is something to be avoided just as the picture has to be hidden away to safeguard the man's jeopardous integrity. Keep away from Africa, or else! Mr. Kurtz of *Heart of Darkness* should have heeded that warning and the prowling horror in his heart would have kept its place, chained to its lair. But he foolishly exposed himself to the wild irresistible allure of the jungle and lo! the darkness found him out.

30   In my original conception of this talk I had thought to conclude it nicely on an appropriately positive note in which I would suggest from my privileged position in African and Western culture some advantages the West might derive from Africa once it rid its mind of old prejudices and began to look at Africa not through a haze of distortions and cheap mystification but quite simply as a continent of people—not angels, but not rudimentary souls either—just people, often highly gifted people and often strikingly successful in their enterprise with life and society. But as I thought more about the stereotype image, about its grip and pervasiveness, about the willful tenacity with which the West holds it to its heart; when I thought of your television and the cinema and newspapers, about books read in schools and out of school, of churches preaching to empty pews about the need to send help to the heathen in Africa, I realized that no easy optimism was possible. And there is something totally wrong in offering bribes to the West in return for its good opinion of Africa. Ultimately, the abandonment of unwholesome thoughts must be its own and only reward. Although I have used the word *willful* a few times in this talk to characterize the West's view of Africa it may well

be that what is happening at this stage is more akin to reflex action than calculated malice. Which does not make the situation more, but less, hopeful. Let me give you one last and really minor example of what I mean.

31 Last November the *Christian Science Monitor* carried an interesting article written by its education editor on the serious psychological and learning problems faced by little children who speak one language at home and then go to school where something else is spoken. It was a wide-ranging article taking in Spanish speaking children in this country, the children of migrant Italian workers in Germany, the quadrilingual phenomenon in Malaysia and so on. And all this while the article speaks unequivocally about *language*. But then out of the blue sky comes this:

> In London there is an enormous immigration of children who speak Indian or Nigerian dialects, or some other native language.[7]

32 I believe that the introduction of *dialects,* which is technically erroneous in the context, is almost a reflex action caused by an instinctive desire of the writer to downgrade the discussion to the level of Africa and India. And this is quite comparable to Conrad's withholding of language from his rudimentary souls. Language is too grand for these chaps; let's give them dialects. In all this business a lot of violence is inevitably done to words and their meaning. Look at the phrase "native language" in the above excerpt. Surely the only native language possible in London is Cockney English. But our writer obviously means some thing else—something Indians and Africans speak.

33 Perhaps a change will come. Perhaps this is the time when it can begin, when the high optimism engendered by the breathtaking achievements of Western science and industry is giving way to doubt and even confusion. There is just the possibility that Western man may begin to look seriously at the achievements of other people. I read in the papers the other day a suggestion that what America needs at this time is somehow to bring back the extended family. And I saw in my mind's eye future African Peace Corps Volunteers coming to help you set up the system.

34 Seriously, although the work which needs to be done may appear too daunting, I believe that it is not one day too soon to begin. And where better than at a University?

Notes

1. Albert J. Guerard, Introduction to *Heart of Darkness* (New York: New American Library, 1950), p. 9.

2. Jonah Raskin, *The Mythology of Imperialism* (New York: Random House, 1971), p. 143.

3. Bernard C. Meyer, M.D., *Joseph Conrad. A Psychoanalytic Biography* (Princeton, N.J.: Princeton University Press, 1967), p. 30.

4. *Ibid.,* p. 30.

5. Frank Willett, *African Art* (New York: Praeger, 1971), pp. 35–36.

6. About the omission of the Great Wall of China I am indebted to *The Journey of Marco Polo* as re-created by artist Michael Foreman, published by *Pegasus* magazine, 1974.

7. *Christian Science Monitor,* Nov. 25, 1974, p. 11.

Reading Critically: Questions for Discussion

1. In the third paragraph, the writer advises "I propose to draw from these rather trivial encounters rather heavy conclusions which at first sight might seem somewhat out of proportion to them: But only at first sight." What is the purpose of this warning? Is it designed to keep the audience from objecting to his conclusions? Is this technique effective? Why do you think it is or isn't?

2. Do you have to be familiar with Joseph Conrad's *Heart of Darkness* in order to appreciate this evaluation or consider it convincing?

3. What is the writer's opinion of *Heart of Darkness?* Is the writer adversarial or conciliatory? Cite specific passages to support your answer.

4. What is the writer's primary purpose? What is his subordinate purpose?

5. How does the writer establish his credibility to address this subject? Does he try to identify with his audience? Does he employ self-deprecation? Does he show that he has no ulterior motivations?

6. To support his claim, the writer offers several quotations from *Heart of Darkness.* Is this evidence sufficient, plausible, and pertinent? Is additional evidence necessary?

7. How does the writer motivate his audience to approve his claim? Does he use statistics, examples, narratives, quotations, similes and metaphors, questions and directions?

Knowledge by Participation and Observation: Position

Life on the Global Assembly Line

Barbara Ehrenreich and Annette Fuentes

Barbara Ehrenreich is a journalist whose works include these coauthored works: The American Health Empire *(1970),* Witches, Midwives and Nurses: A History of Women Healers *(1972), and* For Her Own Good: 150 Years of the

Experts Advice to Women (1979); in addition, she has written Re-Making Love: The Feminization of Sex *(1986), and* Fear of Falling *(1986). Like Ehrenreich, Annette Fuentes is also a journalist concerned with women's issues. She serves as the editor of* Sisterhood Is Global.

"Life on the Global Assembly Line" was printed in Ms. *magazine. In this essay, Ehrenreich and Fuentes question the effects of large corporations when they locate businesses in developing countries and employ laborers—usually women who work for extremely low wages in dangerous workplaces and jobs. As journalists, Ehrenreich and Fuentes draw from their own knowledge of women's jobs and wages in the American workplace and investigate numerous sources to write this essay. In writing for the general readers of* Ms., *the authors document their sources by identifying their sources (i.e., tagging) within their text rather than using footnotes, endnotes, or formal bibliographies.*

1   *In Ciudad Juarez, Mexico, Anna M. rises at 5 A.M. to feed her son before starting on the two hour bus trip to the* maquiladora *(factory). He will spend the day along with four other children in a neighbor's one-room home. Anna's husband, frustrated by being unable to find work for himself left for the United States six months ago. She wonders, as she carefully applies her new lip gloss, whether she ought to consider herself still married. It might be good to take a night course, become a secretary. But she seldom gets home before eight at night, and the factory, where she stitches brassieres that will be sold in the United States through J. C. Penney, pays only $48 a week.*

2   *In Penang, Malaysia, Julie K. is up before the three other young women with whom she shares a room, and starts heating the leftover rice from last night's supper. She looks good in the company's green-trimmed uniform, and she's proud to work in a modern, American-owned factory. Only not quite so proud as when she started working three years ago—she thinks as she squints out the door at a passing group of women. Her job involves peering all day through a microscope, bonding hair-thin gold wires to a silicon chip destined to end up inside a pocket calculator, and at 21, she is afraid she can no longer see very clearly.*

3   Every morning, between four and seven, thousands of women like Anna and Julie head out for the day shift. In Ciudad Juarez, they crowd into *ruteras* (run-down vans) for the trip from the slum neighborhoods to the industrial parks on the outskirts of the city. In Penang they squeeze, 60 or more at a time, into buses for the trip from the village to the low, modern factory buildings of the Bayan Lepas free trade zone. In Taiwan, they walk from the dormitories—where the

night shift is already asleep in the still-warm beds—through the checkpoints in the high fence surrounding the factory zone.

4   This is the world's new industrial proletariat: young, female, Third World. Viewed from the "first world," they are still faceless, genderless "cheap labor," signaling their existence only through a label or tiny imprint—"made in Hong Kong," or Taiwan, Korea, the Dominican Republic, Mexico, the Philippines. But they may be one of the most strategic blocs of womanpower in the world of the 1980s. Conservatively, there are 2 million Third World female industrial workers employed now, millions more looking for work, and their numbers are rising every year. Anyone whose image of Third World women features picturesque peasants with babies slung on their backs should be prepared to update it. Just in the last decade, Third World women have become a critical element in the global economy and a key "resource" for expanding multinational corporations.

5   It doesn't take more than second-grade arithmetic to understand what's happening. In the United States, an assembly-line worker is likely to earn, depending on her length of employment, between $3.10 and $5 an hour. In many Third World countries, a woman doing the same work will earn $3 to $5 a *day*. According to the magazine *Business Asia* in 1976 the average hourly wage for unskilled work (male or female) was 55 cents in Hong Kong, 52 cents in South Korea, 32 cents in the Philippines, and 17 cents in Indonesia. The logic of the situation is compelling: why pay someone in Massachusetts $5 an hour to do what someone in Manila will do for $2.50 a day? Or, as a corollary, why pay a male worker anywhere to do what a female worker will do for 40 to 60 percent less?

6   And so, almost everything that can be packed up is being moved out to the Third World; not heavy industry, but just about anything light enough to travel—garment manufacture, textiles, toys, foot wear, pharmaceuticals, wigs, appliance parts, tape decks, computer components, plastic goods. In some industries, like garment and textile, American jobs are lost in the process, and the biggest losers are women, often black and Hispanic. But what's going on is much more than a matter of runaway shops. Economists are talking about a "new international division of labor," in which the process of production is broken down and the fragments are dispersed to different parts of the world. In general, the low-skilled jobs are farmed out to the Third World, where labor costs are minuscule, while control over the overall process and technology remains safely at company headquarters in "first world" countries like the United States and Japan.

7   The American electronics industry provides a classic example: circuits are printed on silicon wafers and tested in California; then the wafers are shipped to Asia for the labor-intensive process by which they are cut into tiny chips and bonded to circuit boards; final assembly into products such as calculators or military equipment usually

takes place in the United States. Garment manufacture too is often broken into geographically separated steps, with the most repetitive, labor-intensive jobs going to the poor countries of the southern hemisphere. Most Third World countries welcome whatever jobs come their way in the new division of labor, and the major international development agencies—like the World Bank and the United States Agency for International Development (AID)—encourage them to take what they can get.

8   So much any economist could tell you. What is less often noted is the *gender* breakdown of the emerging international division of labor. Eighty to 90 percent of the low-skilled assembly jobs that go to the Third World are performed by women—in a remarkable switch from earlier patterns of foreign-dominated industrialization. Until now, "development" under the aegis of foreign corporations has usually meant more jobs for men and—compared to traditional agricultural society—a diminished economic status for women. But multinational corporations and Third World governments alike consider assembly line work—whether the product is Barbie dolls or missile parts—to be "women's work."

9   One reason is that women can, in many countries, still be legally paid less than men. But the sheer tedium of the jobs adds to the multinationals' preference for women workers—a preference made clear, for example, by this ad from a Mexican newspaper: *We need female workers; older than 17, younger than 30; single and without children: minimum education primary school, maximum education one year of preparatory school (high school): available for all shifts.*

10   It's an article of faith with management that only women can do, or will do, the monotonous, painstaking work that American business is exporting to the Third World. Bill Mitchell, whose job is to attract United States businesses to the Bermudez Industrial Park in Ciudad Juarez told us with a certain macho pride: "A man just won't stay in this tedious kind of work. He'd walk out in a couple of hours." The personnel manager of a light assembly plant in Taiwan told anthropologist Linda Gail Arrigo: "Young male workers are too restless and impatient to do monotonous work with no career value. If displeased, they sabotage the machines and even threaten the foreman. But girls? At most, they cry a little."

11   In fact, the American businessmen we talked to claimed that Third World women genuinely enjoy doing the very things that would drive a man to assault and sabotage. "You should watch these kids going into work," Bill Mitchell told us. "You don't have any sullenness here. They smile." A top-level management consultant who specializes in advising American companies on where to relocate their factories gave us this global generalization: "The [factory] girls genuinely enjoy themselves. They're away from their families. They

have spending money. They can buy motorbikes, whatever. Of course it's a regulated experience too—with dormitories to live in—so it's a healthful experience."

12   What is the real experience of the women in the emerging Third World industrial work force? The conventional Western stereotypes leap to mind: You can't really compare, the standards are so different. . . . Everything's easier in warm countries. . . . They really don't have any alternatives. . . . Commenting on the low wages his company pays its women workers in Singapore, a Hewlett-Packard vice-president said, "They live much differently here than we do. . . ." But the differences are ultimately very simple. To start with, they have less money.

13   The great majority of the women in the new Third World work force live at or near the subsistence level for one person, whether they work for a multinational corporation or a locally owned factory. In the Philippines, for example, starting wages in U.S.-owned electronics plants are between $34 to $46 a month, compared to a cost of living of $37 a month; in Indonesia the starting wages are actually about $7 a month less than the cost of living. "Living," in these cases, should be interpreted minimally: a diet of rice, dried fish, and water—a Coke might cost a half-day's wages—lodging in a room occupied by four or more other people. Rachael Grossman, a researcher with the Southeast Asia Resource Center, found women employees of U.S. multinational firms in Malaysia and the Philippines living four to eight in a room in boardinghouses, or squeezing into tiny extensions built onto squatter huts near the factory. Where companies do provide dormitories for their employees, they are not of the "healthful," collegiate variety implied by our corporate informant. Staff from the American Friends Service Committee report that dormitory space is "likely to be crowded, with bed rotation paralleling shift rotation—while one shift works, another sleeps, as many as twenty to a room." In one case in Thailand, they found the dormitory "filthy," with workers forced to find their own place to sleep among "splintered floorboards, rusting sheets of metal, and scraps of dirty cloth."

14   Wages do increase with seniority, but the money does not go to pay for studio apartments or, very likely, motorbikes. A 1970 study of young women factory workers in Hong Kong found that 88 percent of them were turning more than half their earnings over to their parents. In areas that are still largely agricultural (such as parts of the Philippines and Malaysia), or places where male unemployment runs high (such as northern Mexico), a woman factory worker may be the sole source of cash income for an entire extended family.

15   But wages on a par with what an 11-year-old American could earn on a paper route, and living conditions resembling what Engels found in 19th-century Manchester are only part of the story. The rest

begins at the factory gate. The work that multinational corporations export to the Third World is not only the most tedious, but often the most hazardous part of the production process. The countries they go to are, for the most part, those that will guarantee no interference from health and safety inspectors, trade unions, or even free-lance reformers. As a result, most Third World factory women work under conditions that already have broken or will break their health—or their nerves—within a few years, and often before they've worked long enough to earn any more than a subsistence wage.

16   Consider first the electronics industry, which is generally thought to be the safest and cleanest of the exported industries. The factory buildings are low and modern, like those one might find in a suburban American industrial park. Inside, rows of young women, neatly dressed in the company uniform or T-shirt, work quietly at their stations. There is air conditioning (not for the women's comfort, but to protect the delicate semiconductor parts they work with), and high volume piped-in Bee Gees hits (not so much for entertainment, as to prevent talking).

17   For many Third World women, electronics is a prestige occupation, at least compared to other kinds of factory work. They are unlikely to know that in the United States the National Institute on Occupational Safety and Health (NIOSH) has placed electronics on its select list of "high health-risk industries using the greatest number of toxic substances." If electronics assembly work is risky here, it is doubly so in countries where there is no equivalent of NIOSH to even issue warnings. In many plants toxic chemicals and solvents sit in open containers, filling the work area with fumes that can literally knock you out. "We have been told of cases where ten to twelve women passed out at once," an AFSC field worker in northern Mexico told us, "and the newspapers report this as 'mass hysteria.'"

18   In one stage of the electronics assembly process, the workers have to dip the circuits into open vats of acid. According to Irene Johnson and Carol Bragg, who toured the National Semiconductor plant in Penang, Malaysia, the women who do the dipping "wear rubber gloves and boots, but these sometimes leak, and burns are common." Occasionally, whole fingers are lost. More commonly, what electronics workers lose is the 20/20 vision they are required to have when they are hired. Most electronics workers spend seven to nine hours a day peering through microscopes, straining to meet their quotas.

19   One study in South Korea found that most electronics assembly workers developed severe eye problems after only one year of employment; 88 percent had chronic conjunctivitis; 44 percent became near sighted, and 19 percent developed astigmatism. A manager for Hewlett-Packard's Malaysia plant, in an interview with Rachael Grossman, denied that there were any eye problems. "These girls are used to working with scopes. We've found no eye problems. But it sure makes me dizzy to look through those things."

20   Electronics, recall, is the "cleanest" of the exported industries. Conditions in the garment and textile industry rival those of any 19th-century (or 20th—see below) sweatshop. The firms, generally local subcontractors to large American chains such as J.C. Penney and Sears, as well as smaller manufacturers, are usually even more indifferent to the health of their employees than the multinationals. Some of the worst conditions have been documented in South Korea, where the garment and textile industries have helped spark that country's "economic miracle." Workers are packed into poorly lit rooms, where summer temperatures rise above 100 degrees. Textile dust, which can cause permanent lung damage, fills the air. When there are rush orders, management may require forced overtime of as much as 48 hours at a stretch, and if that seems to go beyond the limits of human endurance, pep pills and amphetamine injections are thoughtfully provided. In her diary (originally published in a magazine now banned by the South Korean government) Min Chong Suk, 30, a sewing machine operator, wrote of working from 7 A.M. to 11:30 P.M. in a garment factory. "When [the apprentices] shake the waste threads from the clothes, the whole room fills with dust, and it is hard to breathe. Since we've been working in such dusty air, there have been increasing numbers of people getting tuberculosis, bronchitis, and eye diseases. Since we are women, it makes us so sad when we have pale, unhealthy, wrinkled faces like dried-up spinach. . . . It seems to me that no one knows our blood dissolves into the threads and seams, with sighs and sorrow."

21   In all the exported industries, the most invidious, inescapable health hazard is stress. On their home ground United States corporations are not likely to sacrifice productivity for human comfort. On someone else's home ground, however, anything goes. Lunch breaks may be barely long enough for a woman to stand in line at the canteen or hawkers' stalls. Visits to the bathroom are treated as privilege; in some cases, workers must raise their hands for permission to use the toilet, and waits up to a half hour are common. Rotating shifts—the day shift one week, the night shift the next—wreak havoc with sleep patterns. Because inaccuracies or failure to meet production quotas can mean substantial pay losses, the pressures are quickly internalized; stomach ailments and nervous problems are not unusual in the multinationals' Third World female work force. In some situations, good work is as likely to be punished as slow or shoddy work. Correspondent Michael Flannery, writing for the AFL-CIO's *American Federationist,* tells the story of 23-year-old Basilia Altagracia, a seamstress who stitched collars onto ladies' blouses in the La Romana (Dominican Republic) free trade zone (a heavily guarded industrial zone owned by Gulf & Western Industries, Inc.):

22   "A nimble veteran seamstress, Miss Altagracia eventually began to earn as much as $5.75 a day. . . . 'I was exceeding my piecework quota by a lot. . . .' But then, Altagracia said, her plant supervisor, a

Cuban emigre, called her into his office. 'He said I was doing a fine job, but that I and some other of the women were making too much money, and he was being forced to lower what we earned for each piece we sewed.' On the best days, she now can clear barely $3, she said. 'I was earning less, so I started working six and seven days a week. But I was tired and I could not work as fast as before.'" Within a few months, she was too ill to work at all.

23   As if poor health and the stress of factory life weren't enough to drive women into early retirement, management actually encourages a high turnover in many industries. "As you know, when seniority rises, wages rise," the management consultant to U.S. multinationals told us. He explained that it's cheaper to train a fresh supply of teenagers than to pay experienced women higher wages. "Older women, aged 23 or 24, are likely to be laid off and not rehired."

24   We estimate, based on fragmentary data from several sources, that the multinational corporations may already have used up (cast off) as many as 6 million Third World workers—women who are too ill, too old (30 is over the hill in most industries), or too exhausted to be useful any more. Few "retire" with any transferable skills or savings. The lucky ones find husbands.

25   The unlucky ones find themselves at the margins of society—as bar girls, "hostesses," or prostitutes.

26   *At 21, Julie's greatest fear is that she will never be able to find a husband. She knows that just being a "factory girl" is enough to give anyone a bad reputation. When she first started working at the electronics company, her father refused to speak to her for three months. Now, every time she leaves Penang to go back to visit her home village she has to put up with a lecture on morality from her older brother—not to mention a barrage of lewd remarks from men outside her family. If they knew that she had actually gone out on a few dates, that she had been to a discotheque, that she had once kissed a young man who said he was a student. . . . Julie's stomach tightens as she imagines her family's reaction. She tries to concentrate on the kind of man she would like to marry: an engineer or technician of some sort, someone who had been to California, where the company headquarters are located and where even the grandmothers wear tight pants and lipstick—someone who had a good attitude about women. But if she ends up having to wear glasses, like her cousin who worked three years at the "scopes," she might as well forget about finding anyone to marry her.*

27   One of the most serious occupational hazards that Julie and millions of women like her may face is the lifelong stigma of having been a "factory girl." Most of the cultures favored by multinational corporations in their search for cheap labor are patriarchal in the

grand old style: any young woman who is not under the wing of a father, husband, or older brother must be "loose." High levels of unemployment among men, as in Mexico, contribute to male resent-ment of working women. (Ironically, in some places the multination-als have increased male unemployment—for example, by paving over fishing and farming villages to make way for industrial parks.) Add to all this the fact that certain companies—American electronics firms are in the lead—actively promote Western-style sexual objectification as a means of insuring employee loyalty: there are company-sponsored cosmetics classes, "guess whose legs these are" contests, and swim-suit-style beauty contests where the prize might be a free night for two in a fancy hotel. Corporate-promoted Westernization only height-ens the hostility many men feel toward any independent working women—having a job is bad enough, wearing jeans and mascara to work is going too far.

28   Anthropologist Patricia Fernandez, who has worked in a *maquiladora* herself, believes that the stigmatization of working women serves, indirectly, to keep them in line. "You have to think of the kind of socialization that girls experience in a very Catholic—or, for that matter, Muslim—society. The fear of having a 'reputation' is enough to make a lot of women bend over backward to be 'respectable' and ladylike, which is just what management wants." She points out that in northern Mexico, the tabloids delight in playing up stories of alleged vice in the *maquiladoras*—indiscriminate sex on the job, epidemics of venereal disease, fetuses found in factory rest rooms. "I worry about this because there are those who treat you dif-ferently as soon as they know you have a job at a *maquiladora*" one woman told Fernandez. "Maybe they think that if you have to work, there is a chance you're a whore."

29   And there is always a chance you'll wind up as one. Probably only a small minority of Third World factory workers turn to prostitu-tion when their working days come to an end. But it is, as for women everywhere, the employment of last resort, the only thing to do when the factories don't need you and traditional society won't—or, for eco-nomic reasons, can't—take you back. In the Philippines, the brothel business is expanding as fast as the factory system. If they can't use you one way, they can use you another.

Reading Critically: Questions for Discussion

1. What is the function of the two stories—of Anna and Julie? Do the sto-ries prove the logic of the writers' claim or motivate their audience?
2. Do the writers anticipate and answer objections to their claim?
3. How do the writers establish their credibility?
4. How do the writers motivate the audience to approve their claim? Do the writers address the audience's self-interest or sense of altruism?

Which is more likely to be effective? Explain your answer.

5. How is this essay organized? Why is it organized the way it is? Would headings serve to clarify the organization? Why don't the writers use headings?

6. In supporting their claim, the writers offer numerical information regarding wages and working conditions. Would this information be easier to read if it were displayed in tables and figures? Would it be more persuasive?

7. How would this essay be different if the writers were addressing business managers instead of working women? If the writers were addressing legislators? Or religious leaders?

PART VII

A Guide to Logic and Reasoning

Formal Logic
Deductive Logic
Inductive Logic

Practical Reasoning

FORMAL LOGIC

Logic is essential to critical thinking, reading, and writing. By studying the principles of formal logic, you develop your ability to analyze claims and identify sufficient, plausible, and pertinent evidence.

In formal logic, the thesis or claim is called the **conclusion** and the evidence is called the **premises.** The relationship of the premises to the conclusion is of two basic types: deductive and inductive.

Deductive Logic

In a **deductive** relationship, if the premises are true, the conclusion is necessarily true. That is, if you approve the premises, you are simultaneously approving the conclusion because the premises imply the conclusion. Consider, for example, the following:

> Because all animals are beautiful and because tigers are animals, tigers are beautiful.

If the relationship is deductive, no new information is discovered. It is only the implications of the premises that are uncovered.

This deductive relationship of premises to conclusion is called a **syllogism.** Syllogisms are classified as categorical, alternative, disjunctive, or hypothetical.

Categorical Syllogisms

A **categorical syllogism** has two premises and a conclusion. The **major premise** introduces the **major term** (the idea that is also the predicate of the conclusion). The **minor premise** introduces the **minor term** (the idea that is also the subject of the conclusion). The middle term is the idea common to the major and minor premises, but omitted from the conclusion. Each term is either **distributed** (including all of the class) or **undistributed** (including only a portion of the class). Consider, for example, the following:

	subject	predicate
Major premise:	All writers enjoy reading.	

	subject	predicate
Minor premise:	Theresa is a writer.	

	subject	predicate
Conclusion:	Therefore, Theresa enjoys reading.	

The major term is *enjoy reading,* the minor term is *Theresa,* and the middle term is *writer.* In the major premise, *writer* is distributed (all writers). In the minor premise, *writer* is undistributed (a single writer).

Premises and conclusions are either affirmative or negative and either universal or particular. Each type of assertion exhibits a unique configuration of distributed and/or undistributed terms:

Type of Assertion	Example	Subject	Predicate
Universal affirmative	All bicycles have wheels.	distributed	undistributed
Universal negative	All bicycles have no eyes.	distributed	distributed
Particular affirmative	Some bicycles have lights.	undistributed	undistributed
Particular negative	Some bicycles have no lights.	undistributed	distributed

In a syllogism, the relationship of the premises to the conclusion is **valid,** or justified if

- the syllogism has only three terms, each occurring twice.
- the middle term is distributed at least once.
- each term that is distributed in the conclusion is also distributed in the premises.
- at least one premise is affirmative.
- a negative premise has a negative conclusion.
- a negative conclusion has a negative premise.

The following are examples of valid syllogisms:

Major premise:	All poets are writers.
Minor premise:	All writers are creative.
Conclusion:	Therefore, all poets are creative.

Major premise:	All writers are creative.
Minor premise:	Theresa is a writer.
Conclusion:	Therefore, Theresa is creative.

Major premise:	No writer is foolish.
Minor premise:	Theresa is a writer.
Conclusion:	Therefore, Theresa is not foolish.

Major premise:	All poets are inspired.

Minor premise: Some writers are not inspired.
Conclusion: Therefore, some writers are not poets.

Notice also that a valid syllogism always has at least one universal premise. In addition, particular conclusions always have at least one particular premise, and universal conclusions always have universal premises only.

The following are examples of invalid syllogisms:

Major premise: All poets are creative.
Minor premise: Theresa is a writer.
Conclusion: Therefore, Theresa is creative.

This syllogism is invalid because it has four terms instead of three.

Major premise: All writers are creative.
Minor premise: Theresa is creative.
Conclusion: Therefore, Theresa is a writer.

This syllogism is invalid because the middle term (*creative*) is never distributed.

Major premise: All writers are creative.
Minor premise: Some writers are not poets.
Conclusion: Therefore, some poets are not creative.

This syllogism is invalid because a term that is distributed in the conclusion (*creative*) is not distributed in the premises.

Major premise: All writers are not foolish.
Minor premise: Theresa is not a writer.
Conclusion: Therefore, Theresa is not foolish.

This syllogism is invalid because none of the premises are affirmative.

Major premise: All writers are creative.
Minor premise: Theresa is a writer.
Conclusion: Therefore, Theresa is not creative.

This syllogism is invalid because the conclusion is negative but neither of the premises is negative.

Major premise: All writers are creative.
Minor premise: Theresa is not a writer.
Conclusion: Therefore, Theresa is creative.

This syllogism is invalid because one of the premises is negative but the conclusion is affirmative.

Alternative Syllogisms

In **alternative syllogisms,** the major premise offers two possibilities. The minor premise denies one of the two choices. The conclusion affirms the remaining choice. Consider, for example, the following:

Major premise:	He always eats fruit or vegetables for lunch.
Minor premise:	Today he ate no fruit.
Conclusion:	Therefore, he ate vegetables.

Major premise:	He always eats fruit or vegetables for lunch.
Minor premise:	Today he ate no vegetables.
Conclusion:	Therefore, he ate fruit.

The following alternative syllogisms are invalid because the minor premise affirms one of the two choices instead of denying it:

Major premise:	He always eats fruit or vegetables for lunch.
Minor premise:	Today he ate fruit.
Conclusion:	Therefore, he ate no vegetables.

Major premise:	He always eats fruit or vegetables for lunch.
Minor premise:	Today he ate vegetables.
Conclusion:	Therefore, he ate no fruit.

Disjunctive Syllogisms

In a **disjunctive syllogism,** the major premise prohibits the choice of both of two possibilities. The minor premise affirms one of the two choices. The conclusion denies the remaining choice. Consider, for example, the following:

Major premise:	She can't be both a doctor and a dentist.
Minor premise:	She can be a doctor.
Conclusion:	Therefore, she can't be a dentist.

Major premise:	She can't be both a doctor and a dentist.
Minor premise:	She can be a dentist.
Conclusion:	Therefore, she can't be a doctor.

The following disjunctive syllogisms are invalid because the minor premise denies one of the two choices instead of affirming it:

Major premise:	She can't be both a doctor and a dentist.
Minor premise:	She can't be a doctor.
Conclusion:	Therefore, she can be a dentist.

Major premise: She can't be both a doctor and a dentist.
Minor premise: She can't be a dentist.
Conclusion: Therefore, she can be a doctor.

Hypothetical Syllogisms

In a **hypothetical syllogism,** the major premise identifies the conditions necessary for a given occurrence. The minor premise either affirms the condition or denies the occurrence. If the minor premise affirms the condition, the conclusion affirms the occurrence. If the minor premise denies the occurrence, the conclusion denies the condition. Consider, for example, the following:

Major premise: If we have liberty, then we will have justice.
Minor premise: We have liberty.
Conclusion: Therefore, we have justice.

Major premise: If we have liberty, then we will have justice.
Minor premise: We have no justice.
Conclusion: Therefore, we have no liberty.

The following hypothetical syllogisms are invalid because the minor premise affirms the occurrence instead of affirming the condition or denies the condition instead of denying the occurrence:

Major premise: If we have liberty, then we will have justice.
Minor premise: We have justice.
Conclusion: Therefore, we have liberty.

Major premise: If we have liberty, then we will have justice.
Minor premise: We have no liberty.
Conclusion: Therefore, we have no justice.

Inductive Logic

The **inductive** relationship points only to the probability of truth. If the premises are true, it is likely that the conclusion is also true. Induction is predictive: that is, given evidence of yesterday's conditions and today's conditions, you try to predict tomorrow's conditions. Inductive logic is thus the basis of scientific reasoning. The inductive relationship of the premises to the conclusion is either categorical, statistical, or analogous.

In a **categorical** relationship, the premises describe specific examined cases and the conclusion offers a prediction regarding all cases:

All patients previously admitted to the clinic have survived; therefore, we believe all patients are likely to survive.

In a **statistical** relationship, the premises describe a specific fraction of examined cases and the conclusion offers a prediction regarding a specific equal fraction of all cases:

> Because 90 percent of the patients we have injected with this new drug have improved, we believe that this drug has promise for 90 percent of all patients.

If the relationship is **analogous,** the premises describe specific examined cases and the conclusion offers a prediction regarding specific unexamined cases. Analogous relationships are either categorical or statistical:

> All of the cancer patients admitted to the clinic have survived. Bill is a cancer patient and thus is likely to survive.

> Of the cancer patients admitted to the clinic, 75 percent have survived. Bill has cancer and so there's a 75 percent probability that he'll survive also.

Erroneous premises and invalid inductive relationships lead to fallacious or deceptive reasoning. Such mistakes of logic are called **logical fallacies:**

Composition is the claim that a characteristic of each part is necessarily a characteristic of the whole:

> Sooner or later humanity will die off because all human beings are mortal.

This claim is fallacious because the mortality of individual humans is different from the extinction of the human species.

Division is the claim that a characteristic of the whole is necessarily a characteristic of each part.

> Because 60 percent of the citizens are registered voters, 60 percent of the people on this campus are registered voters.

This claim is fallacious because 60% is the average of all citizens and this campus might be above or below that average.

Hasty generalization is a claim without sufficient evidence as its basis. For example, if you observe a woman reading a politically liberal magazine such as *Ms.,* it would be fallacious to conclude with only this evidence that the woman is politically liberal. She might be a conservative who is reading the magazine to do research on the political philosophy of liberals. She might have been given a copy of the magazine. Or she might simply be curious to see why *Ms.* is famous. A logical conclusion regarding this woman's political orientation is impossible without more evidence. Similarly, if several Egyptians are impolite to you, it would be fallacious to conclude on the basis of only this evidence that all Egyptians are impolite. A logical conclusion regarding the social habits of Egyptians is impossible without a representative sampling of the Egyptian population.

Accident is the mistake of trying to apply a generalization to exceptional situations. For example, as a democracy we espouse the equality of all people. It would be fallacious, however, if we failed to consider convicted criminals as special cases and imposed no limits on their rights and privileges.

Filtering the evidence is the mistake of consciously or unconsciously omitting information that contradicts your desired conclusion. For example, your research uncovers that women's wages are rising, though the median income of full-time women workers with a college education is still equal to the median average income of full-time men workers with a high school education. Citing women's rising wages and ignoring the comparison of men's and women's wages relative to their level of education, you claim that wage discrimination has stopped. Such a claim is fallacious because you have only incorporated the evidence that supports your claim.

Non sequitur (it does not follow) is the use of irrelevant evidence as the basis of a claim:

> I like this candidate's campaign commercials: she'll be a terrific governor.

This claim is fallacious because it ignores political experience, managerial ability, and positions on major issues—direct indicators of the merits of a candidate. The caliber of a candidate's campaign commercials is itself no way to gauge the caliber of a candidate.

Begging the question is the mistake of assuming the truth of the claim you are trying to prove:

> You can't trust anything he tells you because he's a liar.

This is a circular assertion. While it looks as though it is offering evidence for the claim, the supposed evidence is simply a different way of wording the claim:

> You can't trust anything he tells you because he's a liar (a person who tells you things that you can't trust).

Slippery slope is the assumption of a simple domino-effect on a given issue. A specific action or occurrence is claimed to be undesirable because it will inevitably lead to more undesirable actions or occurrences:

> If we allow doctors to assist terminally ill patients to commit suicide, soon we'll have legalized euthanasia.

This assertion simplifies the cause-effect relationship, ignoring the complex social, political, medical, religious, ethical, and legal influences on this issue.

Hypothesis contrary to fact is the mistake of offering speculation on the impossible as evidence for a claim:

> If men got pregnant, abortion would be a religious ceremony.

Because the condition described is impossible, the consequences are also impossible. Thus a prediction regarding the consequences of impossible conditions has no reliability. Equally fallacious is the following:

> We could have won that game if only Chris had been playing goalie.

The condition described never occurred, leaving the consequences impossible to determine. If you offer additional evidence (e.g., a record of winning whenever Chris has been the goalie), your prediction might acquire a degree of probability, but it is still speculation. This fallacy simplifies the cause-effect relationship: it assumes that the alteration of a particular cause leads inevitably to the alteration of a particular effect.

   Post hoc ergo propter hoc (after this, therefore because of this) is the mistake of assuming that a chronological relationship is also a cause-effect relationship:

> We didn't have this explosion of teenage pregnancies until we started having sex education classes in the schools. If we eliminate the classes, we'll fix the problem.

The introduction of sex education classes has a chronological relationship to the explosion of teenage pregnancies, but that relationship itself is unsatisfactory evidence for the claim that the classes cause pregnancies. Without additional evidence to prove that introducing information on human reproduction causes teenagers to have sexual intercourse, the claim of a cause-effect relationship is dubious. A chronological relationship is a necessary but insufficient condition for a cause-effect relationship.

   Argument from ignorance is the mistake of accepting a claim simply because it has never been disproved or rejecting a claim simply because it has never been proved:

> I believe in ghosts because nobody has proved that they don't exist.

This is a fallacious assertion. It assumes that the absence of evidence against the existence of ghosts constitutes the presence of evidence for the existence of ghosts. Equally fallacious is the following:

> I don't believe in ghosts because nobody has proven that they exist.

This assertion assumes that the absence of evidence for the existence of ghosts constitutes evidence against the existence of ghosts. Logically, the only thing that ignorance allows you to claim is "I don't know."

   False dilemma is the mistake of perceiving or offering only two choices on a given issue:

> Either you're with us or you're against us.

This assertion is a false dilemma because you could be indifferent. Similar is the following:

> If we don't start building more nuclear power facilities, we will all have to sit in the dark.

This assertion is a false dilemma because it fails to consider the variety of available alternatives. We could, for example, develop solar power and wind power as energy sources, or we could improve the energy efficiency of electrical appliances and light bulbs, or we could minimize personal energy consumption.

False analogy tries to justify a claim by declaring that a characteristic of a given subject is also characteristic of a subject with which it has trivial similarities:

> You should have a drink of alcohol every day because it keeps your engine running smoothly.

The implicit analogies here are two: that the human body is like a combustion engine and that alcohol is like a gasoline additive. The human body, however, is quite different from a combustion engine. And the impact that a gasoline additive has on a combustion engine is different from the impact that a daily drink of alcohol has on the human body. The similarities thus are insufficient evidence for the claim.

Two wrongs equal a right is the mistake of trying to justify your inappropriate, illegal or unethical behavior because your neighbor is also guilty of this behavior:

> It's okay to drink and drive because my friends do it all the time.

This claim is fallacious because you assume that the crimes of your friends give you permission to commit a similar crime.

Distortion is offering a biased interpretation of opposing opinions because the biased version is easier to repudiate:

> Environmentalists believe we should stop all logging operations—and lose thousands of jobs—in order to save a couple of owls.

> The loggers just want to keep cutting trees until there are no more trees to cut or owls to kill.

Such gross exaggerations do little to advance the cause or establish the credibility of either side of this issue. If you distort opposing opinions and discredit the distortion, you neither discredit the opposing opinions nor bring credit to your opinion.

Complex question is the practice of composing a question with a built-in or implicit assumption. If you answer the question, you simultaneously affirm the implicit assumption; if you address the implicit assumption, you never answer the question:

> How often have you been asked to stop stealing books from the library?

This question assumes that you are a thief. How do you answer this question without affirming the assumption? Even if your answer is "Never!" you still admit to being a thief. Similar is the following:

> Are you supporting that lunatic antiwar candidate?

This question assumes that the antiwar candidate is a lunatic.

Argument to the person is the practice of trying to discredit a claim by discrediting the person who advances the claim. Consider, for example, the following:

> I wouldn't accept that man's advice on child-care facilities because he was caught for shoplifting.

This is a fallacious opinion because the man's shoplifting conviction has no relevance to his advice on child care facilities. A convicted shoplifter's opinion of child care facilities is potentially as perceptive or valid as the opinion of people who have never been convicted of shoplifting. If the man were a convicted child abuser, however, his credibility on the subject of child care facilities could be appropriately questioned.

Poisoning the well is the practice of assigning a negative label to people of opposing opinions so that either their rejection of this label or their expression of their opinion is viewed suspiciously:

> The people who support bilingualism are the cultural elite.

If the people who espouse bilingualism object to this label, the discussion shifts from advocacy of bilingualism to definitions of *cultural elite*. If the bilingualists ignore the label, however, their silence could be perceived as their admission of its accuracy. The label also intimidates people who might ordinarily support bilingualism, but who dislike the idea of being associated with a cultural elite.

Borrowed prestige is the practice of trying to prove the logic of your claim by associating it with famous people or with ideas or objects that enjoy wide popularity. Figures in the fields of film, music, or athletics, for example, often endorse charitable causes, products, or legislative proposals. Although your favorite singer contributes to a particular charity, drives a certain type of car, or votes for a specific candidate, that is no logical justification for your choosing to contribute to that charity, purchase that car, or vote for that candidate. Equally fallacious is a slogan such as the following:

> Ellipsoid is the official soap of the 1996 Olympics.

This official association with the Olympics is no evidence that Ellipsoid is a superior soap. Similarly, political candidates oftentimes link themselves to the flag or their families to improve their credibility.

Appeal to fear is the practice of trying to win your approval of a claim by emphasizing how dangerous it is for you to reject the claim:

> If you don't have fire insurance, everything you own could go up in smoke.

This slogan tries to sell you fire insurance simply by frightening you with the possibility of catastrophic economic and emotional loss instead of explaining to you with statistics the likelihood of your experiencing a fire and the damage that a typical fire causes. Similar is the following:

> Don't litter! If you do, you'll go to jail.

This slogan tries to achieve compliance with the law strictly through intimidation. A logical alternative would be to explain why littering is illegal.

Appeal to pity is the practice of trying to win your approval of a claim by emphasizing the suffering you will impose on others if you reject the claim:

> If you don't give me a passing grade in this course, I'll lose my scholarship.

The student making this assertion offers no evidence to justify a passing grade, but tries to acquire a passing grade by soliciting the teacher's pity.

Appeal to the masses is the mistake of assuming that the majority has the correct opinion on a given issue:

> Nothing's better for cooking than Quicko, the world's top-selling vegetable oil.

This slogan assumes that popularity equals superiority. Equally fallacious is the following:

> I'm voting for Joanne Pauley because she's leading in the polls.

This voter's decision has no logical basis: he or she is simply adopting the opinion of the majority.

Appeal to tradition is the justification of a claim simply on the basis of historical practice:

> We'll do it this way because we've always done it this way.

While keeping a tradition is often emotionally satisfying, progress is impossible if you never consider new ideas or techniques. The traditional way might do the job, but a new way might be superior. Thus "we've always done it this way" is no reason to continue to do it that way. Evidence of the superiority of the traditional way is necessary.

Appeal to authority is unquestioning dependence on the opinions of specialists or officials:

> Ignore the newspapers! According to the city council, crime in the city is rising.

This assertion assumes the accuracy of the city council's opinion. The city council's perception, however, might easily be biased. If crime is said to be rising, the city council has a justification for hiring more police or raising taxes. Or the city council might simply be looking at old statistics, and new information is available. Unless you give the opinions of specialists or officials a critical review, you are guilty of fallacious thinking.

PRACTICAL REASONING

Practical reasoning is the theory of persuasion of philosopher Stephen Toulmin. Viewing formal logic as unusually complicated and thus impractical for daily communication, Toulmin developed a simpler way of proving that your opinion is logical. In practical reasoning, your thesis or opinion is your **claim.** Evidence for your claim is called the **data.** To show that the relationship of the data to the claim is valid, you explain your **warrant.** You support your warrant with additional evidence or

backing. Often, **qualifiers** are necessary to limit the scope or probability of your claim, data, warrant, or backing. Exceptions or conditions for the claim are the **rebuttal.**

Consider, for example, the following:

Data: This lizard is a green iguana.

Qualifier: Ordinarily,

Warrant: green iguanas are vegetarian,

Backing: according to zoological studies.

Qualifier: It is quite likely,

Claim: as a consequence, that this lizard will thrive on a diet of fruits and vegetables,

Rebuttal: unless you have to boost its protein consumption by feeding it a couple of crickets once or twice a week.

In practical reasoning, the warrant is especially important because it is the bridge linking your claim to your data. While the claim and data are specific, the warrant is typically a generalization—a belief or assumption that could be applied to a variety of similar situations. Ordinarily, different fields of inquiry use different types of generalizations. In science, for example, the laws of physics (e.g., gravity) could serve as a warrant. In engineering, a warrant might be a mathematical formula (e.g., $a^2 + b^2 = c^2$). In legal discussions, a law or a judicial ruling could be a warrant (e.g., *Roe v. Wade*). A political claim might use a philosophical or ethical principle as a warrant (e.g., the right to privacy). In the evaluation of a painting or novel, a prevailing social attitude regarding aesthetic or literary merit could constitute a warrant (e.g., the importance of originality).

Often, a warrant is implied because the principle or generalization is widely established and no explicit identification is thus necessary. Consider, for example, the following:

Claim: Tom deserves a raise.
Data: He's been a major contributor to the company's success this year.

In this case, the implied warrant is a common belief: Contributors to a company's success deserve higher wages.

It is also possible for a writer, through duplicity or negligence, to disguise a frail claim by making a questionable warrant implicit instead of explicit. Consider for example, the following:

Claim: Tom deserves a raise.
Data: He's getting married and starting a family.

In this case, the warrant is a dubious assumption: individuals getting married and starting families deserve higher wages.

For more information on practical reasoning, see Stephen Toulmin's *The Uses of Argument* (New York: Cambridge University Press, 1964).

Index of Key Terms

Planning Your Answers

Translating Your Answers

Reviewing Your Answers

PART VIII

A Guide for Writing Essay Examinations

The objective of essay examinations is to determine your knowledge of a subject as well as your ability to communicate that knowledge effectively in a timed situation.

In essay examinations, your writing is subject to a variety of influences. Because the essay examination is a testing situation, you might be anxious or nervous. A night of studying might leave you physically tired. In addition, because essay examinations are timed writing situations, you often have little opportunity to revise your writing or to consider issues of style, memory, and delivery. Your focus is typically on invention and arrangement: retrieving information appropriate to the question and organizing that information logically.

PLANNING YOUR ANSWERS

Because the essay examination is timed writing, you might be tempted to read the question and immediately start writing your answer to it. Resist this temptation. You are more likely to write a satisfactory answer if you do a little quick planning.

Dedicate ten minutes at the beginning of the examination period to planning your answers to all the questions. If you do your thinking at the beginning of the examination period—while you are still alert—you are more likely to compose answers of uniform quality. In a one-hour examination, for example, after you have been writing for thirty minutes, you are likely to be tired and, as a consequence, thinking less clearly. Such fatigue often causes the later answers on essay examinations to be inferior to the earlier answers.

If your essay examination has several questions, divide the time available to you according to the complexity or weight of the questions. For example, a question that is 25 percent of the examination deserves approximately 25 percent of your time.

Start your planning by reading each question critically to determine the appropriate way to answer it. Is the question asking you for a summary, evaluation, or analysis? If a question asks you to analyze or evaluate a subject and you only summarize it, your answer is inappropriate and thus unsatisfactory. Questions that ask you to summarize assess your ability to retrieve and discuss information covered during class or by assigned readings. Evaluative questions ask you to judge the merits of a subject, weigh advantages and disadvantages, or choose among alternatives. Analytical questions assess your ability to recognize similarities and differences, determine causes, perceive influences, interpret results, consider implications, explain significance, or apply knowledge to specific situations. Consider, for example, the examination questions at the top of the next page.

Once you decide how to answer a question, list your ideas regarding the answer. List only ideas appropriate to the question. If your answer covers unnecessary information, you damage your credibility. Getting this list of ideas on paper or on screen at the beginning of your essay writing

Sample Question	Explanation of Question
Identify and briefly discuss three examples of unsatisfactory hospitality in Homer's *Odyssey*.	This question asks you to summarize. Your task is to choose three episodes and offer sufficient details to prove the episodes are examples of unsatisfactory hospitality.
In Homer's *Odyssey,* which of the adventures of Odysseus on his journey to Ithaca reveals the most about his character? Give evidence to support your answer.	This question asks you to evaluate. Your task is to choose a specific episode and offer sufficient details to justify your choice.
How is the journey of Aeneas in Virgil's *Aeneid* like and unlike the journey of Odysseus in Homer's *Odyssey?*	This question asks you to analyze. Your task is to examine the two journey narratives and specify points of similarity and points of difference. You might also explain the significance of the similarities and differences.

process is important. Listing ideas focuses your attention on the question and stimulates your thinking. This list is also your guide to writing the answer: it serves as a reminder to you of the ideas to discuss and thus allows you to write a thorough answer to the question.

Before starting to write your answer to a question, determine your thesis and organize your ideas. In declaring your thesis, consider how you might adopt or adapt the wording of the essay question itself. This technique keeps you and your answer focused on the question. The following are several possibilities:

Sample Question	Possible Thesis
What are three examples of unsatisfactory hospitality in Homer's *Odyssey?* Identify and briefly discuss each.	A possible thesis is "Three examples of unsatisfactory hospitality in Homer's Odyssey are. . ." Complete this sentence by briefly identifying three examples from your list of ideas.
In Homer's *Odyssey,* which of the adventures of Odysseus on his journey to Ithaca reveals the most about his character? Give evidence to support your answer.	A possible thesis is "Of all of the adventures of Odysseus on his journey to Ithaca, the one that reveals the most about his character is. . ." Complete this sentence by choosing a single appropriate episode from your list of ideas.

Sample Question	*Possible Thesis*
How is the journey of Aeneas in Virgil's *Aeneid* like and unlike the journey of Odysseus in Homer's *Odyssey?*	A possible thesis is "The journey of Aeneas in Virgil's *Aeneid* and the journey of Odysseus in Homer's *Odyssey* have several similarities, including [identify similarities here]. Nevertheless, the two journeys also display a variety of important differences, such as [identify differences here]."

Finish your planning by deciding on a logical way to organize your answer. A disorganized answer damages your credibility. Consider again the examination questions below.

Sample Question	*Possible Organization*
What are three examples of unsatisfactory hospitality in Homer's *Odyssey?* Identify and briefly discuss each.	The answer to this question might be organized chronologically: discuss the three examples in the order of their occurrence. Also possible is a hierarchical organization: start with the example of the most unsatisfactory hospitality and finish with the example of the least unsatisfactory hospitality.
In Homer's *Odyssey,* which of the adventures of Odysseus on his journey to Ithaca reveals the most about his character? Give evidence to support your answer.	The answer to this question might be organized categorically. Start with your choice of episode, progress to your explanation of the characteristics that this episode reveals, and finish with your emphasis on the characteristic or characteristics that *only* this episode reveals.
How is the journey of Aeneas in Virgil's *Aeneid* like and unlike the journey of Odysseus in Homer's *Odyssey?*	This question might be organized categorically: start with the similarities and finish with the differences, or vice versa. You might also organize the similarities and differences hierarchically: start with the most important similarity and finish with the least important (or vice versa); start with the most importance difference and finish with the least important (or vice versa).

As you write your answer to a question, you might think of information pertinent to a later question. Interrupt your writing to add this information to your list of ideas for the later question. Your answer to this later question thus benefits from your writing of the earlier question.

TRANSLATING YOUR ANSWERS

To write your answer, start by introducing your thesis and identifying your major points. You might also number and list your points, especially if you have several to discuss. This introductory paragraph offers a quick preview of your answer, displays your command of the subject, gives you a sense of direction, and establishes the reader's expectations. For example, consider the following introductory paragraph:

> Odysseus has many adventures on his journey to Ithaca, but the adventure that reveals the most about his character is the episode with the Sirens. Because the singing of the Sirens leads sailors to crash their ships on the rocks, Odysseus plugs the ears of his sailors with wax. He leaves his ears unplugged, but ties himself to the ship so that he might listen to the singing without risking his ship. In addition to demonstrating Odysseus's courage, ingenuity, physical strength, and love of his sailors, this episode also shows his adventurous spirit—his desire to experience everything that life has to offer.

Following the introduction, discuss each point, offering sufficient and appropriate information to exhibit your knowledge of the subject and support your thesis. Write a separate paragraph for each major point; this practice visually reinforces the organization of your answer. Transitional words and phrases also serve to clarify your organization and thus simplify reading. For example, if your introductory paragraph promises to cover five points, you might start your discussion of each point by specifying its numerical position within your discussion:

> First, this episode reveals Odysseus's courage. . . .

> Second, Odysseus proves his ingenuity by determining a way to listen to the singing of the Sirens without losing his ship on the rocks surrounding the island. . . .

> Third, the physical strength of Odysseus is obvious. . . .

> Fourth, Odysseus displays love of his sailors by plugging their ears with wax. . . .

> Fifth, better than any of his other adventures on the journey to Ithaca, this episode reveals the desire of Odysseus to experience everything life has to offer. . . .

If time allows, finish your answer by writing a concluding paragraph that summarizes your major points and emphasizes your thesis. This final paragraph is a reminder to the instructor of your command of the subject.

REVIEWING YOUR ANSWERS

After you have written your answers to all the questions on your essay examination, dedicate your remaining time to revising and editing. Is your answer as thorough as possible? Is important information missing? Is your answer specific, clear, and logically organized? Is the wording and spelling appropriate? While writing your answer, for example, you might have accidentally omitted a word essential to the clarity of your explanation or skipped a critical point on your list of ideas. By reviewing your answers, you minimize such errors and the damage to your credibility that such errors could cause.

PART IX

A Guide for Documenting Knowledge by Observation

Depending on the aim, purpose, subject, and audience of your writing task, every text you compose could potentially include knowledge by observation. *Knowledge by observation* refers to information gained indirectly—data learned from other people's experiences and from published materials about subjects.

While it is important for you to adhere to conventions when documenting knowledge by observation, it is equally important for you to research and integrate your source materials effectively. That is, your research should deepen your understanding of your subject, strengthen your evidence and arguments, and lend authority and credibility to your text. Instead of merely offering a string of research findings, however, your text should represent a carefully constructed and reasonably ordered series of source materials that you have been able to analyze and synthesize purposefully.

USING THE KNOWLEDGE CONTINUUM TO AVOID PLAGIARISM

As a writer and researcher, you are obliged to acknowledge the contributions of other people whenever their ideas appear in your text. The sources of these contributions may take many forms: books, magazines, newspapers, interviews, recordings, questionnaires, lectures, electronic documents, television programs, films, letters, formal reports, or teleconferences. And as you discover and arrange these contributions to your essay, it is useful to list key terms in the "knowledge by observation" area of the knowledge continuum. Whenever you refer to ideas that you have mapped in this area of the knowledge continuum, you must credit their sources.

You acknowledge these sources by following a documentation system that is appropriate for the academic discipline and subject you are writing about. One of the easiest ways to determine the documentation system to use for your text is to survey which system your source materials employ. You will find that ordinarily scholars in the humanities prefer an author-page system like that of the Modern Language Association (MLA), whereas those in business and the social sciences prefer an author-year system like that of the American Psychological Association (APA), and those in engineering and technology prefer a numerical system like that of the Institute of Electrical and Electronics Engineers (IEEE). For scholars in science and medicine, the Council of Biology Editors (CBE) offers an author-year system and two numerical systems. Each of these documentation systems is presented in the following pages.

What happens if you fail to credit your sources? You plagiarize. Consider the following explanation of **plagiarism** from the *MLA Handbook* (1977):

> Derived from the Latin word *plagiarius* ("kidnapper" and also "plagiarist" in the modern sense), plagiarism is defined by Alexander Lindley as "the false assumption of authorship: the wrongful act of taking the product of another person's mind, and presenting it as one's own" (*Plagiarism and Originality*

[New York: Harper, 1952], p. 2). Plagiarism may take the form of repeating another's sentences as your own, adopting a particularly apt phrase as your own, paraphrasing someone else's argument as your own, or even presenting someone else's line of thinking in the development of a thesis as though it were your own. In short, to plagiarize is to give the impression that you have written or thought something that you have in fact borrowed from another. Although a writer may use another person's words and thoughts, they must be acknowledged as such. (6)

By using your map of the knowledge continuum (as well as your notes), you can verify which evidence in your essay can be attributed to others and which information derives from your own experiences (knowledge by participation). Instead of using the adage, "When in doubt, document," you can consult your knowledge continuum to ascertain with confidence when you should acknowledge sources.

SELECTING A SUBJECT

In choosing and researching subjects for writing, you might have noticed that you typically start out with a fairly general subject and subsequently refine it, through your research process, into a more specific subject. For example, suppose your initial subject is cancer research. You happen to read the following article in your hometown newspaper:

Scientists Seek Secret of Cancer-fighting Pigs

Jade Boyd

It sounds like the next hit movie for kids—"Tumor-Fighting Ninja Pigs"— starring 600 porkers with disease-fighting superpowers. Actually, it's a National Cancer Institute research project headed by Texas A&M endocrinologist Max Amoss. The cancer-fighting pigs are real.

"I have some animals out there that are 8 years old that were covered with melanomas, and they're living a very pleasant life in a breeding herd," said Amoss, a researcher in A&M's College of Veterinary Medicine.

Amoss' A&M research team and scientists from four other U.S. labs are working together to find out how Sinclair pigs fight off one of the deadliest forms of cancer. Most of the animals develop tumors when they're young, but only about 10 percent die from them.

Skin cancer is the most common form of cancer in the country, and while only 5 percent of the 600,000 cases diagnosed annually are melanoma, it accounts for about 75 percent of all skin cancer deaths. Due to the popularity of tanning, melanoma is 14 times more likely today than it was in the 1930s.

A melanoma tumor is made up of abnormal melanocytes, the cells that produce the skin pigment melanin. The reason this type of cancer is so deadly is that the tumors tend to metastasize, or spread throughout the body.

As in humans, the pigs' melanoma cells do migrate.

"We find melanoma cells in the brain, in the lung, spleen and the liver," Amoss said. "But by and large, the animal doesn't die of metastatic disease, which is what happens in almost any other kind of cancer. These metastatic melanoma cells start to grow and then just stop."

If Amoss and the other researchers can isolate the pigs' secret defense against melanoma, they may be able to transfer it to humans, saving thousands of lives.

There are many questions to be answered before the mystery is solved, though, not the least of which is why the pigs get melanoma in the first place.

For people, the No. 1 contributing factor is overexposure to the sun. But melanoma's relationship to sunlight isn't as easily established as with the more benign forms of skin cancer—basal and squamous tumors. With those types, the more sun exposure you get, bit by bit, over many years, the more likely your chances of developing tumors.

With melanoma, the main risk is for fair-skinned people who get burned.

With the pigs, sunlight has nothing to do with it.

Their tumors start growing before they're born and grow rapidly for about six weeks after birth. Then the tumors slowly fade.

"By six months, in many instances, the tumors have completely regressed," Amoss said.

Boyd, Jade. "Tumor-Fighting Ninja Pigs!" Bryan-College Station Eagle 7 June 1992: A1+.

This article introduces you to an area of cancer research that you had never known about; let's suppose that, during one of your trips home, you decide to visit Dr. Amoss and his laboratory. Your visit is so fascinating that you narrow your focus to cancer research in animals, eventually settling on the subject of melanoma (skin cancer) research in Sinclair pigs. Depending on your aim, you might develop the following subjects using knowledge by observation:

Expressive Aim. Describe the laboratory research on skin cancer or melanoma tumors in Sinclair pigs and consider its possible significance for you, a summertime water safety instructor and a regular patron at tanning salons throughout the fall and winter months.

Referential Aim. Explain melanoma in Sinclair pigs—the disease, the kinds of laboratory experiments being conducted to understand it, and the possible implications of the research findings for humans with melanoma.

Persuasive Aim. Defend or attack the laboratory research being conducted on pigs with melanoma. Consider, for example, whether or not the cost of such research is justifiable given its uncertain relevance to melanoma in humans. Consider also the ethical implications of using animals in laboratory experiments.

A word of advice: Before you start writing any essay—especially one incorporating knowledge by observation—make sure you consider the amount and depth of research necessary, the degree of personal commentary appropriate, as well as the aim, purpose, and audience for the text.

DEVELOPING A WORKING BIBLIOGRAPHY

Once you understand your task, you can determine which invention strategies to use (questionnaires, interviews, surveys, library searches). In Chapter 4, you can locate information about different research methods that can help you develop a working bibliography (a list of books, journal articles, recordings, maps, videotapes, and other sources). You will probably revise your working bibliography frequently during your invention process as you read and analyze the ideas of other people, discovering information that transforms and hones your thinking about your subject. You can compile a working bibliography by recording your references on three-by-five-inch note cards (bibliography cards); more than likely, you will probably first log these sources in your journal as you research and will transfer them to note cards later. Following the documentation style appropriate for your subject, write one bibliography card for each reference. Using cards enables you to alphabetize, locate, add, and delete references easily.

Below is a sample bibliography card that reflects the MLA documentation system:

```
Res/T/352/S85/1982


   Stitch, Ira Eliot, and Delma S. Martinez. Engineering Graphics

      Technology. 4th ed. New York: Synchronous Press, 1982.



   Comment: General manual of engineering graphics for

      students and professionals.  Useful bibliography.
```

If you have access to a computer, you may enter bibliographic entries directly on disk. In this way, you can create a database of sources, easily updating and printing new copies of your working bibliography as you wish.

In fact, special bibliographic programs have been developed to help you compile your bibliography. Intended to be user-friendly, these programs simply present you with pre-designed data forms to fill in. Once you have supplied the necessary information, you select the documentation system for your bibliography or reference list; the computer automatically arranges the information. Some program accessories even allow you to access files from specific databases (e.g., Dialogue, BRS, and MedLARS) and format them according to a documentation style of your choice.

EXAMINING SOURCES

As you examine sources, your job is to determine the information that is appropriate to your essay. You achieve this objective through the following **critical reading** activities: survey, inventory, interpret, and evaluate.

Survey

Before reading, survey the source to determine its major characteristics:

- What is the title?
- Who is the author?
- What is the date of publication?
- How did the author obtain his or her information? By participation? By observation? By participation and observation?
- What are the major and minor headings?
- How is the information organized?
- Are tables and figures included?
- What is the focus or emphasis of the source?

Inventory

After surveying the source, inventory your knowledge and attitudes regarding the author, the subject, and the source:

Author

- What do you know about the author? Does he or she have appropriate qualifications to write on this subject? Has he or she written on this subject previously?
- What is your attitude toward the author? Is he or she a credible source of information?
- How might your knowledge or attitude regarding the author influence your reading? Are you positively or negatively disposed before reading the source?

Subject

- What do you already know about the subject? Do you consider yourself knowledgeable on the subject? Is your knowledge by participation, by observation, or by participation and observation?
- What is your attitude toward the subject? Do you consider the subject important? Do you enjoy learning more about the subject?
- How might your knowledge or attitudes regarding the subject influence your reading? Are you positively or negatively disposed before reading the source?

Source

- What do you already know about this source of information?
- Is it often cited? Have you seen it summarized or reviewed?
- What is your attitude toward this source? Do you have specific expectations?
- How might your knowledge or attitudes regarding this source influence your reading? Are you positively or negatively disposed before reading the source?

Interpret

Once you have surveyed the source and inventoried your knowledge and attitudes, it is time to start reading. As you do, develop a clear understanding of the source by answering the following questions:

- What assumptions does the author make about your knowledge and attitudes regarding the subject? Does the author assume you are familiar with specialized terminology, previous studies, or the history of the subject? Does the author assume you are positively or negatively disposed?
- What is the author's aim and purpose?
- What information does the author provide to establish his or her credibility?
- What is the author's thesis or claim? What evidence does the author provide to support the thesis?
- What information does the author provide to motivate you to accept the thesis?

Evaluate

After reading, evaluate the source by answering the following questions:

- Is the author a credible source of information?
- What do you know about the author that you didn't know before? How has your attitude toward the author changed?
- Is the title clear?
- Is the organization logical?
- Do the headings emphasize the organization?
- Is the wording of ideas appropriate?
- Are tables and figures designed and integrated effectively?
- Is the thesis supported by sufficient, plausible, and pertinent information?
- What do you know about the subject that you didn't know before? How has your attitude toward the subject changed?

- Are you motivated to accept the thesis?
- Does the author achieve his or her objective?
- Has this source satisfied your expectations? Has reading this source been worthwhile?

TAKING NOTES: DIRECT QUOTATION, PARAPHRASE, AND SUMMARY

If you decide that a source has important information, start taking notes. While everyone agrees that note-taking is essential for keeping track of source materials, probably no two writers take notes in exactly the same way. Some use four-by-six-inch lined index cards; others use notebooks or research journals; still others type their notes on their computers. Regardless of the method, all writers need to include in their notes all the information required for documentation and bibliography purposes.

Typically, to take notes effectively and efficiently, you may **paraphrase** (put into your words) or **summarize** (condense) ideas when the original wording is not essential. Occasionally, the original wording captures key ideas so well that you risk losing their import by changing the phrasing. In such cases, a **direct quotation** (word for word) is appropriate. Use quotation marks carefully in your notes to distinguish the information as a direct quotation. Often, quotations may continue to another page in your source; remember to record where the page break occurs. For every note, you should also record basic bibliographic information accurately (author, title, and page numbers).

Now that you know what and when you may opt to quote directly, paraphrase, or summarize, consider the following illustrations of each.

Direct Quotation:

In *A Writer's Repertoire*, Gong and Dragga explain the problem of definition that *rhetoric* presents:

> During the past 2500 years, the word <u>rhetoric</u> has been construed in a great many ways. For some, the term suggests a certain eloquence. For others, it means deceptive ornamentation, as is evident in comments such as "All show, but no substance" and "empty bombast." Passing remarks like these are often attributed to unfulfilled campaign promises made in political speeches, the slick use of language and image in advertising, or eyeball-busting research articles. . . . (8)

(Note: In MLA style, direct quotations that extend more than four lines are indented ten spaces from the left margin and double-spaced; no quotation marks are used. In APA style, direct quotations that are longer than forty words are indented five spaces from the left margin and double-spaced; no quotation marks are used.)

Paraphrase:

According to Gong and Dragga in <u>A Writer's Repertoire</u>, <u>rhetoric</u>, a term over 2500 years old, is not simple to define. Some people may consider rhetoric to refer to language in an honorific sense (well-spoken and articulate). Others, however, think that the word refers to language in a pejorative sense (embellished and misleading). Three examples of the negative meaning associated with the term are broken political pledges, clever phrasing and pictures in advertisements that misrepresent products, and confusing, jargon-ridden academic prose (8).

Summary:

A term used over the past 2500 years, <u>rhetoric</u> can refer to the appropriate and effective use of language; or it can refer to the flowery and deceptive use of language associated with political campaign speeches, misleading ads, and pretentious scholarship (Gong and Dragga 8).

Because of the need to express other people's ideas accurately, you may choose to photocopy key materials—important sources that you anticipate referring to frequently. While photocopying sources helps you gather information accurately and conveniently, do so judiciously: photocopying every source can be expensive, time-consuming, unnecessary, and wasteful.

INTEGRATING SOURCES: TAGGING

To integrate direct quotations, paraphrases, and summaries into your text, use a technique called **tagging.** When you tag, you accomplish the following:

- introduce bibliographical and contextual information into your sentence structure, thereby helping readers' comprehension
- provide readers with smooth and clear transitions, showing how ideas are related and avoiding the impression that you have simply "cut and pasted" a series of other people's ideas together
- reduce the amount of information that you need to include in the parenthetical citation or note
- strengthen the ethos (credibility and authority) of your sources and evidence

Here are some tagging methods you can use to incorporate knowledge by observation into your text:

Tag the entire title of a work:

In <u>The Firm</u>, the plot revolves around . . .

Tag the author's name and credentials:

According to Southern fiction writer Eudora Welty . . .

Hamlin L. Hill, the foremost Mark Twain scholar in the United States, argues . . .

Tag a specific section of a work:

In Chapter 6, Nell Ann realizes Beth had poisoned the aliens.

Tag the publication date of a work:

Published in 1993, the same year the poem was read aloud to the nation,. . .

USING DOCUMENTATION SYSTEMS

Now that you know when to document and how to integrate knowledge by observation into your own text, you are ready to focus on documentation systems. As you will see, every major academic discipline prefers a particular system, and every system differs.

In academic writing that you compose for college classes, ask your instructor or academic department to recommend the documentation system you should follow. Or review the research materials you've been reading for your essay. What is the predominant documentation system used? For journal articles, check the editorial policy concerning the submission requirements. Which system is specified? Of course, you can also go to your college library's reference section to find documentation guides for all academic disciplines.

If you are writing about subjects in the humanities, you will likely use the MLA documentation system. If you are discussing business or the social sciences, the APA system is appropriate. If engineering or technology is your subject, you might prefer the IEEE system. And if you are discussing subjects in science and medicine, you might adopt the CBE system. The full citations for these four reference guides appear below:

Gibaldi, Joseph. *MLA Handbook for Writers of Research Papers.* 5th ed. New York: The Modern Language Association, 1999. (updated information available at www.mla.org)

Publication Manual of the American Psychological Association. 4th ed. Washington: American Psychological Association, 1994. (updated information available at www.apa.org)

Information for IEEE Transactions, Journal, and Letters Authors. New York: Institute of Electrical and Electronics Engineers, 1997. (updated information available at www.ieee.org)

Scientific Style and Format: The CBE Style Manual for Authors, Editors, and Publishers. 6th ed. Chicago: Council of Biology Editors, 1994. (updated information available at www.councilscienceeditors.org)

For most of the writing that you will undertake in this course, these are the four systems that you will want to become most familiar with. Consequently, we end our Guide for Documenting Knowledge by Observation with a brief overview of the MLA, APA, IEEE, and CBE systems.

Humanities: The MLA System of Documentation

In the MLA (Modern Language Association) system of documentation, you identify sources of information in a list labeled "Works Cited." List your sources alphabetically by the author's last name. If no author's name is available, list the source alphabetically by its title.

In the text, cite specific sources parenthetically using the author's last name. If no author's name is available, cite the source by its title. If referring to a particular passage or if quoting a source, also cite specific pages (without using a comma after the the author's name).

Citing Sources

One author:

Collaboration is a dynamic process and typically includes five different operations (Malone 112).

Two authors:

In business and industry, you will find three different types of teams (Larson and LaFasto 61–69).

Three or more authors:

Long and complicated words often cause confusion and misinterpretation (Dobbs, Friedman, and Lloyd 89–91).

Four or more authors:

Collaboration is possible in each of four relationships of time and space (Johnson et al. 16).

Whole source cited:

It is important to distinguish among affective conflict, procedural conflict, and substantive conflict (Putnam).

Multiple sources cited:

Serif type guides the reader's eye from left to right across the page (Burt, 8–9; Zachrisson, 128–131).

Author named in text:

According to Weiss, "difference and struggle are inherently part of the bridge-building of understanding" (46).

Listing Sources

Start the first line on the left margin; indent subsequent lines five spaces. Give the author's last name first, followed by his or her full first name. Place a period after the author's name. Identify the title next, followed by publication information, including the date of publication. Capitalize the

In a variety of academic journals, traditional **footnotes** or **endnotes** substitute for parenthetical citations: sources are cited with a superscript number in the text, followed by a reference either at the "foot" of the page or "end" of the essay. In addition, the superscript numbers might signal **substantive footnotes or endnotes:** explanations or commentaries that appear either at the foot of the page or end of the essay. Consult your instructor or the *MLA Handbook for Writers of Research Papers,* 5th ed., for more information.

If you use a computer, check your word processing program. It may include a footnoting command that enables the computer to automatically place the superscript in the text and to open a "window" or space for you to write in your note. Moreover, whenever you add, delete, or rearrange notes, the program can automatically renumber and reposition your notes and superscripts in your text.

first word of the title, the last word of the title, and the first word after a colon; capitalize all other words with the exception of articles (*a, an, the*), conjunctions (*and, but, or*), and prepositions (*in, of, to*). Italicize (or underline) titles of books and journals. Use quotation marks to enclose titles of journal articles. For the place of publication, identify only the city.

Book, one author:

Crosby, Faye J. <u>Relative Deprivation and Working Women</u>. New

York: Oxford UP, 1982.

Book, four or more authors:

Johansen, Robert et al. <u>Leading Business Teams</u>. Reading:

Addison-Wesley, 1991.

Book, edited:

Barker, Thomas T., ed. <u>Perspectives on Software Documentation:</u>

<u>Inquiries and Innovations</u>. Amityville: Baywood, 1991.

Book, edition other than the first:

Lannon, John. <u>Technical Writing</u>. 6th ed. New York: Harper-

Collins, 1994.

Book, translation:

Vygotsky, Lev. <u>Thought and Language</u>. Trans. Eugenia Hanfman

and Gertrude Vakar. Cambridge: MIT, 1962.

Special guidelines apply to discussions of literary materials:

- Maintain the present tense throughout. The action, characters, published criticism, and so on always occur in the historical present:

    Critics find Oedipus a most complex character. For example, Oedipus kills his father and marries his mother. Assuredly, nothing is simple here. . . .

- Try to tag all direct quotations. When you use quotes by critics, provide their names and give some information about them:

    Cleanth Brooks, a formalist critic, . . .

- Place the date of publication in parentheses after your first mention of the literary work:

    Gertrude Stein wrote *The World Is Round* (1939), a children's book.

- Document literary prose works that might be published in different editions as follows: give the page number first, followed by a semicolon, and then include other identifying information such as book or chapter:

    (280; bk. 2)

- Document classic poems and plays as follows: omit the page number and include the act, scene, or line in the parenthetical reference. This information will enable readers to find the material in different editions. Use arabic numerals throughout unless your instructor asks you to use roman numerals:

    (*Othello* 3.2.24)

- Write out the title of a literary work the first time you mention it; thereafter, use an abbreviation in parentheses. You can adopt the abbreviation you find in your source, or formulate your own from the first letters of the main words in the title:

    I Know Why the Caged Bird Sings (CBS)

- Cite the lines of poems that you refer to, using slashes to indicate line breaks for quotations of two or three lines. For longer quotations, indent 10 spaces from the left margin and double space:

    Dickinson finds her voice when she writes that "Much Madness is divinest Sense—/To a discerning Eye—/Much Sense—the starkest Madness" (lines 1–3).

    The plain and concise language of Dickinson's poetry disguises the emotional power of this simple observation:

    > There's a certain slant of light,
    >
    > On winter afternoons,
    >
    > That oppresses, like the weight
    >
    > Of cathedral tunes. (lines 1–4)

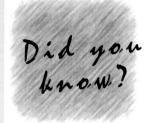

Did you know?

Essay or article in a book:

Van Pelt, William, and Alice Gillam. "Peer Collaboration and the
Computer-Assisted Classroom: Bridging the Gap Between
Academia and the Workplace." <u>Collaborative Writing in Industry: Investigations in Theory and Practice</u>. Ed. Mary M. Lay
and William M. Karis. Amityville: Baywood, 1991. 170–205.

Article in a professional journal, continuous pagination within a
volume:

Flynn, Elizabeth A. "Composing as a Woman." <u>College Composition
and Communication</u> 39 (1988): 423–35.

Article in a professional journal, each issue paginated separately:

Lay, Mary M. "Interpersonal Conflict in Collaborative Writing:
What We Can Learn from Gender Studies." <u>Journal of Business and Technical Communication</u> 3.2 (1989): 5–28.

Article in a monthly or bimonthly publication:

Lavin, Marilyn Aronberg. "Closing the Circle on Piero della
Francesca." <u>Smithsonian</u> Dec. 1992: 122–31.

Article in a weekly publication, author identified:

Reiss, Spencer. "Requiem for a Revolution." <u>Newsweek</u> 18
Jan. 1993: 28–30.

Article in a weekly publication, anonymous:

"Turn On, Tune In—and Order Takeout." <u>Newsweek</u> 9
Nov. 1992: 53.

Article in a daily newspaper, author identified:

Altman, Lawrence K. "Factory Problem Cuts Supply of a Heart
Drug Across U.S." <u>New York Times</u> 6 Jan. 1993, natl. ed.:
A1+.

Article in a daily newspaper, anonymous:

"Cancer Patient Gets Unproven Therapy." <u>Los Angeles Times</u> 6

Jan. 1993: A13.

Review, untitled:

Bolman, Lee G. Rev. of <u>The Charismatic Leader</u>, by Jay A.

Conger. <u>Journal of Management</u> 16 (1990): 678–79.

Review, titled:

Shapiro, Laura. "What's Cooking in the U.S.A.: Tracking the

Adventures of the American Palate." Rev. of <u>Paradox of</u>

<u>Plenty</u>, by Harvey Levenstein. <u>Newsweek</u> 18 Jan. 1993: 53.

Government publications:

United States. Dept. of Commerce. Bureau of the Census. <u>Money</u>

<u>Income of Households, Families, and Persons in the United</u>

<u>States: 1991</u>. Current Population Reports, Series P-60, No.

180. Washington: GPO, 1992.

Computer software:

<u>Microsoft Flight Simulator</u>. Vers. 4.0 Computer software.

Microsoft, 1991. Macintosh, 2MB, System 7.0, disk.

Online Book

Lynch, Patrick J. and Sarah Horton. *Web Style Guide: Basic*

Design Principles for Creating Web Sites. 1997. 3 Feb. 2000

<http://info.med.yale.edu/caim/manual/>.

Online journal article.

Rodrigues, Dawn. "Models of Distance Education for Composition:

The Role of Interactive Video Conferencing." *Kairos* 3.2

(1998). 2 Apr. 1999 <http://english.ttu.edu/kairos/3.2/

features/rodrigues/bridge.html>.

Online newspaper article:

Mirapaul, Matthew. "For Museums, Internet Art is a Tricky Fit."

New York Times on The Web 31 Mar. 2000 31 Mar. 2000

<http://www.nytimes.com/library/tech/00/03/cyber/

artsatlarge/30artsatlarge.html>.

Online document

Nielsen, Jakob. "International Usability Testing." 1997. 15 Mar.

2000.<http://www.useit.com/papers/international_usetest.html>.

Online Posting to a Discussion List:

Schriver, Karen. "Legal Writing Suggestions/Contacts." Online

posting. 24 March 2000. ATTW-L: Association of Teachers of

Technical Writing Listserv. 5 May 2000.

<http;//lyris.acs.ttu.edu/cgi-bin/lyris.pl?enter=attw-l>.

World Wide Web site:

Spinuzzi, Clay. Home Page. 21 Dec. 1999.

<http://english.ttu.edu/spinuzzi> *Dallas Telelearning.* Dallas

County Community College District. 3 Apr. 2000.

<http://www.lecroy.dcccd.edu>.

E-mail message:

Wick, Corey. "Knowledge Management." E-mail to Locke Carter.

30 Oct 1999.

Rickly, Rebecca. E-mail to the author. 9 Aug. 2000

Pamphlet or brochure:

Gate Structured Cell Array (G51005-0, Rev. C). Camarillo: Vitesse

Semiconductor Corporation, 1988.

Presentation:

Berkenkotter, Carol. "Novelty and Intertextuality in Two Biolo-

gists' Experimental Article." Conference on College Composition and Communication. Cincinnati, 20 Mar. 1992.

Unpublished letter:

Smith, Robin. Letter to the author. 9 Oct. 1992.

Unpublished interview:

Dinkins, David. Personal interview. 31 Aug. 1993.

Cisneros, Henry. Telephone interview. 7 Sept. 1993.

Multiple sources by the same author (listed alphabetically by title):

Tebeaux, Elizabeth. "The Evolution of Technical Description in
Renaissance English Technical Writing, 1475–1640: From
Orality to Literacy." Issues in Writing 4.1 (1991): 59–109.

---. "Ramus, Visual Rhetoric, and the Emergence of Page Design in
Medical Writing of the English Renaissance: Tracking the
Evolution of Readable Documents." Written Communication 8
(1991): 411–45.

---. "Toward an Understanding of Gender Differences in Written
Business Communication." Journal of Business and Technical
Communication 4.1 (1990): 25–43.

(Notice that in subsequent references by the same author, the author's
name is replaced by three hyphens.)

Social Sciences and Business: The APA System of Documentation

In the APA (American Psychological Asociation) system of documentation,
you identify your sources of information in a list labeled "References." List
your sources alphabetically by author's last name. If no author's name is
available, list the source alphabetically by its title.

In the text, cite specific sources parenthetically using the author's last
name and the year of publication, separated by a comma. If no author's
name is available, cite the source by its title and year of publication.

If you are emphasizing a particular passage or quoting a source, also
cite specific pages. Use the abbreviation *p.* for a single page and *pp.* for
two or more pages. Use a comma to separate the year of publication from
the citation of specific pages.

Citing Sources

One author:

Collaboration is a dynamic process and typically includes five different operations (Malone, 1991).

Two authors:

In business and industry, you will find three different types of teams (Larson & LaFasto, 1989).

Three to five authors, first citation only:

Long and complicated words often cause confusion and misinterpretation (Dobbs, Friedman, & Lloyd, 1985).

Three to five authors, subsequent citations:

Long and complicated words often cause confusion and misinterpretation (Dobbs et al., 1985).

Six or more authors:

Collaboration is possible in each of four relationships of time and space (Johansen et al., 1991).

Specific passage cited:

Collaboration is a dynamic process and typically includes five different operations (Malone, 1991, p. 112).

Multiple sources cited:

Serif type guides the reader's eye from left to right across the page (Burt, 1959; Zachrisson, 1965).

Author named in text:

According to Weiss (1991), "difference and struggle are inherently part of the bridge-building of understanding" (p. 46).

Listing Sources

Start the first line on the left margin; indent subsequent lines three spaces. Give the author's last name first, followed by the first and middle initials. Identify the date of publication next, in parentheses and followed by a period. Complete the bibliographic reference by identifying the title and other publication information. For titles of books and articles, capitalize only the first word, the first word after a colon, and proper names. Italicize (or underline) titles of books and journals; do not use quotation marks to enclose titles of journal articles. For the place of publication, identify both the city and state (using its two-letter abbreviation), except for major cities such as New York, Los Angeles, and Chicago.

Book, one author:

Crosby, F. J. (1982). Relative deprivation and working women.

New York: Oxford University Press.

Book, three or more authors:

Stanley, L. C., Shimkin, D., & Lanner, A. H. (1985). <u>Ways to</u>
<u>writing: Purpose, task, and process</u>. New York: Macmillan.

Book, edited:

Barker, T. T. (Ed.). (1991). <u>Perspectives on software documenta-</u>
<u>tion: Inquiries and innovations</u>. Amityville, NY: Baywood.

Book, edition other than the first:

Lannon, J. (1994). <u>Technical writing</u> (6th ed.). New York: HarperCollins.

Book, translation:

Vygotsky, L. (1962). <u>Thought and language</u> (E. Hanfman &
G. Vakar, Trans.). Cambridge, MA: MIT.

Essay or article in a book:

Van Pelt, W., & Gillam, A. (1991). Peer collaboration and the
computer-assisted classroom: Bridging the gap between academia and the workplace. In M. M. Lay & W. M Karis (Eds.),
<u>Collaborative writing in industry: Investigations in theory and</u>
<u>practice</u> (pp. 170–205). Amityville, NY: Baywood.

Article in a professional journal, continuous pagination within a
volume:

Flynn, E. A. (1988). Composing as a woman. <u>College Composition</u>
<u>and Communication, 39</u>, 423–435.

Article in a professional journal, each issue paginated separately:

Lay, M. M. (1989). Interpersonal conflict in collaborative writing:
What we can learn from gender studies. <u>Journal of Business</u>
<u>and Technical Communication, 3</u>(2), 5–28.

Article in a monthly or bimonthly publication:

Lavin, M. A. (1992, December). Closing the circle on Piero della
Francesca. <u>Smithsonian</u>, pp. 122–131.

Article in a weekly publication, author identified:

Reiss, S. (1993, January 18). Requiem for a revolution.

    Newsweek, pp. 28–30.

Article in a weekly publication, anonymous:

Turn on, tune in—and order takeout. (1992, November 9).

    Newsweek, p. 53.

Article in a daily newspaper, author identified:

Altman, L. K. (1993, January 6). Factory problem cuts supply of

    a heart drug across U.S. New York Times, pp. A1, A14.

Article in a daily newspaper, anonymous:

Cancer patient gets unproven therapy. (1993, January 6). Los

    Angeles Times, p. A13.

Review, untitled:

Bolman, L. G. (1990). [Review of The charismatic leader]. Journal

    of Management, 16, 678–679.

Review, titled:

Shapiro, L. (1993, January 18). What's cooking in the U.S.A.:

    Tracking the adventures of the American palate. [Review of

    Paradox of plenty]. Newsweek, p. 53.

Government publications:

Department of Commerce, Bureau of the Census. (1992). Money

    income of households, families, and persons in the United

    States: 1991 (Current Population Reports, Series P-60, No.

    180). Washington, DC: U.S. Government Printing Office.

Computer software:

Microsoft Corporation. (1991). Microsoft Flight Simulator. [Com-

    puter program]. Redmond, WA: Author. (Version 4.0,

    Macintosh).

Online book:

Lynch, P J., & Horton, S. *Web style guide: Basic design principles for creating web sites.* (1997) Retrieved February 3, 2000 from the World Wide Web: http://info.med.yale.edu/caim/manual/

Online journal article.

Rodrigues,D. (1998). Models of distance education for composition: The role of interactive video conferencing." *Kairos* 3(2). Retrieved April 2, 1999 from the World Wide Web: http://english.ttu.edu/kairos/3.2/features/rodrigues/bridge.html

Online newspaper article:

Mirapaul, M. (2000 March 31). For museums, Internet art is a tricky fit. *The New York Times on The Web.* Retrieved March 31, 2000 from the World Wide Web: http://www.nytimes.com /library/tech/00/03/cyber/artsatlarge/30artsatlarge.html.

Online document

Nielsen, J. (1997) International usability testing [essay]. Retrieved March 15, 2000 from the World Wide Web: http://www.useit.com/papers/international_usetest.html.

Online Posting to a Discussion List:

Schriver, K. (2000, March 24) Legal writing suggestions/contacts [posting]. Retrieved May 5, 2000 from the World Wide Web: http://lyris.acs.ttu.edu/cgi-bin/lyris.pl?enter=attw-l>.

World Wide Web site (cited in the text only, excluded from the list of references):

Available through the Dallas Telelearning site (http://www.lecroy.dcccd.edu) is information regarding . . .

E-mail message: (cited in the text only, excluded from the list of references):

According to R. Rickly (personal communication, August 9, 2000).

. . . (R. Rickly, personal communication, August 9, 2000)

Pamphlet or brochure:

Vitesse Semiconductor Corporation. (1988). <u>Gate structured cell array</u> (G51005-0, Rev. C). Camarillo, CA: Author.

Presentation:

Berkenkotter, C. (1992, March). <u>Novelty and intertextuality in two biologists' experimental article</u>. Paper presented at the Conference on College Composition and Communication, Cincinnati.

Unpublished letter (cited in the text only, excluded from the list of references):

According to R. Smith (personal communication, October 9, 1994) . . .

. . . (R. Smith, personal communication, October 9, 1994) . . .

Unpublished interview (cited in the text only, excluded from the list of references):

According to D. Dinkins (personal communication, August 31, 1993) . . .

. . . (H. Cisneros, personal communication, September 7, 1993) . . .

Multiple sources by the same author (different years of publication listed chronologically, same years of publication listed alphabetically by title):

Tebeaux, E. (1990). Toward an understanding of gender differences in written business communication. <u>Journal of Business and Technical Communication</u>, 4 (1), 25–43.

Tebeaux, E. (1991a). The evolution of technical description in Renaissance English technical writing, 1475–1640: From orality to literacy. <u>Issues in Writing</u>, 4 (1), 59–109.

Tebeaux, E. (1991b). Ramus, visual rhetoric, and the emergence of page design in medical writing of the English Renaissance: Tracking the evolution of readable documents. <u>Written Communication</u>, 8, 411–445.

Engineering and Technology: The IEEE System of Documentation

If you're using the IEEE (Institute of Electrical and Electronics Engineers) system of documentation, identify sources of information in a list labeled "References." Number and list your sources in the order of their citation in the text. If no author's name is available, list the source by its title.

In the text, cite specific sources by inserting a bracketed number corresponding to the appropriate source in your numbered list of references. If you are emphasizing a particular passage or quoting a source, also cite specific pages. Use the abbreviation *p.* for a single page and *pp.* for two or more pages. Use a comma to separate the number of the reference from the citation of specific pages.

Citing Sources

One or more authors:

Collaboration is a dynamic process and typically includes five different operations [9].

Specific passage cited:

Collaboration is a dynamic process and typically includes five different operations [9, p. 112].

Multiple sources cited:

Serif type guides the reader's eye from left to right across the page [5], [21].

Author named in text:

According to Weiss, "difference and struggle are inherently part of the bridge-building of understanding" [17, p. 46].

Listing Sources

Align the bracketed number on the left margin and the bibliographic information in a column two spaces to the right of the bracketed number. Give the author's first and middle initials before his or her last name. Place a comma after the author's name. Identify the title next, followed by publication information, including the date of publication. Italicize (or underline) titles of books and journals. For titles of books, capitalize the first word of the title, the last word of the title, and the first word after a colon; capitalize all other words with the exception of articles (*a, an, the*), conjunctions (*and, but, or*), and prepositions (*in, of, to*). For titles of journals, magazines, and proceedings, omit articles, conjunctions, and prepositions; capitalize all remaining words; and abbreviate if possible (e.g., *J* for *Journal*). Use quotation marks to enclose titles of journal articles; capitalize only the first word, the first word after a colon, and proper names. For the place of publication, identify both the city and state (using its two-letter abbreviation), except for major cities such as New York, Los Angeles, and Chicago.

Book, one author:

[1] F. J. Crosby, <u>Relative Deprivation and Working Women</u>. New York: Oxford University Press, 1982.

Book, edited:

[3] T. T. Barker, Ed., <u>Perspectives on Software Documentation: Inquiries and Innovations</u>. Amityville, NY: Baywood, 1991.

Book, later edition:

[4] J. Lannon, <u>Technical Writing</u>, 6th ed. New York: Harper-Collins, 1994.

Book, translation:

[5] L. Vygotsky, <u>Thought and Language</u>, E. Hanfman and G. Vakar, Trans. Cambridge, MA: MIT, 1962.

Essay or article in a book:

[6] W. Van Pelt and A. Gillam, "Peer collaboration and the computer-assisted classroom: Bridging the gap between academia and the workplace," in <u>Collaborative Writing in Industry: Investigations in Theory and Practice</u>, M. M. Lay and W. M. Karis, Eds. Amityville, NY: Baywood, 1991, pp. 170–205.

Article in a professional journal, continuous pagination within a volume:

[7] E. A. Flynn, "Composing as a woman," <u>Coll. Comp. Commun.</u>, vol. 39, pp. 423–435, 1988.

Article in a professional journal, each issue paginated separately:

[8]   M. M. Lay, "Interpersonal conflict in collaborative writing: What we can learn from gender studies," <u>J. Bus. Tech. Commun.</u>, vol. 3, no. 2, pp. 5–28, 1989.

Article in a monthly or bimonthly publication:

[9]   M. A. Lavin, "Closing the circle on Piero della Francesca," <u>Smithsonian</u>, pp. 122–131, Dec. 1992.

Article in a weekly publication, author identified:

[10] S. Reiss, "Requiem for a revolution," <u>Newsweek</u>, pp. 28–30, Jan. 18, 1993.

Article in a weekly publication, anonymous:

[11] "Turn on, tune in—and order takeout," <u>Newsweek</u>, p. 53, Nov. 9, 1992.

Article in a daily newspaper, author identified:

[12] L. K. Altman, "Factory problem cuts supply of a heart drug across U.S.," <u>New York Times</u>, sect. A, pp. 1 and 14 , Jan. 6, 1993.

Article in a daily newspaper, anonymous:

[13] "Cancer patient gets unproven therapy." <u>Los Angeles Times</u>, sect. A, p. 13, Jan. 6, 1993.

Review, untitled:

[14] L. G. Bolman, Review of <u>The Charismatic Leader</u> (J. A. Conger, 1989). <u>J. Management</u>, vol. 16, pp. 678–79, 1990.

Review, titled:

[16] L. Shapiro, "What's cooking in the U.S.A.: Tracking the adventures of the American palate"; review of <u>Paradox of Plenty</u> (H. Levenstein, 1993). <u>Newsweek</u>, p. 53, Jan. 18, 1993.

Government publications:

[19] Department of Commerce, Bureau of the Census. <u>Money</u>

Income of Households, Families, and Persons in the United States: 1991. Current Population Reports, Series P-60, No. 180. Washington, DC: GPO, 1992.

Computer software:

[23] Microsoft Flight Simulator (computer software, Macintosh version 4.0). Redmond, WA: Microsoft Corporation, 1991.

Online Book:

[24] P.J. Lynch, and S. Horton, Web style guide: Basic design principles for creating web sites [Online], (1997) [cited February 3, 2000]. Available from <http://info.med.yale.edu/caim/manual/>

Online journal article.

[25] D. Rodrigues "Models of distance education for composition: The role of interactive video conferencing." Kairos [Online], vol. 3, (no.2) (1998) [cited April 2, 1999].Available from <http://english.ttu.edu/kairos/3.2/features/rodrigues/bridge.html>.

Online newspaper article:

[26] M. Mirapaul, "For museums, Internet art is a tricky fit," The New York Times on The Web [Online], (March 31, 2000) [cited March 31, 2000]. available from <http://www.nytimes.com/library/tech/00/03/cyber/artsatlarge/30artsatlarge.html>.

Online document

[27] J. Nielsen, "International usability testing" [WWW page]. Useit.com, 1997 [cited March 15, 2000] Available from <http://www.useit.com/papers/international_usetest.html>.

Online Posting to a Discussion List:

[28] K. Schriver "Legal writing suggestions/contacts," [Posting], (March 24, 2000). [cited May 5, 2000] Available from <http://lyris.acs.ttu.edu/cgi-bin/lyris.pl?enter=attw-l>.

World Wide Web site (cited in the text only, excluded from the list of references):

> Available through the Dallas Telelearning site
>
> > (http://www.lecroy.dcccd.edu) is information regarding . . .

E-mail message: (cited in the text only, excluded from the list of references):

> According to R. Rickly (e-mail message to the author, August 9,
>
> > 2000). . . . (R. Rickly, e-mail message to the author, August
> >
> > 9, 2000)

Pamphlet or brochure:

> [31] "Gate structured cell array." Vitesse Semiconductor Corpora-
>
> > tion, Camarillo, CA, G51005-0, Rev. C, 1988.

Presentation:

> [32] C. Berkenkotter, "Novelty and intertextuality in two biolo-
>
> > gists' experimental article," presented at the Conf. Coll.
> >
> > Comp. Commun., Cincinnati, OH, 1992.

Unpublished letter (cited in the text only, excluded from the list of references):

> According to Robin Smith (letter to the author, October 9, 1994) . . .

Unpublished interview (cited in the text only, excluded from the list of references):

> According to David Dinkins, mayor of New York City (personal
>
> > interview, Aug. 31, 1993) . . .

Science and Medicine: The CBE System of Documentation

If you are using the CBE (Council of Biology Editors) system of documentation, identify sources of information in a list labeled "References," "Cited References." Organize your list of sources in one of the following ways:

- Numbered list: Number and list your sources in the order of their citation in the text.
- Numbered alphabetical list: Number and list your sources alphabetically by author's last name.
- Unnumbered alphabetical list: List your sources alphabetically by author's last name.

If no author's name is available, list the source by its title.

In the text, cite specific sources parenthetically. If emphasizing a particular passage or if quoting a source, also cite specific pages. Use the abbreviation *p* for a single page and *pp* for two or more pages. Use a comma to separate the number of the reference or the name of the author from the citation of specific pages.

If your list of sources is numbered or numbered alphabetical, cite the number corresponding to the appropriate source in your numbered list. If your list of sources is unnumbered alphabetical, cite the author's last name and the year of publication. If no author's name is available, cite the source by its title and year of publication.

Citing Sources

Numbered or Numbered Alphabetical List

One or more authors:

Collaboration is a dynamic process and typically includes five different operations (9).

Specific passage cited:

Collaboration is a dynamic process and typically includes five different operations (9, p 112).

Multiple sources cited:

Serif type guides the reader's eye from left to right across the page (5, 21).

Author named in text:

According to Weiss, "difference and struggle are inherently part of the bridge-building of understanding" (17, p 46).

Unnumbered Alphabetical List

One author:

Collaboration is a dynamic process and typically includes five different operations (Malone 1991).

Two authors:

In business and industry, you will find three different types of teams (Larson and LaFasto 1989).

Three or more authors:

Long and complicated words often cause confusion and misinterpretation (Dobbs and others 1985).

Specific passage cited:

Collaboration is a dynamic process and typically includes five different operations (Malone 1991, p 112).

Multiple sources cited:

Serif type guides the reader's eye from left to right across the page (Burt 1959 Zachrisson 1965).

Author named in text:

According to Weiss (1991), "difference and struggle are inherently part of the bridge-building of understanding" (p 46).

Listing Sources

NUMBERED LIST

Align the number of the source on the left margin and the bibliographic information in a column two spaces to the right of the number. Give the author's last name, followed by his or her first and middle initials. Identify the title next, followed by publication information, including the date of publication. For the title of a book or article, capitalize the first word and all proper names. For the title of journals, magazines, and proceedings omit articles (*a, an, the*), conjunctions (*and, but, or*), and prepositions (*in, of, to*); capitalize all remaining words; and abbreviate if possible (e.g., *J* for *Journal*). For the place of publication, identify both the city and state (using its two-letter abbreviation), except for major cities such as New York, Los Angeles, and Chicago.

Book, one author:

1. Crosby, F J. Relative deprivation and working women. New York: Oxford University Press; 1982. 268p.

Book, two or more authors:

2. Larson C E L Fasto F M J. Teamwork: what must go right, what can go wrong. Newbury Park, CA: Sage; 1989. 150p

Book, edited:

3. Barker T T, editor. Perspectives on software documentation: inquiries and innovations. Amityville, NY: Baywood; 1991. 279p.

Book, later edition:

4. Lannon J. Technical writing. 6th ed. New York: HarperCollins; 1994. 693p.

Book, translation:

5. Vygotsky L. Thought and language. Hanfman Vakar G, translators. Cambridge, MA; MIT; 1962. 168p.

Essay or article in a book:

6.   Van Pelt W, Gillam A. Peer collaboration and the computer-assisted classroom: bridging the gap between academia and the workplace. In: Lay M M, Karis W M editors. Collaborative writing in industry: Investigations in theory and practice. Amityville, NY: Baywood; 1991: p 170–205.

Article in a professional journal, continuous pagination within a volume:

7.   Flynn E A. Composing as a woman. Coll Comp Commun 1988; 39: 423–435.

Article in a professional journal, each issue paginated separately:

8.   Lay M M. Interpersonal conflict in collaborative writing: what we can learn from gender studies. J Bus Tech Commun 1989; 3(2): 5–28.

Article in a monthly or bimonthly publication:

9.   Lavin M A Closing the circle on Piero della Francesca. Smithsonian 1992 Dec: 122–131.

Article in a weekly publication, author identified:

10.   Reiss S. Requiem for a revolution. Newsweek 1993 Jan 18: 28–30.

Article in a weekly publication, anonymous:

11.   [Anonymous] Turn on, tune in—and order takeout. Newsweek 1992 Nov 9: 53.

Article in a daily newspaper, author identified:

12.   Altman L K. Factory problem cuts supply of a heart drug across U.S. New York Times 1993 Jan 6; Sect A: 1 (col 5), 14 (col 1).

Article in a daily newspaper, anonymous:

13. [Anonymous] Cancer patient gets unproven therapy. Los
     Angeles Times 1993 Jan 6; Sect A: 13 (col 2).

Review, untitled:

14. Bolman L G. [Review of The charismatic leader]. J Manage-
     ment 1990 16: 678–79.

Review, titled:

15. Shapiro L. . What's cooking in the U.S.A.: tracking the
     adventures of the American palate. [Review of Paradox of
     plenty]. Newsweek 1993 Jan 18: 53.

Government publications:

16. Department of Commerce, Bureau of the Census. Money
     income of households, families, and persons in the United
     States: 1991. Current Population Reports. 1992. Available
     from: U.S. Government Printing Office. Washington, DC:
     Series P-60, No. 180.

Computer software:

17. Microsoft Flight Simulator. [Computer program]. Redmond,
     WA: Microsoft Corporation, 1991.

Online Book:

18. Lynch PJ, and Horton S. Web style guide: Basic design principles
     for creating web sites [monograph online], 1997 Available from:
     http://info.ned.yale.edu/caim/manual/. Accessed 2000 Feb 3.

Online journal article.

19. Rodrigues D. Models of distance education for composition: The
     role of interactive video conferencing. Kairos [serial online]
     1998; 3(2) Available from: http://english.ttu.edu/kairos/
     3.2/features/rodrigues/bridge.html. Accessed 1999 Apr 2.

Online newspaper article:

20. Mirapaul M. For museums, Internet art is a tricky fit. *The New York Times on The Web* [serial online] 2000 Mar 31. Available from http://www.nytimes.com/library/tech/00/03/cyber/30artsatlarge.html. Accessed 2000 Mar 31.

Online document

21. Nielsen J., International usability testing [essay online]. Available from: http://www.useit.com/papers/international_usetest.html. Accessed 2000 Mar 15.

Online Posting to a Discussion List:

22. Schriver K. Legal writing suggestions/contacts [posting] 2000 Mar 24. Available from: http://lyris.acs.ttu.edu/cgi-bin/lyris.pl/enter=attw-l. Accessed 2000 May 5.

World Wide Web site (cited in the text only, excluded from the list of references):

23. Available through the Dallas Telelearning site (http://www.lecroy.dcccd.edu) is information regarding . . .

E-mail message: (cited in the text only, excluded from the list of references):

24. According to R. Rickly (e-mail message to the author, August 9, 2000). . . . (R. Rickly, e-mail message to the author, August 9, 2000)

Pamphlet or brochure:

25. Vitesse Semiconductor Corporation. Gate structured cell array. G51005-0, Rev C; 1988. Available from: Vitesse Semiconductor Corporation, Camarillo, CA.

Presentation:

26. Berkenkotter C. Novelty and intertextuality in two biologists' experimental article. Paper presented at the Conf Coll Comp Commun Cincinnati, OH: 1992.

Unpublished letter (cited in the text only, excluded from the list of references):

According to Robin Smith (letter to the author, October 9, 1994). . .

Unpublished interview (cited in the text only, excluded from the list of references):

According to David Dinkins, mayor of New York City (personal interview, Aug. 31, 1993) . . .

. . . (H Cisneros, telephone interview, September 7, 1993) . . .

NUMBERED ALPHABETICAL LIST

1. Barker T T, editor. Perspectives on software documentation: Inquiries and innovations. Amityville, NY: Baywood; 1991. 279p.

2. Crosby F J. Relative deprivation and working women. New York: Oxford University Press; 1982. 268p.

3. Larson C E, LaFasto F M J. Teamwork: what must go right, what can go wrong. Newbury Park, CA: Sage; 1989. 150p.

Multiple sources by the same author (different years of publication listed chronologically, same years of publication listed alphabetically by title):

4. Tebeaux E. Toward an understanding of gender differences in written business communication. J Bus Tech Commun 1990; 4(1): 25–43.

5. Tebeaux E. The evolution of technical description in Renaissance English technical writing, 1475–1640: from orality to literacy. Issues Writing 1991a;. 4(1): 59–109.

6.   Tebeaux E. Ramus, visual rhetoric, and the emergence of page design in medical writing of the English Renaissance: tracking the evolution of readable documents. Written Commun 1991b; 8: 411–45.

UNNUMBERED ALPHABETICAL LIST

Start the first line on the left margin; indent subsequent lines five spaces. Give the author's last name, followed by his or her first and middle initials. Identify the title next, followed by publication information, including the date of publication. For the title of a book or article, capitalize the first word and all proper names. For the title of journals and magazines, omit prepositions and articles, capitalize all remaining words, and abbreviate if possible (e.g., *J* for *Journal*). For the place of publication, identify both the city and state (using its two-letter abbreviation), except for major cities such as New York, Los Angeles, and Chicago.

Barker, T. T., editor. Perspectives on software documentation: inquiries and innovations. Amityville, NY: Baywood; 1991. 279p.

Crosby, F. J. Relative deprivation and working women. New York: Oxford University Press; 1982. 268p.

Larson, C.E.; LaFasto, F. M. J. Teamwork: what must go right, what can go wrong. Newbury Park, CA: Sage; 1989. 150p.

Multiple sources by the same author (different years of publication listed chronologically, same years of publication listed alphabetically by title):

Tebeaux, E. Toward an understanding of gender differences in written business communication. J. Bus. Tech. Commun 1990; 1991a; 4(1): 25–43.

Tebeaux, E. The evolution of technical description in Renaissance English technical writing, 1475–1640: from orality to literacy. Issues Writing 1991a; 4(1): 59–109.

Tebeaux, E. Ramus, visual rhetoric, and the emergence of page
design in medical writing of the English Renaissance: tracking the evolution of readable documents. Written Commun.
1991b; 8: 411–45.

Index of Key Terms

Classroom English is the dialect that school teachers, business people, and journalists adopt to do their jobs: it is the dialect of dictionary spellings and grammar books. If you are addressing a specific social, ethnic, or regional group, you might consider using the dialect of that group to communicate your message. If your audience is composed of different groups, however, using the dialect of a single group might cause confusion or damage your credibility. To communicate your message effectively, as a consequence, choose a dialect that has a wider currency. In school and on the job, classroom English is often the appropriate choice.

WORDS

Nouns

Nouns are words that identify people, animals, plants, places, things, or ideas. In sentences, nouns serve as subjects, objects, objects of prepositions, and complements. You distinguish singular from plural nouns by the absence or presence of a plural ending (usually *s* or *es*). Irregular plurals are of five basic types:

	Singular	Plural
en ending	ox, child	oxen, children
no ending	fish	fish
word mutation	goose, mouse	geese, mice
f-v mutation + s	life	lives
foreign plurals	alumnus, crisis	alumni, crises

Attention ESL Writers

Nouns that cannot be counted (called **mass nouns**) have no plural: for example, *milk, biology, attention, spaghetti, malaria.*

In the possessive case, nouns serve as modifiers of nouns, noun phrases, and noun clauses. Use an apostrophe + *s* for singular possessives (*child's*) and for plural possessives without *s* endings (*children's*). Use only the apostrophe for plurals with *s* endings (see "Apostrophes").

	Singular	Plural
Subjects/Objects	engineer	engineers
Possessives	engineer's	engineers'

In a pair or series of nouns, signal individual ownership by displaying all nouns as possessives:

Tim's and Nick's iguanas are sick (Tim's iguanas are sick and Nick's iguanas are sick).

Signal joint ownership by displaying only the final noun of the pair or series as a possessive:

Tim and Nick's iguanas are sick.

Nouns are also either common or proper. **Common nouns** are general identifiers, whereas **proper nouns** are specific names. Proper nouns are capitalized (see "Capitalization"). Check your dictionary or style manual to determine if a given noun is common or proper.

Pronouns

Pronouns substitute for nouns, noun phrases, noun clauses, and other pronouns. The five types of pronouns are personal, relative, interrogative, demonstrative, and indefinite.

Personal Pronouns

Personal pronouns differ according to the following characteristics:

- person: the relationship of the speaker/writer to the subject (first, second, or third person)
- case: function within the sentence (subjective, objective, possessive, or reflexive)
- gender: masculine, feminine, or neuter
- number: singular or plural

The following is a list of the personal pronouns:

Singular	1st Person	2nd Person	3rd Person
Subjective	I	you	he, she, it
Objective	me	you	him, her, it
Possessive	my, mine	your, yours	his, her, hers, its
Reflexive	myself	yourself	himself, herself, itself

Plural	1st Person	2nd Person	3rd Person
Subjective	we	you	they
Objective	us	you	them
Possessive	our, ours	your, yours	their, theirs
Reflexive	ourselves	yourselves	themselves

Notice that no apostrophes are used with the possessive case of personal pronouns. Thus the possessive of *it* is *its* (*it's* is a contraction of *it is*). Notice also the third person reflexives, especially the masculine singular and the plural. While various local dialects use *hisself* and *theirselves,* classroom English uses *himself* and *themselves.*

To substitute effectively for a noun, a personal pronoun has to correspond to the person, case, gender, and number of the noun. Consider, for example, the following sentence:

Linda visits Maria daily. Maria lives on 55th Street.

To substitute for Maria in the second sentence, the personal pronoun must be third person, subjective case, feminine, and singular:

Linda visits Maria daily. *She* lives on 55th Street.

Reflexive pronouns echo a noun or pronoun within the sentence. The reflexive pronoun, therefore, has to correspond to the person, gender, and number of this noun or pronoun. Consider, for example, the following sentences:

Paolo kicked *himself.*

Paolo directed the questions to *himself.*

Paolo is never *himself* with his piano teacher.

Because *Paolo* is third person, masculine, and singular, the reflexive pronoun is also. Notice that the reflexive pronoun always echoes a noun or pronoun within the sentence. In a sentence such as the following, therefore, the reflexive is inappropriate: *She offered it to myself.* In this sentence, the objective case of the personal pronoun is necessary: *She offered it to me.*

Relative Pronouns

Relative pronouns introduce restrictive and nonrestrictive relative clauses (see "Complex Sentences"). The relative pronouns are *who, which,* and *that,* with *who* referring to people and *which* and *that* referring to animals, plants, places, things, and ideas. Ordinarily, *who* and *that* introduce restrictive clauses; *who* and *which* introduce nonrestrictive clauses. Occasionally, *when* and *where* also serve as relative pronouns, introducing either restrictive or nonrestrictive clauses.

Interrogative Pronouns

The interrogative pronouns are *who, which, what, when, where, why,* and *how.* In questions, interrogative pronouns serve as subjects, objects, or modifiers (see "Wh-Questions"):

subject: *Who* delivered the flowers to my office?

object: *Which* of your sisters did you visit this morning? (The subject is *you.*)

modifier: *Why* did you quit your job? (The subject is *you.*)

Demonstrative Pronouns

The demonstrative singular pronouns are *this* and *that;* the plural demonstratives are *these* and *those. This* and *these* identify items near to the speaker or writer in space or time; *that* and *those* identify items distant from the speaker or writer. Demonstrative pronouns substitute for nouns, phrases or clauses:

noun: She usually dislikes *pizza,* but she'll love *this.*

phrase: *Running five miles a day* is terrific: I wish I'd started doing *this* years ago.

clause: *He was divorced five years ago. This* explains why he avoids serious relationships.

Indefinite Pronouns

Indefinite pronouns never refer to specific individuals, items, or ideas. The indefinite pronouns are the following: *many, much, more, most, little, less, least, few, fewer, fewest, both, several, enough, some, somebody, someone, something, any, anybody, anyone, anything, either, neither, one, other, another, none, no one, nobody, nothing.* The indefinite pronouns ending in *one, body, either,* or *other* also have a possessive case, using an apostrophe + *s* (*someone's responsibility, nobody's fault*).

Adjectives

Adjectives modify nouns from two positions within a sentence:

preceding the noun: The *new* machine stopped working.

following the noun: The machine that stopped working is *new.*

To compare two items to each other, use the **comparative** form of the adjective and the word *than:*

Comparatives

1-syllable adjectives:	adjective + *er*	*big, bigger*
	or *more* + adjective	*strained, more strained*
2-syllable adjectives:	adjective + *er*	*funny, funnier*
	or *more* + adjective	*polite, more polite*
3 or more syllables:	*more* + adjective	*specific, more specific*

Consider, for example, the following sentences:

Eduardo is *taller than* Adrian.

This house is *prettier* on the inside *than* it is on the outside.

She is *more industrious than* he is.

To compare three or more items to each other, use the **superlative** form of the adjective:

Superlatives

1-syllable adjectives:	adjective + *est*	*big, biggest*
	or *most* + adjective	*strained, most strained*
2-syllable adjectives:	adjective + *est*	*funny, funniest*
	or *most* + adjective	*polite, most polite*
3 or more syllables:	*most* + adjective	*specific, most specific*

Consider, for example, the following sentences:

Eduardo is the *tallest* of the five children.

This house is the *prettiest* on the street.

She is the *most industrious* teacher at the school.

Several adjectives have irregular comparatives and superlatives: for example, *good, better, best; bad, worse, worst*. In addition, a number of adjectives have no comparatives or superlatives: for example, *several, principal, next, infinite, unique*.

Adjectives are also either common or proper. **Common adjectives** are general modifiers whereas **proper adjectives** are specific names. Proper adjectives are capitalized (see "Capitalization") and have neither comparatives nor superlatives. Check your dictionary or style manual to determine if a given adjective is common or proper.

Numbers

Numbers are of two types: **cardinal numbers** (one, two, three) and **ordinal numbers** (first, second, third). In sentences, numbers function as nouns, pronouns, or adjectives:

noun: The industrious *five* cooperated on this design.

pronoun: *Five* of us cooperated on this design.

adjective: *Five* engineers cooperated on this design.

As nouns and pronouns, numbers have no possessive case; as adjectives, numbers have neither comparative nor superlative forms.

Verbs

Verbs communicate information regarding subjects:

activities: *sing, dig, repair*

processes: *live, age, wither*

sensations: *itch, thirst, smell*

emotions: *love, sympathize, forgive*

perceptions: *know, understand, comprehend*

relationships: *possess, marry, equal*

A number of verbs consist of two or three words: for example, *bring up, break off, break open, come down with, cut loose, face up to, find out, give up, get away with, give out, look down on, look forward to, look into, look over, look up to, make up, put across, put down, put off, put on, put up with, run for, set free, turn on, turn off.*

Verbs are either transitive or intransitive:

Attention ESL Writers

Transitive
(subjects act on objects): The girl delivered the flowers.

Attention ESL Writers

Intransitive
(subjects act without objects): The flowers arrived yesterday.

A verb that links a subject to a noun or adjective following the verb is a **linking verb:**

The woman *is* a doctor.

The man *is* sick.

In addition to *be,* other linking verbs are *appear, become, feel, grow, look, prove, remain, seem, smell, sound, stay, taste, turn.*

English also has **auxiliary verbs:** *be, have,* and *do.* The auxiliaries have no meaning themselves, but serve to communicate the tense, aspect, voice, and mood of accompanying verbs:

We *are* visiting the museum.

We *have* visited the museum.

We *did* visit the museum.

Modals specify conditions regarding the occurrence of verbs:

Modal	Meaning	Example
be going to	intention/prediction	*I am going to drive to school.*
can/could	ability	*I can drive to school.*
have to	necessity/obligation	*I have to drive to school.*
may/might	permission/possibility	*I may drive to school.*
shall/should	intention/obligation	*I shall drive to school.*
will/would	intention/prediction	*I will drive to school.*
must	necessity/obligation	*I must drive to school.*
need to	necessity/obligation	*I need to drive to school.*
ought to	obligation	*I ought to drive to school.*
used to	previous habit	*I used to drive to school.*

Verbs have four characteristics: tense, aspect, voice, and mood.

Tense

Tense is applied to verbs to indicate the relative time of the action or condition. English has two tenses: present tense and past tense. Ordinarily, you signal the past tense either by adding the ending *-ed* (for regular verbs) or by modifying the present tense verb (for irregular verbs).

Present Tense	**Past Tense**
walk	*walked*
bring	*brought*
strike	*struck*
know	*knew*
send	*sent*
go	*went*
do	*did*
am/is/are	*was/were*

Several verbs, such as *cut* or *hit,* display no change across tenses. If you are unsure of how to form the past tense of a verb, check your dictionary.

Use the present tense to discuss existing actions or conditions. Use the past tense to discuss previous actions or conditions.

Aspect

The **aspect** of the verb is the manner of its action: simple, progressive, perfect, or perfect progressive.

Attention ESL Writers

Ordinarily, you will use simple aspect for the majority of verbs. **Simple aspect** is just verb + tense:

Gloria *kicks* the ball.　　　　Gloria *kicked* the ball.

Miguel *drinks* the juice.　　　Miguel *drank* the juice.

To emphasize that a given action or condition is or was ongoing or repetitive, use progressive aspect. The **progressive aspect** consists of *be* + tense + present participle (verb + *ing*):

Gloria *is kicking* the ball.　　Gloria *was kicking* the ball.

Miguel *is drinking* the juice.　Miguel *was drinking* the juice.

Choose perfect aspect to emphasize that a given action or condition is or was already completed. **Perfect aspect** comprises *have* + tense + past participle:

have + tense + verb + *ed/t:*

Gloria *has kicked* the ball.　　Gloria *had kicked* the ball.

have + tense + verb + vowel mutation:

Miguel *has drunk* the juice.　　Miguel *had drunk* the juice.

have + tense + verb + *n/en:*

Laura *has given* the money.　　Laura *had given* the money.

have + tense + verb + vowel mutation + *n/en/t:*

David *has broken* the window.　David *had broken* the window.

have + tense + verb mutation:

Kwan *has taught* the class.　　Kwan *had taught* the class.

have + tense + verb:

The time *has come* for action.　The time *had come* for action.

If a repetitive or ongoing action or condition is or was already completed, use perfect progressive. **Perfect progressive** consists of *have* + tense + the past participle of *be* (*be* + *en*) + present participle (verb + *ing*):

Gloria *has been kicking* the ball. Gloria *had been kicking* the ball.

Notice that if a modal is added, the modal carries the tense:

Gloria kicks the ball.	Gloria *will* kick the ball.
Gloria is kicking the ball.	Gloria *might* be kicking the ball.
Gloria has kicked the ball.	Gloria *could* have kicked the ball.
Gloria has been kicking the ball.	Gloria *must* have been kicking the ball.

Voice

Voice is either active or passive. In **active voice,** the subject of the sentence is active:

subject
Daniel built the bridge quickly.

In this sentence, the subject is *Daniel* and he did the building. In **passive voice,** however, the subject of the sentence is a passive recipient of the action:

subject
The *bridge* was built quickly by Daniel.

In this sentence, the original subject, *Daniel,* is shifted to a position following the verb and the word *by* is inserted. Oftentimes, the original subject is simply omitted (e.g., *The bridge was built quickly.*). The object of the original sentence is shifted to the subject position. The verb changes to *be* + past participle:

be + tense + verb + *ed/t:*

Lew *collects* the cans.	The cans *are collected* by Lew.
Lew *collected* the cans.	The cans *were collected* by Lew.

be + tense + verb + vowel mutation:

Bobbi *sinks* the ship.	The ship *is sunk* by Bobbi.
Bobbi *sank* the ship.	The ship *was sunk* by Bobbi.

be + tense + verb + *n/en:*

Marion *grows* these flowers.	These flowers *are grown* by Marion.

Marion *grew* these flowers. These flowers *were grown* by Marion.

be + tense + verb + vowel mutation + *n/en/t:*

Sara *rides* that horse. That horse *is ridden* by Sara.

Sara *rode* that horse. That horse *was ridden* by Sara.

be + tense + verb mutation:

Jamal *brings* the books. The books *are brought* by Jamal.

Jamal *brought* the books. The books *were brought* by Jamal.

be + tense + verb:

Maggie *cuts* the grass. The grass *is cut* by Maggie.

Maggie *cut* the grass. The grass *was cut* by Maggie.

In addition to the simple passive, a progressive passive and a perfect passive also occur:

progressive passive (be + tense + be + ing + past participle):

The cans *are being collected* by Lew.

perfect passive (have + tense + be + en + past participle):

The cans *have been collected* by Lew.

Notice that passive voice is limited to transitive verbs (i.e., verbs that have objects). Notice also that if a modal is added, the modal carries the tense:

The cans are collected by Lew. The cans *will* be collected by Lew.

Use active voice to emphasize or clarify the agent of action. If the agent of action is unimportant, use passive voice. Keep in mind, however, that passive voice raises the level of reading difficulty (see Chapter 6, pp. 187–188).

Mood

The **mood** of the verb indicates how the writer or speaker perceives the action or condition:

indicative mood: action or condition is a fact

imperative mood: action or condition is a command

subjunctive mood: action or condition is a hypothesis

Ordinarily, the mood of verbs is indicative. **Indicative mood** has a present and a past tense as well as a first, second, and third person, both singular and plural:

	Singular	Plural
Present Tense	I *am* here.	We *are* here.
	You *are* here.	You *are* here.
	He/She/It *is* here.	They *are* here.
Past Tense	I *was* here.	We *were* here.
	You *were* here.	You *were* here.
	He/She/It *was* here.	They *were* here.

Singular verbs accompany singular subjects and plural verbs accompany plural subjects:

singular subject/singular verb: The *book is* here.

plural subject/plural verb: The *books are* here.

In the present tense, all third person singular verbs have *s* endings:

singular subject/singular verb: The *girl likes* the book.

plural subject/plural verb: The *girls like* the book.

Imperative mood has only a present tense and only a second person, singular and plural:

singular: [You] *be* here.

plural: [You] *be* here.

Often the personal pronoun *you* is omitted.

Subjunctive mood is disappearing from the English language. While Spanish and French, for example, have a vital subjunctive mood, English preserves only two basic types of subjunctive expressions:

that subjunctive:

I recommend that he *be* fired.   (instead of indicative *is*)

She asked that he *come* to visit.   (instead of indicative *comes*)

were subjunctive:

I wish he *were* here.   (instead of indicative *was*)

If I *were* you . . .   (instead of indicative *was*)

The subjunctive also occurs in a number of familiar expressions:

So be it.   (instead of indicative *is*)

God *forbid* that. . . .   (instead of indicative *forbids*)

Come this evening, we will . . .   (instead of indicative *comes*)

The subjunctive mood is often used in formal writing. For informal communication, therefore, you might revise to avoid the subjunctive:

I recommend that he *be* fired.	I recommend firing him.
She asked that he *come* to visit.	She asked him to visit.
I wish he *were* here.	I wish he could be here.
If I *were* you . . .	I think you ought to . . .

Verbals

Verbals are verbs that function as nouns or adjectives. Similar to verbs, verbals are either transitive (acting on objects) or intransitive (acting without objects). Verbals are of four types:

Attention ESL Writers

Verbal Type	Function	Example
infinitive (to + verb)	noun	*She asked to leave the room.*
	adverb	*To please his sister, he washed the dishes.*
gerund (verb + ing)	noun	*His job is repairing small appliances.*
present participle (verb + ing)	adjective	*Running all the way, he arrived at his office before nine o'clock.*
past participle (verb + ed/t)	adjective	*Often he would sleep through class, exhausted from his job as a waiter.*
(verb + vowel mutation)		*Rung each morning and evening for 50 years, the school bell cracked.*
(verb + n/en)		*We could be allies, given the right conditions.*
(mutation + n/en/t)		*Kept from his friends, the boy was always lonely.*
(verb mutation)		*The vicious criminal, finally caught by the police, admitted his guilt.*
(verb)		*Hit by a hurricane, the city was severely damaged.*

Often a participle has a subject, creating a verbal phrase that modifies the remainder of the sentence:

The sun starting to shine, she closed the umbrella.

The city was again quiet, *the police officers having stopped the riot.*

His shirt [being] dirty, the man decided to leave. (The word *being* is optional.)

His reputation [being] damaged, the man quit his job. (The word *being* is optional.)

Adverbs

Adverbs modify verbs, adjectives, adverbs, and sentences. Adverbs modify from several positions within a sentence:

Modifying Verbs:

preceding the verb:	The driver *often* stopped the bus.
following the verb:	The driver stopped *often.*
following the object:	The driver stopped the bus *often.*

Modifying Adjectives:

preceding the adjective:	This color is *incredibly* bright.
following the adjective (*enough* only):	This color is bright *enough.*

Modifying Adverbs:

preceding the adverb:	She composed this essay *quite* easily.
following the adverb (*enough* only):	She composed this essay easily *enough.*

Modifying Sentences:

beginning of the sentence: *Ideally,* eligible citizens will register to vote.

Adverbs are of five basic types:

adverbs of time:	today, tomorrow, daily, weekly,
adverbs of location:	here, there, inside, outside, near, far
adverbs of manner:	abruptly, easily, briefly, wisely, slowly, often
intensifiers:	too, very, especially, definitely, always, never
transitions:	however, therefore, as a consequence, thus

To compare two items to each other, use the **comparative** form of the adverb and the word *than:*

Comparatives

early, late, fast, slow, hard, long, quick, soon:	adverb + *er*	earlier, later, faster, slower, harder, longer, quicker, sooner
remaining adverbs:	*more* + adverb	more aggressively

Consider, for example, the following sentences:

He leaves *earlier than* she does.

She works *more efficiently than* he does.

To compare three or more items to each other, use the **superlative** form of the adverb:

Superlatives

early, late, fast, slow, hard, long, quick, soon:	adverb + *est*	earliest, latest, fastest, slowest, hardest, longest, quickest, soonest
other adverbs:	*most* + adverb	most aggressively

Consider, for example, the following sentences:

He leaves *earliest* on Fridays. (Of all the days of the week, he leaves earliest on Fridays.)

She works *most efficiently* in the morning. (Of all the times of day, she works most efficiently in the morning.)

Several adverbs have irregular comparative and superlatives: for example, *well, better, best; badly, worse, worst.* In addition, a wide variety of adverbs have no comparative or superlative forms: for example, *however, very, daily, here, never.*

Prepositions

Prepositions are words that specify relationships, primarily of place, time, cause, manner, and possession. The **object of a preposition** is a noun, gerund, or pronoun. Together, the preposition and its object (as well as modifiers of the object) compose a **prepositional phrase.**

preposition + noun:	The boy *on the bicycle* is my brother.
preposition + gerund:	He exercised *by jogging.*
preposition + pronoun:	This gift is *for you and me.*

A preposition might also introduce a *which* or *whom* clause:

I visited the office *to which he delivered my books.*

She is the doctor *of whom I was thinking.*

A preposition could also come after its object clause, especially if the writing is informal:

I visited the office *[that] he delivered my books to.* (The word *that* is optional.)

She is the doctor *[whom] I was thinking of.* (The word *whom* is optional.)

A preposition describes the relationship its object has to a noun, verb, adjective, or clause within the sentence:

	noun prep phrase
modifying a noun:	I asked the *owner of the store.*

	verb prep phrase
modifying a verb:	I *stopped at the store.*

	adjective prep phrase
modifying an adjective:	I am *afraid of your dog.*

	prep phrase clause
modifying a clause:	*In conclusion, I advise a new policy.*

Attention ESL Writers

Ordinarily, prepositions describe the following five relationships:

Relationship	Prepositions	Example
location	*above, across, along, among, around, at, below, beneath, between, beyond, by, down, from, in, off, on, out, over, to, through, under, up*	The book is *on the desk.*
time	*after, at, before, between, by, for, in, on, since, through, throughout, until, up to, when*	She arrived *in the morning.*
cause	*at, because of, for, from, of, to*	He was dying *of thirst.*
manner	*against, at, by, despite, except, except for, in spite of, notwithstanding, with, without, like*	She was skiing *with a friend.*
possession	*of, with, without*	The office *of the director* is locked.

Coordinators and Subordinators

Coordinators join two or more words, phrases, or clauses, emphasizing their equality (see "Compound Sentences"). In formal communication, the coordinators are *and, but, nor, or,* and *yet.* The coordinators *for* and *so* are typically limited to informal communication.

Subordinators introduce subordinate clauses, emphasizing the dependence or lesser importance of the subordinate clause relative to the main clause of the sentence (see "Complex Sentences"). Subordinators communicate several meanings:

Meaning	Subordinator	Example
time	*after, as long as, as soon as, before, once, since, until, when, whenever, while*	We ought to leave for the airport *as soon as* he arrives with the suitcases.
location	*where, wherever*	*Wherever* I go I always bring my dog.
comparison	*as, as if, as though, as much as, as little as*	We enjoyed reading this book *as much as* we did seeing the film.
contrast	*athough, even though, though, whereas, while*	She enjoys gymnastics, *whereas* he likes soccer.
cause	*because, since, due to the fact that*	*Because* I enjoy bicycling, I ride five miles a day.
effect	*so that, in order that*	She practiced the violin daily *so that* she could receive a music scholarship.
condition	*as, as long as, even if, if, unless*	*If* my sister visits, we might go sightseeing.
manner	*how, however*	He did the job *however* he could.

Determiners

Determiners are the words that introduce nouns and noun phrases. Determiners introduce all nouns and noun phrases except indefinite plural nouns (e.g., *I like dogs.*) and indefinite mass nouns (e.g., *I like milk.*). Nouns referring to specific occurrences of a subject or object are definite (e.g., *She painted this picture.*). Nouns referring to no particular subject or object are indefinite (e.g., *She paints pictures*). Determiners are of four types: articles, demonstratives, possessives, and quantifiers.

Attention ESL Writers

Articles

Articles are definite and indefinite. The **definite article** is *the,* and the indefinite articles are *a* and *an.* For example, *the dog* is a specific dog; *a dog* is no specific dog. Articles have no meaning themselves, but function only to identify the definite or indefinite condition of their nouns.

The **indefinite article** *a* is used with nouns starting with a consonant sound (e.g., *a tree*); *an* is for nouns starting with a vowel sound (e.g., *an orange*). The definite article *the* is spelled identically for nouns starting with vowel sounds and nouns starting with consonant sounds, but the pronunciation differs: "thuh" for consonant sounds and "thee" for vowel sounds.

Demonstratives

The demonstrative determiners are identical to the demonstrative pronouns: *this* and *that* for singular nouns; *these* and *those* for plural nouns.

This and *these* introduce nouns near to the speaker or writer in space or time (e.g., *this* evening); *that* and *those* introduce nouns distant from the speaker or writer (e.g., *that* evening a year ago).

Possessives

The possessive determiners are the possessive case of all personal pronouns, indefinite pronouns, and proper nouns, as well as the relative pronoun *whose:*

personal pronouns:	*my, your, his, her, its, our, their*
indefinite pronouns:	*somebody's, anyone's, each other's*
proper nouns:	*Linda's*
relative pronouns:	*whose*

Quantifiers

The quantifying determiners are words such as *another, any, both, enough, either, few, fewer, little, less, many, more, most, much, neither, no, several,* and *some.*

Interjections

Interjections are various emotional signals and filler expressions: for example, *oh, ah, uh, huh, wow, ooh, ouch, hmmm.* Interjections typically occur at the beginning of a sentence: for example, *Ouch, I hit my finger!* or *Wow, that's a terrific idea!* Ordinarily, interjections are restricted to informal speaking and writing.

SENTENCES

Functions of Sentences

Sentences declare, question, command, and exclaim.

Declaratives

In declarative sentences, three sequences are dominant:

Subject + Verb (+ Adverbial Modifier):	She walked.
	She walked often.
	She walked home.
	She walked today.
	She walked to the store.

Notice that adverbs, prepositional phrases, and nouns referring to times and locations function as adverbial modifiers. Essentially, if the word or phrase answers the questions *when, where, how,* or *why,* its function is adverbial.

Subject + Verb + Object:

subject + verb + object	He liked the book.
subject + verb + object + indirect object	He delivered the flowers to the office.
subject + verb + indirect object + object	He offered his friend a drink.
subject + verb + object + adjective complement	He considered the man devious.
subject + verb + object + noun complement	He considered the man a liar.

Notice that the words following the verb answer the questions *who* or *what* and thus function as objects or complements. A **complement** is a noun or adjective that modifies the subject or object of the sentence.

Subject + Linking Verb + Complement:

subject + linking verb + adjective complement	She is perceptive.
subject + linking verb + noun complement	She is a professional.

Notice that the adjective or noun complement following the verb describes the subject. The verb thus links the subject to this modifier (see page 690).

Two other declarative sequences also occur:

It + linking verb (or the verbs *rain* and *snow*)	It is raining.
	It appears that he is hungry.
	It seems to be time to leave.
	It smells good in the kitchen.
	It rained this morning.

There + *be, appear,* or *seem:*   There is a mistake on this page.

There are mistakes on this page.

There appear to be mistakes on this page.

There seems to be a mistake on this page.

In such sentences, *it* and *there* are meaningless words that fill the subject position of the sentence. The *it* sequence always occurs with a third person singular verb; the *there* sequence occurs with either third person singular (if the noun following the verb is singular) or third person plural (if the noun following the verb is plural).

Questions

Questions are of two types: yes/no questions and wh-questions:

YES/NO QUESTIONS

To ask a **yes/no question,** you have two choices. You could compose a declarative sentence and finish it with a question mark:

She designed this house.   She designed this house?

Or you could start the sentence with a modal or auxiliary verb (see page 690) and finish the sentence with a question mark:

She will design this house.	Will she design this house?
She has designed this house.	Has she designed this house?
She is designing this house.	Is she designing this house?
She should be designing this house.	Should she be designing this house?
She has been designing this house.	Has she been designing this house?
She designed the house.	Did she design the house?

Notice that you always start this type of yes/no question with the modal or auxiliary that carries the tense. Keep in mind that if you are using a modal, the modal carries the tense. Notice also that if the sentence has no modal or auxiliary, you start the sentence with the auxiliary *do,* adding tense to it.

WH-QUESTIONS

You ask a **wh-question** by starting the sentence with the appropriate interrogative word and finishing it with a question mark. The interrogative word might serve as the subject of the sentence:

Who designed this house?

Which deteriorated quicker?

What constitutes the policy?

Or the interrogative word serves as a modifier (either adjective or adverb). In such questions, the subject occurs after a modal or auxiliary:

Whose car has *he* been driving?

Which book is *she* reading?

When is *he* arriving?

Where has *she* served?

Why will *he* leave?

How did *she* build this bridge?

To whom could *he* have written?

For what might *she* have been asking?

Commands

A command uses the imperative mood of the verb. The subject is *you,* either singular or plural.

You be here at eight o'clock. (The subject *you* is explicit.)

Please be here at eight o'clock. (The subject *you* is implicit.)

You intensify a command, adding urgency or emphasis, by ending it with an exclamation mark:

Be here at eight o'clock!

Exclamations

To compose exclamations, you have three choices. You might compose a declarative sentence, ending it with an exclamation mark instead of a period:

A horse is crossing the river!

Or you might compose a yes/no question, ending it with an exclamation mark instead of a question mark:

Isn't that horse beautiful!

Or you might start your sentence with the interrogative *what* or *how,* following it immediately with the topic of your exclamation and ending with an exclamation mark:

noun complement:	What *a swimmer* that horse is!
adjective complement:	How *beautiful* that horse is!
adverb:	How *quickly* that horse is crossing the river!

Types of Sentences

English has four types of sentences: simple, compound, complex, and compound-complex.

Simple Sentences

A **simple sentence** is a single independent clause. A **clause** has a **subject** (a noun or pronoun) and a **predicate** (a verb, verb + object, or linking verb + noun or adjective). The predicate offers information regarding the subject. A clause is **independent** if it communicates a complete idea by itself:

> subject   predicate (verb)
> *The tourists arrive at nine o'clock.*

> subject predicate (verb + object)
> *My sister drives a truck.*

> subject   predicate (verb + complement)
> *This orange is delicious.*

In a simple sentence, compound subjects or predicates are also possible:

> subject   compound predicate
> *The tourists arrive at nine o'clock and leave at eleven o'clock.*

> compound subject   compound predicate
> *My sister and my brother drive a truck and deliver flowers.*

> compound subject   predicate
> *This orange and this apple are delicious.*

If a specific idea deserves the reader's undivided attention, use a simple sentence.

Compound Sentences

A **compound sentence** has at least two independent clauses divided by a comma and joined by a coordinating word (e.g., *and, but, or*):

subject predicate compound subject predicate
Linda smiled, but *Nick and Tim laughed.*

subject compound predicate   subject predicate
He slices the squash and chops the broccoli, or *he cooks the rice.*

subject   predicate subject   predicate
This painting of the ocean is beautiful and *that portrait of a sailor is hideous.*

To divide a reader's attention equally among several ideas, use a compound sentence.

Complex Sentences

A **complex sentence** also has at least two clauses. The **main clause** is independent, but the other clause or clauses are subordinate to the main clause and depend on it to communicate a complete idea. Subordinating words (e.g., *after, as soon as, although, because, before, if, since, though, unless, until, when, whereas, while*) serve to introduce and identify the **subordinate** clause:

main clause   subordinate clause
She lifted weights while he jogged and I practiced my diving.

 subordinate clause   main clause
While she lifted weights, he jogged and I practiced my diving.

 main clause   subordinate clause
Jasmaine and Raj started playing baseball after we watched the World Series.

 subordinate clause   main clause
Before Jasmaine and Raj started playing baseball, we watched the World Series.

 main clause   subordinate clause
Kariesha enjoys gymnastics, though she dislikes the emphasis on competition.

 subordinate clause   main clause
Though Kariesha enjoys gymnastics, she dislikes the emphasis on competition.

To divide a reader's attention unequally among several ideas, use a complex sentence. Use the subordinate clause for the less important idea and the main clause for the more important idea. If the subordinate clause comes before the main clause, this division of importance is emphasized.

It is also possible for a subordinate clause to function as the subject, object, or complement of a main clause. Ordinarily such subordinate clauses are introduced by subordinating words such as *what, which, when, where, who, whom, why, how, however, that, the fact that, if,* and *whether:*

   subject
How we choose the winning candidate is still undecided.

   subject
The fact that he married a doctor could influence the jury's opinion.

object

I asked *if he delivered the materials to my office.*

object

She said *[that] I have to interview the five job candidates.* (The word *that* is optional.)

complement

This project is *what I have been working on each day for two full years.*

complement

Ocean City is *where my family likes to vacation.*

Attention ESL Writers

A **relative clause** is a special type of subordinate clause. Introduced by the relative pronouns (especially *who, which,* or *that*), a relative clause is a clause within a clause. A relative clause offers a piece of information regarding the subject or object of the sentence. This information is either essential to the accuracy of the message or it is optional. If the information is essential, the relative clause is **restrictive** because it limits or restricts the subject or object:

My sister *who lives in Chicago* is a doctor.
(Of all my sisters, the one in Chicago is a doctor.)

He cooked the spaghetti *that he usually serves with a garlic sauce.*
(Of all the types of spaghetti he cooks, he cooked the spaghetti served with garlic sauce.)

Notice that if you eliminate a restrictive clause, critical information available in the original sentence is omitted.

If the information is optional, the relative clause is **nonrestrictive:**

My sister, *who lives in Chicago,* is a doctor.
(My only sister lives in Chicago, and she is a doctor.)

He cooked the spaghetti, *which he usually serves with a garlic sauce.*
(He cooked the spaghetti, and he usually serves it with a garlic sauce.)

Notice that commas are used to divide the nonrestrictive relative clause from the remainder of the sentence and that the words *who* or *which* introduce nonrestrictive clauses. Notice also that a sentence with a nonrestrictive clause could be phrased as a compound sentence. Or the nonrestrictive clause might be displayed as a parenthetical aside. If you eliminate the nonrestrictive clause, you only simplify the sentence: you omit information without changing the meaning of the remaining clause.

If the relative clause is relative pronoun + *be* + noun complement, it is possible to omit the relative pronoun and *be,* leaving only the noun complement. Such structures are called **appositives** because of the adjacent positioning of the two nouns or noun phrases:

restrictive relative clause: My sister who is a doctor lives in Chicago.

appositive: My sister *the doctor* lives in Chicago.

nonrestrictive relative clause: My sister, who is a doctor, lives in Chicago.

appositive: My sister, *a doctor,* lives in Chicago.

Names and titles often occur as appositives:

The director *Spike Lee* is visiting Dallas.

He directed the film *Do the Right Thing.*

Compound-Complex Sentences

A **compound-complex sentence** has coordinated and subordinated clauses:

This city is where I would like to live, but all the houses here are quite expensive.

I just visited my doctor's office, which is in this building on the sixth floor, and the receptionist there validated my parking slip.

Before he registered for this biology class, he reviewed the instructor's teaching evaluations and he examined the proposed syllabus.

PUNCTUATION AND MECHANICS

. Periods

Use a period after a declarative or imperative sentence:

declarative: He repaired the television.
imperative: Repair the television.

Periods also accompany various abbreviations (see "Abbreviations").

, Commas

Use a comma with a coordinating conjunction (*and, but, nor, or, yet*) to divide the two clauses of a compound sentence (see "Compound Sentences"):

Tim built a cage for his iguana, *and* Nick designed a terrarium for his snails.

Use a comma after introductory words, phrases, or clauses:

Ordinarily, he asks permission to leave the office early.

Yes, he always asks permission to leave the office early.

On Tuesdays and Thursdays, he asks permission to leave the office early.

Before leaving early, he always asks the manager's permission.

If he has to leave the office early, he always asks the manager's permission.

Use commas to separate nonrestrictive clauses and appositives from the remainder of the sentence (see "Complex Sentences"):

His niece, *who is a famous photographer,* arrives today.

His niece, *a famous photographer,* arrives today.

If a name is followed by a degree, designation, or title, use commas to separate the degree, designation, or title from the remainder of the sentence:

Eduardo Ramirez, *Ph.D.,* has written a book on the subject of spiders.

Isaac Fields, *Jr.,* is visiting the campus today.

This award is given to Theresa Ricco, *director of advertising.*

Use a comma to separate verbal phrases from the remainder of the sentence (see "Verbals"):

Distracted by the accident on the highway, he missed the exit to Memphis.

The little girl, *singing and dancing merrily,* delighted the visitors.

He arrived at the hospital, *his sister complaining of nausea.*

Use a comma to separate transitional words and phrases from the remainder of the sentence:

In addition, the police never discovered the identity of the thieves.

The police, *as a consequence,* never discovered the identity of the thieves.

The police never discovered the identity of the thieves, *however.*

Use commas to separate quotations from the remainder of the sentence:

She said, *"Your boss is impatient."*
"Your boss," she said, *"is impatient."*

"Your boss is impatient," she said.

Use a comma with coordinated adjectives instead of using the word *and:*

This is a *perceptive and detailed* analysis.
This is a *perceptive, detailed* analysis.

Adjectives are **coordinated** if it is possible to reverse their order without changing their meaning (e.g., *perceptive, detailed analysis* or *detailed, perceptive analysis*). Notice that coordinated adjectives are different from **cumulative adjectives:**

This is a perceptive literary analysis.

The adjective *literary* modifies *analysis* and the adjective *perceptive* modifies the phrase *literary analysis*. Commas never divide cumulative adjectives.

Use a comma after each item in a series (with the exception of the final item):

His favorite foods are *pizza, macaroni and cheese, lobster, and tacos.*

He *washed a shirt, ironed his suit, and packed two suitcases* before leaving for the airport.

Use a comma to separate a day of the week from a day of the month:

The moon landing was on *Sunday, July 20.*

The moon landing was on *Sunday, 20 July.*

If the day is positioned after the month, use a comma to separate the day of the month from the year; if the day is positioned before the month, omit the comma:

The moon landing was on *July 20, 1969.*

The moon landing was on *20 July 1969.*

Use commas to separate a street address from the name of a city and to separate the name of a city from the name of a state, province, or country:

street address, city, state, and zip code: His address is *1221 Athens Street, Kettering, Ohio 45417.*

city, province: We are planning a trip to *Montreal, Quebec.*
city, country: She shipped the materials to *Tijuana, Mexico.*

: Colons

Use a colon after an independent clause to separate it from a list, word, phrase, clause, or quotation that explains, illustrates, or elaborates on the independent clause:

list: Kurt Vonnegut's earliest novels are the following: *Player Piano, Sirens of Titan, Cat's Cradle,* and *Mother Night.*

Eudora Welty has written several terrific books: *The Robber Bridegroom, Losing Battles,* and *The Optimist's Daughter.*

word:	He has a serious disease: leukemia.
phrase:	She travels all over the city either of two ways: riding a bicycle or taking a trolley.
clause:	He answered the telephone nervously: Dr. Cooper was calling.
quotation:	The victim's testimony was unequivocal: "I was hiding in the closet. I didn't see the thief."

Also use colons for the following:

after the identifying headings of a memo: DATE*:*   February 3, 1994
TO*:*   Reader
FROM*:*   Writer
SUBJECT*:*   Using Colons

after salutations of letters: Dear Dr. Cooper*:*
before subtitles: *Editing: The Design of Rhetoric*
within time designations: She arrived at 10:30.

; Semicolons

Use a semicolon to link two closely associated independent clauses:

Building a city recycling facility is critical; the cost is $347,000.

Building a city recycling facility is critical; however, the cost is $347,000.

Use semicolons to separate items in a series if one or more of the items includes a comma:

Katherine Anne Porter has also written *Flowering Judas; Pale Horse, Pale Rider;* and *Ship of Fools.*

He visited *Athens, Georgia; Springfield, Illinois; Waterville, Maine;* and *Salem, Oregon.*

I asked *Mr. Garcia, my immediate supervisor; Ms. Chung, the director of advertising;* and *Ms. Powers, the office manager.*

? Question Marks

Use a question mark after a question:

She designed this bridge*?*

Did she design this bridge*?*

Why did she design this bridge*?*

! Exclamation Marks

Use an exclamation mark to display emotion or give emphasis:

This doctor speaks politely to the nurses*!*

Doesn't this doctor speak politely to the nurses*!*

How politely this doctor speaks to the nurses*!*

Speak politely to the nurses*!*

— Dashes

Use dashes to separate examples, interruptions, and explanations from the remainder of the sentence, but only if you wish to call special attention to this information:

The neighbor arrived with a load of gifts—clothing, towels, candy, and toys.

The neighbor arrived—to my surprise, she was driving a truck—with a load of gifts.

The neighbor—a friend of the mayor's sister—arrived with a load of gifts.

In typing, a dash is either a single long line (—) or two consecutive hyphens (--), with no space either before or after the dash.

( ) Parentheses

Use parentheses to enclose examples, interruptions, and explanations, but only if you wish to emphasize that this information is optional reading:

The neighbor arrived with a load of gifts *(*clothing, towels, candy, and toys*)*.

The neighbor arrived *(*to my surprise, she was driving a truck*)* with a load of gifts.

The neighbor *(*she is a friend of the mayor's sister!*)* arrived with a load of gifts.

The neighbor arrived with a load of gifts. *(*To my surprise, she was driving a truck. And it was a big truck!*)* She delivered clothing, towels, candy, and toys.

Parenthetical information within a sentence starts without a capital letter; omit periods, but include exclamation marks or question marks if appropriate. If the parenthetical information is a separate sentence or series of sentences, start with a capital letter and finish with a period, question mark or exclamation mark, inside the parentheses.

Use parentheses to enclose the years of biographical and historical occurrences (such as dates of birth and death, terms of office, reigns, or wars), but only if such information is optional reading:

> Martin Luther King (1929–1968) received the 1964 Nobel Prize.

> Jimmy Carter was the 39th president of the United States (1977–1981).

> Victoria was queen of England (1837–1901) during the colonization of India.

> World War I (1914–1918) is the subject of the poem "Dulce Et Decorum Est" by Wilfred Owen.

If a sentence identifies a series of items, use parentheses to enclose the numerals or letters that designate the items:

> In psychology class, I have to write (a) a review of literature, (b) a proposal, (c) a comparative analysis of appropriate research methodologies, (d) a summary and discussion of my empirical findings, and (e) a critical interpretation of the significance of my findings.

> She advised that we (1) terminate all part-time sales clerks as soon as possible and (2) hire seven full-time sales clerks and two sales managers.

Use parentheses to enclose cross references:

> Aristotle emphasizes persuasive rhetoric (see page 179).

> Aristotle emphasizes persuasive rhetoric (see also "Audience Analysis").

Use parentheses to enclose MLA, APA, and CBE source citations (see Part IX, pp. 658, 664–665, and 675, respectively)

> Research on page design ordinarily ignores ethical issues (Cooper 65).

> Research on page design ordinarily ignores ethical issues (Cooper, 1991).

> Research on page design ordinarily ignores ethical issues (8).

[ ] Brackets

Use brackets to enclose parenthetical information within parenthetical information:

> He interviewed Jimmy Carter (39th president of the United States [1977–1981] and international humanitarian).

In a quotation, use brackets to modify language, insert explanations, or add capitalization:

He has also written on the subject of war: "Either /humanity/ is obsolete or war is."

According to this writer, "Freedom of speech and freedom of action are *meaningless* /emphasis added/ without freedom to think."

"/W/hile there is a soul in prison, I am not free," he said.

Use brackets to enclose IEEE source citations (see Part IX, p. 670):

Research on page design ordinarily ignores ethical issues /7, p. 124/.

" " **Quotation Marks**

Use quotation marks to enclose the written or spoken words of others:

According to the newspaper, "The city council opposes the building of a trash incinerator."

A city council representative declared, "The city council unanimously opposes the mayor's idea of building a trash incinerator."

"The city council is opposing my proposal to build a trash incinerator," said the mayor.

If the quotation is introduced by the word *that* (either explicitly or implicitly) start the quotation without capitalization:

A city council representative declared *that* "the city council unanimously opposes the mayor's idea of building a trash incinerator."

The mayor said [that] "the city council is opposing my proposal to build a trash incinerator." (The word *that* is optional.)

If a quotation is long (over four lines of type for MLA style, over forty words for APA style), indent the quotation from the left margin (ten spaces for MLA style, five spaces for APA style) and omit the quotation marks (see Part IX, p. 655):

According to the city council:

> The city council unanimously opposes the mayor's idea of building a trash incinerator. Although the proposed incinerator would create approximately 75 jobs, the air pollution from such a facility would also keep other business from locating here and drive off existing businesses.

If you substitute your words to communicate the essence of ideas said or written by others, omit the quotation marks:

According to the newspaper, the city council is against the proposed trash incinerator.

A city council representative predicted that the entire council would vote to reject the trash incinerator.

The mayor said [that] the city council opposes the trash incinerator. (The word *that* is optional.)

Use single quotation marks for a quotation within a quotation:

According to the newspaper, "The mayor said, 'The city council is opposing my proposal to build a trash incinerator.'"

If you quote a conversation, signal a change of speaker by starting a new paragraph:

"Why are you trying to stop the building of the trash incinerator?" asked the mayor.

"It's wrong for the city," answered the editor of the local newspaper.

"Why is it wrong? This facility is likely to create 75 jobs."

"Yes, but the resulting air pollution will keep other businesses from locating here and could drive off existing businesses."

Use quotation marks to enclose titles of articles in magazines, journals, and newspapers; chapters of books; essays; speeches; poems; short stories; and songs:

title of article: She is reading "Computer-Based Instruction and the Humanizing Impulse" in the February issue of *Technical Communication*.

chapter of book: He especially likes the chapter "The Canons of Rhetoric" from your previous book.

essay: We are reading Martin Luther King's "Letter from Birmingham Jail" today.

speech: Martin Luther King's "I Have a Dream" is a brilliant speech.

poem: She thinks Tennyson's "Ulysses" is inspiring.

short story: Are you reading Jackson's "The Lottery" in your English class?

songs: Judy Garland sings "Over the Rainbow" in *The Wizard of Oz*.

Use quotation marks to enclose words with a special or ironic meaning:

She is a "traditional" woman.

This "doctor" has no license to practice medicine.

Keep in mind that periods and commas always go inside closing quotation marks:

He said, "We analyze the chemicals daily to determine their toxicity."

After I finished reading "Chicago," I decided to visit the city.

Colons and semicolons always go outside closing quotation marks:

I enjoyed reading "Ozymandias": it is filled with striking images.

She said again and again that this machine was "clearly defective"; however, she was ignored.

Use dashes inside closing quotation marks to signal that the quotation has been interrupted:

"The winner is—" he started to announce, but she pulled the plug on the microphone.

Ordinarily, however, dashes go outside the quotation marks:

She loved Lennon's music—especially "Imagine"—and listened to it daily.

Question marks and exclamation marks go inside closing quotation marks, but only if applicable to the quoted material:

She asked "Who is the chair of this committee?"

Who composed the lyrics to "Amazing Grace"?

"It is such a surprise to receive this award!" he said.

I can't believe that he said she is "inefficient and ineffective"!

... Ellipsis Points

Ellipsis points are three spaced periods (. . .). Use ellipsis points to signal the omission of words, sentences, or paragraphs from a quotation:

Original Quotation:

Style is the way you speak or write, including your choice of words and your manner of putting words together to compose sentences. Also a style issue is your handling of the mechanical issues of oral communication like pronunciation or of written communication like spelling and punctuation. All your decisions regarding style influence the accuracy and clarity of the information you communicate.

Your vocabulary might be simple or complicated. You might depend chiefly on nouns and verbs to communicate your message or you might use lots of adjectives, adverbs and prepositional phrases.

Your sentences might be simple or complex. You might start your sentences with adverbial clauses or you might avoid relative clauses. You might limit your subjects and objects to nouns and verbals or incorporate clauses as the subjects or objects of your sentences.

You might also spell words according to the way you pronounce the words or you might adopt the dictionary's spelling. You might capitalize words you consider important or comply with the guidelines of a typical style manual. (Cooper 123)

To omit material from the beginning of a quotation, use no ellipsis points and start the quotation with quotation marks:

To communicate effectively, you have to consider "your choice of words and your manner of putting words together to compose sentences."

To omit material from the middle of a sentence, use ellipsis points to signal the omission:

"Style is . . . your choice of words and your manner of putting words together to compose sentences."

To omit material from the end of a sentence, use the appropriate ending punctuation (period, question mark, or exclamation mark) and ellipsis points following to signal the omission:

"Style is the way you speak or write, including your choice of words. . . ."

If the quotation is followed by a parenthetical source citation, position the ending punctuation after the parentheses:

"Style is the way you speak or write, including your choice of words. . . " (Cooper 123).

To omit a sentence or to omit material from consecutive sentences, use ellipsis points to signal the omission:

"Style is the way you speak or write, including your choice of words and your manner of putting words together to compose sentences. . . . [Y]our decisions regarding style influence the accuracy and clarity of the information you communicate."

"Style is the way you speak or write. . . . All your decisions regarding style influence the accuracy and clarity of the information you communicate."

To omit a paragraph or to omit material from consecutive paragraphs, indent the quotation from the left margin and use ellipsis points to signal the omission:

Cooper also address the subject of style:

> Style is the way you speak or write, including your choice of words. . . . Also a style issue is your handling of the mechanical issues of oral communication like pronunciation or of written communication like spelling and punctuation. . . .
>
> Your vocabulary might be simple or complicated. You might depend chiefly on nouns and verbs to communicate your message or you might use lots of adjectives, adverbs and prepositional phrases. . . .

You might also spell words according to the way you pronounce the words or you might adopt the dictionary's spelling. You might capitalize words you consider important or comply with the guidelines of a typical style manual. (123)

' **Apostrophes**

Use apostrophes to signal the possessive case of nouns. Use apostrophe + *s* for singular possessives and for plural possessives without *s* endings. Use only the apostrophe for plurals with *s* endings.

Singular: dog's   child's

Plural: dogs'   children's

Use the apostrophe + *s* to signal the possessive case of indefinite pronouns ending *one, body, either,* or *other:*

someone's responsibility

nobody's business

neither's fault

each other's job

Use apostrophes to signal the missing letters of contractions:

I have	I've
you are	you're
it is / it has	it's
we will	we'll
they are	they're
who is / who has	who's
there is/there has	there's
might have	might've
could have	could've
is not	isn't
are not	aren't

Use apostrophe + *s* to create the plural of letters and of words identified as words. Italicize the letter or word; leave the *s* ending plain:

The *q*'s on this page look peculiar.

She italicized all the *is*'s and *are*'s.

- **Hyphens**

Hyphens often link words to create a single noun or adjective. Guidelines on hyphenation, however, differ from dictionary to dictionary and style manual to style manual. Adopt a single dictionary or style manual appropriate to your aim and audience and check it to determine if a given noun or adjective is typically spelled as a single word, as two words, or as a hyphenated word.

Use a hyphen for the following (unless your dictionary or style manual specifies no hyphen):

noun + participle modifiers preceding a noun:	law-abiding citizen
	grief-stricken spouse
	oil-stained gloves
noun + adjective modifiers preceding a noun:	nutrient-rich soil
	paper-thin slice
	flamingo-pink dress
adjective + noun modifiers preceding a noun:	short-term memory
	low-impact aerobics
	middle-class neighborhood
number + noun modifiers preceding a noun:	sixth-grade class
	25-mile hike
	four-bedroom house
modifying phrases preceding a noun:	trial-and-error learning
	love-it-or-leave-it attitude
	before-the-kickoff jitters
the following suffixes and prefixes:	
-elect:	president-elect
-in-law:	sister-in-law
all-:	all-around athlete
ex-:	ex-president
half-:	half-hearted effort
quasi-:	quasi-scientific research

self-:	self-denial
well-:	well-intentioned

prefixes preceding capitalized words:	pre-World War II weapons
	pseudo-African cooking
	anti-American demonstration

prefixes preceding numbers:	pre-1900 literature
	post-1950 technology
	anti-1980's philosophy

prefixes preceding acronyms and abbreviations:	pre-NFL practices
	non-IBM machines
	anti-U.S. Postal Service

spelled numbers from 21 through 99:	thirty-one
	fifty-seven
	eighty-five

inclusive dates or numbers:	He served as mayor 1980-1990.
	She lived January 13, 1899-April 3, 1968.
	This subject is discussed on pages 213-219.

Use a hyphen to link the numerator and denominator of spelled fractions (unless either is already hyphenated):

two-thirds

eleven-sixteenths

fifteen thirty-seconds

twenty-three fiftieths

Use a hypen to divide a polysyllabic word at the end of a line if the entire word would violate the right margin. Divide the word between syllables, leaving at least three letters on each line. Check your dictionary to verify appropriate division. Never divide single-syllable words, acronyms and abbreviations, contractions, or numerals.

Use *no* hyphen for the following (unless your dictionary or style manual specifies a hyphen):

noun + participle, noun + adjective, adjective + noun, number + noun, and phrase modifiers *following* the noun:

My gloves are oil stained.

Your dress is flamingo pink.

The neighborhood is middle class.

This house has four bedrooms.

She always has jitters before the kickoff.

ly adverb + participle or *ly* adverb + adjective:

partially justified crime

thoroughly researched essay

especially generous sister

adjective or number + possessive:

dying man's confession

two week's severance

miserable day's journey

modifying phrases using non-English words:

caveat emptor philosophy

a priori questionnaire

post hoc ergo propter hoc analyses

modifying phrases using chemical terminology:

carbonic acid gas

nitrogen dioxide poisoning

sulfuryl chloride solution

modifying phrases that are unlikely to be misinterpreted because of wide usage:

life insurance policy

child care facility

prescription drug program

cap **Capitalization**

Capitalize the first letter of proper nouns and adjectives. Check your dictionary or style manual to determine if a given noun or adjective is capitalized. Ordinarily, the following nouns and adjectives are capitalized:

names of people:	Susan B. Anthony César Chávez Frederick Douglass
names of products:	Hoover Kodak Nabisco
titles accompanying names:	President Bill Clinton Senator Diane Feinstein Uncle Roger
planets:	Earth Jupiter Venus
continents:	Africa Asia South America
countries:	Italy People's Republic of China United States of America
geographical regions:	Appalachia Scandinavia the South
states and provinces:	Florida California Nova Scotia
cities:	Chicago Los Angeles New York
bodies of water:	Indian Ocean Mississippi River Niagara Falls
nationalities:	Bolivian Ethiopian Malaysian
languages:	English Japanese Spanish
religions:	Christianity Islam Judaism
holidays:	Independence Day Thanksgiving Valentine's Day
days of the week:	Monday Tuesday Wednesday

months:	August February November
institutions:	Library of Congress Ohio University Smithsonian Institution
organizations:	Apple Computer, Inc. Democratic Party Habitat for Humanity
buildings:	Empire State Building Radio City Music Hall St. Patrick's Cathedral
specific academic departments:	Department of Accounting Department of Electrical Engineering Department of Physics
specific academic courses:	AGRO 4331, Soil and Water Conservation JOUR 3317, Publication Design and Graphics MATH 2300, Statistical Methods

Capitalize the first letter of sentences, including incomplete sentences (e.g., a subordinate clause, relative clause, noun phrase, verb phrase, verbal phrase, prepositional phrase):

complete sentence   **incomplete sentence**
The editor examined the book enthusiastically. And was bitterly disappointed.

complete sentence   **incomplete sentence**
Which color is appropriate on the cover? Red? Yellow? Green?

Capitalize all words in a title except articles, conjunctions, and prepositions. Capitalize articles and conjunctions that occur as the first word of the title or the first word after a colon. Capitalize prepositions that occur as the first word of the title, the first word after a colon, or the last word of the title.

Document Design: A Review of the Relevant Research

Learning Through Interaction: The Study of Language Development

On Writing Well: An Informal Guide to Writing Nonfiction

If you are following APA style, also capitalize prepositions of four letters or more (e.g., *after, before, with, without*). (See Part IX for MLA, APA, IEEE, and CBE guidelines for capitalizing the titles of listed sources.)

ital Italics

Italicize (or underline) the following names and titles:

books:	*Invisible Man*
magazines:	*Vogue*
newspapers	*Washington Post*
professional journals:	*Technical Communication Quarterly*
plays:	*Romeo and Juliet*
long poems:	*The Aeneid*
films:	*Malcolm X*
paintings:	*Mona Lisa*
statues:	*The Thinker*
record albums:	*Thriller*
long musical compositions:	*Messiah*
radio or television series:	*The Simpsons*

Italicize (or underline) the scientific names of plants and animals:

Equus caballus [i.e., horse]

Taraxacum officinale [i.e., dandelion]

Italicize (or underline) non-English words and phrases unfamiliar to English speakers and writers. Check your dictionary to determine if a word or phrase deserves italics; if your dictionary lists it, omit the italics. For example, you ordinarily omit italics for the following:

a posteriori	hors d'oeuvres
a priori	laissez-faire
ad lib	savoir-faire
esprit de corps	per se
ex post facto	vis-à-vis

Italicize (or underline) words, letters, and numbers specified as such:

A definition of the word *rhetoric* is necessary.

The *e* on my typewriter is dirty.

He painted a *55* on the sign.

Italicize (or underline) letters used as algebraic variables and statistical symbols:

$a + b = c/d$

M [i.e., mean]

SD [i.e., standard deviation]

N [i.e., number of individuals in the population studied]

p [i.e., probability of occurrence]

Italicize (or underline) technical terminology that you are introducing or defining:

A *table* is the display of numbers or words in columns and rows. All other illustrations are *figures*.

Italicize (or underline) words that you wish to emphasize.

The mayor never said that *she* opposed this idea. She said a majority of the city council opposed it.

Keep in mind, however, that the more words you italicize, the less emphatic each italicized word is:

The mayor *never* said that *she* opposed this idea. She said a *majority* of the *city council* opposed it.

num Numbers

Check the style manual of your academic field to determine its guidelines on spelling numbers versus using numerals. Always adopt a consistent practice for both cardinal and ordinal numbers.

Ordinarily, you spell the numbers zero through nine and use numerals for all remaining numbers. The following are exceptions to this practice:

Spell all numbers at the beginning of a sentence:

The petition carried 86 signatures.

Eighty-six students signed the petition.

Use numerals for all numbers within a sentence instead of mixing spelled numbers and numerals, unless the numbers occur at the beginning of the sentence:

The subjects were 5 bulls and 21 cows.

Five bulls and 21 cows were the subjects.

Use numerals for all numbers that specify measures of height, length, width, weight, volume, and distance or that specify times, dates, ages, mathematical processes, ratios, scores, and scales, unless the numbers occur at the beginning of the sentence:

height: She is 5 feet, 7 inches tall.

length: He bought 6 yards of this fabric

width:	This box is 9 centimeters wide.
weight:	Your package weighs 7 pounds.
volume:	The dosage was 5 milligrams.
distance:	She walked 9 miles.
time:	He arrived at 7:45.
age:	He is 8 years old.
mathematical processes:	You divide this score by 6 to determine the average.
ratio:	She was elected by a 2:1 ratio.
score:	He scored a 9.95 on the floor exercise.
scale:	This questionnaire uses a 7-point scale.

In writing that includes little numerical information, you might adopt the practice of spelling the numbers zero through ninety-nine as well as numbers ending with *hundred, thousand, million, billion,* etc:

nine

thirty-seven

one hundred

101

two thousand

2341

five million

You would also spell numbers at the beginning of a sentence, and you would avoid mixing numerals and spelled numbers within a sentence.

ab Abbreviations and Acronyms

An abbreviation is a brief version of a word or phrase. It is created from the significant letters of the word or the initial letters of the phrase. An acronym is similar: it is itself a word, created from the initial letters of a series of words (e.g., UNICEF = United Nations International Children's Emergency Fund).

Titles

Abbreviations of titles are always used with people's names, never by themselves:

Personal and professional titles preceding the name are never used with professional titles following the name:

Mr.	Mr. Daniel Driskill
Ms.	Ms. Alice Kozlowski
Mrs.	Mrs. Lydia Garcia, Mrs. Paolo Garcia
Miss	Miss Laura Cooper
Dr.	Dr. Chai-Bo Chao

Professional titles following the name are never used with personal or professional titles preceding the name:

Doctor of Philosophy	Ph.D.	Robin Hibbler, Ph.D.
Doctor of Medicine	M.D.	Linda Fields, M.D.
Doctor of Education	Ed. D.	Umair Khan, Ed.D.
Master of Arts	M.A.	Judith Hoover, M.A.
Master of Business Administration	M.B.A.	Lee Olivarez, M.B.A
Master of Fine Arts	M.F.A	Thomas O'Connor, M.F.A.
Master of Science	M.S.	Manisha Gopal, M.S.
Bachelor of Arts	B.A.	Brian Simmons, B.A.
Bachelor of Science	B.S.	Virginia Powers, B.S.

Personal titles following the name, such as *Jr.* and *Sr.,* may be used with personal or professional titles preceding the name *or* with professional titles following the name:

Dr. Phillip Goss, Jr.   Phillip Goss, Sr., Ph.D.

Time

The following abbreviations often accompany designations of time:

ante meridian	A.M./a.m.	She arrives at 7:45 a.m.
post meridian	P.M./p.m.	Does the film start at 8 p.m.?
before the Common Era	B.C.E.	Confucius lived 551–479 B.C.E.
before Christ	B.C.	Confucius lived 551–479 B.C.
of the Common Era	C.E.	Augustine lived 354–430 C.E.
Anno Domini (in the year of our Lord)	A.D.	Augustine lived A.D. 354–430.

Use time abbreviations to avoid misunderstandings. If no misunderstanding is likely, omit the abbreviations:

He arrives daily at 10 a.m. and leaves at 11 p.m.

He arrived at the restaurant at 11:45 to have lunch with us.

In 44 B.C.E., Julius Caesar was assassinated.

From 55 to 44 B.C.E., Cicero composed six treatises on rhetoric. In 43, he was assassinated.

Augustus reigned as Emperor of Rome from 27 B.C.E. to 14 C.E.

George Washington served as President of the United States from 1789 to 1797.

In a list of information sources, specify the month of publication (if appropriate) by using the following abbreviations:

January	Jan.
February	Feb.
March	Mar.
April	Apr.
May	
June	
July	
August	Aug.
September	Sept.
October	Oct.
November	Nov.
December	Dec.

Organizations

Abbreviations and acronyms are used for various companies, societies, institutions, and agencies, including the following:

American Civil Liberties Union	ACLU
Central Intelligence Agency	CIA
Environmental Protection Agency	EPA
Federal Bureau of Investigation	FBI
General Electric	GE
International Business Machines	IBM
Internal Revenue Service	IRS
Mothers Against Drunk Driving	MADD
National Association for the Advancement of Colored People	NAACP
National Organization for Women	NOW

Occupational Safety and Health Administration	OSHA
Public Broadcasting System	PBS
Radio Corporation of America	RCA
United Nations	UN
United Nations International Children's Emergency Fund	UNICEF

If the acronym or abbreviation is unfamiliar to your readers, introduce the full name of the organization at its first mention and identify the acronym or abbreviation in parentheses. Thereafter, you may use the acronym or abbreviation to refer to the organization:

> This year the National Council of Teachers of English (NCTE) is publishing 25 new books. NCTE publications serve the profession by covering important research findings and effective teaching techniques.

Specialized Terminology

In a wide variety of fields, abbreviations and acronyms are efficient substitutes for long and unwieldy words and phrases. For example, consider the following:

acquired immune deficiency syndrome	AIDS
analysis of variance	ANOVA
chief executive officer	CEO
computerized axial tomography	CAT
deoxyribonucleic acid	DNA
disk operating system	DOS
electrocardiogram	EKG
estimated time of arrival	ETA
extrasensory perception	ESP
graphical user interface	GUI
gross national product	GNP
licensed practical nurse	LPN
lysergic acid diethylamide	LSD
multiple independently targeted re-entry vehicle	MIRV
random access memory	RAM

If the acronym or abbreviation is unfamiliar to your readers, first use the full word or phrase and introduce the acronym or abbreviation parenthetically:

The research on Quality of Working Life (QWL) is often criticized. Studies of QWL, it is said, display little rigor and yield little insight.

Addresses

In addresses on letters, résumés, and envelopes, the following are appropriate abbreviations:

Apartment	Apt.	Georgia	GA
Avenue	Ave.	Guam	GU
Boulevard	Blvd.	Hawaii	HI
Circle	Cr.	Idaho	ID
Lane	Ln.	Illinois	IL
Parkway	Pkwy.	Indiana	IN
Post Office Box	P.O. Box	Iowa	IA
Road	Rd.	Kansas	KS
Route	Rt.	Louisiana	LA
Street	St.	Maine	ME
United States of America	USA	Maryland	MD
Alabama	AL	Massachusetts	MA
Alaska	AK	Michigan	MI
American Samoa	AS	Minnesota	MN
Arizona	AZ	Mississippi	MS
Arkansas	AR	Missouri	MO
California	CA	Montana	MT
Colorado	CO	Nebraska	NE
Connecticut	CT	Nevada	NV
Delaware	DE	New Hampshire	NH
District of Columbia	DC	New Jersey	NJ
Florida	FL	New Mexico	NM

New York	NY	West Virginia	WV
North Carolina	NC	Wisconsin	WI
North Dakota	ND	Wyoming	WY
Ohio	OH	Canada	
Oklahoma	OK	Alberta	AB
Oregon	OR	British Columbia	BC
Pennsylvania	PA	Labrador	LB
Puerto Rico	PR	Manitoba	MB
Rhode Island	RI	New Brunswick	NB
South Carolina	SC	Newfoundland	NF
South Dakota	SD	Nova Scotia	NS
Tennessee	TN	Northwest Territories	NT
Texas	TX	Ontario	ON
Utah	UT	Prince Edward Island	PE
Vermont	VT	Quebec	PQ
Virginia	VA	Saskatchewan	SK
Virgin Islands	VI	Yukon Territory	YT
Washington	WA		

Source Citations and Parenthetical Explanations

Use the following abbreviations to cite and list sources of information and to exemplify or explain ideas in parentheses or in notes:

and others	et al. (*et alia*)
and so on	etc. (*et cetera*)
and the following page	f.
and the following pages	ff.
anonymous	anon.
chapter	ch.
chapters	chs.
circa	c. or ca.
compare	cf. (*confer*)

ed.	editor/edition
eds.	editors/editions
for example	e.g. (*exempli gratia*)
line	l.
lines	ll.
manuscript	ms.
manuscripts	mss.
namely	viz. (*videlicet*)
no date	n.d.
note well	N.B. (*nota bene*)
number	no.
numbers	nos.
page	p.
pages	pp.
revised	rev.
reprint	rpt.
that is	i.e. (*id est*)
the same	ibid. (*ibidem*)
translated	tr. or trans.
versus	vs.
volume	vol.
volumes	vols.

sp SPELLING

Check a dictionary or computerized spell-checking program to verify the appropriate spelling of words. The following words are often spelled inappropriately. The dictionary spelling is given here:

a lot	accessible	achievement
absence	accidentally	acknowledg-ment
abundance	accommodate	
accelerate	accumulate	acquire
acceptable	accuracy	against

all right	cooperation	hospitable
anxiety	curious	humorous
anxious	curiosity	hypocrisy
apparently	curriculum	hypocrite
appropriate	deceive	illiterate
arctic	definitely	immediately
argument	dependent	incidentally
athlete	descendant	incompatible
athletic	develop	indispensable
authoritative	divisible	initiate
auxiliary	ecstasy	innocuous
beautiful	efficiency	inoculate
before	eligible	interrupt
beginning	embarrass	invariable
behavior	environment	irrelevant
believe	exaggerate	irresistible
beneficial	exercise	jackknife
boundary	exhilarating	jealousy
bureaucracy	experience	jewelry
business	extension	kindergarten
businesses	familiar	label
calendar	feasible	laboratory
candidate	feasibility	leisure
cannot	February	length
categories	fictitious	library
changeable	finally	license
characteristic	forcibly	lieutenant
chiefly	foreign	lightning
chocolate	forty	likelihood
column	frightening	livelihood
commitment	gauge	maintenance
committee	generous	mathematics
comparable	generosity	mileage
conceive	grief	miscellaneous
condemn	grievous	mischievous
consensus	guarantee	misspelling
contact	harass	mortgage
convenient	height	necessary

nickel
niece
ninety
no one
noticeable
occasionally
occurrence
opportunity
outrageous
parallel
pastime
permissible
plausible
precede
prevalent
privilege
probably
procedure
proceed
professor
pumpkin
quarantine

questionnaire
recede
receipt
receive
recommend
reminisce
repetition
representative
reservoir
restaurant
rhythm
roommate
sacrifice
sandwich
seize
separate
sergeant
siege
similar
souvenir
strength

subtle
successfully
supersede
supposed to
teammate
temperament
therefore
thorough
through
truly
twelfth
unanimous
undoubtedly
unmistakable
until
used to
vacillate
vicious
villain
Wednesday
withhold

USAGE

Check a dictionary to verify that you are using the appropriate words to communicate your ideas. The following words are often used inappropriately. The dictionary definition is exemplified here:

accept: I *accept* your invitation. [verb]

except: All *except* Laura arrived early. [preposition]

adverse: I missed the meeting because of *adverse* circumstances.

averse: I was *averse* to the original proposal.

advice: I appreciate your *advice*. [noun]

advise: I *advise* you to call a doctor. [verb]

affect:
: The new taxes *affect* all citizens. [verb]

  The students *affect* innocence whenever the teacher is watching. [verb]

effect:
: The medicine has little *effect* on this disease. [noun]

  Their disposal policies *effect* substantial damage to the ocean. [verb]

allude:
: The diaries *allude* to a missing treasure.

elude:
: The thieves might *elude* the police.

allusion:
: I appreciated this book's *allusion* to *Romeo and Juliet*.

illusion:
: He gives the *illusion* of being athletic.

all ready:
: The cook is *all ready* to start.

already:
: I *already* cooked dinner.

all together:
: My family was *all together* on Thanksgiving Day.

altogether:
: She was *altogether* delighted by your gift.

among:
: She has to choose *among* chemistry, physics, and biology. [three or more alternatives]

between:
: She has to choose *between* chemistry and biology. [two alternatives]

amount:
: He witnessed a considerable *amount* of illegal activity. [with mass nouns]

number:
: He witnessed a considerable *number* of crimes. [with plural nouns]

anymore:
: I never see my sister *anymore*.

any more:
: I don't want *any more* trouble.

as:
: He acted *as* a spoiled child would. [subordinator introducing a clause]

  He acted *as* if he were dying. [subordinator introducing a clause]

like:
: He acted *like* a spoiled child. [preposition]

assure:
: I *assure* you that he is coming.

insure/ensure:	Their skill and experience *insure* [ensure] satisfactory service.
insure:	The company will *insure* its building for two million dollars.
awhile:	He stopped and visited *awhile*.
a while:	She arrived *a while* ago. He visited for *a while*. [before *ago* or after prepositions]
bad:	She feels *bad* about causing the accident. [adjective following a linking verb]
badly:	She suffers *badly* since the accident. [adverb]
bring:	She could *bring* me a glass of milk. [to the speaker]
take:	She could *take* you a glass of milk. [from the speaker]
canvas:	He always carries a *canvas* bag to the store.
canvass:	The *canvass* of citizens is still incomplete.
	The managers often *canvass* the sales clerks to solicit their advice.
capital:	The *capital* of Ohio is Columbus. [city]
capitol:	The *capitol* is being painted, including the halls and the offices of the legislators. [building]
censor:	The *censor* judged the film pornographic. [noun]
	The committee might *censor* the film's excessive violence. [verb]
censure:	The city council is considering *censure* of the mayor for unethical behavior. [noun]
	The city council might *censure* the mayor for unethical behavior. [verb]
cite:	Several articles *cite* my research on typography.
site:	This is the *site* of the '96 Olympics.
climactic:	In the *climactic* trial, she accuses the judge of unethical behavior.
climatic:	The meteorologist evaluated the *climatic* information.

complement: This shirt is a nice *complement* to your suit. [noun]

                      This shirt and tie *complement* your suit. [verb]

compliment: You deserve a *compliment* for this delicious dinner. [noun]

                      I must *compliment* you on your cooking. [verb]

conscience: He is a terrible liar and has no *conscience*. [noun]

conscious: He is *conscious* of the importance of this meeting. [adjective]

continually: She *continually* typed the wrong addresses on business letters. [repetitious activity]

continuously: She typed *continuously* for thirty minutes. [uninterrupted activity]

council: The city *council* is meeting tonight. [noun]

counsel: The doctors often *counsel* the patients to exercise. [verb]

                      He ignored my *counsel* regarding his eating habits. [noun]

different than: The two books are more *different than* they are similar.

different from: This book is *different from* that book.

discreet: He is always *discreet* in his conversation and behavior.

discrete: The company has five *discrete* divisions.

disinterested: Because the arbitrator is *disinterested,* she is a fair judge of the situation.

uninterested: He enjoys baseball, but is *uninterested* in soccer.

elicit: The police could never *elicit* the woman's confession.

illicit: She was accused of *illicit* activities.

emigrate: He *emigrated* from Spain.

immigrate: He *immigrated* to Mexico.

eminent: The *eminent* scientist arrives this morning.

imminent: The scientist's arrival is *imminent*.

everyday:	The *everyday* things of life are priceless.
every day:	She visits the library *every day.*
explicit:	The *explicit* warning on the package directs the user to avoid driving while under the influence of this medicine.
implicit:	The *implicit* message of the warning is that this medicine will impair the user's judgment and motor abilities.
farther:	The store is five miles *farther.* [distance]
further:	No *further* evidence is necessary. [degree, quantity, or time]
fewer:	He bought *fewer* tomatoes than you did. [plural nouns]
less:	He bought *less* milk than you did. [mass nouns]
good:	She is a *good* writer. [adjective]
well:	She writes *well.* [adverb]
have:	I could *have* written a letter to you. [modal + auxiliary verb]
've:	I could *'ve* written a letter to you. [modal + contraction of auxiliary verb]
of:	He is the director *of* advertising. [preposition + noun]
	I know *of* a specialist you might ask. [verb + preposition]
imply:	The speakers *imply* that the city manager is a crook.
infer:	The listeners *infer* that a police investigation is necessary.
incredible:	The gymnast's performance during the floor exercise was *incredible.*
incredulous:	The audience was *incredulous* while watching the gymnast's performance.
its:	The iguana closed *its* eyes. [possessive]
it's	*It's* a lovely animal. [contraction of *it is*]

lay: I ordinarily *lay* the pencil on the paper. [present tense]

I *laid* the pencil on the paper yesterday. [past tense]

I often have *laid* the pencil on the paper. [past participle]

lie: I ordinarily *lie* on the rug to read a book. [present tense]

I *lay* on the rug yesterday to read a book. [past tense]

I often have *lain* on the rug to read a book. [past participle]

lead: My mechanical pencil has no *lead*. [noun]

led: I *led* the class yesterday. [past tense of the verb *lead*]

I often have *led* the class.[past participle of the verb *lead*]

leave: I *leave* my dog with my neighbor whenever I go on vacation.

let: I *let* my neighbor play with my dog whenever I am home.

maybe: She is a doctor or *maybe* a nurse.

may be: She *may be* a doctor or a nurse.

passed: He *passed* a gas station five minutes ago. [verb]

He *passed* the ball to his sister. [verb]

past: He walked *past* the library on his way to school. [preposition]

He was hired because of his *past* job experience. [adjective]

He never studied this much in the *past*. [noun]

personal: I received a *personal* invitation.

personnel: This memo is addressed to the *personnel* of the marketing division.

principal: She is the *principal* of the high school.

The *principal* of the loan is $5000.

Drunk driving is the *principal* cause of traffic accidents.

principle: The *principle* of neutrality guides their policy.

quotation: I like this particular *quotation*. [noun]

quote: My teachers often *quote* Einstein. [verb]

raise: I ordinarily *raise* questions. [present tense]

I *raised* questions yesterday. [past tense]

I often have *raised* questions. [past participle]

rise: I ordinarily *rise* at 6:30 a.m. [present tense]

I *rose* at 6:30 a.m. yesterday. [past tense]

I often have *risen* at 6:30 a.m. [past participle]

respectfully: She listened *respectfully* to the boss.

respectively: Maria, Robin, and Bill direct accounting, marketing, and sales, *respectively*.

set: I ordinarily *set* the magazines on the shelves. [present tense]

I *set* the magazines on the shelves yesterday. [past tense]

I often have *set* the magazines on the shelves. [past participle]

sit: I ordinarily *sit* on this chair to play my guitar. [present tense]

I *sat* on this chair to play my guitar yesterday. [past tense]

I often have *sat* on this chair to play my guitar. [past participle]

stationary: That pipe organ is heavy and quite *stationary*.

stationery: I use official *stationery* to write my business letters.

than: This building is bigger *than* that building.

then: I visited this building and *then* that building.

their: This book is *their* favorite. [possessive]

there: The book is *there* on the desk. [adverb]

There is a book on the desk [meaningless word starting a declarative sentence]

they're: This is the book that *they're* reading. [contraction of *they are*]

to:	I am going *to* the store. [preposition]
too:	She is going *too*. [adverb]
	This shirt is *too* expensive. [adverb]
two:	I would like *two* shirts. [number]
weather:	The *weather* here is unpredictable.
whether:	I never know *whether* to expect rain, snow, hail, or sunshine.
who:	*Who* spilled the acid? [subject]
	Who did you interview? [object of verb: informal usage]
	Who did you give the money to? [object of a following preposition: informal usage]
whom:	*Whom* did you interview? [object of verb: formal usage]
	Whom did you give the money to? [object of a following preposition: informal usage]
	To *whom* did you give the money? [object of a preceding preposition: formal usage]
whose	My sister is the engineer *whose* design you admired. [possessive]
who's	My sister is the engineer *who's* joining the company. [contraction of *who is*]
	My sister is the engineer *who's* joined the company. [contraction of *who has*]
your:	She delivered *your* message. [possessive]
you're:	*You're* delivering a message. [contraction of *you are*]

CAUTIONS

run-on Avoiding Run-On Sentences

Avoid linking two independent clauses without appropriate punctuation:

independent clause	independent clause

run-on: *My trip to the zoo yesterday was exciting all the gorillas were either eating or playing*.

Divide the two independent clauses with a period, semicolon, or comma and conjunction.

period:	My trip to the zoo yesterday was exciting. All the gorillas were either eating or playing.
semicolon:	My trip to the zoo yesterday was exciting; all the gorillas were either eating or playing.
comma and conjunction:	My trip to the zoo yesterday was exciting, and all the gorillas were either eating or playing.

Or consider subordinating one of the clauses:

    main clause   **subordinate clause**

My trip to the zoo yesterday was exciting because all the gorillas were either eating or playing.

cs Avoiding Comma Splices

Avoid joining two independent clauses with a comma:

                    independent clause   **independent clause**

comma splice: I arrived at nine o'clock, she departed a few minutes later.

Divide the two independent clauses with either a period, a semicolon, or a comma and a conjunction:

period:	I arrived at nine o'clock. She departed a few minutes later.
semicolon:	I arrived at nine o'clock; she departed a few minutes later.
comma and conjunction:	I arrived at nine o'clock, and she departed a few minutes later.

inc Avoiding Incomplete Sentences

Ordinarily, readers operate on the assumption that sentences will communicate complete ideas. If you substitute an incomplete sentence (a subordinate clause, relative clause, noun phrase, verb phrase, verbal phrase, prepositional phrase) for a complete sentence, you violate your readers' expectations and interrupt their reading process. This interruption is justified if you are communicating information that deserves special emphasis. If no emphasis is necessary, however, avoid the incomplete sentence by linking it to a preceding or following sentence:

Incomplete sentence:

complete sentence   **subordinate clause**
He was anxious to leave the library before six o'clock. Because he
                                          complete sentence
was meeting a friend for dinner that evening. He stopped at a florist shop and bought a bouquet of roses.

Revised:

He was anxious to leave the library before six o'clock because he was meeting a friend for dinner that evening. He stopped at a florist shop and bought a bouquet of roses.

Revised:

He was anxious to leave the library before six o'clock. Because he was meeting a friend for dinner that evening, he stopped at a florist shop and bought a bouquet of roses.

Incomplete sentence:

complete sentence   **relative clause**
He was anxious to leave the library before six o'clock. Which is closing time at the florist shop.

Revised:

He was anxious to leave the library before six o'clock, which is closing time at the florist shop.

Incomplete sentence:

            complete sentence   **noun phrase**
He stopped at a florist shop and bought a bouquet of roses. The ideal gift for his special friend.

Revised:

He stopped at a florist shop and bought a bouquet of roses, the ideal gift for his special friend.

Incomplete sentence:

complete sentence   **verb phrase**
He was anxious to leave the library before six o'clock. Then stop at a florist shop for a bouquet of roses.

Revised:

He was anxious to leave the library before six o'clock and then stop at a florist shop for a bouquet of roses.

Incomplete sentence:

     complete sentence   **verbal phrase**
He stopped at a florist shop and bought a bouquet of roses. After leaving the library and before meeting a friend for dinner.

Revised:

He stopped at a florist shop and bought a bouquet of roses, after leaving the library and before meeting a friend for dinner.

Incomplete sentence:

     complete sentence   **prepositional phrase**
He stopped at a florist shop and bought a bouquet of roses. With the money given to him on his birthday.

Revised:

He stopped at a florist shop and bought a bouquet of roses with the money given to him on his birthday.

Keep in mind that using incomplete sentences could also damage your credibility: readers might interpret this practice as evidence of your inability to write complete sentences. Avoid using incomplete sentences, therefore, unless the writing is obviously informal or unless your readers are already familiar with your writing ability.

shift Avoiding Shifts of Tense

Avoid switching tenses unnecessarily or without appropriate time signals:

Unnecessary shifting:

past tense   **present tense**
I *knocked* on the door and a child *answers*.

Consistent tense:

I *knock* on the door and a child *answers*.

I *knocked* on the door and a child *answered*.

Without time signals:

past tense   **present tense**
We *walked* to the museum. We *drive* to the zoo.

With time signals:

Yesterday we *walked* to the museum. *Today* we *drive* to the zoo.

par Achieving Parallelism

In a list or series of items, use the same grammatical structure for each item. This similarity of grammatical structure is called **parallelism,** and it reinforces for the reader the similarity among the items in the list or series. Consider, for example the following:

> lack of parallelism: She likes reading, to dance, and basketball.
>
> parallelism: She likes *reading, dancing,* and *playing* basketball.
>
> She likes to *read, dance,* and *play* basketball.

Lack of parallelism:

This week I have the following objectives: (1) I would like to finish the research for my psychology project; (2) start my English essay; (3) my statistics course has a quiz, and I still have studying to do; and (4) reading six chapters for my history class.

Parallelism:

This week I have the following objectives: (1) *finish* the research for my psychology project, (2) *start* my English essay, (3) *study* for my statistics quiz, and (4) *read* six chapters for my history class.

s-v agr Achieving Subject-Verb Agreement

Singular verbs accompany singular subjects and plural verbs accompany plural subjects (see "Verbs"). If a subject and verb are separated by words or phrases, pay special attention to the possibility of subject-verb disagreement. In such cases, you might unintentionally allow the verb to agree with an intervening noun instead of with the subject:

Subject-verb disagreement:

The *books* that she located yesterday on the third floor of the library probably *was* yours.

Subject-verb agreement:

The *books* that she located yesterday on the third floor of the library probably *were* yours.

Subject-verb disagreement:

The *book* of famous quotations, cliches, jokes, and proverbs *make* for amusing reading.

Subject-verb agreement:

The *book* of famous quotations, cliches, jokes, and proverbs *makes* for amusing reading.

Keep in mind that if the subject is modified by the word *each* or *every,* the verb is singular:

Each student *has* a book.

Every student *has* a book.

If the subject of the sentence is *each,* the verb is singular:

Each of the sisters *is* invited.

If the subject of the sentence is *none,* the verb is either singular or plural:

None of the sisters *is* going.

None of the sisters *are* going.

In a *there + be* sentence, the verb is singular if the noun following *be* is singular, and the verb is plural if the noun following *be* is plural:

There *is one question* that I still have to answer.

There *are two questions* that I still have to answer.

n-p agr Achieving Noun-Pronoun Agreement

Singular pronouns substitute for singular nouns and plural pronouns substitute for plural nouns (see "Pronouns"). If a noun is singular and preceded by an indefinite determiner (*a* or *an*) or modifiers such as *typical* or *average,* pay special attention to the issue of noun-pronoun agreement. While indefinite nouns are grammatically singular, often their meaning is plural. For informal writing, as a consequence, you might choose a third person plural pronoun (*they, their, them*) instead of a third person singular pronoun (*he, his him, she, her, it, its*), especially if several words or phrases separate the noun and pronoun:

Informal:

The average *actor* is poorly paid but loves *their* profession nevertheless.

An *actor* is trained to speak clearly and loudly, but sometimes in this theater I have trouble hearing *them.*

In formal writing, you would use a singular pronoun or change the noun to the plural to maintain noun-pronoun agreement:

Formal:

The average *actor* is poorly paid but loves *his or her* profession nevertheless.

Actors are trained to speak clearly and loudly, but sometimes in this theater I have trouble hearing *them.*

Or you might change the wording of the sentence to avoid the noun-pronoun issue altogether:

The average actor is poorly paid but loves the acting profession nevertheless.

An actor is trained to speak clearly and loudly, but sometimes in this theater I have trouble hearing what is being said on stage.

In formal writing, if a noun is modified by the word *each* or *every,* the pronoun is singular:

Each student has *his or her* books.

Every student has *his or her* books.

For informal writing, a plural pronoun is often used:

Each student has *their* books.

Every student has *their* books.

In formal writing, a pronoun referring to the word *each* is singular:

Each of the students has *his or her* books.

For informal writing, a plural pronoun is often used:

Each of the students has *their* books.

A pronoun referring to the word *none* is either singular or plural:

None of the students has *his or her* books.

None of the students have *their* books.

ref **Avoiding Unclear Pronouns**

Using a pronoun as a substitute for a noun is effective only if it is immediately clear which noun is being substituted. Consider, for example, the following:

Unclear:

The doctor informed the patient that she was a friend of his sister.

In this sentence, *she* and *his* offer two possible meanings:

The doctor informed the patient that she [the doctor] was a friend of his [the patient's] sister.

The doctor informed the patient that she [the patient] was a friend of his [the doctor's] sister.

If a pronoun is preceded by two or more nouns or pronouns of the same person (first, second, third), number (singular/plural), gender (male, female, neuter), and case (subjective, objective, possessive), check for ambiguity (see "Pronouns"). If you notice an unclear pronoun, either repeat the appropriate noun, substitute a synonymous word or phrase, or change the wording to avoid the ambiguity:

Unclear:

She stopped at the *store* for a *bottle of aspirin* and a *copy of Newsweek,* but she didn't have enough money to pay for *it.*

Repetition of noun:

She stopped at the store for a bottle of aspirin and a copy of *Newsweek,* but she didn't have enough money to pay for *the Newsweek.*

Substitition of synonymous word or phrase:

She stopped at the store for a bottle of aspirin and a copy of *Newsweek,* but she didn't have enough money to pay for *the magazine.*

Change of wording:

Stopping at the store, she bought a bottle of aspirin. She also wanted a copy of *Newsweek,* but didn't have enough money to pay for it.

dm Avoiding Dangling Modifiers

A dangling modifier has no appropriate subject to modify. Consider, for example, the following:

Dangling:

After riding a bicycle for twelve miles, the ice water was invigorating.

In this sentence, the rider of the bicycle is never mentioned. The phrase *after riding a bicycle for twelve miles* thus has no appropriate noun to modify and is considered dangling.

To avoid dangling modifiers, always specify the subject of a modifying word or phrase:

After riding a bicycle for twelve miles, *Robin* thought the ice water was invigorating.

mm Avoiding Misplaced Modifiers

A misplaced modifier is subject to misinterpretation. Consider, for example, the following:

Ambiguous:

Lydia asked Marco privately to report the results of his investigation.

In this sentence, it is unclear if Lydia asked privately or if Marco was to report privately. To avoid possible misinterpretation, position modifiers as close as possible to the word being modified:

Lydia privately asked Marco to report the results of his investigation.

Lydia asked Marco to report privately the results of his investigation.

Index of Key Terms

EPILOGUE

You're at the close of this writing course, an exploration of the territory of rhetoric. Before you end this time with your instructor and classmates, however, we wish to ask you a favor.

In a "Write More About It" section in Chapter 3, p. 59, we requested that you record comments and complaints in your journal. We forecasted that, in the Epilogue, we would ask you to use your observations to write a letter to us—Gwendolyn Gong and Sam Dragga, c/o HarperCollins College Publishers, 10 East 53rd Street, New York, NY 10022-5299—with your suggestions on how we might improve this book. We are asking you to write that letter now.

From your comments, we will learn how to strengthen this "draft" of *A Writer's Repertoire* in future revisions. That is, your feedback will enable us to expand our own writing and teaching repertoires. Through our own writing experiences, we gain knowledge by participation; from your essays and letters, we gain knowledge by observation. As a consequence, the next students we teach and the next "draft" of this textbook will be informed by knowledge gained by both participation and observation. Our journey in the territory of rhetoric continues.

Credits

Index